Alan Palmer was educated at B̶a̶n̶c̶r̶o̶f̶t̶'̶s̶ ̶S̶c̶h̶o̶o̶l̶, Woodford Green, and at Oriel College, Oxford. He was head of the History Department at Highgate School from 1953 to 1969 when he gave up his post to concentrate on historical writing and research. Alan Palmer lives in Woodstock, Oxfordshire.

By the same author

The Gardeners of Salonika
Yugoslavia
The Penguin Dictionary of Modern History 1789–1945
Napoleon in Russia
The Lands Between: a history of East-Central Europe since the Congress of Vienna
Metternich
Alexander I: Tsar of war and peace
Frederick the Great
The Life and Times of George IV
Russia in War and Peace
The Kings and Queens of England
Bismarck
The Kaiser: warlord of the Second Reich
The Princes of Wales
The Penguin Dictionary of Twentieth-Century History
Who's Who in World Politics
The Chancelleries of Europe
An Encyclopedia of Napoleon's Europe
Crowned Cousins: the Anglo-German royal connection
The Banner of Battle: the story of the Crimean War
The East End: four centuries of London life
Bernadotte: Napoleon's Marshal; Sweden's King
Kemal Ataturk
The Decline and Fall of the Ottoman Empire
Dictionary of the British Empire and Commonwealth

Co-author with C. A. Macartney: Independent Eastern Europe, A History

Co-author with Prince Michael of Greece: Royal House of Greece

Co-author with Veronica Palmer: Quotations in History
Who's Who in Shakespeare's England
Royal England
Who's Who in Bloomsbury
The Pimlico Chronology of British History

TWILIGHT

of the

HABSBURGS

The Life and Times of

EMPEROR FRANCIS JOSEPH

————————

Alan Palmer

To Anna, László and Judit,
Győrgy and Eszter,
in gratitude and affection

A PHOENIX GIANT PAPERBACK

First published in Great Britain by Weidenfeld & Nicolson in 1994
This paperback edition published in 1997 by Phoenix, a division of Orion Books Ltd,
Orion House, 5 Upper St Martin's Lane, London WC2H 9EA

Second Impression 1998

A CIP catalogue record for this book is available from the
British Library.

ISBN: 1 85799 869 3

Printed and bound in Great Britain by
Butler & Tanner Ltd, Frome and London

CONTENTS

Map of Austria Hungary 1878–1918		vi
Illustrations		vii
Family tree of the Habsburgs		viii
Preface		x
1	Schönbrunn 1830	1
2	A Biedermeier Boyhood	12
3	Year of Revolution	28
4	Apotheosis of the Army	49
5	Marriage	64
6	'It Is My Pleasure . .'	80
7	Italy Without Radetzky	98
8	'Power Remains In My Hands'	114
9	In Bismarck's Shadow	130
10	The Holy Crown of St Stephen	148
11	Facing Both Ways	165
12	A Glimmer of Light	180
13	The Herzegovina and Bosnia	195
14	Father and Son	214
15	Golden Epoch	228
16	Mayerling and After	246
17	Spared Nothing	267
18	The Belvedere	286
19	Two Journeys to Sarajevo	300
20	War	325
21	Schönbrunn 1916	340
22	Into History	345
	Notes and Sources	350
	Alternative Place Names	374
	Index	375

Germans Magyars Czechs Slovaks Croats Serbs Slovenes Italians Roumanians Poles Ruthenes

RUSSIA

ROUMANIA
Bucharest
Ruschuk

BULGARIA

100 miles
50
0

GALICIA
Czernowitz
BUKOVINA
Lemberg
Przemysl
Cracow
Vistula

KINGDOM OF HUNGARY

TRANSYLVANIA
Cluj
Debrecen
Maros
Orsova
Arad
Temesvár
Szeged
Gödöllő
Budapest
Tisza
Komárom
Győr
Bratislava
Sopron
Mayerling
Balaton

SILESIA
MORAVIA
Olmütz
Brno
Znaim
Reichstadt
Königgrätz
BOHEMIA
Prague
Plsen
Vltava
Elbe
Konopischt

LOWER AUSTRIA
UPPER AUSTRIA
Vienna
Linz
Passau
Danube
BAVARIA
Munich
GERMAN EMPIRE

STYRIA
Graz
Salzburg
SALZBURG
Ischl
CARINTHIA
Klagenfurt
CARNIOLA
Ljubljana
GORZ
Gorz
Trieste
ISTRIA
Pola
Venice

TYROL
Innsbruck
Bolzano
VORARLBERG
SWITZERLAND
Verona
Milan
Po
Garda
ITALY

CROATIA
Zagreb
Rijeka
SLAVONIA
Sava
Drava
Pécs
Drava
Zadar
Split
DALMATIA
Lissa
Dubrovnik
Kotor
Adriatic Sea

BOSNIA
Sarajevo
HERZE-GOVINA
Mostar

SERBIA

SANJAK OF NOVIBAZAR
MONTENEGRO
ALBANIA

Danube

Austria Hungary 1878–1918

ILLUSTRATIONS

Maps in text
Francis Joseph's Vienna (c. 1900) 75
Francis Joseph and the Solferino Campaign 1859 106
Francis Joseph's Europe (frontiers 1878–1912) 208

Plates between pp 116 and pp 117
Schönbrunn[1]
Archduchess Sophie[3]
Radetzky[3]
Francis Joseph as Hussar officer[1]
Emperor and Empress, 1855[2]
Elizabeth on horseback[1]
Elizabeth and dog[2]
Francis Joseph and two of his children[2]
Francis Joseph as huntsman[2]
Francis Joseph and companions during hunting trip[2]
View of Schönbrunn through avenue of trees[1]
Emperor's visit to the pyramids[2]

Plates between pp 212 and pp 213
Acclamation of Hungarian parliament[2]
Mayerling[1]
Court ball[2]
Archduke Francis Ferdinand and family[1]
Francis Ferdinand[1]
Stephansplatz, Vienna[1]
Kaiservilla at Bad Ischl
Villa Schratt at Bad Ischl[1]
Katharina Schratt[1]
Francis Joseph with nephew, Charles I, 1894
Francis Joseph at wedding of Charles and Princess Zita[1]
Emperor in old age[1]
Funeral procession of Francis Joseph[1]
Francis Joseph in his study at Schönbrunn[2]

[1] Weidenfeld & Nicolson archive   [2] Mansell Collection   [3] Austrian National Library

Unacknowledged photographs are taken from private collections. The publishers have attempted to trace copyright owners. Where inadvertent infringement has been made they apologise and will be happy to make due acknowledgement in future editions.

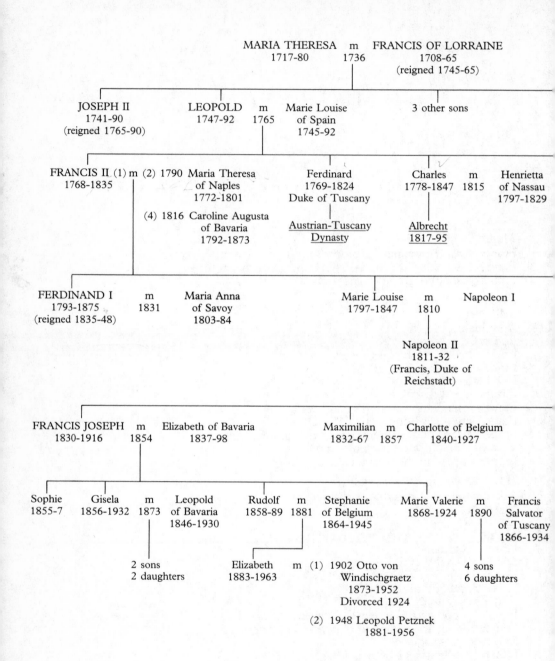

MARIA THERESA   m   FRANCIS OF LORRAINE
1717-80   1736   1708-65
(reigned 1745-65)

JOSEPH II — LEOPOLD   m   Marie Louise   3 other sons
1741-90   1747-92   1765   of Spain
(reigned 1765-90)   1745-92

FRANCIS II (1) m (2) 1790   Maria Theresa   Ferdinand   Charles   m   Henrietta
1768-1835   of Naples   1769-1824   1778-1847   1815   of Nassau
               1772-1801   Duke of Tuscany   1797-1829

(4) 1816 Caroline Augusta   Austrian-Tuscany   Albrecht
        of Bavaria   Dynasty   1817-95
        1792-1873

FERDINAND I   m   Maria Anna   Marie Louise   m   Napoleon I
1793-1875   1831   of Savoy   1797-1847   1810
(reigned 1835-48)   1803-84

                                            Napoleon II
                                            1811-32
                                    (Francis, Duke of
                                    Reichstadt)

FRANCIS JOSEPH   m   Elizabeth of Bavaria   Maximilian   m   Charlotte of Belgium
1830-1916   1854   1837-98   1832-67   1857   1840-1927

Sophie   Gisela   m   Leopold   Rudolf   m   Stephanie   Marie Valerie   m   Francis
1855-7   1856-1932   1873   of Bavaria   1858-89   1881   of Belgium   1868-1924   1890   Salvator
                       1846-1930   1864-1945   of Tuscany
                                                              1866-1934

            2 sons   Elizabeth   m   (1)   1902 Otto von   4 sons
           2 daughters   1883-1963   Windischgraetz   6 daughters
                                             1873-1952
                                             Divorced 1924

                                (2)   1948 Leopold Petznek
                                       1881-1956

Rulers in Vienna capitalised. Note: Francis II was
the second Holy Roman Emperor of that name but
the first emperor of the new style Austrian empire.

Simplified genealogical table of the Habsburg dynasty

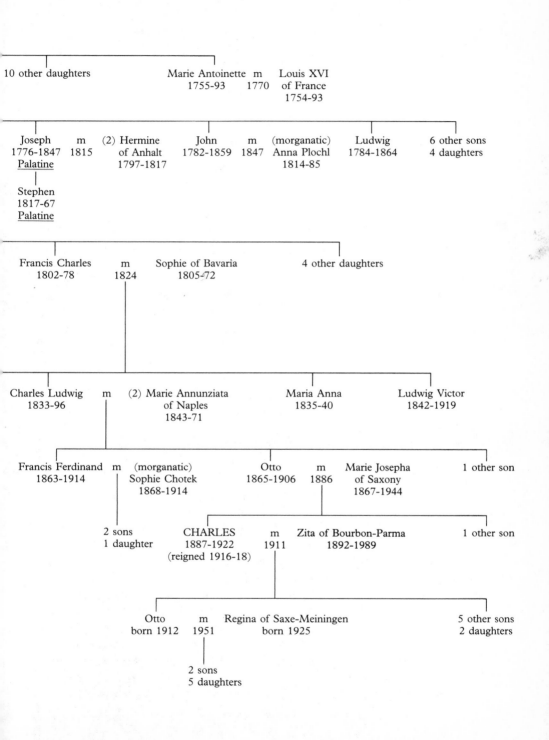

PREFACE

Francis Joseph, who was born in the summer of 1830, ruled Austria and much of central Europe from December 1848 until his death in November 1916. Had he lived eleven days more, he would have been on the throne for sixty-eight years. No other emperor, empress, king or queen exercised full sovereignty for so long; for, though Louis XIV was titular King of France for seventy-two years, he remained under the regency of his mother during the first eight of them and left the management of affairs to his ministers for the next eight. Francis Joseph, on the other hand, began to mould his form of paternalistic autocracy at the age of eighteen, and he was still looking for ways to sustain his inheritance when he entered his eighties.

Longevity gave the Emperor links between a remote past and a puzzling future. He received his baptism of fire in 1848 under the command of Radetzky, who had fought in Ottoman Serbia before the French Revolution transformed the nature of warfare: he lived long enough to try to comprehend the talk of army pilots standing beside their flying machines at Wiener Neustadt. In an early portrait Francis Joseph perches happily on the lap of his first cousin the Duke of Reichstadt, son of the great Napoleon: in a late photograph he has at his knee the infant Archduke Otto, who was to sit in the European Parliament as the Iron Curtain rusted away and whose many years as head of the House of Habsburg have exceeded even the span of his great-great-uncle, the subject of this biography.

But there is far more of interest in Francis Joseph's life than the sheer passage of time. He was brought to the throne by army leaders anxious to sustain the monarchy at the end of a year of revolution and he never forgot the circumstances of his accession. Yet politically he was no obscurantist. At the height of his reign he showed greater foresight than almost all his ministers and generals. An overwhelming sense of dynastic responsibility made him a cautious reformer who was surprised by new ideas, but he was willing to think them over and use them if he did not see them as a threat to the well-being of the multinational community over which he presided. He was not the remote, cardboard cut-out figure of historical legend, a humourless bureaucrat able to endure personal tragedies because he lacked the human warmth to feel their impact deeply. Nor was his intelligence so limited as some writers insist; for, while he rejected pretentious intellectualism with brusque common-sense honesty, he took pains to master several languages and to perfect an astonishingly detailed memory.

Shyness and inhibition made him publicly aloof, and only gradually – long after his death – has the publication of letters and diaries confirmed the agreeable simplicity of his inner character. Like Queen Victoria, he was a compulsive writer of letters but, in contrast to her (and her grandson in Berlin) he never became a natural correspondent, with a spontaneous style in which the ink brims over with underlining. Rather he was a chronicler, choosing to narrate what he saw and did each day in long accounts to the three women who were closest to him: his mother, Archduchess Sophie, who died in 1872; his wife and first cousin, the Empress Elizabeth, who was assassinated in 1898; and the actresss, Katharina Schratt, whose intimate companionship for over thirty years he valued too dearly to cheapen by a physical relationship. It has been a pleasure, in writing this biography, to read the printed editions of these letters, and I feel a deep sense of gratitude to their editors: Franz Schnürer, Georg Nostitz-Reineck, Jean de Bourgoing and Brigitte Hamann. Count Egon Caesar Corti made the first detailed studies of the Emperor-King and his family, using sources which in some cases were lost during the Second World War, and no one can attempt an assessment of Francis Joseph's qualities without quarrying into Count Corti's pioneer works. While writing this biography I was deeply conscious, too, of how much my interest was stimulated many years ago by the late Dr C. A. Macartney, with whom I once had the privilege of collaborating on a preliminary study of independent Eastern Europe.

Long ago I realized that in histories of central Europe the rendering of proper names poses problems for English readers and leaves an author liable to accusations of bias favouring one or other nationality of the region. In this book I have, in general, followed the principle of using the familiar, modern form of a place name, readily identifiable in today's atlases, even though it may be anachronistic to write of 'Bratislava' or 'Ljubljana' etc. during the earlier part of Francis Joseph's reign. Readers will find alternative place names given in an appendix. Dynastic names are anglicized, thus 'Francis' for 'Franz' and 'Charles' for 'Karl', but I have retained the name 'Ludwig', as I do not think the English equivalent

'Lewis' would be readily recognizable when applied, for example, to the eccentric rulers of Bavaria. Somewhat illogically, I refer to Francis Joseph's soldier cousin as 'Archduke Albrecht', partly to distinguish him from other princely Alberts – but also, I suspect, from force of habit, after passing the Archduke Albrecht Monument on the Augustinerbastei so many times.

I wish to acknowledge the gracious permission of Dr Otto von Habsburg to make use of material from his family archives in Vienna, and especially for allowing me access to the journals of Archduchess Sophie. I would like also to express my gratitude to the General Director of the Haus-, Hof- und Staatsarchiv and his staff – notably Dr Elisabeth Springer – for their patient advice during my visits to the Minoritenplatz. There are others, too, in Austria to whom I am indebted for kind assistance, though unfortunately I do not know their names. I remember, with particular thanks, the lay sister at Mayerling who drew my attention to the fresco above the high altar.

In England, I feel a particular debt to Lord Weidenfeld for suggesting, in an inspirational flash, that I should write a life of the Emperor Francis Joseph, a task which has given me much pleasure. Good fortune brought me the editorial aid of Christopher Falkus, a friend with long experience of historical biography. I am grateful to him, to Catherine Lightfoot, editorial co-ordinator at Orion House, and to John Mclaughlin and Charlotte Bruton for their wise counsel. The staffs of the Bodleian Library and the London Library have once again offered me ready help, much appreciated. Since my wife, Veronica, accompanied me on more than a dozen trips to the former Habsburg lands, she has been able to give me advice, chapter by chapter. She also undertook the formidable task of indexing the book at a time of considerable difficulty for her. Even so, these instances of practical help constitute only a small part of the support she has given to me during this absorbing enterprise. My greatest debt remains, as ever, to her.

For more than twenty years we have enjoyed the friendship and frequent hospitality of a Hungarian family, in four generations. Their companionship, in person or by letter, has warmly enriched our experience and broadened our understanding of central Europe, past and present. Sadly, the head of that family, László Szőke Snr., a doctor who served devotedly the young people of the Hatvan district, died prematurely four years ago. In dedicating this book to his widow Anna, and to his sons, László and György, and their wives, I wish also to honour his memory.

Alan Palmer
Woodstock, July 1994

Chapter 1

SCHÖNBRUNN, 1830

The summer residence of the Habsburgs lies barely three miles from the centre of Vienna. Like Versailles, Schönbrunn was originally a hunting lodge; it was converted into a palace by the Empress Maria Theresa, to whose achievements it offers a finer memorial than any sculptured statue in a city square. Yet unlike Versailles, which the greatest of revolutions had left forlorn and neglected, Schönbrunn remained the home of a reigning dynasty. It was, of course, more modern than Louis XIV's prototype; and, in an odd way, it was more elegantly easy-going and self-assured, despite over fourteen hundred rooms and a long facade stretching for an eighth of a mile towards the slopes of the Wienerwald. No steep angled chapel roof buttresses Schönbrunn into oppressive grandeur, as at Versailles, for Maria Theresa's feeling for natural spaciousness ensured that the palace would always look subordinate to the landscaped parkland behind it. In August 1830, fifty years after Maria Theresa's death, the ochre stonework was still new enough to glow with pristine splendour in the sunshine. At sixty-two the reigning emperor, Francis I, could remember how on sunny days in her last years his grandmother would sit beneath the open arcade of the palace, facing the clipped hedge-shaded walks which led to the newly completed colonnade of the Gloriette. A box holding state papers was strapped to her chest so as to form a portable desk, and to them she would turn conscientiously, oblivious of the bustle around her. It was rarely quiet at the palace which the most businesslike of empresses had created.

All that, however, was by now more than half a century ago. Recent history associated Schönbrunn in name with a foreign conqueror rather than with Maria Theresa. For on three occasions – before and after Austerlitz, and following his hard-won victory at Wagram – Napoleon I made the palace his headquarters. Ironically, it was in one of Maria Theresa's exquisite salons that an Austrian plenipotentiary was forced to sign the peace treaty of 1809, which cost her grandson more thalers than his treasury could afford, lost him three and a half million subjects, and forced what remained of the Habsburg Empire into dependence upon France. That humiliating episode passed swiftly, and within six months Emperor Francis's daughter, Marie Louise, became Napoleon's second wife; but the defeat at French hands left scars which the reversal of Habsburg fortunes in the campaigns of 1813–14 never healed. For two generations men and women who remembered the shock of occupation dominated Viennese society, with the poet and dramatist Franz Grillparzer outstanding among them. The public figures of the war years survived the return of peace. In 1830 Emperor Francis was still on the throne; and Metternich, the Rhinelander whom Francis appointed foreign minister while the French were in Schönbrunn, was still Chancellor of his empire.

There were other reminders of the occupation, too. Gilded French eagles, mounted on Napoleon's orders above the pyramidical columns of Maria Theresa's time, continued to overlook the palace courtyard (as they do today). Since both empires made proud use of eagle symbolism, it was tempting to leave them in place even if, in heraldic ornithology, the *Aquila Bonaparta* has a single head while the Habsburg species boasts two. More romantically evocative than gilt symbols was the Eaglet himself. For *l'Aiglon* – 'the Son of the Man' and Marie Louise – had his home at Schönbrunn, although for much of that summer he was at Baden. The boy, who upon his birth in 1811 was proclaimed King of Rome, had been parted from his father before his third birthday and educated as a Habsburg 'Serene Highness'. His baptismal name was dropped in favour of 'Franzl', the German diminutive of his second name, and at the age of seven he was created Duke of Reichstadt. Though Emperor Francis petted this first-born grandson, enjoying long walks and talks through the parkland of Schönbrunn, Franzl's status was anomalous. Occasionally, he seemed placed on a pedestal; when in 1826 the Viennese artist Leopold Fertbauer was commissioned to paint 'Emperor Francis and his Family', the fifteen year old Reichstadt was placed at the centre of the group, between his grandfather and Marie Louise, so that the eye at once focuses on him. In Court precedence, he ranked immediately after the Habsburg archdukes. But Reichstadt's origins continued to worry Chancellor Metternich, who made certain that his secret police kept the intelligent young man insulated from Bonapartism and its agents. Not surprisingly, Reichstadt was eager to shake off Court restraint. If he could not return to France as Napoleon II, he hoped to serve in his grandfather's army. Although Franzl was delicate, he was promised a colonelcy in the foot guards at the age of twenty.

Yet, however generous the Emperor's sympathy with a half-Bonaparte might be, he was preoccupied with the immediate prospects of his own dynasty. For although fifty-two Habsburg archdukes and archduchesses had been born in the past hundred years, the future succession remained in doubt. Francis had married four times and fathered thirteen children, but only two sons and five daughters survived infancy; all were the offspring of his second wife, Maria Theresa of Bourbon-Naples, who was doubly a first cousin. Such inbreeding had disastrous genetic consequences. Francis's heir, Crown Prince Ferdinand, was a good and amiable simpleton and an epileptic, with no inclination to marry. The Emperor's other surviving son, Archduke Francis Charles, was a kindly nonentity, slightly brighter in intellect than his brother but dominated by his wife, Archduchess Sophie, who was a daughter of King Maximilian I, head of the Wittelsbach dynasty and the first sovereign King of Bavaria. If anyone could give the dynasty a new lease of life, it was Archduchess Sophie, as all Vienna recognized. She, too, is prominent in Fertbauer's group canvas, almost edging out her sister-in-law, poor Marie Louise; and in these sultry August days of 1830 Sophie's well-being was Emperor Francis's chief concern.

Over the centuries Habsburg and Wittelsbach had frequently intermarried. Indeed, the reigning Empress-consort – Francis's fourth wife, Caroline Augusta – was Sophie's half-sister. Officially the Church frowned on such a relationship, but between Francis Charles and Sophie there was no close consanguinity, and their wedding in Vienna in November 1824 was welcomed as yet another affirmation of the links between the two principal German Catholic dynasties. Disappointment followed; for in her first five years of married life the Archduchess suffered a succession of miscarriages: would she prove barren, like her half-sister? But when, early in 1830, pregnancy was confirmed, the Archduchess – who was still only twenty-five in that January – began writing back to her mother in Munich with calm confidence. Before the end of the month she was even prepared to give Monday, 16 August, as her child's probable birthday.

Sophie was reluctant to abandon her social life. But fate was against her. There was little gaiety in Vienna that winter: a bitter February, with the Danube frozen, gave way to a thaw on the last night of the month and unprecedented flooding, with loss of life in the low-lying suburbs, on the eve of *Fasching*, the pre-Lenten carnival. Briefly, after Easter, Sophie was able to go to the theatre and opera, but at the end of April the Emperor's doctors clamped down on her movements. Despite particularly pleasant weather, for the next fourteen weeks she was expected to remain at Schönbrunn, walking gently in the gardens, with no exciting distractions permitted. To climb the sloping path up to the Gloriette colonnade, 150 feet above the parterre, was inadvisable. The Archduchess may, too, have avoided the western side of the park, near the zoological gardens; for a tale, which Sophie's letters show troubled her over several years, maintained that her husband's youngest sister Archduchess Marianna – only seven months older than Sophie – owed the hideous disfigurement of her face and her virtual imbecility to a pre-natal incident when her mother was startled by an escaped orang-utang while walking in the gardens. In 1830 Archduchess Marianna was still living at Schönbrunn, a rarely seen presence secluded in the labyrinth of smaller rooms.

The Emperor's concern for his daughter-in-law's health is understandable. His fear of madness, deformity or epilepsy increased as her time of confinement drew nearer. Most of her days were spent in the pleasantest wing of the palace, her bedroom on the first floor of the east terrace looking directly out across the main courtyard. Yet if Sophie hoped for privacy she was disappointed. Even the relatively human task of getting born could not pass without ritual observance; and by mid-August the pregnant Archduchess was the light around whom the planetary Habsburg Court revolved. On the Monday afternoon – 16 August, as Sophie predicted – her child's birth seemed imminent. The principal midwife told Archduke Francis Charles he would be a father that evening; the Archduke duly informed the Emperor in Vienna; and Francis at once left for Schönbrunn. The palace became a hive of activity, with bustle and confusion everywhere. Prayers for the mother's safe delivery were offered up in the chapel; but still the Archduchess was not in labour. Members of the family hurried to the bedroom; Court officials and well-wishers from high society waited in crowded antechambers, an initial noisy excitement giving way to a no less noisy impatience. Many were still there twenty-four hours later, by which time the midwives had wisely decided against giving any more forecasts. In the chapel, votive candles were lit once again.

By Tuesday the Emperor was so nervously restless that he refused to go to bed, spending a fitful night on a sofa. As ever, dutiful functionaries sought to emulate their sovereign's example and slept wherever they could. Apparently in all this suspended animation no chronicler bothered to notice the expectant father – that was Archduke Francis Charles's fate throughout his life. By eight on Wednesday morning, when cries from within the bedroom let her audience know that the Archduchess was at last in labour, the palace corridors were full of weary men and women. At a quarter to eleven the shrieks ceased. A few moments later Empress Caroline Augusta brought them her half-sister's good news: 'It's a son – and a healthy, well-formed child, too,' she announced. Francis Joseph – throughout his reign the most punctilious of timekeepers – had arrived on Wednesday, 18 August, some forty hours behind schedule. Not that the long wait mattered now; his tired grandfather was delighted. Although

4

technically third in line of succession, from that moment onwards the newcomer was treated as an Archduke destined soon to rule.

He was born into the most historic dynasty on the continent. The House of Habsburg had provided Germany with twenty emperors and gave rulers to Spain, the Netherlands and much of the Italian peninsula. From 1438 until its abolition in 1806, the 'Holy Roman Empire of the German Nation' was virtually a Habsburg hereditary possession, and in 1792 Emperor Francis had been duly crowned in Frankfurt as 54th successor to Charlemagne. But Francis was under no illusions; he needed more precisely defined authority than this curious relic of feudal obligations could provide. Within ten weeks of his coronation, a republic was proclaimed in France. The revolutionary upheaval and Napoleon's subsequent imperial aspirations, made him seek a new title which would assert his sovereignty over all the Habsburg lands, and in April 1804 he was proclaimed 'Francis I, Emperor of Austria'.

In many respects Francis's new realm was a hasty improvisation; and the changing fortunes of war delayed a final settlement of its frontiers until 1815 when the map of Europe was redrawn at the Congress of Vienna, under the chairmanship of his foreign minister, Prince Metternich. The Empire of Austria became the largest country in Europe apart from Russia, spanning the centre of the continent. It linked in common allegiance to the dynasty towns as far distant as Milan in Italy and Czernowitz (now Chernovtsy) in the Ukraine. All of present-day Austria, Hungary, the Czech Republic, Slovakia, Slovenia and Croatia fell within its frontiers at the time of Francis Joseph's birth. So too did such cities as Lublin in Poland, Cluj and Timişoara in Roumania, and Venice, Verona, Mantua and Trieste in Italy. In the provinces of Lower Austria (around Vienna) and Upper Austria (around Linz) the population was almost exclusively German, while in Lombardy and Venetia it was overwhelmingly Italian. Everywhere else the nationalities were mixed; even in Vienna there was a considerable Czech minority in the outer districts. Germans could be found in every province; they constituted about a fifth of the total population of the empire – in 1830 some 6.5 million out of a total 34 million. Sometimes the Germans were a majority in a province, as in Tyrol (with an Italian minority) or in Styria and Carinthia (Slovene minorities); but often they were so concentrated as to form Teuton islands in a Slavonic, Magyar or Roumanian sea. The empire could therefore never be described as a Germanic institution, even though German was the first language of sovereign and Court. Throughout Francis Joseph's reign his empire was always to have more Slavs – Czechs, Slovaks, Croats, Serbs, Slovenes, Ruthenes, Ukrainians, Poles – than Germans or Magyars or Latins (Italians and Roumanians).

But on 18 August 1830 it was German Catholic churches around Schönbrunn that first celebrated the good news from the palace. Bells rang in jubilation in neighbouring Hietzing. Soon they were pealing in Vienna, too. Guns thundered a first royal salute; crowds streamed into the outer palace courtyard at Schönbrunn, cheering with satisfaction and waving flags. Archduchess Sophie was far from popular in the capital, where her peremptory manner and Bavarian Sunday piety aroused a certain mistrust. But, for the moment, that hostility was forgotten. The birth of the young Archduke provided an excuse for more celebrations in Vienna's Augarten and Prater, the open land which the 'reformer emperor' Joseph II (Maria Theresa's son and Francis's uncle) presented to the city. In this vast area south of the Danube there were already some forty restaurants or taverns, certain to attract good custom on a warm summer evening.

Prince Metternich heard of the Archduke's birth while working in his study at the state chancellery in the Ballhausplatz. The gun salutes must have pleased him – 'I have a great weakness for the sound of cannon', he once confessed – but there is no evidence he showed any great interest in the news from Schönbrunn. He was, of course, glad that Archduchess Sophie could bring new hope to the dynasty he served, for he recognized that hereditary kingship was the best constituted source of authority for the rule of law in a post-Jacobin age. But, while Emperor Francis had been impatient for the birth of a Habsburg grandson, his Chancellor was looking farther afield, anxiously waiting on events hundreds of miles from Vienna. More than once Metternich lamented living in such an 'abominable epoch'. Reports from France and from several of the Italian states left him in little doubt that the 'tranquillity and repose' which he believed essential were about to be disturbed yet again by violent assertions of popular sovereignty. To combat the moral anarchy of Revolution he urged collaboration between the three eastern autocracies – Austria, Prussia and Russia.

Metternich never expected to be in Vienna when Francis Joseph was born. Arrangements had been made for him to conduct government business that August from Königswart, his country estate in Bohemia. But while he was there, late in the evening of 4 August, he received news through the courier service established by the Rothschild brothers to serve their banking interests: on 27 July the people of Paris had risen in revolt against the reactionary policies of their Bourbon king, Charles X. Metternich was shocked by the news, briefly collapsing in despair. But he soon rallied: 'When Paris sneezes, Europe catches cold', he was heard to remark. There could be no summer holiday in the quiet of Königswart that year. He set off back to Vienna at the end of the first week in August and was at his desk in the Ballhausplatz long before Archduchess Sophie went into labour.

His forebodings were justified: Europe did, indeed, catch cold. On the day Francis Joseph was born, the last legitimate Bourbon King of France, newly landed in England, was on his way to exile in Edinburgh; and the Archduke's first months of infancy coincided with a period of protracted tumult across the continent. In Paris a Constitutional Charter provided for Louis Philippe, head of the Orleanist branch of the Bourbons, to accede as 'King of the French by the Grace of God and the Will of the People'. When Francis Joseph was nine days old, rioting in Brussels and Liège marked the outbreak of a national revolution against Dutch rule in the Belgian provinces which, as Emperor Francis and his Chancellor could well remember, had been the 'Austrian Netherlands' less than forty years earlier. Before the end of September, rulers were dethroned in Brunswick, Hesse-Cassel and Saxony, where German liberals followed the example of the French and Belgians in demanding constitutions; and it became clear that, before the winter was over, there would be grave unrest in Italy, where Metternich had sought to stamp out the embers of a national patriotism fired by Napoleon. But the most dramatic challenge to Metternich's European system came in the last days of November, when an army revolt in Warsaw sparked off a national insurrection in Poland. The uprising was aimed principally at the Russian puppet 'Congress Kingdom', created at the end of the Napoleonic Wars. But as Russia, Prussia and Austria had jointly partitioned historic Poland in the eighteenth century, and some two million Poles lived within the Habsburg Empire, what happened in Warsaw mattered deeply in Vienna. The revolt placed the Polish Question firmly back on the agenda of Europe. It was to remain unresolved throughout Francis Joseph's lifetime: indeed, the search for a solution became the last diplomatic problem to trouble him in his dying days.

No echo of these events disturbed life in the young Archduke's nursery, where Sophie remained proudly protective of her infant son's interests. There was little trouble in the heart of the Habsburg Empire: Metternich's chief of police, Count Sedlnitzky, reported all was quiet in the Austrian lands, apart from habitual grumbling at heavy taxation; even in Galicia the Poles made no open moves to aid their compatriots in Warsaw. But before the end of the year Archduchess Sophie was disturbed by one unexpected aspect of Metternich's policy. At first it seemed harmless enough: the Chancellor began to encourage the Emperor to affirm the status of his eldest son, Ferdinand, by presenting him for coronation as King of Hungary at a meeting of the bicameral Hungarian Diet in the autumn. There were plenty of occasions in Hungary's past when the sovereign's designated successor had been crowned while his predecessor was alive. But Metternich had another purpose in advocating the coronation: if Francis showed a special regard for his Magyar subjects, he hoped that their spokesmen would respond by authorizing the recruitment of additional soldiery from the Hungarian counties.

All went as well as Metternich had hoped, perhaps even better. Less than six weeks after Francis Joseph's birth, his simple-minded uncle was crowned King of Hungary at Pressburg, the fortress city some 40 miles down the Danube from Vienna, known as Pozsony to the Hungarians and Bratislava to the Slovaks (whose capital it is today). Ferdinand fulfilled his duties adequately and with a certain pathetic dignity, thanks to the careful guidance of his father's sixth brother, Archduke Joseph, Palatine of Hungary for the past third of a century. The Diet agreed to authorize the enlistment of 28,000 recruits in return for procedural concessions, notably the use of the Magyar language rather than Latin in official communications. Here too, as in Poland, was a pointer to future problems; the 'language question' was to be raised time and time again during Francis Joseph's reign.

Barely a month after Ferdinand's return from Hungary, it was made known at Court that the imperial physician, Dr Stifft, had become convinced there were no medical reasons why the Crown Prince should not marry. The news, totally unexpected, startled Archduchess Sophie; if Ferdinand married and had a son it was unlikely that either her husband or her child would become Emperor. More disturbing still was the announcement in December of the Crown Prince's betrothal to Maria Anna of Savoy. Only after Dr Stifft had assured Sophie that it was unlikely the Crown Prince would ever 'make any attempt to assert his marital rights' was the Archduchess mollified. When Ferdinand and Maria Anna were married in Vienna at the end of February 1831, she felt a genuine sympathy for the bride, coupled with indignation over Metternich's cynical manoeuvres. No one in the imperial family really believed that poor Ferdinand's disabilities would allow him to accept the strains of married life. These doubts seemed confirmed when the Crown Prince took to his bed on the day after the wedding. His bride – kind at heart, dutiful and singularly plain – was left with the doubtful consolation of accompanying Sophie on an evening visit to the Schönbrunn nursery, where she could admire the wonder child in his cot. Metternich, it was thought, wished to safeguard Ferdinand's succession, confident that a figurehead sovereign would leave the business of government in his experienced hands.

Despite her worry over Metternich's intentions, the Archduchess was more immediately concerned with the health of her child. To her great relief, throughout his first winter, Francis Joseph remained astonishingly robust and lively, by Habsburg standards. He had golden curls and a rosy complexion: 'a strawberry ice with a topping of whipped cream', was Reichstadt's happy description of his infant cousin. But before the boy's first birthday Sophie was seized by a fear common that year to families in every social class throughout central Europe. For during 1830 the first great cholera epidemic had been advancing remorselessly across Russia, causing near panic in Moscow in October and sweeping into Russian Poland, where it killed the Tsar's brother and his wife, and the Russian commander-in-chief. By the early spring of 1831 cholera had reached Galicia, soon crossing into the northern counties of Hungary, where it was especially virulent. So gravely did the disease strike Hungary as a whole that, during the year, it was to claim the lives of 1 in 25 of the population.

Early in July 1831 cholera was confirmed in central Vienna. Archduchess Sophie was thoroughly alarmed: 'God's scourge of the cholera threatens us', she had already warned her mother. The imperial family gathered in Schönbrunn, cordoned off from the evil-smelling River Wien – virtually an open sewer in the 1830s – and from all contact with the city. In Vienna the authorities responded to the epidemic much as if it were the plague: isolation was imposed with such rigour that cholera made less impact on the city than in London a year later. Nevertheless both Sophie and her husband were eager to get away from the capital. The Archduchess had a firm belief in the therapeutic qualities of the Salzkammergut's saline springs and at the end of July, husband, wife and child set out for Gmunden and the clear mountain air of Ischl, farther up the valley of the Traun.

The village of Ischl had prospered in the previous century, when wealthy salt refiners built elegant houses along the north bank of the River Traun and raised a fine parish church, at much the same time as Maria Theresa was watching the scaffolding come down from the Gloriette at Schönbrunn. In 1821 a fashionable Viennese medical practitioner, Dr Wirer, began to praise the saline waters of the Traun valley. Sophie was impressed by Wirer's 'discovery'. She visited Ischl after the last of her miscarriages and fully agreed with Wirer. Ischl delighted her, reminding her of home; and small wonder, for the Bavarian mountains she had known in her girlhood are an extension of the same alpine range. On this first visit with her child, she told her mother (in English) of Francis Joseph's high spirits, describing to her how he would sit astride a huge, good-tempered dog belonging to the director of the salt works, riding the hound like a pony. In later years Francis Joseph made Ischl his summer holiday home for as much of July and August as official duties would permit. Seventy years after this nursery visit 'dear Ischl, so beautiful and so green' could lift his tired spirits, much as did the magic of Osborne for the widowed Queen Victoria.

Before the autumn rains came, Archduke Francis Charles took his wife and child northwards to Bohemia. Prague was officially free of cholera, and the family stayed for some weeks in the Hradčany, where a royal palace of some 700 rooms was stamped with the unmistakable embellishments of Maria Theresa's reign. From the Hradčany, the family moved southwards to Laxenburg, on the Danubian plain barely ten miles from Vienna. Laxenburg was a natural hunting-ground, where the child grew accustomed to the sound of his father shooting wild duck around the lakes in the well-timbered parkland. But before Christmas they were back in the capital. As spring approached in 1832, they prepared to return to Schönbrunn.

By then, Sophie was again pregnant, her baby due early in July. During these months of waiting, she became less self-centred. More and more she wrote and spoke about Franzl Reichstadt. So much was he in her thoughts that gossip then and in later years suggested the young and romantic Duke was father of the child she was expecting. Such an easy assumption of an improbable sexual relationship fails to understand the nature of the attachment binding the Archduchess to the twenty-one-year-old Eaglet. At heart both Sophie, as a young woman, and poor Franzl remained interlopers at the Habsburg Court. Her character was shaped by a typical Wittelsbach mixture of family ambition, dreamy melancholia and realistic common sense to which, in an intellectually lack-lustre Court, she added a cautiously restrained mental curiosity. Misfortune had made Reichstadt devious, shyly hesitant, and suspicious of those around him, but he was highly imaginative and eager to discover if he had inherited the creative genius which lifted his father so far above the mediocre talents of the other men in the Bonaparte clan. In the winter before Francis Joseph was born, the Archduchess was frequently escorted to the opera and theatre not by her philistine husband but by her nephew; the two outsiders came to trust each other, sharing enthusiasms and exchanging ideas freely. Their confidences were those of a brother and an elder sister rather than of lovers.

Tragically, Sophie's second pregnancy coincided with the relentless advance of Reichstadt's tuberculosis; and it was the knowledge that she was creating life, while disease was eating away his health which accounts for the devotion she showed to her young companion at this time. Some rooms in her own apartments at Schönbrunn were given over to him, so that he could catch the lingering sunshine in the late afternoon that spring. So long as she could do so, Sophie would visit the sickroom on Reichstadt's bad days and read to him, even though at times she was overcome by the heat of the room. 'How tragic it is to see someone so young and beautiful slowly wasting away', she wrote to her mother in Munich, 'At times he looks as if he were an old man'.

He had helped amuse Francis Joseph in that first year in the nursery, and Sophie believed there was a deep bond of affection between the two cousins. In June she took the 'little one' with her on a brief visit to the Schönbrunn sickroom because, as she told her mother, Franzl Reichstadt 'so desperately wanted to see him, as he is so much alone'. The young man's condition grew worse but he rallied, as if he was determined to cling to life until Sophie had her baby. On 4 July – a humid Wednesday morning – the Archduchess paid her customary visit to the sickroom, but the heat was too much for her, and she did not stay long. Later in the day the midwives were once more on duty, and on the Friday Sophie's second son was born; he was called Ferdinand Maximilian (although the first name was rarely used). A few doors away, in what had once been Napoleon's study, Reichstadt heard the news of Max's arrival, and smiled with evident satisfaction. He never saw the boy – a cousin destined to become disastrously ensnared by a Bonapartist misadventure in Mexico while still only in his thirties.

Reichstadt never saw Maximilian's mother again, either. For, though Archduchess Sophie's confinement had been much easier this time, she collapsed physically and mentally when the ordeal was over. Her doctors would not allow her to leave her bedroom for three weeks. Early on 29 July, the third Sunday after Maximilian's birth, Archduke Francis Charles broke to his wife the news she had dreaded: only a few minutes before, he had been with his sister Marie Louise at Reichstadt's bedside, as the Eaglet's lungs gave up the fight for life. Now there was only one 'Franzl' in the palace. Rather strangely, within an hour of her son's death, Marie Louise was with his young cousin in the nursery above the Schönbrunn guardhouse. To the one-time Empress of the French there was comfort in the chatter of a little boy who could not probe memories half-forgotten of loyalties half-fulfilled.

Chapter 2

A BIEDERMEIER BOYHOOD

Regimentation and orderliness shaped the daily life of the young Arch-dukes from their first weeks in the nursery. Their father had little influence on his boys' upbringing, though he was later to impart to his eldest son the skills from which he acquired so many hunting trophies. Inevitably it was Archduchess Sophie who set the form and pace of Francis Joseph's education, a responsibility she fulfilled with methodical care, knowing that, in contrast to her own girlhood in Munich, he would gain little intellectual stimulus from the Court life around him. Sophie was proud to play the Emperor-maker, conscious – perhaps too conscious – that her hands possessed the strength to mould the Monarchy.

The Archduchess held no theories of her own on education. For, though the most cultured woman to brighten the Court for many decades, she was in no sense a child of the Enlightenment. Music and the arts could count on her patronage, and with Reichstadt she read and discussed novels and poems upon which the Imperial Censorship frowned. But she was a conventionally devout Catholic, sentimentally pious and always respecting her spiritual confessor, Abbot Joseph von Rauscher. Sophie knew that her son's active imagination should be cultivated, but she took care to see that any sign of enthusiasm was held in check: for it was essential he should learn to show iron self-respect in the face of adversity. From Sophie's letters to her sister in later years it is clear that she gave top place in any ideal curriculum to linguistic skills.

Even in infancy, the Archdukes had their own household. Both were entrusted to the care of the same governess ('Aja'), Baroness Luise von Sturmfeder, a spinster with a firm and equable temperament, sixteen years older than Sophie, and herself the sixth child in a family of eleven, from the lesser Prussian nobility. Her young charges remained personally devoted to the Baroness, whom they affectionately called 'Amie'. As she also won and retained the trust of the boys' mother, she must have been a woman of good sense and tact. Subordinate to the Aja were a nurse, an assistant nurse, a cook, a chamberwoman, a general purpose maid, a scullery maid and two footmen. Much detail of these early years can be reconstructed from an edited selection of Luise von Sturmfeder's dotingly reverential jottings, published some forty years after her death, but while Francis Joseph was still on the throne. Her diary vividly recalls exaggerated fears over minor happenings, such as the near panic at Schönbrunn one afternoon in early November when 'Franzi' arrived back from a walk in the park with his hands blue as no one had given him gloves. We learn from Baroness von Sturmfeder and from the Archduchess's correspondence of Franzi's happy disposition, of his delight in looking down from a gallery on his first masked ball and of seeing his father riding back from a hunt, and of the pleasure he gained from the tambourines and toy drummer-girl left as presents beneath a Christmas tree when he was still too young to talk. As the young Archdukes passed from infancy into boyhood, their mother's letters show the difference in temperament between the brothers. For, while Max became fascinated by the animals, birds and flowers at Schönbrunn and Laxenburg, his elder brother absorbed the soldierly ceremonial around him. With sentries pacing beneath the nursery window each day and the sound of bugle calls from neighbouring barracks thrown back by the palace walls, it is hardly surprising if, from birth, Francis Joseph seemed a natural parade ground officer. In Austria, unlike Prussia or Russia, there was no tradition of educating the heir to the throne first and foremost as a soldier.

A well-known portrait by Ferdinand Waldmüller shows the future emperor at the age of two, wearing a frock but holding a toy musket in his right hand, with a child's helmet above his blonde curls, and his left hand firmly grasping by its wooden head a carefully carved officer doll in trim white uniform. By the age of four he was often dressed up in uniform himself, while toy soldiers became his principal playthings: his Christmas presents in 1834 included a large model of the palace guard from his grandparents, and a hand-painted set of officers and other ranks in finest parade ground order. Boyhood letters to Max, when the brothers were separated by illness or the demands of family itineraries, mention bombardments of forts in the nursery, but the toy soldiers were not mere playthings. Gradually Francis Joseph built up a collection in which every regiment of the army was represented; soon he came to know the detail of every uniform. Not one of these toy soldiers was broken.

'No peace at all around the little ones', Archduchess Sophie complained often enough, especially after the birth in July 1833 of Charles Ludwig, her third son in three years. A daughter, baptized Maria Anna, followed Charles Ludwig in October 1835, but she was extremely delicate. To her mother's grief she soon showed signs of epilepsy and she was to die shortly after her fourth birthday. But, apart from this tragedy to a much-loved little sister, Sophie's sons had a happy childhood. At Ischl they wore *lederhosen* and followed a simple life in contrast to the traditionally strict Court etiquette of Vienna. In practice, however, the 'Spanish' ceremonial stiffness had eased under Emperor Francis and there was a certain cosy domesticity during the winter months.

In the third week of December 1834 Francis Joseph was allowed to join his grandparents at dinner in the Hofburg. His mother was well satisfied with her son's natural confidence in what to a four year old might well have proved a disastrous ordeal. Franzi was, of course, used to the presence of his imperial grandfather. The old Emperor had never stood aloof from childish pleasures and often visited the nursery, chatting happily with the boy who would eventually succeed to his crowns. But by that December everyone at the Hofburg sensed he was unlikely to live much longer; a note of valedictory gloom runs through the pages of more than one diary chronicling events at Court that winter. Stories began to circulate in Vienna which emphasized the middle-class bonhomie the Emperor readily affected and which always pleased his subjects. It was said that he had complained openly of the 'silliness' of the government's censorship. There was a slightly mocking undertone to the phrase '*Der gute Kaiser Franz*', which was so often heard in Vienna in the early 1830s; but there was a loyal affection in it, too.

'Good Emperor Franz' survived the Christmas of 1834 and the bitterly cold January which followed. On 12 February, with his grandson standing briefly beside him, he looked down benevolently at the Court Ball which celebrated his sixty-seventh birthday. Eleven nights later the Emperor and Empress went to the Burgtheater. On that Monday a sharp north wind was blowing into the city from the frozen plains beyond the Danube; less than forty-eight hours after leaving the Burgtheater the Emperor was confined to bed with pneumonia. Archduchess Sophie was touched by her son's concern; for when, on Thursday, Franzi heard his Grandpapa was so ill that he could drink only tea, he decided, in a nice gesture of family solidarity, that it was his duty also to drink nothing but tea. Over the weekend the Emperor's strength rallied, but by Monday afternoon it was clear he was sinking fast, and his grandson was taken on one last visit to the sick room; he died that night, in the small hours of 2 March, plunging Vienna into mourning on the last day of the Fasching carnival.

The imperial titles passed to the unfortunate Crown Prince Ferdinand. But on his deathbed Francis had signed two documents, addressed to his successor: one enjoined Ferdinand to defend and uphold the free activity of the Roman Catholic Church; the other was a political testament, insisting that Ferdinand should 'not displace the basic structure of the

State', and should take 'no decision on public affairs . . . without consulting
. . . my most faithful servant and friend Prince Metternich'. More surprising than this recommendation was the dying Emperor's counsel over
dynastic questions. Francis I was survived by six brothers, three of whom
were far abler than himself: Archduke Charles, respected throughout
Europe as a military commander; Archduke Joseph who showed rare
skills of diplomatic tact as 'Palatine' (governor) of Hungary; and Archduke
John, who was a good soldier and a discriminating patron of the arts
in Graz (where he delighted the Styrians, and shocked his family, by
morganatically marrying the daughter of the village postmaster of Bad
Aussee). But Francis's political testament passed over all three gifted
Archdukes and recommended as Ferdinand's guide the youngest of the
brothers, Archduke Ludwig, dull and unmarried. To Sophie's dismay,
the testament gave no status to Francis Charles, the heir apparent. Not
that she had any illusions over her husband's abilities: she merely wished
him at the centre of affairs as trustee for their eldest son's interests.

Francis I's death made an impression on a small boy of five. His uncle
Ferdinand, the new Emperor, was kind and gentle but a pathetic sight on
those rare occasions when he took the salute or wore the robes of sovereignty. By contrast, the young Francis Joseph conjured up in his mind
an image of his grandfather as an ideal ruler, though in reality he had
been a very ordinary monarch – and knew it. 'My son has still no
attachment so strong as that which he bears to the memory of his grandfather', the Archduchess told Frances Trollope two years later. But the
first months of the new reign coincided with the emergence of Francis
Joseph from the nursery to the schoolroom. Count Heinrich Bombelles,
who became his principal tutor was a soldier-courtier, trained as a diplomat. Metternich warmly approved of Bombelles: 'one of the few men
who thought as I thought, saw as I saw, and wished as I wished', he recalled
a few years later. Bombelles was assisted by Count Johann Coronini-
Cronberg, who as personal Chamberlain was primarily responsible for
the young Archduke's military training. The Coronini family estates were
in Gorizia, a province part-Italian and part-Slovene. Coronini was a good
horseman, stiffly unimaginative and, like so many senior officers, totally
non-national; he was a servant of the dynasty rather than in any sense an
'Austrian' by sentiment or conviction. Since Francis Joseph's main interest
as a boy was in soldiering, Coronini had a greater influence in shaping
his character than did Bombelles.

It was, however, Bombelles who presented the Archduchess with the
first of several elaborate programmes of study. Her eldest son would be
expected to progress from 18 hours a week spent over his books at the
age of six to 36 or 37 hours at the age of eight, 46 hours at eleven, and

between 53 and 55 hours a week at the age of fifteen. As an educational programme, the scheme had grave defects, even by the standards of the time: there was too much rote-learning, too little emphasis on how to think, and – apart from his brothers – virtually no contact with other youngsters in a classroom. Despite half a century of social upheaval there was little difference between what Francis Joseph was learning in the late 1830s and what his grandfather had been learning sixty years before, except for increased attention to minor languages within the Empire. Training in spiritual matters was entrusted in the first instance to a Court chaplain, Joseph Colombi, but the Archduchess sought advice from the ultramontane Abbot von Rauscher, who personally supervised the young Archduke's instruction in moral philosophy from the age of fourteen onwards. By then, too, the Bombelles scheme had been revised by Colonel Franz von Hauslaub, but not in any liberal spirit; Hauslaub's programme was specifically designed to include 'instruction in military science.'

This programme of education remained far narrower than the syllabus followed by Albert of Saxe-Coburg some twelve years earlier and was in marked contrast to the precepts laid down by Baron Stockmar in 1842 for the Prince of Wales. Even in Berlin the future Emperor Frederick – fifteen months younger than Franzi – was, thanks to his mother's insistence, receiving a more liberal and scientific education to offset his Potsdam military training. Fortunately, while every lesson in history, philosophy and Christian apologetics emphasized to Francis Joseph the divine omnipotence of kingship, he was also taught that imperial sovereignty carried obligations and that it was his duty to protect his subjects from injustice as well as to uphold monarchical rule. Neither character nor training inclined him to despotism.

Francis Joseph showed greater academic promise in boyhood than the familiar word portraits of the mature Emperor would lead one to expect. He was a good linguist. Even before his eighth birthday he was writing letters in French to his mother which seem to have been his own work, for he asks the recipient to let him know if his grammar or choice of words are at fault. Occasionally, too, he lapsed into a German phrase, as if he could not think how to express himself in French. In 1841 he was sufficiently confident in the language to tell his mother what he regarded as an amusing incident: the noise made by the boys at their early morning gymnastics in Schönbrunn aroused his widowed grandmother's septuagenarian chamberlain whose anger, while draped in a dressing-gown, 'made us laugh'. By that spring Francis Joseph was already learning Magyar and Czech as well as French; before the end of the year he had begun Italian, too. A thin veneer of classical studies soon followed, with a little Latin acquired at twelve and less Greek at thirteen.

He possessed a natural aptitude for drawing. Some sketches made in northern Italy soon after his fifteenth birthday, and later printed, may well have been touched up by the lithographers who reproduced them: a priest astride a donkey outside an inn looks almost too carefully well-fed and the fetlocks of a horse in a second drawing seem professionally tidy. But, though the draughtsmanship may not be entirely original, the composition of the sketches is good, and it is interesting that earlier scribbles in the margin of letters to Max show a similar sense of fun and attention to detail. Francis Joseph had a sharp eye and a ready perception of the ridiculous. He enjoyed, too, a finely appreciative sense of landscape, simply and naturally expressed in his boyhood letters to his mother. When in the early autumn of 1844 he travelled to the Vorarlberg and the Tyrol, it is hardly surprising to find him as excited by a steamboat trip on the Bodensee as any other fourteen year old would have been, but his greatest enthusiasm was reserved for the magnificent alpine scenery around Merano, Bolzano and Innsbruck. In particular, he admired the Stubaital, 'the loveliest valley I have seen'.

Yet, though both Archdukes responded warmly to the beauties of nature, their mother feared they would become as antipathetic to the finer aspects of cultural life as their father. They liked the theatre (as had Francis I); it is true that early letters show more interest in the mechanics of scene changing than anything on the stage, but this is hardly surprising among boys of their age. Their mother, however, sought to counter incipient Habsburg philistinism by welcoming selected writers and performers into the family circle. Thus the three Archdukes listened to Hans Christian Andersen telling them his stories in the Hofburg itself, and much later – when Francis Joseph was fifteen – Jenny Lind was treated as a personal friend by the Archduchess, who vainly hoped that the soprano's presence at Schönbrunn would break through Max's wall of tone deafness and arouse in her elder son a taste for harmonies more rhapsodic than the steady beat of a military march. Nothing could make Francis Joseph appreciate good music. He did, however, enjoy dancing, even as a boy: 'Tomorrow Papa is giving a Ball in the Gallery, where 20 couples will be able to dance to the enlivening strains of Herr Lanner's music', runs an excited letter to Maxi in May 1841; and other correspondence and diary entries show that he took the floor himself at an early age. He liked going to the ballet, too, when he passed into adolescence. During Fanny Elssler's short season at the Karntnertortheater in the spring of 1846 he saw her dance in *La Esmeralda, La Jolie Fille de Gand* and in a showy divertissement of Jules Perrot, *La Paysanne Grand Dame*. Like his cousin Reichstadt before him, he became an Elssler fan, continuing to acclaim the ballerina on her return to her native city until she retired, three years after his accession.

In admiring the dancer-actress from Gumpendorf the young Francis Joseph was following the fashionable taste of the Viennese public. So it was, too, with much else that he liked and disliked. This was a period of theatrical achievement but not of great innovative drama, as in the previous decade. Joseph Schreyvogel, the modernizer of the Hofburg Theatre, died when Francis Joseph was still a baby, and Grillparzer gave up writing plays when his comedy *Weh dem, der lügt!* flopped in March 1838. During the early years of Emperor Ferdinand's reign, the theatre-going public enjoyed the Volkstücke dialect plays at the Theater an der Wien and the Theater an der Leopoldstadt, the earlier refinements of traditional comedy lapsing into farce, liberally intermingled with song. The almost insatiable demand for these Volkstücke plays was matched by the mounting popularity of the rhythmic, gliding music of Joseph Lanner and the elder Strauss: it was a happy culture, if not a subtle one, and Francis Joseph shared it to the full. Long after he reached maturity he would use Viennese dialect phrases in conversational moments of relaxation; but this particular habit is more likely to have come from the affectations of an officers' mess in his adolescence than from early days in the nursery. Luise von Sturmfeder was too conventional a Prussian to tolerate vernacular usage.

In the late 1850s a more earnest generation began to ridicule the style of life which had prevailed at the end of Francis I's reign and throughout the early years of his successor. *Fliegende Blätter*, a humorous journal published in Munich, invented a naive character called Gottfried Biedermeier, the 'worthy Meier' (which, sometimes as Maier or Meyer, is one of the commoner surnames). He was first portrayed as a poetaster, perpetrating sentimental verse, some of it the genuine surplus doggerel of a well-meaning village schoolmaster in Bohemia. Sustained satirical attacks were then mounted on all that Biedermeier was held to represent: the virtues of thrift, diligence and cleanliness; the limited vision of an unambitious middle class content to seek a quiet life in comfortable domesticity. From Bavaria these lampoons crossed into Austria, where the emerging tastes of a thriving middle class had set new fashions in provincial cities, as well as in Vienna. Nowadays the graceful paintings, furniture and porcelain of the Biedermeier era, with its decorative clocks, lyrical landscapes and smug portraiture are accepted as a cheerful expression of bourgeois faith in stability and progress. But at the height of Francis Joseph's reign 'Biedermeier' was a term of amused contempt, the elevation of mediocrity into a generalized style of expression. The myth became rapidly extended until the dismissive adjective 'Biedermeier'

began to be applied retrospectively to all the decorative arts and architecture, painting and music which emerged from the new social order
after the Napoleonic Wars. An Age of Stifled Revolt could not forgive the
Biedermeier era for being an Age of Acquiescence. From so preposterous
a misreading of recent cultural history it was easy enough for the youthful
intellectuals of the early 1870s to scoff at their sovereign's limited attain-
ments: Francis Joseph became a Biedermeier figurine in uniform, exalted
in his polished saddle astride a horse groomed to perfection.

The caricature was, of course, unfair. It ignored the Emperor's sense
of duty and discipline, the inner conviction that accession to the throne
required an immolation of personality for fear that any display of feeling,
or any impulsive action, might impeach the dignity of monarchy; his
character was more clearly defined than he would reveal on public
occasions. But the Biedermeier image was not entirely false. From his
letters it is clear that the interests which Francis Joseph retained in later
life were shaped by the fashions of his boyhood. This is not surprising:
temperament and taste always respond more readily to the contemporary
mood than to the formal teaching of precepts in an improvised code,
however well intentioned. Twelve years of Francis Joseph's early life were
spent in absorbing the facts presented to him by his tutors but, apart from
a desire to widen his vocabulary in the four foreign languages he studied,
there was no stirring of intellectual curiosity. By the age of eighteen a fine
memory was excellently trained. The mind, however, was not disposed
to analyse ideas or to question acknowledged truths.

These limitations remained with Francis Joseph throughout his life.
They explain why his inclination was towards chatter rather than serious
conversation, why he respected musical virtuosity and not originality in
composition, and preferred tableaux vivants to histrionic declamation on
the stage. But his education made him a perfectionist in matters of detail,
and he expected high standards; a slipshod performance of Schiller at the
Burgtheater would incur an imperial rebuke, especially if an actor forgot
his lines. Despite his boyhood skill at drawing, he never pretended to be
a connoisseur of the visual arts. Painters, he instinctively felt, should
be decorators, their pictures celebrating military victories or faithfully
reproducing the colour and contours of familiar landscape, notably in
the Salzkammergut. His mother had admired the works of Ferdinand
Waldmüller and Peter Fendi, who depicted the Archdukes in their infancy
with cosy sentimentality. Waldmüller, in many respects the archetypal
Biedermeier artist, received imperial patronage for the first quarter of
Francis Joseph's reign; and, though Fendi died six years before his
accession, the Emperor approved of the work of his pupils, notably
Friedrich Treml. There was, however, another side to the Fendi school

of painting, not without influence on Francis Joseph; for Fendi could record domestic incidents among the poor in Vienna's outer suburbs without resorting to contrived or condescending pathos. This aspect of the Biedermeier tradition Francis Joseph, too, absorbed. It helped sustain embers of compassion which a less reserved monarch would have kindled into human warmth of feeling.

That human warmth, so rarely shown by Francis Joseph after his accession, was still present when the fourteen-year old Archduke took part in his first military review. On the eve of his thirteenth birthday he became colonel-in-chief of the Third Dragoon Regiment, and in late September 1844 he was considered sufficiently proficient as a horseman to ride at the head of his regiment when it was participating in exercises in Moravia, close to the historic battlefield of Austerlitz. The Dragoon officers were impressed by their honorary colonel. Archduke Albrecht – himself only twenty-eight – wrote to Francis Joseph's father praising his cousin's 'natural friendliness' and tact, his ability to speak easily when in company with the regiment while maintaining 'a certain bearing and dignity such as I have never seen at his age'. When, a year later, the three young Archdukes – Franzi, Maxi and Charles Ludwig – were sent on an official tour of Lombardy-Venetia, Francis Joseph again scored a personal success. Their host was the most respected veteran commander in the Habsburg army, Field Marshal Radetzky, who had fought against the Turks nearly sixty years before and, as Austrian chief-of-staff in 1813, drew up the strategic plans for the campaign which culminated in Napoleon's defeat at Leipzig. Now, with equal application, he staged military reviews, firework displays and exhibitions of horsemanship for his young imperial visitors; there were conducted tours of the defensive bastions of the Quadrilateral, the fortresses Radetzky was modernizing at Peschiera, Mantua, Legnano and in Verona itself. From the Roman arena in Verona the Archdukes watched a military reconnaissance balloon ascending into the sky. Radetzky was convinced of the importance of aeronautics. Four years later he authorized the first use of airborne missiles, with explosive balloons released from the mainland to harass Italian patriot insurgents besieged in Venice.

The presence of the Archdukes in Verona, and later in Venice, posed a security risk, even though Radetzky himself thought it unlikely that Italian hostility to Austrian rule would endanger their lives. He was right. Girls threw flowers from balconies of the houses in central Verona and thousands of Venetians cheered the three brothers as they were escorted down the Grand Canal by a small fleet of gondolas, late on a warm September evening. The combination of torchlit palaces, bells ringing out from a hundred churches, moonlight over the lagoon, and – for the first ever time – gas lamps in the Piazza San Marco excited Francis Joseph, and (as he also wrote to his mother) he was gratified at finding the four bronze horses, filched from Byzantium by a thirteenth century Doge and carried off to Paris by General Bonaparte, 'back in their rightful place' above the central doors of the basilica. There were no patriotic liberal protests in Venice, whose citizens were criticized in the more ardently nationalistic towns of central Italy for their lukewarm response to the national cause.

If their journey was intended to introduce the Archdukes to the complexities of the Italian problem, it failed. The Kingdom of Lombardy-Venetia was the most highly industrialized region of the Monarchy at that time, a development which, over the following three years, heightened the struggles between the north Italian peoples and their sovereign's representatives. But, not surprisingly, the young Archdukes kept away from Milan, where anti-Austrian feeling was already intense, and they saw nothing of industrialized Lombardy. Apart from the military instruction accorded to Francis Joseph by Radetzky's staff, the boys were essentially tourists on an educational holiday, an experience which made the most sensitive of the three brothers, the thirteen-year old Maximilian, an Italophile. Francis Joseph – older, more suspicious by temperament, and ready to accept unquestioningly all he was told by the veteran Marshal and his staff – did not share his brother's enthusiasm for everything south of the Alps. Francis Joseph recognized that there was a natural antipathy between German-Austrians and Italians. Yet he failed to understand how deeply the people of Lombardy and Venetia resented the presence of the Austrian 'whitecoats' among them. One in three of the infantry battalions under Radetzky's command at the time of the imperial visit were Italian, and the Marshal assumed that their military honour would ensure their lasting loyalty. In 1848 Francis Joseph was both surprised and disillusioned by what he regarded as a rebellion in his imperial uncle's Italian-speaking kingdom. Almost half of Radetzky's Italian infantrymen fought against the dynasty, a transfer of allegiance which hardened the mood of the old Marshal in the last years of his long life and intensified the young Emperor's hostility to the Italian cause.

From the daily journal she began to keep in 1841, it is clear that Archduchess Sophie was amused rather than perturbed by the totally different response of her sons to their brief visit to Lombardy. In that autumn of 1845 Italy was not yet a pressing problem for the government in Vienna; the agitation against the Habsburg yoke only became dangerous in the peninsula as a whole after the election of the allegedly liberal pope, Pius IX, in the following June. The Archduchess was determined that Francis Joseph should be well-versed in current problems, for ten years of Ferdinand's nominal reign had convinced her – and most of the Court –

that the accession of a young and assertive emperor could not long be delayed. Sophie remained in close touch with political affairs, her influence strengthened by the firm backing she received from the long-suffering Empress Maria Anna, who was painfully aware of her husband's inability to understand state documents or political argument.

Sophie's ambitions never again sustained so sharp a blow as the rebuff of 1835, when Emperor Francis's will excluded her husband from the central council of government. There followed some eighteen months of political in-fighting, in which Archduke John methodically and unobtrusively undermined the primacy of Metternich. By Christmas 1836 the Archduchess was satisfied by the creation of a 'Staatskonferenz' – a virtual Council of Regency – consisting of Archdukes Ludwig and Francis Charles, Chancellor Metternich and minister of state Count Kolowrat-Liebsteinsky, a great Bohemian landowner, whose skilful financial retrenchment over the previous six years made him a potential challenger to Metternich's long ascendancy. So intense was the antagonism between the two statesmen that the Staatskonferenz was threatened with permanent paralysis. If the Archduchess may be believed, effective government was possible only through the enterprise and initiative of Francis Charles: 'Whenever a decision has to be taken, Uncle Ludwig needs my husband's support to counter his modesty and timidity', she claimed. There is no other evidence that Francis Charles played so active a role in government. He may, however, have been encouraged by his wife and the more far-sighted 'absentee' Archdukes – his uncles Joseph, Charles and John – to stiffen Ludwig's resistance to Kolowrat; for only a stubbornly obtuse chairman, deaf to plausible argument, could have checked a Minister of State who showed such super-efficient mastery of detail at the council table.

So weak was the centre of government that, in practice, the day-to-day running of the Monarchy depended on the rulings of a larger council of seventeen specialists, co-opted from the principal departments of state, rather than on the Staatskonferenz itself. But, ultimately, executive authority remained vested in the Staatskonferenz; and in this political confusion the role of the Archduchess Sophie, speaking ventriloquially at the conference table through her husband, became all important for Metternich, despite his earlier misgivings at the prospect of a Bavarian-born princess meddling in government. From the closing weeks of 1836 until the opening months of 1848 there was, accordingly, a tacit pact of political convenience between Archduchess and Chancellor; the way would be smoothed for the early accession of Sophie's eldest son, under the veteran statesman's tutelage.

As parents, Metternich and Sophie encouraged a certain companionship between their children. For, although the Chancellor was sixty-seven in 1840 and a grandfather, he was also the father of four youngsters: his second wife had died within a fortnight of giving birth to their only child, Richard (eighteen months older than Francis Joseph), but in 1831 he married for the third time. Princess Melanie Metternich, a Zichy-Ferraris by birth, was the same age as the Archduchess, and in six years she became the mother of a daughter (named after her) and three more boys, one of whom died in infancy. Melanie was imperious and supremely tactless, a natural sparring partner for the Archduchess Sophie. But she saw the social advantages of close association with the dynasty. Her journal entry for 8 May 1838 records Franzi's first train journey (on the earliest completed section of the Vienna-Brno line) and her determination that the young Metternichs would not miss such an occasion: 'Went with the children and mother to look at the locomotive. Clement had been on a trip by train along with the Dowager Empress, Archduchess Sophie, the Archdukes – among whom we found even the little Archduke Francis Joseph – and Count Kolowrat. The excursion by this new device was eminently successful and everyone was well pleased with it.' At Christmas 'the little Archduke' and his two brothers were invited to the children's ball at the Chancellery, a regular event in their lives over the next few years. Richard Metternich and his half-sister would always be among the selected group of boys and girls invited to the archducal birthday parties at Schönbrunn.

The youngsters never became close friends, as children or as adolescents. Francis Joseph fettered his leisure hours, exhorting himself to work harder, even on days when most boys were content to enjoy themselves. His journal for 18 August 1845 reads: 'My birthday, and more important still my fifteenth. Fifteen years old – only a little more time to go to get educated! I must really pull my socks up (*muss ich mich sehr anstrengen*), really mend my ways!'. These resolutions, it should be added, did not keep him away from a birthday stag-hunt with his father. He cannot have been such a really impossible prig for, though he may have felt inadequate beside the precocious Metternichs, he could make friends of his own choosing. Closest among them, from the age of sixteen onwards, was his cousin, Prince Albert of Saxony, but at twelve or thirteen he liked to play with 'Charly' and 'Franzl C.', the sons of his instructors, Bombelles and Coronini; they remained his personal companions until the upheaval of 1848. Dénes Széchényi, a young offshoot of the large and culturally distinguished Hungarian family, joined his circle of intimates when Francis Joseph was sixteen. So, too, did 'Eddy' Taaffe, a mischievous lad with a keen sense of fun, three years his junior. Eventually Taaffe won a slightly puzzled respect in Europe as Count Eduard Taaffe, the part-

Irish nobleman who 'muddled through' as Austrian prime minister for fourteen years. But in the 1840s he was the young Archduke's riding companion, his skill sharpening Francis Joseph's desire to raise the standard of his horsemanship even higher. By contrast, Richard von Metternich was staid and studious, the dutiful son of his father, just as Francis Joseph was a dutiful son of his mother. In this relationship there could be mutual respect, but never easy understanding. For a few months, immediately following the Archduke's seventeenth birthday, they were jointly initiated into statecraft by Richard's father at weekly sessions in the state chancellery. But, by then, Prince Metternich's hold on European affairs was weakening. It is doubtful if either young man profited greatly from such high-powered instruction. In all, there cannot have been more than twenty hours of these tutorial sessions.

In Hungary, the Habsburg lands whose peoples most resented the Chancellor's centralist theories of government, Metternich made use of Francis Joseph even before he became his occasional pupil. Hungary was constitutionally unique, a kingdom within the Empire which possessed an elective system of county government as well as its bicameral Diet; and members of the Diet jealously safeguarded its ancient right to accord its sovereign the Hungarian soldiery and revenue his ministers required only in return for royal approval of its laws. The emergence of a Hungarian reform movement, moderate in the 1820s but intensely nationalistic twenty years later, convinced Metternich of the need to 'so manipulate the constitution that it becomes possible to govern Hungary in the regular manner' (as, in 1841, he told a session of the Ministerial Council, the seventeen specialists who advised the Staatskonferenz). Thereafter Metternich sought to create a neo-conservative political group of Hungarian magnates, who would emphasize loyalty to the Habsburg dynasty. He intended this creed to serve as an alternative to the Magyar patriotism so warmly invoked by the popular idol, Lajos Kossuth, and accepted by many Hungarian noble families as well as by the middle classes in town and country. When in the second week of January 1847 Archduke Joseph died, after half a century in Hungary, Francis Joseph was sent to Ofen (Buda) for the Palatine's obsequies, with Bombelles to advise him. The young Archduke's evident progress in learning Magyar and his tact and apparent interest in all that he saw in this first brief journey into the Hungarian lands made a favourable impression, which Metternich was determined to exploit.

Yet there could be little doubt of the real feelings of the Hungarians; a fortnight after Francis Joseph's visit to Buda, students across the river in Pest set fire to the German theatre, burning it to the ground. To send the Archduke back to Buda in the autumn as Ferdinand's representative at the installation of the new Palatine – Joseph's son, Stephen – showed great confidence in his bearing and personal nerve. On this occasion he delivered a speech in Magyar which was well received, even by Kossuth personally. A few weeks later Francis Joseph was among the Hungarians once more, on this occasion at Bratislava for the opening of the momentous Diet, which was to be dominated by Kossuth and his radical reformers. Even in the Diet's honeymoon days, when defiant rebellion was still a long way off, Francis Joseph could sense the mounting excitement, the 'terrific agitation' as he wrote at the time. When revolution shook the Monarchy a year later, he was not so much taken by surprise as puzzled by its persistence. He had seen for himself more of the troubled regions of the empire he was to inherit than historians generally acknowledge. But mere acquaintance does not in itself bestow insight.

By now he was spending less hours in the study. Often in the spring and summer of 1847, and increasingly during the winter, he was in uniform. All too frequently he would have a black armband around the sleeve of his white tunic, for there was a high Habsburg mortality rate in the eleven months after the Palatine's death. In early May Francis Joseph was at the head of his regiment for the funeral of the great army commander, Archduke Charles; six months later he attended the funeral of his host on the moonlit gondola procession in Venice, Archduke Charles's third son, Frederick, the nominal commander-in-chief of the Imperial navy; and Francis Joseph went into mourning yet again shortly before Christmas, when his aunt Marie Louise was buried in the family vault of the Kapuzinerkirche. But he was also experiencing – and enjoying – military life away from the parade ground. That autumn he joined his regiment for field exercises in Bohemia, staying on the Taaffe family estate and meeting, for the first time, Prince Alfred Windischgraetz, the commanding general in Prague. At seventeen he was making high claims on his reserves of confidence, assuming a dignity of bearing in the regiment which concealed the diffidence he felt among contemporaries whose upbringing had been less carefully regulated than his own.

Archduchess Sophie's diaries record a mother's pride in her eldest son, slim and handsome in his Hussar uniform. But she was never dotingly foolish; there were blemishes on that proto-imperial image, and she knew it. In his mother's company – and even more under the disparaging gaze of Melanie Metternich – Francis Joseph became woodenly self-conscious. He was too stiff and lifelessly impassive during receptions at Court, the Archduchess complained. With the best of intentions she set about overcoming his inhibitions. Early in December 1847 she hit upon a fitting solution. Amateur theatricals had been a popular feature of German Court life for over a century: why should not Francis Joseph immerse himself in some light-hearted comedy? A romping role, full of wit and humour, played privately in the Hofburg before the imperial family, the Metternichs and other luminaries of Court would teach him how to present himself happily and easily. The Bertrams of Mansfield Park, in Jane Austen's novel, chose Augustus Kotzebue's *Lovers' Vows* for their amusement, and it was to Kotzebue that the Archduchess, too, turned; he had, after all, been director of the Hofburg Theatre long before that unfortunate day in 1819 when he was assassinated as a police spy by a German theological student in Mannheim. But Sophie settled, not for *Das Kind der Liebe* (*Lover's Vows*), but for the, sightly older, five act farce *Wirrwarr* (*Confusion*). Her eldest son could play Fritz Hurlebusch, a country squire's roguish heir and ward.

Francis Joseph disliked the idea intensely. From a reading of the play, one sympathizes with him: Hurlebusch is a habitual joker, amiably polite in the family circle, while throwing aside sardonic comments to the audience; in the final scene he must hide under a table, where he hears his cousin Babet, who had spurned his advances, avow her secret love for him; the curtain falls as they are about to marry and live happily ever after. Francis Joseph told his mother that Maximilian was ideal for the role and coveted it, but she was adamant: Richard Metternich could be in the cast; Dénes Széchényi and Charly Bombelles, too; Marie Széchényi was to play Babet; and, at fourteen, Charles Ludwig might be the night-watchman; but Franzi was to play Hurlebusch. Not even the death of Marie Louise could save her nephew from the stage debut he dreaded; the performance was not cancelled. It was postponed until the end of court mourning.

Wirrwarr was duly presented in the Alexander wing of the Hofburg at 10 pm on 9 February 1848. 'A wonderful production', the Archduchess noted in her diary. She said nothing of Francis Joseph's acting. Nor did Melanie Metternich in her journal, though she questioned the choice of title: why 'confusion' at such a time in the Monarchy's history? From the awed admiration with which Francis Joseph later commented on good theatrical presentation, he probably hated every minute on the stage, though he dutifully learned his lines. None of Hurlebusch's waggishness was grafted on to his character, perhaps fortunately. Yet the evening of theatricals proved a turning-point in his life. Never again did he need to accept his mother's ruling on how to present himself. Events overtook his adolescence. Five weeks after watching the play, the Metternichs were fugitives from revolution, hurrying westwards to find sanctuary in England; and within 300 days of his curtain-call, the reluctant actor was to receive the homage of his father and mother, his brothers and all the paladins of the army as their sovereign emperor. Effectively *Wirrwarr* marked the end of Francis Joseph's childhood.

Chapter 3

YEAR OF REVOLUTION

A persistent legend maintains that throughout the winter of 1847–8 Francis Joseph's mother sought the downfall of Metternich and a transition to constitutional government. 'Events enabled a court faction, led by Archduchess Sophie, to pressure Emperor Ferdinand into jettisoning Metternich', a distinguished modern American historian has written. So, certainly, Princess Metternich believed when she looked back on the recent past from the bitterness of exile; she convinced herself that the Archduchess let Kolowrat know he could count on support from a 'dynastic Opposition' if he tried to defeat the Chancellor's proposals at meetings of the Staatskonferenz. She may well have held dark suspicions of a dynastic intrigue as early as the second week in February, when the two women sat watching the private theatricals in the Hofburg; for by then *The Sybilline Books out of Austria*, an anonymous pamphlet blaming Metternich for the sterility of Austrian politics, was the talk of the salons. Rumour correctly identified the author as Captain Moehring, tutor to the five sons of the Viceroy of Lombardy-Venetia, Archduke Rainer. More sensationally the pamphlet carried a dedication to Archduchess Sophie. Could Moehring have put her name forward in such a way without foreknowledge of her convictions? It seemed unlikely.

Yet the dedication, like so much that happened during the spring, took the Archduchess by surprise. There is no evidence she was ever prepared to make any active move against Metternich, nor did she show sympathy for Kolowrat, the ambitious spokesman of a particularly narrow circle of German-Bohemian landowners. Throughout the 1840s she had kept abreast of Europe's affairs. Family letters afforded her an insight into Germany's problems: a half-brother was King of Bavaria; her twin sister was Queen of Saxony; and their elder sister was married to Frederick William IV of Prussia. As well as these private sources, she read the main German newspapers and several French periodicals, defying the Austrian government's clumsy censorship. She was aware of the mounting discontent: the impatience of the younger generation of politicians with Metternich's negative conservatism; the widespread resentment at the arbitrary imposition of taxes; the confusion caused by the election of a so-called 'liberal Pope'. Within the Monarchy she could see for herself the spread of a linguistic, cultural nationalism and the growing frustration of the commercial class in many towns at the bureaucratic barriers hampering the spread of trade. By Christmas 1847 the Archduchess was deeply pessimistic: 'God knows what the future holds for our poor country', she wrote in her journal. But gloomy jottings in a diary are a sign of passive fatalism rather than active conspiracy. Sophie, and the Court with her, waited anxiously upon events.

So, for that matter, did Metternich. On 2 January 1848 he drew up his 'political horoscope' for the year: radical forces would emerge and throw society into confusion, he predicted; the danger-spot was Italy, he insisted, and more precisely Rome. He dismissed the significance of events in Germany or France and the familiar problems of Hungary. At first it seemed as though he was right. Reports reached Vienna of insurrection in Sicily, the grant of a constitution in Naples, and the spread of a liberal agitation through Tuscany and the Papal States. But when, on the last Sunday in February, it was confirmed that Radetzky had proclaimed martial law in Lombardy-Venetia there were also rumours in Vienna of a revolution in France. Next morning – Monday, 28 February – there was a rush of panic selling as soon as the stock exchange opened. By Wednesday the Chancellor, still as imperturbable as ever, felt he should reassure his luncheon guests. Were he to be dismissed from office, he explained, Revolution would have come to Vienna; and that, of course, as he assumed every visitor to the Ballhausplatz must realize, was unthinkable.

Meanwhile the Hungarian Diet, whose opening ceremonies Francis Joseph had attended in the city now known as Bratislava early in November, remained in session. It was on Friday, 3 March, that, with news of the fall of the monarchy in Paris confirmed, Lajos Kossuth made the most historic of all his speeches to the Lower House of the Diet. He urged the establishment of a virtually autonomous Hungary, with a responsible government elected on a broad franchise. It was not a fiery call to arms. He spoke respectfully of the dynasty as a unifying force, welcoming in particular the first steps taken by Archduke Francis Joseph to win the love of the nation; but Kossuth was not the man to compromise. To safeguard Hungary's historic rights for all time, it was essential to change the character of government in the Monarchy; and he called for 'general constitutional institutions which recognized the different nationalities'.

Reports of Kossuth's proposals soon reached Vienna. They produced a triple response: a plea for civil rights and some form of parliamentary government from the Diet of 'Lower Austria' (*Nieder Oesterreich*), the province including the capital and its suburbs; petitions to Emperor Ferdinand from several professional bodies, seeking the removal of police surveillance; and demonstrations by university students for the abolition of censorship, more freedom in education, and liberty of public worship. For the first time there were signs of dynastic Opposition to the Chancellor, but it was not inspired by Archduchess Sophie. She was increasingly alarmed by the unrest: as early as 9 March she recorded in her journal the fear that Vienna would soon suffer the horrors experienced by Paris in 1793 (though one would have thought 1792 a more alarming parallel). It was the popular and pragmatic Archduke John rather than Sophie who began to rally the dynasty; 'Uncle Johann' was induced by a member of the Lower Austrian Diet to come up to Vienna from Graz in the hope that he would give sensible advice to the Staatskonferenz. John found, as he wrote, that Metternich 'was the only person to whom you could talk and he remained convinced he could handle the situation by writing memoranda and delivering long speeches. Everyone else was impossible'.

The events of 1848 were to mould Francis Joseph's character and determine the pattern of his life. But at first, during these heady days of March, there was little change in his customary Hofburg routine. On Sunday afternoon (12 March), while the students awaited news of a petition presented to Ferdinand by two liberal professors, Francis Joseph escorted his mother through the gardens, strolling down to the bastion of the old palace, where they were seen and cheered by some of the demonstrators. There was no positive response from the Court and overnight the mood of the students turned uglier. By nine on Monday morning thousands were gathering outside the Landhaus in the Herrengasse, where the Lower Austria Diet was to meet. A Tyrolean with powerful lungs read Kossuth's speech in a German translation, amid repeated cheers and angry calls for Metternich's resignation. A second deputation went to the Hofburg and the Emperor summoned his Chancellor to the palace soon after midday. But Metternich did not intend to surrender office: he was prepared to talk to the leaders of 'the rabble'; but he urged his fellow councillors to stand firm. It was decided that the thirty-year old Archduke Albrecht, as military commandant of Lower Austria, should close the city gates, for there were rumours of a general attack on property by unemployed labourers squatting outside the walls. When Albrecht's men sought to clear the Herrengasse, some shots rang out: a student and two artisans lay mortally wounded on the cobbles; a journeyman weaver died from a broken skull; and an elderly woman from an almshouse was crushed to death when the demonstrators fled in panic down the narrow street.

The sound of shooting could be heard in the Hofburg, where there was already great confusion. Archduchess Sophie – who had to allow 13, 14 and 15 March to pass before finding time to write up her journal – gathered her sons around her protectively in one room, suddenly emphasizing the immaturity of Francis Joseph, of whose manliness in uniform she had been so proud over the past year. Empress Maria Anna, a close friend ever since she came to Vienna as Ferdinand's bride, was by now convinced of the need for her husband's abdication and assumed that Francis Charles would renounce the succession in favour of his eldest son. But Sophie insisted that the time had not yet come for such a dramatic palace revolution. During Monday afternoon she met Prince Windischgraetz, the commanding general in Bohemia who – though on a purely private visit to Vienna – was summoned to the palace when it was feared Albrecht's inexperience might put the fate of the dynasty at risk. To Windischgraetz Sophie carefully explained that Francis Joseph had not yet attained his majority, 'being more or less still a child'. 'We must set things in order first, before letting him take the reins', she added.

For most of this historic Monday 'the child' was therefore necessarily an onlooker. But not entirely so. During the early evening Archduke Ludwig, the customary chairman of the Staatskonferenz, at last turned against Metternich and asked for his resignation. The Chancellor refused to go unless his sovereign and the Archdukes in line of succession should personally absolve him from the oath he had taken before Emperor Francis's death that he would give loyal support to Ferdinand. Such a gesture of absolution required the presence of both Francis Charles and his eldest son around the Staatskonferenz table; and in this curious way Francis Joseph was ushered into the inner counsels of government. From that moment until his death in 1916 he remained close to the heart of affairs.

Metternich's resignation was announced at nine o'clock on the Monday evening, even though it was Tuesday afternoon before he was able to slip quietly away from the capital with his family. Archduke John returned to Graz, confident he could check the spread of unrest through Styria. Nominally Windischgraetz was given full powers to keep order in the capital, but he never exercised them; unexpectedly Francis Charles emerged as chief spokesman for the government, effectively succeeding Ludwig as chairman of the Staatskonferenz. It was Francis Charles who summoned a special conference, at eleven on Tuesday night, at which he spoke in favour of a constitution; once the Emperor had made such a great concession, Francis Charles argued, all later political demands could be refused on the grounds that these matters must wait until agreement had been reached on the basic instrument of government. The Archdukes Francis Joseph and Albrecht, as well as Windischgraetz and Kolowrat, were present at this conference. Significantly Archduchess Sophie, though not herself present, made it clear that she was unhappy over her husband's proposal; she did not wish to find that, when their son came to the throne, his freedom of action would be constrained by any earlier concessions. Nothing, however, was done that night; far better wait until the celebrations of the Chancellor's fall were over and the popular agitation died down.

Accordingly, on Wednesday afternoon, Francis Joseph joined his father and Emperor Ferdinand for a carriage drive through the inner city which was to test the public mood. That morning the Palatine had arrived in the capital with a large deputation from the Hungarian Diet, intensifying the widespread excitement. There were cheers once more, especially for the good-natured 'Kaiser Ferdl', but outside the Hofburg itself the crowd seemed sullenly suspicious. The drive settled doubts left unresolved at Tuesday night's conference. Some two hours after the carriage's return, a mounted herald rode out to the Michaelerplatz and proclaimed the Emperor's resolve to convene a constituent assembly 'as speedily as possible'. Cabinet government came to Austria on the following Monday, with the appointment of Kolowrat as head of a 'responsible ministry'.

Metternich's fall meant different things to different groups of people, but most hailed it as the end of a supranational repressive system. The pace of revolution quickened, notably at Bratislava where, in the last week of March, the Hungarian Diet carried through a series of sweeping constitutional changes which required their sovereign's assent to the establishment of responsible government in the historic Lands of the Hungarian Crown, too: there would be a Hungarian minister of war, a Hungarian minister of finance and a Hungarian minister 'resident around the King's person'. When the Palatine brought details of these proposed reforms to Vienna the Court complained that, if they became law, the Magyars would share nothing with the other peoples of the Monarchy except the person of the sovereign.

These demands were bad enough for the Court in Vienna. Yet however vexatious they might be, Hungary's striving for independence was at least a recognizable cause, steeped in past history. Other nationalities posed unfamiliar problems or raised old questions in a new form: thus Cracow, a 'free city' until absorbed into the Empire in 1846, remained a seedbed of Polish patriotism; and there was uncertainty over the loyalty of the Roumanian and Serbian minorities. In Zagreb representatives of the

'Triune Kingdom of Croatia, Slavonia and Dalmatia' asserted claims for acceptance of their national identity in a continued voluntary union under the Hungarian crown and reigning dynasty, but they unanimously entrusted executive authority and military command to their chosen governor (*Ban*), Baron Josip Jellaçić; while in Prague the Czechs put forward demands which threatened the power of the great landowners, the German magnates of Bohemia and Moravia. Nor could Vienna entirely escape the Pan-German enthusiasm, which surfaced so dramatically in Berlin and Frankfurt.

In one form or another, each of these issues continued to confound politics throughout Francis Joseph's life and reign. But the most immediate problems were raised by the Italian Question, as the exiled Chancellor had foreseen. The eruption of radical rebellions in Milan and Venice made the Risorgimento a sustained threat to Habsburg primacy in the peninsula. Less than a fortnight after Metternich's fall, King Charles Albert of Sardinia-Piedmont felt in honour bound to answer the call of Italian patriots for a crusade which would sweep the whitecoats back across the Alps. It was this challenge which thrust Austria into war for the first time in a third of a century.

The Austrian army, accustomed to quelling isolated rebellions in the cities of the peninsula, was surprised by the extent of the anti-Habsburg rising. By the third week in March Radetzky, who had already evacuated Milan and fallen back on the fortresses of the Quadrilateral, was appealing to Vienna for military aid; he could count on only 50,000 loyal troops to hold Verona, Peschiera, Mantua and Legnano and protect his communications from Venetian raiders at the head of the Adriatic and guerrilla attacks in the South Tyrol. But before the army could receive reinforcements the Piedmontese claimed a victory, at Goito on 8 April. In Vienna the Kolowrat government seriously considered granting Lombardy independence and Venetia autonomy, in the hopes that the troops deployed in the peninsula could be used to maintain order elsewhere in the Monarchy. But, from a sense of pride and prestige, the army would not willingly pull out of so familiar an arena of battle. Archduke Albrecht, whose father had fought against Bonaparte with distinction in northern Italy half a century before, left Vienna to command a division of Radetzky's army. Understandably Francis Joseph, who was intensely proud of his Hussar commission, wished to accompany his cousin to the Italian Front.

Not yet, however. To his mother's evident relief, the government needed Francis Joseph in Vienna, where the removal of press censorship was stimulating the growth of radical journalism. An uneasy calm prevailed with sudden displays of dynastic loyalty which may – or may not – have been sincere in intention. Thus when Archduchess Sophie and her son took an afternoon drive down the Praterallee they would hear the coffee-house orchestras suddenly switch from a popular tune to the Habsburg anthem, *Gott erhalte Franz den Kaiser*, as the carriage approached and there would be cheers from the townsfolk out walking. But many stolidly respectable Viennese families were ready to affirm their Pan-Germanic sentiments and copied the university students by wearing the black, red and gold cockades of the Frankfurt liberals. Politically, these were confusing days.

By early April Kolowrat seemed about to quit office in despair, although he did not resign until the middle of the month, largely because it was by no means clear who – or what – would succeed him. Meanwhile, to appease the radical trouble-makers, he encouraged Baron von Pillersdorf, his minister of the interior, to go ahead with the preparation of a con-stitution for early publication and discussion. Both Francis Charles and Francis Joseph were asked to examine Pillersdorf's first drafts and amplify his proposals, if they wished, but neither father nor son made any written comment on what was to them an alien document, difficult to com-prehend. Yet, though it was clear Francis Joseph remained ill-prepared for such matters, the Kolowrat government persevered with the attempt to draw him gradually into political life; and on Thursday, 6 April, he received his first official post, Governor of Bohemia.

Kolowrat assumed that the appointment would enable the young Arch-duke to complement Windischgraetz's military authority, perhaps even to contain it, for the civilian landed magnates of the northern provinces felt a certain mistrust of their colleague's ambitions. But Francis Joseph had no chance to familiarize himself with the tasks ahead of him. He was at once plunged into the complex problems of Czech government. A group of 'German Bohemians resident in Vienna' was quick to seek the new *Statthalter*'s protection for the German language in Bohemia's schools. He received a deputation, but the meeting with Francis Joseph was unproductive, one delegate sadly admitting that the great hope of the dynasty 'did not appear to know what it was all about'. Kolowrat seems to have had second thoughts; for on Saturday morning the ministers went back on Thursday's arrangements. 'In the circumstances ... it would be better' for the Archduke 'not to hurry to take up his appointment', they declared.

Hungary's affairs were more pressing; and on Tuesday Francis Joseph was on his way down the Danube by steamer, accompanying Emperor Ferdinand and his own father to Bratislava for the closing of the Reform Diet. In later years the champions of the dynasty regarded Ferdinand's speech at the ceremonies on the following day as a humiliating surrender to the demands of the revolutionaries, for he gave formal consent to all the thirty-one measures enacted by the Diet over the past six months. Yet at Court there was some hope that these April Laws would give the Monarchy an effective balance of government: there is no evidence that Francis Joseph disapproved of the attempts by his cousin, the Palatine Archduke Stephen, to strike a working compromise with Kossuth and the parliamentarians. The liberals in Vienna were optimistic, too; once again warm cheers greeted the imperial carriages as they sped back to Schönbrunn from the Prater landing-stage after the steamer's return from Bratislava on 13 April. But the Palatine had his critics. Archduchess Sophie consoled herself with the curious constitutional doctrine that, although her son might have witnessed Ferdinand's acceptance of the April Laws, he had not given the reforms his assent and was not therefore bound to uphold them. She noted with approval the subsequent decision of Archduke Stephen's Chamberlain to resign office because he thought the Palatine too sympathetic towards Magyar nationalism. Soon she found room for the ex-Chamberlain, Count Karl Grünne, in her personal service. He was a forty year old devout Catholic, more stolidly conservative in politics than Bombelles, and in character and training a parade-ground officer certain to win her eldest son's warm regard.

On 19 April – Wednesday in Holy Week, and also Emperor Ferdinand's birthday – the Archduchess received a visit from Windischgraetz, who was about to return to Bohemia. The sixty-one year old Prince, who in his boyhood had witnessed the flight of French emigrés from the Revolution, expressed doubts over the wisdom of having the imperial family grouped together in the capital during Easter week: it was a time of traditional open air gatherings in the Prater and this year, on the Tuesday, the text of the Pillersdorf constitution would be published. He therefore warmly backed Francis Joseph's plea to be allowed to join Radetzky's army in Italy, and the Archduchess relented. She had never met the old Field Marshal, but she wrote a letter to him on Easter Eve, expressing confidence in the troops under his command and commending her eldest son to his safe-keeping: 'He is a good and honest boy', she wrote, 'and ever since his childhood has set his heart on a soldier's career'.

Francis Joseph travelled slowly down to the Italian Front, stopping overnight at Salzburg, Innsbruck and Bolzano on the way. He reached field headquarters in Verona before dawn on Saturday, 29 April. Next morning he rode out beside Radetzky to reconnoitre the Piedmontese positions south-west of Verona. 'My most precious possession, my life-blood, I entrust to your faithful keeping', Sophie had written in her letter to the Field Marshal.

One's sympathies go out to the veteran commander, with such new and unwanted responsibility thrust into his hands. On that same Sunday his troops, dangerously depleted in strength, suffered a rebuff at Pastrengo; and he was painfully aware that they were facing a well-equipped Piedmontese army supplemented by 5,000 enthusiastic volunteers from Tuscany, and awaiting the coming of several thousand men from the Papal States and a large contingent of Neapolitans who were on their way northwards. It is true that, though heavily pressed at Peschiera, the Austrians still held the Quadrilateral fortresses. Moreover, at the turn of the month, Radetzky was encouraged by news of the appointment in Vienna of a vigorous war minister, General Count Latour-Baillet, who made the sending of reinforcements to Italy a matter of urgency. But, for the moment, the Field Marshal could grumble at having his headquarters littered with sword-rattling princelings; for the five young Archdukes already there were now joined by the great hope of the dynasty, full of fire and fervour, eager – as he told his mother – to see 'the Piedmontese swept from our two provinces' and 'the double-headed eagle flying over Turin'. He was attached as an ordnance officer to Baron d'Aspre's corps, covering the approaches to Verona from Mantua.

Francis Joseph received his baptism of fire on 5–6 May, when the Piedmontese army launched three stubborn assaults on the Austrian positions in the suburban village of Santa Lucia. The Archduke was well to the north of the centre of the fray but several cannon-balls fell close to him; he remained cool and totally unperturbed, though urged to seek cover. The victory came as a great morale booster for Radetzky's troops and for dynastic loyalists throughout the Monarchy. Santa Lucia was no Austerlitz or Leipzig; no one reckons it among history's bloodier battles and there were less than 350 Austrian casualties, dead, wounded and missing. But the Santa Lucia positions were strategically important: had the defences been breached, the key fortress of Verona would have been in danger.

To a seventeen year old Hussar, barely two months out of the schoolroom, this experience of battle was a great occasion. 'For the first time I have heard cannon-balls whistling around me and I am perfectly happy', he wrote to his mother. But thereafter discreet postings kept him away from the firing line. He had, however, an opportunity to meet Radetzky's protégés, his 'military children'. Among them were an intrepid brigade commander, Prince Felix Schwarzenberg, and a gifted regimental officer who despised military theorizing, Colonel Ludwig von Benedek. Yet the Archduke's chief service was as a correspondent, someone to emphasize to the Court that, given reinforcements, victory would come swiftly and decisively. Radetzky suspected the government of seeking a compromise settlement, ceding Lombardy to Piedmont. This suspicion seemed confirmed when, as the month ended, he was forced to pull out of Peschiera.

By then, Vienna was again in revolt. Pillersdorf's constitution seemed inadequate, for it did not even specify who would have the vote. On 10 May radical student leaders set up a Central Political Committee and five days later columns of students and labourers marched through the inner city carrying a 'storm petition', demanding a constituent assembly elected by universal male suffrage. The government, short of reliable troops and alarmed by the rapid growth of a National Guard loyal to the Central Committee, capitulated; and on Tuesday, 16 May, the people of Vienna were informed that the Emperor had accepted the student demands, even promising that, from Thursday onwards, the National Guard should share sentry duty at the palace with the regular garrison.

These concessions alarmed both the Empress Maria Anna and Archduchess Sophie. Parallels with the great French Revolution were in everyone's mind: there were rumours of a student mob planning to force an entry into the Hofburg, set it ablaze, and murder the imperial family. 'Here we are held like a mouse in a trap', the Archduchess declared; they would wriggle free before the first National Guard sentries went on duty. On Wednesday the Emperor and Empress set out for an afternoon drive; and so, soon afterwards, did Francis Charles, Sophie and their younger children. But this time the carriages did not make for the Prater; they turned westwards out of the city and through the suburbs. In France, fifty-seven years before, Emperor Ferdinand's great-aunt and her royal husband had been ignominiously intercepted at Varennes and returned as virtual captives to Paris. Now, in this year of revolution, the Habsburg refugees were taking no chances. Their carriages sped throughout that night and all Thursday until, in the failing light of their second evening, they reached Innsbruck. There, behind the familiar yellow ochre stonework of a far smaller Hofburg, the Court was to remain in residence for the next three months.

Francis Joseph warmly approved of the move to Innsbruck; it left the family free from any threat of intimidation by radical students in the capital. Indirectly, however, it also ended his participation in the Italian campaign. Now that he had won wide respect as a courageous young officer under fire, there was a good case for bringing him back to Court and grooming him for the tasks which would confront him after his accession. He might, it was felt, take up his post as Governor of Bohemia; and he certainly needed to be abreast of affairs in Hungary, where Count Lajos Batthyány was striving to keep in office the loyal constitutional government envisaged by the April Laws. By the second week in June Francis Joseph was in Innsbruck.

Sophie was relieved to have her 'most precious possession' restored to her unharmed. She was pleased, too, a week later, when her sister Ludovika, Duchess in Bavaria, arrived in Innsbruck with her daughters Helen, fourteen, and Elizabeth, ten. It was the first time Francis Joseph had met his Bavarian cousins; they seem to have made no impression upon him whatsoever. Elizabeth ('Sisi') fascinated his younger brother, Charles Ludwig, but the Santa Lucia veteran had no time to spare for a little round-faced girl, who was still so much a child that she brought with her in the coach a pet dog and a cageful of canaries. Day after day the Archduke seemed content to remain closeted with General Grünne, whom Sophie induced her son to appoint as his personal chamberlain. Grünne confirmed the High Tory prejudices which Francis Joseph absorbed at Radetzky's headquarters: to both men 'constitutions' were the invention of the devil. When a deputation from Vienna persuaded Ferdinand to appoint Archduke John as his personal representative in the capital, Francis Joseph echoed his mother's disapproval of such contact between dynasty and rabble.

While the Bavarian Princesses were staying at Innsbruck the Court received the first news of effective military backing for a counter-revolution. Not surprisingly it was Windischgraetz, the military commander in Bohemia, who seized the initiative. For several weeks in the late spring he had sought full powers from the government to stamp out the embers of revolt in the capital and the more restless cities of the Empire, but his pleas had always been rejected. In June, however, unrest in Prague gave him the opportunity to strike a blow for the old order at a time when elections for a constituent Reichstag were taking place throughout the Austrian lands.

During the Metternich era Prague was never reckoned one of the more explosive cities of the Empire. Local magnates from German princely families backed a Czech cultural and antiquarian movement which was, at times, sentimentally Slavophile but never aggressively Panslav in sentiment. The growth of factory industries had thrown many home craftsmen out of work and by late May 1848 there was high unemployment in the mills because the delivery of American cotton, normally landed at Trieste, was disrupted by the fighting in the north of Italy. Yet politically Prague remained true to the dynasty, mistrusting 'the rebellious people of Vienna'. When on 1 June a Slav Congress was opened in the city, its leaders wished to emphasize to Ferdinand the loyal support of Slavonic peoples of his Empire, and their conviction of the need for an 'Austria' freed from dependence on Germans and Magyars. Other nationalities proved less cool-headed than the Czechs: Poles, Slovaks, Ruthenes, Serbs, Slovenes and Croats all had different objectives, while radical delegates from outside the Monarchy urged support of Panslav ambitions which presupposed a need to dissolve the Empire entirely. The Congress got out of hand, and Windischgraetz put his troops on the alert, a provocative move with fatal consequences. Clashes between the army and demonstrators became serious on 6 June, and over the following days there were some four hundred casualties in a series of confused skirmishes at hastily improvised barricades. Among the dead was Windischgraetz's wife (who was also a sister of Felix Schwarzenberg); she was hit by a stray bullet as she stood at her window, trying to observe what was happening in the narrow streets below. This misfortune settled Windischgraetz's line of conduct. He refused to receive two missions of would-be mediators sent from Vienna and began shelling central Prague. The city surrendered unconditionally to Windischgraetz on 16 June: martial law was imposed; and military tribunals meted out harsh punishment. The 'conqueror of Prague' received, not a reprimand for insubordination, but a warm letter of gratitude signed by Emperor Ferdinand. From St Petersburg came further congratulations and a high military decoration; Tsar Nicholas I saw himself as the custodian of the old order now that Metternich was gone, and he recognized in the army commander of Bohemia a natural ally against Revolution.

Archduchess Sophie welcomed the news from Prague: had she not emphasized to Windischgraetz in March the 'need to set things in order' before her son came of age? Sophie remained in close touch with Windischgraetz. She was heartened, too, by the attachment to the Emperor's suite of Felix Schwarzenberg, as spokesman for 'Papa' Radetzky and the army in Lombardy-Venetia. That, after all, was the decisive battle-front: 'All Austria is in thy camp' ran a line in Grillparzer's famous ode to Radetzky, published in the *Donauzeitung* of 8 June; and Schwarzenberg emphasized the truth behind the poetic apostrophisation. Certainly after 25 July, when Radetzky defeated the Piedmontese army at Custozza, there was no more talk, either among the ministers in Vienna or at Innsbruck, of seeking a compromise peace with King Charles Albert. Within a fortnight the whole of Lombardy had been cleared of the invaders and Charles Albert was glad to accept an armistice. This was a decisive moment in the counter-revolution. Latour, the war minister, no longer had to find troops to send down to Verona; there was some prospect that, in the near future, units could be withdrawn from Italy to restore order elsewhere in the Monarchy.

Meanwhile, three days before Radetzky's victory, a newly elected assembly (*Reichstag*) met in Vienna's imperial Riding School. Delegates came from every part of the Empire, except Lombardy-Venetia and Hungary (which had its own Diet, opened by the Palatine Archduke Stephen in Buda early in July). Although there was friction between some

39

national groups in the Reichstag and scuffles broke out in the narrow streets around the Riding School, there seemed no threat of further violence in the capital. The most lasting achievement of the Reichstag – the emancipation of the peasantry from feudal dues and obligations – was carried through peacefully in the second week in August. Archduke John, the ministers and the deputies, all urged the Court to return to the capital, and Ferdinand and the Empress duly left Innsbruck as soon as the report of the armistice with Piedmont was confirmed. Francis Joseph accompanied them as far as Ischl where, with Grünne now acting as his chief adviser, he called on Archduke Ludwig, who chose to remain in the Salzkammergut and leave affairs of state to more active members of the family. Not entirely, however. News of a plan for Francis Joseph to visit England, where Metternich had settled in exile, stirred him into strong opposition: it would be far better for Franzi to wait upon events in Austria, he told Sophie.

It was therefore at Schönbrunn that Francis Joseph passed his eighteenth birthday and reached the age of majority. Outwardly there was nothing unusual about the day itself or the festivities which continued for much of the week. From his parents he received a gift of two beautifully decorated meerschaums, for he was already a habitual pipe-smoker; he attended a Te Deum and a military parade to celebrate the victory in Italy. Yet affairs were far from normal. Tension remained high: the troops drawn up for inspection came, not only from historic regiments in the garrison, but from units of the National Guard, the citizen militia established in March; and a relaxed day with his younger brothers at a village festival was cut short by a plea from Grünne to return to the palace, as there were clashes between unemployed and soldiery in the poorer districts of Vienna. Worse rioting followed in mid-September, when the University was put into a state of indefinite vacation in the hope of dispersing the students and keeping them away from allegedly left-wing academics. The Reichstag, too, came under suspicion when by a narrow majority it threw out a proposed vote of thanks to Radetzky, for his victories in Italy. The rebuff angered the veteran Field Marshal. Unlike his colleague in Bohemia, Radetzky liked to stay so far as possible above politics, but he resented this gesture by the Reichstag; he told war minister Latour – himself a General of the old school – that he would never tolerate attacks on the honour of the officer corps, and he expressed alarm at the prospect of decisions over the future of the army passing into 'the hands of mere boys and contemptible agitators'.

There was no precedent for a military coup in the whole history of Imperial Austria. Over-ambitious generals had been effectively discouraged for the past two centuries, deterred perhaps by the fate of

Wallenstein in the Thirty Years War. Yet by September it seemed clear to outside observers – including the British ambassador – that the future of the Monarchy depended on its military commanders and, allegedly, on a camarilla of generals and courtiers with influence over the young Archduke. Here the key figure was thought to be Windischgraetz: he insisted on holding autumn manoeuvres in Moravia, thus massing a large army within a few days march of Vienna; and he strengthened his links with the Court through the appointment in late August of a trusted staff officer, Prince Joseph Lobkowitz, to serve as adjutant-general to the Emperor. Recent historical scholarship has played down the role of the camarilla, emphasizing the discord between the rival commanders, but Windischgraetz personally had little doubt of his objective. He would lead a counter-revolution, designed to perpetuate aristocratic rule in central Europe through the agency of the Habsburgs. He presented Lobkowitz with a contingency plan in case the imperial family had to flee the capital a second time: no more slipping away to the alpine provinces, as in May; 'the Emperor and all the imperial family' must head northwards 'by way of Krems to Olmütz, not in flight, but under the protection of the army'. 'Then', Windischgraetz added in confidence, 'I shall conquer Vienna, the Emperor will abdicate in favour of his nephew, and I shall proceed to occupy Ofen (Buda)'.

Hungary determined the pace of events that autumn. Throughout the summer the Hungarians behaved with exemplary loyalty, within the constitutional structure of the April Laws: Archduke Stephen remained Palatine; Count Lajos Batthyány served as prime minister of a coalition which included the cultural 'father of his people' István Szechényi and the cautious lawyer Ferencz Deák as well as the more radical Kossuth. In early June Batthyány travelled to Innsbruck, where he promised to raise funds for 40,000 recruits to swell Radetzky's army in Italy. Yet, though their prime minister might be treated with respect, the Court looked on all Hungarians with suspicion. If the Batthyány ministry made the April Laws really work, then the centre of the Habsburg Monarchy would effectively shift from Vienna to Buda, with the Magyar magnates succeeding to the privileged position held by the Germanised Bohemian nobility. It was therefore in the Court's interest to encourage the discontented non-Magyar peoples of historic Hungary, both 'backward' nationalities like the Slovaks and historically more assertive communities, such as the Roumanians of Transylvania and the militant Serbs of the Voivodina, where the Serbs could count on covert backing from Belgrade. Fighting spread across southern Hungary in the second week of June and continued intermittently throughout the summer.

The key figure in these troubled south-eastern lands of the Monarchy was Colonel Josip Jellaçić, the Ban of Croatia. At midsummer the Court at Innsbruck disavowed the Ban as a disobedient and independently minded troublemaker, but he received some encouragement and funds from Latour, officially for the well-being of the 'frontier folk', military families settled along the historic Croatian-Bosnian borderland. The worsening situation in southern Hungary bolstered the Ban's status, making him indispensable to the so-called camarilla in Vienna. He was promoted General and on 11 September led a Croatian army across the River Drava and marched swiftly northwards to Lake Balaton, having achieved a working alliance with some 10,000 Serbian irregulars in the east. This South Slav ('Yugoslav') invasion rallied the Hungarian parliamentarians who, on Kossuth's prompting, voted funds for an army of Home Defence, numbering 200,000 men. The Palatine's well-intentioned appointment of Count Lamberg to negotiate with Jellaçić went tragically wrong; on 28 September a nationalistic mob in Pest seized and lynched Lamberg. Archduke Stephen, who was in Vienna, had already determined to step down as Palatine because of the hostility he encountered at Court; and Batthyány also resigned soon afterwards. The fate of Hungary was in the hands of Kossuth, as head of a Committee of National Defence.

Francis Joseph, with Grünne at his elbow, was well briefed on events in Hungary, receiving Jellaçić's proclamations as soon as they reached Vienna and passing them on to his mother (who, in her journal, already called the Ban of Croatia 'that admirable Jellaçić'). Emperor Ferdinand, at Latour's prompting, issued a manifesto on 3 October giving Jellaçić command of all troops in Hungary and proclaiming him as representative of the sovereign in the absence of a Palatine. This appointment soon proved an embarrassment. Hungarian resistance stiffened north of Balaton, thanks largely to the enterprising young General, Arthur Görgei. After three days of heavy fighting, the Croat army was in urgent need of reinforcement. Latour ordered a regiment to be sent by rail from Vienna into Hungary on the morning of Friday, 6 October. The troops mutinied. There was shooting at the railway station. By midday rioting had spread to the centre of the city.

As in March and in May, the imperial family was gathered in the Hofburg. Alarming reports reached Lobkowitz, who was entrusted with their safety. Angry groups of workers and students were hunting for the two most unpopular men in Vienna: Alexander Bach, a liberal reformer who had accepted office as minister of justice; and Latour, the war minister. Bach escaped the mob: he changed into women's clothes but, refusing to shave off his moustache, was induced to accept the role of gentleman's gentleman instead. Latour was tricked into emerging from the war ministry and was seized by the mob who repeatedly stabbed him, stripped him naked and strung him up on a lamp post in the square known as Am Hof. News of this bestial murder, less than a quarter of a mile from the Hofburg, convinced Lobkowitz of the need to get his charges out of Vienna. They left under heavy escort at half past six on the Saturday morning.

Once clear of the city, the imperial 'caravan' (as Archduchess Sophie called it) moved slowly, conscious that Windischgraetz's troops were heading southwards to give the family greater protection and restore order in the capital. Sunday was spent at Sieghartskirchen, barely twenty miles west of Vienna, and it was not until the following Saturday morning that the caravan reached its destination, the garrison town of Olmütz (now Olomouc), a natural centre for the fertile farms and small industries of northern Moravia. The imperial family occupied the palace of the Prince Bishops, a spacious Baroque residence built some 180 years previously. Both the German townsfolk and the Czech peasantry in Moravia were as effusively loyal to their 'honoured guests' as the people of Innsbruck had been a few months before. In later years Francis Joseph remained suspicious of Vienna's artisans and students and continued to look on Hungarians and Italians as natural rebels – but not the good folk of Moravia, the Salzkammergut or the Tyrol.

The sudden departure from Vienna and the week-long journey through an army massing to avenge the murder of Latour and the alleged affronts to the dynasty left a deep impression on the Archduke's mind. Once again he was, in his own eyes, a professional soldier; he chafed at the restraints which prevented him from marching 'to conquer Vienna' beside Windischgraetz (whom Emperor Ferdinand created a Field Marshal two days after the Court reached Olmütz). By the last week in October the new Field Marshal concentrated 59 battalions of infantry, 67 squadrons of cavalry and 200 guns on the outskirts of the capital. There he joined forces with Jellačić, who was glad to have sound strategic reasons for leading his Croats westwards out of Hungary as Magyar resistance stiffened. The Honved, an essentially National Defence force, was reluctant to cross the frontiers of historic Hungary in pursuit of Jellačić, but its commanders raised the hopes of the beleaguered Viennese by tentatively probing forward as far as Schwechat – where Vienna's airport now stands – before falling back at the approach of the main Austrian army.

By 31 October Vienna was in Windischgraetz's hands. The Field Marshal set up his headquarters in imperial Schönbrunn, while Jellačić's ill-disciplined troops were left to break down the last improvised barricades in suburban Leopoldstadt. Almost a quarter of Vienna's inhabitants had fled the city before Windischgraetz tightened the noose, many heading northwards to Moravia; but some two thousand Viennese per-

ished in the fighting, and twenty-five alleged ringleaders were subsequently shot. Throughout the winter the city remained under strict
military control.

Windischgraetz was dictator of the Monarchy in all but name. For him
it was enough to be invested by Emperor Ferdinand 'with the necessary
plenipotentiary powers to restore peace in My realm'. Outwardly the
months of November and December 1848 marked the apogee of Habsburg militarism; and in several provinces there was a brief popular cult
of WJR, a symbolic trinity of soldierly saviours and of the dynasty, formed
by the initials of Windischgraetz, Jellaçić and Radetzky. But, in reality,
the three generals had little in common: Jellaçić, a far inferior soldier,
was mistrusted politically by both colleagues; Radetzky complained that
Windischgraetz's politics were impossibly reactionary; and Windischgraetz, for his part, undervalued the victor of Custozza's generalship.
The WJR combination never sought to establish a purely military oli-
garchy for the Empire as a whole. Ministerial government had not been
swept away: the septuagenarian diplomat Baron Wessenberg, appointed
prime minister in July when Pillersdorf retired from the political stage,
followed the Court to Olmütz, and he was joined there by most of the
cabinet. Nor were the delegates to the constituent assembly sent about
their business: the Reichstag sitting in the Vienna Riding School was
prorogued on 19 October, with its members given a month to make their
way to Moravia, where the assembly would reopen at Kremsier. This was
a town some 25 miles south of Olmütz in which the Prince-Bishop had a
summer palace, with large halls and galleries to accommodate the deputies. Yet in one respect, Windischgraetz left a decisive imprint on active
politics in Moravia: once Vienna was in his hands, he secured the nomi-
nation of Felix Schwarzenberg as prime minister in succession to Wessenberg. For Windischgraetz's political future this was a mistake. If
Schwarzenberg felt any obligation at all towards the mythical WJR trinity,
it was to the old Field Marshal he had served in Italy rather than to his
brother-in-law.

Francis Joseph, though steeling himself to show no strong feelings
over any question, liked and respected the forty-eight year old brigade
commander whom he had first met in the forts outside Verona. Schwarzenberg was a Byronic cavalry officer beginning to look slightly seedy
from the ravages of typhus. He had been a career diplomat and still
possessed ideas of his own as well as the skill to express them convincingly.
To come from the most illustrious family still in attendance at Court was
also an advantage for him. 'A man of authority, but in no sense an
absolutist', Metternich's protégé Baron Hübner wrote contentedly in his
journal after hearing Schwarzenberg expound his views for the first time.

He was strongly opposed to Windischgraetz's extreme Toryism and, since he was more sympathetic towards constitutionalism than Grünne, he slightly broadened Francis Joseph's political horizon during those weeks at Olmütz when Windischgraetz's star seemed in the ascendant. Above all, Schwarzenberg acknowledged that his experience of domestic politics was limited: and in Olmütz he looked for advice to Count Francis Stadion, a genuine believer in parliamentary government, and the lawyer Alexander Bach who, though regarded as a renegade by Vienna's radicals, was one of the ablest administrators who ever operated Austria's cumbersome bureaucratic machine. When Schwarzenberg announced his cabinet on 21 November, he found in it posts for Stadion (Interior) and Bach (Justice) as well as for Baron Bruck (Commerce), the entrepreneur who had already created for Austria a new port at Trieste. Unlike the Empress and Archduchess Sophie, who still believed Windischgraetz was the soldier-statesman of the coming reign, Schwarzenberg saw no reason to look to the WJR combination for guidance. And, under his tutelage, neither did Francis Joseph.

Windischgraetz, in Vienna, remained unaware of the day to day shifts in power and influence at Olmütz. He did not realize how rapidly Schwarzenberg established an ascendancy at Court. Long ago both men had agreed that Ferdinand should abdicate in favour of his nephew; and Schwarzenberg accepted office only on the understanding that a change of emperor was imminent. Empress Maria Anna and Archduchess Sophie also recognized that the time had come for Francis Joseph's accession. But the long-suffering Empress retained a certain pride. She did not wish to see her husband nudged off the throne for a new monarchy based upon popular sovereignty. An act of abdication must condemn the revolutionary leaders who had induced Ferdinand to whittle away his powers, she insisted; and she wished it to emphasize that, in renouncing the throne, Ferdinand was ensuring that his nephew could begin his reign unfettered by concessions exacted from his predecessor. Windischgraetz fully agreed with the Empress. He assured her of his conviction that the Schwarzenberg government would respect her views: 'You need have no scruples over advising the Emperor to abdicate', he wrote.

Schwarzenberg did not see political life in such simplistic terms. Neither the Empress nor Windischgraetz seem to have known of the speech he delivered to the Reichstag at Kremsier five days after becoming prime minister, when he told the deputies that the government wished 'to place itself at the head of' the movement in favour of representative institutions. 'We want constitutional monarchy sincerely and unreservedly', Schwarzenberg declared. Perhaps he even meant it, for there was no reason why a 'constitutional monarchy' need necessarily concede popular sovereignty. But the speech made no attempt to condemn the Revolution; the prime minister's sentiments had little in common with the straightforward Toryism shared by Maria Anna and her sympathetic correspondent in Vienna.

On the evening of Friday, 1 December, Windischgraetz and Jellaçić arrived in Olmütz from the capital, knowing that the change of monarch was imminent; the third paladin, Radetzky, could not leave the Italian war zone. In the evening Windischgraetz discussed the Abdication Act and the accession ceremonies with Schwarzenberg. He seemed satisfied by all he was told, for Metternich's close assistant, Kübeck, had drafted a stern preamble to the Act, denouncing the sins of Revolution.

The presence of the Court in Olmütz had drawn the diplomatic corps to northern Moravia, and the town was already packed. It was clear some ceremony was to take place next day, for the garrison was ordered to turn out in full-dress uniform at half past nine. Few people were in the secret, certainly not Archduchess Sophie's younger sons: Maximilian, not unreasonably, assumed that his brother was to be invested as Governor of Bohemia-Moravia. There was an element of improvisation right up to the last moment. Only on Friday morning was it agreed in talks between the prime minister and the Emperor-to-be that he would retain his two baptismal names as sovereign, reigning as 'Francis Joseph I' rather than as 'Francis II' (as styled in the first draft of the proclamation): both men liked to associate 'good Kaiser Franz' with the reformer emperor, Joseph, who was also an active soldier.

The date chosen for the ceremony was hardly auspicious: 2 December was the anniversary, not only of an upstart Emperor's coronation in Paris, but of the humiliating defeat he inflicted a year later on the Austrian and Russian armies at Austerlitz, scarcely thirty miles away from Olmütz. But, for different reasons, both Windischgraetz and Schwarzenberg were in too much of a hurry to worry about anniversaries: the Field Marshal wished to march on Buda before winter made the roads impassable; and his brother-in-law believed he could curb the giddier flights of constitutional fantasy at Kremsier by emphasizing that there was, once again, a central authority prepared to exercise real powers.

Only a small gathering of people witnessed the ceremonies in the salon of the Prince-Bishop's palace on that Saturday morning: the imperial family, the government ministers and the two soldier paladins. With a weary voice, halting between words and placing emphasis at times on the wrong syllables, Emperor Ferdinand read out the Abdication Act which Schwarzenberg handed to him. Windischgraetz, who was not listening carefully, thought the reading took less time than he had anticipated, and when he received the official copy of the gazette he was able to see why;

for Kübeck's preamble condemning the revolution had dropped out of the speech. 'Important reasons have led Us to the irrevocable decision to lay down Our Crown in favour of Our beloved nephew, Archduke Francis Joseph ...', Ferdinand declared, surrendering his Austrian imperial titles and the crowns of Hungary, Bohemia, and Lombardy, although retaining the personal style and dignity of Emperor. Schwarzenberg read Archduke Francis Charles's formal renunciation of his claims, with its assertion that, at this grave moment in the dynasty's history, a younger person was needed on the throne; and family, generals and ministers gave homage to their new sovereign lord. 'It is thanks to you that all this is possible', Francis Joseph said, simply enough, to Windischgraetz. Afterwards Ferdinand recorded all that he remembered in his journal: 'The function ended with the new Emperor kneeling to his Emperor and master – that is to say myself – and asking for a blessing, which I gave by laying my hands upon his head and making a sign of the Cross'. Sophie heard Ferdinand say, 'God bless you, Franzi. Be good. God will protect you. I'm happy about it all'. Then, as Ferdinand wrote in his journal, 'We went away to our room ... and heard Holy Mass in the chapel of the Bishop's Palace ... After that I and my dear wife packed our things'.

At two in the afternoon Emperor Ferdinand and Empress Maria Anna left for Prague and took up residence in the Hradschin Castle. Meanwhile in Olmütz Francis Joseph's accession was proclaimed to his subjects with a flourish of trumpets outside the Rathaus and again on the steps of the cathedral. Schwarzenberg later read a proclamation of accession to the Kremsier Assembly: 'Long Live the constitutional Emperor, Francis Joseph' responded Franz Smolka, the Speaker of the Reichstag, with conviction. Only from Hungary came the firm voice of dissent: the change of throne was 'an affair of the Habsburg family', Kossuth insisted. Hungary would acknowledge no other King until a successor swore to uphold the constitution as defined in the April Laws and received on his head the Holy Crown of St Stephen.

Legend depicts Francis Joseph as returning from the ceremony with the sad comment, 'Farewell my youth', and bursting into tears. Perhaps so; though, for the past nine months, moments of light-hearted frivolity were already rare; and thus life continued for him. He remained at the heart of the family circle in the Prince-Bishop's apartments, along with his mother and father and three brothers. But, long before dawn each morning, the Emperor was working at his official papers. For a fortnight he buried himself in documents of state, trying to make sense of reports from his commanders in the field and sending off holograph letters to the sovereigns of Europe. On 16 December came the grave news that Windischgraetz had led an army of 52,000 men eastwards into Hungary, confirming that the Monarchy was racked by civil war. That evening the self-control which was second nature to the young ruler momentarily broke, exacting a curious price. A ball thrown to one of his brothers by the six-year old Archduke Ludwig Victor cracked a mirrored door in the episcopal palace. The boys, fearing a scolding or worse, appealed to Francis Joseph for sympathy and support. Unexpectedly the Emperor felt an urge to join in their romp. Turning to his mother, he asked for her permission to smash the door down; and, with astonishing indulgence, the Archduchess allowed her children to do as they pleased. A frenzy of glass-breaking followed, until the door was shattered. '*Sa Majesté se donna à coeur joie*' ('His Majesty went at it to his heart's content'), Sophie wrote in her diary that night. What the Prince-Bishop said is not on record.

Chapter 4

APOTHEOSIS OF THE ARMY

Army officers had brought Francis Joseph to the throne, and for the first months of his reign the future form of the Monarchy remained in their hands. Windischgraetz's invasion of Hungary from the west held promise of a speedy victory, especially as Jellaçić seized the opportunity to launch a second offensive on the southern front. By 5 January 1849 the Austrians controlled Buda and Pest, forcing Kossuth to move his revolutionary government 120 miles eastwards to Debrecen. 'Whoever today holds the capital in his hands is master of the land', Windischgraetz proclaimed. Offers by a Hungarian delegation to discuss a compromise settlement were contemptuously brushed aside: there would be no negotiations with 'rebels', Windischgraetz insisted. At the end of the third week in January the emperor approved an official bulletin for publication in Monday's *Wiener Zeitung* which proclaimed the glorious conclusion of the campaign in Hungary. Thus, within fifty days of his accession, the paladins handed Francis Joseph the swift and tidy victory he had sought, achieved with little cost in men or material. Or so it seemed.

Meanwhile, Vienna and Prague remained under martial law, the Court was still at Olmütz, and in neighbouring Kremsier deputies continued to dabble with constitutional drafts. 'Our Reichstag at Kremsier has become very docile', Schwarzenberg smugly told Windischgraetz on the day his troops entered Pest: 'Every victory, every step forward in Hungary, broadens its political horizons and adds more maturity to its capacity for law-making'. But a week later the prime minister's tone changed. For the deputies were not marionettes, responding to his pull of the strings; in Kremsier, as earlier in Vienna, they were concerned with fundamental principles of government; the Emperor enjoyed sovereignty through the will of the people rather than 'by grace of God', they declared. Such doctrines smacked of political heresy. 'In the last few days the Reichstag has shown itself so naturally malevolent that any hope of reaching the planned objective, the working out by it and with it of a constitution, is fast disappearing', Schwarzenberg wrote to his brother-in-law; and grimly Windischgraetz responded, 'If they will not hear of the grace of God, they must learn of the grace of cannon'.

But neither Francis Joseph nor his ministers would let Windischgraetz's guns loose on Kremsier. They preferred a political solution, and by the end of January the government had an alternative constitution ready, in case the deputies remained tiresome. Stadion, as minister of the interior, collaborated with Alexander Bach, the minister of justice, to produce a draft constitution which would be centralist and pan-monarchical in character, while providing both for a bicameral elective parliament and a Reichsrat, a council of advisers to the Emperor nominated by himself. For the moment, however, the Kremsier deputies were allowed to continue with their debates: Schwarzenberg had assured his brother-in-law that no constitution would be presented for the Emperor's signature without field headquarters' approval, and Windischgraetz remained opposed to all talk of parliamentary government. Moreover, despite January's confident bulletin in the *Wiener Zeitung*, there was still no prospect of imposing a unitary constitution on the whole of the Monarchy: General Görgei was massing the Honved volunteers along the line of the Tisza; General Damjanics held in check the Austrian-Serbian-Croatian force in southern Hungary; and Jozef Bem, the exiled Polish General who had offered his services to Kossuth, was virtually master of Transylvania and even led a foray into the Bukovina. With such uncertainty around the eastern frontiers, it was felt at Olmütz better to wait upon Windischgraetz, even though there was some disquiet over the slowness with which he responded to Görgei's continued challenge. No doubt, in time, the saviour of Prague and Vienna would give his blessing to a modified draft of Stadion's constitution, and present his Emperor with a positively final victory in Hungary.

In the last days of February the Austrians inflicted a tactical defeat on the Honved at Kapolna, forcing Görgei back across the River Tisza and silencing Windischgraetz's critics. Three days later the Kremsier deputies completed work on a draft constitution which promised the establishment of a democratic multi-national empire (though not in Hungary, where it was assumed the April Laws still prevailed): 'All political rights emanate from the people', the Kremsier blueprint declared, defiantly. The deputies hoped the constitution would be approved by the Emperor and published on 15 March, the first anniversary of Metternich's overthrow. But Francis Joseph would have none of it. Rather than allow 'the people' to assert their sovereignty, he backed Stadion's proposals and on Sunday, 4 March, formally approved the centralist constitution drafted a few weeks earlier. On Tuesday Stadion himself travelled to Kremsier to let the deputies know that the Emperor had graciously endowed his subjects with a constitution which rendered their continued labours superfluous. The Reichstag was dissolved, he announced; they could all return to their families. By Wednesday morning a battalion of grenadiers was patrolling the streets of the little town, while sentries paced the silent galleries of the Prince-Bishop's palace.

Within three weeks Francis Joseph was celebrating a genuine military victory; but not against Kossuth. On 14 March Charles Albert of Sardinia-Piedmont unexpectedly denounced the Armistice. Six days later he attacked the Austrian positions in Lombardy. It was a brief campaign, decided as early as 23 March by Radetzky's crushing response to the would-be invaders on the battlefield of Novara, some ten miles inside Piedmont, a disaster which led Charles Albert to abdicate that same evening. The octogenarian Radetzky became once more the hero of the hour at Court: why, it was asked, had not Windischgraetz, who was twenty-one years his junior, shown a similar initiative in Hungary? Grünne, the Emperor's military adjutant, was no great champion of Radetzky, but he was by now even more critical of Windischgraetz for failing to mop up the Magyar rebels he so despised; and Schwarzenberg, long impatient of his brother-in-law's political obscurantism, was irritated by Windischgraetz's constant pleas to seek help from Tsar Nicholas in stamping out the Hungarian insurrection. Emperor and government were 'absolutely opposed to foreign aid in restoring order within the monarchy, even when the source was so intimate and friendly an ally', Windischgraetz was told, before the battle of Kapolna. His influence at Court, paramount five months before, was fast slipping away as Damjanics's southern army launched a successful flank attack on Austrian positions around Szolnok, forcing Windischgraetz to pull his forward troops back across the open steppe-land of the Alföld towards Pest and the Danube.

Far worse followed a month later. Görgei, moving swiftly across the featureless countryside in a scimitar manoeuvre, came down from the north on Komarom, threatened the main artery between Vienna and Hungary, and compelled Windischgraetz to abandon Pest. The Hungarian successes prompted Kossuth to make the decisive break with the Habsburgs. On 14 April the independence of Hungary was at last proclaimed in the Calvinist church at Debrecen, with Kossuth recognized as Regent President of the Kingdom.

Military defeat sealed Windischgraetz's fate. In the third week of April he was replaced by Baron von Welden: 'I . . . rely on your patriotism and self-sacrificing devotion to my house and to Austria to accept this step, which causes me endless pain', Francis Joseph wrote in the letter informing Windischgraetz of his recall. The proudest High Tory in central

Europe dutifully accepted his dismissal, but he did not hesitate to let the Emperor know he thought he deserved better treatment 'for the sacrifices I have made for the Imperial House'. In the remaining thirteen years of his life he continued to blame his brother-in-law for his humiliation.

Windischgraetz's bitterness was intensified by Welden's total failure to check the Hungarian advance. By late April the Austrians were back to the lines they held five months earlier, before the march into Hungary. Welden remained in command of the army for only five weeks. Before the end of May he was himself superseded by Baron Julius von Haynau. The new commander was one of Radetzky's most competent generals but, as the 'beast of Brescia', he was already notorious abroad for cruelty to men, women and children across northern Italy.

Like many of his contemporaries, Windischgraetz had assumed that his Emperor remained a cipher, responding to ideas put before him by Prince Schwarzenberg or Count Grünne, or even by his mother. But Francis Joseph had acquired remarkable self-confidence in the past twelve months; he was hungry for authority and eager to accept responsibility. The Emperor presided over meetings of his ministers in person, until Schwarzenberg himself was heard grumbling privately, more than once, that he had not intention of being a mere 'hack' for the throne: 'No one knows better than I how many ministerial proposals he sends back on the ground of faultiness', he complained to Metternich in the following summer. There were moments when Francis Joseph affected a family sentimentality which pleased his mother: thus, when she went with his brothers to Prague soon after Easter in 1849, she received a letter from him emphasizing how much he missed her company, especially at the breakfast table, where he was accustomed to joining her after several hours of early morning tedium at his desk. But already the young Emperor was acquiring an iron reserve of character, a conscious awareness of sovereignty. The sentimental note to his mother was written soon after he had penned that hardest of all letters, in which he sacked the saviour of the monarchy from his military command.

For Francis Joseph there was no distinction between the prestige of the army and of the crown. Like his first prime minister – and in sharp contrast to his two predecessors on the throne – he was rarely seen in public out of uniform. The ideal of the Russian and Prussian autocracies, in which the sovereign was accepted as a Supreme War Lord, appealed to him. On the last day of April the war minister in Vienna was notified that the Emperor, who was still at Olmütz, had taken over the supreme direction of the army and was setting up a personal military chancellery. But no Supreme War Lord could conduct military affairs from the heart of Moravia. On the following Saturday Francis Joseph arrived back in

Vienna by the train from Brno and went into residence at Schönbrunn. It was thirty weeks to the day since Lobkowitz's hussars had escorted the imperial 'caravan' out of the troubled city.

In those seven months much had changed in the capital. The Viennese themselves, though vexed by the retention of martial law, were politically quiet and complaisant now that Windischgraetz had been rusticated to his estates and 'that admirable Jellaçić' was back in Zagreb, working for the creation of an 'Illyrian Kingdom' under Habsburg suzerainty. But, as General Welden could still warn Schwarzenberg, 'the fate of the capital city, and with it that of the Monarchy, hangs in the balance'. For the Hungarians, who had threatened outlying Schwechat in the autumn, were once more a mere forty miles away from the outer villages; and there is ample evidence from contemporary journals and diaries of a near-panic in government circles during the first week of May. Until the Hungarian insurrection was suppressed there could be no return to normal life; and so long as Hungary asserted its independence of Habsburg rule, the institutions promised to the Empire as a whole in Stadion's centralist constitution could exist only on paper. A peaceful settlement was even more pressing now than at the Emperor's accession.

Barely a week after returning to Vienna, Francis Joseph left Schönbrunn to spend three days with his troops along the border with Hungary. His presence put heart into his sadly depleted army at a time when he was especially anxious to emphasize the bonds linking Emperor and soldiery. For, shortly before leaving Olmütz, he at last took a step which Windischgraetz had long recommended, but which he and Schwarzenberg consistently rejected: on 24 April the Emperor agreed to seek Russian help. A few days later, in a personal letter to Tsar Nicholas I, he urged the immediate despatch of a Russian expeditionary force which would destroy that 'rendezvous of the lost children of all ill causes ... and, above all, the eternal Polish conspirators enrolled under the banner of Kossuth'; only thus, Nicholas was told, could the 'glorious fraternity' in arms of the Habsburg and Romanov empires 'save modern society from certain ruin, ... uphold with firm resolution the holy struggle of the social order against anarchy' and 'prevent the Hungarian rebellion from becoming a European calamity'. The plea was eloquently phrased, but at great cost to the young Emperor's dignity. Schwarzenberg had always insisted that for governments to seek foreign assistance in order 'to restore order in their own house' was to risk losing 'all credit, both domestic and foreign'. Much of Francis Joseph's behaviour through the second half of the year sprang from the pique of a young ruler at having to reveal to the doyen of autocrats how defective was the army in which he took such exaggerated pride.

Soon after his visit to the Front, he set off for Warsaw and a conference with the Tsar and Marshal Paskevich, his Viceroy in Poland. It was not the first time the two rulers had met. When Tsar Nicholas paid a surprise visit to Vienna soon after Emperor Francis's death he had taken tea with Archduchess Sophie and affectionately bounced her eldest son on his knees. Ten years later they met again, with the Tsar on this occasion admiring the young archduke's bearing as a Lieutenant of Dragoons. The Tsar did not anticipate much satisfaction from the Warsaw meeting or from the proposed intervention in Hungary: 'I see only envy, malice and ingratitude ahead', he told Paskevich, ' and I would certainly not interfere ... if I did not see in Bem and the other rascals in Hungary not only enemies of Austria but also ... villains, scoundrels and destroyers whom we must root out for the sake of our own tranquillity'. But when Francis Joseph reached Warsaw, at the start of the fourth week in May, he scored a striking personal success. The visit coincided with bad news from Hungary, where the garrison, which had held out on Buda's Castle Hill after Windischgraetz ordered the general retreat, was forced to surrender to Görgei's troops on 21 May. Nicholas was impressed by his guest's calm dignity: 'The more I see of him and listen to him, the more I am astonished by his good sense and by the soundness and rectitude of his views', the Tsar told his wife. Francis Joseph emphasized the importance of upholding monarchical solidarity so as to safeguard 'order and justice' across Europe. But however much these sentiments might please the Tsar, nothing could speed up Russian mobilization. Six weeks elapsed between the Tsar's approval of intervention and the southward movement of Paskevich's cumbersome army, which was ravaged by cholera.

The delay at least allowed Haynau to take the initiative and push Görgei's vanguard back from the Austrian border. Against the advice of both Schwarzenberg and his own mother, Francis Joseph again visited the Front in June, accompanied on this occasion by his brother Maximilian. Schwarzenberg, who from his days at Verona well knew the Emperor's imperviousness to danger, accompanied the imperial party, 'fussing around him like an old hen with a prize chick', as Archduke Max wrote back to their mother: 'The Emperor was splendid, always to the forefront of the battle; you can imagine the soldiers' enthusiasm at seeing him sharing their danger and fatigue'. On 29 June he led his troops into the town they knew as Raab (now Győr) across a bridge already licked by flame; 'the burning bridge of Raab' became a set-piece of Habsburg legend, as prone to artistic licence as the famous assault by Napoleon on the bridge of Lodi in his first Italian campaign. By 9 July when, to Schwarzenberg's relief, Francis Joseph and his brother were safely back at Schönbrunn, the Hungarians were in full retreat.

Most of the fighting in that summer was between Haynau's army and the Honved units, for the Hungarians skilfully avoided pitched battles with Paskevich's Russians. But when, in the second week of August, independent Hungary could hold out no longer and Kossuth escaped to Turkey, it was to the Russians that General Görgei capitulated at Vilagos, not the Austrians. Paskevich's subsequent message to Tsar Nicholas, 'Hungary lies at the feet of Your Majesty', was doubly unfortunate: it used courtiers' licence, for some citadels held out for several weeks; and it infuriated Francis Joseph, his government and his generals, all of whom regarded the Russian presence as supplementary to their own efforts.

There followed a bleak two months in the history of Hungary and of Francis Joseph's style of government. At first the Emperor left Haynau to punish his rebellious subjects but, knowing the General's notorious reputation for brutality, he gave orders that no death sentences were to be executed without authority from Vienna. Haynau was aghast at such restraints; he protested that to be an effective deterrent 'Justice' needed swift implementation on the spot; and in this instance Haynau was supported by the prime minister. Legend maintains that, when urged to show mercy in Hungary, Schwarzenberg replied, 'Yes, it is a good idea, but we'll have a little hanging first'. Although the remark is apocryphal, it conveys the sad essentials of a policy of repression to which Francis Joseph weakly assented. The requirement that death sentences needed endorsement from Vienna was revoked; and it was not until the last days of October that the Emperor curbed Haynau's powers, insisting (despite the general's further protests) that there should be no more executions. By then 114 Hungarians had been shot or hanged. Among them were thirteen generals, executed at Arad on 6 October: those who surrendered to the Russians were hanged, while those who gave up their swords to the Austrians had the privilege of being shot. General Görgei, under the personal protection of Tsar Nicholas, escaped with banishment to Carinthia; he was still alive when Francis Joseph began his last year on the throne. The Emperor hardened himself against appeals for clemency not only from the former Palatine, Archduke Stephen, but even from his brother Maximilian. The execution of Count Lajos Batthyány, prime minister of Hungary under the April Laws, was particularly resented. More fortunate were 75 Hungarian magnates who had safely fled the country and were symbolically hanged in effigy. Among them was Count Gyula Andrássy.

Görgei capitulated at Vilagos on 13 August. Fifteen days later the Republic of St Mark surrendered to Radetzky, and the Austrians re-entered Venice, which had been tightly blockaded for almost a year, enduring a steady – though erratic – bombardment since early May.

Radetzky, who had twice concluded armistices with Piedmont and on both occasions showed a wise moderation, did not exact vengeance on the city or its defenders, for he had more foresight than either Haynau or Schwarzenberg. Alone among the military paladins the veteran Field Marshal's reputation was untarnished. In Venice his qualities were not appreciated; only a single Italian – a priest – was in the Piazza San Marco when he made his formal entry into the city. But in Vienna, where war with the Italians stirred deeper feelings than the civil war with Hungary, Radetzky remained a popular idol. On the last day of August in 1848 a 'Grand Impressive Victory Festival ... in Honour of our Courageous Army in Italy and to benefit the Wounded Soldiers' had been held, and for the occasion Johann Strauss 'the Elder' composed a march dedicated to the man of the hour. When, thirteen months later, the capital honoured the twice victorious Field Marshal with a banquet in the Hofburg, it was expected that Strauss would provide a 'Radetzky Banquet March' to complement this earlier work. That second march was never completed; for Strauss fell gravely ill with scarlet fever and died three days later. But the most famous and liveliest of his marches was played at the celebratory banquet; and in the years ahead it was played again and again. No tune became more popular with the Emperor than the *Radetzky March*.

There was a serious purpose behind Radetzky's visit to the capital; for the imperial army needed re-structuring now that it was under the Emperor's personal command and serving soldiers deplored the influence on Francis Joseph of Count Grünne, a staff officer who had seen no active service. To their relief, Radetzky's prestige enabled him to persuade the Emperor to appoint Baron Hess as Quartermaster-General and his personal chief-of-staff, a post the Field Marshal assumed would check the ascendancy of the military chancellery and prevent the rapid promotion of Grünne's nominees to high command. 'Hess is clever, industrious and absolutely convinced that control of the army should be in my hands', Francis Joseph reported to his mother, in a note which shows how well Radetzky had emphasized the qualities most likely to appeal to his sovereign. But, although the Emperor, his QMG and the head of his military chancellery all worked in harmony for some months, Hess was never able to dislodge Grünne entirely, for the Count remained a favourite of Archduchess Sophie. She approved of Grünne's innate conservatism, shared his anti-Hungarian prejudices, and was glad if his devout Catholicism strengthened Francis Joseph's personal religiosity. The Archduchess's whims had little impact on day-to-day politics – Schwarzenberg made certain of that. But at Court it was different. Grünne and his circle would refer to Sophie privately as 'our Empress', and she basked in her status as First Lady of the Monarchy.

In one respect her tastes left a lasting mark on inner Vienna at this time. The private apartments of the Hofburg, though perfectly adequate for the Emperors Francis and Ferdinand, had long seemed drab to her eyes. Once peace and order returned to the Monarchy, Francis Joseph willingly agreed to her suggestion that she should supervise their redecoration. By the following spring the inner rooms of the Hofburg were as impeccably baroque as she could induce mid-century craftsmen to design them. For the Archduchess, dignity could never be compromised for the sake of modernity.

When, in November 1849, Baron von Kübeck was invited to dine with the Emperor and his parents, the Hofburg apartments were not ready and the family was at Schönbrunn. Kübeck, the painstaking civil servant who became Metternich's financial counsellor, was not impressed by the table-talk that evening: 'the apotheosis of the army', he wrote gloomily in his journal. Yet can he really have been surprised? Schwarzenberg was himself a soldier as well as a diplomat. He believed that, even if other institutions failed the Habsburgs, the Emperor should always be able to depend upon his army to maintain order at home and give purpose and meaning to the demands of Austria's diplomatic envoys abroad. Francis Joseph, for his part, had made it clear within a few weeks of his accession that, as he regarded the army as the most important manifestation of state power, he would keep it under his personal control.

From exile in England and Belgium, Metternich's letters criticized Schwarzenberg's inclination to rattle the sword: why had he failed to give the Emperor an alternative to the military regimes which still controlled the great centres of the Monarchy? In the winter of 1849–50 martial law prevailed in Prague and Cracow as well as in Vienna; Radetzky had been re-appointed military and civilian Governor of Lombardy-Venetia on 17 October; Haynau was confirmed as military Governor of Hungary on the same day, with the country divided into six military districts, each under the control of a general. A similar administration functioned in Transylvania, while from Zagreb Jellaçić continued to control Croatia and its frontier marchlands, although mistrusted by Vienna for his 'Illyrianism'. The Stadion Constitution was neither scrapped nor implemented. It was ignored.

For Schwarzenberg such matters were overshadowed by an unresolved problem threatening war along yet another border: how should the Emperor respond to the German Question and, in particular, to the mounting rivalry between Prussia and Austria? Germany's national revolution, symbolized by the attempts of the Frankfurt Parliament to draw up a constitution for a united Germany, lost all impetus when in April 1849 King Frederick William IV of Prussia turned down the offer of the crown of a liberal 'small' Germany, which would have excluded the Germanic lands of the Habsburg Monarchy. Throughout the summer Tsar Nicholas I, an anxious observer of all that was happening in central Europe, assumed that General von Radowitz (Prussia's prime minister) and Schwarzenberg would both wish to restore the old German Confederation which had functioned in the Metternich era. In this he was mistaken. Schwarzenberg at first hoped for a Greater Austrian Confederation, one which would recognize the pre-eminence of the Habsburgs over all central Europe, Germanic and non-Germanic. Radowitz, on the other hand, favoured the establishment of an enlarged German Confederation, organized in two loosely integrated units: there would be a small 'Germany', dominated by Prussia, and the Habsburg Monarchy, serving as an ally and economic partner. To advance this policy Radowitz set up an embryonic confederation, the Erfurt Union, in March 1850. Radowitz's initiative was unpopular with the rulers of Bavaria, Saxony, Hanover, and Württemberg as well as with the government in Vienna, and yet for several months it seemed possible that Prussia would risk a war to impose the Erfurt Union on Germany, assuming that Francis Joseph could not spare troops from Hungary and Italy to meet the threat.

At heart Schwarzenberg was more concerned over the shaky state of Austria's finances than over the possibility of defeat by Prussia. Already military expenditure was twice as high as in the last years of the Metternich era. A long war would bring state bankruptcy and was out of the question, but in the autumn of 1850 he seemed willing to take a gamble on a brief campaign: there was even some skirmishing between Prussian and Austrian units in a dispute over the right to give 'protection' to the Elector of Hesse against his more rebellious subjects. Ultimately, however, both Frederick William IV and Francis Joseph shrank from such a 'war of brothers': Radowitz was dismissed, and Schwarzenberg held in check by the young Emperor's firm resolve to keep the peace. On paper the Austrians gained a diplomatic victory; for a compromise settlement was reached at Olmütz, in late November: the Erfurt Union was dissolved and a new Prussian prime minister, General von Manteuffel, agreed to Schwarzenberg's sponsorship of a series of conferences in Dresden to discuss the future of Germany.

But at Dresden Schwarzenberg was convincingly defeated. The other German states, though wary of Prussia, equally mistrusted an army-run Austria: they rejected proposals from Vienna for a strong executive authority to be set up by the German Confederation and they refused to allow the Austrian Empire, as a single entity, to join the Zollverein, the German Customs Union. The best Schwarzenberg could achieve was a

Prusso-Austrian mutual defence pact, signed on 16 May 1851, valid for three years and renewable thereafter.

When the Dresden Conference opened in late December 1850 Schwarzenberg had urged his Emperor to propose the establishment of an all-German parliament. But Francis Joseph was aghast at the suggestion and brought his prime minister sharply to heel, and during these long months of confrontation with Prussia he became increasingly uneasy over Schwarzenberg's general policies. He would always defend the good name of the army, dismissing complaints of harsh conduct as malicious gossip, and Schwarzenberg found that, over military matters, he invariably met a stubborn hostility to change. In particular the Emperor long chose to give Haynau the benefit of the doubt when the prime minister denounced the Governor-General's ruthless policies in Hungary. Reluctantly Schwarzenberg had to turn to Grünne for support on this issue, knowing that the Count's duties as military adjutant ensured he was in constant attendance on the Emperor and that casual conversation would influence him more than matters raised in any formal audience. Haynau had been Radetzky's nominee rather than Grünne's, and the Count held no brief for him. The joint campaign succeeded. In June 1850 Haynau was abruptly recalled from Hungary.

Yet, though Grünne and Schwarzenberg might ally against an independently-minded general, their political views were poles apart. Despite the disdain with which Schwarzenberg had sent the Kremsier Reichstag about its non-business, he looked upon representative institutions with limited powers as safety-valves for an over-centralized monarchical system. But he knew he was inexperienced in domestic affairs and, with Stadion out of his mind and in an asylum, he became dependent for technical advice on one-time liberal reformers like Alexander Bach and Baron von Schmerling, men whose presence was barely tolerated at Court, even though they were by now firm upholders of the established order. No one was more hostile to the ministers than the egregious Grünne. For, while Schwarzenberg still paid lip-service to constitutionalism, Grünne was at heart an absolutist. It was natural for Grünne to encourage Francis Joseph to indulge his current inclination and create a Russian-style autocracy in Vienna.

The Emperor never intended to put the Stadion constitution into full operation. But he was prepared to establish a Reichsrat, the nominated council of advisers which Stadion had envisaged (and which strongly resembled the Tsar's Council of State). In late October 1850 he entrusted Kübeck with drafting statutes to define the form and purpose of the Reichsrat; and on 19 November he was more specific. Kübeck was told that the Emperor wished the Reichsrat 'to supersede, and in some ways replace, the Constitution'; the advisory council would thus afford the Monarchy a firm basis of government, which would encourage foreign bankers to give Austria the credit essential for the reconstruction of the Empire after years of upheaval. This made good sense to Kübeck, and he dutifully did all that was expected of him. Understandably, his ideas provoked strong opposition from the prime minister and his colleagues in the government. The draft statutes were, in effect, a constitutional counter-revolution and discussions continued for several months. It was clear that the nominated Reichsrat would abolish ministerial responsibility which, so Kübeck argued, was a pernicious concept rooted in popular sovereignty. Once again ministers would become mere servants of the Emperor, reduced to the status of departmental chiefs, as at the height of the Metternich era. So drastic were these proposals that, in the last week of June 1851, Kübeck noted in his diary that Francis Joseph was 'apprehensive of the possible resignation of Prince Schwarzenberg'. But if he went, who would take his place? Kübeck, the provincial tailor's son, was already the Emperor's choice as chairman of the Reichsrat. There was, however, as court and politicians well knew, a more illustrious elder statesman hovering in the wings. News had just reached Vienna that Prince Metternich, though not yet on Austrian soil, was back on his estate in the Rhineland.

Francis Joseph was spared the need to look for a new chief minister. For, though other members of the government left office, both Schwarzenberg and Bach were prepared to stay on, accepting most of the proposed changes. Four decrees, printed in the official gazette on 26 August 1851, revoked basic reforms conceded at Olmütz: out went ministerial responsibility and innovations in municipal administration and the legal system; while a Reichsrat committee would re-assess the remaining promises of the Stadion constitution. Francis Joseph's own views may be gathered from a letter sent on that Tuesday to his mother: 'When you read the *Wiener Zeitung* you will see that we have taken a big step forward', he wrote, 'We have thrown all that constitutional stuff overboard, and Austria has only one Master. Now one must work even harder. After three years we have almost reached the point we wanted to, thank God'. For a young ruler, just twenty-one and only now trimming a thin moustache for the first time, the tone of the letter rang with astonishing self-confidence.

Some of Francis Joseph's optimism derived from the reports with which Schwarzenberg regularly fed him. More than once Kübeck's journal grumbles at the prime minister's glowing accounts of progress in the previously disaffected regions of the Monarchy. But the Emperor did not entirely rely on his diligent desk reading. He was by now travelling increasingly across his empire: northwards to Prague and the Bohemian cities, to all the German-Austrian provinces, and, more than once, southwards to Trieste, Lombardy and Venetia. 'The farther I went from Vienna, the better I found the attitude', he wrote to his mother from Trieste, 'In Graz quite good and calm. In Laibach [Ljubljana] excellent, just as though there had been no revolution, and here all is enthusiastically Austrian.' Only in the capital was he uneasy: 'Here the mood grows worse every day, but the people are sufficiently cunning to avoid an armed clash', he told his mother in September 1850, 'On Sunday a great church parade on the glacis, just to let the dear Viennese see that troops and cannon still exist.' And yet, even when living among these 'cunning people', he found moments of relaxation: no one could recall a more light-hearted carnival than in February 1851, with the Emperor continuing to gain real pleasure from dancing at the numerous balls. At times he liked to escape from it all to Laxenburg, while Ischl remained a favourite retreat. He found solace from the problems of government by stalking chamois or stag in the mountains and using his sharp eye and steady hand to bring down the black alpine wood grouse he would often hunt at sunrise.

By now his brother and one-time companion Maximilian had decided to serve as a naval officer; he made a villa above Trieste his home. The Habsburgs had long neglected their fleet and Maximilian sought to interest the Emperor in the service, either by letter or by word of mouth when he was on leave. In May 1850 Francis Joseph spent a 'delightful night' at sea off Venice and he was with the Adriatic squadron again in the following March as well as visiting Venice in September 1851, during a protracted tour of the Italian provinces. But an unfortunate experience in March 1852 confirmed his prejudices against the navy. While sailing in the northern Adriatic aboard a steam-powered warship, the Emperor and his brother were caught in a violent storm which raged for twenty-six hours and wrecked one of the smaller vessels in the squadron. The naval authorities were blamed for putting to sea at such a time of unruly winds and waves and thus endangering the lives of both their sovereign and his brother, the heir-apparent. To Maximilian's intense chagrin, the navy was thereafter treated as an auxiliary of the army, despised by the veteran generals at the war ministry and at Court. Only in the autumn of 1854, when the twenty-two year old Archduke was himself promoted to Rear-Admiral and appointed commander-in-chief, were serious attempts made to modernize the fleet.

While the Emperor was in northern Italy in September 1851, the Metternichs returned to Vienna after three years of exile. Francis Joseph paid an unheralded private visit to the ex-Chancellor at his villa on Sunday, 3 October, and Melanie arrived home from Mass to find him 'asking Clement's advice on a great many topics'. But the Emperor was readier at asking advice than at heeding it. Shortly before Christmas he sent Metternich Kübeck's latest draft proposals for the Reichsrat. An accompanying note, from 'your faithful pupil and friend', invited comments; and, in his leisurely way, Metternich began to prepare a 2,000 word memorandum, urging the setting up of provincial consultative diets, from which spokesmen would be chosen to serve in the Reichsrat.

He was still working on the memorandum when it was overtaken by events. For Francis Joseph was in too much of a hurry to await the considered verdict of the doyen of elder statesmen. On New Year's Eve – Sylvesterabend in German-Austria – the so-called 'Sylvester Patent' was made public. It comprised three pronouncements, in the form of a message from the Emperor to his chief minister: the Constitution of March 1849 was abolished, without ever having been put into practice; 'fundamental rights', conceded by the Emperor under threat of revolution, were annulled (though freedom of worship was guaranteed and no attempt was made to re-impose feudal obligations on the peasantry); and centralization of the administrative system was completed by the abolition of all locally elected councils and the application of Austrian codes of law to every part of the Monarchy, including Hungary. Now at last Francis Joseph had achieved his first ambition. He ruled as a benevolent soldier autocrat, Austria's Tsar in his own right, not the nominee of a military camarilla. In St Petersburg the Russian Tsar warmly approved. On the desk of his St Petersburg study, Nicholas I kept a statuette of the young man whom he liked to regard as not so much Metternich's pupil as his own.

Schwarzenberg adapted himself to this newest shift of constitutional emphasis with no great heart-searching. He remained prime minister, as of right. Everyone knew he was more interested in statecraft than in forms of government. At fifty-one he was still looking to the future. With railways and the electric telegraph linking Vienna more closely to other capitals, he dreamt of seeing the city accepted as the natural centre of Great Power diplomacy. But the strain of government was taking more out of him than he recognized. The Metternichs, the Radetzkys and, indeed, the Habsburgs themselves enjoyed longevity; the Schwarzenberg family did not. On 5 April 1852 he was felled by an apoplectic stroke as he buckled himself into a tight-fitting hussar uniform for a court ball.

Francis Joseph genuinely mourned the soldier-statesman. Over half a century later, he recalled Schwarzenberg as 'my greatest minister'. A well-known lithograph shows him kneeling beside the deathbed, with Archduke Charles Ludwig, Count Grünne and Alexander Bach sharing the grief of their sovereign, who is said to have been in tears. 'I must make an effort not to lose my composure', he wrote next morning to his mother, who was in Graz; 'I must uphold the principle of order, which cannot be allowed to sink into the grave with this great man.' These were fine sentiments, no doubt; more practical ones followed. 'Now I shall have to do more things myself, for I cannot rely on anybody as I used to rely on Schwarzenberg', the Archduchess was told. And in a revealing after-thought her son added, 'Perhaps that is all to the good'. For the next seven years Francis Joseph was to rule without a prime minister.

Chapter 5

MARRIAGE

For Archduchess Sophie the death of Felix Schwarzenberg intensified a personal dilemma of which she had been uneasily conscious over many months. She knew she fulfilled the role of First Lady in the Empire excellently, adding a lustre to Court life unknown for thirty years. The heads of distinguished families served as Grand Master of the Household, Grand Chamberlain, Master of the Horse, and so on; but it was the Archduchess who made certain that the Court machine purred smoothly. The Emperor's daily timetable was submitted to her for approval: she said where and when meals were to be served and, in the last resort, she decided such tricky matters as the guest list at the imperial table or the floral decorations for State and Court Balls during carnival time. She ensured that a new and young Emperor rode in smartly refurbished carriages, with coachmen and postilions once more elegant in the yellow imperial livery, for she believed in parading the triumph of counter-revolution for all Vienna to observe, and to accept as right and natural. These tasks would increase if her son's insistence on being both head of the army and head of the government reduced still more the time he gave to the outer trappings of royalty.

Yet the Archduchess was only an Acting First Lady. Her son would soon have to marry, as she sadly recognized. If the future of the Monarchy looked assured in 1851–2, what of the future of the dynasty? Had well-placed guns killed both her elder sons at Raab in the summer of 1848, or had they perished at sea in that storm in the northern Adriatic, the task of moulding an Emperor would have begun all over again, with the succession passing to the Archduke Charles Ludwig. This was a challenge no bereaved mother could contemplate. She remained deeply concerned over Francis Joseph's safety. His courage was admirable: unflinchingly he set out on long visits to inner Hungary, Transylvania and Croatia soon after Schwarzenberg's death. But was this headstrong bravery foolhardy? He seemed at times to be courting assassination. Sophie, despite her superficial silliness of sentiment, was a realist at heart. There was no doubt in her mind that Francis Joseph needed a bride and children to safeguard the succession. The intrusion on his daily life of family responsibilities might mellow that stern sense of duty to the state which made the Emperor so much more like an institution than the father of his peoples.

In adolescence Francis Joseph had absorbed Catholic doctrines on the sanctity of family life, with moral precepts given him by Rauscher or Colombi and endorsed by his mother. Like most children of his day, whether noble or commoner, he received no sex instruction whatsoever, and he may well have been surprised by some aspects of barrack life when he was first attached to the Hussars. But he was a normal and healthy full-blooded young man and in the following winter it was left to Count Grünne to rectify lapses in the Emperor's education, with the apparent approval of the Archduchess. Gossip later elaborated a *Giselle*-esque sequence of secret assignations in deepest Bohemia during army manoeuvres. Perhaps there was some basis for these tales but, if so, the girl whom Grünne vetted for his sovereign would have been a 'hygienically pure' countess rather than a simple, starry-eyed peasant. Whatever the truth about these well-regulated escapades, it is at least clear that Francis Joseph was not without some sexual experience before he set out in earnest to look for a wife.

Inwardly he had already convinced himself that he would choose a companion whose charm and qualities appealed to him alone. He would, he thought, ignore the promptings of his mother or her trusted agents at Court; and, almost inevitably, his first attachment startled both the Archduchess and Grünne. For, at the time of Schwarzenberg's death, he was captivated by a beautiful young widow, Princess Elizabeth of Modena, a first cousin five months his junior in age but already the mother of a two year old daughter. What alarmed Sophie was not the Princess's tragically brief experience of married life but her childhood background, for she was a daughter of Archduke Joseph, the long-serving Palatine of Hungary; she was therefore a half-sister of that Palatine-Archduke Stephen, whose fair-mindedness towards the Hungarians had caused Grünne to resign from his service. Briefly Francis Joseph's infatuation for his cousin seemed likely to soften his attitude towards his Hungarian subjects. In the spring of 1852 he appeared at a state ball in Hungarian Hussar's uniform and allowed the Csardas to be danced at Court in Vienna for the first time in five years. But the romantic attachment did not last out the summer. It is probable that the entrenched anti-Hungarian prejudices of Sophie and the Court were too formidable a challenge for the young widow to face; two years later she married another first cousin,

Archduke Charles's second son, and settled down happily enough in Moravia.

In the autumn Francis Joseph visited Berlin. At Charlottenburg he met the King of Prussia's niece, Anna. Politically a Prussian marriage appealed to the Austrian foreign minister, Count von Buol-Schauenstein, and his mentor, Metternich; dynastic links would ease Austro-Prussian relations after the tension of the Schwarzenberg years. But by Christmas it was clear the Prussian marriage project was a non-starter. There were three grave obstacles to any such union: Anna's staunch Lutheranism; her prior betrothal to the widower Margrave of Hesse; and the fierce opposition to an Austrian connection of the old guard of Prussian conservatives. With Berlin off the list, Archduchess Sophie encouraged her son to go to Dresden and court Princess Sidonia, one of the six sisters of his close friend and cousin, Albert of Saxony. But Sidonia's health was poor and, in contrast to Elizabeth of Modena and Anna of Prussia, she seemed awkward and low-spirited: there was no Empress in the making to be found at Dresden.

After these setbacks it was natural for Sophie to return to the fond hopes of earlier years and dream of arranging yet another Habsburg-Wittelsbach marriage. Letters to her sister Ludovika, in Bavaria, gave due attention to what Sophie believed were Francis Joseph's likes and dislikes in a woman: graceful movement, a ready smile, lightness of laughter and, above all, confident horsemanship: 'There is nothing the Emperor admires more in a woman than an elegant seat on a horse', reported Sophie. At once Ludovika insisted that her elder daughter, Helen, should take more riding lessons. But 'Néné' would never match the skills of her sister 'Sisi' in the saddle.

Francis Joseph had shown no interest in his Bavarian cousins since their brief visit to Innsbruck, and he does not seem to have suspected his mother of rekindling the Wittelsbach flame that winter. During the first months of 1853 he was again up to his eyes in desk-work: there were long despatches for him to consider from London, Paris, St Petersburg and Constantinople over the evident weakness of Ottoman rule in the Balkans, and in particular the harsh treatment of Christian communities in Bosnia; and there was a renewal of Italian nationalistic feeling in Milan. He remained in residence at the Hofburg after the Carnival season was over, taking regular walks around the old fortifications for exercise in the afternoons. It was while he was strolling beside one of the outer bastions on the second Sunday in February, that Janos Libenyi, a twenty-one year old tailor's apprentice, attacked him from behind, thrusting a long knife into his collar. Fortunately the heavy golden covering embroidered on the stiff collar of the Emperor's uniform deflected the blow, saving him from death but leaving him bleeding from a deep cut. A civilian passer-by, Dr Joseph Ettenreich, came to his assistance while his military aide, Count Maximilian O'Donnell, seized Libenyi and held him until police guards took him into custody: 'Long live Kossuth', Libenyi shouted (in Magyar), as he was led away. Francis Joseph insisted that the police should not maltreat him on the spot, but when the young Hungarian was condemned to death, there was no reprieve and he was hanged on Simmering Heath. Characteristically the Emperor granted a small pension to his would-be assassin's mother.

The attempt on Francis Joseph's life aroused widespread sympathy for him in Vienna. The churches were crowded that evening as rumours spread through the city and suburbs. Archduke Maximilian, serving with the naval squadron at Trieste, was so alarmed by the news that he hurried to the capital; he found his brother in bed with a high fever, but so angry at the sudden arrival of the heir-presumptive in his bedroom that he gave him a good dressing-down for leaving the fleet without permission. Despite this rebuff, the Archduke was deeply affected by the attempt on his brother's life and launched an appeal for subscriptions to build a thanksgiving church, close to the site of Libenyi's attack. Maximilian did not live to see the church completed, but the tapering twin spires of the neo-Gothic Votivkirche remain a familiar feature of Vienna's skyline, a graceful monument to the uncertainties of those first years of the reign.

The Emperor's narrow escape from death stirred sentiments of loyalty in the capital as well as in more distant provincial cities, where his popularity had never been in doubt. Despite his courage and fortitude on the day of the attack, he suffered from delayed shock and was weak from the loss of blood. It was almost a month before he was able to leave the Hofburg. When, on 12 March, he drove in a Victoria carriage to St Stephen's Cathedral for a service of thanksgiving at his recovery, crowds along the street gave him an enthusiastic reception. It is said that, on this occasion, he resolved to relax the military regime which still ordered affairs in both Vienna and Prague, but the restrictions of martial law were not finally lifted until early September.

Francis Joseph was soon himself again. In the second week of May he was host to King Leopold I of the Belgians, who had known Vienna before and during the Congress. The Emperor's bearing and personality made a deep impression on the King, a shrewd judge of character. 'There is much sense and courage in his warm blue eye, and it is not without a very amiable merriment when there is occasion for it', Leopold wrote to his niece Queen Victoria on returning to Brussels, 'He is slight and very graceful, but even in the mêlée of dancers and Archdukes, and all in uniform, he may always be distinguished as the *Chef* [dominant man].

'This struck me more than anything, as now at Vienna the dancing is also that general mêlée which renders waltzing most difficult. The manners are excellent and free from pompousness or awkwardness of any kind, simple, and when he is graciously disposed, as he was to me, *sehr herzlich und naturlich*' (very cordial and unaffected) ... 'I think he may be severe *si l'occasion se présente*' (if called upon to be so); 'he has something very *muthig*' (mettlesome; self-assured). 'We were several times surrounded by people of all classes, and he was certainly quite at their mercy, but I never saw his little *muthig* expression changed either by being pleased or alarmed.'

Franz Grillparzer, with a poet's instinct for deeply felt sentiments, celebrated the Emperor's escape by addressing a short ode of thanksgiving, not to the wounded convalescent, but to his mother. Libenyi's knife thrust on 18 February shocked the Archduchess; in the last years of her life she never let the anniversary pass by without giving thanks in her diary for her son's preservation that Sunday. The attack intensified her determination to see her son married soon; family life, she believed, would domesticate the imperial institution, thereby making it more acceptable and secure. In June an invitation was sent to Duchess Ludovika in her summer residence at Possenhofen. Sophie suggested that her sister might leave the delights of the Starnbergersee for a few days in August and bring her two elder daughters through the mountains to the Salzkammergut to help celebrate their cousin's twenty-third birthday. The roads were not difficult in summer; and, as it happened, Ischl was actually nearer to Possenhofen than to Vienna.

Despite his insistence that he would not be pushed into marriage, on this occasion Francis Joseph welcomed his mother's initiative. As he regarded himself as the paramount German prince, he had never seriously considered looking outside the German dynastic system for a bride, for his passing infatuation with his widowed Habsburg cousin seems basically to have sprung from a rush of carnival blood to the head. At nineteen his Bavarian cousin Helen was the right age for him; close consanguinity never troubled him or his mother – doubts over such matters could be set aside by papal dispensation. At Innsbruck she had meant nothing to him, a sharp-featured and slightly morose youngster, with little enough to say for herself. Yet by now there seemed nothing but praise for Néné's qualities, even from the Austrian envoys in Munich. So eager was Francis Joseph for the meeting that he insisted on having the speediest horses from the Schönbrunn stables saddled for the journey to the Salzkammergut. With Grünne as his travelling companion he reached Ischl in nineteen hours rather than the usual day and a half.

By contrast, Duchess Ludovika and the Princesses Helen and Elizabeth arrived an hour and a half late, for it had been a wet August in the mountains, and rain and mud slowed down their coachmen. Even so, they outpaced the carriage containing their luggage boxes, and Ludovika was travel weary and ill-at-ease when, on the afternoon of 16 August, she brought her daughters to join the Archduchess and her sons for tea, with Ludovika's elder sister, Queen Elise of Prussia (Elizabeth's godmother) also there. Socially it was not the easiest of family gatherings. Néné, fully aware of the plans made for her, succumbed to an embarrassed shyness and could only exchange conventional pleasantries with Francis Joseph. Sisi, on the other hand, had no such high expectations to inhibit her. She behaved naturally, her oval face alive with changing expression as she speedily took up the childhood friendship with Charles Ludwig which so amused the family at Innsbruck five years before. The tense awkwardness of a contrived reunion thawed. Yet even before dinner was served that evening both the devoted Charles Ludwig and Sisi herself realized that the Emperor had grown tired of small talk with Néné. Instead, he was fascinated by her sister's untarnished elfin qualities, by the long auburn hair and the challenge of those dancing eyes, quizzically unfathomable beneath straight, black eyebrows. Throughout the meal he seemed to be looking intensely at Sisi, who had always hated to be drawn into the limelight and lapsed into a silence. That evening Charles Ludwig, with a sad pang of jealousy, reproached his mother: 'Mama, Franzi likes Sisi very much, far more than he does Néné. You'll see; he will choose her rather than the elder one.' This, the Archduchess thought, was sheer nonsense: 'What an idea!', she replied, 'As if he would look twice at that little imp!'

But Charles Ludwig was right. When next day Francis Joseph saw his mother before breakfast he could talk of nothing except Sisi's natural charm. The Archduchess's diary – with these pages more faded than any others, as if they had been read and re-read time and time again – still conveys her son's excitement that morning. She urged him to be in no hurry, not to rush matters, for there was no need for an immediate betrothal. It was no use; her son had fallen irretrievably in love with his cousin. Even in the sober light of a rainy morning, the passion was still there; and in seeking to refute his mother's arguments, he sought to express himself in a poetic lyricism remote from every earlier experience in his life. The words are trite and the imagery ludicrous, but there is no questioning the sincerity of his emotions. He could not accept his mother's contention that she was too young for him. 'No, see how sweet Sisi is!', he insisted, 'She is as fresh as a newly peeled almond, and what a splendid crown of hair frames such a vision! How can anyone help loving such tender eyes and lips like strawberries!'. The Archduchess was reluctant to give up the fight. 'Don't you find Helen intelligent, and with a beautiful slim figure, too?' she claims to have asked her son. 'Yes', came the reply, 'but, although she is pretty and agreeable enough, she is serious and tongue-tied. Now, Sisi- Sisi – there is something really attractive; that modest girlishness; and yet such high spirits!' The Emperor was not infatuated. He was bewitched.

Not that Elizabeth consciously strove to enchant him. She was puzzled and surprised by his attention. At the first ball in Ischl, which both Archduchess Sophie and Duchess Ludovika had expected to be a triumph for Helen, it was with Sisi that the Emperor insisted on dancing the cotillion; and he presented her with every bouquet. Her governess asked her if she was surprised by this gesture: 'No', she replied, 'only embarrassed.'

By the morning of Francis Joseph's birthday, the Archduchess acknowledged defeat. Carefully planned dynastic marriages had a habit of going slightly awry: fourteen years previously Queen Victoria chose 'dear Albert' rather than his elder brother, Ernest (whom her half-sister had thought more suited for her); and now Francis Joseph was attracted to Elizabeth with a not dissimilar stubborn intensity of passion. Yet there was an all important difference between the two royal romances: Albert of Saxe-Coburg was twenty at the time of his betrothal, mature beyond his years and trained to assume responsibilities greater than any son of a minor German princeling might be expected to encounter; Elizabeth of Bavaria, who would not be sixteen until Christmas Eve, still romped like a child, and was, as yet, totally uncoached in the role of Empress. Francis Joseph brushed aside these objections and others, too. By the time he had spent most of his birthday in her company and sat beside her as he was serenaded by Tyrolean singers in the early evening, he was convinced he had met his bride. All he would concede in conversation with his mother was that 'My position is such a difficult one that God knows it can be no pleasure to share it with me.' He insisted that no one should put pressure on the young Elizabeth to accept him as a husband. She must weigh up such matters herself, he said, with what he assumed to be a kindly understanding of his cousin's dilemma.

Yet he had not even begun to understand her temperament. When Francis Joseph was fifteen he could pen a diary entry regretting the speedy passage of time, which left him with only a few years in which to mend his ways and complete his education. Happily, at that same age, Elizabeth was untroubled by so priggish a conscience, though she remained dutifully devout in her strictly religious observance. But Elizabeth was a puzzling girl, with a character much more high-powered than her aunt appreciated. She was a romantic, already given to writing verses which were restlessly pining rather than sentimental in form. When happy she was young enough to radiate a spontaneous joy in living, a natural antidote to Francis Joseph's cool, disciplined professionalism. But she was a creature of impulse. Often her response to events or to meeting people was either a passionate enthusiasm or a long and childish hatred. At Ischl, in these perplexing days she needed good advice. 'Yes, I am already fond of the Emperor', she told her governess, 'But if only he were not an Emperor!' she sighed.

Her mother and her aunt, though disappointed that Helen had been brushed aside, were too committed to the idea of a Bavarian marriage not to encourage Elizabeth; and Sophie, ignoring the truculent set of her niece's stubborn chin, thought Sisi still young enough to be moulded into character. The Archduchess carefully noted her response to all that was happening: her resentment of the hovering presence of the sardonic Count Grünne beside the Emperor on their expeditions, and the moments when she seemed awkward, diffident and shy; and Sophie's journal also records Elizabeth's significant reply to the good wishes of Countess Esterhazy, the Court Mistress of the Robes: 'I shall need a great deal of indulgence at first'. Everyone at Ischl spoke of the Princess's marvellous good fortune. Had her father, an eccentric and wildly independent hedonist, accompanied his daughters to the Salzkammergut he might have given wise counsel to his favourite child. But would he have advised her to turn her back on the greatest marriage in Catholic Europe? As it was, he was consulted by telegram. Willingly, he gave his approval.

Officially the betrothal was made public at the end of Mass in Ischl's parish church. Francis Joseph led Elizabeth by the hand to the altar steps, presented her to the priest as 'my future wife', and asked for his blessing. The *Wiener Zeitung* carried the news next day, prompting a rash of speculative artistry by painters who had never seen the Bavarian princess but cashed in on local knowledge of the Salzkammergut to give their work scenic verisimilitude. For the rest of August the Emperor lingered happily at Ischl, on fine days showing Sisi the countryside he particularly liked. 'It is lovely to see such youthful radiance shining in such a wonderful landscape', Queen Elise remarked after the whole party dined beside the Wolfgangsee.

'It was hard and depressing to make the leap from the earthly paradise of Ischl to a desk-bound existence and masses of state papers, with all the cares and troubles they bring me', sighed Francis Joseph in a letter to his mother as soon as he was back in Vienna. The romantic idyll had come in the midst of a grave international crisis, with Russian troops threatening to invade the Ottoman Empire and controlling the lower waters of the Danube. Throughout the eight months of his engagement to Elizabeth, it was the Emperor's misfortune to be plagued by elaborate memoranda, some expressed at great length by the indomitable elder statesman, Metternich. To what extent should Austria assert independence of Russia? Was it possible to benefit from dynastic goodwill without lessening the Empire's protective influence over Catholic communities in the western Balkans?

The Tsar gave him little peace. Nicholas was even willing to travel down from Warsaw for several days of top-level talks. Accordingly, less than a month after saying farewell to Elizabeth at Ischl, Francis Joseph was back in northern Moravia, riding beside the Tsar as the two sovereigns inspected troops encamped outside Olmütz, and their foreign ministers sought compromise solutions of the long-term disputes between Russia and her Ottoman neighbour. There followed a brief, and unconvincing, show of solidarity by the three eastern autocrats in Warsaw, where the Emperor found the King of Prussia as reluctant as himself to join the Tsar in a formal military alliance. Then, as soon as he could decently escape from Poland, Francis Joseph was on his way to Bavaria to see the Princess at Schloss Possenhofen, her much-loved home on the Starnbergersee. With her family he would go into residence in Munich, where he could pay his respects to yet another cousin, Maximilian II, King of Bavaria.

Possenhofen – 'Possi' as the place was affectionately called – remained tucked away from the outside world; and this seclusion enabled Francis Joseph and Elizabeth to find even more satisfaction in each other's company than at Ischl. It was while riding beside the Starnbergersee that the Emperor discovered for the first time how fine a horsewoman he was marrying, as skilled a rider sidesaddle as anyone in Europe. The brief visit to Munich was more trying: Elizabeth could not disguise her boredom at having to receive the whole diplomatic corps, assembled to offer felicitations on her forthcoming marriage; and when the Emperor and Princess entered their box at the opera house, the reception was so rapturous that Sisi was overcome with shyness and sought to sink back into the shadows rather than face the appraising eyes of Munich high society. However, at the Court Ball on the following night she carried herself with a natural dignity and poise. Francis Joseph remained enchanted by her, although he was surprised at the casual indiscipline of life at his fiancée's beloved Possi. The tone of his letters to Archduchess Sophie was ecstatic: 'I love Sisi more every day and feel more certain than ever that there is no other woman who would suit me as well as she', he wrote with refreshing simplicity.

He returned to Vienna in the last week of October to find the international crisis intensifying day by day. Already the Russian and Ottoman armies were in conflict along the lower reaches of the Danube, and on the last day of November a squadron from Sebastopol destroyed the Sultan's fleet at Sinope. No one doubted that France and Britain would soon become involved in a war to deny Russia naval mastery over the Black Sea and the Straits. The Austrians were subjected to intense diplomatic pressure from both sides, and the Emperor presided over a succession of cabinet meetings to discuss ways of safeguarding commercial and strategic interests along the Danube, while stopping short of a war which would have brought the Monarchy close to bankruptcy. Yet, despite these worries, Francis Joseph was able to reach Munich in the small hours of 21 December, in good time to celebrate Elizabeth's sixteenth birthday.

On this occasion the couple exchanged portraits, each having been painted on horseback. And for Christmas itself there were flowers brought by express courier from the hothouse conservatories at Schönbrunn, together with a green parrot – a present which especially delighted Elizabeth, and which she was to insist on being brought back to her in Vienna before her wedding. Archduchess Sophie sent a fine garland of roses which, with a tactful gesture, Elizabeth held with her left arm while posing for a birthday portrait by Franz Hanfstaengel. A slight note of Elizabeth's wilfulness crept into Francis Joseph's reports to his mother, though he assured her that Sisi's teeth were now admirably white; back at Ischl in the summer, Sophie had mentioned to Ludovika that she thought them too yellow. Detailed arrangements over the wedding were settled, for the most part, by the two mother-sisters; and in March, barely a month before the marriage, Francis Joseph came once more to Munich, bringing the diamond and opal necklace the Archduchess had worn at her own wedding and now wished to pass on to the future Empress.

This third visit to Bavaria in six months emphasizes Francis Joseph's extraordinary ability to keep a public and a private life detached in his mind. He was still effective head of the government and head of the army, and in Vienna he recognized that, as in the first months after his accession, the Austrian Empire stood at a crossroads in its affairs. Count Buol, faithfully echoing the views of Metternich, sought to follow the policy of 1813; he would stay clear of war until Austrian intervention could be decisive. But there was, too, a powerful military party in the capital, pro-Russian in sentiment and recommending an alliance with St Petersburg on the assumption that Austria would receive a free hand in the western Balkans and the certainty of continued partnership against revolutionary liberalism. As so often when his generals spoke out, Francis Joseph found in their arguments much to attract him. In the end, however, he backed Buol. Nevertheless he accepted the need for partial mobilization, and throughout the celebrations of the following weeks, his troops stood on the alert in Galicia and along the Empire's eastern borders.

Would the marriage have been postponed had Austria gone to war? Did the thought of Possenhofen and his marriage compact tilt the balance of judgment towards peace and arbitration? It is hard to say. At all events, he was able to put such grave issues out of his mind once he travelled to Bavaria. To his mother he wrote back from Munich, much as he had done ten years before, when first excited by the mountains of the Tyrol: 'It was a wonderful sunny day', he reported, describing how he joined his aunt Ludovika, Sisi, Néné and four other cousins, 'all bundled into one carriage so as to drive off to Possenhofen. The snow-covered mountains reflected in the deep blue lake looked near enough for us to be on their slopes, and clouds of wild geese were flying over the water'; and he added, 'It was all very jolly, especially after dinner when the youngsters had more champagne than they were accustomed to drinking.'

On Thursday, 20 April 1854, an offensive and defensive alliance between Austria and Prussia was concluded in Berlin, a key treaty which was to help localize the Crimean War. Yet, however important this pledge of 'intimate understanding' between the two sovereigns may have become, it aroused little interest at the time in the German lands and even less in Austria. For on that same Thursday Princess Elizabeth left Munich for her marriage on the following Monday, and during the rest of the month there was a constant round of festivity in Vienna and many other cities of the Empire, too. It was hoped finally to heal the bitterness left by the revolutionary years. Church charities in the worst ravaged lands received a gift of 200,000 florins. The Magyar nobility were invited to send delegations to the marriage ceremony and receptions, wearing what Archduchess Sophie sourly called their 'fancy dress costumes', while the Emperor-bridegroom granted an amnesty for 380 political offenders and promised that, from 1 May, martial law would be lifted in Lombardy-Venetia.

In Vienna itself, every effort was made to encourage Prater gaiety and to restore the neo-classical image of an imperial capital city. Streets and squares were to be decorated with flags and flowers and illuminated on the eve of the wedding as well as on the day itself. 'Several nobles have gone to an enormous expense in the external decoration of their palaces', reported Thomas O'Brien, the (frequently sardonic) correspondent of *The Times*, adding that 'the Papal Nuncio has taken advantage of the festive occasion and had his palace whitewashed, of which kind attention it has been in very great need for many long years'. In planning the ceremonies old traditions were maintained: the bride would, as was customary, go into residence at the Theresianum in Wieden as soon as she arrived in the capital and, like other imperial brides, she would be officially

74

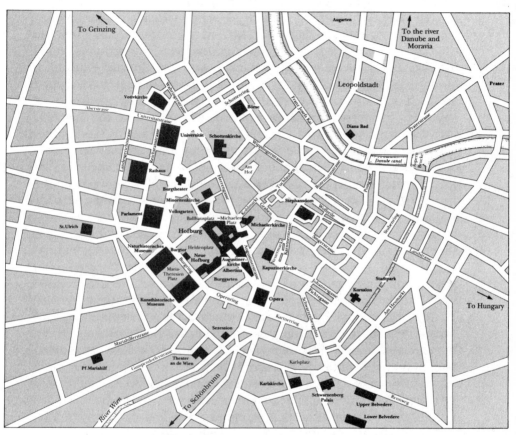

Francis Joseph's Vienna (c. 1900)

received by the city authorities on the day before the wedding. But there were novelties, too. Elizabeth was to come down the Danube aboard a paddle-steamer, named after the Emperor. And, having welcomed her to Austrian soil at Linz on the Friday evening, he would then travel back to Vienna in time to greet her on Saturday afternoon at an ornate landing stage constructed on the quayside at Nussdorf.

Even before Elizabeth left Munich, an ominous incident in Vienna was noted down by the Archduchess in her journal. Sophie's half-sister, the widowed Dowager Empress Caroline Augusta, had come up to the capital from Salzburg where she had lived for most of the nineteen years since her husband's death. Leaning forward to inspect a beautifully shaped diamond tiara which was to be Francis Joseph's wedding present to his bride, the poor woman's mantilla was caught on one of the diamond stars and, as she stepped back, the tiara went crashing to the ground. Fortunately the court jeweller succeeded in repairing the damage before Elizabeth arrived in Vienna and there is no evidence that she ever discovered what had happened. Thereafter, however, all went well with the arrangements, except that it took the paddle-boat half an hour to moor at Nussdorf because of the strong current in the Danube.

The Times correspondent was at the quayside to comment on all that happened. As soon as the landing bridge touched the vessel, Francis Joseph 'rushed on board and, in the presence of a vast crowd of onlookers, tenderly embraced and kissed his bride. The youthful Monarch yielded entirely to the dictates of his feelings, taking no pains whatever to conceal the delight he felt at the safe arrival of the Princess, whose hand he never quitted until he placed her in the carriage in which she drove with the Archduchess Sophie to Schönbrunn ... The Princess Elizabeth smiled and bowed to her future subjects as if every face on which her eye rested belonged to an old and valued friend. Some straightlaced critics would have preferred a more dignified and reserved deportment, but what has a young girl of 16, whose heart is overflowing with love and kindly feeling, to do with dignity and reserve?'. And, with some satisfaction, Thomas O'Brien observed that 'the military colouring which for so many years has been given to everything here was entirely wanting'. But the army was there in strength on the following afternoon, when the Princess made her grand entry into Vienna, taking two hours to cover the densely packed mile and three-quarter route from the Theresianum to St Stephen's Cathedral. The procession, so O'Brien reported, 'was headed by 2 or 3 squadrons of lancers'; and, remembering that *The Times*'s readers would have the war with Russia in their minds, he added, 'Would that the Allies had a dozen such regiments in Bulgaria!'.

The wedding was solemnized at four o'clock in the afternoon on

Monday, 24 April, in the Augustinerkirche, the fourteenth century court church in the shadow of the Hofburg. The imperial couple were married by the Archduchess's spiritual adviser, Joseph Othmar von Rauscher, who had been consecrated Archbishop of Vienna in the previous year. More than 50 mitred bishops formed a huge semicircle around Rauscher as the rings were exchanged and saluting cannon on the Augustinerbastion fired the first salvoes to join the pealing church bells in letting Vienna know that Austria had a new Empress. Rauscher, an ambitious prelate with a cardinal's red hat in his sights, made the most of the occasion by delivering a thirty minute address on the virtues of family life – a sermon 'evidently too long for at least one of the parties present', *The Times* archly reported.

There followed a fifty yard procession down the carpeted street to the Hofburg, where for two hours the Emperor and Empress were expected to receive the loyal homage of their guests: princes and princesses, dukes and duchesses, the old aristocracy and the new and the surviving military paladins, Radetzky, Windischgraetz and Jellaçić. At last, between ten o'clock and eleven, dinner was served, purely for the family. The bride, however, had little appetite. She had seen Habsburg court life only on holiday in Ischl; the reality in Vienna stifled her. Nor were the wedding festivities yet complete. One traditional ceremony remained, duly noted by the Archduchess with the slightly prurient sentimentality so typical of her journal entries: Ludovika 'and I escorted the young bride to her room. I left her with her mother and waited in the anteroom, next to the great chamber in which was the marriage bed. I then fetched my son and led him to his young wife, as I now accepted her to be, so as to wish them a good night. She hid her natural loveliness, for only a wealth of beautiful free-flowing hair buried in her bolster caught my eye, like a frightened bird lying low in its nest'.

Such intrusiveness came naturally to the Archduchess, and she thought nothing of Elizabeth's shy discomfiture. Nor, indeed, did Francis Joseph himself. Some twenty years later, when the Empress could rely on her own hand-picked ladies in waiting, she told them of the embarrassments she experienced in these first weeks of married life: there was no honeymoon; and she was horrified to find she could never rely on having a private breakfast with her husband in the mornings. Perhaps she exaggerated the extent to which Francis Joseph was, in domestic matters, still under his mother's thumb. But there can be no doubt of the lack of privacy at such an intimate time. Once more, the evidence is there, in Sophie's journal: 'Tuesday, 25 April . . . We [the two mother-sisters] found the young pair at breakfast in the lovely writing-room, my son radiant and full of himself, a picture of happiness (God be thanked). Sisi was deeply affected as her mother embraced her. At first we wished to leave them alone, but the Emperor stopped us with a heart-warming summons back again'. There was one question to which both mothers anxiously sought an answer. Elizabeth had no intention of satisfying their curiosity. But in such matters Francis Joseph understood the older generation better than the younger. On Thursday, 27 April, the Archduchess's journal records that Elizabeth had excused herself from the communal breakfast; and later the Emperor came to his mother privately, and let her know that 'Sisi had fulfilled his love'.

Francis Joseph did his best to make his sixteen-year old wife happy. The international crisis ruled out any honeymoon distant from Vienna, he insisted. But, just as he had sought to amuse her with a new parrot before their marriage, so on the Saturday after the wedding he escorted her to the Prater for a command performance by the Circus Renz, the finest display of trick horsemanship in the world: sixty horses; a firework display; more than forty balloons released into the night sky; twelve greys and twelve blacks dancing a horse quadrille; and Ernst Renz himself giving a superlative exhibition of *haute école* on his Arab mare. 'It really was too lovely for words', Sisi was heard to remark to her husband as she left; and she added, 'I really must get to know that man Renz'. Such a suggestion shocked her mother-in-law.

Next morning Elizabeth's mother, father and sister left Vienna to return home. The Emperor, though still puzzled by the child bride's reactions to what seemed to him the natural way of life in the capital, recognized that she was close to physical and nervous collapse. On that Sunday afternoon he acted decisively: his spell of formal residence in the capital was over; he would take his bride fifteen miles out into the country at Laxenburg, and travel every morning into the Hofburg, returning to his wife each evening. Sisi, so he told his mother, was overtired; and no doubt she was, at least within the Hofburg. But she was fit enough to go out riding that same evening. Laxenburg, with its grotto and Gothic bridge and the small wooded lake dotted with artificial islands, lacked 'dear Possi's' spaciousness; but to get into the saddle again after eight crowded days in Vienna brought an almost electric vitality back into her being. She became once more the firebird, as entrancing as at Ischl.

This was, of course, the conduct of a spoilt child, as Francis Joseph knew at heart. But, though rigidly bound by disciplined codes of behaviour himself, he was ready to show a generous complaisance towards his wife's moods. And thus, almost casually, he set standards to which he was to adhere in later years, too. For however much her self-indulgent whims might try his patience, throughout their married life the Emperor loved Elizabeth's individuality so intensely that he never tried in earnest to curb the firebird's flight.

Chapter 6

'IT IS MY PLEASURE . . .'

Francis Joseph was trained to fulfil dutifully whatever tasks circumstances dictated to him, and he possessed an iron constitution anyone might envy. Throughout his life he remained astonishingly fit, rarely needing medical care once he shook off spells of faintness which occasionally afflicted him in early manhood. Yet, despite these advantages, there can be little doubt that he found the first years of married life supremely taxing. Increasingly stern portraits follow each other through the late 1850s: the mouth becomes harder set and side-whiskers, first cultivated in 1855, offset a hairline which photographs show fast receding by the end of the decade. The strain is not surprising. Other people might pursue professional careers and find relaxation in private domesticity: an Emperor of Austria could not expect to have his days so tidily divided, not even if newly married and still in his early twenties. The nature of imperial kingship obliged the young ruler to function at an extraordinary number of levels within a short span of time: as supreme autocrat, he was responsible for deciding issues of peace and war which could enhance or destroy the dynastic heritage handed down to him; as the living embodiment of a divinely instituted sovereignty, he was the ceremonial light around whom the planetary pageant of Court revolved; and as self-appointed president of the council of ministers he was, for much of the day, a desk-bound notary-extraordinary, with reports and memoranda to be read, and decrees and commissions awaiting his signature of authority. To this burden of work there was added each evening the task of placating an adolescent bride, who was bored with Laxenburg, angered by ladies-in-waiting she had not herself chosen, and quite incapable of understanding why her husband should remain so long at the Hofburg, immersed in the humdrum business of government.

Since the Emperor remained passionately in love with his wife, he dealt patiently and sympathetically with her grievances. They would ride together at the weekends and one day he took her with him to the Hofburg, but the experiment was not a success; Elizabeth became ill-at-ease once she was left in what still remained so visibly the home the Emperor's mother had created. Some twenty years later Elizabeth would list the Archduchess's enormities for her chosen companions to hear and record: the rebukes for troubling Francis Joseph with petty matters in these months of crisis; the astonishment that she should wish 'to chase after her husband, driving here, there and everywhere as if she were a young subaltern'; and, conversely, the insistence that an Empress could not expect privacy, that she must not remain hidden away from her husband's subjects in the inner gardens of Laxenburg. The Archduchess, in her 'malice' (*bosheit*), exaggerated trifles, so Elizabeth complained.

Many of these tales find echoes in Sophie's correspondence. It is clear that at times she could be tiresomely silly, especially in the late summer and autumn of 1854 once Elizabeth was known to be pregnant. Old worries surfaced again, including the pre-natal misfortune which had allegedly disfigured Sophie's sister-in-law, Marianna: 'I feel that Sisi should not spend too much time with her parrots', the Archduchess wrote to Francis Joseph, 'If a woman is always looking at animals in the first months, the children are inclined to resemble them. Far better that she should look at herself in the mirror, or at you. *That* would have my entire approval'. Yet there is no malice and little envy in the Archduchess's writings. Her diary preserves the proud – and sometimes exasperated – affection she felt towards Elizabeth. She rejoiced over the success of a state visit to Bohemia and Moravia made by the Emperor and Empress soon after their marriage, and her journal entry for 15 June 1854 is full of praise for Elizabeth's bearing in the solemn Corpus Christi Day procession through the heart of Vienna: 'The young couple looked perfect, inspiring, uplifting. The Empress's demeanour was enchanting; devout, quite wrapt in humble meditation.'

Not all of the Emperor's preoccupations were so solemn. Thus, in a note to his mother a fortnight later, he apologized for not having written to her earlier in the day by explaining that on his journey back from the capital, he had gone to Mödling, a small town three miles from Laxenburg, and 'for the first time swam' in the 'swimming-school' there. Occasionally he went shooting and in late July, to Elizabeth's great relief, they were able to get away to Ischl. Yet in that summer of 1854 there could be little holiday.

Increasingly, week by week, it seemed as if Austria must be swept into 'the war in the East'. For over nine months the army had been mobilized in Slavonia and Transylvania and, shortly before his wedding ceremonies, the Emperor agreed that the Third Army in Hungary should be placed on a war footing. By the middle of May the Fourth Army, too, was fully mobilized in Galicia – and the whole military budget set aside for the year 1854 was already used up. Responsibility for all military dispositions lay with the Emperor, who had kept the post of minister of war vacant since the previous spring as he had no intention of allowing his authority as supreme master of the armed forces to be questioned. Grünne, head of the military chancellery, would speak for the army and navy at ministerial conferences, though General Hess was also normally present as Master of the Ordnance.

Francis Joseph did not appreciate the full significance of the policies he advocated that summer. He sought independence, allowing Austria to work with the British and the French, or to put forward a specifically Austrian solution to Balkan problems – and perhaps to German affairs – if Tsar Nicholas could be induced to abandon his role as 'gendarme of Europe'. At heart he believed he was fulfilling the testament of Schwarzenberg in freeing Austria from a dangerous dependence upon Russia and recovering the Empire's key position as arbiter of the balance of power on the continent. But he was wrong, as eventually he came to recognize. Since he could never collaborate with governments who gave sanctuary to radical exiles from Hungary and Lombardy-Venetia, the Empire would not so much gain independence as drift into dangerous isolation. In effect, Francis Joseph gave an impetus to the diplomatic revolution which was soon to bury the last relics of the Holy Alliance, abandoning the ideal of peace through collective responsibility which had been pursued by Europe's statesmen, however imperfectly, for the past forty years.

Yet, at the time, the policy made good sense. The Emperor accepted the political strategy first recommended to him by his foreign minister, Count Buol, earlier in the spring: Austria would avoid entanglement in any war in the East, but put pressure on St Petersburg to force the Russians out of Moldavia and Wallachia, the Sultan's semi-autonomous 'Danubian Principalities', occupied in the previous summer; Austrian troops might then, it was hoped, police the Principalities, standing guard along the lower Danube. Their presence would create a buffer between the Russians and their Ottoman enemy; it would also ensure that, in any postwar treaty, Austria could insist on international guarantees of free navigation along the great river.

On 29 May 1854 Francis Joseph, who would shortly be leaving Vienna for the state visit to Bohemia, convened a ministerial conference. At the head of the agenda was the need to settle details of an ultimatum which would require Russian evacuation of Moldavia and Wallachia on the grounds that the peaceful development of the Principalities was essential to Austria's vital interests. The conference minutes show that General

Hess was firmly opposed to sending any form of ultimatum whatsoever: Austria, he argued, was as yet unprepared for war on a battlefront stretching from Cracow, around the foothills of the Carpathians and across to the Danube delta. The Emperor, however, was convinced the Russians would not fight, for they too could not face a general war in the heart of the continent. Accordingly Francis Joseph overruled Hess's objections, but he also insisted that his ambassador in Constantinople should be instructed to seek an agreement with the Sultan authorizing Austrian troops to enter Moldavia and Wallachia as a guarantee that the Russians would not return there. The ultimatum was duly despatched to St Petersburg five days later. It required the Russians immediately to end military operations in Bulgaria, south of the Danube, and agree on talks to decide an early date for evacuation of the Principalities.

Tsar Nicholas, who for a year had conducted an increasingly acerbic correspondence with Francis Joseph, was infuriated by the ultimatum. With a characteristically dramatic gesture, he turned a portrait of the young Emperor to the wall and wrote across the back, *Du Undankbarer* ('You Ungrateful Wretch'); and he seriously considered rejecting the ultimatum. But not for long. Francis Joseph was right. Nicholas's generals could wage a localized war around the Black Sea, but they dared not risk opening up a new front in Europe. In August the Russians evacuated the Principalities. By the Convention of Boyadji-keuy, negotiated and ratified before the end of June, the Austrians were thereupon able to occupy Moldavia and police Wallachia jointly with the Turks, although no Austrian units were stationed in Bucharest itself.

Briefly, Francis Joseph believed Austria might gain even more from the war, possibly the permanent incorporation of the Principalities in his Empire. Early in October he explained to his mother that 'despite the political confusion, I am full of hope for, as I see it, if we act strongly and energetically, only good can come to us from this whole eastern affair. For our futures lies in the East, and we are going to push back Russia's power and influence behind the frontiers from which, solely through the weakness and disunity of earlier times, she was able to advance so as to work slowly but surely for ruin, perhaps unconsciously on the part of Tsar Nicholas'. Already Buol had moved as closely as possible to France and Great Britain; a formal alliance was under discussion; and, in consultation with the French, Buol formulated a peace programme – 'the Four Points' – which included a European guarantee of the Principalities and free navigation on the Danube, as well as assurances over the future of the Bosphorus and Dardanelles and of the status of the Sultan's Christian subjects which were of more immediate concern to the western allies. Francis Joseph personally would not have shrunk from waging war in the East. In the late summer of 1854 he ordered General Hess to prepare contingency plans for an attack on Russia next spring, with the main thrust coming between the rivers Bug and Vistula, and on 22 October the Emperor authorized total mobilization, even though Hess still thought he was setting the Monarchy on a dangerous course. There followed conferences in the Hofburg on 26 October and 15 and 17 November at which it was made clear to Francis Joseph that, although Archduke Albrecht shared his bellicosity, his ministers were inclined to agree with General Hess. Could troops be spared from Lombardy-Venetia, for Radetzky had already written personally to the Emperor in August asking for the return of a brigade which was on its way to Galicia? Could the Monarchy sustain the cost of war without plunging into state bankruptcy? And – the most telling of arguments – now that the arena of battle had shifted away from Bulgaria to the Crimea, was there a change of emphasis in the whole purpose of the war? A Lower Danubian War was a matter of deep concern to Austria: a Crimean War, fought primarily over the question of naval power in the Black Sea, was not. At the end of November 1854 Francis Joseph acknowledged the good sense of these arguments; there was to be no more contingency planning for a spring campaign in Poland.

Nevertheless Buol, always ready to assert Austria's importance as a Great Power, still occasionally pirouetted on the brink of war. On the sixth anniversary of Francis Joseph's accession a new Treaty of Vienna bound the Empire in alliance with Britain and France 'in case hostilities should break out between Austria and Russia', but it did not commit Francis Joseph to entering the conflict. Intermittent peace talks continued in Vienna, with Lord John Russell and the French Foreign Minister, Drouyn de Lhuys, attending an abortive conference which met under Buol's presidency in March and April. Russell, writing home to the British foreign secretary, reported that he found Francis Joseph's 'manner singularly agreeable, his countenance open and prepossessing' and added, somewhat patronizingly, that he showed 'an intelligence and a firmness of purpose which may enable him to rule with ability and success'; and Drouyn, too, was impressed by the Emperor's sincerity. But nobody had a good word to say for Buol. Although Austrian mobilization tied down in Poland a considerable Russian army which would otherwise have been deployed in the Crimea, the general feeling in Paris and London was that the Empire sought the fruits of victory without having to fight for it. This conviction was increased when financial necessity induced Francis Joseph to stand down his reservists at midsummer in 1855, a time when the British and French were mounting their most costly assaults on Sebastopol. At the start of the following year, it was under threat from Austria of an immediate declaration of war that the Russians finally agreed to end the fighting. But the ultimatum came too late to boost Austria's prestige; for, though the peace preliminaries were signed in Vienna, the Peace Congress was to be held in Napoleon III's Paris.

Once his minister's had persuaded him not to risk full-scale participation in the war, Francis Joseph seems to have lost interest in the 'eastern affair', despite his recent assurance to his mother that it was where 'our future' lay. He was, after all, first and foremost a German prince, constantly concerned over Prussia's reactions to the turn of events. Moreover his freedom of initiative remained limited by the circumstances of his accession. The autocratic system improvised by Schwarzenberg was still on trial. Much of the resistance to any forward policy in the east sprang from ministerial doubts whether the centralist forces upon which the regime depended for success were strong enough to check simultaneously national and social opposition, wherever it might occur. In many regions of Hungary, for example, the gentry and townsfolk remained passively uncollaborative, ridiculing the efforts – and decorative uniforms – of administrative officials drawn from other parts of the Monarchy who were unable to speak or understand their language. The Croats, who had expected much from Baron Jellaçić's loyalty to the dynasty, found themselves little better off than their Magyar neighbours. It is true that, so long as the industrial boom of the early 1850s provided jobs in the mills and factories, the urban areas of Austria and Bohemia-Moravia were quiet and contented, while the peasants were satisfied with the great land reform of 1848 which freed them from feudal obligations (though not until 1853 was their legal status as freeholders finally determined). So long as there was a surface prosperity, and a reasonably efficient administrative bureaucracy, Francis Joseph had no need to fear any challenge to the system; but throughout this 'decade of absolutism' he had to move with extreme caution: the Monarchy could not hope to survive another 1848. Fortunately the Emperor's confidence in his ability to fulfil his mission as a ruler remained undented.

He made no change in his circle of close advisers. Over most issues he still respected Grünne's opinions, though the Count was under a cloud in the autumn of 1854 because of allegedly pro-Russian inclinations. And only rarely did the Emperor question the stern rule of Radetzky in northern Italy, for he shared the respectful awe in which the army was encouraged to hold its legendary hero. As Governor-General of Lombardy-Venetia Radetzky lived in vice-regal splendour at Monza, the royal palace eight miles north of Milan which had been built for Francis Joseph's great-uncle in the heyday of benevolent despotism, and the Field Marshal had also been assigned 'perpetual' personal apartments in the Vienna

Hofburg. His administration was unimaginative and illiberal rather than harsh, but he was far too old to modify well-tried policies to meet the changing needs of the two provinces. Yet not until Radetzky entered his ninetieth year did the Emperor begin to heed the advice of those who favoured a more conciliatory attitude towards his Italian subjects.

The most outspoken advocate of a new approach was the heir to the throne, Archduke Maximilian. It was in September 1854, when Grünne was out of favour, that Francis Joseph had made his eldest brother a Rear Admiral and commander-in-chief of the navy, an appointment which pleased their mother and caused dismay among the old guard of military paladins. The Archduke, with his headquarters at Trieste and all the resources of the old Venetian naval yards to draw upon, at once began to seek money and imperial backing for the modernization of the fleet as a matter of urgency; and he received it. At Maximilian's insistence a new naval base was created in the fine natural harbour of Pola, while in the Trieste dockyards a 91-gun warship, her wooden hull protected by iron plates and her design incorporating the lessons learnt from the fighting in the Black Sea, was built and ready for launching in little more than a year. The navy remained a subordinate department of the Ministry of War and, almost inevitably, the warship was named *Radetzky*.

However much the old Marshal might merit this honour, the liberal-minded Archduke continued to chafe at the inadequacies of his government in Lombardy-Venetia. Maximilian had been an Italophile since boyhood and, as a naval officer, he came to like and respect the Triestini. On the outskirts of the city he built his dream villa, the castellated palace of Miramare, at far greater cost than he could afford but in confident expectation that this beautiful stretch of Adriatic littoral would remain as much a Habsburg possession as Laxenburg or Schönbrunn; this was a reasonable assumption, for Trieste had been in Habsburg hands since 1382, apart from the interlude of Napoleonic upheaval. In visits back to Vienna during 1854 and 1855, Maximilian stressed the importance of Trieste and the loyalty of the Slovene and Italian population throughout Istria. But Francis Joseph remained sceptical over his brother's assumption that the establishment of a benevolent regime in Milan and Venice, where the population was overwhelmingly Italian, would bring as good results for the Monarchy as in Trieste, where Slovenes pushed the Italians into a minority. For the moment there would be no change in the responsibilities of either Radetzky or Maximilian.

The Emperor already appreciated the significance of Trieste both as a port, set to challenge Marseilles and Genoa for the commerce of southern Europe, and as a Habsburg outpost beyond the Alps and the mountains of Venezia Giulia. The whole region formed, together with Gorizia and

Carniola, a separate administrative 'crownland', totally independent of Lombardy-Venetia. In his first years on the throne it would, indeed, have been difficult for Francis Joseph not to give some attention to the likely future of the region for Baron von Bruck, the far-sighted Rhinelander whose financial wizardry had converted what was little more than a fishing harbour into a major port, served until the spring of 1851 as minister of commerce in the Schwarzenberg government. Under Bruck's auspices, the Emperor visited Trieste in May 1850 to lay the foundation stone of the railway station, although it was not until June 1857 that the vitally important strategic link with Vienna was completed. The Semmering Pass section, a pioneer engineering achievement, was ready by the autumn of 1854. By then, however, the *Sudbahn* was in financial difficulties and work was further delayed by the difficulty of cutting through the mountains between Ljubljana and the coast. That the line was finished at all was largely thanks to Bruck's persistence, for the Baron returned to the administration in May 1855 as minister of finance and masterminded the implementation of a Railway Concession Law, approved by the Emperor in the previous year and authorizing the sale to private companies of an extensive network of state lines.

Francis Joseph remained impressed by Bruck's understanding of monetary matters and, on his return to office, allowed him virtually a free hand to reform the fiscal system and ensure the solvency of the Empire. Bruck did nothing to curb the money supply but imposed heavier taxation and improved the exchange rate by putting on sale state property and bonds. Within two years Bruck had come nearer to his ideal of a central European free trade area based upon Vienna, for in 1857 a currency treaty provided for monetary union between the Empire and the Prussian-dominated *Zollverein*. But Bruck's most lasting achievement in these years was the establishment of a Vienna-based credit institution. In the summer of 1855 he convinced Francis Joseph that the surest way to stimulate private industry and safeguard the imperial state finances was by establishing a bank, backed by the Rothschilds and with its investments confined within the borders of the Monarchy. Once the Emperor was won over to his arguments, Bruck sought the help of Anselm Rothschild, and the two financial experts moved quickly, not least through fear of French competition: the *Oesterreichische Creditanstalt für Handel und Gewerbe* (Commerce and Trade) received a charter on the last day of October 1855; shares were made available for public subscription on 12 December; and by the end of the month, when the board of directors of the Creditanstalt met for the first time, the share value had more than trebled, heralding almost two years of golden harvest for speculators. The bank's founders steered investment towards large-scale development of private enterprise, especially for railways and public works.

This apparent improvement in the availability of credit may finally have induced Francis Joseph to approve a project long under consideration. The possibility of razing the remaining ramparts of Vienna, and thus encouraging the outward spread of the city so as to include the cluster of suburbs immediately behind its walls, was first mooted by bankers and industrialists when he was a boy of nine, though the Volksgarten had been laid out, on the site of a fort destroyed by Napoleon I, a few years before he was born. Military diehards in the bureaucracy strongly opposed any such change: how could the centre of imperial power and the residences 'of the most prosperous and contented subjects of the State' be safe-guarded against looting and attack by 'the brutal, licentious general trade and factory people' except by strong fortifications? Even Francis Joseph, who at first agreed with such a view, was forced to admit that the experience of 1848 did not support the argument at all; the military experts now contended that, so far from providing the Court with a safe refuge, the old bastions had enabled the radical revolutionaries to hold out even longer against Windischgraetz, Jellaçić and the regular army.

On the eve of his marriage, when so many post-revolutionary restraints were being relaxed, the Emperor began to waver. He conceded the prin-ciple that the inner fortifications need no longer be preserved, provided demolition was, in each instance, related to the completion of earthworks for an outer girdle of defences. This cumbersome relationship held good for three years. But practical necessity was already forcing changes around the glacis: on 24 April 1856, for example, the Emperor and his brothers attended the laying of the foundation stone for the Votivkirche, built at the point along the ramparts where Libenyi had sought to assassinate Francis Joseph.

There was, too, as so often in Austrian history, an architectural chal-lenge from France for the Viennese to emulate. These were the years when Napoleon III and Baron Haussmann opened up Paris, thrusting broad boulevards with straight vistas through the old quarters of the inner city. Archduke Maximilian, sent to Napoleon's Court in May 1856 with his brother's congratulations on the birth of the Prince Imperial, was deeply impressed by what was going on around him: a historic city, little changed in six centuries, would soon be basking in the spacious dignity of an artificially created planned capital, like St Petersburg. If long, open avenues were the hallmark of imperial grandeur then, potentially, Vienna possessed an advantage over Paris; for in the Habsburg capital there was no need to sweep away picturesque winding-streets or demolish homes in districts where there was already a shortage of housing for a rapidly growing population. In Vienna, it would be enough to raze the bastions, fill in moats and ditches, and level the glacis. Then the architects and planners, bankers and contractors could compete for the privilege of constructing on this readily prepared surface a wide, circumambient boulevard, more a horseshoe than a ring, which would provide the imperial city with a parade prospect of public buildings.

Five days before Christmas in 1857 the Emperor made his great decision, taking both Alexander Bach (his minister of the interior) and the department of engineers by surprise. A letter-patent, using the characteristic phrasing of benevolent autocracy, informed Bach: 'It is My Pleasure that, as soon as possible, preparatory work should begin on the extension of the inner city of Vienna so as to establish an appropriate link with the suburbs, and that, at the same time, consideration should be given to the regulation and embellishment of My Residence and My Capital'. And he added, 'I give My Permission to abolish the walls and fortification of the inner city, as well as their surrounding ditches.'

Unfortunately the momentous decree coincided with a tightening of credit, following several crises of nerves on Wall Street, in the banking houses of London, Paris and Frankfurt as well as Vienna. But seven weeks after the decree was signed, a government commission invited architects to draw up plans for expanding and 'embellishing' the city; and within two months the first ramparts came down and a fine avenue was laid beside the Danube Canal. Work continued throughout the most critical years of the Emperor's reign. It was easy enough to extend the Volksgarten and create a Stadtpark, which was opened to the townsfolk in 1863 and covered waste ground between one of the eastern bastions of the wall and the River Wien. Even the Ringstrasse itself was completed by the spring of 1865 when Francis Joseph and Elizabeth drove along the boulevard in a flower-bedecked coach on May Day. But the great buildings came later in the reign: the Opera House, begun in 1861, was not opened until 1869; the two museums (Kunsthistorisches and Natural History) went up between 1872 and 1881; Parliament and the Rathaus were not finished until 1883; and work on the Burgtheater dragged on from 1872 until 1888. The process begun at Francis Joseph's 'pleasure' in those closing days of 1857 transformed the Austrian capital into a city as spacious and beautiful as any in Europe. No other missive sent from Emperor to minister had such enduring consequences as that letter-patent to Bach.

Foreign observers, reporting to their governments in the mid-fifties, attached greater importance to a far different initiative by the Emperor, the conclusion of a Concordat with Rome. Some diplomats thought that the privileged position which he gave to the hierarchy was the tired gesture of a harassed young man anxious to please his mother. But this view (which has influenced several historians) is misleading. Francis Joseph had always been dutifully devout, accepting from Colombi and Rauscher in his boyhood the current assumptions of a reactionary Church: lay control of moral teaching led to atheism and the break up of society; the only hope of crushing the demon of revolution was to acknowledge the sovereignty of Holy Church over all temporal rulers. The circumstances of Francis Joseph's accession made him even more inclined to respect the Church's code of government.

The famous Napoleonic Concordat of 1801 had taken several months of preparation: the Austrian Concordat took six years. Within six weeks of coming to the throne Francis Joseph received a petition from Cardinal Schwarzenberg (brother of the then head of government) seeking imperial authority to convene a conference of bishops who would recommend to their sovereign the conclusion of a Concordat with the Pope. The bishops' conference opened in Vienna on 30 April 1849, the day the Emperor assumed supreme command of the army, and it was still in session when he returned to Schönbrunn from Olmütz a week later. Cardinal Schwarzenberg and Rauscher between them were convinced that they possessed sufficient influence over government and Court to sweep aside all concessions made to modern thought by the Emperor Joseph II seventy years before; they sought to bind the Empire in a spiritual tutelage unknown since the Counter-Reformation. A working agreement was reached with the government as early as April 1850, and in July 1851 the Jesuits were allowed back into the Empire after a lapse of nearly eighty years. The death of Felix von Schwarzenberg did not impede the discussions over a formal treaty with the Holy See, for the bishops could still count on support from several government ministers, notably Bach and the equally devout minister of education and religious affairs, Count Leo Thun-Hohenstein.

Even so, the proposals put forward by Rome were so overbearing that Francis Joseph jibbed at accepting them; the terms of the treaty had not been settled when Rauscher preached his thirty minute sermon at the Emperor's marriage. But the Holy See was adamant: the Austrians gave way over eleven points on Church-State relations and seven on doctrine, some of which even Rauscher queried. The state surrendered all control over the Church and its relations with Rome, left to the Church the right to punish priests guilty of civil offences, and agreed to allow marriage laws to be interpreted by ecclesiastical courts. The hierarchy was given the right to ban books on moral or religious grounds, while the clergy exercised supervisory rights over education at all levels. The state recognized Church property as sacrosanct and inviolable, and undertook not to alter confessional laws without the Church's consent, while the Emperor promised not to tolerate derogatory remarks against the faith or Church institutions.

When, on 18 August 1855, Francis Joseph sent a telegram of thanks to his mother at Ischl for her birthday greetings, he added the information, 'Today the Concordat was signed'; and there is no doubt that, even if the Archduchess was not the prime mover in seeking an understanding with Rome, she found the news gratifying. Over purely political affairs she had long ceased to have any real influence, but she remained the matriarch of the dynasty, the most formidable figure in the family. It was not in Sophie's nature to question the fundamental values upon which her life was modelled. For her the indisputable truths of the Church emphasized the role of the family, and her diary jottings reveal a genuine gratitude for the God-given understanding of mind and spirit vouchsafed to her at the Habsburg Court. Read in retrospect, the simple sincerity of her sense of mission softens this tone of self-righteousness, which is present in her letters as well as in her journal; but it is easy to see how, in life, the practice of her precepts must frequently have made the Archduchess intolerable. Familiarity with the ways and wiles of her niece and daughter-in-law strengthened her inner satisfaction at having been a wiser mother than Ludovika. It also convinced Sophie of the need to regulate the nursery routine of her grandchildren and supervise the matchmaking of her remaining sons.

Sophie had suffered several miscarriages in her earliest years of marriage. But all seemed to go well for Elizabeth. On 5 March 1855 she had her first child, a girl rather than the Crown Prince needed to guarantee the succession to another generation; and almost inevitably the baby was named Sophie. Within five months the Empress was again pregnant: a second daughter, the Archduchess Gisela, was born on 12 July 1856, at Laxenburg. Should Elizabeth continue to give birth to girls, the succession would pass to Francis Joseph's brothers and any male descendants they might have; for, despite the reverence shown to the memory of Maria Theresa, legalistic pedantry ruled out the accession of a sovereign's daughter. The Archduchess Sophie intensified her matchmaking and, soon after Gisela's birth, pulled off a second family triumph: Archduke Charles Ludwig, disappointed in his childhood attachment to Sisi, was betrothed to yet another first cousin, Princess Margaretha, the fifth daughter of Sophie's sister, Queen Amalia of Saxony; and in November 1856 they married in Dresden.

The youngest son, Ludwig Victor ('Bubi'), was only fourteen in 1856, but he was already his mother's spoilt pet, with no interest in girls, then or in later years. A more immediate family problem was the Archduke Maximilian, ten years older than Bubi. The independently minded Maximilian was at first disinclined to be pushed into marriage. On his sea voyages he fell in love with Princess Maria Amalia of Brazil, who, though a granddaughter of Archduchess Sophie's eldest sister, was also a great-granddaughter of the Empress Josephine. Sadly, the Princess died from consumption in Madeira before their betrothal was announced. Maximilian then followed his mother's advice and visited Brussels in late May 1856 to meet Princess Charlotte, the only daughter of King Leopold I of the Belgians. A link between the Habsburgs and the newest Catholic kingdom in Europe had been established in 1853, when Leopold's eldest surviving son, the Duke of Brabant, married the Palatine Archduke Joseph's youngest daughter; and Sophie was impressed by what she heard of the Court at Brussels and of the intelligent, pretty and deeply religious Princess Charlotte in particular. But Maximilian remained in no hurry to marry. Charlotte may have found the sailor Archduke a romantic figure but, though he treated her graciously, he was not excited by her presence, as he had been in his brief courtship of poor Maria Amalia. He resumed his naval duties at Trieste and Pola, concentrated on the building of Miramare and in October sailed off with the fleet down the Adriatic. Their engagement was not made public until December, after Charles Ludwig had returned with his bride from Saxony.

The Emperor and Empress were away from Vienna in that month; they spent much of the autumn and winter of 1856–7 undertaking state visits to the southern provinces of the Monarchy. A week in Styria and Carinthia early in September was followed by a nine day visit to Ljubljana and Trieste in October and by four and a half months of formal residence in Lombardy-Venetia. The Carinthian expedition was in part a holiday, allowing both Francis Joseph and Elizabeth to relax and find a natural exhilaration in the mountain scenery of the Grossglockner. Relations with the matriarch in the Hofburg had become strained over the previous year, and Elizabeth insisted on having the children's nursery removed from the immediate proximity of their grandmother's apartments to the imperial wing of the palace. On returning from Carinthia, Francis Joseph wrote more firmly to his mother than on any earlier occasion: he deplored her habit of virtually confining the two little girls to her own rooms and bringing them out as show pieces, for he had a horror of having them turned into vain little madams. Specifically he asked her 'to treat Sisi indulgently when she is perhaps too jealous a mother – she is of course so devoted a wife and mother'. He backed Elizabeth in her determination to take little Sophie with them on the journey to Italy, arguing that the child, who was delicate, would benefit from the warmer winter climate south of the Alps: Grandmamma demurred.

When riding in the Prater, or at ceremonial occasions in Vienna, the

Empress often seemed ill-at-ease, reluctant to have prying eyes staring at her. But in Styria, Carinthia and Carniola she was free of such inhibitions. Her gracious charm and beauty readily aroused popular enthusiasm. It was therefore hoped that in northern Italy her personal magnetism would offset the hostility which it was assumed would be aroused by the presence of her husband. This, however, was asking a lot from Elizabeth. Resentment at individual acts of harsh repression over the past eight years continued to smoulder in Venetia and even more in Lombardy. When, on 25 November, the Venetian State Galley bore the Emperor, Empress and infant Archduchess to the landing stage in front of Doge's Palace there were no cheers. As Francis Joseph inspected the Guard drawn up in the Piazza San Marco, only the orchestrated hurrahs of the troops broke the cold silence. A gala at the Fenice Theatre was half empty, and three out of every four Venetian patricians declined the imperial invitation to the first Court reception. There was a mood, not so much of rebellion, as of proud indifference among the people of the old republic.

The Emperor had not realized the extent to which the army retained administrative control over the two provinces. He was glad he went to the Italian provinces, as he later told his mother, 'for it was high time to clean up the mess in Verona', still the centre of military command for the region. Within ten days of arriving in Venice he gave approval to a widespread amnesty and to measures providing for the restoration of sequestered property and encouraging the return of political exiles. Rumour rightly credited the Emperor with planning a general administrative change of system; and by Christmas the atmosphere in Venice had become less tense; Emperor and Empress were applauded when they entered the Fenice, now full to capacity. To win and retain the confidence of the Venetians was a hard task; but for Francis Joseph the burden was eased by Elizabeth's attention to small details, and in particular, her tact in persuading him to accept petitions from men and women in the crowd, ignored by his military suite. But when, in early January, the imperial couple moved into Lombardy the good work had to begin all over again. In Bergamo the police hurriedly erased graffiti proclaiming, 'The Emperor arrives at 1500. We will get him at 1600'. Elizabeth's most winning charms could not thaw the hostility in Brescia, while in Milan some patrician families sent surrogate servants to a gala at the Scala, providing them with gloves of purple or black, the shade of mourning. Only an administration genuinely sympathetic to Italian culture and the needs of the local community could even hope to coax the Lombards back from the seductive nationalism of Cavour in neighbouring Piedmont.

It was clear that Radetzky would have to go. As soon as he landed in Venice, Francis Joseph saw that the Governor-General was in his dotage –

'horribly changed and in his second childhood', he wrote back to his mother nine days later. But who would take his place? It took nearly three months for Francis Joseph to reach a solution which had already occurred to such disparate foreign observers as Lord John Russell and King Leopold. On 1 March 1857 it was the Emperor's 'pleasure' to announce publicly in Milan that the Archduke Maximilian would succeed Radetzky as Governor-General of Lombardy and Venetia. Characteristically, however, he did not wish to offend senior officers by giving the military command to a reforming 'Sailor Archduke', and Maximilian was therefore given far less power than Russell or King Leopold had envisaged. The Archduke was a purely civilian viceroy: the army would be commanded by Field Marshal Count Gyulai von Maros-Nemeth, a nominee of Grünne whose inadequacies Radetzky had been too old to perceive. At heart Francis Joseph was uneasy over the arrangement: 'I feel a little happier, but not fully reassured. Everything remains very uncertain ...', he told his mother next day, 'Let us hope Maxi's tact will do some good.'

The Emperor and Empress arrived back in Vienna on 12 March, convinced that their long residence in the troubled provinces had proved a successful experiment. 'On the whole Sisi and I have enjoyed our stay', Francis Joseph insisted. At once they planned a further expedition. Elizabeth wished to know about Hungary: she admired Magyar horsemanship; she found several of the Hungarians at court to be lively and interesting companions; and, even before leaving Bavaria, she had begun to learn their language. Now she persuaded her husband to encourage further reconciliation with his Hungarian subjects by planning a month's visit to the kingdom. And this time, ignoring renewed protests and well-intentioned advice from Archduchess Sophie, both little girls were with their parents when, on 5 May, the Danube steamer brought them to Pest.

A state entry into Buda followed, across Adam Clark's suspension bridge and up the steep, cobbled streets to the royal palace above the river. That night the bridge was festooned with lights while an enterprising Levantine financier paid for an ambitious firework display to welcome Hungary's King and Queen. Once again there was an amnesty and the restoration of confiscated property; and once again Elizabeth set about pleasing all whom she was allowed to meet. But Francis Joseph himself was less inclined to forgive and forget than in Italy. He scarcely bothered to flatter national susceptibilities. Similarly, many of the greater families remained irreconcilable – for it was, after all, only seven and a half years since the royal prime minister and the president of the upper house of parliament were shot and Hungary's generals publicly hanged at Arad.

Sentimental writers claim that Elizabeth fell in love with Hungary at first sight and the Magyar people at once took 'Erzsebet' to their hearts.

In reality, after the first two days, she was distracted by mounting worries over the health of her children, although she resolutely sought to give the Emperor the support he needed. Gisela went down with measles but was soon well on the way to recovery. Her two-year-old sister Sophie, who was more delicate, caught the measles and seemed so weak that the parents postponed their departure for inner Hungary. On Saturday, 23 May, with Sophie said to be out of danger, Francis Joseph and Elizabeth set out for the pustza plains of the north-east, leaving the children in the palace at Buda. By Thursday the royal progress had reached Debrecen, the Calvinist city in north-eastern Hungary where in 1849 Kossuth had proclaimed the deposition of the dynasty. There they received a telegram summoning them back to Buda, 140 miles away, which they reached soon after ten next morning. Nothing could be done to save the poor child's life. 'Our little one is an angel in heaven', Francis Joseph was forced to telegraph to her grandparents late that night, 'We are crushed'.

The Hungarian royal progress was cancelled. Back at Laxenburg, Elizabeth shut herself up, full or remorse for having taken the child with them to Buda in the first place, and then for having set out for Debrecen. The tragedy confirmed Archduchess Sophie's worst fears: children should be kept in the nursery, not carried on long journeys to strange cities. Francis Joseph went back to Hungary later in the summer to complete the tour of the kingdom: but it was ten years before Elizabeth could face the prospect of returning to Buda.

This first personal disaster of the reign cast a shadow over the summer of 1857, for the Empress remained secluded and in deep mourning. She would ride and walk alone, her mind dazed, her nerves numb, her eyes lustreless. Francis Joseph was infinitely patient, but so concerned was he for her health that he pressed Ludovika to come from Bavaria and draw her back to the serenity of daily life in the peace of Laxenburg. These days of anguished introspection could not be prolonged; in early August the Court had to come out of mourning and greet Maximilian and Charlotte, as they passed through Vienna after their marriage in Brussels. The Empress dutifully stood beside her husband at the magnificent reception at Schönbrunn, ethereally lovely in white and as silent as an apparition. Her sombre mood did not help the Belgian Princess transmute into an Austrian Archduchess; and it is possible Elizabeth saw no reason to assist her make the change.

Archduchess Sophie, with whom Elizabeth had little contact during these months, travelled up to Linz to welcome her new daughter-in-law to the Empire. She was pleased to find her both good-looking and sharply intelligent. 'Charlotte is charming, beautiful, attractive, and full of love and affection for me', she wrote in her diary on 4 August, 'I thank God from the bottom of my heart for the delightful wife Max has found and for the wider family they will give us.' The Archduchess already assumed Sisi would have no son and the succession pass to Maximilian and the children whom she was sure that the robust and sensible Charlotte would bear. By contrast, so fitfully did Elizabeth's light flicker, that it was doubtful if she could ever again glow with the ecstasy of happiness fulfilled.

The Emperor and Empress remained deeply conscious of their loss. Six months after Sophie's death Francis Joseph could write to his mother telling her that when, 'yesterday', they saw Gisela sit for the first time in her sister's 'little chair in my study, we wept together'. But this shared sense of bereavement enabled him to show a sympathetic understanding of Sisi's grief: the love that had blossomed at Ischl proved resilient and enduring. By Christmas the Empress knew she was for the third time pregnant: might the baby come on her husband's twenty-eighth birthday? Not quite. The child was born at Laxenburg on 21 August. 'Not exactly beautiful, though well-built and sturdy', Francis Joseph told his parents. Beauty was of little importance this time; what mattered was the child's gender; and Elizabeth had given birth to a son who, on the following Sunday, Cardinal Rauscher baptized Rudolf Francis Charles Joseph. If, as at the imperial wedding, he preached too long on the spiritual rewards of a virtuous family life, on this occasion neither father nor mother grudged the cardinal his pious platitudes.

Towns and villages from Galicia to Lombardy duly celebrated the Crown Prince's birth with festoons of patriotic bunting. There was a further amnesty, and gifts by the child's father to charitable bodies in widely separated regions of his Empire. In Vienna itself Francis Joseph endowed the Rudolfspital, a general infirmary for a thousand patients 'irrespective of family origin and religion'. Some of the rejoicing was officially sponsored, some spontaneous and some commercially opportunist. Josef Strauss soon had a *Laxenburger Polka* on sale and, as the Emperor lost no time in giving his son honorary rank in the 19th Infantry Regiment, the Strauss family made certain that regimental bands would be playing '*The Austrian Crown Prince's March*' long before His Imperial Highness learnt to walk. Yet there was, too, in these August days of 1858 a slightly portentous sense of occasion, perhaps because it was three centuries since an imperial baptism had honoured the founder of the dynasty. Much was expected of the Crown Prince, as the imperial director of theatres speedily acknowledged. On the stage of the Burgtheater a tableau vivant was mounted: with a golden pen the Muse of History inscribed on a huge marble slab the date of Ruldolf's birth; then she declaimed: 'Here stand engraved Year and Day. The rest of this tablet shall be left empty, for space I must leave to record there the famous deeds which, I foresee, he shall accomplish.'

Chapter 7

ITALY WITHOUT RADETZKY

On 18 January 1858 the most impressive military funeral procession ever seen in Vienna made its way across a silent city to the Nordbahnhof. Field Marshal Radetzky, who had died in Italy, was to be interred on the Heldenberg in Lower Austria; and the Emperor wished his subjects to honour their hero in a solemn pageant to match Great Britain's tribute to the Duke of Wellington five winters before. On that November morning in London the weight of the funeral chariot proved too great for the rain-sodden roadway down the Mall, and sixty men and twelve dray-horses had to strain at cables and traces before the cortège could resume its progress towards St Paul's. Francis Joseph would not risk a similar embarrassment on the icy glacis: the Marshal's body was borne in a hearse, not a funeral chariot; but 40,000 men – as many as he commanded on the Italian battlefields – were put on parade, with the Emperor himself riding at their head.

A British diplomat, who some forty years later came back to Vienna as ambassador, watched from a window in Leopoldstadt as the cortège went by, with 'light flakes of snow whirled about by the bitter gusts of wind'. In his memoirs Horace Rumbold was to recall:

No sound but the rumble of the artillery wagons, the tread of the battalions, the clatter of horses' hoofs, the clanking of spur and scabbard, the roll of muffled drums, and – most striking to me of all – the music of the bands playing a solemn strain which seemed strangely familiar and yet had a new and unaccustomed rhythm. Some clever Capelmeister had had the simple, but ingenious, thought of adapting old Strauss's brilliant Radetzky march to a minor key and a dirge-like measure, and, as regiment after regiment filed by, there came up through the frosty air a fresh wail of this famous melody, with just enough of its old original fierceness and wildness left in it to carry the mind back to the days when they had hoisted the octogenarian into his saddle at Custozza or Novara, the troops, as they passed him cheering like mad for 'Vater Radetzky'.

Although old Metternich was still alive, penning memoranda for the

Emperor in his villa off the Rennweg, everyone recognized that the Marshal's death marked the true passing of an era. The Italian Question was once again posed acutely. Cavour's statesmanship and economic policies, together with the increased influence of Sardinia-Piedmont after the kingdom's participation in the Crimean War, made it essential for the Habsburgs to offer a solution of their own, as Francis Joseph had himself recognized when he made Maximilian Governor-General in the previous spring. But the Archduke felt increasingly frustrated. Until the last months of his viceregal term, Radetzky's prestige enabled him to show a certain independence, modifying general policies laid down in Vienna so as to suit the needs of the two Italian provinces (though not always wisely). As Maximilian reminded his mother in a letter, 'For loyalty's sake, Radetzky was disobedient'. Such independence was denied a young and inexperienced Archduke.

Yet Maximilian was astute and perceptive. He spoke Italian fluently and his first speeches emphasized the attachment his great-grandfather, Leopold II, felt for his Tuscan lands at a time when in Turin the House of Savoy-Piedmont showed little feeling for the cultural traditions of Italy. He accomplished much in a short span of time: he secured the establishment of a discount bank to help the silk industry, caught in a severe depression; he saw to it that Milan, like Paris and Vienna, was given a public works programme, with a new square in front of the Teatro alla Scala, and plans for setting off to greater advantage the facade of the cathedral by more than doubling the size of the Piazza del Duomo (a project begun eighteen years later); and he encouraged agrarian enterprises, such as draining the Piano di Spagna marshland at the head of Lake Como. When heavy rain led the Po and Ticino to burst their banks in October 1857, Maximilian supervised some of the relief work, towards the cost of which he contributed money from his personal funds. In Venetia he achieved less, partly through bad harvests, but also because the Venice Arsenal suffered from the loss of naval work he had already assigned to Trieste and Pola. Nevertheless, the record of his first nine months as Governor-General was impressive, not least because of his skill in persuading his brother to sign pardons for over a hundred political prisoners outside the provisions of earlier amnesties. Politically he would have liked to go further: he urged Francis Joseph to seize the initiative and summon a congress of Italian princes at Monza where they might consider the development of specifically Italian railway and telegraph networks and a customs union to match the German Zollverein. But, in Vienna, Buol joined the Emperor's closest advisers in opposing so radical a programme. At such a congress what, they wondered, could be expected from the House of Savoy? And who would speak for the Papal States? Nothing more was heard of the proposed congress.

Yet the Italian Question remained in urgent need of solution. In the week of Radetzky's death and funeral all the European governments were assessing the significance of the Orsini plot in Paris. On 14 January three bombs were thrown at Napoleon III and the Empress Eugenie as their carriage arrived at the Opera House in Paris. Eight people were killed and over a hundred badly injured by this terrorist outrage. The French police had little difficulty in placing responsibility on four Italian exiles led by Count Felice Orsini, a former Mazzinian governor of Ancona who had escaped from the Austrian prison fortress of Mantua five years before. At first it was widely assumed the outrage would put an end to the overt patronage given by Napoleon III to the Italian national cause since the Crimean War. Cavour, who was alarmed by Maximilian's growing popularity and hoping to retain the sympathy already shown by western liberals for the Risorgimento, sent a message to his agents in Lombardy: 'It is urgent that you bring about the reimposition of a state of siege in Milan.' The subsequent publication in the official French gazette of Orsini's letter to Napoleon, appealing to him to follow his uncle's example and liberate Italy from Austrian rule, did not save the Count from execution but it made him a patriot martyr throughout the peninsula, thereby forcing Maximilian's administration on the defensive. But the Archduke refused to retreat into a purely repressive policy. He came to Vienna in July 1858, with proposals for giving Lombardy-Venetia an autonomy unknown anywhere else in the Monarchy. Once again, Francis Joseph was not unsympathetic to his brother's recommendations: he authorized minor reforms in taxation and the system of enforcing military service; but both Grünne and his ministers convinced the Emperor that any major political concession would prompt similar demands from Magyars, Croats, Poles, Czechs and every other nationality, making it hard to prevent the Empire's disintegration.

While Maximilian was travelling back to Monza in the third week of July 1858, Cavour was in France where he met Napoleon III secretly at Plombières, the small spa in the foothills of the Vosges; a verbal agreement, defined more precisely on paper later in the year, promised French support to Sardinia-Piedmont in a campaign to end Habsburg rule in the peninsula, provided Austria could be provoked into launching the war. Cavour's visit soon became known, and over the following three weeks newspapers in Turin, Vienna and London speculated about the talks. Few commentators doubted the two high-level conspirators regarded Austria as their natural enemy. Maximilian, however, wished to press ahead with his limited programme of reforms, particularly in education, and there is some evidence from both Russian and British diplomatic sources that – as Cavour had feared – the Archduke's lenient policies were winning back support for Austrian rule, at least in Lombardy. In Vienna, on the other hand, Maximilian's opponents insisted that reform would weaken the Austrian hold on the provinces. Count Thun-Hohenstein, as minister responsible for education and religious affairs, even encouraged Francis Joseph to wonder if his brother was seeking the crown of Lombardy for himself. Reports of injudicious remarks by both Maximilian and Charlotte criticizing official policy reached Vienna.

On 15 September 1858 Archduchess Margaretha, the eighteen year old wife of Charles Ludwig, suddenly died from a mysterious fever while on a visit to Monza. This latest domestic tragedy intensified the gloom within the imperial family. Charlotte, who like Margaretha remained childless, was especially depressed. The Emperor, pained by the mischievous tales of his brother's open dissent, encouraged Maximilian to go on leave with his wife; and they sailed down the Dalmatian coast to Corfu, discovering yet another idyllic retreat, a ruined monastery on Lacroma, the island off Dubrovnik. When, in late November, the Archduke returned to Milan, he found the Lombard people frigidly unco-operative in his ventures, and he was alarmed at the 'complete chaos' around him. Any confidence he had felt in Count Gyulai as military commander was gone, and he asked the Emperor for more powers in case of war or rebellion. But Francis Joseph refused. In a long and ominous letter on 26 December he explained that he could not risk exposing the Archduke's reputation to the uncertainties of the battlefield; for the moment he was to remain in Milan, carrying out imperial decisions whether or not he agreed with them. Should war come, he might again take command of the fleet in the Adriatic. 'This is the most difficult time I have experienced', the Emperor wrote, 'I am counting, with the firmest confidence, on your loyal support.'

Six days later Napoleon III startled Europe's chancelleries by his famous greeting to the Austrian ambassador, Joseph von Hübner, at the New Year's reception in the Tuileries: 'I am sorry that our relations with your government are not as good as in the past, but please write to Vienna and assure the Emperor that my personal sentiments towards him have not changed.' At first Hübner saw nothing menacing in this urbane and largely meaningless observation, but long before he could send any formal message back to Vienna, the Paris Bourse was full of alarming rumours that the tone of Napoleon's remarks confirmed the imminence of war in northern Italy. Share prices tumbled, first in Paris, later in London and Vienna. At the Hofburg, Grünne urged the despatch of reinforcements to Lombardy. When, two and a half weeks later, King Victor Emmanuel assured his parliament in Turin that he could not 'close his ears' to 'the cry of anguish' reaching him from the oppressed peoples of Italy, Francis Joseph was convinced that war must follow south of the Alps as soon as the winter snows receded and the passes were once more clear.

A wiser, more experienced ruler would have checked the drift into a conflict from which little was to be gained; the Monarchy could not stand the cost of mobilization, let alone the losses in men and material from a long campaign. The ingenuity of Bruck, and the backing given to Austria's currency by the great banking institutions, had allowed the Empire to stave off state bankruptcy after spending so recklessly in 1854–55 for the war in the east which never came. Even so, the military budget for 1857 had been more than halved. But Francis Joseph ignored the lesson of the 1854–55 crisis; he had – at least in these years of unfettered autocracy – a simplistic, old-world belief in treating military threats from abroad like a challenge to a duel, with the honour of the dynasty at stake.

As war loomed in March 1859 Napoleon III seemed to draw back from the brink, and his foreign minister supported Russo-British proposals for a congress to solve the Italian Question without recourse to war. Yet even though Britain, and probably Prussia, would have supported Austria at such a congress, this diplomatic initiative did not appeal to Francis Joseph, who feared international pressure might force him to concede territory – a humiliating prospect. Ten thousand volunteers from all over Italy were in Turin, shouting for war against Austria, and Francis Joseph insisted on regarding them as a serious threat. He warned Maximilian in Monza that he intended to force Piedmont to disarm and told him to 'be ready to send your wife from Italy at a moment's notice'. Charlotte left Milan on 19 April, officially to observe a penitential Holy Week in Venice.

It was at a ministerial council in the Hofburg on Tuesday, 19 April, that Francis Joseph finally decided to risk a war. Next day the Archduke learnt by telegraph he had been relieved of his gubernatorial responsibilities, all powers passing to Gyulai as commander-in-chief. Less than 48 hours later – by then it was Good Friday morning – the Austrian envoy in Turin presented Cavour with an ultimatum: war would follow in five days time unless the Piedmontese army was withdrawn from the frontier in Lombardy and reverted to a peacetime footing. Cavour rejected the ultimatum. By Wednesday, 27 April, Austria and Sardinia-Piedmont were at war; and, after some days of characteristic indecision, on 3 May Napoleon III issued a proclamation calling on the French people to march with him beside Piedmont against the tyranny of Austria. By letting the ultimatum go off to Turin, Francis Joseph thus sprang the trap set for him at Plombières.

Not all the fault lay with the Emperor. His foreign minister had served at the Austrian Legation in Turin and believed that he understood both Cavour and his policy. Throughout the critical weeks Count Buol argued that the Piedmontese were bluffing and that Austria could rely on threats from Prussia to prevent Napoleon III from denuding his eastern frontier so as to wage a campaign south of the Alps. Archduke Albrecht was sent to Berlin to co-ordinate Austrian and Prussian military moves, and as late as 6 April Buol assured the Emperor that he was certain of Prussian support, thereby neutralizing French military backing for Piedmont: Buol argued that, without the prospect of aid from Napoleon, the Piedmontese would meekly accept Austria's demands. Incredibly, Francis Joseph took Buol at his word. To save money, he allowed the ultimatum to be presented in Turin without first ordering the full-scale mobilization which both Grünne and Hess thought essential. If Buol's prediction was correct and Cavour climbed down, the Emperor would gain a prestigious victory on the cheap. If Buol was wrong, he was courting a swift defeat and financial disaster.

In Berlin Archduke Albrecht found the Prussians unresponsive. As Metternich had reminded Buol in memoranda which the foreign minister chose to ignore, neither Prussia nor any other member of the German Confederation was under any treaty obligation to assist Francis Joseph unless he became engaged in a purely defensive war. But Prince Regent William gave Albrecht some slight grounds for hope: Prussia was, after all, an independent Great Power and might be tempted to threaten France, provided the Austrians allowed Prussia a freer hand in purely German affairs. Francis Joseph, by now as angry with Prussia as Nicholas I had been with the Austrian 'ingrate' five years before, offered no tempting concessions; and when the first French army corps headed for the Alpine passes, there was no corresponding movement of Prussian troops across the Rhine and the Moselle.

In January 1858 Rumbold had admired the 'absolute perfection of military trim and equipment' with which Francis Joseph's 'renowned regiments' escorted Radetzky's hearse across Vienna. Fifteen months later Feldzugmeister Gyulai's staff looked no less impressive as they watched five corps, drawn from all the nationalities of the Monarchy, and a crack German-Austrian cavalry division cross the River Ticino to invade Piedmont. But, as Gyulai well knew, these troops belonged to what was essentially a parade-ground army. Numerically they should have had little difficulty in preventing the Piedmontese from emerging from their alpine passes into the plains. But their commander-in-chief was in no hurry. Between Cavour's rejection of the ultimatum and Gyulai's review of the troops beside the Ticino four days elapsed, with no action whatsoever. Gyulai was without a war plan and scarcely on speaking terms with his chief-of-staff. He was also short of rations, support wagons, bridging equipment and trained gun teams for his artillery. An inconclusive month went by, with Gyulai's vanguard at one time advancing to within fifty miles of Turin and encountering little opposition. But the Feldzugmeister was worried by reports that day by day the French were bringing guns, wagons and horses over the Little St Bernard and Mont Cenis passes down to the Po at Chivasso. Fearing that his left flank was over-extended and exposed, on 2 June he ordered the army to pull back out of Piedmont. He would await the enemy east of the Ticino, on Austrian soil.

This aimless marching and counter-marching confirmed Francis Joseph's early suspicions that things were going desperately wrong. At council meetings during the first months of the year Grünne and Hess had urged caution, suspecting that the army was not ready to face a war that spring. They thought (rightly) that, as yet, the single track railway from Vienna to Trieste could not cope with urgent military traffic. Moreover, as Maximilian's reports consistently emphasized, there was still no line linking Trieste to Venice, seventy miles away. Yet both the Emperor and his military advisers were shocked by Gyulai's inability to retain control of an army when faced by unexpected hazards. The late spring of 1859 was exceptionally wet: in early May the Po was already fifteen feet above its normal level; roads were deep in mud, and many of the open fields treacherously swampy. Conditions had been as bad in 1800, during the weeks before Marengo. On that occasion the rivers remained in flood until mid-June, forcing both Bonaparte and the Austrian commander, the septuagenarian General Melas, to adjust the disposition of their troops so as to concentrate on the retention of key bridgeheads. But Gyulai, who had never previously commanded an army in the field, learnt no lessons from the Marengo campaign. The incessant rain and mud demoralized him. By the third week in May Gyulai's desperate telegrams to Vienna convinced Francis Joseph he would have to travel down to the battle-front himself.

He had wanted to leave the capital as soon as it was known that Napoleon III would take command of the Franco-Piedmontese army in person. But Francis Joseph was hampered by the nature of the autocratic structure he had himself created. When he had gone to the front in Hungary ten years before, Schwarzenberg was still chief minister, shaping policies while his sovereign was with the troops. Now, however, he had no chief minister. He had lost all confidence in Buol as soon as it became clear that Prussia would not be entering the war, and Buol was ready to quit office by the end of the first week in May. But who should take his place? So desperate was Francis Joseph that, on several days, he sounded out the Empire's eldest statesman, on one occasion staying for three hours at the villa on the Rennweg. It was largely on Metternich's advice that Francis Joseph appointed Count Rechberg to succeed Buol on 15 May, the old Chancellor's eighty-sixth birthday. Rechberg, a fifty-three year old diplomat of Bavarian origin, was an expert in German affairs and the last of Metternich's protégés. So highly did the Emperor rate the new foreign minister's qualities that he immediately authorized him to act as interim president of the council of ministers as well. A few days later Francis Joseph asked Metternich to draw up secret contingency plans for a council of regency for Crown Prince Rudolf and a memorandum on how the Monarchy might be preserved without an active sovereign on the throne. But these tasks were beyond the ex-Chancellor: his health gave way, and he died on 11 June without drafting this last political testament.

Archduchess Sophie reluctantly accepted the need for the Emperor to go down to Verona once more. Elizabeth did not: his wife and children needed him in Vienna, she insisted. When she found her husband adamant, she begged to be allowed to accompany him to headquarters, again without success; and when at last, on 29 May, he left Vienna, she wept quite openly, like any other young wife seeing her husband off to the wars. The Archduchess disapproved: 'Poor Sisi's scenes and tears only serve to make life even harder for my unfortunate son', she noted in her journal. No sooner had the Empress returned to Schönbrunn from the station than she wrote to her husband, again seeking permission to join him. Long letters followed, almost every day of the campaign. In reply, her harassed husband found time to send Elizabeth seventeen letters in the forty days he was in Italy, most running to a thousand words, several to far more. By contrast his aunt, Marie Louise, had received only scribbled notes of some one hundred words from the great Napoleon as he marched on Moscow.

Francis Joseph, accompanied by both Grünne and Hess, reached Verona late on 30 May, having spoken briefly to Maximilian at Mestre on the way. 'My dearest angel Sisi', the Emperor wrote next morning, 'I am using the first moments after getting up to tell you once again how much I love you and long for you and the dear children . . .'; and after describing to her the journey, telling her that he was now 'in the selfsame room we shared together', and complaining that 'it rains here every day', he praised what he had seen of the army and referred optimistically to Gyulai's success in beating off attacks on his outposts. By then Gyulai had more than 110,000 front-line troops available to check an enemy attempt to penetrate Lombardy, four times as many men as the defenders of Marengo at the start of the century.

A note of disquiet crept into the Emperor's second letter to Elizabeth,

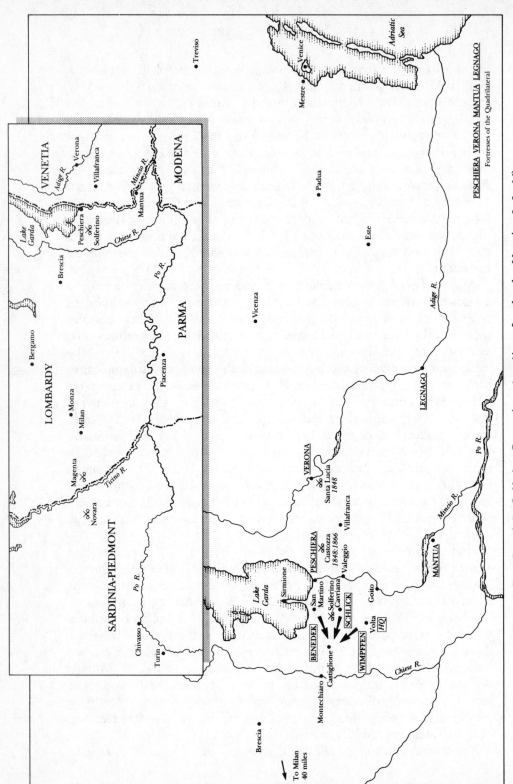

Francis Joseph and the Solferino Campaign 1859 (inset Lombardy–Venetia 1848–66)

dated 2 June. Her latest plea to be allowed to join him was firmly set aside: 'In headquarters which are on the move there is no place for women. I cannot set my army a bad example; and I don't myself know how long I shall be here . . .'; and he hinted that he would soon need to take over the operational command of the army himself. In reality, matters were far more serious than he appreciated. The first clashes had shown French gunnery to be superior to Austrian. Now it became clear that Gyulai's inexperienced sappers underestimated the strength of viaducts and bridges to resist the charges they had laid in them.

On 4 June what began as a sharp engagement between patrols west of the small town of Magenta for bridges over the river Ticino and a neighbouring canal soon developed into the biggest battle fought in Europe for forty-five years. Territorially the fighting was inconclusive on that Saturday for, though the Austrians eventually pulled back from Magenta railway station after twelve hours of bloodshed, Gyulai still commanded the main route towards Milan, twelve miles to the east. His army had, however, suffered over 10,000 casualties, more than twice as many killed and wounded as the French. By now the rains of the previous month had been succeeded by the customary scorching heat of a Lombard summer, and his men were weary, hungry and demoralized; he feared that in a second day's fighting they would be scattered like chaff across the plain. Overnight he decided to abandon Milan and retreat to the River Mincio, around Mantua, where his new positions would be covered by the good, solid fortresses of the Quadrilateral. Francis Joseph was amazed at Gyulai's decision. He sent Hess to field headquarters in the hope that the retreat could be halted. But Hess reported that any attempt to check the retreat of the weary troops short of the Mincio might prove disastrous. On 8 June Francis Joseph, still in Verona, was appalled to learn that Napoleon III and Victor Emmanuel II of Sardinia-Piedmont had entered Milan in triumph. One of the Emperor's aides, sent out to discover Gyulai's intentions, found the commander-in-chief apparently unruffled; he was comfortably housed, with good cooking and a chance to play cards after dinner. Yet Francis Joseph hesitated to get rid of him. Hess, who had served Radetzky brilliantly as a chief-of-staff and was now the Emperor's right-hand man, feared that it would be dangerous for the dynasty if Francis Joseph took command in the field and suffered military defeat. Not until further reinforcements reached the Quadrilateral, giving the Austrians a good prospect of victory under wise leadership, was Gyulai dismissed. On 16 June, at half past one in the afternoon, as Francis Joseph meticulously noted, 'I was driven to Villafranca, where I had summoned Gyulai, and gave him the formal order of dismissal. He was very grateful for it . . .'

News of Magenta and the fall of Milan had caused consternation in Vienna. A sustained press campaign was mounted against the whole absolutist system. Indirectly the Emperor himself came under criticism – particularly as patron of the despised Grünne – and as early as 9 June the council of ministers decided it was their 'sacred duty' to warn Francis Joseph of the mood in Vienna. It was agreed that, if the agitation continued, Rechberg should go down to the war zone and warn the Emperor of the disaffection in the capital; but not yet.

Francis Joseph had, however, sensed the danger already. A letter to the Empress sent soon after Magenta shows a rare impatience with her reports of bickering with the Archduchess and with her failure to do anything useful: 'My dearest one and only angel,' he wrote, 'I beg you, for the love you still have towards me, to pull yourself together. Show yourself in the city now and again, visit hospitals and institutions. You've no idea what a great help that would be to me. It would lift the spirits of people in Vienna and keep up morale, which I so urgently need now.' Throughout these critical weeks her whims continued to worry her husband: how she would eat scarcely any food, and sit up late at night reading or writing letters; and how, during these midsummer days, she would take long rides on her favourite horse, once covering some twenty miles without a stop. Sometimes she was accompanied by her head groom Harry Holmes, a forty-nine year old skilled horseman from the English Dukeries, but these excursions brought a stern reproof from Verona: 'I cannot allow you to go out riding alone with Holmes, that just won't do at all', Francis Joseph insisted. With great relief he heard that Elizabeth did, indeed, visit the capital occasionally. He was pleased to learn that she had converted part of Laxenburg into a hospital for wounded officers, in whose welfare she took a personal interest.

Hess, now chief-of-staff to the Emperor, recommended that the army should move forward from Gyulai's line along the River Mincio to the Chiese, a parallel river some eighteen miles to the west; and for the first two days after superseding Gyulai, Francis Joseph travelled widely so as to get to know the villages, farms and vineyards of this undulating countryside south of Lake Garda. He returned to Verona on the evening of 19 June for what he described as a 'long' meeting with Rechberg, who updated him with news from Vienna and assessments of unrest elsewhere in the Monarchy, notably in Hungary. Francis Joseph believed a battle was imminent, and his letters show a quiet confidence. On Thursday evening, 23 June, he set up headquarters at Valeggio, on the River Mincio some five miles south of Peschiera. His advance troops had still not reached the Chieso, but Valeggio was a good vantage-point: headquarters looked out towards the steep hills around the villages of Cavriana and

Solferino which commanded the plain sloping gently down to Castiglione and eventually to the crossing of the Chieso at Montechiaro. Although Francis Joseph did not know it, Napoleon III had moved French head-quarters forward from Brescia to Montechiaro that night.

Francis Joseph was to remember Friday, 24 June, 1859, as 'a harsh, bitter day'. It was the only time he led his army in a major battle against foreign enemies; and he was defeated, with more than 22,000 of his troops left dead, missing or seriously wounded. Yet the day had begun for him as undramatically as its immediate predecessors during the campaign. He was, as usual, up early to attend to his correspondence but when, soon after eight o'clock, he took his breakfast, he could hear a desultory exchange of gunfire, which grew steadily in intensity: the opposing armies had stumbled across each other as they advanced over the plain, and there was firing along an unusually broad front. At nine o'clock, with breakfast over, the Emperor decided to set out for Cavriana and see what was happening. Remarkably it took another two hours before headquarters appreciated that the full force of the two armies were engaged in battle.

By then Francis Joseph had assumed overall command of the 129,000 troops massed to the west of the Mincio. They were deployed in what might be regarded as a classical defensive position, ready to meet the advance of a slightly larger enemy force, and throw it back towards Milan. General Wimpffen, commanding the three corps of the First Army, was to attempt a turning movement from the left, aiming to reach Castiglione: the four corps of General Schlick's Second Army were to check and repulse the French centre by using the natural escarpment of Solferino; and General Benedek, commanding the largely independent 8 Corps, would engage the Piedmontese on the extreme right of the plateau before the village of San Martino. Francis Joseph established his field head-quarters at Volta, on the left of the battlefield, almost fifteen miles from Benedek.

Only once before, at Leipzig in 1813, was a European battle fought over so great an area and with such large numbers of men to control. On that occasion the opposing commanders were soldiers of great experience, yet even they had found the task virtually beyond them, making Leipzig a victory of attrition rather than a striking triumph of arms. Both Francis Joseph and Napoleon III had received a baptism of fire before Solferino, but they remained textbook generalissimos skilled in parade-ground sol-diery; they were accustomed to assessing army manoeuvres but not to improvising and executing a co-ordinated strategy dependent on reports from sectors spread across a wide battlefront. The French dutifully stuck to their task; they threw in column after column of infantry to support the guns bombarding Solferino itself; and on the Austrian side Wimpffen mounted two conventional attacks against the French right.

Under the midday heat the fighting was intense but indecisive, with over a quarter of a million men and some 40,000 horses in action. By two o'clock in the afternoon, however, the hilltop defences of Solferino had suffered an intense battering, while Wimpffen's cavalry were exhausted, and the corps commanders were painfully conscious of their lack of reserves. An hour later the French tricolour was flying over the ruined village of Solferino, while from his headquarters at Volta Francis Joseph could see that in the plain Wimpffen's exhausted men had been forced to give ground. Fifteen miles away, almost out of touch with headquarters, Benedek's 8 Corps had spent the morning beating off successive Piedmontese attacks. Had Benedek been able to count on receiving cavalry reinforcements, he was in a position to thrust forward and threaten the main French army with encirclement. But, at half-past three, to his dismay he received from headquarters not the promise of additional cavalry, but an order for all troops to pull back to the protection of the Quadrilateral.

Shells had begun to fall close to the Emperor's headquarters, confirming the enemy's steady and relentless advance across the plain. 'So I had to give the order to retreat' Francis Joseph wrote to Elizabeth on the following Sunday from Verona, thirty miles east of the battlefield:

I rode into Volta, where I stopped briefly, and then through a fearful thunderstorm to Valeggio, from where I drove to Villafranca. There I spent a horrible evening, amid a confusion of wounded, of refugees, of wagons and horses, in which it took a great effort to establish any semblance of order. I was asleep for four hours and at dawn travelled here by railway ... That is the sad history of a terrible day on which much was achieved, but fortune did not smile on us. I have learnt much from what I have experienced, and I know what it feels like to be a beaten general. The grave consequences of our misfortune are still to come, but I put my trust in God and do not feel myself to blame for having made any faulty disposition of troops.

This claim was justified. It might, however, be argued that he had broken off the action prematurely and, in particular, that his judgment of the battle wavered under the shattering news that the 19th and 34th Hungarian Infantry Regiments had deserted, almost to a man, during the day. Kossuth, it was reported, had come to Genoa and was raising a Hungarian Legion to recover the kingdom's lost liberties. The multi-national structure of the Monarchy left Francis Joseph unsure of the loyalty of certain units. The German-Austrian and Czech regiments had fought valiantly, and they fell back on the fortresses of the Quadrilateral still in good order. From the Venetian troops there was no real threat of mutiny either, though many Lombards had gone over to the Italian national cause. Although less than six per cent of the rank and file deserted during the campaign, contingents coming from the eastern half of the Monarchy were less reliable than those from the west and north and, after the terrible losses of Solferino, there was little fighting spirit left in any of the South Slav regiments, whether they were raised in Croatia or along the (predominantly Serb) frontier zone to the east. But Hungary remained the greatest uncertainty of all. Francis Joseph knew that Kossuth had been received by Napoleon III in the first week of May; and a German-Austrian and Czech army corps, whose presence in Lombardy would have tilted the numerical balance of forces in Austria's favour, remained in Hungary throughout the war. A French squadron sailed up the Adriatic, ready to support followers of Kossuth in Dalmatia and thus fire the fuse of a Magyar rebellion. But, perhaps fortunately for the Hungarian peoples, no spark of revolt was ignited that summer.

Francis Joseph was deeply shaken by the carnage at Solferino. Archduke Maximilian, who had been at his brother's side ever since the dismissal of Gyulai, wrote to Charlotte on the day after the battle: 'I had never much hope of the outcome, but I did not imagine it would follow so swiftly or be quite so overwhelming. The retreat during the evening formed a scene of desolation I shall never forget. The sight of all the wounded was terrible'. Nevertheless the Emperor was at first prepared to continue the war: the Quadrilateral remained the strongest defensive system in the world; and he was certain Napoleon III would not risk throwing weary troops against the defences of Verona. He had still not entirely given up hope that 'the despicable scum' in Prussia would 'stand by us in the end'; and Prince-Regent William did, indeed, order the massing of six army divisions along the Rhine frontier on the day that the battle of Solferino was fought. If the Austrians had been prepared to allow the Prince-Regent to command all the northern troops of the German Confederation, the Prussians would have marched on Paris. But, though Maximilian liked to pose as an Austro-Italian prince, Francis Joseph still saw himself as the residual legatee of the old Empire of the German Nation: better accept, at least temporarily, the loss of Lombardy than help Lutheran Prussia achieve primacy in Germany.

He was right in assuming that Napoleon III would hesitate before committing his army to a long campaign of probing at the Quadrilateral. Like Francis Joseph and Maximilian, Napoleon was appalled by the horrors of the battlefield, much as his uncle had been after the terrible losses at Eylau. He was worried, too, by the attitude of the Prussians and in particular by threats from Berlin that if a national insurrection flared up in Hungary, Prussia would force France to make peace with Austria so that the German Powers could work together against the spread of revolution. Napoleon, aware that he was becoming involved in problems beyond his control, decided to end the war as speedily as possible. 'I can't hang on in this position', his cousin heard him say, 'I must get out of here'.

In one of her letters the Empress Elizabeth had raised with Francis Joseph the possibility that he might hold talks with the Prince-Regent of Prussia, as a means of putting pressure on France. 'A meeting with the Prince of Prussia, such as you mention, is not on the cards', he replied on 8 July, 'but it could be that another meeting is in store for me which I dread, namely one with that arch-scoundrel Napoleon ... At present Napoleon seems to possess a deep desire for an armistice and for peace ... The evening before last I had already gone to bed when the arrival of General Fleury, aide-de-camp of the French Emperor, was announced ... I leapt out of bed, had myself got into uniform and welcomed the General, who brought me a handwritten letter from his Emperor in which he proposed to me a ceasefire' on land and sea. Next morning Francis Joseph had answered Napoleon: he welcomed a ceasefire pending negotiations and was willing to meet Napoleon to discuss an interim settlement of the Italian question. On 8 July the armistice became effective.

Three days later Francis Joseph set out from Verona soon after dawn, with a group of senior officers, escorted by a squadron of the Imperial Uhlans. A mile to the east of Villafranca he was received by Napoleon III, at whose side he rode into the town, dismounting outside the house which had so recently been his headquarters. In 1807 two opposing emperors – Napoleon I and Tsar Alexander I – surprised the world by meeting on a raft at Tilsit to end a long war and reverse the alliance system, making Russia France's ally rather than her enemy. The Villafranca meeting was intended by Napoleon III to suggest parallels with Tilsit: once more two emperors would startle Europe by coming together privately and deciding the fate of the continent – although, as usual, Napoleon was in far too much of a hurry to spare such matters more than a few hours of conversation. He wished to shun possible mediation by Prussia, Russia or Great Britain and confound the calculations of the European chancelleries with the possibility of a Franco-Austrian detente. Unlike Tilsit – or Plombières – the meeting with Francis Joseph was given great publicity. Journalists were encouraged to clamber round the rubble and craters of Villafranca in search of good copy.

Within a couple of days, Europe's newspaper public could read how Napoleon III and Francis Joseph had gone alone, without advisers or interpreters, into a ground floor room where they talked for about an hour, apparently taking no notice of reporters peering through the windows. They sat at a table smoking cigarettes, and talking fluently in either French or German. No maps were unrolled. Occasionally they would jot down notes on sheets of paper. One journalist claimed to have seen Napoleon III nervously fraying some flowers, and he was certainly less at ease than Francis Joseph; a few days later he admitted to the British ambassador in Paris that, while talking to Francis Joseph, he had no idea 'who ruled what in the various Italian duchies'. By eleven o'clock the meeting was over. The journalists learnt that the emperors had agreed on a preliminary peace. They favoured the creation of an Italian Confederation under the Pope; the cession to France (for transfer to Sardinia-Piedmont) of all of Lombardy, except the fortresses of Mantua and Peschiera; the inclusion of Venetia, which would remain an Austrian possession, in the Italian Confederation; the return of the rulers of Tuscany and Modena to their duchies; 'indispenable reforms' in the Papal States; and a general amnesty 'to persons compromised by recent events'. Refinement of these terms would be made in a definitive treaty later in the year.

Francis Joseph was well satisfied with his morning's work. After signing the 'preliminary peace' he rode beside the 'arch-scoundrel' a short distance down the familiar road towards Valeggio. The two emperors parted courteously, still scrutinized by journalists for whom such occasions remained a novelty. Francis Joseph then returned swiftly to Verona. Three days later he was back in his capital. He had fared better at Villafranca than he dared to hope after conceding defeat on the battlefield. All Radetzky's fortresses in the Quadrilateral remained in Austrian hands, providing him with bases from which he might launch a war to avenge Solferino. He was resigned, for the present, to accept a loss of territory; 'We shall get that back in a couple of years', he was heard to remark a few days later. But in Vienna he found Rechberg still uneasy over the falling prestige of the dynasty. The lost campaign in Italy pierced the mystique of military autocracy cultivated so carefully for the first ten years of his reign. In Prague his uncle Ferdinand, the kindest of ex-emperors, read of the cession of Lombardy and observed, 'Even I could have managed that!'. To win back and hold his subjects' regard Francis Joseph needed to follow retreat in Italy by a phased withdrawal from absolutism in the Monarchy as a whole.

Chapter 8

'POWER REMAINS IN MY HANDS'

Despite the warnings given to him at Verona by Rechberg, the Emperor was shaken by the coolness with which he was received in Vienna on his return from the war. There were no spontaneous cheers in the street and several instances of men failing to raise their hats in respectful salute as his carriage sped by them. The newspapers were, of course still censored, although less strictly than at the peak of the Metternich era, and readers could catch ominous growls emerging from their loosely muzzled columns. The liberal *Neues Wiener Tagblatt*, knowing it could not attack Francis Joseph in person, was outspoken in criticizing his closest advisers, especially Grünne, whom it described as 'a behind-the-scenes head of government' with 'the authority of a Vice-Emperor'. More serious than the press attacks were police reports of assassination threats: some may merely have originated in hotheaded talk after too much drink, but an alleged plot by a footman at the Hofburg who wished to murder both the Emperor and the Archduchess Sophie caused greater concern at Court.

Characteristically, Francis Joseph shrugged off any risk to his person. He stayed away from Vienna, however, for he did not want foreign observers reporting to other governments on what were, in effect, silent demonstrations of disapproval when Emperor or Empress appeared in the capital. Yet, at a time when (as he said) 'our land is suffering from deep wounds', his diligent conscience would not permit him to relax. He therefore changed the normal pattern of Court life: no birthday vacation at Ischl this year, and no lengthy residence at Schönbrunn, for the palace was too public. Instead, he shut himself up at Laxenburg through the last scorching weeks of a sultry summer. The parkland was good for shoots and short rides, but for the most part he chose to immerse himself in the study of memoranda and reports of the 'unfortunate but glorious campaign'. After that shattering experience, he found it hard to feign once more the ebullient self-confidence which had carried him through the first years of his married life. At Laxenburg a morose husband joined a wife who, though still devoted to him, was accumulating more and more grievances over the role she was called upon to play at Court

As early as 15 July Francis Joseph presided over a ministerial Council, the first inquest into what had gone wrong. Later that day he published the so-called Laxenburg Manifesto in which, after informing his subjects of the preliminary peace terms, he held out a promise of reform. He would, so the Manifesto ran, use the 'leisure' hours granted to him by the ending of the war to bolster the Monarchy's welfare 'by a suitable development of its rich spiritual and material resources, and by modernizing and improving the legislature and administration'. But he was in no hurry to complete the changes. During the next five weeks the Council never met once. Two unpopular figures disappeared from the public eye: Bach resigned as minister of the interior at the end of July; while Grünne attended no more meetings of the Council and, in October, accepted the largely honorific Court post of Master of the Horse. A new team of ministers was announced on 21 August: Rechberg remained in charge of foreign affairs as well as being effective prime minister; the indispensable Baron Karl von Bruck looked after finance, trade and communications; and Count Goluchowski, Governor of Galicia for the past ten years, became minister of the interior. Never before had a Polish aristocrat received so high an appointment in Vienna.

Briefly the Emperor seemed to be flirting with liberalism. This was an illusion. He was impressed by a memorandum presented to him by Baron Bruck: it recommended the introduction of constitutional government, with both communal assemblies and an enlarged Imperial Council, and religious concessions to curb the powers enjoyed by the Catholic hierarchy under the Concordat and increase the civic rights of the Protestant and Orthodox churches, so influential among the nationalities around the fringe of the Monarchy. But though Francis Joseph summoned Bruck to Laxenburg to discuss these proposals, over one point he remained adamant: he would never grant a constitution; there must be no more Kremsier play-acting. It was thus impossible for him to accept a genuinely liberal programme of reform. He mistrusted any proposal which might have limited his sovereign powers over the army or foreign affairs. On the other hand, he respected Bruck's judgment of affairs and he agreed with him that local assemblies in the provinces might have a valuable administrative function. He therefore sounded out two highly trusted members of the dynasty, his cousins the Archdukes Albrecht and Rainer; both emphasized the need for something to be done to calm the mounting political excitement in Hungary. Significantly, Francis Joseph took little notice of Maximilian. There had been a brief meeting with him and Charlotte, under Archduchess Sophie's auspices, but Max's ideas remained too drastically reformist, and a popular cult in Buda and Vienna of the 'liberal Archduke' – together with a certain jealousy between Sisi and Charlotte – heightened Francis Joseph's doubts.

Bruck had given the Emperor the views of a bourgeois Protestant: Goluchowski was an astute, Jesuit-educated Catholic, whose religiosity ensured that his political opinions were treated with some indulgence by Archduchess Sophie. For Goluchowski 'Germanization' was the curse of the Monarchy. If he favoured any system of government at all, it was a multi-national benevolent aristocracy. By contrast Rechberg, though a Metternichian conservative in general policy, had the faults and virtues of a slightly pedantic bureaucrat. He acknowledged a need for the Emperor's government to consult the peoples of the Monarchy over regional and local problems, but his main concern was with Austria's status as a European Great Power. In particular, he wished to define anew the traditional Habsburg role in Germany. None of these three ministers – Bruck, Goluchowski, Rechberg – would support a second round of war in Italy.

Nor, indeed, after November, when the Peace Preliminaries were defined more precisely by the Treaty of Zurich, did Francis Joseph want another campaign. He could see that the intensity of Italian nationalist feeling had already ruled out many proposals conjured up so easily in the tobacco smoke of Villafranca; and he did not want to become involved more deeply in the affairs of the peninsula so long as they were in such a state of flux. The army needed to be re-equipped, notably with better rifles and field guns. Before facing new battles, he wished to be certain of the loyalty of all his nationalities.

The first of the reforms promised in the Laxenburg Manifesto were announced on 23 August and followed Bruck's recommendations closely. Local assemblies (*Landtage*) were to receive increased administrative powers; and the Protestant and Orthodox Churches were promised greater freedom. In November Francis Joseph approved proposals to abolish many of the remaining restrictions on the Jewish communities of the Empire (a topic Bruck had not raised in his memorandum). Before the end of the year the Emperor established a State Debt Committee, to examine the financial structure of the Monarchy, for he agreed with Bruck on the need to re-assure foreign investors. Finally, on 5 March 1860, it was announced that an enlarged Reichsrat (to comprise 20 notables appointed by the Emperor and 38 elected representatives from the *Landtage*) would meet in Vienna at the end of May, with the immediate task of settling a national budget. Apart from a group of Magyar magnates, the Hungarians were slow to respond to Francis Joseph's modest reform programme; and the Viennese liberals were suspicious of Goluchowski

Schönbrunn, the enormous 'summer palace' built by Maria Theresa in the 18th century, birthplace of Francis Joseph and chief residence of the Habsburg rulers of a great multi-ethnic empire. In the foreground are the gilded eagles.

Archduchess Sophie of Bavaria, the power behind the throne at the time of her son Francis Joseph's accession and whose ambitions for him were a constant theme of Habsburg politics.

Field marshal Radetzky, one of the greatest of Francis Joseph's commanders, whose control of Italy held back the forces of nationalism at a critical time and inspired the world-famous Radetzky March by Johann Strauss. Radetzky retired in virtual senility at the age of ninety-one.

Young Francis Joseph in his uniform as a Hussar officer prior to his accession. He was trained to love soldiering, uniforms and the military dignity of the dynasty, and this picture reminds us of the dashing figure which contrasted so strongly with the many later images of Francis Joseph as 'elder statesman'.

The Emperor with his young bride Elizabeth, 1855, a year after their marriage. He remained captivated by her throughout their long years of marriage, though her own wayward temperament, not helped by the interfering bossiness of Archduchess Sophie, placed many strains upon them.

Elizabeth's life-long riding skills entranced her husband, and she was acknowledged as one of the most accomplished horsewomen in Europe.

Alongside her passion for horses, Empress Elizabeth was a dog lover too. This photograph shows Elizabeth, in her thirtieth year, with her favourite hound 'Shadow'.

The Emperor with two of his children, Archduchess Gisela and Crown Prince Rudolf, in 1860. The photograph was sent by Francis Joseph to Elizabeth while she was convalescing in Madeira.

Only rarely did the Emperor escape the cares of state. He was a hunting enthusiast, however, and this picture was taken during one of his escapes from the business of government.

Francis Joseph and his companions picnic during a hunting expedition at Gödöllo, in the Habsburg Kingdom of Hungary.

A view of Schönbrunn, taken from the point at which the Emperor first encountered Anna Nahowski.

On his visit to mark the opening of the Suez Canal, the Emperor climbed the pyramid of Cheops, a not inconsiderable achievement despite helping hands.

as an aristocrat, a clericalist, and a Pole. But there were hopes of Bruck and Rechberg together introducing some form of central representative government.

Bruck, however, was dead before the 'Reinforced Reichsrat' met. The enquiry into the lost war had revealed peculation and corruption in high places, with the Quartermaster-General of the army the chief culprit, although he committed suicide before the inquiries were complete. Among financial figures arrested were several directors of Trieste companies with whom Bruck was once linked; and in mid-April 1860 Bruck was summoned to give evidence at the trial of an eminent banker accused of embezzling government funds (and eventually found innocent). The sustained smear campaign by Bruck's enemies made him offer his resignation to the Emperor, on the grounds that a finance minister should not in any way be associated with a trial of this nature. In a private audience, the Emperor assured Bruck that he enjoyed his complete confidence, and he persuaded him to stay in office. But Francis Joseph always remained brutally unimaginative in handling personal relationships. Others at Court – almost certainly Grünne among them – suggested that Bruck was right: he should give up such a sensitive office while the inquiries were continuing. On the evening of 22 April, Bruck returned with his family from a theatre visit to find awaiting him a brief note from the Emperor: 'As you requested, I have decided to put you on the retired list for the time being'; and he was told that one of his senior officials, Ignaz von Plener, would succeed him as minister of finance. So shaken was Bruck by this curt message that he seized his razor and cut his throat. Subsequently, a detailed investigation of the Baron's papers and documents exonerated him from all scandal.

Bruck's suicide deepened Austria's chronic financial crisis, for his prestige among Europe's bankers had been high, and the exchange rate of the thaler fell sharply at the news of his death. Never again would Francis Joseph find such a far-sighted economist to manage the Monarchy's finance and commerce. Politically, too, his death was ill-timed. When the Reinforced Reichsrat began, very cautiously, to discuss a more representative system of government, the balance was tilted in favour of the aristocratic federalism favoured by Goluchowski and a group of Hungarian 'Old Conservatives'.

Francis Joseph was angry that the topic had been raised at all: 'I cannot allow any curtailment of monarchical power through a constitution', he told his ministers in June, 'I would face any storm rather than that. The possibility may not even come up for discussion.' At Reichsrat sessions two Archdukes and Cardinal Rauscher tried to ensure that the Emperor's wishes were observed, but without success. In the last week of September the Reichsrat presented two recommendations to the Emperor: a majority report favoured federalism; a minority report recommended centralized government under an even larger Reichsrat. The Emperor accepted both documents but, for over a fortnight, remained silent about them. He had, however, agreed to meet the rulers of Russia and Prussia in Warsaw on 21 October to discuss a common autocratic Front against the Italian Risorgimento and other manifestations of national liberalism. There was – so he was told by Count Szécsen, spokesman for the Magyar Old Conservatives – a danger of unrest in Hungary if he did not give the Reichsrat a clear answer. On the other hand, Szécsen assured the Emperor that if his compatriots knew their historic Diet was to be restored, they would co-operate with the other nationalities and treat the Monarchy as a unitary state. Francis Joseph did not want his standing at the Warsaw meeting weakened by reports of trouble in Hungary, for that would recall too sharply the first months of his reign. Accordingly, he appointed Szécsen a government minister with the task of drafting, within a few days, 'a new settlement for the Empire as a whole' based upon the recommendations sent to him by the majority in the Reichsrat.

It was a tough assignment. Yet, after consulting Rechberg and Goluchowski, Szécsen completed his task some thirty hours ahead of Francis Joseph's departure for Warsaw. The 'October Diploma' was a fundamental law which strengthened the provincial Diets, giving them legislative authority over matters previously determined by ministers of the interior. It provided for them to send delegates to the Reichsrat, which would be recognized as the principal legislature of the Empire. Supplementary to the basic Diploma were more than twenty 'Sovereign Rescripts' which established electoral bodies to prepare for the Diets in the various provinces – thereby tacitly sanctioning open discussion in towns where, for twelve years, a discreet instinct of well-being had precluded political debate. On paper, at least, the Emperor had abandoned absolutism, while still avoiding use of that accursed word 'constitution'.

'We are certainly going to have a little parliamentary life, but the power remains in my hands', Francis Joseph wrote to his mother, a few hours before leaving for Warsaw. His confidence re-assured the Archduchess, who had read the details of the October Diploma earlier that day. The past twelve months had been hard for her. She had seen earlier protégés, like Grünne and his nominees, discredited and the political clericalism which brought about the Concordat called in question. It was a blow to her that she could not smooth down the mounting mistrust between her eldest sons for, though she thought Franzi right and Max wayward, her second-born child was her favourite. Saddest of all to the Archduchess was the rift with her niece and daughter-in-law, which broadened every week.

The worst disputes concerned the upbringing of the Crown Prince. Archduchess Sophie remained convinced that Elizabeth was too immature to supervise the education of the heir to the throne. As soon as Rudolf left the cradle, his grandmother planned for him precisely the same early training as she had laid down for Francis Joseph and Maximilian. Over such matters the Emperor did not question his mother's wisdom. At heart he, too, still looked upon 'my heavenly Sisi' as a child-wife, his 'one and only, most beautiful angel'; he seems indeed always to have loved an immaturity of spirit she never completely shed. But the Empress was too strong-willed to remain a pet. She resented 'interference' in the nursery routine and, in her indignation, convinced herself that her mother-in-law would stop at nothing to humiliate her. This was unfair: there are many instances in Sophie's journal of sympathy and affection for the niece whose moods she could never understand. Yet the Archduchess must have been a trying companion with whom to share a palace, for her approbation tended to spice Bavarian sentimentality with an astringency all her own: thus, on 24 December 1859, she could describe 'Sisi at a Christmas party for her 22nd birthday, looking as delicious as a sugar bonbon, in a strawberry pink dress of watered silk (*moiré*)'. Was this praise, or criticism of the young Empress's dress sense?

At all events, by the following autumn, when her husband was trying to make up his mind over 'the new settlement for the Empire', Elizabeth had lost much of that bewitching vitality on which her strained nerves had drawn in the first years of marriage. Her reluctance to eat more than a few mouthfuls of the meals set before her – a trait which first caused concern while Francis Joseph was in Verona – had grown into a positive loathing for all food. Each day she would take vigorous exercise on gymnastic apparatus; she feared that she would soon look like her sister Néné, whom she considered overweight but who was, in reality, a comfortably proportioned mother, happily married to the Prince of Thurn and Taxis.

In a modern adolescent a similar instance of eating very little and constantly fighting an imaginary weight problem might well be diagnosed as a form of anorexia nervosa. But in 1860 the science of human behaviour was still in its infancy. That the Empress was ill, there was little doubt. When she took a holiday at Possenhofen in mid-summer her mother and brothers were deeply worried; she was 'a bean-pole', Ludovika told her. As for the cough which she could not shake off, that seems to have been as much a nervous gesture as a symptom of trouble in the throat or lungs.

Elizabeth certainly had grave matters on her mind. Everyone at Possenhofen was concerned over the future of her eighteen year old sister, the Queen of Naples, who bravely decided to stiffen her weak-kneed husband's resistance to the menace of Garibaldi and his thousand redshirts. Elizabeth found it galling that, because of Austria's losses in the Solferino campaign, the Emperor would not sanction intervention in southern Italy. Francis Joseph joined her at Possenhofen in late July; he enjoyed playing billiards with his Bavarian kinsfolk and he was glad to relax in the family circle; he expressed admiration for the Queen of Naples's fighting spirit, but nothing could induce him to send ships or men or material to uphold the independence of the Two Sicilies. And, at this very moment of disillusionment with her soldier husband idol, Elizabeth's enemies at Court seem to have made certain that she picked up rumours of his passing attachment to a Polish countess, resident in Vienna during the previous winter and spring. Whether there was any truth in these tales remains unclear: from Marie Walewska onwards, seductive Polish countesses flit across historical romance at the drop of a fan. But, given the circulation of these rumours, it was unfortunate to have chosen Warsaw for a summit conference that autumn.

The Warsaw meeting, which formally opened on 22 October, was unproductive. Prince-Regent William of Prussia and Francis Joseph treated each other with a cool, mutual suspicion, while Alexander II was too concerned with Russia's internal affairs to trouble himself over a revival of 'the revolution' and the alleged need for the Holy Alliance powers to crusade against liberalism in Italy. Alexander was not sorry to disoblige Francis Joseph, for bitterness over Austria's 'ingratitude' during the Crimean War lingered on. The sudden death of Alexander II's mother gave the Tsar an excuse to cut the meeting short and return to St Petersburg. By 28 October Francis Joseph, too, was back in his capital. He found Sisi in a state of nervous collapse.

A modern biographer of the Empress has claimed that, while her husband was in Warsaw, Elizabeth decided to seek the opinion of an outside physician on the state of her health. 'Heavily veiled and under an assumed name, the doctor may not have guessed at her identity and therefore told the truth, namely, that she was suffering from an unpleasant and contagious disease. To learn that Francis Joseph had not only been unfaithful but had contaminated her as well would have filled her with such horror and disgust, as to explain, not only her behaviour at the time, but her whole attitude in the future.' No authority is given for this tale, the details of which sound highly unlikely. More probably, with winter approaching after months of worry and frustration, the Empress experienced on a greater scale than in earlier years the claustrophobic escapism that had in the past impelled her to ride long distances non-stop in a single day. It would seem that Elizabeth was suffering from a mental illness rather than from any disease, and that the physical symptoms she showed were attributable to emotional causes. 'I must go far, far away, right out of the country', she told Francis Joseph. Villas in Istria or the southern Tyrol were too accessible. She wanted a remote island where no one could reach her. Madeira was her choice. Reluctantly, but with the tolerant kindness he reserved for Sisi, Francis Joseph concurred.

An official medical bulletin informed the public that Her Imperial Majesty was suffering from a grave infection of the lungs which required her to winter in a warm climate. Archduchess Sophie seems to have known nothing of the illness, nor did she hear in advance of the plans for rest and recuperation. 'I was shattered by the news' she wrote in her journal on the last day of October; she could not understand why Sisi wished to leave her husband and children 'for five long months'. As no Austrian ship was said to be ready or available for the voyage to Madeira, Queen Victoria put her royal yacht at the disposal of the Empress. Francis Joseph accompanied Elizabeth through Bavaria and as far as Bamburg. She then travelled on to Antwerp with her personally selected ladies-in-waiting and equerries and with the foreign minister's brother to act as a personal secretary. The Emperor paid a brief courtesy visit to the King of Württemberg in Stuttgart and by the end of the week was back at Laxenburg.

The mystery of the Empress's illness remained unresolved. A fringe observer with a long experience of royal maladies attended her at Antwerp. 'Yesterday before daybreak I ... paid the Empress a visit, and then I took her to your beautiful ship', King Leopold wrote to Queen Victoria, on 22 November, 'She was much struck with it ... I saw the Empress already dressed for her departure, but I think there is something very peculiar about her, which is very pleasing (*sic*). Poor soul, to see her go away under, I fear, not very safe circumstances, as she coughs a great deal, quite grieves one'. The wintry voyage down the Channel and across the Bay of Biscay was exceptionally rough. While most of the imperial suite were seasick, Elizabeth developed a hearty appetite for meals cooked and served by the Royal Navy, her own chef being far too ill to attend to her delicate needs. For several weeks after landing at Madeira, she revelled in the delights of the island like a child on a seaside holiday. And then, as Christmas and her birthday approached, she became bored and depressed once more. 'She often shuts herself up in her room and cries all day ... She eats alarmingly little ... the whole meal, consisting of four courses, four sweets, coffee etc. does not last more than twenty-five minutes', her secretary wrote back to Vienna in a private letter. Not all these details were made known to Francis Joseph but, as the year ended, it became increasingly clear to him that, so far from finding reassuring relief in Madeira, Sisi still believed herself wracked by an illness that tormented her spirits.

This protracted crisis in his private affairs coincided with the most perplexing political problems Francis Joseph had as yet encountered. Szécsen had assured him that the October Diploma would be well received in Hungary. He was wrong. The group of Magyar Old Conservatives at the Vienna Court had no following in Hungary. As soon as self-government was re-introduced into the Hungarian counties, there was a rush of patriotism to the head throughout the kingdom and a firm refusal in the towns and the countryside to pay any taxes unless the validity of the constitutional concessions granted in April 1848 was acknowledged. Some districts in Hungary, mocking the whole system, nominated absentees as their 'elected' representatives; the names put forward included, not only Kossuth, but even Napoleon III and Cavour. Nor were the Hungarians the only nationality to find the October Diploma inadequate: the Germans thought it too feudal, too clericalist, and too sympathetic to the Czechs (who, for their part, complained that the Diploma failed to acknowledge Bohemia's historic State Rights); and the Poles felt aggrieved because Goluchowski did not secure for Galicia the privileged status which they maintained Szécsen had won for Hungary. With every nationality disgruntled, Francis Joseph's 'little parliamentary life' proved stillborn.

On 14 December 1860, eight weeks after the Diploma was announced, Goluchowski arrived at his ministerial office to find a letter of resignation awaiting him on the desk, ready for his signature. Szécsen, too, was unceremoniously dropped; immediately after Christmas Francis Joseph held conversations in Vienna with two much respected Hungarian reformers, the lawyer Ferenc Deák and the novelist Baron Josef Eötvös. Both men had been moderate liberals in 1848–49 and both had important roles to play in the course of the coming decade, but for the moment their chief value was in giving their sovereign some insight into genuine Hungarian hopes and fears, rather than the rarefied feudalism of the Old Conservatives.

Francis Joseph was not prepared to tear up the October Diploma – why publicly admit political bankruptcy? He chose instead to have the Diploma's proposals 'elucidated' by a supplementary series of enactments announced on 27 February 1861, and therefore known as the 'February Patent'. These modifications were primarily the work of Baron Anton von Schmerling, a liberal who had once chaired the Frankfurt Parliament, and who took the place of the ousted Goluchowski (although in the first week of February Archduke Rainer officially took over as head of the government). They preserved the institutions proposed by the October Diploma but changed their composition and responsibilities, so as to make the new system more centralized. A bicameral Reichsrat was created, with the lower house comprising members sent to Vienna from the provincial diets under an indirect electoral college system of representation. To the disquiet of many professional army officers, this nominated chamber of deputies was intended to have control over the military budget. But the Emperor was not surrendering his prerogatives. Once again he rigidly insisted that real power remained in his hands: under no circumstances, he told his ministers when the February Patent was under discussion, must they allow the lower chamber to trespass into matters left properly to the foreign ministry and the army High Command. As the legislative programme of the following four years shows clearly enough, Francis Joseph retained a right of veto over contentious legislation and used it freely. He neither liked nor trusted parliaments, but he was prepared to let public opinion have a safety-valve if it minimized the risk of a democratic explosion. The Reichsrat was opened on 1 May with a speech from the throne in the ceremonial Redoutenhalle of the Hofburg. Thereafter parliamentary business was transacted in a specially constructed wooden building, popularly dubbed 'Schmerling's theatre': there seemed no point in commissioning a permanent chamber.

On that May Day of 1861 the Empress was in Seville. She had left Madeira three days before, having decided of her own volition to end the self-imposed exile. Her homeward voyage took her briefly to Malta and then to Corfu, where the beauty of the island entranced her. At last she reached Trieste and, on 18 May, joined Francis Joseph, Maximilian and Charlotte at Miramare, the Archduke's villa outside the city. She seemed fully recovered in health when she completed the journey by train to Vienna. But old grievances returned swiftly. Why was she at once absorbed into the routine of Court life, resuming the formal receptions which she found so tedious in the past? Why were Gisela and Rudolf expected to adhere to so rigid a daily programme that their mother seemed like a visiting guest to her own children? Nursery routine centred upon Grandmama and her two nominees, Countess Sophie Esterházy (the Empress's Mistress of the Robes ever since her wedding) and Baroness Caroline Welden, Rudolf's Aja. At almost three years old, the Crown Prince was devoted to 'Wowo', as he called the Baroness all his life.

The well-ordered life at the Hofburg became intolerable for Elizabeth within a matter of days. Less than a week after landing at Trieste, her health gave way again. Court receptions and state dinners were cancelled. Hurriedly she was moved out to Laxenburg, with her doctors in attendance. Had her recovery been more apparent that real? Or, as the more cynical Viennese began to speculate, was her illness less real than apparent? Soon she was refusing most of the food cooked for her, and her personal physician said she was feverish. In tears, she begged Francis Joseph to allow her to go away once more: not to Madeira, but down the Adriatic, back to the sunshine and peace of Corfu. Though wretchedly depressed himself, Francis Joseph as usual let her have her way. On 23 June he travelled to Trieste with her, leaving Maximilian to take her to Corfu, aboard an Austrian vessel. The fever had gone down and her appetite was picking up again even before she reached Corfu. When she disembarked, it was six weeks to the day since her first visit to the island.

Francis Joseph realized that this second flight of the Empress cast doubts on the future of Court life in Vienna, and indeed on the survival of his marriage. He therefore insisted on regular medical reports from Corfu and sent special couriers down the Adriatic to see what was happening on the island; some emissaries, notably Grünne, were poor choices. Far more welcome to Elizabeth was a visit from her sister, Helen of Thurn and Taxis, in August. When she passed through Vienna a month later Princess Helen urged Francis Joseph to travel to Corfu himself. He was at once attracted by the suggestion. Even though he had amused himself shooting and stalking deer with Helen's husband while she was staying with Elizabeth, he had spent a laborious summer trying to hold in check the mounting German liberalism in 'Schmerling's theatre' while encouraging his ministers to find new ways of asserting Austrian primacy within the German Confederation. Moreover Hungary remained a problem. Despite Deák's calming influence, the Hungarians still refused to take part in the Reichsrat's deliberations, while in Zagreb a new Croatian patriot, Ante Starčević, began to campaign for 'Croatia's historic rights'. Even had Elizabeth not been in Corfu, an escape to the peace of the Ionian Islands would have been welcome.

'I should like to spend early October paying a rapid visit of a few days to my dear Sisi in Corfu', the Emperor felt obliged to explain to his mother on 30 September, 'I feel the greatest longing to be there after such a long separation'. He arrived a fortnight later; soon he was writing back to the Archduchess in rhapsodies over the beauty of 'this earthly paradise'. The short sojourn in Corfu was the only occasion Francis Joseph visited territories which acknowledged Queen Victoria's sovereignty, for the Ionian Islands had been a British protectorate since the Congress of Vienna; and it is inevitable that, though he paid tribute to Corfu's scenic delights, he was more interested in the way the British had modernized the Venetian fortifications and developed the shipping facilities than in the laurel-woods, cypresses and craggy blue coves which so uplifted Elizabeth's spirits. The visit enabled husband and wife to talk long and calmly, with Francis Joseph showing great patience. He tempted her to return home with messages from the children as well as personal pleas, emphasizing his own need for her company. Elizabeth remained concerned for the well-being of the Empire, recognizing the validity of her husband's argument that her absence lowered his prestige as head of a historic dynasty. She kept up her regular lessons in the Magyar language as well as improving her Italian, and now sought to learn modern Greek, too. But she firmly refused to go back to Vienna, believing that to go into residence at the Hofburg again would lead to social disaster. The most she would concede was an agreement to winter in Venice, where she could hope to see Gisela and Rudolf occasionally, free from the brooding presence of their grandmother.

To have the Empress resident in Venice promised some political advantages, as Francis Joseph was quick to perceive. If his ministers were to concentrate on German affairs and on seeking an accommodation with the Hungarians, then it would be as well to preserve peace along the Monarchy's southern borders. Francis Joseph consistently deluded himself over Italian affairs. When the Kingdom of Italy was proclaimed in March 1861 he refused to acknowledge the new state, even arguing that the sentiment of nationalism in the peninsula was a fleeting enthusiasm which would soon give way to indignation over conflicting local interests. He believed Venetia was not quite lost to the Empire; the merchant class, with their traditional shipping interests in the Levant, might have more to gain from the improved railway network of central Europe than they could expect from competition with neighbouring commercial communities in the new Italy. Five years previously, Sisi's tact and charm melted the glacial patrician attitude of the old republic's ruling class towards the first imperial visit. Was there still a dormant strain of spontaneous wizardry crushed within her temperament? Moreover, if she became the First Lady of Venice, spending a Christmas season in the city for the second time in her life, she might well recover the social confidence which had always deserted her at the Hofburg and Schönbrunn.

In fact it was too late for any Habsburg to win acceptance. Elizabeth arrived in Venice at the end of October 1861 and remained in the city for six months. Never was she able to arouse any show of loyal support from her husband's Italian subjects. To them she was an outsider, a visitor wintering on the lagoon. Elizabeth's children were brought to her, and Francis Joseph paid several visits: 'They appear to be as much in love as in the first days of their marriage', Baron Hübner observed when he passed through Venice shortly before Christmas. Yet Elizabeth continued to worry the Emperor: the Crown Prince's trusted 'Wowo' earned her grudging approval, but she found Countess Sophie Esterházy as insufferable as ever, constantly insisting that the regime laid down by the Archduchess for the children's upbringing must be observed, even when they were away from Vienna.

In January the Emperor at last agreed to Elizabeth's request for the removal of the Countess from her household, after nine years in office. Henceforth the Empress would have around her only women she had chosen herself. But the dismissal of the Countess temporarily widened the rift with the Archduchess, for Sophie Esterházy was her closest friend and confidante. The Emperor could see that Sisi was not yet able to return to Vienna; and her behaviour seemed increasingly odd. She had started collecting a picture album of the (allegedly) most beautiful women in Europe, even asking her husband to use the services of the Austrian ambassador in Constantinople to obtain likenesses of the women of Sultan Abdulaziz's harem. These portraits she would study in admiration or envy. They brought little pleasure. According to her ladies-in-waiting, she again spent long hours alone in her room in tears. As spring approached, the reports sent back to Vienna and Possenhofen made Elizabeth seem so unwell that Duchess Ludovika took the most sensible decision ever recorded of her; she travelled down by train to Venice and, after lengthy consultation with Francis Joseph, whisked her daughter back to Bavaria for medical advice from Dr Fischer, who had cared for her in childhood.

The Emperor spent much of the late spring and summer of 1862 considering reforms in the judiciary and in banking and taxation, put before his ministers by the Reichsrat. He was faced, too, by an unexpected problem over which there were long family discussions. Since the previous December Napoleon III had been pursuing a forward policy in Mexico, where the radical government of Benito Juarez had suspended payments due on foreign debts. Although Mexico's financial viability was of great concern to France, and to a lesser extent to Spain and Britain, it did not touch any vital Austrian interests. But Napoleon believed that a monarchical Mexico, ruled by a European prince with the support of France, would open up a Latin American market to European commerce and political influence at a time when the United States was weakened by the Civil War. At Napoleon's prompting the property-owning clericalist party in Mexico was prepared to invite Francis Joseph's eldest brother to become sovereign of a new empire.

At first Maximilian, a restless romantic at heart, was inclined to accept the offer from Mexico, but he hesitated over leaving the exquisite home he had created at Miramare and he was conscious of the strong opposition of most of his family and his oldest advisers. Francis Joseph himself wavered: he acknowledged that opponents of the Mexican venture had a good case, but he knew that Maximilian and Charlotte had received some encouragement from Brussels, London and Paris to press for the creation of a dynastic satrapy within the Monarchy; better their hopes of a royal title should be realized outside Europe than in an autonomous kingdom of Greater Venetia or a virtually independent kingdom of Hungary. Moreover, though Francis Joseph looked on Napoleon as a 'rogue', he accepted that collaboration with France would help Austria emerge from politically dangerous diplomatic isolation. Yet he could not make up his mind. He was still uncertain over the course he should pursue in Mexico – or the merits of the Reichsrat's reform programme – when, in mid-July, he travelled to Possenhofen to judge for himself the true state of Elizabeth's health.

Here at least he received clear, and reassuring, advice. Dr Fischer was less gloomy than the Austrian physicians. No Bavarian Court doctor, accustomed to Wittelsbach eccentricities, tended to take alarm at relatively mild manifestations of nervous tension in any member of the family; and the doctor could find nothing wrong with the Empress's lungs or with her constitution in general. He was mainly concerned over her anaemia, a condition for which he recommended annual courses of hydropathic treatment at Kissingen. She had recently returned from a visit to the spa when Francis Joseph arrived at Possenhofen, and he was delighted by her progress. But, when it was suggested that the Empress might go back with her husband to Ischl, her ankles puffed up and she seemed once more a sick woman. Yet he was not despondent – merely, as he said at the time, 'hungry and thirsty for mountain hunting and mountain air'. For this deprivation he speedily found a simple remedy. As ever, it was the wildlife of the alpine crags and woodland which gratified the imperial craving for good sport.

Francis Joseph was soon back in Vienna; and, fortunately, too. For Elizabeth was unpredictable. Suddenly, without any warning to her ladies-in-waiting, she arrived by train in the capital on Thursday, 14 August, accompanied by her favourite brother, Karl Theodore. The Archduchess Sophie was in the Salzkammergut, where she had the tact to remain for several more weeks. Elizabeth was thus settled at Schönbrunn for the celebrations of her husband's thirty-second birthday and her son's fourth birthday three days later. The people of Vienna, by no means sympathetic to the Empress over the previous two years, welcomed her with as warm a reception as on the eve of her wedding. Their enthusiasm may have been genuine, but it was perhaps influenced by some liberal newspapers which gave the (over-simplified) impression she was at heart a progressive in conflict with a clericalist, reactionary mother-in-law. On the Sunday after her return – the eve of Francis Joseph's birthday – the imperial couple were serenaded by a choir of three hundred singers, and when dusk fell there was a torchlight procession in which between 14,000 and 20,000 people took part.

Elizabeth was extremely nervous, as her ladies soon discovered. For the next four or five months she wanted some member of her Bavarian family with her, either her brother or one of her sisters. But, as each week passed and Elizabeth remained still in residence, Francis Joseph became more optimistic. With his wife beside him and his mother discreetly absent, he found a new delight in playing the role of family father. Soon after Sisi's return, he took the four-year old Crown Prince with him for the annual inspection of the Wiener Neustadt military academy. He made certain that Rudolf was in uniform, just as he would himself have been at that age. When the cadets raised their caps to give three cheers for their Emperor, and Rudolf followed their example, Francis Joseph found the occasion so moving that tears came into his eyes. For several minutes he could not speak.

In many ways the Emperor remained a simple regimental officer who doted on wife and son and was, at heart, as sentimental as his mother. Yet an inbred conservative acceptance of the demands of duty and a pride in dynastic honour made him acutely conscious of the momentous responsibilities he bore. When he assured the Archduchess that 'power remains in my hands' he was satisfying not only his mother but his own conscience. Gradually, however, some principles she had instilled into him were modified, perhaps to a greater extent than he realized. As yet he would make no concession to the growing popular awareness of nationalism throughout his Empire, rightly perceiving that so powerful a force for change represented the negation of the Habsburg ideal. But, under the influence of Schmerling and the German-Austrian bourgeois liberals, his resistance to parliamentary politics at least began to show a certain elasticity of prejudice. When the Reichsrat ended its first session, a week before Christmas in 1862, he had accepted reforms of the commercial code as well as laws improving personal civil rights, freedom of the press, reform of local administration and the competence of the law courts. But perhaps the most interesting comment on the barely perceptible modifications to the form of the Monarchy came on the eve of the new session of 'Schmerling's theatre'. For on 26 February 1863 a gala performance took place at the opera house in Karntnertor to celebrate the second anniversary of the February Patent. The Emperor, who had at first been so alarmed at the intrusion of the Patent on his sovereign authority, was in the opera house that evening. Beside him, 'radiant and smiling' as foreign envoys noted, was his Empress, returning at last after three years to grace Court Balls and public receptions with her charm. What no ambassador could have predicted that February was how, in little over three more years, Elizabeth would possess the vision and skill to coax Francis Joseph into accepting the greatest of all changes in the structure of his Empire.

Chapter 9

IN BISMARCK'S SHADOW

In September 1862, while the Austrian Court was waiting anxiously to see if the Empress would settle once more in Vienna, the monarchy in Prussia faced a major political crisis. King William I – as the Prince Regent became on acceding in 1861 – shared Francis Joseph's belief that matters relating to the army remained within the sovereign's prerogative and were not subject to parliamentary debate. This contention had kept the King in conflict with liberals in the Berlin *Landtag* since his accession, for William sought army reforms, based upon three years of conscript service, while his parliament refused to authorize funds for changes which they feared would intensify the autocratic character of Prussian government. So disheartened was William by the protracted dispute that he was contemplating abdication when, on 22 September, General von Roon persuaded him to receive in audience the Junker diplomat, Otto von Bismarck, who convinced the King he could form a government which would raise the funds for the reforms without sanction of parliament. Bismarck thereupon became both head of the government in Berlin and foreign minister, responsibilities he held for twenty-eight years.

Francis Joseph had met Bismarck as early as June 1852 when he was sent to Vienna for a brief spell as acting ambassador. The Emperor was in Hungary that month and, after paying his respects to Archduchess Sophie and Metternich, the thirty-seven year old Prussian took the paddle-steamer down the Danube for an audience at the royal palace on Buda hill. The Emperor, Bismarck told his wife, 'had the fire of a young man of twenty, together with sober-minded self-possession'; in other letters Bismarck commented on his self-confidence and on his 'engagingly open expression, especially when he laughs'. At the time, Bismarck made little impression on Francis Joseph: he was, after all, only a stop-gap envoy, seconded from diplomatic duties in Frankfurt. But in 1854, and again in 1859, it was realized in Vienna that Bismarck had greater influence on the shaping of Prussian diplomacy than his duties as an executant of government policies warranted. Bismarck and his circle of Junker conservatives were blamed for Prussia's lack of response to Austrian initiatives both in the Crimean War and in the Magenta-Solferino campaign. It was accordingly with a certain apprehension that Francis Joseph and his ministers greeted the formation of a Bismarck government. On the other hand, there was a widespread feeling that, in defying the Prussian *Landtag* with such contemptuous insolence, the newcomer was courting disaster.

When he received his appointment Bismarck was serving as ambassador in Paris and, in October, he returned briefly to France to present letters of recall to Napoleon III. While in Paris he sought out Richard Metternich, Francis Joseph's envoy to the French Court: Prussia intended to secure political, economic and military primacy in northern Germany, Bismarck insisted in conversation; he preferred to attain this position through an understanding with Austria, he added, but if the government in Vienna opposed his policies he would resort to 'any means without scruple' to ensure Prussian leadership. There was, of course, nothing new in proclaiming such an objective, merely in Bismarck's hectoring tone. A few weeks later, on 5 December, Bismarck had the audacity to propose to Count Alois Károlyi – the Magyar magnate who was Francis Joseph's envoy in Berlin – that the time had come 'for Austria to shift her centre of gravity from Germany to Hungary'; once that was achieved Francis Joseph could count on full Prussian support in Italy and south-eastern Europe, but he warned Károlyi that if Austria rejected his overture Prussia would side with France in any future European crisis.

Neither conversation impressed Francis Joseph or his ministers. Prussia's tone and tactics varied from day to day, sometimes wooing, sometimes cajoling and sometimes threatening Austria: 'It is truly astonishing how swiftly Herr von Bismarck moves from one extreme position to another diametrically opposed to it', Károlyi observed in January. But when Bismarck began to bully the smaller German states into accepting a commercial treaty with France which was hostile to Austria's interests, Rechberg and Schmerling took him more seriously. They had already advised the Emperor to support a reform programme, aimed at re-asserting Habsburg leadership of a 'modernized' German Confederation by bringing together delegates from the German and Austrian *Landtage* in a federal parliament. Francis Joseph was hesitant: he did not want to advance the cause of parliamentarianism; and, though always thinking of himself as a German prince, he had the good sense to appreciate the dangers of identifying himself too closely with any particular nationality in his Empire. But in the summer of 1863 he was tempted by a project raised, in the first instance, by Elizabeth's brother-in-law, Prince Maximilian of Thurn and Taxis: the reigning monarchs of the German states would be invited to Frankfurt for a *Fürstentag*, a 'Conclave of Princes', where the future of the Confederation could be discussed by the rulers themselves rather than by their ministers. At such a gathering the princes might well offer the crown of a revived German Empire to the head of the senior dynasty. In late July Francis Joseph made up his mind. On 3 August he paid a courtesy call on William of Prussia, who was taking the waters at Bad Gastein, and invited him to a congress of princes to meet in less than a fortnight at Frankfurt.

The German Princes accepted the invitation, but William temporized. He disliked hustle; he did not fancy the pomp and pageantry of a princely conclave at any time, least of all in August. At sixty-six he was old enough to remember the humiliations inflicted on his father by Napoleon I at the Dresden Congress of rulers. William's doubts were fed by Bismarck, who opposed any initiative taken by the Habsburgs: no acceptance and no final refusal was sent. Francis Joseph, however, was optimistic. He was sure of his fellow German Princes. 'It is the last chance for Germany's rulers, faced by revolution, to save themselves', he told his mother on the eve of departure. His letter rang with cheerful confidence: he felt invigorated by carefree days with Sisi, Gisela and Rudolf in the woods near Schönbrunn, 'the children bathing delightedly in the marvellous water'. When he reached Frankfurt there was still no sign of William, but the Princes warmly welcomed the Emperor and agreed to send their own invitation to the King, who was at Baden-Baden, less than three hours distant by train. King John of Saxony travelled there with a unanimous request that William should join his brother sovereigns.

William was impressed: 'Thirty reigning Princes and a King as a messenger! How can I refuse?', he pointed out to his prime minister. But Bismarck was adamant: to attend the congress would acknowledge Habsburg leadership in Germany; to stay away would wreck Vienna's plans and affirm Prussia's status as a Great Power in Germany and Europe. After a melodramatic dispute which dragged on until midnight, Bismarck had his way. In a letter to the King of Saxony, William politely but firmly rejected the invitation of the 'thirty Princes'.

Without Prussian co-operation there could be little prospect of federal reform or of an imperial coronation. Yet Francis Joseph's visit to Frankfurt was not wasted. The congress forged a loose bond between the Princes, with the Emperor himself accepted as the vital link. Despite William's absence, German affairs were discussed at some length. So long as Bismarck continued treating the Berlin *Landtag* with contempt, Austria appeared less reactionary than Prussia and there was, too, a certain feeling that a multinational institution like the Habsburg Monarchy was better suited to promote unity among the German states than was a narrowly Junker-led Prussia. Francis Joseph and Rechberg were even prepared to champion causes of prime concern to the German states but of little interest to Austria – notably the rights of the German-speaking population in the Danish duchies of Schleswig-Holstein, a topic raised intermittently at Frankfurt over the past fifteen years. Then, too, there was the Polish question. The congress met during the national-liberal insurrection in Russian Poland, which began in January 1863 and reached its peak in March. Most German states were anti-Russian over Polish affairs, but not Prussia. Yet while Bismarck still used the political jargon of the Metternich age, Francis Joseph joined the other states in showing some sympathy towards the Poles, despite his Galician possessions. Not surprisingly, the Princes followed Austria's lead in promoting federal reform. Francis Joseph's warm reception at Frankfurt and in southern Germany, emphasized Bismarckian Prussia's isolation.

So, indeed, Queen Victoria believed. On his way home to Vienna Francis Joseph broke his journey at Coburg, where the widowed Queen was on a protracted visit. It was a curious first meeting. Three days previously the Queen had given luncheon to William of Prussia; she loathed Bismarck and his policies, but she sympathized with the King and convinced herself that he had been kept away from the Frankfurt *Fürstentag* because the Austrians were set on deliberately snubbing Prussia. Francis Joseph was puzzled; he told his mother that, though the Queen was 'very gracious', she became 'quite grumpy . . . inclined to have some bees in her bonnet'. The truth was that Victoria thought her son-in-law, Crown Prince Frederick, might soon succeed his ageing father, and she did not want to see his reign open with Prussia confronting a bloc of Austrian-led states.

She need not have worried: not only did William have almost a quarter of a century ahead of him on the throne but, as natural conservatives, both Francis Joseph and Rechberg were determined to shift their policy so as to work with Prussia in matters of joint interest. When, in the closing months of the year, the simmering Schleswig-Holstein question boiled over, German nationalist sentiment in the Confederation as a whole favoured military intervention against Denmark. So, too, did Bismarck's Prussia – though with narrower objectives. Francis Joseph thereupon assumed the role Queen Victoria had pressed upon him at their Coburg meeting; he made certain that, if the German Confederation had to oppose Denmark, the smaller states could at least rely on the backing of both Prussia and Austria. Saxon and Hanoverian troops entered Holstein in the last days of the old year; the Prussians followed a few weeks later, and on 1 February 1864 the Prussians and Austrians jointly marched into

Schleswig. Gradually the larger German Powers took matters into their own hands. In late February it was primarily the Prussians who invaded the Jutland peninsula, while an Austrian naval squadron effectively neutralized the Danish fleet. Little more was heard of Saxon or Hanoverian or Bavarian policies. The future of Schleswig-Holstein was left to British mediation at the conference table and to the diplomatic ingenuity of Bismarck and Rechberg. This was not the happiest of solutions, but there was satisfaction in Vienna that, at all events, Austria and Prussia were working in partnership, despite the rift of the previous summer.

With hindsight, it is clear that relations with Prussia should have been Francis Joseph's constant concern, once Bismarck had begun to press Austria to shift her 'centre of gravity'. But, like Alexander II and Napoleon III, the Emperor underestimated Bismarck: the brash Junker was boasting or bluffing or both, he assumed. A ruler in Vienna could not give more than a cursory glance northwards to the Baltic; Hungary was a more pressing topic than Schleswig-Holstein; and the Emperor continued to question much of the work put before him by Schmerling and the moderate Austrian reformers. There was, too, another problem which could no longer be shirked. The successful naval challenge in northern waters was a tribute to the spirit of enterprise fostered by Archduke Maximilian during his years as commander-in-chief of Austria's small fleet. Yet ironically this achievement came at a time when Maximilian had little opportunity to follow the fortunes of Admiral Tegetthoff's squadron. For in these early months of 1864 the Archduke had to make the supreme decision of his life. A Mexican crown was his for the taking. Should he accept an unstable throne in a distant continent or remain second in line of succession in Vienna?

In the previous August, a week before the German Princes began their deliberations in Frankfurt, Maximilian received a telegram at Miramare from Napoleon III informing him that in Mexico City a 'national assembly' had proclaimed him as Emperor. There was nothing to prevent the Archduke from rejecting the Mexican crown: his father-in-law, King Leopold, though supporting this particular project, had once declined to become the first sovereign of an independent Greece; and several of the Princes at Frankfurt took the opportunity to express doubts over the wisdom of allowing one of their number to become so closely associated with what was, in origin, a neo-Napoleonic project; Archduchess Sophie, Empress Elizabeth, and even Emperor Ferdinand in Prague urged Maximilian to have nothing more to do with Mexico. Reports reaching Europe indicated widespread support in the country for Juarez's republicanism and confirmed that President Lincoln (whose armies were gaining the upper hand in the war against the Confederates) remained hostile to the creation of a new empire in the Americas. Moreover, it became clear that the 'national assembly' which chose the Archduke as sovereign represented, at best, the will of the capital and its surrounding villages. In these circumstances why did Maximilian remain in contact with the Mexican monarchists? Was his obstinacy fed by the ambition of his wife, as his mischief-making youngest brother insisted in a letter to their mother? Perhaps so. Maximilian was not a political schemer; he liked flowers, and seascape gardening. He is said to have remarked to a friend at Miramare, 'If I heard that the whole Mexican project had come to nothing, I should jump for joy – but what about Charlotte?'.

What about Francis Joseph, for that matter? There is no doubt that over Mexico the Emperor behaved equivocally. In letters to Archduchess Sophie, written as early as August 1863, the 'Mexican business' appears as a tiresome distraction from more urgent questions: at heart he disliked the project and mistrusted its patron, 'that man in Paris who, in the last analysis, is the chief enemy of us all'. Yet at no point did he urge Maximilian to give up on the idea entirely, as both Rechberg and Richard Metternich assumed he would do. This failure to intervene decisively has been seen as proof that he welcomed the opportunity to ship a popular brother off to another continent. Consciously or sub-consciously, such motives may have helped shape the Emperor's policy. But these theories over-simplify a complex relationship in which both brothers were troubled by uncertainty. Maximilian, for example, had a higher regard for Napoleon III than did the Emperor; and yet, despite his hostility to Bonapartism, Francis Joseph was alive to the merits of an Austro-French entente in European affairs; he was disinclined to offend the 'man in Paris'. After their earliest talks on the project, Francis Joseph did all he could to please the Archduke. He allowed recruiting in Austria of volunteers who would serve Maximilian in a Mexican imperial army and he put funds at his brother's disposal. Occasionally both Francis Joseph and Maximilian looked upon Mexico as a lost Habsburg inheritance: the first European sovereign of the Aztec lands had been their ancestor, the great Charles V. It has been easy for people, puzzling over the brothers' behaviour, to lose the sight of that particular thread in the web Napoleon III wove around Mexico.

There is another explanation of Francis Joseph's conduct. Knowing Maximilian's character so well, he may have believed that outright opposition would intensify the Archduke's determination to accept the crown; he therefore resorted to less direct methods of persuading him to give up the idea, heavy-handed though they proved to be. Thus in January 1864 Maximilian received a memorandum, drawn up by Rechberg at the Emperor's request, in which it was made clear to the Archduke that, should he go to Mexico, he would lose his rights and titles in Austria, a deprivation which would extend to his heirs, if Charlotte had children. Maximilian protested vigorously at these proposals, which seem to have taken him by surprise. Supposing a disaster struck the dynasty, with both Francis Joseph and Rudolf dying; surely he would then reign as Emperor of both Mexico and Austria? The constitutional experts gave him no encouragement. He was even more outspoken in March, when the original conditions – together with a stipulation that he could no longer receive his annual allowance as a Habsburg prince – were presented in a 'family treaty', which he flatly declined to sign.

At this point Francis Joseph offered him a dignified line of retreat: 'If you cannot consent to this renunciation and prefer to refuse the crown of Mexico', he said, 'I will myself notify foreign countries of your refusal, and in particular the imperial sovereign in France'. But the Archduke believed his honour was involved; there were angry scenes between the two brothers, before Maximilian and Charlotte left Vienna for Miramare with the Act of Renunciation unsigned. A Mexican deputation was on its way from Paris. Already Austrian and French warships were moored off Trieste, ready to escort the newly created Emperor and Empress to Veracruz. But would they sail? For a few days it seemed likely that, even at this late hour, the Mexican project might become one of those rare opportunities which history had the good sense to miss.

Charlotte, however, would not give up the prospect of a crown. She became her husband's emissary, taking the train back to Vienna for prolonged talks with her imperial brother-in-law. She gained some success, securing an amendment to the family pact by which her husband kept his annual income as a Habsburg prince: much of the money was to go towards the upkeep of Miramare, which would be the Mexican sovereign's private retreat in Europe. Her return to Trieste was soon followed by the arrival there of Francis Joseph himself, accompanied by no less than seven Archdukes and his principal ministers. For two hours the brothers remained in the library of Miramare, locked in private conversation. Once, at least, distant observers believed they saw the Archduke on the terrace, looking out to sea, deep in thought. Might he still decide to remain in Europe?

On Saturday, 9 April, he took his irrevocable decision. The Act of Renunciation was signed. There were tearful farewells on the station platform. By Monday he was so deeply affected by the strain that his doctor declared he was suffering from a 'feverish chill' and the departure for Mexico was postponed. Not until the following Thursday did the joint Austro-French flotilla sail out into the Adriatic and set course for Civitavecchia, with a papal blessing awaiting their Mexican Majesties in

Rome. At last, on 28 May 1864, the flotilla reached Veracruz, the port Cortes had dedicated to the 'True Cross' in the year that Charles V was crowned emperor. Back in Austria people soon lost interest in Mexico. Except in the navy, it proved astonishingly easy to forget the most handsome of the archdukes.

Maximilian's departure enabled Francis Joseph to give his attention once again to Schleswig-Holstein, and to German affairs in general. By mid-April the fate of the Duchies was really settled, although an armistice was not signed until 12 May; and the failure of a conference in London led to a second campaign in June and July. No one doubted that the days of Danish sovereignty over a unitary Schleswig-Holstein were over. But the character of the dispute kept changing rapidly. The smaller German states had long maintained that the rightful ruler of Schleswig-Holstein was Frederick, Duke of Augustenburg, who was strongly (if belatedly) supported by the Austrians in the third week of May at the London conference. But by early summer, first Rechberg and later Francis Joseph realized that Austria and Prussia were no longer equal partners, acting as allies in the name of the German Confederation: Bismarck had broken loose on his own, and he was treating Augustenburg's claims with contempt. The geographical position of the Duchies ensured that, over this diplomatic problem, Prussia held the initiative. There was an open cynicism in Bismarck's way of doing business which alarmed Rechberg and puzzled the Emperor: Bismarck might suggest to Austria that 'it was time to begin a policy of mutual compensation', but where? And at whose expense?

Yet, while Francis Joseph deplored Bismarck's methods, he was convinced that 'alliance with Prussia is the only sensible policy' (as he told his mother), and his foreign minister agreed with him. Rather strangely, though a signed convention regulated military dispositions during the campaigns, no formal alliance existed at that moment; and when, in late July, Bismarck travelled to Vienna for talks with Rechberg, the Austrians sought to revive the treaty relationship which had bound the two Powers during the Crimean War and in earlier years, too. But Bismarck was wary of alliance fetters. He preferred to strike specific bargains. Not for the first time, he hinted that Prussia would help Austria recover her primacy in Italy – but only provided he received a free hand in Germany.

Closer acquaintance with Bismarck did not reassure Francis Joseph: why did he persist in 'speaking recklessly and exaggeratedly, trying to frighten people with words'? But the Emperor welcomed King William's decision to visit Ischl in mid-August, and he invited him to celebrate the success of Austrian and Prussian arms in the Duchies by a state visit to Vienna. Although his chief minister would be in attendance, it was hoped that sovereign-to-sovereign talks might draw direct answers to questions of policy rather than the evasive replies with which Bismarck delighted to mystify diplomats who sought enlightenment.

Francis Joseph was at Penzing station to greet the King and Bismarck when – on Saturday, 20 August – they arrived in Vienna, and he escorted them to neighbouring Schönbrunn. On Wednesday there was an excursion to Laxenburg, with boat trips to visit the pseudo-Gothic follies built on the lake islands (for, architecturally, they resembled William's familiar waterfront on the Heilige See, outside Potsdam). But much of the four-day state visit was spent in political discussion at Schönbrunn. Bismarck was prepared to let his hosts do the talking. If Austria allowed Prussia to acquire the duchies what compensation would she receive, asked Rechberg? Help in winning back Lombardy? Retrocession of part of Silesia annexed by Frederick the Great, suggested Francis Joseph? But the recovery of Lombardy would necessitate a major war against France, a challenge neither the Austrian nor the Prussian general staff was prepared to face at this stage; and King William had no intention of handing over land acquired by the most illustrious of Hohenzollerns.

On the final day of talks Francis Joseph at last asked William directly about the future of the northern duchies: did he wish to annex Schleswig-Holstein, or merely secure commercial and strategic concessions for Prussia within them? Reluctantly, and without consulting Bismarck, the King gave his reply: 'I am not exactly thinking of absorbing Schleswig-Holstein. I have no right to the duchies and cannot therefore lay claim to them', he said. This was a startling admission, a conscientious statement of principle which effectively deprived both Bismarck and Rechberg of any opportunity to strike bargains over the duchies; for how could William's chief minister barter territory over which his King denied possessing any rights? Little more could be said around the conference table at that moment. Hurriedly it was agreed that Austria and Prussia should maintain military administration in their respective zones within the duchies until a more definite solution could be found. Rechberg's hopes of securing a lasting treaty relationship, with the Habsburg lands joining the Zollverein common market on an equal footing with Prussia, began to seem totally unrealistic.

The Schönbrunn talks confirmed Francis Joseph's belief that direct contact with Prussia's sovereign could effectively counter Bismarck's schemes. Rechberg's days as foreign minister were numbered. It was not simply that the Emperor lost confidence in his minister's ability to draw Prussia into partnership by conciliatory gestures. More precisely, he felt no need for a minister who possessed ideas of his own. Rechberg had wished to resign in the previous year but had remained in office because his imperial master made it clear he could see no distinction between a minister who, of his own volition, sought to leave office and an officer who deserted his post. By the autumn of 1864, however, Francis Joseph was so confident of his authority within Germany that he was prepared to shape policy himself on a monarch-to-monarch basis, accepting advice from specialist experts in the Ballhausplatz if he chose, but ignoring their views should he believe he might reach an accommodation with King William personally. Accordingly, on 27 October Rechberg was induced to resign, largely through the machinations of two counsellors he had long mistrusted: Ludwig Biegeleben, a conservative Catholic from Darmstadt who was strongly hostile to Prussia; and the fitfully eccentric Count Moritz Esterházy, whom Francis Joseph made minister without portfolio. Briefly the Emperor even considered naming Esterházy as Rechberg's successor. More wisely, he appointed Count Alexander Mensdorff-Pouilly, a soldier-diplomat of fifty who had survived twenty-two battles and two difficult years as ambassador in St Petersburg with equal credit.

The newcomer was respected by the German Princes both for his personal qualities and for his lineage – Mensdorff's mother had been Princess Sophie of Saxe-Coburg and Gotha, thus making him a nephew of the King of the Belgians and a first cousin to Queen Victoria. Like the paladins of 1848–49, he was by conviction *schwarzgelb*, a 'black and yellow man' (the name, derived from the colours of the dynasty, given to devotees of the Habsburg cause). He was not a forceful personality; if a lowly official brought a document or file to his study in the Ballhausplatz, the minister 'would accompany him back to the door and open it himself', a colleague recalled long afterwards. So courteous a gentleman could hardly oppose policies commended by an Emperor whom he was to serve almost too loyally over the following years. At heart Mensdorff understood the nature of the Monarchy better than most of his successors: Austria 'was an empire of nationalities', he told the British ambassador; if concessions were given to any one nationality the whole structure would be in danger; in Transylvania there was 'a considerable Roumanian population' he pointed out; and 'the Prince of Serbia might also claim the Serbs in Austria'.

Yet, as Francis Joseph by now recognized, one 'nationality' within the empire was unique. Alone among his subjects the Magyars of historic Hungary had no 'mother country' beyond the frontier to which they might turn for cultural backing or political assimilation. But the exiled Kossuth was still a danger, as likely to respond to Bismarck's blandishments as he did to those of Napoleon III. It was natural for Francis Joseph to give fresh thoughts to a settlement with Hungary. He had made some progress towards winning the support of Deák and the Hungarian moderates in 1860–61. Now, on Moritz Esterházy's prompting and with the encouragement of Archduke Albrecht, he secretly sent an emissary to Deák shortly before Christmas in 1864 to see yet again if there could be a reconciliation with Hungary. Talks continued slowly well into the new year. They were sufficiently promising for the Emperor to believe that time was on his side, if only the critical confrontation with Prussia could be delayed. Accordingly, while making every effort to win support from the other German states during the summer of 1865, Francis Joseph sanctioned a policy of appeasement towards Prussia. No one in Vienna was prepared to face the prospect of a fratricidal war in Germany so long as there was still the risk of an uprising in Hungary's Danubian heartlands: better to play for time and accept an interim settlement of the dispute over the Duchies. The Convention of Gastein (14 August 1865) provisionally assigned Schleswig to Prussia and Holstein to Austria, while allowing Prussia to fortify Kiel as a naval base, construct a canal across Holstein to link the Baltic and the North Sea and maintain two military roads through Austrian-administered territory. Only Francis Joseph's desire to postpone the conflict until the Monarchy was ready for war justified the signing of such a disadvantageous convention.

He did not fear another military disaster. On the eve of the Danish war he had written to the commanding Austrian General urging him to lift morale by reviving 'the old Radetzky spirit'; and the Austrians acquitted themselves well, whereas the Prussians at first made little impact on the Danish fortified positions. In 1865 he returned from the autumn manoeuvres more than ever convinced that his army could defeat the Prussians. He was especially pleased with improvements in gunnery, notably the replacement of smoothbore cannon by rifled forward-loading light field guns, and he welcomed a change in the side weapons of crack hussar, dragoon and uhlan regiments which marked the end of long outdated pistols. Over military equipment Francis Joseph was less conservative than many senior officers. The new infantry drill manual incorporated lessons learnt from the 1859 campaign, notably the importance of massed bayonet charges. In April 1865 the Emperor watched trials of the needle gun, a breech-loading rifle fired from a lying position, and he appreciated its potential value for the infantry. But where could money be found to equip the army with this new weaponry? Defence expenditure had been cut by almost a third in the four years leading up to the Danish War, largely in response to complaints of military extravagance by a finance committee of the Reichsrat.

To the Emperor this committee seemed to represent all that was unacceptable in parliamentary institutions. With the German liberals still cavilling over funds for rearmament, he made up his mind to get rid of

Schmerling and dissolve his 'theatre', too. In late July 1865 a Bohemian aristocrat, Count Belcredi, was appointed to form a new government; only Mensdorff and Esterházy survived from Schmerling's administration. Six weeks later the Reichsrat deputies were sent about their business: an imperial manifesto declared the February Patent indefinitely 'superseded'. Not that Francis Joseph wished to revert to autocracy. The manifesto anticipated a new political structure for the Monarchy; talks would begin with a Hungarian Diet and spokesmen for other lands and provinces would be consulted about constitutional change in due course. Elections for the Hungarian Diet took place in November. On 14 December Francis Joseph himself opened the first session, with a speech in Magyar.

War did not seem imminent when, on 20 January 1866, the Emperor met the British ambassador. He was in an optimistic mood: 'There were no serious complications on the European horizon for the time being', he told the ambassador, and 'he was confident that the year would unfold quietly and peacefully and that Austria would therefore be able to devote itself almost entirely to its internal affairs'. Nine days later Francis Joseph and Elizabeth went into residence at Buda, remaining in Hungary until 5 March. But military affairs were rarely far from his mind: on the day he spoke so reassuringly to the British ambassador he also gave orders for the infantry to be equipped with the breech-loader needle guns he had seen tested in April. The Austrian ordnance system was, however, a cumbersome machine. Five weeks elapsed before the minister of war drew the Emperor's attention to the regrettable fact that a cheese-paring budget provided funds for only 1,840 new rifles – not enough for a single regiment to begin training with the needle guns. By contrast, each 'regular' Prussian infantry regiment and many militia units were already armed with breech-loading rifles.

Relations between the occupation armies in Schleswig-Holstein remained strained throughout the winter, the tension responding to political manoeuvres at Frankfurt, where Francis Joseph continued to be accepted as rightful leader of the German Princes. Yet it was not until late March that Bismarck's activities caused alarm at the Hofburg. He was known to have links with Hungarian émigré dissidents, and on 21 March Károlyi reported that a high-level Italian military mission was in Berlin. Soon afterwards General von Moltke went to Florence – Italy's interim capital – where, on 8 April, a secret military convention threatened Austria with war on two fronts.

The precise nature of the Prusso-Italian relationship remained unknown in Vienna, but by mid-April Italian troops began massing in Lombardy, half the pincer grip with which Bismarck intended to loosen the Monarchy. Briefly Francis Joseph tried to keep the grasping claws apart by proposing that both Austria and Prussia should reduce the strength of their armies within the German Confederation, a move which he thought King William would welcome. But on 20 April the Austrian general staff presented the Emperor with a memorandum pointing out the need for mobilization in the south, so as to discourage the Italians from entering Venetia. Mobilization in the Habsburg lands was always a slow process. Against Mensdorff's advice, Francis Joseph gave way to his generals; on 21 April he ordered the mobilization of the Army of the South, with Archduke Albrecht in command. Since Bismarck insisted on holding his King to the new commitments to Italy, the call to mobilization along Austria's southern border made certain that all attempts to defuse the tension in Germany itself were doomed.

If there was to be a war, the Emperor was determined to avoid one great mistake he had made seven years before. On this occasion, rather than risk juggling with fortune as a commander in the field, he would remain in the capital, co-ordinating grand strategy. The most respected officer in his empire, General Ludwig von Benedek, 'the new Radetzky', was given command of the Army of the North. An inspired appointment, it was felt; as good as having another 40,000 men in the front-line, declared Bavaria's chief minister. Only Benedek himself demurred. He knew, he said, 'every tree on the road to Milan' but he was unfamiliar with the mountain barriers and plains of central Europe, where Frederick the Great and Napoleon had won and lost reputations. Yet as a stern Calvinist from western Hungary, Benedek dutifully bowed himself to accept the destiny which God and his Emperor imposed upon him. To compensate for his unfamiliarity with Bohemia and Moravia Benedek appointed as his chief-of-staff General Gideon Krismanić, a former head of the army's topographical bureau. Krismanić was recommended to Benedek by Archduke Albrecht, who had found his map-reading skills useful on manoeuvres. Neither the Emperor nor his senior military advisers realized how cautiously defensive were the slow workings of Krismanić's mind.

In mid-May Francis Joseph became impatient. By now he was convinced the Austro-Prussian struggle in Germany would have to be resolved that summer. 'Better a war than prolongation of the present situation', he wrote to his mother on 11 May, 'In any case we must have a result, after spending so much money and making so many sacrifices.' At ministerial conferences he realistically assessed his options. Over one important calculation there was general agreement: Austria might defeat Prussia and Italy together, especially if the campaign in the south could be swiftly decided; but Austria could never hope to defeat the combined forces of Prussia, Italy and France. Something therefore had to be done to buy off that rogue in Paris. In early June Napoleon III hinted to Richard Metternich that Bismarck was prepared to offer an adjustment of the frontier in the Rhineland in return for a Prusso-French alliance, but Metternich saw that French neutrality could be bought for the right offer, a token acknowledgement of Napoleon's decisive role in the Italian peninsula. When the French attitude was reported back to Vienna Francis Joseph reluctantly accepted that the Monarchy might well have to give that acknowledgement and let Venetia go. He was, however, stubborn: no direct negotiations with Italy, for he refused to recognize the unified kingdom; and no surrender of Venetia without a fight, for he believed that if the Austrians could gain a victory in the field against Victor Emmanuel's army, the defeat would prevent the Italians from persisting with future demands for other Italian-speaking regions, such as Trieste and its hinterland or the southern Tyrol. The Emperor therefore authorized Metternich to take up the Venetian question with Napoleon III: if Austria defeated Prussia, Francis Joseph would surrender Venetia to Napoleon III (for handing over to Italy), provided he kept France neutral, would guarantee Austria's remaining Italian-speaking lands, and would accept a new settlement in central Europe (probably including the return of Silesia as compensation for the loss of Venetia). On 12 June a treaty embodying these conditions was signed in Paris.

War followed swiftly, with Bismarck repudiating the authority of the German Confederation on 14 June and Prussian troops crossing the borders of the smaller German states two days later. Though Napoleon III envisaged a long war which France would finally settle by armed mediation, military experts in Paris and London as well as Vienna expected an Austrian victory before the autumn. William Howard Russell, the doyen of war reporters, was impressed by Benedek's cavalry, 'the finest by many degrees I ever saw'. No one doubted Archduke Albrecht's skills, and rightly. Within little over a week he telegraphed the Emperor to inform him that the southern army had defeated the Italians at Custozza, the village between Verona and Mantua where Radetzky had gained a decisive victory eighteen years previously. That was the news Francis Joseph wanted to hear, and all Vienna with him. More ominous was the paucity of information from Benedek and the Army of the North.

Benedek and Krismanić established their headquarters at Olmütz on 26 May. Francis Joseph and Crenneville (head of his military chancellery) anticipated that Benedek would move north-westwards from Moravia, carrying the war into the German lands while the Prussians were still engaged with the armies of the smaller German states. When, a fortnight later, there was no sign of any move towards the frontier, the Emperor sent one of his ablest adjutants, Colonel Beck, to Olmütz to stir the northern army into action. But Beck could not make any impression on Benedek and his staff on this occasion, or indeed on a second short visit a few days later. Krismanić insisted that it would be dangerous to take up positions along the frontier until the whole army was massed around Olmütz, a slow task since the military concentration was dependent upon the efficient working of a single railway. Eventually, with nearly 200,000 men and 770 guns at his command, Benedek crossed from Moravia into Bohemia, two days after the Prussians invaded Hanover, Bavaria and Saxony. The first skirmish – on 27 June, near the border of Silesia – ended in a minor Austrian victory; but along the main sector of the front it seemed impossible to halt the Prussian advance, for the rapid and accurate fire power of the needle gun wrought havoc among the massed Austrian formations. On 30 June Colonel Beck arrived again at Benedek's head-quarters on a mission from the Emperor to discover why his huge Army of the North did not engage the enemy in strength.

Beck found Benedek in the fortress of Königgrätz, now the Czech town of Hradeć Kralove. On the previous day the army had suffered a triple setback, with heavy casualties from Prussian artillery at Königinhof and Schweinschädel and a more serious defeat at Gitschin, where a crack Austrian regiment had only been saved from disaster by the intervention of their Saxon allies. Benedek summoned a war council at which he explained to Beck that, since his army was so badly mauled, he had no hope of victory. At Beck's insistence, a telegram was sent directly to the Emperor: 'I beg Your Majesty to seek peace at any price urgently. Catastrophe for the army is unavoidable.' Colonel Beck set out at once for Vienna.

The telegram caused consternation at the Hofburg. It was followed by a second one, from Beck to Crenneville: 'Armistice or peace imperative because withdrawal is hardly possible. My heart is broken, but I must report the truth'. Heads were cooler in Vienna than in Königgrätz: there was no evidence of a 'catastrophe'; the army was not encircled; reinforce-ments would soon be heading northwards from among Albrecht's vic-torious troops. Francis Joseph's reply was swift and terse: 'Impossible to make peace. I authorize a retreat in good order, if it is unavoidable', he wired, adding at Crenneville's suggestion, 'Has there been a battle?'. But, though standing firm in central Europe, Francis Joseph finally accepted that he did not have the resources to retain his hold on the Italian peninsula. On 2 July Napoleon III was invited to arrange a ceasefire with King Victor Emmanuel, on the understanding that Venetia would be surrendered whatever happened in Bohemia. The Emperor had decided he needed Albrecht, as well as his troops, in the northern theatre of war if Bismarck's machinations in Germany were to be frustrated.

Benedek spent much of the first two days of July in the saddle, taking stock of his resources. Morale was not so bad as he had feared. He decided to lead his army out from the fortress of Königgrätz, cross the Elbe, and take up positions in the hilly ground east of the river Bistritz, between the villages of Sadowa and Chlum. Early on 3 July the telegraph in Vienna reported that a great battle had begun: never before in European history had such vast numbers contested a single battlefield. Throughout the day the Emperor anxiously awaited wires from Benedek's headquarters. At noon the outcome was still in doubt; the Prussian advance was checked by Austrian artillery fire. But at seven in the evening the dreaded news reached the Hofburg: during the afternoon the Prussian Second Army, commanded by Crown Prince Frederick, had reached the battlefield from the east, forcing the Austrians to abandon their defensive positions in order to avoid encirclement. The battle was lost. 'Fragments of regiments' were seeking safety behind the Elbe, W. H. Russell was to tell his *Times*'s readers a few days later: they were no longer crack troops but merely 'the debris of the army'.

Francis Joseph resolved to continue the fight. He had hopes that Napoleon could be tempted to threaten Prussia along the Rhine and he knew that he would soon have sufficient troops, brought by railway from the south, in order to defend the capital. As a precaution, Elizabeth and the children were sent to Buda and, for the first time in his reign, he was protected by a cavalry escort each day as his carriage carried him from Schönbrunn to the Hofburg for a succession of critical conferences. There were some ominous shouts of 'Long Live Emperor Maximilian' – a sentiment for which, of course, no sceptical Viennese could be accused of showing disrespect towards the dynasty. Not least among the ironies of that summer was the news wired to the Emperor by Admiral Tegetthof on 20 July from Spalato: his ironclads had that morning scattered a larger Italian squadron attempting to seize the island of Lissa; and, in the most memorable episode of modern Austria's naval history, the *Re d'Italia* was rammed and sunk at the height of the battle by Tegetthof's flagship, which bore Maximilian's name. The victory of Lissa made no difference to the outcome of the war; but it gave the Austrians a new hero, an admiral to place on a pedestal rather than a soldier. And it asserted a naval supremacy in the Adriatic which was to be upheld throughout Francis Joseph's reign, and beyond.

Six days later Archduke Albrecht at last took command of Benedek's beaten army, which had fallen back south of the Danube at Bratislava. But the fighting was by then over. Bismarck, who was intent on avoiding a harsh peace likely to perpetuate hostility between Austria and Prussia, succeeded in inducing a reluctant King William to abandon his hopes of entering Vienna in triumph at a time when the most advanced Prussian outposts were on the edge of the old Napoleonic battlefield of Wagram, some 14 miles from the Hofburg itself. A five-day ceasefire along the Danube was agreed on 22 July, while peace terms were discussed. They were more moderate than Francis Joseph had feared, as he told Elizabeth in a letter written hurriedly at six o'clock next morning: 'Whether it is asked of us or not, we shall withdraw completely from Germany – and after what we have seen of our dear companions in the German Confederation, that's a piece of luck for Austria', he wrote ruefully. A preliminary peace was agreed at Nikolsburg on 26 July: apart from Holstein and the cession of Venetia, Francis Joseph lost no territory. He accepted an obligation to pay a war indemnity, the dissolution of the German Confederation and its replacement by a North German Confederation, established under Prussian auspices, and by a Southern German Union from which Austria was excluded. Prussian troops would withdraw from Austria as soon as a final treaty was concluded. The definitive peace was embodied in the Treaty of Prague, signed on 23 August. By the beginning of September the troop trains were heading back across the frontier.

For the second time in seven years Francis Joseph had begun and lost a war. Once again, his subjects held him in low esteem, as he well knew. Yet if he thought he was in any way to blame for the disaster he did not admit it. Poor Benedek was made a scapegoat for the lost battle. As an honourable man, he accepted his misfortune because – as he once told his wife – to justify his conduct would 'be of service neither to the Emperor nor to the army'. While the war was in progress it became fashionable to attribute Prussia's military success to the wonder weapon, the needle gun, while later commentators stressed the genius of Moltke as a staff officer capable of transporting and deploying the huge number of conscript troops in a modern army. The Emperor's greatest folly was his assumption that Austria was in any better position to win a war on two fronts than in the days when his grandfather had faced the challenge of the first Bonaparte.

In an odd way, Francis Joseph sensed the omnipresence of the past. For him the Seven Weeks War came not so much as an isolated conflict as an episode in some long historical serial. He had no doubt of the real villains. They were Austria's neighbours, whose rulers and governments wished to manipulate the popular belief in nationalism. 'We have fallen a victim to refined double-dealing', he wrote to his mother from Schönbrunn the day before the peace treaty was signed. 'Everything was fixed between Paris, Berlin and Florence. As for us, we were very honest, but very stupid.' 'This is a life and death struggle which is not yet over', he added, rallying to that awe-inspiring sense of vocation which was his strength and his misfortune. 'When the whole world is against you and you have no friends, there is little chance of success, but you must go on doing what you can, fulfilling your duty and, in the end, going down with honour.'

Chapter 10

THE HOLY CROWN OF
ST STEPHEN

At Easter in 1865 Archduchess Sophie gave 'praise to God a thousand times over' in her journal for good news which Francis Joseph told her on the eve of his eleventh wedding anniversary; his relations with Sisi had 'at last' reached a peak of reconciliation, or so he 'virtually assured' her. Despite ever returning doubts over Elizabeth's fitness to share her son's great inheritance, the Archduchess was genuinely pleased: happy domesticity around the throne made for contentment in the Monarchy as a whole, she believed.

Everyone could see that Elizabeth had gained poise and authority. Those anxious weeks before Christmas in 1862, when she still needed a brother or sister beside her to face life at Court, seemed far away now. Annual cures at Bad Kissingen, supplemented each morning by carefully regulated gymnastic exercises, strengthened her physically, and her daily life had acquired a purpose and structure. New acquaintances won her trust; notable among them were the principal coiffeuse of the Burgtheater, Fanny Angerer (who became Fanny Feifalik on her marriage a few years later) and young Ida Ferenczy, from a Hungarian lower gentry family at Kecskemét, who in November 1864 was appointed 'Reader in Hungarian to Her Majesty' and was soon accepted as a close confidante. New interests held Elizabeth's attention, enabling her to rein in her impulse to escape on horseback for long, lonely rides in the open countryside. She worked hard at perfecting her Magyar, as Francis Joseph proudly reported to his mother in the autumn of 1863; and she read good literature seriously, enabling her to improve the quality of her own poetry. In the spring of 1863 Fanny Angerer evolved a style of plaiting the Empress's auburn hair which restored a pride in her personal appearance. Such vanity was no doubt deplorable, as she may well have reflected; but, if the Empress lacked confidence in her own appearance, how could she assert her personality either within the family or at Court? In October 1864, when Elizabeth thought her beauty in full blossom, she sat for Franz Winterhalter. A famous portrait shows the Empress in a white ball dress studded with embroidered petals and crowned by the elaborately plaited hairstyle, decked on this occasion with diamond stars. Winterhalter succeeded in making her look both magnificently imperial and shyly imperious. But at the same time Winterhalter painted two more portraits of Elizabeth, each with her hair hanging down over shoulders loosely draped by a simple flowing white gown. These portraits Francis Joseph kept on the wall of his study for the next half-century of his life.

Returning self-confidence bred self-assertiveness. Elizabeth showed her strong will in the first instance over the upbringing of the Crown Prince, although she was slow to respond to a mounting personal crisis. The nursery routine originally instituted, at Francis Joseph's request, by Archduchess Sophie had been modified when Elizabeth secured the dismissal of Sophie Esterházy as head of her household and Rudolf was happy under the daily supervision of his Aja, 'Wowo' von Welden. He was an intelligent child but delicate: an alarming bout of typhoid fever in December 1863 left him frail and in the following summer he suffered concussion after falling from a tree. In his seventh year he was removed from his Aja's keeping and assigned his first tutor, Major-General Ludwig von Gondrecourt, a bachelor of whose high moral principles the Archduchess warmly approved.

As a field commander in the Danish campaign Gondrecourt won a reputation for using shock tactics. These he now applied to his young charge, whom he convinced himself needed toughening up. On one wintry morning Rudolf was forced to drill in the snow long before dawn; and when Gondrecourt thought the boy unduly timid, blank cartridges were fired without warning in his room to test his reactions, an experiment which may have had disastrous psychological effects on the Crown Prince in later life. In the spring Rudolf was again seriously ill, probably with diphtheria; Caroline von Welden personally begged the Emperor to curb the sadistic streak in his son's tutor, which she believed was weakening the boy's constitution. But the Emperor, who could remember his own Aja's affectionate interest in her boys once they left the nursery, played down her concern. Then, at last, Elizabeth intervened. She discovered that Gondrecourt had taken Rudolf to the Lainzer Tiergarten, an imperial game reserve a few miles from Schönbrunn. There Gondrecourt left the boy alone, behind a locked gate, and shouted at him 'Look out, a wild boar is coming!' – at which warning the boy's nerves gave way entirely. So angry was his mother when she heard of this experiment that she told the Emperor outright, 'Either Gondrecourt goes or I go'. The family were at Ischl at that moment, where they had recently celebrated the two birthdays, the Emperor's thirty-fifth and Rudolf's seventh. Yet still Francis Joseph hesitated.

Elizabeth, however, held the whip hand. It was just four months since Francis Joseph had told his mother of the new intimacy of their family life and he was still enchanted by Winterhalter's recent portraits. Now she went to her room at Ischl and sent her husband a virtual ultimatum, in which she did not mention Gondrecourt by name:

'I wish full and unlimited powers shall be accorded me in all matters concerning the children, the choice of their household, of their place of residence, and complete control over their upbringing; in short I alone must decide everything about them until they attain their majority. Furthermore I wish that all matters concerning my personal affairs, such for example as the choice of my household, my place of residence, all changes in domestic arrangements etc., etc., shall be left for me alone to decide'.

Francis Joseph capitulated. The firm, but sympathetic, General Joseph Latour von Thurnburg, was appointed tutor to the Crown Prince, while Gondrecourt received command of an army corps in Bohemia (where unimaginative generalship cost his men heavy casualties outside Königgrätz). Although the Emperor did not formally countersign the 'ultimatum', he was ready to observe the spirit of the agreement, except when he considered his wife's choice of residence dangerous to herself personally or an embarrassment to affairs of state. Elizabeth, for her part, loyally supported him for thirty years of mixed fortunes, even if her restlessness of spirit too often took her from his company.

Until now she had shown no interest in politics, apart from ineffectually seeking support for her sister in Naples. But over Hungary Elizabeth felt strongly, despite the tragic death of little Sophie in Buda. When Francis Joseph opened the Hungarian Diet in December 1865 he agreed that a Hungarian deputation might travel to Vienna and invite their Queen to make a second visit. She received the deputation at the Hofburg on 8 January 1866, wearing Hungarian national costume and addressing the magnates in clear and fluent Magyar. Towering over his companions, and magnificent in their fur-trimmed robes, was Count Gyula Andrássy whom Elizabeth now met for the first time. At forty-two he was a romantic hero who expected to be lionized, but he was, too, supremely accomplished in the art of pleasing women. Elizabeth was captivated. The dark, slender aristocrat, exuding a refined charm which lightly dispelled her shyness, personified the idealized Hungary of her imagination. She respected Deák, but she liked to believe that in Andrássy she had found a genius to reconcile the husband she loved to the people with whom she so passionately identified herself. Andrássy, sensing the political value of Elizabeth's capacity for admiration, remained level-headed: was it, perhaps, with gentle irony that he hailed his queen as 'our lovely Providence'? At all events she accompanied Francis Joseph to Hungary before the end of January. For five weeks she endured (as she wrote to Rudolf) 'a most unrestful time', going to the riding school every morning and attending balls, dinners and receptions she would have avoided in Vienna. 'With her courtesy, tact and discretion as well as her excellent Hungarian, Sisi is a great help to me', Francis Joseph wrote to his mother halfway through his visit.

She was a great help to him again during the dark summer days of war, endlessly visiting hospitals around Vienna and making a point of speaking to wounded Hungarians in their own language. A few days after König-grätz Elizabeth travelled to Pest, ostensibly to see the hospitals within Hungary, too. She was met at the railway station by Deák and Andrássy who explained to her the dangers of allowing Bismarck to exploit the Kossuthite radicals and emphasized to her the need for Francis Joseph to give a gesture of re-assurance to the moderate Hungarians at this time. She then went back to Vienna, reported their remarks to her husband, urged him to send for Andrássy and collected Gisela and Rudolf before settling with them at the Villa Kochmeister, in the hills behind Buda. Her letters begged Francis Joseph to 'do something', consoling herself (as she told him) with the thought that even if nothing happened she would 'be able to say to Rudolf one day, "I did everything in my power. Your misfortunes are not on my conscience".'

This appeal, backed by news that Andrássy was taking the night train to Vienna and would await a summons from the palace, was irresistible. Francis Joseph assured her by coded telegram that he was sending for Deák – who was in a remote region of Hungary – and asked her to be discreet in her contacts with the Count. But eventually, at five in the morning of 17 July, he sent his 'beloved angel' the message she confidently awaited: 'Today I am expecting G. A. I shall listen to what he has to say quietly, letting him do the talking and then sounding him out to see if I can trust him ... The old man [Deák, aged 63] can be here tomorrow or the day after.' After ninety minutes of discussion with Andrássy, the Emperor thought him 'good, honourable and highly gifted' but 'wanting too much and offering too little'. Deák, whom he received on 20 July (the day of the battle of Lissa), showed greater consideration than Andrássy for the political needs of other regions of the Monarchy. Yet, though the Emperor believed Deák to be 'honest and devoted to the dynasty', he told Elizabeth that he felt he should talk again to Andrássy, with whom he hoped to take up 'the threads of the negotiations' once 'this luckless war' ended. Francis Joseph seems to have wished to draw up a settlement with

Andrássy – politically more flexible than the legalistic Deák – which would, however, be based upon the 'old man's' principle that Hungary should ask for no more after the war than before it. Yet he understood, as Elizabeth did not, that he would have to move slowly. The Emperor's personal sympathies were with his chief minister, Belcredi, who favoured careful consultation, stage by stage, with the Landtage and the institution of an 'extraordinary Reichsrat', which would need to approve any new status given to Hungary. Such a process was far too pedestrian to satisfy the Empress.

With the return of peace Elizabeth overplayed her hand. She continued to urge her husband to appoint Andrássy as his foreign minister, and she declined to leave the Villa Kochmeister and return to Vienna where the air was unhealthy, she said. Why should not the dynasty have a Laxenburg type residence near to the capital in Hungary, she asked? She had visited a temporary hospital established in a chateau at Gödöllö, some twenty miles north of Pest. It lay in parkland between a ridge of low hills and the wild Puszta steppes, the traditional picturesque Hungary of colourful costumes and fine horses. Elizabeth wondered if Francis Joseph might like to purchase Gödöllö. Andrássy, with whom she sometimes went riding, welcomed the idea.

The Emperor did not. A passing acerbity sharpens his replies to all her suggestions. How could he risk offending his German-Austrian and Slav subjects under Prussian occupation by handing over the conduct of foreign affairs to a Magyar magnate? 'It would be in conflict with my duty to adopt your exclusively Hungarian viewpoint', she was told. He urged her 'not to look over [Gödöllö] as if we were going to buy it, for at present I have no money and we shall have to cut back drastically in these hard times'. Yet he was genuinely worried to learn that Elizabeth was again setting out on long cross-country rides, as in 1859; and a rare note of melancholic loneliness saddens his letters. To reassure him – perhaps to ease her own conscience – Elizabeth returned to Vienna for his birthday on 18 August. But she would not stay. To her mother-in-law's consternation Elizabeth hurried back to the Villa Kochmeister to join her Hungarian friends for the national festival on St Stephen's Day (20 August), which was followed by Rudolf's birthday. Belcredi was aghast at such partisan support of Hungary by the First Lady of the Monarchy.

Francis Joseph could not find it in his heart to be annoyed with Sisi for long. He desperately needed her support, as his letters continue to show. For in late August another, totally unexpected, problem surfaced to vex him in this 'loathsome summer'. Prussia's military ascendancy indirectly called in question the future of Maximilian's empire in Mexico, for Napoleon III had decided he needed back in France the expeditionary force which formed the core of the monarchist army. Common sense inclined Maximilian to abdicate, but his Empress persuaded him to hold on to his throne while she returned to Europe in order to rally support for the monarchist cause. Thwarted in Paris – and as yet showing no public sign that her mind was deteriorating – Charlotte made her way to Miramare, sailing into Trieste where Tegetthoff's victorious squadron lay at anchor, expecting an imperial visit, which was now cancelled. 'At present I cannot go to Trieste', Francis Joseph complained to Elizabeth on 26 August, 'Her Mexican Majesty ... is due to appear there at any moment, so I prefer to remain here, rather than make the journey. Come back soon, my angel.' He had not yet seen his brother's wife; he sought Elizabeth's moral backing before facing a family meeting which he dreaded, for Austria could spare no aid for the unfortunate Maximilian. A week later Elizabeth was home in Vienna with the children. Had she closed up the Villa Kochmeister from fear of the cholera, across the river in Pest? Or did she respond to her husband's plea for help in handling Her Mexican Majesty? As with so many of Elizabeth's sudden decisions, no one knows. At all events there was no meeting with Charlotte.

Politically Francis Joseph immersed himself in the Hungarian Question. He would not contemplate appointing Andrássy to the foreign ministry, but with sovereign-to-sovereign diplomacy shown as ineffectual, he wanted a more forceful man at the Ballhausplatz than Mensdorff. Even before Elizabeth returned from Buda, he was in touch with Baron Ferdinand Beust, foreign minister of Saxony on the eve of the Seven Weeks War but dismissed from office at the insistence of Bismarck as a condition of peace. Beust, a hard-headed realist rather than a doctrinaire upholder of outmoded concepts, supported Francis Joseph's German policy before the war, partly because he believed in reforming the German Confederation but largely because of his hostility to Prussia. Although Beust was a liberal and a Protestant, the Emperor respected his loyalty and his talents as a diplomat, which were also commended by Crown Prince Albert of Saxony, Francis Joseph's cousin and close friend. As a possible minister in Habsburg service, Beust had the inestimable advantage of no commitments or group affiliations within the Monarchy, though he soon showed a certain contempt for the Slav peoples, whether western or southern. Francis Joseph explained his immediate objectives to Beust as early as 1 September 1866: he wanted internal peace among the nationalities of the Empire in order to raise the Monarchy once more to the status of a European Great Power; he wanted to improve Austrian contacts with the southern German states to keep them clear of Prussia's orbit; and he intended to give up all ideas of waging war 'for a long time ahead'. After nine weeks of thought and preparation Beust took over the foreign ministry from Mensdorff at the end of October, working in uneasy partnership with the autocratic federalist Belcredi, who remained titular head of the government.

A few days later the Hungarian Diet began a new session. Francis Joseph gave an assurance that he would soon authorize the establishment of a responsible Hungarian administration and appoint a prime minister for the first time since his accession. Deák, whose followers formed the majority party in the Diet, was willing to take part in constitutional discussions but thought himself too old for active politics and recommended Andrássy as head of government. But there was still powerful opposition in Vienna both from Belcredi's circle, who continued to seek the postponement of final decisions until the meeting of an 'extraordinary Reichsrat', and from the army chiefs. Shortly before Christmas, Francis Joseph took the unusual step of sending Beust to Buda-Pest, confident that his foreign minister would reach an agreement with Deák and Andrássy which Belcredi could never even have contemplated committing to paper. The Emperor sought the best of both worlds: 'The government can never satisfy every national group', he told the ministerial council on 1 February 1867, 'That is why we have to rely on those who are strongest ... and they are the Germans and Hungarians'. He retained Belcredi as prime minister in Vienna because he hoped that he would soothe the ruffled feelings of the Bohemian and German-Austrian aristocracy. But for Beust the situation was becoming impossible; he mistrusted the tactics of Belcredi and Archduke Albrecht. After seven weeks as imperial go-between he demanded a free hand; and on 7 February, 'with tears in his eyes', Francis Joseph therefore asked Belcredi to hand over his responsibilities to the Saxon newcomer. As his deputy Beust secured the appointment of Count Taaffe, the Emperor's boyhood friend, (who remained at the heart of Austrian government for twenty-six years). Andrássy became Hungary's prime minister eleven days later.

The final settlement of 1867 (*Ausgleich*, 'Compromise': or in Hungary, *Kiegyezes*) was speedily worked out by Beust and Andrássy, in consultation with Deák. It was discussed by the Hungarian Diet over the following three months and enacted as 'Law XII' in the last week of May. As an outsider, Beust accepted a fact of political life which the Emperor's Austrian subjects were reluctant to acknowledge: Royal Hungary was a historical entity with an ancient constitution only recently suspended, while other Habsburg lands were provinces of an improvised Empire searching for a cohesive constitutional pattern. Beust could therefore strike a bargain with national leaders who knew precisely what they wanted, even if most Hungarians were to complain that the Compromise merely satisfied their minimum political needs and Deák was disowned by the staunch Kossuthites.

Some Habsburg provinces – notably Bohemia, Moravia and (rump) Silesia, the 'Lands of St Wenceslas's Crown' – could claim historic rights older than those of Hungary though far longer in abeyance, and when Francis Joseph told Beust that he sought internal concord between the nationalities he was conscious of being titular King of Bohemia as well as Apostolic King of Hungary. But Czech nationalism only blossomed in Prague under the next generation, fifteen or twenty years after the Compromise. Czech political leaders were narrowly pan-Slav in sentiment in 1867, and Bohemia was still dominated by the German land-owning minority; there was no single-minded spokesman in Prague with whom Beust could have negotiated a settlement even if the Emperor had wished it. More vociferous were the Croats, another historic nationality with a certain claim on Habsburg gratitude. But Beust felt no obligation towards Jellaçić's compatriots and saw no reason to listen to their complaints. They had experienced a form of 'dualism' in partnership with Hungary from 1102 to 1526, and the terms of the *Ausgleich* left them to strike their own bargain with Buda-Pest.

Territorially Beust's greatest difficulty in Vienna was to overcome the hostility of the army leaders to the inclusion in Hungary of the former 'Military Frontier', for these lands had been virtually colonized by the army since the ejection of the Ottomans. But the Andrássy government received authority over the old frontier regions and Transylvania, too. Francis Joseph made his consent to Law XII conditional on the willingness of the Hungarian parliament to settle a subsidiary 'Compromise' with Croatia and to pass a Nationalities Law, recognizing the principle of national equality. But once parliament began work on the implementation of these details there was no reason to delay royal assent, which was given at the end of July, five months before the basic constitutional laws for the remaining 'kingdoms and provinces' of the Habsburg Monarchy were even promulgated in Vienna.

The *Ausgleich* left defence and foreign affairs as the joint concern of Hungary and 'Austria' (i.e. the rest of the Monarchy, or as it was often called 'Cisleithánia', the region west of the River Leitha). These matters were placed under a common Austro-Hungarian minister. There was also a 'common' finance minister, although he became a spokesman rather than a decision-maker, since the raising and collection of taxes was the responsibility of the separate finance ministers in the two halves of the Monarchy. The economic provisions of the settlement – a quota system to meet common expenditure, trade, the monetary system, and trunk railway construction – were to be regulated once every ten years, a provision which in practice established a pattern of decennial political crises, recurring when the 'economic compromise' came up for revision or renewal. It was also agreed that the problems arising from the common matters – defence, foreign affairs, and joint finance – would be considered by 'delegations', to be nominated by the parliaments in Vienna and Buda-Pest. The delegations would meet in separate assemblies, summoned alternately to the two capital cities of the Monarchy. Hungarian politicians complained that ministers had to present government proposals to Francis Joseph before making them known to parliament, thus giving the sovereign a veto on what was to be discussed as well as on the final form of legislation. But in 1867 these restraints on Hungary's autonomy seemed slight, especially to the other nationalities within the Monarchy. As Andrássy admitted, 'We are paying 30 per cent of joint expenditure and enjoy similar rights to those who pay 70 per cent'; and on a map the bargain looked even more striking than in any commercial balance sheet. The Compromise ensured that the lands of 'the Holy Crown of St Stephen' formed a unitary kingdom considerably greater in extent than Royal Hungary as recognized in 1848 by the April Laws.

That Holy Crown, surmounted by a primitive Cross, was about to become the centrepiece of a ceremony essential to the new relationship between the people and their king, the first modern coronation held in Buda-Pest. Patriotic legend had long ascribed a unique status to the royal regalia. In the year 1000 the fifth chieftain of the Arpád dynasty, Stephen, applied to Pope Sylvester II for recognition as a Christian King, receiving back from Rome a crown and a cross, which were venerated as testimony of royal sovereignty over the Danubian plains in which the Magyar hordes had made their homes. By the fourteenth century the Apostolic Cross and Holy Crown – given additional dignity by a lower circlet of Byzantine origin – were accepted as mystical symbols of national unity. A doctrine formulated by Stephen Werboczi in the sixteenth century maintained that the actual political entity of Hungary was latent in the Holy Crown, becoming corporate through the mystic relationship between the sovereign who wore the Crown and the nobility who paid homage to the king. An elaborate ritual of coronation was observed at Bratislava for 'King' Maria Theresa in 1741, for her grandson Francis in 1792, and for his son Ferdinand six weeks after Francis Joseph's birth.

With Kossuth's proclamation that the Habsburgs had forfeited the throne, possession of the Holy Crown assumed additional significance. Faced with defeat in August 1849, Kossuth buried it beneath a mulberry tree two miles north of Orsova, near the defile of the Iron Gates on the Danube. From this remote location it was recovered three years later by the Austrian authorities, acting on a tip-off from an indigent émigré.

Thereafter, to the disgust of his Hungarian subjects, Francis Joseph retained the Crown in Vienna. Now that a new contract defined the King's prerogatives and obligations, Andrássy was determined to give fresh emphasis to Werboczi's curious doctrine by treating the Holy Crown with particular reverence, as if to atone for its recent indignities. A chapel was built on the site of the mulberry tree near Orsova and elaborate preparations made for the crowning. Early in March 1867, long before the Diet gave final approval to the *Ausgleich*, it was agreed that Saturday, 8 June, would be Coronation Day.

Traditionally, consorts were crowned in later ceremonies. But on arriving at Buda-Pest in March Francis Joseph found that the revised ritual provided for Elizabeth's coronation immediately after his own. At the same time Andrássy told him that, to mark their joy at the reconciliation with the sovereigns, the Hungarian people had bought a summer residence for presentation to them: Gödöllö could be their home, as soon as renovation of the 120-year-old mansion was completed. 'I can hardly wait ... for the moment when we are ready to live there', Elizabeth wrote excitedly to her husband on hearing the news. By now she worked at improving her Magyar for hours on end each day. Her enthusiasm for everything Hungarian was taken up by young Rudolf, who idolized Andrássy. Among the Crown Prince's private papers are some, heavily corrected, letters written by him in Magyar that year and a remarkably good sketch of a dashing horseman with wild curly hair and straggly beard, beside which was written the inscription 'Count Andrássy, Ischl, 1867'. When, in the second week of May, Hungary's Queen formally went into residence at Buda-Pest for the coronation season the Crown Prince wrote to ask if there had been 'a right good cheer' as she arrived in the city. His mother's response left no doubt of the Hungarian people's goodwill towards her.

Elizabeth remained in Hungary throughout the month. There was a succession of entertainments to attend – horse races, the theatre, court receptions. But Francis Joseph had to journey back more than once to Vienna. His enjoyment of the summer was darkened by the climax of the Mexican misadventure. Charlotte's mind, brooding over the past and in anguish for the present, lost all power of reason and she remained remote from outward life at Miramare. Meanwhile, in Vienna there was total uncertainty over what was happening in Mexico itself. American reports suggested that Maximilian had been captured by the victorious Juarez and was to be put on trial for treason against the Mexican Republic. President Andrew Johnson, King William of Prussia and Garibaldi were among those who sent pleas to Mexico's republican master; and in the hopes of encouraging Juarez to put his prisoner aboard a ship for Europe,

Francis Joseph re-instated 'the ex-Emperor of Mexico' as an Austrian Archduke before he left for the coronation in Hungary. Perhaps he even believed there might come a time when Max would settle again at Miramare to write his memoirs, but there was an ominous lack of reliable news from across the Atlantic. 'Should the King of Hungary hear of his brother's death, the coronation will not be postponed, but the fêtes and rejoicings will be abandoned', *The Times* correspondent reported authoritatively.

Mexico was not the only shadow to fall over the festivities. Late on Thursday, 6 June, Francis Joseph learnt of another family tragedy. A few days previously Archduke Albrecht's eighteen year old daughter Mathilde, seeing her father approaching and knowing he did not approve of women who smoked, hid a cigarette behind her back. She set fire to her dress, dying from her burns on that Thursday morning. The Court went into mourning for the pathetic young Archduchess and some festivities involving members of the dynasty were cancelled but, with the ceremonies due to begin in less than forty-eight hours, nothing could check the cycle of celebration on either bank of the Danube. The twin cities of Buda and Pest were packed. Among the visitors were foreign newspapermen, for the first time given an opportunity to report all the spiritual self-indulgence of a Hungarian coronation.

In England *The Times* offered readers a four column account on the following Wednesday, some 5000 words of colourful prose written immediately the coronation was over, while 'the centre of the world is just for the time this capital of Hungary on the lordly Danube'. The morning's events had begun with a royal procession from Buda palace along the crest of the hill to Trinity Square and the coronation church of St Matthias, with Andrássy as acting palatine going slowly ahead of the King and carrying St Stephen's Holy Crown reverently on a velvet cushion. Imaginative readers could picture the Hungarian magnates 'mounted, with ostrich and golden pheasant and argus plumes', tunics frogged with 'chevrons of solid silver', and with saddles so splendid that 'whole fields of cloth of gold must have been cut up for shabracks'.

Other newspapers – in Paris particularly – carried full accounts of the crowning itself and of the Coronation Mass, for which Franz Liszt had composed a new setting. *The Times*'s readers could read the prayers in the original Latin (small print only), and a list of dignitaries, before their correspondent was once more entranced by 'white horses and black uniforms' and 'white uniforms and black horses' as a 'dazzling procession' wound its way down the steep hill to the 'yellow Danube'. Francis Joseph, wearing the crown and with the 800-year old faded mantle of St Stephen on his shoulders, rode through the narrow streets and led the cavalcade across the cobbles of the Chain Bridge in to Pest and half a mile along the quay downstream, where an artificial mound made from clods of earth from every county in Hungary stood outside Pest's old parish church. Francis Joseph set his horse up the mound, steadied it on a levelled platform and, brandishing a sword towards the four points of the compass, vowed to protect the Hungarian people and their constitution. The ceremony was 'gone like a beautiful dream', reported *The Times*, 'The crowned King of Hungary ... has passed out of sight just like the hero of some gorgeous fairy spectacle who vanished behind the wings as the audience are dispersing in great contentment.'

Soon afterwards an observant eight-year-old was induced by his tutor to commit to paper a less ethereal impression of the day's events. Rudolf's 400 word account is with the Crown Prince's papers; it is unlikely to have been touched up by Latour since it preserves at least four spelling mistakes in it. At seven in the morning, so Rudolf wrote, 'we went downstairs ... and we were a long time looking for our coach as the square was full of Lifeguards, Archdukes and horses, and among them the King's white coronation steed'. In the church he saw 'many magnates, officers, the Primate and several Catholic and Greek bishops and many other priests ... Mama sat on a kind of throne and Papa went to the altar where a great deal of Latin was said ... Then the mantle was wrapped around him and the Primate gave him the sword and made three strokes ... Afterwards the drums rolled out and Andrássy and the Primate placed the crown on Papa. Then Papa received in his hands the orb and sceptre. Papa and Mama at this point went up to the throne and Andrássy walked out into the middle of the church and three times shouted "*Eljen a kiraly*" [Long Live the King] ... 'A lot more Latin was said' as 'Mama went to the altar' for the Crown to be held over her head. 'We' then joined her 'in a glass coach' and went by steamer down river to see 'Papa spur his horse very nicely at the gallop up the Coronation Mound'. In the evening there was a banquet.

There were banquets on other evenings, too; for the coronation festivities continued for five days and nights. A Coronation Offering of a silver casket containing five thousand gold ducats was accepted by Francis Joseph from Andrássy and then, on the Count's advice, handed back by Their Majesties to the Hungarian people for the support of the widows and orphans of Honved fighters killed in the 1848–9 battles with the Austrians. 'Were it in our power to do so, we two would be the first to recall Lajos Batthyány and the martyrs of Arad to life', Elizabeth told one of Hungary's former rebel bishops. Reconciliation was in the air everywhere, it seemed – although, to this day, the walls of the room at the Hofburg where Francis Joseph presided over meetings of ministers display paintings of his army's victories over the Hungarians at Komárom and Temesvár.

After the Coronation, Francis Joseph and Elizabeth went straight to Ischl to enjoy a holiday with Gisela and Rudolf. They were at Ischl when, on 19 June, Maximilian was executed by firing squad at Queretaro, allegedly for sanctioning the killing of Mexican republicans soon after his arrival in the country. Archduchess Sophie had a premonition of her son's fate on the day that he died but, in Ischl, a strange optimism lingered; the last information, from the American Secretary of State, held out some hopes of a release. News from Mexico took well over a week to reach Europe and Francis Joseph still knew nothing of what had happened at Queretaro when, on 27 June, he heard of the sudden death of his sister-in-law Helen's husband, the Prince of Thurn and Taxis. With Elizabeth, he travelled to Regensburg to console Helen and accompanied her to the family home. It was therefore in Bavaria, three days later, that he received the first telegram giving the dreaded news of Maximilian's execution. He hurried back to Vienna to join his two brothers in seeking to comfort their parents. Although she had suspected the worst, confirmation of her fears numbed Sophie's response to everyday life. She lost her appetite for politics, only seeking to hear from Austrian officers who had been with her second son in these last terrible months. Gradually she gained new fortitude from what she heard: the last entry in her journal that year mourned the loss of 'my beautiful son', but she also gave proud 'thanks to God for the calm valour' with which he met his death.

Francis Joseph ordered Admiral Tegetthoff to sail for Veracruz and receive Maximilian's remains and transport his coffin to Trieste. To humiliate Austria still further, Juarez refused to release the body until the end of November and it was not until February 1868 that the whole imperial court attended the state funeral in the capital. Meanwhile the Emperor had continued policies essential to Austria's well-being, but which his mother thought deplorable. More and more, Austrian businessmen were looking to the Balkans, fearing a loss of outlets in newly unified Italy and Prussian-dominated Germany. As early as 27 July, despite the deep mourning of the Court, the Emperor entertained at Schönbrunn Sultan Abdulaziz and two Ottoman Princes, the future Sultans Murad V and Abdulhamid II. They were travelling back to Constantinople from the great Paris Exhibition, where they were among Napoleon III's guests when the news of Maximilian's execution broke in France. Even more embarrassing to Francis Joseph was a request from Napoleon III himself to be allowed to come to Vienna and offer his condolences. Only the persistent pleas of Beust that Austria needed France to serve as a buttress in western Europe if the Monarchy were to look to the East persuaded the Emperor to be host to 'that rogue'. Not, of course, that he would see him in Vienna nor in Ischl, where his mother and father were nursing their grief. Reluctantly the Emperor settled for a meeting in Salzburg during the third week of August.

Francis Joseph had difficulty in persuading Elizabeth to leave Ischl for Salzburg. She was feeling unwell, she told him; 'Perhaps I am with child.' But, for once, he was unsympathetic: Richard Metternich's letters from Paris had made it clear that Eugenie would accompany Napoleon and was especially eager to meet Elizabeth. Reluctantly she agreed to make the, relatively short, journey and on 18 August the two sovereigns and their consorts greeted each other, amiably rather than cordially, amid the trappings of a grand state occasion. Salzburg was illuminated, with beacons on the surrounding mountains; a banquet was held in a neighbouring castle; the Burgtheater company travelled down from Vienna to present the dramatic poem *Wildfeur*. Political speculation centred on the negotiation of an anti-Prussian alliance while society amused itself by wondering who was the more elegant, Eugenie or Elizabeth? Nothing was resolved, either in diplomacy or the imperial beauty contest. Francis Joseph had no intention of risking a third war in Europe, least of all with the devious Napoleon III as an ally; but he was willing for Beust and Metternich to linger in Salzburg for further talks with French diplomats. The Austrian Court, seeing the Empresses together, felt that Elizabeth carried herself more naturally. On the other hand, Eugenie won praise from Beust for her tact and from Archduchess Sophie for the unaffected sincerity of her condolences; and she even wished to travel privately to Ischl to see the grief-stricken Archduchess. 'The Empress was most gracious', Sophie noted in her journal, her minuscule writing still shaky from emotion.

Beust, who liked fine distinctions, claimed that Austria and France were 'linked together but not bound together'. This union he sought to nurture. With Metternich's support, he persuaded Francis Joseph to accept an invitation for a return State Visit in October. This time, however, Elizabeth would not accompany him; the pregnancy, which in August had seemed a mere excuse, was now confirmed. 'Heaven is once again blessing my marriage, and the gentle hope which is thus offered me imposes the greatest prudence', Elizabeth explained to Eugenie. However, for a journey to Paris in these last weeks of the Great Exhibition, Francis Joseph found willing companions; all were male. Archduke Charles Ludwig, who had married for a second time in 1862, was prepared to leave his wife with their young Archdukes, Francis Ferdinand and Otto; and his youngest brother, Ludwig Victor, also raised no objection to a dutiful fortnight in Paris. And Count Beust – now officially ranked as

Chancellor – felt bound to serve as attendant minister.

The Austrians reached Paris on 23 October. 'I expected much, but I am really thunderstruck by the conquering beauty of it all', Francis Joseph wrote to Elizabeth next morning. Letters, sent almost every day, show his delight in the visit. Although on All Souls Day he remembered at Mass 'both the Maxs' (his dead brother and Maximilian of Thurn and Taxis), he writes for most of the time in holiday mood, intrigued by all he saw, amused by gossip which would not have reached him at home. Eugenie, he wrote on 28 October, 'is mainly concerned in holding King Ludwig [of Bavaria] at arm's length; he has been here three days now and keeps on trying to steal a kiss from her. Apart from that, he is as merry as a cricket'. The next letter reported that Eugenie had 'made a date with Ludwig. Today she is going up with him in the balloon which makes daily ascents from the Exhibition Gardens. There is little risk, as the balloon is a captive one; but the Emperor is to know nothing about it, all the same. *You* would not do that kind of thing behind *my* back.'

A fatherly pride asserted itself: 'The little Napoleon is a bright fellow but a very puny lad. We've got something to show better than that.' Occasionally, too, Francis Joseph laughed at himself. 'At half-past eight I was at the Théatre Français where a long play was performed very well, but I slept a lot and came home at half past eleven', he told her on 26 October, not mentioning the title or the dramatist's name. Next day he was pleased; he had stayed awake through *Mignon* at the Opéra Comique. But two nights later 'the new opera *Romeo and Juliet* at the Théatre Lyrique' proved too much for him: 'I slept very well again', he admitted, though this time he did let Elizabeth know the composer's name – 'Gounaud' (*sic*). It is fair to remember that Francis Joseph was following an exhausting programme of sightseeing, often accompanying Eugenie, as when they went to the Trianon and the Conciergerie, honouring the memory of Marie Antoinette, his grandfather's aunt. And even on holiday Francis Joseph rose early. Most letters were written before six in the morning.

Politically little was achieved by the visit, though Beust's activities kept Bismarck guessing. Francis Joseph was happy to be reunited with his family at 'dear Possi' before returning to work in the Hofburg in the second week of November. Austrian domestic problems awaited him. After six months of intermittent debate a parliament representing the provinces of Cisleithania had produced a series of five constitutional laws which, together with the Hungarian 'Compromise', determined the basic political structure of the Monarchy throughout Francis Joseph's life, and beyond. These measures were approved by the Emperor four days before Christmas and became known as the 'December Constitution'. They introduced the principle of ministerial responsibility, though they safe-guarded the sovereign's prerogative in matters of defence and foreign affairs. The Reichsrat would have two chambers: an Upper House (*Herrenhaus*) of archdukes, ancient nobility, archbishops and certain princely bishops together with members nominated for life by the Emperor: and a Lower House (*Abgeordnetenhaus*), of some 200 deputies chosen by the provincial diets – a system already being challenged before the end of the year and soon modified. Francis Joseph was not displeased by these December Laws: he still had the power to appoint or dismiss ministers (whose responsibility to parliament involved no more than a threat of impeachment for illegal actions); his assent was needed before a bill became law; and he could reject a measure even if it had been passed by both houses. Moreover, Article XIV re-affirmed the concept of 'emergency government' by the Emperor or his nominees. This prin-ciple had been recognized in earlier constitutional drafts, but it was now slightly curbed by an insistence that any emergency measure lapsed if not approved by the next parliament within four weeks of its opening. Yet despite his general satisfaction it was a troubled Christmas for the Emperor that year. Already the Lower House was preparing an attack upon clericalism and, in particular, upon the Concordat of 1855. The domestic peace he believed so essential to recovery would need to be bought with liberal concessions which he was far from certain his con-science would permit.

The Empress did not share her husband's fears. She remained passion-ately Magyarophile in political sentiment and cultural taste. By now she spent as little time as possible in the Hofburg. Nor was she happy at Schönbrunn where, as in her earlier pregnancies, she complained of prying eyes critically staring at her as she took the walks her physicians demanded. Over Christmas she finally decided that her child would be born in Hungary; if she had a boy, he would be named Stephen, after Hungary's first saintly king. The announcement that her confinement would take place in Buda was not made until 5 February, since it was feared (rightly) that it would be extremely unpopular in Vienna. But, with Andrássy's backing, the Empress again had her way. Except, that is, in one respect. For when the child was born in the royal palace of Buda on 22 April, she was a girl, Marie Valerie.

Elizabeth was not disappointed. She claimed that, for the past two months of pregnancy, she was convinced she would give birth to a girl. The Crown Prince was healthy, and so there seemed no urgent need for a second son. Valerie would become, she thought, the family's Hungarian pet, learning Magyar as her first language. Francis Joseph, too, was pleased to be a father again. Rudolf and Gisela, left behind in Vienna, were told in a letter from Papa that they now had a 'beautiful' sister, with 'great, dark blue eyes', so sturdy that 'she hits out vigorously with her hands and feet'. Not surprisingly, the two elder children drew closer together, resenting the fuss being made of the pampered intruder.

Chapter 11

FACING BOTH WAYS

By the summer of 1868 Francis Joseph had lost that 'open and pre-possessing countenance' Lord John Russell commended thirteen years before. His chin remained beardless but, as if to compensate for the loss of hair on the crown of the head, he grew a thick moustache, longer than in later portraits, while the light brown side-whiskers cultivated early in the reign were by now so luxuriant that they obscured much of the collar, straggling down almost to the lapels of his tunic. Though he was not yet forty and still slim and upright in uniform, the face caught by four photographers that year shows streaks of middle-age, with lines of care discernible below the eyes, and with mouth and chin set in a slanting glance, coldly pensive in repose. He kept himself fit: he had cut down his smoking considerably, and he took plenty of exercise, not simply in the saddle, but by stalking in the mountains when he had the opportunity and by swimming; 'the swimming school' at Mödling, 'which I visit every day, is a great blessing', he was to write to his mother two years later, when pressure of work kept him deskbound well into August. Yet it is not surprising if there was a careworn maturity in his general disposition. For, incredible though it seems, Francis Joseph was already the doyen of continental secular sovereigns (although two minor German Princes had ruled their Grand-Duchies for a slightly longer span). Of Europe's crowned heads in 1868, only Queen Victoria was on the throne at his accession; even Napoleon III did not become Prince-President of France until eighteen days after the hurried ceremony at Olmütz.

This prematurely long experience of public affairs had united with an unimaginative conservatism of spirit to mould a temperament which varied little throughout the second half of Francis Joseph's life. He was slow to come to terms with reality and abandon the chimeric illusions of Metternich's day, with their sense of Habsburg mission in Germany and in Italy; and it could be argued that he never completely freed himself from their influence. His mind remained unreceptive to new ideas, many of which he did not even begin to comprehend. This stunting of intellectual capacity hardened innate prejudices: he never lost an interest in art, but he liked painters to show a neo-baroque approach to their subjects, and he wasted little time on innovations in style or technique. In politics he hankered for the absolutism of the Schwarzenberg era. He continued to mistrust parliamentarians, whether from the chambers in Vienna or in Pest; and on several occasions his choice of prime minister in Cisleithania ignored the prevailing inclination of the Austrian politicians.

On the other hand, the bigoted clericalism of his earlier years mellowed. When, in September 1867, an episcopal conclave submitted an address urging the Emperor to uphold the Concordat and condemn liberal demands to free the Church from state control, the bishops were sharply rebuked for making the government's task difficult; they should not excite public opinion; far better that they should tackle questions of conscience 'in a conciliatory spirit of understanding'. With Archduchess Sophie withdrawing from active political life, the septuagenarian Cardinal Rauscher's influence over her eldest son declined. When in May 1868 the Austrian liberals introduced legislation permitting civil marriage, withdrawing the Church's monopoly of jurisdiction in matrimonial affairs, and freeing education from clerical control, the Emperor did nothing to curb these concessions or a further educational law twelve months later.

The Empress, on a private visit to Rome in December 1869, was present at the opening of the Vatican Council. From her raised and enclosed box she felt swamped by the 'ocean of mitres' beneath her and stayed for only one of the seven hours given to the ceremonies. Next day she sent her husband a gently irreverent account of her audience with Pius IX: all 'that down-on-the-knees-shuffling-around' was 'quite comical', she wrote. Not that either Francis Joseph or Elizabeth became any less devout in their religious practices: on Maundy Thursday each year, the Emperor and Empress penitentially washed the feet of more than a dozen elderly pensioners brought to the Hofburg from Vienna's almshouses; and the imperial family continued to observe the public acts of reverence at Easter and Corpus Christi. The Emperor certainly did not intend to accept the growth of a conflict between the Church and secular authority. When, in July 1869, Bishop Rüdiger of Linz was sent to prison for instigating a breach of the peace by an intemperate attack on the new liberalism, Francis Joseph intervened: the Bishop was swiftly pardoned and released. The Austrian episcopate recognized the sincerity of their Emperor's delicate search for a middle way, and at the sessions of the Vatican Council Cardinals Rauscher and Schwarzenberg, together with the Croatian bishop Strossmayer, were outspoken critics of papal claims of supremacy. Francis Joseph and his closest spiritual advisers considered that the proclamation of papal infallibility on 18 July 1870 provided the pontiff with an unprecedented excuse for interfering in the Monarchy's affairs; and within a fortnight Francis Joseph agreed that the Concordat of 1855 should be considered null and void. 'The annulment of the Concordat was hard for me', he assured his mother, but he put all the blame on the wrong headedness of Rome: 'One might despair of the Church's future, if one could not hold firmly to the belief and hope that God will safeguard His Church from further mischief.'

Naturally Francis Joseph recognized that the *Ausgleich* modified the character of the Monarchy. He was fully prepared to spend more time in Hungary and, though he never liked the palace on Buda's Castle Hill, he came to enjoy the weeks of royal residence at Gödöllö almost as much as did Elizabeth. Yet it is clear that the Hungarian Compromise was, for him, a beginning rather than an end. He officially notified Chancellor Beust in November 1868 that his titles were now 'Emperor of Austria, King of Bohemia, etc. and Apostolic King of Hungary'. His grandfather had been crowned in Prague as early as August 1792, barely eight weeks after his Hungarian coronation, and there is no doubt that Francis Joseph intended to follow this precedent as closely as possible – always provided he could reach a political agreement with Bohemia's Germans and Czechs.

When Francis Joseph visited Prague in June 1868 to open a new bridge, he conferred with the veteran Czech historian, Palácky, as well as with his son-in-law, the far less accomplished nationalist spokesman, Franz Rieger. But neither Czech leader possessed the authority of Deák in Hungary nor the political dexterity of Andrássy. Rieger had been in Moscow in 1867 for the first Pan-Slav Congress and he was not prepared to make the concessions which Francis Joseph sought for Bohemia's Germans. Czech nationalism, quiescent for several years, had received a fillip earlier in the spring when the foundation stone was laid in Prague for a National Theatre, and feeling in the Czech provinces became so intense that in the autumn a state of siege was once more proclaimed in Prague. The building of the magnificent neo-Renaissance theatre on the banks of the river Vltava was not completed until 1881, and its construction served as a symbolic inspiration for the next generation of Czech patriots. To emphasize their distinctive 'West Slav' nationality Rieger made certain that all Czech deputies absented themselves from the Reichsrat in Vienna for the first twelve years of its existence. The almost forgotten Emperor Ferdinand and his devoted Maria Anna – 'their Prague Majesties' – could be certain of a polite reception on their walks in the gardens of the Hradčany castle, but Francis Joseph saw that he could not count on the Czechs responding as festively as the Hungarians to another Habsburg coronation.

Nevertheless he persevered in his attempts to secure an agreement with the Czechs. In September 1868 he tried the gambit which had succeeded at Buda-Pest and sent Beust for private talks with the Czech leaders. This was a tactical error: most Slavs, and particularly Czechs, were antipathetic to the Chancellor; and the immediate consequence of Beust's secret mission was the resignation of the Austrian prime minister, who complained that he had not been consulted. Taaffe took over as head of the Austrian government, while the Emperor continued to look for some respected figure who would coax the Czechs into co-operation. Having tried a Galician landowner, Count Alfred Potocki, whose federalist ideas proved unpopular, he eventually turned to one of the Austrian provincial governors, Count Charles von Hohenwart, who at first seemed to make some progress in discussions with Bohemia's politicians. The Czechs themselves at last drew up a series of 'Fundamental Articles', providing for the autonomy of Bohemia, followed the Hungarian model, and in the third week of September 1871 Francis Joseph sent a message to the Bohemian Diet in which he declared 'We gladly recognize the rights of this Kingdom and are prepared to renew that recognition in a coronation oath.' But this gesture provoked a violent reaction. The largely German-Austrian students of the University of Vienna protested so vigorously that there was a threat of riots in the capital; the Silesians complained that, though loyal German subjects of the Monarchy, they were being sacrificed to the Slavs of Prague; the Poles of Galicia saw no reason why the Czechs should receive special treatment; and Andrássy, invited to give his views at a specially convened Crown Conference, declared that the granting of concessions to the Czechs made civil war likely. 'Are you willing to carry through the recognition of Bohemian state rights with cannon?' he is said to have asked Hohenwart, 'If not, do not begin this policy.' Possibly Andrássy spoke less dramatically than this dire warning would suggest. But, at all events, the policy of satisfying the Czechs was abandoned. Hohenwart resigned. Francis Joseph found yet another princely Austrian to head the government of Cisleithania. There was no more talk of a coronation in Prague.

In Francis Joseph's boyhood the Monarchy had been concerned primarily with the German lands in the north and the Italian peninsula in the south. Metternich used to maintain that 'Asia begins at the Landstrasse', the highway eastwards from Vienna – and Asia held no interest for him whatsoever. But this blinkered approach was out of date even before Metternich fell from power. As early as 1837 a pioneer Austrian steamship service linked Trieste and Constantinople; and, after the unrest of 1848–49, improved navigation on the Danube, soon followed by the lifting of most restrictions on foreign banking in the Ottoman Empire, resulted in the growth in Vienna of a lively commercial interest in Near Eastern affairs. Defeat by Prussia in 1866 and the cession of Venetia intensified the need for the Monarchy to face both ways. Francis Joseph's ministers began to show a new sensitivity over what was likely to happen in south-eastern Europe. In 1869 the 'Krisvosije Rising', a series of armed disturbances over conscription in the mountain villages around Kotor, was treated as a major insurrection by the military chiefs in Vienna, not least because the long-neglected Gulf of Kotor seemed potentially the finest harbour for a fleet in the southern Adriatic. At the same time Beust, as Imperial Chancellor, showed an accommodating liberality towards the Balkan peoples: he offered financial assistance to Montenegro, encouraged the Turks to remove their last garrisons from three Serbian fortresses, acted as a mediator in a constitutional dispute between the Serbs and their nominal Ottoman suzerain in Constantinople, and gradually broke down the hostility of government ministers in Vienna and (less successfully) in Buda-Pest to the attempts of the Roumanians to assert their full independence. Very slowly, and with much argument, Beust convinced his colleagues of the value of giving support to a Franco-Belgian consortium which wished to construct a railway from Vienna through the Balkans to Salonika. Completion of this line would, he hoped, ensure that Austria kept a profitable hand on Ottoman trade with Europe.

It was Beust, too, who in 1869 persuaded Francis Joseph to attend the opening ceremonies of the Suez Canal. The invitation was given by Khedive Ismail of Egypt when the Emperor entertained him at Laxenburg in the first week of June. Until he went to the Paris Exhibition Francis Joseph had crossed the Monarchy's frontiers only to visit other German Princes or meet successive Tsars. Now Beust urged him to emphasize Austria's interest in the Near East, not merely by going to Egypt, but by paying a courtesy call on the Sultan in Constantinople, a gesture no Christian monarch had ever made while on the throne. Gradually the itinerary of the 'Imperial Tour in the East' grew longer, until it included other first occasions for a Habsburg sovereign, too: a river trip through the Iron Gates to the lower Danube; a visit to Athens; and a journey to Jerusalem. Originally it was assumed that the Empress Elizabeth would accompany her husband, but she shrank from accepting such a burden of official festivities; the need to appear in public ceremonially so often was more than she dared to face. Young Valerie needed her mother, she maintained; and there were Gisela and Rudolf to be considered, too, she remembered. Unkind gossip insisted that Elizabeth decided against the trip on learning that Eugenie would formally open the Suez Canal, for she could not face a second round in the so-called beauty contest with her alleged rival. At the last moment, when Elizabeth was preparing to say goodbye to Francis Joseph at Gödöllö, she seems to have regretted her decision, but there was no way in which the elaborate arrangements for a six week tour could be adjusted to accommodate her whims.

Not since his accession had Francis Joseph benefited from such an enjoyable and enlightening experience as these travels 'in the East', and yet their significance has been ignored by many later commentators on his reign. He sent Elizabeth twelve letters, with entries written up day by day; for the most part, they read like a travel diary, some 20,000 words long. They enable us, for once, to penetrate the formal mask which, as an essentially shy individual, Francis Joseph created to protect the private face of Empire from public gaze. Their style is a curious mixture; the astonished enthusiasm of an innocent abroad mingles with military assessments from a veteran inspector-general. Sometimes the sheer beauty of the scene overwhelms him; then, a few lines later, he notes the number of gun salutes or the bearing of the jäger battalions, cavalry and field artillery of the Sultan's army on parade.

Francis Joseph reached Turkish soil on 27 October, landing at Ruschuk, the river port of Ottoman Bulgaria. The welcoming ceremonies passed with routine familiarity, but, as he drove into the town, his interest quickened. 'It was a beautiful oriental picture, and I was in the midst of Turkish life, in the World of the East. For me the suddenness of the adventure and the swift change of scene was like a dream.' But when he wrote those words he was already on the Bosphorus: 'I am in Stamboul!', he exclaimed, 'To describe what I am seeing and feeling is beyond me. Only one thought is in my mind, the wish that you were here; my one hope is that you may be able to see it all: this setting for a city; these waters; these palaces; the glorious sunsets; the cypresses; the fleets of boats; the hurly-burly of people in every colour of costume; the women, unhappily veiled but with such eyes that you can only regret they should so be; and as for this air!' His room in the 'imperial palace of Besiktas' amazed him: 'The bed would hold at least three people, and one cannot help constantly thinking of all that must already have happened in it.' He knew his wife's interests, however, for next day he said, 'Soon after I had written to you, I began my sightseeing with the Sultan's stables. I feel certain that's what you would have done'; and he told her about the Sultan's thirty-year-old favourite grey and his 800 mounts, and how even his 'little prince' had 150 horses. Sultan Abdulaziz, so he assured Elizabeth, was 'the most charming host imaginable.'

After four more days off the Golden Horn the imperial yacht *Greif*, followed by two other Austrian ships carrying Francis Joseph's suite and accompanying ministers (including Beust and Andrássy), steamed out into the Sea of Marmora, for the Dardanelles and ultimately Piraeus. 'Here Leander swam to Hero, here Xerxes built the bridge over which he marched against the Greeks, here Lord Byron swam across', wrote the Emperor, stirred by the romantic associations of the Hellespont. As the *Greif* sailed along the coast of Attica he was delighted to see, 'to the right an ancient Greek temple to Diana on a promontory' (the Temple of Poseidon at Sounion, perhaps?). His letters left no temple undescribed, no glory from the monumental past unilluminated. But they carried, too, a modern touch: 'From Piraeus we went by railway in ten minutes to Athens across quite well cultivated plains, with olive-trees, vines and figs'. Francis Joseph was as meticulous an observer as any note-taker employed by Karl Baedeker.

'Four days at sea to reach Jaffa!', he warned Elizabeth in advance. When he landed in the Holy Land he was once again entranced by his surroundings. His party was guarded by several hundred Ottoman soldiers, moving slowly forward in a caravan of camels, while Bedouin horsemen on their lively greys served as outriders. On seeing Jerusalem for the first time, he sank to his knees in prayer. Then, over another four days, he visited the holy shrines in the city and at Bethlehem, went out to Jericho and the Dead Sea, stopped at the River Jordan, and, loaded with relics and holy water bottles, set off back to the coast, bivouacking in tents with their canvas embroidered with gold and silk designs. A lively swell made embarkation difficult: 'I made the trip out to the *Greif* from Jaffa in a small boat manned by local people, and the hoisting aboard in a sling, as horses are, is something I shall never forget for the rest of my days, and I would not do that kind of thing again for a million.' But, at last, on 15 November the three Austrian vessels moored off Port Said, where the official opening ceremonies of the canal were to begin next day.

The principal guest had already been in Egypt for a month, having left Paris nearly four weeks before Francis Joseph set out from Gödöllö. 'So now you are happily united with your beloved Empress Eugenie', Elizabeth wrote to her husband in a lightly mocking tone, 'It makes me very jealous to think of you playing the charmer for her benefit while I sit here all alone and am not even able to take my revenge'. Francis Joseph's response was tactful, though hardly gallant; Eugenie, he informed Elizabeth, 'had grown quite stout and was losing much of her beauty'. The opening ceremonies were, however, Eugenie's great personal triumph. The construction of the Suez Canal had been masterminded by her cousin, Ferdinand de Lesseps, and the whole enterprise was sponsored by the French imperial establishment. It was right for her to be accorded the honours of the occasion, since, as Napoleon III was suffering from stone in the bladder, there could be no question of his coming to Egypt. The French yacht *L'Aigle* headed the procession of ships down the canal, with Francis Joseph following aboard *Greif*; then came a line of nearly forty other vessels, which set out at fifteen minute intervals. Overnight the flotilla anchored in the Bitter Lakes before completing the second stage of what by now Francis Joseph had decided was a 'monotonous' journey down to Suez. At Ismailia there was a Grand Ball – '*Schrecklich*!!' (Frightful), he wrote. There were several thousand people there, so he reported; some were 'quite ordinary guests', including 'Riciotti Garibaldi, the son of the famous Garibaldi'. Eugenie, in a bright red dress and with a crown on her head, entered the ballroom on Francis Joseph's arm. He was, others noted, very attentive to her needs. It was impossible to dance or to make much progress. 'In all our minds there was only one thought: *Aussi mocht ich*' ('Let's get out of here' in Viennese dialect); 'The Empress and I did all in our power to get supper started, which we were bound to wait for, as the most magnificent preparations had been made, and the menu included more than 30 dishes. The meal seemed endless . . . I came back aboard *Greif* at 2 in the morning and slept like a log.'

Cairo was more to his liking: 410 mosques, he noted down carefully. Less pleasing was gala night at the new 'Italian Theatre' opera house beside the Nile: 'everyone in white ties' for an occasion which 'cost the Khedive the devil of a sum': 'Act 4 (*sic*) of *Rigoletto*', followed by 'the ballet of *Giselle*, to which I gave my support for only the first act, as I then fell asleep'. Best of all Francis Joseph enjoyed the opportunity to climb the pyramid of Cheops, the highest at Ghiza; this feat he achieved in seventeen minutes, having found that 'my rock-climbing experience stood me in good stead'. 'One Bedouin took me by the hand, another followed so as to push me from behind when the blocks of stone were too high to scramble up, though this was needed only five or six times', he explained to Elizabeth; and he added, 'The Bedouins are very agile, strong and self-assured. As they mostly only wear a shirt, when they are climbing they leave a lot exposed, and that must be the reason why English women so happily and frequently like to scale the pyramids.'

From Cairo it was back to the *Greif* at Alexandria and so, by way of Crete and Corfu, home to Trieste. There Francis Joseph was to see Elizabeth again. Not, however, at the happiest choice of rendezvous: for, with Charlotte in a private asylum in her native Belgium, Miramare had become an Austrian imperial villa, and it was in the rooms Maximilian had designed, looking out on the gardens to which he had given such thought, that his brother and sister-in-law were re-united. Even then, their meeting could be little more than a passing encounter, for during the later stages of her husband's tour, Elizabeth decided she was needed by her sister, the exiled Queen of Naples, who was expecting her first child in Rome; and, accordingly, the Empress had merely stopped briefly at Miramare while travelling to the papal city (and to that opening ceremony of the Vatican Council). Francis Joseph, who landed at Trieste pleasantly elated by all he had seen and done, soon found himself once more 'in harness', to use Elizabeth's phrase. She, on the other hand, avoided public life well into the New Year; from Rome she went directly back to Hungary, and then with her two daughters to Merano; it is hardly surprising if when, in March, the Empress at last returned to the capital, an ironical newspaper article referred to her as 'the resident guest in the Vienna Hofburg'. By then, of course, Francis Joseph had recounted his traveller's tales many times over. Like the gifts he brought with him, their father's adventures excited Rudolf and Gisela at Christmas, and he found he could still share his knowledge of a wider world with his mother, though it was clear her powers of assimilation were beginning to fail.

This new awareness of Eastern affairs soon became of great importance in his shaping of policy. But, for much of 1870, he was compelled to look to the West and the North. There remained a powerful pressure group in the war ministry who hankered for a war of revenge against Prussia. To them the great virtue of Francis Joseph's travels in the East had been the visible signs of friendship and support he extended to Eugenie at Port Said and Ismailia. Unofficial conversations between French staff officers and Austrian representatives were held from time to time during the closing months of 1869, and in February 1870 Baron Franz Kuhn, the first Austro-Hungarian war minister, informed the French military attaché in Vienna that, should France and the Monarchy find themselves at war with Prussia, he could guarantee an army of 600,000 men would be fully mobilized within six weeks. A month later Archduke Albrecht, as titular Inspector-General of the Imperial and Royal army, paid a much publicized visit to Paris, where he unfolded a grand strategic plan to the French minister of war. Provided France kept the Prussians engaged for six weeks and mounted an offensive in the general direction of Nuremberg, the Austrians (and he hoped an Italian expeditionary force) would cross into Saxony, raise the south German states and join the French in a march on Berlin which would destroy Bismarck's Prussia. The French, however, were doubtful of Albrecht's master-plan, not least because of the six week delay it imposed; and when, early in June, a French general returned Albrecht's visit, he received a clear impression that Francis Joseph had no desire whatsoever to risk another war.

This assessment of the Emperor's attitude was perfectly correct. Twice already he had allowed his ministers and generals to hustle him into disastrous wars. Experience made him cautious. Moreover, he could see that there was a conflict around the conference table between Albrecht and Kuhn. Their advice was inconsistent. If the Archduke rattled his sabre, Kuhn insisted that the work of years in preparing the army to face its great challenge was not yet finished. When Kuhn changed his position and began to urge that Austria-Hungary could not stand aside from a coming 'struggle involving all Europe', Albrecht circulated a critical pamphlet, technically anonymous: the army, so the pamphlet asserted, was short of modern weapons, and the parsimony of the war ministry meant that it was ill-equipped for any mobile campaign in the field. Understandably, at this point, the Emperor decided to order an inquiry into the readiness of his troops for war; this task he entrusted to Beck, who had served Francis Joseph so well in the Seven Weeks War, that he was appointed chief of the military chancellery.

Ultimately Beck agreed with Albrecht rather than Kuhn; but before these quarrels could be resolved, the Emperor and all his ministers were shaken by the sudden deterioration in Franco-Prussian relations over the so-called Hohenzollern Candidature for the Spanish throne. On 15 July Richard Metternich was surprised to be informed in Paris that war was certain; 'If Austria realizes what is best for her, she will march beside us', he was told. But Francis Joseph was not going to have questions of peace or war decided for him in Paris. Hurriedly he summoned a council of ministers for 18 July, the day before formal hostilities began between France and Prussia.

Francis Joseph presided over the council himself, and spoke at some length. Beust confirmed that Austria-Hungary retained a free hand and that the French had taken no notice of Austrian pleas not to allow the Hohenzollern Candidature to become transformed into a German national issue. Andrássy thought Russia posed a greater threat to the Monarchy than Prussia, for he maintained that Pan-Slav hotheads were in the ascendant at St Petersburg. If Austria-Hungary was committed to a campaign in southern Germany, the Russians would seize the opportunity to stir up the southern Slavs and press forward with plans to dominate the Balkans and the lower Danube. Kuhn, who had circulated a memorandum in advance of the conference favouring immediate intervention, made a fiery speech which stressed the need for Austria to prevent the permanent siting of Prussian garrisons along the River Inn. Archduke Albrecht wanted immediate mobilization but when, later in the day, he took the chair at a second ministerial conference, there was a strong feeling in favour of neutrality. As a gesture of reassurance towards Andrássy, Francis Joseph ordered defensive measures to be taken along the Monarchy's 500-mile frontier with the Russian Empire.

Before the war began, Beust hoped his influence in Saxony would keep the southern German states from giving military support to the North German Confederation. Here, however, he was wrong. The appeal of German national sentiment was too strong. On 27 July Archduchess Sophie's journal echoed the feeling of the Court: deep sorrow at the 'sad enthusiasm' with which the German states were falling in beside Prussia to fight against the old enemy beyond the Rhine. When, nine days later, press reports indicated that Bavarian units in the Prussian Crown Prince's Third Army were marching on Strasbourg, the Archduchess despaired of her homeland: 'This is the ruin of Saxony and Bavaria', she wrote, 'May God help them.'

Francis Joseph remained at Schönbrunn, presiding over five ministerial conferences in twelve days once the German invasion of France began in earnest. Church-State relations were also discussed at these meetings, for the outbreak of war had coincided with the declaration of papal infallibility. By the end of the first week in August he had little doubt that an Austro-Hungarian entry into the war would be disastrous. After a long conference on 9 August, he stopped all preparations for an imminent campaign. Kuhn thought Austria-Hungary should take advantage of Prussia's pre-occupation with the West by marching into Silesia and recovering lands lost to Frederick the Great. But Francis Joseph was more sympathetic to Beust's argument that the Monarchy stood to gain influence and prestige by staying out of the war and coming forward as a mediator. A ministerial conference on 22 August duly endorsed the policy of armed neutrality – but with a wary eye kept on the Russians, for Tsar Alexander II had complained of hostile troop movements in Galicia. Francis Joseph took note of a warning from Andrássy which confirmed the impression he had formed during his journey to Ruschuk and the Bosphorus: 'Austria's mission remains, as before, to be a bulwark against Russia', the Hungarian prime minister declared, 'Only so long as she fulfils this mission does her existence remain a necessity for Europe.' The army corps in Galicia was kept on the alert.

Yet Francis Joseph could hardly turn his back on what was happening in the West. 'The catastrophes in France are frightful and offer no comfort for our future', he wrote to his mother on 25 August. Worse soon followed: the French defeat at Sedan on 1 September; Napoleon III's capture; the proclamation of a republic in Paris. 'How Eugenie must regret the timidity and vacillation of her husband!' Archduchess Sophie observed. Another long ministerial council on 11 September reviewed the situation gloomily. Beust was sent to Munich in the hopes that, at this late hour, he could persuade the south Germans to stay outside a Prussianized nation state. But even Beust, with all his understanding of German affairs, could achieve nothing. 'I see a very dark future, even more dismal than the present', Francis Joseph admitted to his mother at the end of October. Twelve weeks later a German Empire, from which the Austrian lands were excluded, was proclaimed in the Hall of Mirrors at Versailles. The Habsburgs seemed finally to have lost their voice in German affairs. Not everyone in Vienna was willing to accept the change. Archduchess Sophie, though recognizing the newly elevated status of the ruler in Berlin, denied him his full title: the last volumes of her journal refer to William I simply as the 'Prussian Emperor'.

A second humiliation buffeted Habsburg pride within a few weeks of the ceremony at Versailles. Francis Joseph and his ministers were convinced that Alexander II would take advantage of the European crisis to assert Russia's Great Power status. Rather curiously they seem to have believed he would order his troops into Moldavia and Wallachia, brushing aside the tenuous existence of a semi-independent Roumania. Accordingly when, in November 1870, Russia abrogated the clauses of the Treaty of Paris providing for the demilitarization of the Black Sea, Beust and Andrássy were in a sense relieved, for the Tsar's army would not now be on the move. At a conference on 14 November Francis Joseph agreed with Beust's contention that there could be no question of war with Russia, but it was subsequently agreed that, should there be an international conference over Black Sea problems, Austria-Hungary would seek special status so as to counter-balance Russia. But when, in February and March 1871, these matters were aired at a conference in London, Beust's proposals were totally ignored; even the Sultan's representatives preferred to rely on Germany and Great Britain. Diplomatically the Habsburg Monarchy had been left isolated by the Crimean War and the Treaty of Paris: now, after the Franco-Prussian War and the denunciation of the Treaty of Paris, the Habsburg Monarchy was isolated again.

Beust, however, was a resilient statesman. The definitive peace treaty between the German Empire and France was signed at Frankfurt on 10 May 1871. Eight days later Francis Joseph received a memorandum from Beust setting out a strategy to enable Austria-Hungary to become Europe's pivotal Great Power once more: the Emperor should seek reconciliation with the new German Empire. Side by side the governments of Berlin, Vienna and Buda-Pest could form a central bloc across Europe, ready if necessary to put out feelers to St Petersburg and revive the old understanding between the three northern courts or to unite against revolutionary republicanism should it triumph in France (for Beust was writing while the Communards still held Paris). There must be no more talk of revenge for 1866: on the contrary, the Emperor should realize that Bismarck had created a national empire which might appeal to the

German population of the Monarchy, and thereby threaten its very existence.

Although before the end of the year Francis Joseph was to turn against
Beust, for the moment he was willing to accept the principles of the
memorandum. Chancellor Beust and Chancellor Bismarck met three
months later; and on 11 August Emperor Francis Joseph was on the
railway platform at Wels to greet Emperor William I as he made his way
to Gastein. It was not the first contact between the two sovereigns since
Königgrätz: they had briefly exchanged cold courtesies at Oos in October
1867, when Francis Joseph's train crossed Prussian territory on the way
to Paris. But at Wels there was some amiable conversation, and the two
Emperors travelled together across the mountains to Ischl, before William
went on to Gastein. The reconciliation was carried further when they met
again on 6 September in Salzburg. So far, so good; but Francis Joseph
had his doubts. Was Beust the best man to carry out the policies he had
recommended? Could he subdue his old hatred of Bismarck, for example?
Conversely was he still too southern German in his approach to the
problems of the Monarchy and, in particular, to the position of the Czechs
in Bohemia? In the late autumn Francis Joseph resolved to make one of
the sudden and ruthless changes of minister for which he was by now
becoming notorious. On 1 November the Emperor asked Beust for his
resignation as Imperial Chancellor, the title disappearing with the departure of its holder to serve as ambassador in London. At last Francis Joseph
implemented the 'preposterous' suggestion which Elizabeth had put
forward five years before: on 9 November Gyula Andrássy moved into
Metternich's old room looking down on the Ballhausplatz. For the first
time, the Monarchy was to have a Hungarian magnate as foreign minister.

Elizabeth was pleased at the appointment. Yet she was less elated than
before her coronation. Her liking for Hungary, its people, language and
culture, was undiminished; she now included among her close companions both Ida Ferenczy and the highly intelligent and perceptive
Countess Marie Festetics, a confidante of Andrássy. She continued, too,
to enjoy hunting at Gödöllö, where Andrássy was a frequent guest. But,
after the birth of Marie Valerie, Elizabeth lost her interest in politics,
never very great. Once again she earned frowns of disapproval at Court.
At the height of the Franco-Prussian War her strong will made her decide
that, for reasons of health, she must spend most of the winter at Merano,
with little Valerie and at first with Gisela, too. 'My poor son', Archduchess
Sophie commented in her journal, on hearing that Elizabeth was heading
for the southern Tyrol a such a time. Three weeks later the Archduchess
transcribed an unctuous letter she had received from Rudolf, which she
seems to have commended: 'So in these difficult days poor Papa must be

separated again from darling Mama', wrote the twelve-year-old Crown Prince, 'I am only too happy to accept the noble duty of being the sole support of my dear Papa.' Sophie was fond of her grandson; and there is no doubt that he warmly returned her affection. But in his unhappiness can the boy really have been such an insufferable prig? Did she attribute to him her own sentiments, or was he astute enough to play on her feelings?

In that winter of 1870–71, and in the next, the Archduchess seemed to recover much of her old vigour, making a final bid to preside over high society in the capital. She was, after all, only in her mid-sixties. Every Friday evening she held a dinner-party at the Hofburg, but she did not like new fashions or new ideas. Least of all, could she accept the need for the Monarchy to face both ways, for she deplored the intrusiveness of all those Hungarians at Court. When she entered up her diary on New Year's Eve in 1871 – eight weeks after Andrássy became foreign minister – she followed her usual practice and looked back on the past twelve months. This time she wrote with unaccustomed bitterness: 'liberalism', she complained, was triumphant; and she regretted the omnipresence of its 'worthless shining lights'. 'May God have pity on us!' she added.

It was nearly half a century since Sophie had left Munich for Vienna. Early in 1872, to her great surprise, she learned of the prospect of yet another dynastic link between the Wittelsbach and Habsburg families. At fifteen the Archduchess Gisela was betrothed to Prince Leopold of Bavaria, her second cousin twice over. 'As there are so few Catholic princes, we had to try to secure the only one to whom we might give Gisela with any confidence', Francis Joseph told his mother on 7 April. Sophie was fond of Gisela, who had been an attentive grand-daughter; she also liked Prince Leopold; but she wrote firmly in her journal, 'This marriage is no match'. Elizabeth, too, had doubts, insisting that Gisela was too young – though she was almost exactly the same age as Elizabeth had been when she became Francis Joseph's fiancée. It was accepted that the marriage would not take place for another year, the Empress's critics insisting that, in her craving for eternal youthfulness, Elizabeth wished to put off the reality of becoming a grandmother as long as possible.

Archduchess Sophie did not live to see Gisela married. On Monday, 6 May, she was up at half-past five to set out on a day-long expedition. It was a sharp spring morning and she caught a chill which, at the end of the week, became dangerously bronchial. On Saturday 11 May she began to write up her journal; the effort was too much for her; and, after a few lines, the entry breaks off abruptly. Not that the curtain was to fall suddenly on her. For more than a fortnight she lingered in a sick-room, while her family converged on Vienna, finally gathering in the Hofburg around her.

As Sophie grew weaker, Elizabeth kept a constant vigil, while Francis Joseph put Maria Theresa's rosary in his mother's hands. When at last the Archduchess died – on the afternoon of 28 May 1872 – the Empress had been at her bedside for eighteen hours, contrite for the worry which her wilful ways once caused the dying matriarch. Francis Joseph, deeply shaken by the loss of a mother who was his greatest confidante, admired his wife's dutiful dignity in mourning. Elizabeth's temperament possessed a bewildering facility for swift changes of mood, and he appreciated the sorrowful sympathy which there is no doubt she genuinely felt for all the family around the deathbed. Yet, once the funeral was over, and Sophie's body lay in the vault of the Capuchin church beside the tombs of Maximilian and the Duke of Reichstadt, old convictions sprang readily back into place. Over the following months the Empress liked to gossip about the recent past with her Hungarian ladies-in-waiting, recounting at considerable length the enormities of misunderstanding committed by a bullying mother-in-law in the first years of her married life. Marie Festetics made a careful note of the Empress's spate of reminiscence. Fortunately Francis Joseph was never to read them; the 'dearest, darling angel Sisi' stayed secure on her pedestal in his fondest beliefs.

Chapter 12

A GLIMMER OF LIGHT

The mood of Vienna in Archduchess Sophie's last five years of life changed dramatically, season by season. At first, in 1867, the city was stunned by the lost war against Prussia, slow to accept dethronement from its European eminence. The carnival festivities were muted that winter; it seemed fitting to hold concerts rather than encourage an irresponsible gaiety by the customary series of sparkling balls. Out at the Dianabad-Saal in Leopoldstadt on the middle Friday of *Fasching* – 15 February 1867 – the Vienna Men's Choral Society offered a new choral work, commissioned from Johann Strauss 'the Younger' and frequently changed by him in form and character. It was still without a title when the programme was announced, although words had been found for 'Opus 314' by Joseph Weyl, a member of the Society with a gift for turning out verses for any occasion. This time they were good ones. 'Why are you Viennese sad?', Weyl asked, in effect, 'Why shrug your shoulders in despair? Don't you see a glimmer of light? Carnival time is here; let's be merry and gay'. To this challenge Strauss's music duly responded, a few bars of wistful prelude swiftly giving way to what a leading music critic at once hailed as 'a truly splendid waltz'. Not that Strauss was in the Dianabad-Sall that evening to conduct it. He was with his orchestra at the Hofburg, fulfilling obligations accepted four years previously when he first became *Hofballmusik-Direktor* at Francis Joseph's Court. In the composer's absence the Society's chorus-master, Rudolf Weinwurm, took the baton; and the most famous of Viennese waltzes, hurriedly entitled *An der schönen blauen Donau*, was played for the first time not by Strauss's fiddlers but by the orchestra of the König von Hannover Infantry Regiment, then at barracks in the city.

Three weeks later Johann Strauss conducted the definitive version of *The Blue Danube* in the Volksgarten. Thereafter the waltz was treated as a composition either for piano or for full orchestra; its origins as a choral work were largely ignored until eventually in 1890 Franz von Gernerth, another member of the Men's Choral Society, wrote the anodyne travel commercial which has endured for more than a century. But Joseph Weyl's original satirical verses proved extremely apt. He had told the people of Vienna to forget their misfortunes; and this they had good reason to do in the months which followed that première in the Dianabad-Sall. So, too, did the townsfolk of many other commercial centres in the Dual Monarchy. For during the first six years of its existence Austria-Hungary was unexpectedly blessed with an economic miracle. State finance, held for so long in the shadow of imminent bankruptcy, emerged to such astonishing prosperity that between 1869 and 1872 each annual budget closed with a surplus of public funds.

There are many reasons why the 'glimmer of light' so soon became open sky. The abandonment of forward policies in Germany and Italy, together with apparent constitutional stability in the two halves of the Monarchy, helped spread a business confidence which the politicians' skill in remaining at peace in 1870 seemed to justify. Investment came from Britain, the United States and northern Germany, helped by freer trade conditions and the prospect of better banking facilities. More than four hundred banks were founded in the Monarchy as a whole during the six years following the *Ausgleich*, and government approval was given for twenty-nine new railway companies. Nor was this economic progress limited to industry. While there was a rapid spread of factories – with a jump in production figures for coal and pig-iron – agriculture, too, flourished. Yet in this instance the success was, perhaps, a shade fortuitous. A succession of fine summers in central Europe produced bumper harvests in the rich Danubian basin at a time when the yield in western Europe remained low. Surplus cereals were exported at a good price, particularly wheat from Hungary and, to a lesser extent, rye from Cisleithania. There was an astonishing leap in the cultivation of sugar-beet in Bohemia and Moravia, with a consequent rise in the export of refined sugar, particularly to Germany. Moreover in these pre-phylloxera years – and especially in 1868 – the vineyards around Vienna, in Dalmatia and in central Hungary benefited from the weeks of summer sunshine. It is fitting that when, in February 1869, Johann Strauss completed a second waltz for the Vienna Men's Choral Society he should have chosen to honour 'Wine, Woman and Song'.

Like their Emperor, the joint-stock companies looked eastwards; and they were impressed by the prospects for the future. Danubian shipping improved year by year. No one doubted that there were good opportunities for investment in Rumelia ('European Turkey'), Anatolia and the Levant, especially after the collapse of the Second Empire and Napoleon III's speculative ventures; in 1871 two rival institutions – a Banque Austro-

Ottomane and a Banque Austro-Turque – were opened at Constantinople within a few months of each other. But the boom left its most permanent mark on the great cities of the Monarchy, where rash speculation led to equally rash building projects. The demolition of the mediaeval walls of Prague in 1867 enabled a 'new town' to grow rapidly, facing the royal city across the river Vltava; but there were several instances of sharp practice in municipal administration, with the alleged venality of one or other group of developers exaggerated by their political opponents. In Vienna the Imperial Opera House was at last completed in the spring of 1869, ready for opening by the Emperor on 25 April in a gala occasion of pomp and ceremony – even if Francis Joseph did slip away after Act I of *Don Giovanni*. The Opera House had always been intended to serve as a showpiece for a city dedicated to music; but it was anticipated that there would be around the Opera a long line of public buildings, embodying in stone the dignity of a great empire. As yet, however, the Opera stood in haughty isolation; for it was the grandiose palaces of the newly wealthy barons of finance which were spreading rapidly along the Ringstrasse, not the pedimented majesty of imperial institutions.

On the surface, these boom years were happily relaxed. The confidence in stability which encouraged investors also reassured many ordinary wage-earners, in town and country. Once again, all classes of people could be found enjoying themselves in the open spaces of the capital, perhaps sampling the fairground pleasures of the Wurstelprater, or quieter moments in the relatively new Stadtpark, where in winter a frozen lake beside the River Wien was a delight for skaters; and it is no accident that this period saw the beginning of the golden years of Viennese operetta, an entertainment by no means reserved solely for the fashionable élite. Yet urban life did not glow so warmly in every level of society. There was an ugly sprawl of wretched homes around most towns, more evident in centres like Brno and Pilsen than in Vienna. And from the capital itself came warning signs; a workers' demonstration through the snow and slush of a bleak Monday morning in December 1869 threw a momentary shadow across preparations for the most affluent Christmas in three decades.

There were warning voices, as well; and to at least one of these the Emperor gave careful attention. Albert Schäffle, a Protestant Württemberger from the University of Tübingen, had recently received a professorial chair at the University of Vienna, where his lectures on the capitalist order of society aroused widespread interest. Professor Schäffle was a democratic conservative, a critic of free-trade liberalism who believed, ideally, in universal male suffrage as a means of holding in check what he called 'the rule of money dressed up in intellectual garb'. He believed, too, in the virtues of an aristocratic federalism which would promote racial equality between the nationalities of the Monarchy; and it was no doubt for this reason that in October 1870 the Emperor invited Schäffle to the Hofburg to explain his theories in a private audience. He came twice, virtually giving Francis Joseph two hours of tuition in ideas totally new to him. The Emperor was impressed. On 6 February 1871 Professor Schäffle was appointed minister of commerce and agriculture. Here, it seemed, was a specialist who could ensure that the economic miracle was not fraudulent.

Schäffle found Francis Joseph 'invariably objective and sympathetic', he wrote in his memoirs some thirty years later. The Emperor would examine 'everything put before him ... conscientiously and in detail ... without prejudging the matter'. Probably Francis Joseph learnt a great deal from the professor, notably his conviction that universal male suffrage was a force for stability rather than change; but the experiment of an academic economist in politics was not a success. Though Schäffle understood trade and investment better than any minister since the unfortunate Bruck, he lacked the Baron's dexterity or his practical experience in handling big business. By the autumn of 1871 the joint opposition of German-liberal newspapers, the 'kings of the Stock Exchange', and the more restrained criticism of his federal ideas from Andrássy left Schäffle isolated. On 13 October the professor offered his resignation, thankfully retreating to the relative calm of academic life. His immediate successors gave no indication that they realized the boom years might soon give way to recession. The Emperor, somewhat bewildered by the seven month experiment, placed all his trust in Andrássy who, on being appointed to succeed Beust at the foreign ministry, also became the co-ordinating Austro-Hungarian minister of finance.

Andrássy looked forward, with habitual confidence, to an era of continued peace and prosperity. Peasants were told they might sow their seeds without fear of finding their holdings ravaged by war; the townsfolk were assured they could continue to build houses, for nothing was going to destroy their homes. He warmly backed plans, already put forward, to hold a World Exhibition in Vienna in 1873, convinced that a great fair of this nature would allow other countries to see the material progress made by the Dual Monarchy in six years.

Francis Joseph agreed with him. He welcomed the chance to be host to his fellow rulers, letting them judge for themselves the vitality of the Habsburg lands. Sovereign and minister knew that such an enterprise would steal a march on Bismarck's Germany, putting Vienna ahead of Berlin; for among Europe's capitals as yet only London (1851, 1862) and

Paris (1855, 1867) had promoted these international shop-windows of industry and commerce. Each exhibition had been larger than its predecessors, with Napoleon III's 'greatest show on earth' in the Champ-de-Mars twice the size of the original Crystal Palace in Hyde Park. Vienna, it was agreed, must present an even greater world fair; 280 acres of the Prater would be set aside for its pavilions, an area five times as big as anything that had gone before. Hotels, pensions, restaurants, cafés and taverns sprang up in and around the capital with astonishing rapidity. More than 6 million people had come to London's Great Exhibition in 1851 and 9 million to Paris in 1867. It would have seemed unpatriotic for any citizen of Vienna to expect less than 20 million visitors by the end of the year, when the Silver Jubilee of Francis Joseph's accession was due to be celebrated.

The naturally sceptical Viennese made fun of the massive rotunda, 312 feet in diameter, going up in their Prater. It was crowned by a cupola which reminded them of a whirl of cream added to an iced cake, for images of confectionery sprang readily to mind. But when to this rotunda were added 28 temporary pavilions and a long central arcade, and when thousands of applications for exhibition stands began to reach the city, the whole enterprise was viewed with new respect. The final catalogue listed 15,000 Austrian exhibitors, nearly 7,000 German, 700 from the United States, and some 27,000 applications for stands from 37 other countries, including Japan. Such a concourse would make the Congress of Vienna seem in retrospect like a village market. A Jewish schoolboy, about to celebrate his seventeenth birthday and go to university, feared the Exhibition might distract him from the qualifying examination he was due to take in June. 'When ... the *Matura* is over, I intend to go there every day', he wrote to a friend, but he could not resist looking in twice before his 'day of martyrdom'. Not that it mattered: he passed 'with flying colours'; indeed, for his translation of 33 verses of *Oedipus Rex*, the examiners gave Sigmund Freud their highest commendation.

Before the opening of the World Exhibition there was an imperial curtain-raiser, which budding radical intellectuals like Sigmund Freud scorned. On 20 April Archduchess Gisela – who was ten weeks younger than Freud – married Prince Leopold of Bavaria in the Augustinerkirche, the parish church of the Hofburg, with Cardinal Rauscher once again officiating. Almost inevitably the bride was upstaged by her mother, who in her obsessive cult of beauty was determined to look even younger than her thirty-five years. In a dress embroidered with silver and with a diamond crown surmounting her thick carpet of hair, Elizabeth moved with great dignity down the aisle, for she now knew how to convey a presence which she had never possessed at her own marriage. Nobody seems to have noticed what her shy and pleasant daughter wore. As usual the festivities began well ahead of the wedding-day. At the Burgtheater there was a gala performance of *A Midsummer Night's Dream* – 'Am I, then, the ass?', Prince Leopold asked his Elizabeth; and on 17 April the Emperor, Empress and Crown Prince accompanied the bridal couple to a grand ball given by the city of Vienna at the concert-hall of the Musikverein. The celebrations started with Johann Strauss conducting the Vienna Philharmonic in a waltz composed for the occasion and entitled, rather oddly, *Wiener Blut* (Vienna Blood).

Not everyone was happy on the wedding day. Next morning's *Neue Wiener Tagblatt*, a sympathetic newspaper, commented on the Crown Prince's wretchedness at the railway station as the imperial family said farewell to Gisela and Leopold. Would many boys, approaching their fifteenth birthday, have wept so openly at their sister's departure for a home barely nine hours distant by train? Rudolf, who seems only to have been told the 'facts of life' a few months before, may have been academically precocious but he remained emotionally immature, slow to acquire that public mask of self-control which his father habitually donned. Yet, at parting from Gisela, even Francis Joseph is reported to have had tears in his eyes, as if he felt she had reached womanhood before he really came to know her.

Eleven days later – on Thursday, 1 May, like London's great festival in 1851 – the Emperor opened the World Exhibition in the Prater. At least three witnesses of that earlier May Day ceremony – the Prince of Wales and the Crown Prince and Princess of Prussia – were also present in Vienna twenty-two years on. Unlike Queen Victoria, however, Francis Joseph had the weather against him. 'The 1st of May was a day of well-nigh Siberian cold with a most democratic rain drenching roads and meads', wrote Sigmund Freud, who was there to see the carriage procession drive by, 'No one, with the exception of a few street urchins who sat in the trees, broke into shouts of joy at the sight of the Apostolic Highnesses, while His Majesty's humble and obedient subjects took cover under their umbrellas and hardly raised their hats'. Rain could not spoil the pageantry inside the rotunda where Archduke Charles Ludwig, as Imperial Patron of the Exhibition, delivered a formal speech of welcome before his brother, the Emperor, declared it open to the public. Beside Francis Joseph, Elizabeth and Rudolf on a huge dais, banked with flowers, were the heirs to the thrones of Britain, Prussia, Denmark, and Belgium, together with their consorts, and an array of what Freud irreverently called 'foreign princes . . . made up exclusively of mustachios and medals'. Crowned heads of state were booked to come in an exhausting but, for the most part, well-regulated sequence of visits spread over the following five months: King Leopold II of Belgium in May, Tsar Alexander II in June, Shah Nasr-ed-Din of Persia in early August, swiftly followed by the King of the Hellenes, King Victor Emmanuel II of Italy in late September, and the German Emperor William I four weeks later. And there were the ruling princes of Roumania, Serbia and Montenegro to be entertained, and a special emissary from the Sultan, too. Not all were welcome guests: it says much for Andrássy's powers of persuasion that, in the interests of diplomacy, Francis Joseph should have been so well-disposed towards his old adversary from Turin. Nor, as yet, was he entirely reconciled to the Hohenzollerns; a German state visit required a courtesy donning of the helmet, tunic and trousers of the Prussian Guard Grenadier Regiment, of which Francis Joseph remained honorary colonel-in-chief – 'I felt like an enemy to myself', he would grumble when about to go on parade in German uniform. He was happier with his guests from Württemberg and Saxony.

The World Exhibition was dogged with misfortune, starting with an opportunist strike of fiacre drivers and, more grievously, an early cholera scare in the city which turned into a serious epidemic claiming over 2,500 victims. But, for an enterprise planned to promote industry and commerce, the worst setback of all was *Der Krach*, the sudden collapse of the Vienna stock exchange a week after the opening of the Exhibition. Professor Schäffle's grimmest fears were realized: credit resources were hopelessly over-stretched. On 8 May it was admitted that a hundred traders on the Bourse were insolvent. There was a rush to dispose of stock and shares as bubble companies failed hour by hour on that day and the next, 'Black Friday'.

Almost every company caught in the crash was of recent growth: 62 Viennese credit banks founded in the past five years were forced to close and 45 in the provinces; but of 11 older, well-established banks in Austria, only one went into liquidation. There was, as always in such scandals, a wave of suicides among ruined speculators (including one high-ranking general). Subsequent inquiries revealed corruption in high places: the German liberal, Karl Giskra, once an opposition deputy fiercely critical of military budgets and in 1868–70 the minister for home affairs, was totally discredited; and so was a leading member of the Emperor's military chancellery. No one suggested corruption within the imperial family but Francis Joseph's profligate brother, Archduke Ludwig Victor, had speculated wildly – in part with a legacy from his over-indulgent mother – and he lost the equivalent of two years income (in the values of the early 1990s roughly £200,000 or $280,000). Work stopped on many buildings in the Ringstrasse. When on 14 June the Emperor laid the foundation stone of the new Rathaus, people doubted if public funds would allow the completion of Friedrich Schmidt's neo-Gothic monument to his city's self-confident grandeur; and it was, indeed, another nine years before the council's halls and chambers came fully into service.

Ultimately the worst sufferers from the *Krach* were some of Francis Joseph's loyalist subjects, good church-going lower middle-class families tempted into investment by the bright prospects of the boom years. Also pathetically hit were the workers in new factories and casual labourers forced into unemployment by an abrupt halt to building projects and the sudden abandonment of railway lines along tracks no longer needed. The long-term consequences of Black Friday ran deeper than Court or Government appreciated at the time. A relentless search for scapegoats encouraged the spread of both socialism and anti-semitism over the following ten to fifteen years.

A poor summer gave way to a worse autumn: rain ruined the harvest of cereals in both Cisleithania and Hungary; the phylloxera disease began to attack the vines; and valuable timber from the great forests was lost through a species of beetle which bored deeply into good bark. Far fewer visitors came to Vienna than had been anticipated; and the takings at the World Exhibition fell disappointingly low. This run of misfortune troubled Francis Joseph greatly, not least because he always had to minimize its gravity to his eminent guests. The need for frequent ministerial councils, together with the state visits, meant that he was able to escape for only a short holiday, joining Elizabeth at Ischl in August. The strain was also beginning to tell on the Empress. Public appearances remained irksome to her but, realizing the importance of the World Exhibition to her husband in person and to the Monarchy as a whole, she was resolved to give Francis Joseph the support he needed. From Ischl she returned to Schönbrunn at the end of the second week of September, ready to greet King Victor Emmanuel; but on the eve of his arrival she collapsed with gastric fever and spent the following ten days in bed. The illness caused a ripple of friction in her relationship with Andrássy who, knowing Elizabeth's resentment at the ousting of her sister from Naples, believed her indisposition had sprung from pique. But any doubt that she was genuinely unwell was removed when she failed to attend the grand horse show in the Prater. At last in October the imperial family escaped to Gödöllö. Even in these much-loved surroundings her recuperation was slow. Francis Joseph became alarmed: her medical attendants were puzzled by the symptoms, as they had been thirteen years before. She did not look ill but he was afraid that, if Hungary failed to stir Elizabeth, her wander-lust might soon beckon her once more. As yet, however, her physical frailty ruled out foreign travel.

She was well enough to accompany Francis Joseph back to Vienna in time to celebrate the Silver Jubilee of his accession. Exactly a month earlier, on 2 November, the World Exhibition in the Prater had closed its gates, after attracting seven million visitors rather than the twenty million anticipated by the optimists. Already it was clear that the final balance sheet would show a deficit of some fifteen million gulden (about three million dollars at that year's exchange rate). With this newest loss added to the financial embarrassment of Black Friday, it is hardly surprising if the mood of the Silver Jubilee celebrations was austerely chastened.

Nevertheless Vienna did at least acknowledge Francis Joseph's twenty-five years of political improvisation. The streets of the capital were decorated with bunting and discreetly illuminated. On the evening of 1 December the Emperor and his son drove around the Ringstrasse in an open victoria, with the Empress following in a closed carriage. A spotlight from a balcony in the Schwarzenberg Platz picked out the victoria as it crossed the square; the crowd could clearly see the Emperor and the Crown Prince acknowledging their cheers; but the Empress was hardly visible, no more than a graceful silhouette behind the frosty glass of a fiacre's window. Next day, the actual anniversary of the ceremony at Olmütz, the generals and their commander-in-chief exchanged compliments in the Hofburg, with Rudolf standing in uniform beside his father while Archduke Albrecht offered the congratulations of his brother officers. Momentarily, as in the first years of the reign, imperial majesty seemed once more an apotheosis of the army. In the evening, with Elizabeth beside him, Francis Joseph attended a gala performance of *The Taming of the Shrew* at the Stadttheater, where a company directed by Heinrich Laube had enjoyed great success that season. Critics and audience welcomed Laube's new production, but what impression this lively presentation of Shakespeare made on Francis Joseph remains unclear. Though he summoned Laube to the imperial box, he seems only to have managed a conventional 'It was very lovely; it has given me much pleasure'; ever since the architect of the Opera killed himself on hearing disparaging remarks about a building the Emperor thought too dumpy, Francis Joseph's public comments had remained cautiously muted. He did not send for the principal performers, nor even commend the star of the evening, but her time was to come. For the role of Kate was played by a fair-haired grocer's daughter from Baden whom Francis Joseph had never seen before. Her name was Katharina Schratt, and in later years she became the Emperor's warmest friend. In 1873, however, that was unthinkable; a blonde stage-idol of twenty, whose photograph brightened several shop windows along the Kartnerstrasse that December, had no place amid the solemn decor of the Hofburg.

The Empress herself still found the Hofburg oppressive, at least so long as she had to fulfil official engagements there, while her husband was in residence. Immediately after the jubilee celebrations she returned to Gödöllö; and it is hardly surprising if, as in the spring of 1870, the liberal Press wrote, with gentle reproof, of her strange desire to prefer the wintry charms of a Hungarian hunting lodge to the delights of the Austrian capital. The tone of the newspapers annoyed the Emperor (though they were far milder than the attacks on 'England's future king', on sale at London bookstalls in that same month). When journalists from an eminently respectable professional association in Vienna presented Francis Joseph with their jubilee congratulations, the Emperor pointedly emphasized that he considered the private lives of the imperial family a topic on which newspapers should neither comment nor speculate.

Had he in mind the immediate past or the immediate future? Early in the New Year – on 8 January 1874 – Francis Joseph became a grandfather. Princess Gisela's daughter was named Elizabeth after her grandmother, who at once left for Munich, remaining in Bavaria for a fortnight. The Empress was far from pleased at becoming a grandmother fifteen days after her thirty-sixth birthday; her failure, in the months before Christmas, to shake off the effects of gastric fever may well have come from a subconscious sense of dented vanity. 'Gisela's child is unusually ugly, but very lively – not a thing to choose between her and Gisela', Elizabeth wrote back to Rudolf, in Magyar, with a marked lack of maternal solicitude. Francis Joseph was more philosophical; 'Only 44 and already a grandfather!', he sighed, needlessly adding seven months to his age. But at the Court Ball on 5 February – at which the Empress looked 'radiant with youth and beauty' – he showed an active heartiness Vienna had not seen for many years.

Francis Joseph needed every moment of happy relaxation he could find in that winter. Domestic politics were especially perplexing. In Hungary there was a grumbling conflict with the subject nationalities, which was exacerbated by demands from the younger parliamentary deputies that Magyar should be the exclusive language in service on the kingdom's rapidly growing railway system. Francis Joseph instinctively sensed danger in these policies. Moreover, now that Deák had retired and Andrássy was serving in Vienna, he found it difficult to work in partnership with the political spokesmen in Buda-Pest.

He felt more personally involved in narrowly Austrian affairs. A general election in Cisleithania in the autumn of 1873 showed a slight swing to the so-called 'Progressives' and 'Viennese Radicals', but it was not enough to displace the predominantly Austro-German Liberal government, headed by Prince Auersperg. The Liberals followed the scrapping of the Concordat by a series of mildly anti-clerical reforms: a Religious Fund was levied on ecclesiastical property; the State asserted a right to intervene in the education and appointment of priests; and legal guarantees were given to churches and religious groups other than Roman Catholics. But Francis Joseph was unhappy at the draft 'Confessional Laws' promulgated on 21 January 1874. He had already told the council of ministers that he could only approve of absolutely essential changes in the relations of Church and State; care must be taken, he urged, to resist the temptation to placate extremist groups in parliament or among the journalists. He refused to approve a Bill which would have put monasteries and other religious houses under strict state control, and he encouraged the upper chamber to throw out proposals to facilitate 'mixed marriages' between Catholics and non-Catholics. When, in March 1874, Pius IX even warned the Emperor that, in permitting anti-clerical legislation, he was risking excommunication, Francis Joseph could rightly claim that he was promoting calm and dispassionate discussion of the new relationship between Church and State while also protecting traditional Catholicism against modern secular heresies. The German *Kulturkampf*, then being waged so vigorously in Berlin and the Rhineland, would find no echoes inside the Dual Monarchy.

Andrássy, as foreign minister, wished Francis Joseph to remain on good terms with Pius IX, for the papacy was an international institution. But he also sought collaboration with the Italians, who had occupied Rome in September 1870, making the Pope a virtual prisoner within the Vatican. This desire to placate both Romes was politically embarrassing. Courtesy required the acceptance and fulfilment of invitations given to the Emperor by foreign sovereigns during their visits to the World Exhibition; and among these invitations was one from Victor Emmanuel II. But Francis Joseph would not go to the Italian capital, for fear of offending Pius IX. Careful diplomacy delayed the Austrian return state visit until April 1875 and, by then, an alternative rendezvous to Rome had been found. It says much for Francis Joseph's spirit of magnanimity, that he agreed to become the King of Italy's guest in Venice, a city where he had twice been received as sovereign – though never so warmly as on this occasion.

More pressing than the need to please the ruler of Italy was an urgent gesture of reassurance to the Tsar, who mistrusted Austria-Hungary's Balkan policies. Accordingly for a fortnight in February 1874 Francis Joseph endured 'the shivering climate' of Russia. As well as political discussions with the Tsar's veteran Chancellor, Gorchakov, he was expected to attend a succession of lavish entertainments and banquets in St Petersburg, where Alexander II was, at the same time, host to his Danish and English relatives by marriage. Among the visiting guests was the much-maligned Prince of Wales, whose skill in stalking a bear and shooting it in the head the Emperor greatly envied. Four days later, on 18 February, Francis Joseph, with Andrássy beside him, emulated the achievement of 'Wales', a clear note of triumph running through the letter in which he let Elizabeth know of his success. The Prince of Wales's reports home showed great delight in a bear-hunt in which no less than eighty beasts were killed. But it is characteristic of Francis Joseph that he should have preferred the concept of single combat involved in a bear hunt to the mass slaughters to which the Prince and so many owners of Europe's great estates were accustomed.

While Francis Joseph was in Russia the Empress stayed at the Hofburg, partly to counter a mood of resentment that the imperial family had deserted the capital during *Fasching*. It was then that she participated in a well-authenticated episode which reads like a hack's libretto for a sadly unoriginal operetta. On the last day of carnival – as it happened, the night before her husband's bear hunt – Elizabeth went in disguise to the masked ball at the Musikverein, accompanied by Ida Ferenczy who, by the simple expedient of tapping a good-looking man on the shoulder, found for her an agreeable companion. Fritz Pascher was an aspiring civil servant, ten years junior to the Empress. So sure of herself was Elizabeth that, claiming to be a visitor to Vienna, she quizzed the man on the feelings of the people towards Court life in general and their Emperor and Empress in particular, receiving from him the most diplomatic responses. With incredible naiveté, Elizabeth convinced herself that Fritz Pascher did not know her identity and would continue to think of her romantically as his lost yellow domino from the masked ball. She even sent letters to him, signed 'Gabrielle' and allegedly written in London. These letters she entrusted to her sister Marie, the exiled Queen of Naples, who had leased a house in England. Queen Marie, entering into the spirit of the game, arranged for replies sent by Herr Pascher to the General Post Office in London to be collected on her behalf and duly posted them back to 'Gabrielle' in Vienna.

Her secret was well kept. Newspaper proprietors would not have wished their reporters to pry behind the masks at a Vienna ball and Pascher was a perfectly honourable man who made no attempt to exploit 'Gabrielle's' folly. He kept the letters, not making them public until shortly before his death, some sixty years later. For the Empress the evening was an innocent diversion which she did not forget. Her creative mind returned to the masked ball when she was writing sentimental verses some twelve years later, and she told her younger daughter about her brief encounter. Francis Joseph, however, knew nothing of it.

The escapade was a symptom of Elizabeth's mounting restlessness.

Soon after Francis Joseph's return from Russia she left for Bavaria and completed arrangements to follow her sister Marie to England. Archduchess Marie Valerie, by now aged six, was a frail child, suffering from a bronchial weakness, and Elizabeth told Francis Joseph that she needed a holiday by the sea, somewhere with the sun shining but the heat not too intense for the child's comfort. As usual, he allowed Elizabeth to follow her own wishes. She therefore asked Beust, who was serving as ambassador in London, to find a suitable home for a six week summer visit; and on 2 August 1874 the 'Countess von Hohenembs' and her daughter reached Steephill Castle, Ventnor.

The mock-Gothic castle, high above Ventnor's terraced seafront, was in many ways ideal for a summer holiday. For an Empress seeking seclusion, Ventnor had one great disadvantage, however: within hours of her arrival, she was visited by Queen Victoria who was in residence at Osborne, ten miles away. To the amazement of the Queen's Household, Elizabeth subsequently twice declined a royal invitation to dine at Osborne: her health was too poor, it seemed. This unaccustomed rebuff did not incline Victoria to look with particular sympathy on Andrássy's attempts to strengthen Austro-Hungarian contacts with Great Britain. Nor was the Queen mollified by news that the Empress's health was so much better that she felt able to spend the fourth week of August at White Lodge, Richmond, seeing London as a guest of the Duke and Duchess of Teck. By the time Elizabeth returned to Steephill, Queen Victoria had gone to Balmoral. But the Empress was sure that she knew a way of improving Anglo-Austrian relations: 'What a pity you cannot come!', she wrote to her husband, 'After these manoeuvres – of which I thank you for the list of details – you could actually take a fortnight off, see London, make a hurried excursion up to Scotland to visit the Queen, and then hunt a little in the neighbourhood of London. There are good horses for us here and everything to go with them, so it would be a pity not to make use of them'.

It is easy to scoff at the Empress's suggestion. Like most royalty, her husband's itinerary was worked out months in advance: why should he throw over a carefully prepared programme to canter beside Elizabeth in Rotten Row or follow her to Rutland and chivvy foxes from their coverts in the wolds? Yet the idea was not so preposterous as it seems. As a young sovereign, betrothed to a bewitching cousin, he had at times broken loose, hurrying from Warsaw to see her in Bavaria. She knew that the army manoeuvres were to be held around Brandeis in Bohemia during the second week of September and he had no pressing commitments for the remainder of the month. Moreover he had, from time to time, shown some interest in making a visit to England, a project first broached before his accession, during the Year of Revolutions. Elizabeth closed her letter with gentle irony: 'Do think it over for a day or two before, with your usual tendency to play safe, you say "No"'.

Francis Joseph never came to England. No persuasive prompting from Sisi helped him shake off the harness of state. After visiting the Bohemian capital and attending the army manoeuvres he had sporting trips of his own arranged at home, he explained. Elizabeth did not arrive back in Austria until the autumn leaves had fallen, having lingered in Bavaria on the way home. She enjoyed this first contact with English life and particularly with the horsemen of the Midland shires; and she was determined to return. There was no diminution of affection between husband and wife; no intentional separation; only the gradual drifting apart of a wanderer and a self-fettered slave.

While the Empress was riding with the hounds at Belvoir, her husband had been welcomed to Prague, more warmly than in many years. 'God Bring Him Luck' ran the inscription in Czech across a triumphal arch erected outside the railway station and decorated with garlands of flowers and rich green foliage; and there were elaborate decorations, too, down the long length of the former horse-market, which would soon become socially upgraded as Wenceslas Square. He was, of course, not the only Emperor in the city. Germans and Czechs still held Emperor Ferdinand in high regard and, after a quarter of a century, were accustomed to his presence in the Hradčany. In the following April they put out the flags once more for Ferdinand's 82nd birthday. But it was for the last time. Ferdinand died ten weeks later – on 29 June 1875 – and his body was brought back to Vienna for burial in the vault beneath the Kapuzinerkirche. Empress Maria Anna lived on in Prague, surviving her husband by nine years.

In one respect Emperor Ferdinand's death changed the lives of both Francis Joseph and Elizabeth. When he abdicated in 1848 Ferdinand had retained his personal funds, making him the wealthiest member of the dynasty. After legacies providing for the widowed Maria Anna, the residue of Ferdinand's great fortune was left to Francis Joseph who suddenly found himself as rich as any ruler in Europe. Ferdinand's financial advisers had been too shrewd to play the stock market during the boom years and his money was left untouched by the *Krach* and the subsequent depression. The size of his inheritance took Francis Joseph by surprise: 'From now I am a rich man', he remarked to his military adjutant: no personal financial worries need trouble him any more, whatever the mood of parliament might be.

Yet the habits of forty years of cautious spending died slowly. Unlike his brothers Maximilian and Ludwig Victor, he was by nature parsimonious. In the whole of his life there is not a single occasion when Francis Joseph might be accused of personal extravagance. He kept a good cellar and enjoyed good (mild) cigars; he gave his patronage to artists of whom he approved; and he made certain that the best horses were bought for his stables and the best equipment for days when he would go stalking in the mountains. But, apart from the formal banquets, his meals were frugal, he spent his working days wearing the service uniform of an infantry lieutenant, and his palaces remained sparsely furnished. In the Hofburg he slept on an iron bedstead with a camelskin cover, and he used pitchers and bowls for the cold water douche with which he began each morning. In Schönbrunn there was an imperial bedroom with solid jacaranda-wood twin beds and with wall coverings and curtains of blue Lyonnaise silk, first hung in the year of his marriage and not replaced. Although the palace was said to include 1441 rooms and 139 kitchens, Francis Joseph never had a bathroom installed in the imperial apartments at Schönbrunn; he frowned on these luxurious modern inventions.

He was not, however, personally mean. Within days of inheriting this great wealth, he tripled the annual allowance of 100,000 florins assigned to the Empress since their marriage. At the same time he gave her a capital sum of two million florins, which some of the best bankers in central Europe invested wisely for her, mainly in the more profitable railway projects and Danube Steamship Company. He showed, too, a great indulgence towards her passion for building villas of her own and for purchasing the finest thoroughbreds for her to ride to hounds. She never doubted his personal devotion to her. Whether such open-handed generosity made for contented domesticity is open to question. During the ten years after he inherited Ferdinand's fortune Francis Joseph found his leisure hours increasingly spent in solitude and quiet seclusion. The glow of family life chilled rapidly. In the Austrian provinces his subjects began to speak respectfully of 'the old Emperor' while he was still in his fifties.

Chapter 13

THE HERZEGOVINA AND
BOSNIA

During the first twenty-five years of his reign Francis Joseph came to know almost every province of his Empire. He possessed palaces or official residences in Lower Austria, Hungary, the Tyrol, Salzburg and Bohemia as well as villas at Ischl and outside Trieste. On several occasions he visited Istria, Carinthia, Carniola, Croatia and Moravia; and he travelled to Galicia, Silesia and Transylvania, too. But there remained one province which he had seen only from the sea, a distant blur on a hazy horizon. The Dalmatian coastal strip from north of Zadar down to Kotor, a region long dependent upon the Venetian Republic, had been assigned to the Austrian Empire by the peace settlement after the Napoleonic Wars but was never visited by a reigning Emperor. Early in March 1875 General Rodić, the Governor of Dalmatia, formally invited Francis Joseph to make an extensive tour of the province. It was decided that, after his April meeting with Victor Emmanuel II in Venice, he would spend a month visiting every important town on the coast and several offshore islands. 'Dann brennts!' ('Then there'll be a blaze!'), commented General Anton Mollinary, the army commander in Zagreb, when Rodić told him of the Emperor's plans. Rodić smiled knowingly, and said nothing.

Neither general anticipated trouble in Dalmatia itself. There was a strong movement in the province for union with Croatia rather than for continued government directly from Vienna, but it was unlikely to provoke unrest. Uppermost in Mollinary's mind was the political confusion across the Dalmatian frontier, in the Ottoman provinces of Herzegovina and Bosnia. They were separated from the coastal strip by the Dinaric Alps, a limestone karst curtain which virtually isolated the interior from the Adriatic. Yet, though both provinces acknowledged the Sultan's distant sovereignty and were predominantly Islamic in culture, the people were racially southern Slav, kinsfolk of the Orthodox Serbs and Catholic Croats. Indeed, it was said the purest form of Serbo-Croat language was spoken around Mostar, the 'thoroughly Turkish' capital of Herzegovina.

The twin provinces shared a legacy of history as bleak as the mountain ranges which dominated this north-western extremity of the Balkans. They were steeped in legends of heroism and treachery from a bloody past. Before the Sultan's armies overran Bosnia in the summer of 1463 the region had known two centuries of feudal independence; it was the homeland of a schismatic church which, though technically Catholic, owed little allegiance to Rome. Attempts by the Catholic soldiery of mediaeval Hungary to march southwards and stamp out such eccentric beliefs provoked strong resistance and began a conflict which ultimately weakened Bosnia's opposition to the coming of Islam. In many instances the landowners helped the Ottomans, finding that if they accepted Islam they were able to hold on to their estates and feudal privileges. The peasantry were severely taxed and, until 1676, they had to surrender a fixed tribute of boy slaves to serve as infantrymen in the Janissary corps, but they were allowed to retain Christian beliefs, with their religious practices determined by the Serbian Orthodox Church.

To the south-west of Bosnia, an even more barren region, originally known as Hum, served in the fifteenth century as an outpost of Catholic Christendom in the struggle against the invaders. In 1448 the Holy Roman Emperor Frederick III, wishing to stiffen Christian resistance to the Muslim invaders, bestowed a new title on the feudal master of Hum, creating the tough warlord Stephen Vukčić 'Duke of St Sava'. It became natural to refer to these lands as 'the Duchy' – in German, *Das Herzogtum* – a term corrupted into 'the Herzegovina'. It was a German-Slavonic hybrid word, with the definite article soon falling out of common usage. The name has survived even though Vukčić's successors wielded weaker swords than the proto-duke and within forty years Herzegovina was, like Bosnia, overrun by the Sultan's armies. In Herzegovina, too, the Orthodox Church flourished among the peasantry, but there was also considerable Catholic influence, kept alive by the Franciscans who, soon after the fall of Constantinople, had received a charter from Mehmed II giving them a privileged status in the western Balkans.

For four centuries, the twin provinces of Bosnia-Herzegovina formed the north-western frontier of the Ottoman Empire, isolated from the Mediterranean world and yet far enough from Constantinople to show a contemptuous indifference to the reforms of successive Sultans. Real power in the provinces was long exercised by a *kapetane* of forty-eight native Bosnian beys; they still wielded a capricious authority during the first year of Francis Joseph's reign. Not until March 1850 were they finally defeated by an Ottoman army, after a three day battle on the shores of Lake Jezero. Even then conditions in the provinces remained anarchic. Until 1852 the Sultan's governors had sought to rule Bosnia from their fortress at Travnik, while the beys were in control of a town some 60 miles to the south, originally called 'Bosna Sarayi' (Bosnian Palace), a name swiftly modified in general usage to Sarajevo. Access northwards down the river Bosna to the Pannonian plains and southwards along the valley of the river Neretva to Mostar and the Adriatic made Sarajevo a more important city, politically and commercially, than Travnik or any other town in the western Balkans.

At Francis Joseph's accession neither Herzegovina nor Bosnia were provinces a neighbour might covet. Their economic potential was limited. Even in the spacious valleys of northern Bosnia, opening out on to the plains, farming methods remained backward and unrewarding. In several mountainous districts there were rich mineral deposits, with mines partially developed by the Turks. Only heavy investment and skilled engineering could enable these resources to be exploited; and it was questionable whether the yield would justify the expenditure. Yet as early as 1854 the war ministry in Vienna prepared detailed plans for the seizure of Bosnia-Herzegovina; two years later Radetzky urged Francis Joseph to put these plans into operation. It was not that the Austrian generals wished to see the provinces annexed for their own sake; their concern was to protect Dalmatia by securing a land route to safeguard garrisons holding Zadar, Sibenik, Split, Dubrovnik and Kotor in case of a blockade by sea.

A renewed plea for action was made a few years later, when Admiral Tegetthoff urged the Emperor to absorb the hinterland of Dalmatia. His reasoning differed from that of the generals. After his victory at Lissa Tegetthoff discounted the likelihood of an enemy blockade; he saw the Dalmatian anchorages as outlying naval stations for an Austrian fleet sailing into the Mediterranean, and he wanted improved overland communication between the heart of the Monarchy and the fine harbours on the eastern side of the Adriatic. In 1869 General Beck, as head of the Emperor's military chancellery, returned to the familiar theme in a memorandum which stressed yet another reason for annexing the provinces: the need to prevent their falling into the hands of the two Southern Slav principalities, Serbia and Montenegro, should the Ottoman Empire collapse. He was afraid the principalities might become Russian puppets, easily manipulated in Great Power politics to serve the interests of the Tsars. Beck would not be content with Bosnia-Herzegovina: he wanted the annexation to extend eastwards so as to include the Sanjak of Novibazar, a corridor of land separating Serbia from Montenegro. The Sanjak would, he believed, provide a natural route for the construction of a railway down to Salonika, the great Macedonian port on the Aegean Sea.

With these frequent pleas for action reaching him from military leaders whose views he respected, it is surprising that Francis Joseph held back for so long. At the root of his hesitancy lay deep uncertainty over the Southern Slav problem. In 1848–49 Jellaçić, and many of his compatriots in Habsburg service, had believed in an 'Illyrian' kingdom within the Monarchy, which would include Croatia, Dalmatia and the Serb areas of southern Hungary. Ideas had changed during the past thirty years. There were still 'Illyrians', and some intemperate 'Greater Croatia' fanatics followed Ante Starcević; but in 1861 a member of the *Sabor* – the Croatian Diet – had used a new corporate term to describe his kinsfolk; he had spoken of the 'Yugoslavs' (South Slavs), and by the end of the decade the Yugoslav ideal was in the ascendant.

Throughout the third quarter of the century the Southern Slav cause was vigorously championed by an outstanding churchman. Joseph Strossmayer was Bishop of Djakovo from 1849 until his death fifty-six years later and, in western Europe, won the respect of liberals like Gladstone and Lord Acton for his opposition to papal pretensions at the Vatican Council. But in south-eastern Europe Strossmayer's reputation rested on his devotion to the Southern Slav ideal; he founded a Yugoslav Academy at Zagreb in 1867 and a university in the same city seven years later. The Bishop's concept of Yugoslav union embraced, not only the south-eastern provinces of the Habsburg Monarchy and the principalities of Serbia and Montenegro, but the whole of Ottoman Bulgaria as well. He ignored the divisions separating Catholic Croats and Slovenes from Orthodox Serbs, Montenegrins and Bulgars – a distinction, not simply of religious traditions, but even of alphabet and orthography. Although Francis Joseph respected Strossmayer's learning, he remained puzzled by the affiliations of a movement which stressed what was common to Slavs both inside and outside the Monarchy. 'But is he a patriot for me?', Emperor Francis once asked, on hearing a certain Austrian praised as a 'good patriot'. Similar nagging thoughts seem to have troubled Francis's grandson as he observed Strossmayer's cultural activities.

Nor was Francis Joseph alone in these doubts. Strossmayer commanded a great following in Croatia itself, among the Franciscans of Herzegovina, and throughout much of Dalmatia, though not within the influential Italian trading communities represented in the Dalmatian Landtag. On the other hand, his Catholicism made Strossmayer's Yugoslav ideal suspect to successive princes in Serbia and Montenegro and to Bulgarian national leaders who looked for inspiration to a Moscow Slavonic Benevolent Committee established under the Tsar's patronage. The greatest hostility towards Strossmayer's Yugoslav ambitions came from Buda-Pest. After inducing the *Sabor* to approve the *Nagodba* (the Hungaro-Croatian political Compromise of 1868), no Magyar spokesmen would accept any policies which might increase the number of Slavs owing direct allegiance to Francis Joseph as sovereign, for if there were more Slavs brought into the Monarchy the delicate balance between the two master peoples – German-Austrians and Hungarians – would suffer. Andrássy agreed with this sentiment; but it did not prevent his authorizing expenditure of funds to promote Strossmayer's propaganda activities within Bosnia-Herzegovina – the building of Catholic churches and schools would counter the influence of Holy Moscow and the Orthodox priesthood. Grudgingly Andrássy recognized that, if forced to choose between political campaigners, he preferred Yugoslavs to Panslavs.

These nice distinctions were difficult for Francis Joseph to comprehend. When General Rodić had joined Beck in urging the Emperor to make a tour of inspection, Andrássy as usual objected. He did not, however, press the point. 'The Dalmatian trip is a Cisleithanian affair with which I have nothing to do', he remarked to the German ambassador, a shade too ingenuously. Although Andrássy might have been uneasy, he recognized that conditions for such a visit were more favourable than in earlier years. For, by 1875, there could be no doubt that his careful diplomacy had improved Austria-Hungary's standing with the Great Powers and her immediate neighbours. On 6 June 1873 a treaty signed by Francis Joseph and Tsar Alexander II – generally known as the 'Convention of Schönbrunn' – pledged the two Emperors to prior consultation over 'any question on which their interests disagreed'; and four months later the German Emperor, William I, also signed this Convention, thus creating a loosely knit 'League of the Three Emperors'. There was, moreover, closer contact than during the Beust era with both Great Britain and Italy. Finally, in 1868 Andrássy had planted in Belgrade a trusted Magyar agent – Count Benjamin Kállay – who, during the following seven years, secured such influence over Prince Milan Obrenović that by 1875 his political opponents in Serbia were convinced the young prince was in Habsburg pay. If Mollinary was right in suspecting that Francis Joseph's tour of Dalmatia would start 'a blaze', then Andrássy might legitimately feel he had taken every precaution to dampen the tinder and prevent the flames from firing the Balkans as a whole.

Kállay also kept Andrássy informed over the general state of affairs in Bosnia: the province 'is in a state of latent rebellion', he reported as late as the third week in February 1875. There were grievances over agrarian conditions and the harsh incidence of taxation; the discontent was fed by secret societies, backed by the Serbian 'liberal' politicians or by Russian agitators or, especially in Herzegovina, by the Montenegrins. Armed defiance of Ottoman officialdom was traditional in the mountains: 'Blessed is the rifle fired for national freedom' ran a ballad created in

Herzegovina in that year of revolt. It would have been as well to keep the Emperor away from a region where even the most harmless gestures were accorded a special significance. But, like Andrássy, Kállay realized that once Governor-General Rodić had formally invited his sovereign to Dalmatia, nothing could persuade Francis Joseph not to see for himself the southern outposts of the Empire.

The Dalmatian visit marked a historic turning-point in Habsburg policy, with more lasting effects than Kállay, Rodić or Mollinary anticipated. For the first twenty years of his reign Francis Joseph had looked, first and foremost, to Germany and Italy, like Metternich before him. There then followed a brief period, starting with his journey to the East, when the Emperor remained unsure of Austria's true mission. Finally, for the last forty years of his reign he looked determinedly to the East, partly across the Carpathians and towards the mouth of the Danube, but even more to the Balkans and, beyond the mountain ranges, to the two largest Ottoman cities in Europe, Salonika and Constantinople. That last phase dates from 10 April 1875, when Francis Joseph landed from the warship *Miramare* at Zadar and was received by the civil and military dignitaries of his Dalmatian lands.

From the outset the visit attracted the attention of the press, both in Vienna and abroad. The Emperor's letters home gave detailed accounts of welcoming parties, with children 'of Valerie's age' presenting bouquets of flowers beneath triumphal arches in Sibenik or Split and in far smaller towns and villages. As usual Francis Joseph enjoyed his days at sea and what was, in effect, a round of imperial sightseeing, notably at Diocletian's palace. There is no suggestion, in the account of his movements which he sent regularly to Elizabeth, that he was aware of the visit's political implications. His letters describe how he went inland from Split to Imotski, close to the Ottoman frontier; there he received in audience a mixed group of 'Turks' and Franciscans in 'blue pantaloons'; 'A very odd sight', he observed. Two days later he followed the river Neretva from its mouth up to Metković and to 'the border on the road to Mostar'. Here, too, he received a warm welcome. Did he realize how sensitive were conditions in this frontier zone?

By 28 April, when he reached Dubrovnik, he must have sensed the political tension. For there were Franciscans in Dubrovnik in close contact with their brethren in Herzegovina: they did not disguise their hopes that, if Austria-Hungary absorbed the twin provinces, the Emperor would protect the Christian religion and end an allegedly corrupt system of government. 'The local demonstration ... appeared to me ... thoroughly Slavish', reported the British consul, 'the imperial visit having been, so to speak, utilized to express the popular native feeling of Pan-Slavism supreme in these parts'. Reports reaching Constantinople of Francis Joseph's triumphal progress so alarmed the Sultan that he ordered his *vali* (governor) in Bosnia, Dervis Pasha, to travel down to the coast and greet the Emperor. Dervis was accorded an audience but had little to say for himself; it was a cold, formal occasion.

Far livelier were the Emperor's two visits – by land and by sea – to the Boka Kotorska (Gulf of Cattaro). He received, so he told Elizabeth, 'a great many deputations'; and on 3 May the thirty-three year old Prince Nicholas of Montenegro, a ruler 'of purest Serbian blood' who enjoyed the confidence of the Herzegovinian clans, came down the mountain paths from his capital at Cetinje to talk to Francis Joseph about the plight of his kinsfolk across the Ottoman frontier. The two men had already met in Vienna, when the Prince was a guest at the World Exhibition. But this time he brought with him 'a large following of military chieftains, senators and adjutants'. What aroused particular interest abroad on this occasion was the presence beside Prince Nicholas of his father-in-law, the colourful Petar Vuković, a formidable warlord hand-in-glove with the most rebellious Herzegovinian clansmen. Francis Joseph told Elizabeth he was glad to find Prince Nicholas 'an excellent man ... very well disposed' towards Austria. Of Petar Vuković the Emperor said nothing; but he showed his goodwill towards the Montenegrins by riding up the slopes of Mount Lovcen and crossing the frontier into Prince Nicholas's eyrie.

After thirty-three days in Dalmatia Francis Joseph arrived back in Vienna in mid-May. His tour of inspection clarified his mind. He was impressed by what he had seen of the Venetian legacy along the Adriatic coast and he understood the advantages of securing the mountainous hinterland. Moreover he was by no means averse to acquiring new provinces for the Empire, compensation for his lost Italian possessions. Mollinary was told to hold himself in readiness to command an army of occupation should Bosnia-Herzegovina appear to be slipping from the Sultan's shaky grasp.

A month after the Emperor's return one of the Franciscans who had crossed the frontier to acclaim him at Metković was murdered, allegedly with Dervis Pasha's compliance. The clan leaders at Nevesinje, barely 20 miles from the frontier districts so recently visited by the Emperor, rose in revolt; they knew they could count on supplies from Prince Nicholas, brought in by sea at Utorina on the Boka Kotorska, an anchorage serviced by the Montenegrins which the Austrians made no attempt to close. By the third week in July the Herzegovinian clansmen were raiding Muslim villages and attacking Muslim caravans wending their way along the Neretva valley to Mostar. The 'blaze' was well alight. Rodić confidently recommended rapid intervention so as to secure Bosnia and Herzegovina for the Monarchy, while in Zagreb Mollinary put the final touches to his plans. But from Vienna there came no order to occupy the provinces.

Francis Joseph habitually listened to the views of those around him, though he might frequently ignore them. So long as he was in Dalmatia he had been in the company of officers who were eager for decisive action in the Balkans. Mollinary, a Croat by origin, and Rodić, a Dalmatian Slav, were soldiers who tended to rattle their sabres precipitately at wild rumours from across the Ottoman frontier. By contrast, in Vienna, Francis Joseph could rely on sound advice from a foreign minister who saw the Herzegovinian revolt in a wider context. He began to have second – or, more accurately, third – thoughts. Emperor and minister were agreed on the need to avoid a general war. Andrássy studied reports of what had happened in the Neretva valley, assessed the impact of the revolt on the Monarchy's relations with Russia and Germany, and sensed danger. Even so, he did not foresee a diplomatic crisis which would pre-occupy Europe's chancelleries for more than four years.

At times during that long period of tension Andrássy's patience was severely taxed. The first proposal he received from the Russian Chancellor dismayed him, for Gorchakov wished to establish an autonomous Bosnia-Herzegovina. To Andrássy this solution seemed an invitation to per-petuate anarchy, with Muslim, Catholic and Orthodox sects ravaging provinces which no central government could hope to control. By the end of the year, however, he had regained the diplomatic initiative: Gorchakov backed the 'Andrássy Note', a series of proposed reforms in the admin-istration of Bosnia-Herzegovina which was circulated to the Great Powers on 30 December 1875 and nominally accepted by the Ottoman authorities six weeks later. But, with the coming of spring, the crisis worsened. On 2 May 1876 a new revolt broke out in several Bulgarian villages deep in the Rhodope Mountains. The insurgents committed atrocities which were equalled or surpassed by Ottoman militia (*basçi bozuka*) anxious to suppress Panslavism in a region far nearer to Constantinople than the troubled valleys of Bosnia. Newspaper denouncement of the activities of the *basçi bozuka* was to shock British (and American) opinion during the fourth week of June, but before the ghastly reports appeared in print there had been a palace revolution in Constantinople, with Sultan Abdulaziz deposed and Turkish liberals demanding the grant of a constitution. Serbia and Montenegro, seeking to exploit the embarrassment of the new Sultan's government, declared war on the Ottoman Empire in the first days of July 1876. At this point it seemed essential for the League of the Three Emperors to co-ordinate policy if the war was to remain localised. Francis Joseph sent Archduke Albrecht to Berlin for talks with William I and Bismarck, while the Tsar and his Chancellor also travelled to the German capital, and Gorchakov asked urgently for a meeting with the other member of the League. Accordingly Francis Joseph invited the Tsar to meet him in Bohemia during his circuitous journey home from Berlin.

On the morning of 8 July Francis Joseph greeted Alexander II and the Tsarevich on the railway platform at Bohmisch-Leipa, some 80 miles north of Prague. It was a hurried conference, Andrássy plying Gorchakov with questions during the five mile coach drive to the imperial chateau of Reichstadt. To the relief of both Francis Joseph and his minister, it was clear that neither the Tsar nor his Chancellor sought a Russo-Turkish war. The so-called 'Reichstadt Agreement', concluded later that day, guaranteed that if the Ottoman armies defeated the Serbs and Montenegrins, Austria-Hungary and Russia would ensure that there would be no changes made in the existing boundaries. Should Serbia and Montenegro force the Sultan to sue for peace, the Ottomans would be virtually expelled from Europe. There were some discrepancies between the Austro-Hungarian and Russian versions of the Reichstadt Agreement, particularly over the precise line to be followed by new Balkan frontiers if Turkey were defeated, but the general pattern was clear enough: Russia would recover southern Bessarabia (modern Moldova) and Austria-Hungary would annex Bosnia; Greece would gain Thessaly and Crete; Serbia and Montenegro would expand so as to meet along a common frontier in the Sanjak of Novibazar; Bulgaria and Albania would receive autonomy. According to Andrássy's notes, Austria-Hungary would also acquire Herzegovina. To his great satisfaction, he thought he had successfully ruled out the possibility of a large Slavonic state in the Balkans – as, indeed, Gorchakov warned the Serbian minister in St Petersburg a fortnight later. Francis Joseph, too, was pleased with the Reichstadt Agreement, believing it would help him acquire the twin provinces without risking war with Russia. An amicable meeting with William I at Salzburg in August ensured that League diplomacy remained in concert.

No one at Reichstadt or Salzburg anticipated that the Serbs and Montenegrins would crumble so soon. Once the Ottoman commanders gave up playing at politics and began a series of counter-attacks, the would-be invaders fell back rapidly. By the end of October the Russians were seriously considering intervention in the Balkans in order to save their Orthodox brethren from Ottoman retribution, and St Petersburg peremptorily ordered the Turks to agree to an armistice with Serbia. So far, Alexander II had carefully kept Francis Joseph informed of each step he was contemplating. But over the winter of 1876–77 the safeguards of the Reichstadt Agreement were increasingly called in question. More and more the Tsar was listening to influential Panslavs, notably General

Nikolai Ignatiev, his ambassador in Constantinople. 'I much desire that we shall reach a general agreement', Alexander II publicly announced in Moscow as a Great Power conference on Ottoman reform was about to open at Constantinople: but he added, 'If this is not possible ... then I firmly intend to act independently ... and may God help us to fulfil our sacred mission'. By Christmas a Russo-Turkish war seemed imminent, although Francis Joseph and Andrássy believed, perfectly correctly, that the Tsar preferred a peaceful settlement of the Eastern Question.

In Hungary there was strong support for the Turks. A judiciously timed restoration of trophies looted from the famous royal library of Matthew Corvinus when the Ottoman armies first advanced across the Danubian plains strengthened the Turcophile inclination of the people during the Eastern Crisis; and there was, too, a fiercely anti-Russian mood seeking 'a war to revenge Vilagos' (as Beck warned Francis Joseph). By contrast, military circles in Vienna favoured close co-operation with St Petersburg: for them the Reichstadt Agreement – a bilateral understanding to which Germany was never invited to subscribe – promised a reversion to a more traditional form of conservative diplomacy. General Beck argued in favour of close co-operation with Russia. For him step-by-step bargaining over complementary expansion in the western and eastern Balkans would secure for Austria-Hungary control over the land-route to Salonika.

A joint memorandum, drawn up by Archduke Albrecht and General Beck, was presented to Francis Joseph in November 1876. It was a strong plea to avoid conflict with Russia: Napoleon's 1812 campaign had shown that there could be no swift decision in the East because of the size of the Tsar's Empire and its reserves of manpower. 'A well-developed industrial state, dependent on universal military conscription, cannot accept the strain of long wars ... There Russia enjoys an advantage over every other Power. Least of all, therefore, should Russia's nearest neighbour, half-encircled Austria-Hungary be among the first to take the field for she cannot, like the Western Powers, withdraw from a war when she thinks fit. Rather she should preserve her full strength to the end, and then the decision will lie in her hands'. This advice – reminiscent of Austrian policy in 1813 and again in 1855 – carried considerable weight with the Emperor and, in essentials, was close to Andrássy's reasoning even though, as a Magyar, the foreign minister was distrusted by both Albrecht and Beck. In January and March 1877 further secret agreements – the Budapest Conventions – provided for Austro-Hungarian benevolent neutrality should Russia be forced into war with the Ottoman Empire; the Tsar agreed that Francis Joseph would have a free hand in dealing with Bosnia-Herzegovina and that, in any re-drawing of Balkan frontiers, 'the establishment of a great compact State, Slav or otherwise, is out of the question'.

Francis Joseph was accustomed to evaluating differing opinions on foreign affairs presented to him in memoranda from his ministers or around the council table. He knew, too, that policy would invariably be criticized in the more radical newspapers. But during the Eastern Crisis he was disturbed by a new development. The German liberals in the lower house of the Reichsrat wished to ensure that parliament was consulted over the shaping of policies which might determine issues of peace or war. In October 1876 no less than 112 deputies signed a demand for a debate on foreign affairs. The Emperor was outraged. The Austrian government had no constitutional right to be consulted over such matters, let alone the deputies in parliament. Foreign policy was the Emperor's prerogative. When, at the height of the crisis, an Austrian minister tactfully explained to his sovereign that the German liberals were uneasy over aspects of Andrássy's policy, he received a sharp rebuff: 'You are constantly talking of Andrássy's policy. It is *my* policy; do not forget it'. There was no debate on the Eastern Crisis in either chamber of the Reichsrat.

Sultan Abdulhamid II, who succeeded his brother Murad at the end of August 1876, refused to bow to foreign pressure and accept a programme of reforms imposed by the European Great Powers. With the coming of spring in 1877 Tsar Alexander II was resigned to the inevitability of a conflict which Ignatiev and the Panslavs had sought to thrust upon him for so long. On 24 April 1877 Russia declared war on the Ottoman Empire and the Tsar ordered his armies to march southwards 'for Orthodoxy and Slavdom'. Towards neither of these causes could his brother sovereign in Vienna feel the slightest sympathy. For the remainder of the year, however, Francis Joseph received reassuring messages from St Petersburg. In the last week of July, when Russia's armies were checked by the stubborn Ottoman defence of Plevna, the Tsar specifically emphasized his intention to observe the Reichstadt Agreement. There would be no permanent military occupation of Bulgaria, Alexander declared, and no encouragement in the Balkan lands of any dangerous 'democratic' movements.

Once the fortunes of war changed, a different note came into the exchanges between St Petersburg and Vienna. In the second week of December, when the last resistance of Plevna was finally broken, the Tsar's messages began to sound ominous. The Serbs, who re-entered the war in that week, would need some territorial reward in northern Bosnia, he claimed; and a Russian army would have to police Bulgaria for at least two years. A month later Francis Joseph, while acknowledging that the

Ottoman Empire had not completely disintegrated and that he could not therefore expect implementation of the precise terms discussed at Reichstadt, hoped that the basic principles behind the agreement and the Budapest Conventions would be accepted. Austria-Hungary was, he said plainly, opposed to any occupation of Bulgaria; and if Russia retained newly liberated southern Bessarabia, the Monarchy would expect to absorb Bosnia.

On 15 January 1878, even before Alexander could reply to this message, Francis Joseph presided over a gloomy conference of ministers in Vienna. The news from the theatre of war was disturbing. The Russians were already in Sofia and advancing on Adrianople; it seemed likely they would be at the gates of Constantinople by the end of the month. Andrássy thought some token military demonstration should be made in order to assert the prestige of the Dual Monarchy, but he found Archduke Albrecht hostile to any anti-Russian move. A further ministerial conference, on 24 February, considered the Tsar's lack of positive response to the Emperor's message. War, it was decided, was out of the question: to risk a protracted campaign was to invite state bankruptcy; even brief operations in the Balkans would require additional funds; nobody could predict the consequences of challenging an Empire with such a lengthy shared frontier as Russia. Only peaceful diplomacy could benefit Austria-Hungary.

As early as 28 January Andrássy wrote to Károlyi, the ambassador in Berlin, setting out the stark alternative in Austro-Russian relations of 'conflict or conference'. Gorchakov, as well as Bismarck, also favoured a settlement of the Eastern Question agreeable to Europe as a whole, and throughout February there was talk among the diplomats of a possible conference, with Baden-Baden as a likely venue. Briefly it seemed possible that Francis Joseph would host a second Congress of Vienna, but in early March it was finally settled that the Powers would meet in Berlin, although the mediatory prestige of summoning the Congress was accorded by Bismarck to Andrássy. Even so, when the invitations went out from Vienna on 6 March, it was questionable whether the other Powers would accept them and it seemed highly improbable that any Congress could stitch together a lasting treaty. Too many governments had objectives of their own in the Ottoman lands to make the attainment of diplomatic compromise easy.

Fortunately for Andrássy the terms of the Russo-Turkish peace treaty signed at San Stefano on 3 March became common knowledge to the European chancelleries by the middle of the month and proved generally unacceptable. Russian field headquarters had not even referred back to the foreign ministry the details of the conditions foisted upon the Sultan's representatives. On paper San Stefano was a triumph for General Ignatiev, the apotheosis of Panslavism; but it ran completely counter to the Reich-stadt Agreement and all the subsequent exchanges between Alexander II and Francis Joseph. A big, satellite Bulgaria encroached on the western Balkans and the probable railway route to Salonika; no territorial com-pensation was offered to Austria-Hungary. In St Petersburg more mod-erate counsellors than Ignatiev realized the folly of San Stefano and were prepared to use the terms of the treaty as bargaining counters for a wiser settlement. Andrássy took heart. With great difficulty in the third week of March he persuaded the Austro-Hungarian Delegations to approve a vote of credit of 60 million florins without indicating in advance whether he intended to use it for a war against Russia or for the occupation of Bosnia-Herzegovina. By the end of the month he was certain he could satisfy the Monarchy's immediate needs in the western Balkans and preserve his sovereign's independence and authority within the League of the Three Emperors.

Francis Joseph, too, still anticipated that he would gain Bosnia-Her-zegovina. Although in mourning for his father – who died on 8 March – the Emperor gave a courteous welcome to Ignatiev, whom the Tsar sent to Vienna on 27 March in the hope that the general could reconcile the Austrians to a Russian military presence in Bulgaria and assure them that St Petersburg would raise no objections to any action taken by the Government in Vienna to secure the twin provinces. Detailed discussions between Ignatiev and Andrássy encouraged the Austrians, but the Rus-sian's brief visit – he was only in Vienna for four days of talks – was neither a social nor a political success. Even after returning to St Pet-ersburg, Ignatiev continued to intrigue, unsuccessfully, against Andrássy, hoping to install a more compliant foreign minister in the Ballhausplatz, perhaps General Mollinary. His activities were so maladroit that he streng-thened rather than weakened Andrássy's position. Francis Joseph was not going to have his foreign minister pushed aside by that 'notorious father of lies', as he told his friend, Albert of Saxony, that the Turks called the Russian envoy.

The Congress of Berlin – a thirty day gathering of Europe's leading statesmen in late June and early July 1878 – was an outstanding personal success for Andrássy, greater indeed than Francis Joseph appreciated at the time. He worked in amicable partnership with the British foreign secretary, Lord Salisbury, and he was accepted by Bismarck as a trusted personal friend. The revised map of eastern Europe satisfied his objectives more closely than he had dared to hope. By the Treaty of Berlin the new principality of Bulgaria was cut to one-third of the size outlined at San Stefano while, on a proposal put forward by Salisbury, the Congress gave Austria-Hungary a mandate to occupy and administer Bosnia-Her-

Francis Joseph's Europe (Frontiers 1878–1912)

zegovina in order to end the endemic state of civil war between the Muslim and Christian peoples of the twin provinces. With some difficulty Andrássy secured treaty recognition of Austria-Hungary's right to station troops in the Sanjak of Novibazar and safeguard communications along the strategic corridor which separated Serbia from Montenegro and gave Bosnia access to the East. At the same time he courted the backing of Serbia and Roumania, both by successfully championing their claims to total independence and by securing territorial concessions for them: the Serbs gained Niš, the Roumanians acquired more of the Dobrudja than under the treaty of San Stefano. Austria-Hungary also secured the sole right to keep clear the lower waters of the Danube, thus ensuring the ready movement of barges and river boats down the great waterway. Serbia and Bulgaria accepted obligations to complete their railway systems in such a way as to ensure links with the Austro-Hungarian network.

Andrássy's sole failure at the Congress was with the Turks. Under pressure from Sultan Abdulhamid and from the *seyhulislam* (head of the Muslim hierarchy in his Empire) the Ottoman delegates refused to permit Francis Joseph's troops to enter either Bosnia or Herzegovina, let alone garrison the Sanjak. Only when Andrássy gave a secret pledge that the Sultan's sovereign rights would not be impaired and that an occupation should be regarded as a temporary necessity, did they consent to sign the treaty; details would eventually be settled in a bilateral Austro-Turkish convention.

'The joining of the two provinces to the Monarchy has overjoyed Papa, as we all knew it would', Crown Prince Rudolf told his old tutor, 'I believe that in Bosnia and Herzegovina he is aiming at compensation for Lombardy and Venetia'. Yet Andrássy did not come back from Berlin with two provinces ready to serve on a plate for Francis Joseph's consumption. He wanted the Ottoman Empire, as well as the newly independent Balkan states, to look to Austria-Hungary both commercially and as a safeguard against further Russian encroachment. He was accordingly just as eager to hold the military aristocrats in check as he had been three years before. There was, he told them, no need for a menacing deployment of troops: far better wait for Ottoman acquiescence before crossing the frontiers; and then simply send in 'two companies of soldiers headed by a military band'.

Francis Joseph held his men back for a fortnight after the signing of the Berlin Treaty. This was a grave mistake: the Turks were still smarting from the humiliating treatment their delegates had received as supplicants at the Berlin Congress (especially from Bismarck); they had no intention of concluding a supplementary agreement with Austria-Hungary at such a time. If the Austrians had moved forward in 1875, after the excitement of the Emperor's Dalmatian visit, the occupation might have been carried through without arousing much immediate opposition. But by the summer of 1878 the Bosnian Muslims had formed their own Home Defence Militia, strengthened by well-armed Turkish troops in mutiny against the Sultan's authority. When the Austro-Hungarian army crossed the frontiers on 29 July it met strong resistance in a terrain ideally suited for defensive operations based upon the Turkish forts built to command the valleys.

Beck and Mollinary had settled for rather more than 'two companies and a band': a force of some 85,000 men entered the two provinces. Within ten days the army was in considerable difficulty; Archduke Johann Salvator (of the exiled Tuscan branch of the imperial dynasty) and the brother of the King of Württemberg, who were serving in a crack regiment, were fortunate to survive an ambush near Jajce on 7 August; and, although plans had been made to present Francis Joseph with a symbolic gift from Sarajevo on his birthday, the Emperor was forced to summon an emergency ministerial council to decide on the course of action in the western Balkans. It took twelve weeks of campaigning before the last Muslim garrison in Bosnia surrendered. By then the army of occupation came to nearly 160,000 men and the Government in Vienna reluctantly had to seek another 25 million florins from a Reichsrat still complaining that it had no voice in the shaping of foreign policy. By the end of the third week in October, when an uneasy peace descended on the provinces, the Imperial and Royal Army had officially sustained over 5,198 casualties, although the actual figure seems to have been almost twice as large; 3,300 killed, 6,700 wounded and an extremely high level of sickness in all units. To Andrássy's dismay Francis Joseph now began to demand the outright annexation of Bosnia-Herzegovina claiming that, after such sacrifices, they belonged to the Monarchy by right of conquest.

'The Emperor does not understand the Eastern Question and he will never understand it', an exasperated Andrássy complained to the Empress Elizabeth. The Muslims in Bosnia were always revolting against the Sultans and they would remain rebels until given orderly government: offensive action against them was readily understood in Constantinople. But to annex the provinces would offend the Sultan and cost Austria-Hungary influence throughout the Near East. Moreover once the provinces were incorporated in the Monarchy the balance of historic nationalities established in 1867 would be lost for all time and Strossmayer's Yugoslavs would become the chief beneficiaries from annexation. Five days after the army first occupied Sarajevo, Andrássy begged the ministerial council in Vienna strictly to observe the letter of the Treaty of

Berlin; and he returned to this theme at other conferences during the winter months.

The strain of continuous office was getting too much for him. When, in 1871, as Hungary's prime minister, he took over the foreign ministry Andrássy was in the habit of doing handstands on Metternich's old desk, so his official biographer claims; but it seems unlikely he was still fit and agile after twelve years at the centre of affairs. For the moment, however, he would not contemplate retirement. He was determined to see the parliaments in Vienna and Budapest give formal support to the Treaty of Berlin (which the Emperor himself speedily ratified). It was not that he felt any responsibility towards parliamentary deputies. As ever, he was concerned with more general questions: obstruction in the Reichsrat delayed any final settlement of the Bosnian question. For so long as the German liberals in Vienna continued to snipe at the autocratic control of foreign affairs, the Ottoman government declined to discuss outstanding questions over the fate of the provinces. At last, in March 1879, the Hungarian and Austrian parliaments approved the Treaty. On 21 April a formal agreement concerning the occupation and administration of Bosnia-Herzegovina was concluded between the Austro-Hungarian and Ottoman governments. The map of the western Balkans now followed the line Andrássy had been seeking for the past four years. He was tired; his estates in Hungary had long been neglected. Within a month of the Austro-Turkish convention he offered Francis Joseph his resignation.

It was refused. The Emperor, angered by the attempts of the German liberals in the Reichsrat to raise issues which encroached on his prerogatives, was contemplating a major switch in Austrian domestic policy, with a reversion to a more conservative and aristocratic administration. He did not want Andrássy to go at such a time, for his departure might be interpreted as a gesture of appeasement towards his political enemies in the Reichsrat. Andrássy therefore agreed to stay in office until later in the year. It was a difficult summer. The League of the Three Emperors seemed to fall apart, with the Tsar showing increasing hostility towards the German Chancellor and the Russians exploiting their privileged position in the eastern Balkans to the discomfiture of Austrian commercial interests. When, at the beginning of August, Francis Joseph completed his change in Vienna by asking Count Taaffe to form a government, Andrássy again asked to resign. He suspected that Taaffe would seek support from the Czechs, and he was not prepared to fight yet another political battle to curb Slav influence in Vienna. On 6 August Francis Joseph agreed that Andrássy could retire in two months time, long enough for him to prepare Baron Heinrich Haymerle, his right-hand man at the Berlin Congress, as a successor.

Unexpectedly, in these last weeks of office, Andrássy achieved a diplomatic victory which, only twelve months earlier, would have seemed improbable. The news of Andrássy's impending departure filled Bismarck with alarm. He, too, suspected that a Taaffe administration might be sympathetic to the Slavs; and he had no wish to see the Reichstadt partnership revived and perpetuated, with Francis Joseph and Alexander II maintaining a basically anti-German entente. Hurriedly therefore he arranged to meet Andrássy at Gastein on 28 August to clarify the situation. Relations between Berlin and St Petersburg remained tense that month: Alexander II complained of a succession of minor affronts by the German Chancellor, and the General Staff in Berlin were disturbed by Russian military movements in Poland. To Andrássy's surprise, when he met Bismarck at Gastein the Chancellor proposed the conclusion of a defensive alliance between Germany and Austria-Hungary, aimed at protecting both empires from a Russian attack. As Andrássy emphasized to Francis Joseph, provided that Bismarck did not subsequently add impossible conditions, this was too good an opportunity to miss.

Francis Joseph welcomed the project. It had a familiar look, a modernized version of the Prusso-Austrian partnership of earlier years. To his satisfaction, Bismarck personally was prepared to come to Vienna in September to complete the negotiations with Andrássy; and it was rumoured (rightly) that when William I demurred from authorizing the conclusion of a secret anti-Russian alliance, Bismarck bluntly informed his sovereign that he could choose between accepting Austria-Hungary as an ally or finding a new Chancellor. The treaty, valid in the first instance for five years, was duly signed in Vienna on 7 October 1879 by the Austro-Hungarian foreign minister and the German ambassador. Next day Andrássy retired into private life.

None of Francis Joseph's other foreign ministers shaped policy so decisively and personally as Andrássy: none left such an enduring mark on the Monarchy's history. The Austro-German alliance survived until the collapse of the Habsburg and Hohenzollern Empires at the end of the First World War, a conflict of which the immediate cause lay in unrest among the Yugoslavs of Bosnia-Herzegovina. Yet it would be a mistake to blame Andrássy for later catastrophes. The terms of the treaty signed by him were strictly defined and, like all previous alignments, limited in time. In 1879 Bismarck's Germany was the suitor, not Austria-Hungary, but this relationship did not last. Whenever ministers and diplomats were faced with renewal of the treaty they accepted it as natural that Germany should be the senior partner in the alliance. Francis Joseph never gained the decisive voice in Europe's affairs which Andrássy's final achievement seemed momentarily to promise him, for Bismarck soon realized that his

On 8 June 1867, the Austrian Empire became the Dual Monarchy of Austria Hungary. Here, Francis Joseph stands beside the new Queen of Hungary to receive the acclamation of the Hungarian Parliament.

The ill-fated hunting lodge at Mayerling where the scandal and tragedy which took the lives of the Emperor's son Rudolf and his young mistress Mary Vetsera remain largely inexplicable to this day.

Francis Joseph receives guests at a Court ball. The glitter and ceremonial of Habsburg Imperial life was one of its chief characteristics, yet did much to alienate the Empress who never disguised her dislike of the formality with which she was surrounded at Court.

Archduke Francis Ferdinand with his wife Sophie and their three children, Maximilian, Ernest, and Sophie.

Francis Ferdinand, heir to the Habsburg throne after the suicide of Crown Prince Rudolf at Mayerling. He himself never entered into his inheritance, assassinated at Sarajevo in a sequence of events that led directly to World War One.

Vienna's Stephansplatz, circa 1900. Habsburg power remained intact, but in fact the dynasty which had ruled so much of Europe since the thirteenth century now had less than twenty years before its extinction.

The Kaiservilla at Bad Ischl, a favourite retreat for both the Emperor and Empress.

The Villa Felicitas, Katharina Schratt's home at Bad Ischl, where Francis Joseph was a frequent, and often inconveniently early, caller on his friend.

Katharina Schratt, the actress who became 'friend but not lover' to the far older Emperor and whose close association with Francis Joseph was actively encouraged by Empress Elizabeth, possibly because she was aware that Katharina gave Francis Joseph a domestic peace which she was incapable of providing.

Francis Joseph with his great-nephew, who in 1916 succeeded him as Charles I, last of the great Habsburg rulers. A photograph taken by Charles's mother, outside Cannes, 9 March 1894.

October 1911: the old Emperor at the wedding reception on the balcony at Schwarzau, the castle in Lower Austria, where his great-nephew Charles married Princess Zita of Bourbon-Parma.

'The old gentleman'. The octogenarian Emperor passes the 16th-century Schweizertor, as he walks to his apartments in Vienna's inner Hofburg.

The end of an era. The funeral procession of Francis Joseph, 30 November, 1916. It is headed by Emperor Charles and Empress Zita (heavily veiled), with Crown Prince Otto between them; the rulers of Bavaria, Saxony and Bulgaria follow.

In his study at Schönbrunn, shortly before his death. He always wore uniforms, except when taking a holiday abroad or in the mountains, but for everyday work he would choose the simple service tunic and trousers of a junior officer.

immediate fears were groundless; he did not need the protection of an ally against an aggressive Russia.

Even less was Andrássy responsible for later events in Bosnia-Herzegovina. His policy for the western Balkans assumed the continuing Austro-Hungarian patronage of a client Serbia, while he was so intent on maintaining good relations with the Ottoman Empire that he even drafted a memorandum for his successor suggesting the conditions under which the provinces might eventually be evacuated and allowed back to the Sultan in full sovereignty. Meanwhile, occupied Bosnia-Herzegovina fell administratively under the authority of the joint Austro-Hungarian minister of finance, who from 1882 until his death in 1903 was Kállay, Andrássy's former representative in Belgrade and the author of a history of Serbia. He became the outstanding proconsul of the two provinces, much as Lord Cromer was the supreme proconsul of British-occupied Egypt, and Kállay consistently followed Andrássy's principles: no region in the Balkan lands made such rapid material progress as Bosnia-Herzegovina, but careful attention was always given to Serb susceptibilities and respect was consistently shown for Islam and its teachings. Only after Kállay's death did Francis Joseph resort to policies which had seemed obvious to him from 1875 onwards. Bosnia-Herzegovina was annexed to the Monarchy in October 1908 and relations with neighbouring Serbia allowed rapidly to deteriorate. Andrássy's careful balance, delicately maintained for so long by Kállay, was irretrievably lost by Francis Joseph's later advisers. As Andrássy had predicted, the Emperor never came to understand the Eastern Question.

Chapter 14

FATHER AND SON

On 2 August 1878, four days after the Imperial and Royal Army entered Bosnia, Crown Prince Rudolf began his active military career, serving in the Prague garrison as a colonel attached to the 36th (Bohemian) Infantry Regiment. Technically his links with the army went back twenty years, for his father appointed him honorary colonel-in-chief of the 19th Infantry Regiment when he was two days old. But Francis Joseph wished his son to have proper military training and service experience: he was therefore not expected to serve in his 'own' 19th regiment, nor was he posted to a fashionable unit of Dragoons or Hussars, for most cavalry officers came from the great aristocratic families and the Emperor thought it undesirable for him to be associated with a socially exclusive set. Rudolf agreed with him. He was content to learn soldiering in a workaday regiment of the line, where there would not be too many noble titles in the mess.

General Latour von Thurmburg, the Crown Prince's principal tutor for twelve years, had done his work well. By 1878 Rudolf was an intellectually curious young man, with keen scientific interests, particularly in ornithology. Barely four months before taking up his post in Prague, the Crown Prince shocked the spiritual authorities at Court by attending a lecture in Vienna given by Dr Ernst Hackel, a Darwinian whose views were unacceptable to all the Church leaders. Later that year Rudolf invited the eminent zoologist Alfred Brehm to accompany him on a short expedition to observe animal and bird life in the Danubian river forests of southern Hungary. With Brehm as his consultant, Rudolf published an account of the expedition *Funfzehn Tage auf der Donau* (Fifteen Days on the Danube) that sold better than the title deserved; the author's anonymity was only lightly veiled.

This book, in itself over 300 pages long, was not the Crown Prince's first printed work that year. Shortly before Christmas in 1877 he had accompanied Elizabeth to England. He was a social hit both with the Queen Victoria and with the Prince of Wales: each thought Rudolf 'very pleasing', though Queen Victoria was worried that he 'looks a little over grown and not very robust'. Then, while the Empress enjoyed herself as 'Queen of the Chase' in Northamptonshire, her son set off on an instructive tour, accompanied by a much respected liberal economist, Carl Menger. The Crown Prince met Disraeli, now Lord Beaconsfield, visited the industrialized Midlands and North, southern Scotland, and crossed to Dublin, too; and he made careful notes of the 'English' way of life, whether in the Houses of Parliament, or Billingsgate fish market, the Lancashire mills or newly municipalized Birmingham, or staying with the premier peer of Scotland in east Lothian. After six weeks of travel he sent Latour a long account of his impressions, on notepaper with a 'Queen Railway Hotel, Chester' letterhead: 'I am ... really enthusiastic about England, though I do not fail to recognize grave and very obvious drawbacks in the country', he wrote, 'Life here is magnificent, and I am trying to acquire as much knowledge as possible'. He was fascinated by the role of the aristocracy, the concept of a Tory and a Whig nobility, both socially acceptable, both with patronage in the Commons, both aware of their tenants' needs. Within a few weeks a 50-page pamphlet, *The Austrian Nobility and its Constitutional Mission* 'by an Austrian', appeared in Munich. Subject matter and sub-title – 'A Call to Young Aristocrats' – again left little doubt of the author's identity.

At first Francis Joseph treated his son's intellectual pursuits with paternal indulgence, perhaps even with pride. Latour, who was ten years older than the Emperor, retained his confidence. Francis Joseph supported him against sniping criticism at Court of the unorthodox interests which his old tutor had encouraged the heir to the throne to pursue. Most ruffled of all these conservatives was Archduke Albrecht, Inspector-General of the army since 1867, a hard disciplinarian with no son of his own, who looked out unsmilingly on the younger generation of Archdukes from behind the thick steel rimmed glasses of a graceless pedagogue. Already, in 1876, 'Uncle Albrecht' had sought Rudolf's views on their ancestor, the Emperor Joseph II, and he mistrusted signs of incipient liberalism in his great-nephew's judgments on the past. General Beck shared the Archduke's fears: 'The young, over-excited mind of the Crown Prince, the immaturity of his way of thinking, the extravagance of his undoubtedly high intelligence, make me worry that he will assimilate ideas and tendencies which would not be compatible with the conservative character of a future monarch', Beck wrote in his journal. The military chancellery as a whole was convinced that army service would enable Rudolf to shake off his 'extravagant' ideas. General Beck, meeting the heir to the throne for the first time after he had taken up his post at Prague was satisfied with his progress: 'I have been studying the Crown Prince at Gödöllö', Beck wrote to his wife, 'His mind bubbles over and he wears his heart on his sleeve and has not yet digested many of the liberal teachings of some of his tutors; but otherwise love will soon be his chief preoccupation'.

Beck was not far off the mark. There is a persistent tale that, soon after arriving in Prague, Rudolf was entranced by the beauty of a Jewish girl, who died young and whom he long mourned. But he certainly took his military duties seriously. Within five weeks of joining the regiment he was on manoeuvres under the vigilant eye of Uncle Albrecht. He was attracted, too, by a new intellectual challenge: he had written about ornithology and politics; now he would also become a military historian. 'I shall not be in Vienna for the Hofball', he wrote to Count 'Charly' Bombelles, his father's boyhood friend, who had succeeded Latour as head of the Crown Prince's official household. Instead of leading the traditional defile of Archdukes and Archduchesses into the Rittersaal ballroom, Rudolf chose to immerse himself in study; and with some success. On two consecutive Sunday evenings in March 1879 he lectured the officers of the Prague garrison on the Prussian victory of Spicheren, nine years before. The finest modern book on the Franco-Prussian War devotes 14 pages to the battle: Crown Prince Rudolf's analysis ran to 88 double-sided sheets.

'I am glad I have the lecture behind me', he told Latour on 4 April. He had felt uneasy about it, for he was aware of pinpricks of envy among the more senior of his brother officers. But he was not going to behave like the other Archdukes, he explained: 'Thank God I do not feel within me the call to follow the so-called accustomed paths, the foolish everyday life of my relatives with their blinkers'. He wished to throw himself 'heart and soul into the army, and not just the gaiter legging aspects, but so as to use my head . . . These days one must work to deserve to hold a high position; merely to sit in Vienna and keep up a dignified attitude and not know the people, how they are and what they feel, that does not fit into our century'.

These good intentions may have been influenced by a lingering picture of an idealized 'England'. Yet they were hard to uphold. Temperament inclined Rudolf to evenings of amorous amusement, a flaw of character to which the worldly-wise Charly Bombelles, unlike Latour, gave free rein. Already, before going to Prague, Rudolf had acquired a certain notoriety among the courtesans of the capital. He was reluctant to abandon his friends for too long – 'all the beautiful women of Vienna whom I have so much loved', as he called them in a draft will signed eleven days after penning those fine sentiments in his letter to Latour. As heir to the throne he had, of course, duties to perform; and it was these dynastic obligations which brought him back to the Hofburg that spring. On Thursday, 24 April, 1879 Francis Joseph and Elizabeth were to celebrate their Silver Wedding; and at the start of the week the family gathered in the capital for four days of festivity.

The Silver Wedding has a firm place in Viennese popular folklore. It is associated, however, less with the Emperor and Empress than with Hans Makart, the supreme decorative artist of Ringstrasse Vienna, whose allegorical friezes and historical canvases brought a Romantic exuberance to the walls of the new mansions transforming the central city. Makart was entrusted by the Lord Mayor, Julius von Newald, with supervising the costumes, floats and procession of a great historical pageant, which would look back through three and a half centuries to the opulent Flanders of Emperor Charles V. Representatives of every trade and craft, some 10,000 people in all (according to the newspapers) passed in salute before an Imperial Pavilion set up at the side of the Ringstrasse, close to the Hofburg. At the head of the procession, immediately behind the heralds, rode Hans Mackart with a brocaded costume and plumed hat modelled on Rubens originals. The procession, announced for Saturday, 26 April, was postponed because of heavy rain; and it is the Sunday which is still remembered as *Makart-Festzug Tag* (Makart Procession Day), more than a century later.

The imperial family's personal celebrations took place earlier in the week. On the wedding anniversary itself there was a service of thanksgiving in the Votivkirche; and on the previous evening Archduke Charles Ludwig – twice widowed during those twenty-five years, and by now married to Maria Theresa of Portugal – was host at a reception in which he arranged for the staging before his brother and sister-in-law of a series of historical tableaux. Each figure from the past was played by an Archduke or Archduchess. Many of the decorations and costumes were brought for the occasion from the great museums, even from the *Schatzkammer* (Imperial Treasury). In the first scene the Crown Prince, robed to represent his thirteenth century ancestor Rudolf I, wore the real crown of the Holy Roman Empire. He was soon back again, first as Charles V and then as the victor over the Turks, Charles of Lorraine.

'A lasting family celebration for all the peoples of my empire' was Francis Joseph's verdict on his Silver Wedding week. Elizabeth was less pleased: according to one of her nieces the Empress found the protracted festivities exhausting and regarded Makart's procession as an impertinent public intrusion into private affairs. She was more concerned with the future of the dynasty and the search for an acceptable daughter-in-law. Not that Rudolf was in any hurry to settle down. He visited Lisbon and Madrid, gave serious thought to a Spanish Infanta (too plain), and travelled to Dresden, where he momentarily considered a Princess of Saxony (too fat). By the end of July he was back with the 36th Infantry

Regiment at Mnichović, outside Prague; and in his father's birthday promotions' list he was confirmed as commanding officer of the regiment. On 28 August he led his men on parade before their Emperor: 'My most ardent wish has been fulfilled', he told Bombelles; 'I belong to the army heart and soul'. So might his father have written at twenty-one.

Prague was an attractive city, one of the most desirable postings for a young officer. It was also politically a sensitive city during the four years in which the Crown Prince served there. Comments in his correspondence with Latour leave little doubt that he gained greater insight into the problems of the Monarchy than had he remained in Vienna: a twelve-sheet letter in October 1878 shrewdly assesses the effects of the military moves in Bosnia on the Slav peoples, especially on Croat-Magyar relations; while three months later Rudolf filled fourteen pages with an analysis of the current political situation, particularly the growing challenge of social democracy. But it was the Czech problem which most interested him; and Francis Joseph, who was hoping for several years of calm under a government headed by his friend Eddy Taaffe, was pleased that his son should be stationed at such a time in Prague.

At first Rudolf approved of Taaffe's policy. The Count, who was to remain Austria's prime minister from 1879 until 1893, began his term of office with gestures of goodwill towards the peoples of Bohemia and Moravia: language decrees raised the official status of spoken and written Czech in the two provinces; reforms increased Czech representation in the provincial Landtage; and the 500-year old University of Prague was divided into parallel foundations, one German and the other Czech. The promise of these concessions attracted the Bohemian parliamentary parties back to the Reichsrat in Vienna in September 1879, for the first time in sixteen years, strengthening Taaffe's support against the German liberals. But thereafter the Count temporised. No single nationality within the Monarchy was favoured, for that, he thought, accorded with Francis Joseph's wishes and he always saw himself as an executant of his sovereign's will rather than the originator of new policies. Taaffe preferred, as he once said, 'to keep all the nationalities of the Monarchy in a balanced condition of well modulated discontent'. Eduard Herbst, a German-Bohemian parliamentarian bitterly critical of Taaffe's 'weakness' over the Czech Question, complained that the prime minister was constantly 'muddling through' and the phrase stuck, until people believed Taaffe had used it himself. Yet, however pedestrian his style of government, the early 1880s were not entirely barren years: Taaffe introduced improvements in education and social reforms to protect industrial workers; and he persuaded Francis Joseph to accept an extension of the franchise, which gave the vote to the wealthier peasants in the countryside and to small property owners in the towns. Both groups were natural supporters of Taaffe's 'Iron Ring' coalition of conservative Germans and moderate Slavs. In the general election of 1885 their votes strengthened Taaffe's hold on parliament.

Long before then the Crown Prince had lost patience with Taaffe, deploring in particular his sympathy for the more obscurantist Church leaders. At fifteen and sixteen Rudolf had written for his tutor essays which, when published long after his death, read like proclamations of romantic liberalism. But it would be a mistake to deduce from these adolescent airings of the mind that he was constantly in revolt against his father and the whole structure of the Monarchy; and it is too easy to antedate family friction. There was no rift between father and son during Rudolf's first eighteen months with the regiment. At that time Francis Joseph was amused by the attempts of social climbers to ingratiate themselves with the heir to the throne. He did not blame Rudolf, and for the most part he condoned their activities, but one woman went too far, he thought. At Gödöllö, shortly before Christmas 1879, he observed to the Empress's lady-in-waiting, Marie Festetics, that he found the behaviour of Baroness Helene Vetsera 'unbelievable'; 'She is always in close pursuit of' the Crown Prince, 'Today she has actually sent him a present', he exclaimed. The Baroness was a daughter of the Levantine banker Themistocles Baltazzi, who had grown rich from the concession to collect tolls on the bridge linking Stamboul and Galata, in the heart of Constantinople; Helene had made a good marriage to a diplomat at the Austrian embassy in the Ottoman capital. She was eleven years older than the Crown Prince, with two sons and two daughters, Hanna and Mary. Countess Festetics, who jotted down the Emperor's remarks, disliked Helene Vetsera intensely and distrusted her, as he well knew. So, too, did many other ladies at Court.

It would have been inappropriate for his mother or father to reproach Rudolf too severely for his wayward behaviour. The Empress courted admiration, flirting decorously with skilled horsemen at home and abroad, provided they were good-looking. Like her royal Tudor namesake, Elizabeth resented any inclination of her courtiers (male or female) to marry and lead an independent life. Yet, though she would exercise her tantalizing wiles beguilingly in England and Ireland or among her hunting friends at Gödöllö, there was always an element of caprice and pretence in her conduct, and tales of her infidelities which titillated the scandalmongers were probably fictitious.

Francis Joseph, on the other hand, was in these years deeply entangled in the seamiest personal relationship of his life. One morning in June 1875, soon after returning from Dalmatia, he was taking his customary early exercise in the Schönbrunn parkland when he met a young and attractive blonde, who was standing beside the artificial 'Roman ruin' statuary about a quarter of a mile from the palace. It is probable that Anna Nahowski, the newly married sixteen year old wife of a railway official, had every hope of accosting the Emperor: for why otherwise did she, too, decide to take a walk on her own at 6 A.M. in the vicinity of Schönbrunn, where Francis Joseph was known to be in residence? Her tactics were successful. Throughout the months when Elizabeth was in Bavaria or Greece, France or England or Ireland, the Emperor looked for consolation to the plump, blonde Anna and found it. A compliant husband welcomed the steady flow of generous gifts to his wife which enabled the Nahowskis to set up house in Hetzendorf's Schönbrunner Allee just three summers after that first meeting. By 1884 the family could afford to acquire and renovate a large villa in fashionable Hietzing, along what is now Maxingstrasse, overlooking Schönbrunn Park. To this considerable status symbol they eventually added a summer residence at Trahutten, high in the Styrian Alps. It is hard to believe that the businesslike Anna, meticulously noting down in her journal thirteen years of visits, kindled flames of passion; at best she offered the comforting warmth of passing sensuality to a middle-aged man isolated from human contacts. Before the end of the decade, she became an embarrassment for him. But there was no public speculation about the affair; discretion, and ready money, kept the secret for a hundred years or more.

By contrast, there was such widespread gossip about the Crown Prince that it seemed essential for him to find a wife soon, in the hopes of encouraging him to accept the disciplined conventions of married life. Early in 1880 Count Bohuslav Chotek, the Austrian Minister in Brussels, accordingly approached King Leopold II to arrange for Rudolf to meet his younger daughter, Princess Stephanie. The last Belgian marriage had ended disastrously with Maximilian dead in Mexico and Charlotte – Stephanie's aunt – incurably insane. If Rudolf married Stephanie there would be a bond of consanguinity, missing on the earlier occasion: Stephanie's mother, Queen Marie Henrietta, was a Habsburg princess by birth, the youngest daughter of the Palatine of Hungary, Archduke Joseph; she had been among the family guests in Vienna at the Silver Jubilee celebrations. With no great enthusiasm, Rudolf travelled to Brussels in the first week of March 1880. Princess Stephanie, having been told by her father that it was her parents' wish that she should become Empress of Austria and Queen of Hungary, was summoned into his presence, and did not think of challenging her father's decision. She was a gangling 15-year-old, with flaxen hair, plump cheeks and small eyes set close together. Two days after this meeting, on 7 March, Rudolf sent out the telegrams announcing his betrothal. Latour got the news in Vienna soon after eight in the morning, and was pleased. Countess Festetics records that when the Empress received her telegram – at Claridge's Hotel in London – she turned white before letting her know of the betrothal. 'Thank God, it is not a calamity', the Countess said, with relief. 'Please God it does not become one', Elizabeth grimly replied.

'Comely, sensible, good and very distinguished looking', was Rudolf's first verdict on his fiancée in a letter to Latour of less than 70 words. But after his mother had broken her journey home at Brussels and spent four hours with her son and future daughter-in-law, Rudolf became more sure that he had taken the right step: 'I feel intoxicated with happiness and contentment', he told Latour on 11 March, lapsing into informal hand-writing for the first time in a letter to his old tutor rather than using the traditional *Schrift*. Once back with his regiment he was delighted with his reception in Prague: 'The town is decorated with flags. Everything is very correct; no Slav flags, no German; one Belgian; otherwise gold, red and white everywhere.' 'The patriotism here is colossal', he let Latour know in the first week of April, 'Bohemia and Prague have received me as a man betrothed in marriage most graciously and heartily, from top nobility down to the poorest of workers. Never before have I felt such gratitude and love for the townsfolk as in these days ... Whatever the situation, I shall remain a true friend and supporter of this good and beautiful country'. There was no direct criticism of his parents over the following months, only genuine pleasure when he joined his mother in Hungary and found her taking a more active role in social life than in Vienna: 'Tomorrow is the Red Cross meeting', he wrote to Latour from Budapest on 8 June, 'The Empress will herself preside'. It was fitting for Elizabeth to be patron of a society which owed its origin to revulsion at the appalling carnage of Magenta and Solferino.

Rudolf's wedding, originally planned for the summer of 1880, was postponed until the following spring when it was found that Stephanie had not yet begun to menstruate. The Crown Prince remained for the most part in Prague, while his mother again travelled to England for much of the hunting season, staying in Cheshire until March, when she went to Aintree to see the Grand National steeplechase. Rudolf became rapidly disenchanted with the Taaffe government, blaming his father for allowing 'the blacks' (obscurantist spokesmen for the Church) to increase their influence in education. At the same time he privately criticized his mother, now 'an idle, though thoroughly clever, woman'. In a letter to Latour of the second week in February 1881 he showed particular antipathy towards the septuagenarian Cardinal Archbishop of Prague, Prince Frederick von Schwarzenberg, who sought to restrict the Sunday recreational pursuits of the garrison officers and was known to have complained that the heir to the throne frequently kept company with free thinkers and Freemasons. Taaffe, Rudolf argued, had become as illiberal as the Cardinal, while deluding the Czech parliamentarians into believing they enjoyed his support: 'Both feudal gentlemen owe allegiance to no nation', Rudolf told Latour; they 'are dragging the Czech people down into the mud with them', exploiting the Czechs 'for the sake of reactionary and obscurantist aims'. 'The great Slav race, for whom I have much sympathy', he maintained, '. . . are liberal, and the day must come when they will totally disown these gentlemen'. As for himself, Rudolf declared, 'I don't hide the fact that I have no sympathy at all for the Church's pretensions to influence the state ... I would far rather send my children to a school with a Jewish headmaster than to a school whose headmaster is a priest, an out-and-out supporter of black tendencies'. No heir to the throne since Joseph II had been so suspicious of the conventional Church dogmas which Francis Joseph so confidently accepted. Rudolf was by nature too much a talker to confine these opinions to his private letters. Elizabeth, abroad until a month before the wedding, knew nothing of her son's mounting anger. If Francis Joseph saw any danger signals, he ignored them.

Princess Stephanie spent her first night on Austrian soil at Salzburg and arrived in Vienna on 6 May 1881, four days before the wedding. The popular festivities followed as familiar a pattern as the marriage ceremony in the Augustinerkirche, though the guest list was even more striking: it included both the future King Edward VII and his Prussian nephew, the future Kaiser William II. Rudolf's personal enemy, Cardinal Prince Schwarzenberg, officiated at the wedding, with more than twenty other prelates to assist him. Johann Strauss dedicated his *Myrthenblüthenwalzer* to Stephanie, while Eduard Strauss composed another waltz, *Schleier und Krone* (Veil and Crown). Like his parents, the Crown Prince and his bride spent their first days of married life at Laxenburg. The Empress did not seek to interfere, probably from the kindest of motives, for Elizabeth had vivid recollections of old embarrassments caused by her mother-in-law. But if the Empress did not fuss around them, nobody else did, either. According to Stephanie's memoirs, unseasonal snow was falling when they reached Laxenburg: it was dispiriting to step out of the carriage and be met 'by a breath of air as cold as ice in a cellar', while the predominant smell was 'of mould': 'No plants, no flowers to celebrate my arrival ... no carpets ... no dressing-table, no bathroom, nothing but a wash handstand on a three-legged framework'. She and her husband had 'little to say to each other; we were virtual strangers'. The Crown Prince, recklessly loquacious in familiar company, could think of nothing to

interest a gauche princess six years his junior. Did he know that his
mother had already dubbed her daughter-in-law 'the plain bumpkin' (*das
hässliche Trampeltier*)?

All too often, tales of marital discord spring from incidents inflated in
reminiscence and recollected in adversity. So it is with the traditional
legends of Rudolf and Stephanie's early life together. The evidence of his
letters suggests a far happier association. After a week in Laxenburg,
they travelled to Budapest, where the Crown Princess was fêted as a
granddaughter of the most popular of Palatines. Then back to garrison
duties in Prague, where he found Stephanie ready to share his interests.
She accompanied him on official visits and occasionally on hunting
expeditions and shoots, too. Her vitality of spirit quickened once she
gained a solid foothold in Rudolf's topsy-turvy life, as army officer and
heir apparent.

In the first year of marriage, he seems to have discussed politics with
her. Six months after the wedding he completed the draft of a long
memorandum 'On the Present Political Situation In Austria', which he
sent to his old tutor, for comment: the Crown Prince was dismayed by
the spectacle of parliament and, in particular, by the way in which Taaffe
had to strike bargains with political parties which drew their support from
the nationalities rather than from the peoples of the Monarchy as a whole;
only through the creation of unified Liberal and Conservative parties, with
leaders and rank-and-file drawn from all the nationalities in Cisleithania,
would it be possible for 'Austria' to secure an orderly administration as
coherent as in Hungary. After Latour had replied to Rudolf, praising his
political good sense, the Crown Prince wrote back, again at great length,
emphasizing how much he had gained from Stephanie's companionship.
'I have never been as happy as I was last summer when, surrounded by
domestic bliss, I could settle down quietly to the preliminary studies'.
Ought the memorandum to be presented to the Emperor, he asked
Latour? 'Might I from then onwards be treated distantly, coldly and
sternly; and might this attitude be extended to my wife! She is bright,
very observant and sensitive; full of ambition; she is a granddaughter of
Louis Philippe (*sic*) and a Coburg! Need I say more. I am very much in
love with her, and she is the only person who could lead me much astray!'
This is a strangely different Stephanie from the bumpkin lampooned by
the Empress and her ladies-in-waiting. The real Crown Princess, her
character in many ways still unformed, must be hidden somewhere
between these extremes of impression.

Rudolf's letter – which was written on the 33rd anniversary of the
Emperor's accession – also contained the sharpest assessment of his
father's personality put down on paper since Francis Joseph's boyhood:

'Our Emperor has no friend, his whole character and natural tendency do not permit it. He stands lonely on his peak; he talks to those who serve him of their duties, but he carefully avoids any real conversation. Accordingly he knows little of what people think and feel, their views and opinions. Only those people now in power have access to him, and they naturally interpret matters in the way that is most satisfying for them. He believes we live in one of the happiest periods of Austrian history, he is habitually told so. In the newspaper he only reads the passages marked for him in red and so he is cut off from every human contact, from all impartial and genuinely loyal advice ... There was a time when the Empress ... talked to the Emperor about serious matters, prompted by views diametrically opposed to those he held. These times are past. The great lady no longer cares for anything but sport; and so this source of outside opinions, which were on the whole tinged with liberalism, is now also closed ... Three or four years ago the Emperor was, to some degree, already liberal and reconciled to the nineteenth century. Now he is once again as he was in poor Grandmama's time: bigoted, gruff and suspicious'.

This pen-portrait of his father was unduly harsh. Francis Joseph was indeed eminently isolated, a lonely figure at the head of a spreading dynasty. But it would be wrong to suggest that his political outlook had changed with the contraction of his circle of advisers and confidantes. The Emperor never moved either towards or away from liberalism. Like George Canning earlier in the century, he believed in 'men' rather than in 'measures'; he might appoint a liberal prime minister, provided he was not too doctrinaire; or he might choose a great landowner, if his concepts of political obligation were not too narrow. His ideal remained someone who was not so much a party leader as 'an Emperor's minister'; hence his long support for Taaffe.

There is no evidence that Francis Joseph ever received the Crown Prince's memorandum on the political situation in Austria. This is hardly surprising since, quite apart from Rudolf's fear of his father's cold reaction to such an initiative, the original draft was already out of date when he first sent it to Latour for comment, and he seems to have decided to shelve the matters it raised. For, during the period when Rudolf was preparing the memorandum, the constitutional structure agreed in 1867 was temporarily out of balance. Beust and Andrássy had made certain that the principal government official for the Monarchy should be the common minister for foreign affairs, who was also titular minister of the Imperial and Royal Household and, in the Emperor's absence, presided over the common ministerial council, the Monarchy's 'cabinet'. But from 1879 until 1881 Andrássy's nominee as foreign minister, Heinrich Haymerle, did not have the force of character to maintain this primacy in government. Haymerle was a skilled and patient diplomat. After fifteen months of negotiation he achieved a considerable success. By the secret

League of the Three Emperors' alliance treaty of June 1881 he won from Germany and Russia virtual recognition of Austro-Hungarian supremacy over the western Balkans, including the eventual annexation of Bosnia-Herzegovina. In return Francis Joseph pledged the Monarchy's benevolent neutrality should either of his partners be at war with a fourth Power (other than Turkey). The Crown Prince, like his father, believed during these years that foreign policy remained the prerogative of the Emperor and his chosen minister, and he saw little reason to complain of Haymerle's activities. Disquiet over future trends of policy accordingly led Rudolf to concentrate his criticisms on Taaffe or his Hungarian counterpart Kálmán Tisza, for unlike the foreign minister they were personalities in their own right. Both prime ministers remained in office until after Rudolf's death, but before the end of the year 1881 the balance of the constitutional machine had been corrected; and the Crown Prince increasingly found a new source of dissatisfaction, this time in the Ballhausplatz.

When Haymerle died suddenly, on 10 October 1881, Francis Joseph chose as his successor Count Gustav Kálnoky, the ambassador in St Petersburg, a gifted and hard-working diplomat. Despite his Magyar-sounding name, Kálnoky was a German Moravian landowner, an aristocrat of strong convictions. He was determined to formulate policies himself, after having fed his sovereign with such expert advice from the leading ambassadors that the Emperor was unlikely to question his decisions. This show of expertise so impressed Francis Joseph that Kálnoky remained at the Ballhausplatz for fourteen years, far longer than any other incumbent during the reign. But the Crown Prince did not share his father's admiration for the foreign minister. Kálnoky's ascendancy coincided with a widening of Rudolf's range of interests. A week after Haymerle's death Carl Menger, the economist who had accompanied the Crown Prince on his English tour, introduced to Rudolf an outstanding journalist, Moriz Szeps, editor-in-chief of the *Neues Wiener Tagblatt*, selling some 40,000 copies each day, a good circulation at that time in Austria. By the following spring Rudolf was in regular correspondence with Szeps, who had influential contacts abroad, especially in Paris; his daughter, Sophie, was shortly to marry Paul Clemenceau, brother of Georges Clemenceau, the radical 'Tiger' (with whom, in May 1880, Szeps had had the first of several long interviews). Soon Szeps was to replace Latour as the chief recipient of the Crown Prince's political observations; and in early 1883 the *Neues Wiener Tagblatt* became an unofficial forum in which Rudolf could air his ideas, occasionally through anonymous articles written by himself.

He went to elaborate lengths to keep these contacts secret, for he knew that, on the pretext of protecting him from assassination, the police authorities kept him under virtual surveillance. Letters were carried to Szeps's elder daughter, Bertha, by Karl Nehammer, Rudolf's trusted personal servant who, having shaken off police shadowers by swift changes from tram to tram, would arrive at Bertha Szeps's home posing as her masseur. Conversations with Szeps took place late at night when Rudolf was in Vienna; his guest would be led to the Crown Prince's apartments in the Hofburg through servants' quarters, which were entered through an inconspicuous door on the ramp leading up to the Albertina Collection. When Clemenceau came to Vienna for his brother's wedding, it was by this route that Szeps escorted him to meet the Crown Prince. Yet despite his precautions, the police kept themselves in touch with Rudolf's activities. Taaffe saw no reason to worry the Emperor with the reports they passed on to him.

Thanks to Archduke Albrecht and to Beck (who became Chief of the General Staff in 1881) Francis Joseph had some idea of Rudolf's political contacts; and he strongly disapproved of them. If he had known how deeply the Crown Prince was also interesting himself in journalism, then Rudolf would certainly have been received 'distantly, coldly and sternly'. As it was, the Emperor treated him with indulgence so long as his marriage with Stephanie was not in question. Francis Joseph recognized that he shared Elizabeth's temperament to a greater extent than did their daughters. He possessed Sisi's romanticism and caprice, sometimes enchanting, but often indifferent to the sensitivity of others. But whereas his mother was a cultural dilettante, enraptured by Heine and the dream-world of Greek mythology, the Crown Prince liked to dabble in politics. 'Like his mother', Rudolf's sister-in-law recalled forty years later, 'he had a way of talking that held everybody, and a facility for setting all about him agog to solve the riddle of his personality'.

Occasionally, Francis Joseph was uneasy over the Wittelsbach strain in Rudolf's character. But though the Crown Prince for some five years before his marriage had cultivated a rarefied friendship with his kinsman, the Wagner-omane Ludwig II, the Bavarian king's ill-formed ideas had little influence upon him. To Francis Joseph's great satisfaction, so long as he was stationed in Prague, Rudolf outwardly showed every sign of becoming a good regimental officer, with no alarming eccentricities.

Despite the bitterness which runs through so many pages in the Crown Princess's published memoirs, surviving letters suggest that after two years of marriage Rudolf and Stephanie had achieved a mutual understanding which seemed improbable, given their differences of temperament and background. Szeps noted that Stephanie would be present at some of his early conversations on political topics with her husband; she did not always remain silent. The Crown Princess might enjoy ceremonial occasions more than Rudolf did, and far more than Elizabeth. But that was no fault in the wife of an heir to the throne; indeed, Stephanie's willingness to be present at Court functions won her Francis Joseph's warm approval. Rudolf remained happy in their home in Prague's Hradčany palace. When, after two and a half years of marriage, it was confirmed that Stephanie was pregnant, he hurried to Vienna to tell his father the good news in person.

This journey, too, won Francis Joseph's approval. He saw it as proof of his son's growing sense of dynasty. Just as Elizabeth once planned to give the name of Hungary's patron saint to the second son she never had, so Rudolf in his letters to Stephanie would refer to her coming child as 'Vaclav' (Wenceslas), the patron saint of Bohemia. Was this a private joke between husband and wife, or was it evidence of the Crown Prince's genuine admiration for the Czechs and their historic traditions? There is no indication that the Emperor knew of these exchanges; however, he suddenly approved of new military duties for the Crown Prince, making it certain that Rudolf would be in Lower Austria and not in Bohemia when the child was born.

There was to be no Archduke Wenceslas. On 2 September 1883 Crown Princess Stephanie gave birth at Laxenburg to a strong and healthy daughter. 'Never mind, a girl is much sweeter', Rudolf is reported to have told his wife, who was disappointed not to give the dynasty a male heir. Almost inevitably the Archduchess was named Elizabeth; and she became a favourite of her grandfather. Within the family she was known by the affectionate Magyar diminutive, 'Erzsi'. For, by Francis Joseph's reckoning, there could be no second 'Sisi'.

Chapter 15

GOLDEN EPOCH

For Austria-Hungary the 1880s were a time of promise left unfulfilled. In these years the Monarchy flowered in rich blossom soon blighted by the cold realities of social discontent. There was, at first, an increased prosperity and general stability; the astonishingly rapid growth of railways brought a semblance of economic unity to the Empire as a whole. By the winter of 1885–6, the budget was balanced in both parts of the Monarchy. At the same time, there was a far greater migration of the peasantry to the towns than in the troubled years immediately before Francis Joseph's accession. In central Vienna alone the population increased by 15.5 per cent during the 1880s, with an even larger growth in the inner suburbs. Ultimately urbanization proved a more significant development than the market integration of the economy. In the second half of the decade new mass movements, whose demagogic leaders pandered to popular prejudice and resentment, began to threaten the balance of parliamentary politics so carefully contrived by Taaffe as 'Emperor's minister'. But, before social discontent became a serious threat to stability, the solidly secure wealth of the middle classes provided money to spend on public and private buildings, on the visual arts and on theatre and music. There was a brief golden epoch of decorative pleasure and entertainment in the principal cities, and especially in Vienna, Budapest (a single municipality since 1872), and Prague.

Vienna remained the music capital of central Europe throughout the 1880s. Music could be heard, not only in the concert halls and opera houses, but in parks, wine gardens and beer cellars. Bruckner and Brahms were in their prime; Hugo Wolf, a prolific composer of Lieder, became an influential music critic for a Viennese weekly periodical in 1884; Gustav Mahler completed his first symphony before the end of the decade; while in Prague Dvořák was succeeding Smetana as the musical voice of the Czech people. Popular taste remained lightweight. Operetta flourished, particularly at the Theater an der Wien, where the triumph of

Franz von Suppé's *Bocaccio* in the winter of 1879–80 was followed by Karl Millöcker's *Der Bettelstudent* (Beggar Student), a great success at Christmas four years later. Hungarian audiences, too, enjoyed their light music; and Johann Strauss's *Gypsy Baron*, which delighted the Viennese in October 1885, received an even warmer reception at its Budapest première in the spring.

The artistic taste of the public continued to favour the exaggerated decorative style popularised by Hans Makart, even after his death in 1884, although floral designs and bouquets replaced the neo-Rubens inspiration of the Silver Wedding procession. The most enduring achievements of the decade were architectural. These were the years of the second phase of Ringstrasse building, heavy facades embellished by sculptured figures and offset, where open spaces permitted, by solemnly formal statuary. The Rathaus was finished in 1883 and the massive new home for the University some fourteen months later, fittingly at a time when its faculties of medicine and economics had won great respect throughout most of Europe and north America. Opposite the Rathaus work was in progress for most of the decade on a neo-Renaissance Burgtheater, which in 1888 replaced the smaller, much-loved baroque court theatre in the Michaelerplatz. The pretentions of Viennese architecture were matched by similar ambitious projects in Budapest: thus Austria's neo-classical *Parlaments-Gebaude* was completed in 1883, the year in which work started on its Hungarian counterpart, the grandiose parliament house on the Pest bank of the Danube. Prague, too, was given a neo-Renaissance palace: in 1885 work began on the Bohemian Museum, which was to dominate the newly landscaped Wenceslas Square; it was completed within five years. Trieste had a facelift to celebrate the city's quincentenary in 1882, while in Zagreb the cathedral and many public buildings were given the stamp of neo-Gothic modernity after an earthquake in November 1880 had rocked the Croatian capital and wrecked much of the old town.

Throughout this brief golden epoch, Francis Joseph remained a passive observer of the changes around him. He enjoyed the spectacle of Court balls and welcomed the succession of Strauss waltzes; he was glad to visit the theatre, provided a play did not tax his mind too severely; but he was hesitant over criticizing musical or artistic trends which he knew he had little hope of understanding. Yet he left a mark on the imperial capital, and indirectly on provincial centres which looked to Vienna for inspiration. For there is no doubt that Francis Joseph liked the neo-baroque style of architecture. When consulted over the siting of official buildings around the Ring, he favoured a disciplined orderliness which would preserve distant vistas. The elegant spaciousness of inner Vienna owes more to Francis Joseph's instinctive feeling for landscape than historians who deride his 'heavy and lifeless' lack of taste are prepared to concede.

In 1857 Francis Joseph took the initiative in transforming Vienna into a metropolis with his order for the walls and bastions of the city to be razed to the ground. Thirty years later he was still encouraging the growth of the capital. When, on 30 September 1888, he opened the Turkenschanzpark in Döbling, the Emperor welcomed the completion of this first municipal-sponsored parkland in the suburbs as a step towards the creation of a Greater Vienna, with the last internal barriers swept away; and, as a plaque in Turkenschanzpark still records, two years after his speech the integration of capital and suburbs was, indeed, finally achieved. But after a third of a century on the throne, Francis Joseph asserted his sovereignty less openly than in the early years of the reign. Letters Patent no longer appeared in print with the ringing autocratic decisiveness of the Bach era. Although there was no diminution in the reality of imperial power, during the 1880s the initiative in government lay with Taaffe, Kálmán Tisza or Kálnoky who were, at least in theory, dependent upon the support of the lower house of parliament, both in Cisleithania and Hungary. All matters concerning the army remained within the Emperor's prerogative, and he continued to take the final decision over foreign affairs. By now, however, Francis Joseph was acting circumspectly. In middle age he came to learn more about the practice of politics from that pliable improviser, Eddy Taaffe, than he had gathered in his youth from Metternich's occasional tuition.

Francis Joseph's compulsive sense of duty ensured that he fulfilled every task expected of him. He was at the festivities to mark the completion of the new University buildings in Vienna and he joined Burgermeister Eduard Uhl for the opening of the new Rathaus. He showed respect for musical genius by visiting the workroom of the sculptor, Heinrich Natter, from whom a monument to Joseph Haydn had been commissioned, soon after Natter first began shaping the marble. It was not that Francis Joseph was prepared to express an opinion on the design; he merely wished to inspect progress on a work of art under imperial patronage. Two years later, he duly unveiled the statue outside Haydn's parish church of Mariahilf. A similar sense of obligation ensured that he never missed the international art exhibitions at Vienna's Künstlerhaus in the Karlsplatz. At a time when Elizabeth was abroad, he dutifully accompanied Rudolf and Stephanie to Budapest for the Hungarian Landesexhibition; a less diligent monarch might well have been content to leave the show of royal support for the exhibition to the Crown Prince and Princess. The truth was that, though he might attend fewer ministerial conferences than in the 1850s and 1860s, he was still setting himself an impossibly high standard of duties to fulfil. Not least among them was the punctilio with which he observed royal courtesies. When Queen Victoria, travelling incognito by railway from Florence to Potsdam, passed through the Tyrol she was surprised to find Francis Joseph on the station platform at Innsbruck to greet her. She was even more astounded to learn that the Emperor had made an overnight train journey of 350 miles solely in order to exchange these brief pleasantries with her.

So long as his ministers enjoyed their sovereign's confidence Francis Joseph actively supported them with personal diplomacy. Often this required a conference with his fellow autocrats, as in the early years of his reign; and he was prepared to make a winter journey into Russian Poland to meet his old adversary, William I, and the new ruler of Russia, Alexander III, at the hunting-lodge of Skierniewice in order to uphold Kálnoky's faith in Bismarck's League of the Three Emperors. Sometimes he had to curb old prejudices so as to facilitate tactical shifts of policy. Although sensitive over matters of sovereignty, he agreed to recognize Milan Obrenović as a King in Belgrade rather than a Prince so as to strengthen Austria's hold on a client Serbia; and when Kálnoky persuaded Francis Joseph of the need to expand the Dual Alliance of 1879 with Germany into a Triple Alliance with Italy, the Emperor swallowed his misgivings over the House of Savoy's appropriation of papal Rome and entertained King Umberto and Queen Margherita on a four day state visit to Vienna. Yet, despite the conclusion of the Triple Alliance in May 1882, Francis Joseph had few illusions over the real feeling of Italian patriots towards the Habsburgs and he was not surprised when, five months later, the police discovered a plot to assassinate him during a tour of the southern provinces. Since Taaffe had already emphasized the need for imperial participation in the quincentenary celebrations at Trieste so as to counter the pro-Italian sentiment in the Monarchy's third largest city, Francis Joseph went ahead with the planned journey despite police fears of further dangerous conspiracies.

The visit did nothing to improve Austro-Italian relations, as both Taaffe and Kálnoky had hoped: the subsequent execution of the principal conspirator, Guglielmo Oberdank, gave the irredentists a martyr-hero whom they idolised for the rest of the decade, despite the formal alliance partnership of Vienna, Berlin and Rome. In retrospect, the most significant aspect of the Trieste quincentenary was the presence in the city of the Empress as well as of the Emperor. For Elizabeth, like Francis Joseph, observed a code of duty, though one of her own making. In 1881 she had gladly handed over some of her drearier responsibilities as First Lady to Crown Princess Stephanie: now she surprised Taaffe with her insistence on joining Francis Joseph at Miramare. It was characteristic of

Elizabeth's concept of dynastic obligation that, while willingly shirking the round of social trivialities in the capital, she had no hesitation in sharing with her husband the dangers of a visit to his remaining Italian provinces. A similar sense of duty once made her cut short a hunting season in England so as to help Francis Joseph comfort the victims of the floods at Szeged; and she had been beside him in the harrowing aftermath of the fire at Vienna's Ringtheater in December 1881, a disaster in which several hundred members of the audience perished. Among the victims was Ladislaus Vetsera, the eldest brother of ten-year old Mary.

The Ringtheater tragedy came barely a week after the Crown Prince wrote the long, critical letter to Latour in which he complained that his mother no longer cared for anything except hunting. This was unfair, as Rudolf must have realized when the family came together at Christmas for Elizabeth's 44th birthday. His mother still spent several hours each day ensuring that she looked young, but she was far less agile than in the first years she went riding in England. Soon she would be forced to curb her constant craving to leap into the saddle; she might even, so her husband hoped, give up those long weeks of foreign travel. No one expected the Empress would be content with fulfilling public duties in the Hofburg or Schönbrunn, and she was always restless at Laxenburg (which, some months later, was badly damaged by fire while the Crown Prince was in residence). But Francis Joseph believed Elizabeth might enjoy the happiness of semi-retirement in a new home on the edge of the Vienna woods. Ever since their first years of marriage, they had gained particular pleasure from rides in the parkland at Lainz; and in the autumn of 1881, Francis Joseph agreed to have a small villa built in a secluded part of the Lainzer Tiergarten. It was intended as a family lodge, free from court ceremonial, tucked away from the public gaze, with life at least as intimate as at Gödöllö, Elizabeth's favourite royal residence. Francis Joseph would pay for the villa from his personal funds and present it as a gift to his beloved Sisi.

The prospect of privacy in a home only a short carriage drive from the parade-ground pomposity of Schönbrunn delighted the Empress. To relieve the boredom of public life she enjoyed creating a poetic fantasy world in which she would identify herself with Shakespeare's queen of the fairies, and she duly called her husband's gift 'Titania's enchanted castle' – a villa in a wood near Vienna made a fine substitute for a flowery bed in a wood near Athens. But there was no Oberon to conjure up a dream palace at the wave of a wand. Prosaically, her generous husband commissioned Karl von Hasenauer, architect of the Burgtheater and many of the museums around the Ring, to design a two-storeyed 'hunting lodge in the imperial and royal Tiergarten'. His first plans were ready for scrutiny in mid-December 1881, when it was accepted that the house would not be ready for occupation for four or five years. Work began in the spring, with the original design of symmetrical stables and guardhouses modified, to lessen the formal appearance of the villa.

Francis Joseph suffered an early disappointment. For the prospect of becoming chatelaine of an enchanted castle seems to have revived Elizabeth's desire 'to wander everywhere swifter than the moon's sphere'. Even before the workmen began clearing the site of the villa, she was off to England for one last month of following the hounds, with a stag hunt at Chantilly on her way home. By now, however, she was riding far less, for she suffered from the first twinges of sciatica. Yet the threat of physical weakness served to intensify her eccentricities. Francis Joseph thought he was giving a splendid horsewoman a hunting lodge of her own; the original plans provided for a small riding school as well as extensive stables. But he still did not understand his wife's temperament. Between 1882 and 1885 Elizabeth's interests changed more dramatically than her way of life. Abandonment of the saddle did not domesticate her. What had begun as a hunting lodge in the Tiergarten became a villa named after Hermes, the winged messenger of the Gods and patron of travellers.

The transformation was gradual. At first Elizabeth persisted with gymnastic exercises every morning. This was to be expected; Francis Joseph had seen to it that the draft plans included a personal gymnasium, next to the Empress's washroom. By the autumn, however, she was supplementing her morning exercises with daily fencing lessons. Soon she began to undertake long excursions on foot, especially when she was visiting her native Bavaria or the Salzkammergut. In the second week of June 1883 she insisted on covering the 22 miles from central Munich to Feldafing on the Starnbergersee on foot along a military road with little shade and under a blazing sun; she protected herself with a parasol, and completed the self-imposed route march in seven hours. To the Empress's exhausted attendants her pace seemed more of a trot than a walk. At Ischl a month later she set herself a target of seven and three-quarter hours walking each day, ordering wagons to follow her, with chairs for the ladies-in-waiting. A 23-mile round trip up the wooded Langbathtal kept Elizabeth walking for almost nine hours. Crown Princess Stephanie's memoirs recall how 'the Empress would never stop for a midday meal, and at the most would drink a glass of milk or some orange juice'. All this activity did not benefit her health. To Francis Joseph's consternation, Elizabeth became pale and thin.

Her mother and father (both by now in their mid-seventies) and her sisters were also alarmed. They were puzzled over changes in her attitude to people. To their surprise she formed a close attachment to her cousin,

King Ludwig II of Bavaria. She had been fond of him in his boyhood but observed his erratic behaviour after his accession with mounting indignation. Now she sympathised with him, as he mourned the death of his idol, Richard Wagner. Long talks with Ludwig in 1883 convinced Elizabeth that he was, like her, a poetic soul sustained by the beauty of a dream world of the imagination. Ludwig told her that he saw himself as an eagle, with his throne the high crag of a mountain; she came to see herself as a seagull, at liberty to glide unrestrained over the oceans. Small wonder if her family was worried.

Other changes were less disturbing. Elizabeth began to read more deeply than for many years. Her passion for the poetry of Heinrich Heine reached a new intensity. With the encouragement of her younger daughter, she once more scribbled verses down on paper. Often she consciously echoed Heine, but sometimes she achieved a certain originality, allowing her pen to sublimate the flow of romantic fancy in which she exulted. With renewed energy, she expanded her education. She was, of course, still Titania, but the fairy queen had a wider vision now; for, with the rediscovery of poetry, came a revived enthusiasm for classical Greece. Soon she was learning Homer by heart and, inspired by Schliemann's excavations at Troy, Mycenae and Tiryns, she planned a fourth cruise down to Corfu and beyond. Achilles became her particular hero. When she ordered a copy of Herterich's statue of the dying warrior for the Miramare gardens, it was clear her interests had gone beyond the dogs and horses and huntsmen that filled her idle hours when she first sought a homely villa in the Lainzer Tiergarten.

To respond fittingly to Elizabeth's quicksilver enthusiasms would have been a hard task for any husband. Francis Joseph did his best to please her. Fortunately they retained their shared love of horses, even if he was often alarmed by the risks she took in the saddle. He was prepared to accept her cult of Titania, though after accompanying her to see *A Midsummer Night's Dream* for the first time he had confided to his mother that it was 'rather boring and very stupid'. He was irritated by her admiration for Heine, a dangerous radical by the reckoning of Metternich's censors in the Emperor's youth; but he allowed her a statue of the poet in the grounds of their home at Ischl. Her delight in romantic classicism left him unappreciative; 'I find it hard to imagine what you can find to do with yourself in Ithaca for so many days', he wrote when Elizabeth was at last hot on the trail of Odysseus in his native island. Yet, despite this cold douche, 'the main thing is that you are well and happy' he added.

It was in this mood that Francis Joseph continued to indulge her whims over the interior decoration of the Hermes Villa. She might have her

Titania frescoes and her Pompeian murals in the washroom. Above the pediment of the gymnasium door two centaurs achieved curvets worthy of the finest Lippizaners in the Spanish Riding School; and when the Empress awoke in the morning, there above her she could see Zeus's chariot emerging from billowing clouds painted on the bedroom ceiling. It was all rather overdone, as Francis Joseph knew. But he felt bound to consult his artistic advisers, and Hans Makart's taste prevailed. Some of the old egoist's protégés – notably the brothers Gustav and Ernst Klimt – showed an enlightened initiative, adding a touch of grace to elegance robbed of delicacy. But under Makart's influence a home planned as a simple lodge became a compact and cluttered chateau, rich in colours, marble reliefs, thick carpets and heavy drapery. Even today, when the villa is in effect an art museum, the ornate ceiling of 'the Emperor's workroom' stands out in striking contrast to the simple white stucco of his study at Schönbrunn.

On 24 May 1886 Francis Joseph, Elizabeth and the Archduchess Marie Valerie visited the completed Hermes Villa, though another year elapsed before they went into residence. The Emperor admired its finery but was heard to remark 'I shall always be afraid of spoiling things'. The Empress was delighted by the garden. For the rest of her life, she was glad to seek the seclusion of the Tiergarten. But her horizon had broadened by now. Barely two years after this first visit she let her husband know that she wished to have a small palace dedicated to Achilles built for her on Corfu. 'That will do me no good with the Viennese', Francis Joseph confessed privately; but it was a long time since he had denied his wife any request. Elizabeth was duly promised her Achilleion.

When the Empress had resumed her travels in 1882 Francis Joseph sank back into accustomed habits. At Ischl he donned leather shorts, green jacket, thick woollen socks, mountaineer's boots and Tyrolean hat; out came hunting rifles and cartridge belts and he would stalk the mountain slopes for as many weeks as official duties permitted. In the autumn he hunted at Gödöllö or at Mürzsteg, a lodge in Styria about halfway between Semmering and Graz. It was in Vienna that he suffered most from social isolation; he might shoot at Lainz, or ride in the Prater, or take solitary walks around the Laxenburg parkland. But for long weeks he was denied all family life.

At Schönbrunn he could at least still seek the company of Anna Nahowski. His visits became especially frequent in 1884 when – still aged only 25 – she moved to her spacious new house at Hietzing, opposite to the side gate of Schönbrunn's 'Tyrolean Garden'. In the welfare of one of Anna's children, Helene (who was to marry the composer, Alban Berg) he took some interest, giving the mother the very considerable sum of

100,000 Gulden when, in 1883, the girl was born. But though Anna might satisfy Francis Joseph's physical desires, she seems to have been a young woman of limited interests: did they ever have a real conversation? There is no doubt that he tired of her and it is probable that, as he grew older, he found the twenty-nine year gap in their ages increasingly exacting, although he did not finally break with Anna until the end of the decade. However, about the time of Helene Nahowski's birth, he met for the first time the actress he had seen play Kate in *The Taming of the Shrew* ten years before; and soon his friendship with Katharina Schratt was to give him greater solace and a wiser human understanding than any other relationship he experienced.

Fortune had buffeted Katharina Schratt since her early success at the Stadttheater. In September 1879 she married Nicholas Kiss von Itebbe, a handsome Hungarian, who lived well beyond his means in a fourteen room apartment in Vienna's Gumpendorferstrasse. Katharina retired from the stage and a son, Toni, was born in the following summer. But in 1882 Nicholas Kiss, heavily in debt, fled from his creditors, leaving Katharina to face the bailiffs. The Viennese theatres refused to re-engage her. For a year she played in New York, leaving Toni with her parents at Baden; but she was back in the Monarchy by the following spring; an aristocratic admirer found her playing in a company at Czernowitz, a garrison town in the Bukovina, almost on the Russian frontier. Monetary help and graceful hospitality from wealthy friends enabled her to settle again in the capital: Eduard Palmer, presiding director of a mining company, became her financial adviser and helped her to gain admittance to the Burgtheater within six months of being Czernowitz's leading lady. New entrants to the imperial theatre were received in audience by the Emperor. The natural freshness and vivacity of Katharina at this meeting made an impression he never forgot. He began making frequent visits to the Burgtheater. It was noticed he always chose nights when Frau Schratt was listed to appear.

They do not seem to have met again until February 1885, when the Emperor was observed in long conversation with the actress at the annual Industriellenball in the Hofburg's Redoutensaal. Katharina was by no means blind to her opportunities for advancement, for in the following summer she accepted a seasonal engagement at Ischl, where Francis Joseph was accustomed to celebrate his birthday. And on 17 August 1885 the Crown Prince and Crown Princess, Prince Leopold of Bavaria and Archduchess Marie Valerie accompanied him to the Ischl Kurhaustheater for a birthday eve entertainment: Katharina Schratt as Rosel in Ferdinand Raimund's *Der Verschwender* (The Spendthrift), a musical tale of virtue triumphing over a husband's fecklessness. The theme ran close to the actress's heart. Nine days later she appeared before her Emperor and the Tsar in a one-act comedy presented by the Burgtheater company as a command performance in Kremsier during the Austro-Russian summit conference in the Moravian archbishop's summer palace. That evening, at Alexander III's insistence, all three leading actresses joined the Emperors and Empresses for supper.

Elizabeth noticed Francis Joseph's partiality for Katharina Schratt's company, and there is no doubt that she encouraged the attachment. At times she felt remorse for constantly seeking to escape from sharing the Emperor's monotonous round of duty; he deserved lively companionship. She may, perhaps, have known of the Nahowski ménage in Hietzing and have sought a social arrangement less dangerously compromising for her husband. But she will also have been influenced by her current idolization of Heine: in the last year of his life the poet had been cheered and inspired by the platonic friendship of Elise Krinitz, a young social gadfly whom he nicknamed 'La Mouche'; and eighteen months before the Kremsier meeting Krinitz had published, under the pseudonym Camille Selden, her reminiscences of the months when she so successfully lightened Heine's deep depression. Elizabeth read everything she could obtain written by Heine or about Heine. What could seem more natural to her than to look for an Austrian 'mouche' who would brighten her husband's lonelier days? She commissioned a portrait of the actress from Heinrich von Angeli, an artist to whom the Emperor frequently gave his patronage; she would present the painting as a gift to her husband, just as he had presented her with a home in the Lainzer Tiergarten. On 21 May 1886 – three days before Elizabeth became chatelaine of the Hermes Villa – Katharina Schratt was at Angeli's studio when, to her genuine surprise, the Empress brought her husband to inspect progress on the portrait. Sovereign and actress chatted together informally while Elizabeth took a gracious interest in Angeli's other canvases. Two days later Francis Joseph, signing himself 'Your devoted admirer', sent Katharina the first of more than 500 letters. Over the following thirty years, they were to serve as a safety-valve for the suppressed tensions of his inner self.

For the Emperor and Empress the completion of the Hermes Villa and the commissioning of the Angeli portrait were welcome diversions from a protracted international crisis which threatened to plunge Europe into war. At Kremsier Francis Joseph and Kálnoky emphasized their hopes for continued good relations with Russia while Tsar Alexander III re-affirmed his confidence in the League of the Three Emperors, Bismarck's method of maintaining collaboration between the eastern autocrats through a system of common self-denial. But Crown Prince Rudolf – and, rather unexpectedly, his mother – mistrusted the sincerity of the

Tsar's protestations of friendship. A month before the Kremsier meeting Rudolf had written to Latour strongly criticising Kálnoky's appeasement of Russia in the Balkans. He failed to appreciate the delicate nature of Kálnoky's balancing act in the East. In particular, he underestimated the importance of his achievement in drawing Roumania into a secret defensive alliance against Russia in October 1884, with Germany underwriting the treaty.

The Eastern Question was posed again sooner than either Rudolf or his father anticipated. Shortly before the Kremsier meeting Francis Joseph received at Ischl Prince Alexander of Battenberg who, with the backing of the Great Powers, had become sovereign prince of the small Bulgaria created at the Berlin Congress. In September 1885 Alexander showed his independence by proclaiming the 'union of the two Bulgarias', thus linking the predominantly Bulgarian Ottoman province of Eastern Rumelia with his principality. Thereupon neighbouring Serbia, alarmed by the shift of power in the Balkans invaded Bulgaria, only to be defeated by Prince Alexander at Slivnitza (17 November 1885). In this sudden crisis Francis Joseph and Kálnoky strove to keep the peace; they held Austria-Hungary to a common policy of mediation agreed by her partners, Germany and Russia. But their judicious statesmanship was far from popular in the twin capitals of the Monarchy. Andrássy, who was contemplating a return to public life, sent Francis Joseph a long memorandum recommending the imposition of a settlement of Balkan frontiers which would be agreeable to political and commercial interests in Vienna and Budapest.

Neither the Emperor nor Beck, his Chief of the General Staff, were prepared to risk a war in which they could not count on unqualified German support. Not least among their considerations was the mounting threat of two popular mass movements within the Monarchy: the demagogic Pan-German followers of George von Schönerer opposed the dynasty and its chief pillars, the army and the Catholic Church, and would have exploited any rebuff, military or diplomatic; and there had already been two large-scale socialist demonstrations in Vienna. By using diplomatic pressure to halt the Bulgarians after Slivnitza, Kálnoky patiently defused the crisis. A series of ambassadorial conferences in Constantinople patched up the Balkan frontiers by the following spring; and, despite the lobbying of the Russophobes in Vienna, the League of the Three Emperors remained in being, offering Austria-Hungary a certain security in the north and the east.

It was therefore with some confidence of a peaceful summer that, in June 1886, Francis Joseph and Katharina Schratt compared their planned itineraries. She told him of her intention to take the waters at Karlsbad and spend most of July in the Salzkammergut, having leased a villa at

Frauenstein, above St Wolfgang. The Emperor informed her that he would be at Ischl in early July and would visit her holiday home, since St Wolfgang was only an hour's carriage drive along the shore of the lake. This excursion Francis Joseph duly undertook, inviting himself to breakfast at half-past eight in the morning almost as soon as Katharina had completed the long journey south from Bohemia. From surviving letters of that summer and nostalgic references in later correspondence it is clear that over the following weeks he profited from her infectious gaiety, discovering how to chatter over trivialities in an easy, intimate manner he had not experienced since boyhood. He would invite himself to breakfast once or twice a week. On these occasions, despite the time of day, Katharina would slip into a light comedy role, vivacious, sharp-witted and enlivened by mimicry. The best performances of Katharina Schratt's career may well have been at her breakfast table on these mornings in July and August 1886. There was no amatory intimacy: he enjoyed 'sitting together chatting in the comfortable room at Frauenstein' too much to risk cheapening the honour of his newly found friend. Moreover he had not finally broken with Anna Nahowski – whom he was to visit at Hietzing on 23 August, only a few days after his return to Schönbrunn.

The Empress, having kindled the romantic glow of friendship, was not at Ischl in July to watch it burn with a steady flame. That summer brought her little joy. From May onwards, she awaited the unfolding of the year with trepidation, for she had come across an adage predicting that a late Easter brings sorrows before Christmas; and Easter Day fell on 25 April in 1886, the latest possible date in the Christian calendar. At the end of the first week in June she travelled to Bavaria, accompanied by her younger daughter, Valerie. She was therefore at Feldafing on the west shore of the Starnbergersee when the life of her cousin King Ludwig ended in tragedy. On the late evening of 13 June, two days after he had been put under physical restraint for his mental aberrations, the bodies of Ludwig and his attendant doctor were found on the eastern side of the Starnbergersee, almost opposite to Feldafing.

The news was broken to Elizabeth by her elder daughter, Gisela, at breakfast next morning. It was assumed that the King had thrown himself into the lake and that the doctor had died trying to save him. But in the course of the day Elizabeth became deeply agitated: had Ludwig been trying to swim across the lake to her, as the one person who could sympathise with the fantasies of his mind? That night Valerie was shocked to find her mother distraught, lying on the floor of her room. For several days Elizabeth would burst suddenly into tears and accuse the Bavarian authorities of complicity in Ludwig's murder. Often her talk seems to have lacked coherence: Titania was transformed into an ageing Ophelia.

Francis Joseph sent the Crown Prince to represent the Monarchy at Ludwig's funeral. Rudolf was alarmed by his mother's protracted grief and agitation: it was clear to poor Valerie that her brother, though comforting and charming in his manner, was wondering if Mama, too, suffered from the mental instability of the Wittelsbachs; and to what extent were these disorders hereditary? Once she recovered her general composure similar doubts began to trouble Elizabeth. Much of the poetry she wrote in the remaining months of the year showed an obsession with death. At the same time she became fascinated by the problems of the mentally disturbed. A fortnight before Christmas, without consulting Francis Joseph, Elizabeth made a surprise visit to Brundlfeld, the principal asylum serving Vienna; this was the occasion of the well-known encounter with an inmate who insisted that she was the true Empress Elizabeth and that the visitor who received all the honours was an impostor.

During these closing weeks of the year Francis Joseph was preoccupied with renewed tension in the Balkans. The Russians, having decided that Alexander of Battenberg was by nature too independent to serve their interests, kidnapped the Prince in mid-August. At first it seemed as if there would, for once, be no acute crisis. To the Emperor's satisfaction Kálnoky treated this latest coup in Sofia in a firm and conciliatory manner: the Russians were induced to release the Prince and allow him to cross into Austria; but it was agreed in Vienna and in St Petersburg that, for the sake of European peace, 'the Battenberg' should abdicate and allow the Bulgarian parliament to elect another Prince. But, to Francis Joseph's dismay, Alexander III almost immediately sent his aide-de-camp General Kaulbars to Sofia as a personal envoy; and Kaulbars was expected to browbeat and bully the Bulgarian politicians into electing a ruler nominated by the Tsar. 'Unthinkable for Austria-Hungary', Kálnoky declared, fearing that a Russian puppet in Bulgaria would ensure Panslav control over all the Balkans, including non-Slav Roumania, Austria-Hungary's secret ally. Francis Joseph agreed with his minister; in Budapest both Tisza and Kálnoky made threatening speeches; and for two months it seemed probable that the Crown Prince's preventive war pressure group in Vienna would persuade the Emperor to throw caution to the winds. But he was an older, sadder and wiser commander-in-chief than in the days of Buol and Gyulai. Bismarck would do nothing to help his ally; though Kálnoky received some diplomatic support from the British, it was clear that in a general war, the Imperial-Royal Army would have to fight the Russians alone. Thankfully, late in November the Tsar summoned Kaulbars back to the capital. But the Russian foreign ministry had no contact with Francis Joseph's ambassador in St Petersburg; it was as if the two Empires had severed diplomatic relations, an embassy official complained in late December.

Christmas at the Hofburg was gloomy. Francis Joseph had for company a sad Empress, suffering from sciatica and aware she was entering her fiftieth year, and a Crown Prince who showed his impatience at what he still regarded as the indecisive political leadership of his father's ministers. Valerie, her mother's constant solace, was with her parents; but the Archduchess too was unhappy, complaining in her journal of Rudolf's sarcastic manner when conversation turned to finding a suitor for her. Gifts and greetings from Katharina Schratt brought Francis Joseph a childlike pleasure on Christmas Eve; a note of thanks next day emphasized his eagerness to see her star in a worthwhile role: 'I am always pleased when I see your name on the posters or learn from the advance circular that you are to play' in a particular production. A week later, however, he too was depressed. Lack of news from St Petersburg and close proximity to Rudolf's sustained sabre-rattling may well account for the tone of his New Year's Day letter: 'God grant that the year now beginning will be peaceful', Katharina was told, 'Unfortunately at the moment the prospect is poor. I could then hope that last summer's lovely time would be renewed in this year, too, and I would realize the longed-for joy of being able to be near you again, to talk to you again. In these days of deep trouble and heavy work, the recollection of the wonderful times past and the hope of their return come as rays of light for me'.

Elizabeth's 'New Year's Night' poem also anticipated a general war; and at a Crown Council on 7 January Francis Joseph told his ministers that, though he wished to maintain peace, 'all necessary measures are to be taken' in case there should be 'a sudden deterioration of the political situation in the near future'. But Russia did not want a war. Cool, calm deliberation triumphed. By midsummer the danger was over. Although the League of the Three Emperors might be dead, Kálnoky could offer his master three gains from the protracted crisis: a close understanding with Great Britain concerning Mediterranean problems; a renewal of the alliance with Roumania (though there was constant friction between Budapest and Bucharest over commercial tariffs); and a renewal of the Triple Alliance (Germany, Austria-Hungary, Italy) even if the Italians insisted on a supplementary agreement promising 'reciprocal compensation' for territorial gains in the Balkans.

Francis Joseph was not entirely sure if the final settlement of Bulgaria's dynastic problem was to the Monarchy's advantage. For in early July 1887, Sofia's parliamentary deputies unanimously elected an Austrian cavalry officer, Prince Ferdinand of Saxe-Coburg, as their new ruler. 'Illegal', the Russians complained, 'a worthless comedy staged by the most wretched rabble'. Francis Joseph was not displeased at Russia's discomfiture but he, too, was uneasy over the election: Ferdinand had hardly distinguished himself in the 11th Hussars, and the Emperor thought him effeminate, lacking that strength of character he so respected in King Carol I of Roumania. These considered judgments on the Prince may have owed something to the discovery that he had recently sought Frau Schratt's companionship at Karlsbad. But Francis Joseph acknowledged that Ferdinand was unlikely to become a Russian catspaw. As Kálnoky pointed out, the new Prince was a Roman Catholic and he came from a branch of the Coburgs who had augmented their funds by marrying into the extremely wealthy Hungarian princely family of Kohary. Moreover, as a relative of Queen Victoria, Ferdinand might afford the British new reasons for interesting themselves in the maintenance of Balkan stability. Yet, though Francis Joseph learnt to respect 'Foxy Ferdinand's' political dexterity, he never liked him. A certain restraint may have sprung in part from jealousy over Katharina Schratt's lifelong friendship with her 'brotherly friend' in Sofia. Ferdinand was, after all, more than thirty years his junior – and nearly eight years younger than Katharina herself.

Early in July 1887 Francis Joseph's 'longed-for joy' was, as he had hoped, fulfilled; once more he could relax at Ischl while Katharina was at Frauenstein. In that year he had as yet seen little of the Empress, for soon after Carnival time she was on her travels again: down to southern Hungary and into Roumania; then, after a brief family reunion at the Villa Hermes, up to Hamburg in order to visit Heine's sister and across the North Sea for a month on the Norfolk coast. There was a strange contrast in their lives that July. While Francis Joseph was enjoying the coffee and rich pastries Frau Schratt's cooks had ready for him each morning, Elizabeth would come down to Cromer beach from the small bow-windowed hotel annexe she had rented on the cliffs. At Frauenstein the Emperor (as his later letters show) would explain 'how a military manoeuvre is performed' to an actress who, in her turn, amazed him with the tittle-tattle of stage rivalries. On Cromer sands, the Empress would settle in solitary simplicity under her lace parasol, glance out across the same sea that had inspired Heine, and scribble verse after verse on her notepads. She completed 28 poems at Cromer, a literary output which astounded Valerie when a few weeks later her mother read her the verses. Elizabeth was attracted by the quiet little Norfolk town with its church tower landmark; she enjoyed her sea trips and was fascinated by tales of lost villages which had fallen under the waves as the coast was eroded. She wrote sympathetically of a nun whom she saw sitting each day on the shore, and she wrote angrily of a man who persisted in turning his binoculars on her from the clifftop – the verse even threatens she will lift up her skirts and reveal more than the peeping Tom ever expected. But, all in all, her Cromer poems – good, bad, or indifferent – reflect a welcome contentment. She was in a happy mood for the first time since the tragedy of Ludwig. To Francis Joseph's relief she agreed to travel to the Isle of Wight for a courtesy call on Queen Victoria; she would be at Ischl for his birthday. 'My infinitely beloved angel, your dear letter made me very happy', he replied. But from Ischl, a few weeks later, one last poem – *Ruckblick* (Backward Glance) – recalled the 'fine days' she spent at Cromer.

Once back in Austria the Empress amused her ladies (and mildly embarrassed Valerie) by snide remarks over Katharina's robust figure. The Emperor's devotion to his friend ran deeper than Elizabeth had thought possible during their visit to Angeli's studio; and her feelings towards Katharina may have been a shade less generous than is suggested by those open avowals of friendship which her husband found so gratifying. Some verses have survived which mock Francis Joseph's delight in what Elizabeth implies was a feigned simplicity of manner on the part of the actress. But she, too, needed Frau Schratt – for by mid-October the Empress was off again, sailing down to Corfu. It was good to know her husband would not fret in her absence. Almost every letter from him during this period of separation refers to walks or talks with the 'War Minister' (their code-name for Katharina) or includes news from the Viennese theatre world. When Elizabeth rejoined him at Gödöllö in time for St Catherine's Day (25 November) it was she who ordered champagne to drink the absent friend's health on her saint's day. 'I was really surprised to see champagne glasses set on the table', the Emperor wrote to Katharina, 'We do not usually permit ourselves the luxury of this wine'.

There runs through Francis Joseph's letters in this second winter of close friendship an apologetic strain of self-depreciation, mingled with happiness at his good fortune: 'To see you again would make me happy, but of course only if it pleases you, if you feel well and if you can spare the time', he wrote; and 'With what delight I saw you look up several times to my window', after he had watched her cross an inner courtyard of the Hofburg on her way to early Mass. A fortnight later he proclaimed 'Were I not so old and had no cough, I could shout with joy at the idea of meeting you again tomorrow – I hope'. These manifestations of persistent calf-love nearly 40 years since he had said 'Farewell my youth' induced Katharina Schratt to send Francis Joseph, who was in the castle at Budapest, a carefully phrased 'letter of meditation' (*Gedankenbrief*) for St Valentine's Day in 1888 in which she offered to become his mistress. He was flattered ('especially when I look into the mirror and my old wrinkled face stares back at me') and he told her openly, what 'you must at least guess ... that I adore you'. But he insisted that their relationship 'must remain for the future as it has been until now', for 'I love my wife and do not wish to abuse her confidence and her friendship with you'. He added, 'I am too old to be a brotherly friend, but treat me as a fatherly friend'. The letter determined the form of their friendship and therefore made it happier and easier in the future. As he admitted a few days later, 'Frankness is best ... and now it will save me from that stupid jealousy which so often plagues me'. Then he looked out of his window above the Danube in Budapest, saw snow falling and added wistfully, 'If we were walking in Schönbrunn and the slope above the Tyrolean Garden was again slippery, perhaps I might be permitted to take your arm'.

These exchanges with Katharina lifted the Emperor's spirits as the golden epoch approached what he regarded as its climax. For in that spring Vienna's Ringstrasse would be completed and on the anniversary of Maria Theresa's birth he would unveil a huge monument to his great-great-grandmother in a square between museums newly built to house the Empire's finest collections of natural history and art. He intended the ceremony on 13 May to serve as a salute from the dynasty to the woman whose courage had saved the Habsburg crown.

Unexpectedly Francis Joseph, too, needed courage that spring. For while he was still in Budapest, the submerged tensions in a cosmopolitan city came to the surface in Vienna and plunged the capital into a series of street demonstrations which bordered on riot. The *Neues Wiener Tagblatt* – of which the Crown Prince's friend, Szeps, was the editor – believed it had a journalistic scoop on 8 March: the morning edition announced the death of William I and printed an obituary when the octogenarian German Emperor still had another twenty-four hours of half-existence to endure. The paper's action was interpreted by the Pan-Germans in Vienna as an insult to the first sovereign of a unified Germany; and, with Schönerer at their head, a group of Pan-Germans burst into the newspaper's editorial offices and threatened the staff with violence. Schönerer was a member of the lower chamber of parliament but so disgusted were his colleagues at this behaviour that the House immediately withdrew his immunity from arrest; he was charged with unlawful entry into the *Tagblatt*'s office and sentenced to five months solitary confinement and five years loss of civic rights. The Pan-Germans were indignant. On the evening before the monument was unveiled, thousands of Schönerer's supporters marched along the Ring, passing the draped statue and shouting, 'Down with the Habsburgs! Down with Austria! Down with the Jewish Press! Long live Germany!'. There were fears the Emperor might be insulted in a further demonstration next day. A celebration of the past seemed threatened by an ominous portent – just half a century before the Anschluss.

Never before and never again was there so great a dynastic parade in Vienna. No less than 66 Archdukes and Archduchesses joined the Emperor and Empress for the ceremony. As well as the élite regiments with their bands and the pick of Viennese choirs to sing a *Te Deum*, all the pupils from the Theresian Academy were mustered on parade to honour their founder: 'How handsome they looked!', the Emperor commented soon afterwards. He scorned all thought of insult. Despite the deprecatory comments on his appearance in his private letters, he was still an impressive figure: straight-backed, in a tight-fitting white tunic above scarlet trousers, he looked taller and far younger than he appeared to the townsfolk of Ischl who saw him on the days when he liked to set out for the mountains. Elizabeth, despite hating public occasions, was so moved by the unveiling ceremony that she sought to capture the emotions of the day in a long poem. She was not worried for her husband's well-being: the crowd's ovation emphasized the widespread rejection of Schönerer's mob violence. But Elizabeth was suddenly alarmed by her son's appearance: Rudolf was pale, his eyes were dull and restless, and there were deep shadows beneath them. 'Are you ill?', she asked. 'No, only tired and exhausted', Rudolf replied. She seems to have assumed he was worried over the threats to his liberal and Jewish friends; for she said no more to her son.

Francis Joseph was pleased with the ceremony. The weather was splendid; no member of the family excused himself or herself from the parade; and Kaspar von Zumbusch, who designed and created the monument, had a fine achievement to his credit, with Maria Theresa's counsellors and generals grouped respectfully on the plinth below her. It was right that the crowds should applaud and cheer when their Emperor shook hands with Kaspar. Only one disappointment slightly marred Francis Joseph's day: 'Though you had kindly pointed out to me the privileged stand for spectators, because of the distance and the great mass of people, it was impossible for me to identify you there', he wrote to Katharina Schratt before breakfast a couple of days later. 'Although I especially looked that way, as you perhaps noticed, I had to content myself with a feeling you were there and knowing you were quite close'. But, as he reminded his friend, there would be the banks of the Wolfgangsee in the hot summer months ahead.

Chapter 16

MAYERLING AND AFTER

'On Monday, I will settle at Mayerling', Crown Prince Rudolf told Bombelles on the last Wednesday in July 1887; 'It will suit me very well'. In retrospect the comment seems heavy with portent, for within eighteen months his death at Mayerling was to give the place a tragic notoriety which still provokes occasional headlines in Vienna's tabloid press. But there was nothing sinister in Rudolf's message. The forested hills around Baden and Mödling, less than 20 miles from the capital, had long attracted him. He appreciated the leafy silence of the woods; he once wrote perceptively of their beauty, of changing shades of green in beeches and oaks, 'on a beautiful June evening, when the last rays of the sun throw a golden light on the rounded crest of the hills'. Like other visitors to the region, he was intrigued by relics of its tumultuous past: an isolated watchtower against Turkish invaders standing above the valleys, as if it were a landscaped Gothic ruin; or a monastery set among the lower meadows, enabling (as Rudolf wrote) 'the Angelus to ring out in resonant tones from the lofty spires' and mingle 'with the melancholy sound of the shepherd's horn'. In this enchanting woodland he sought a secluded and compact home. He found it at Mayerling, where a fifteenth century chapel and pilgrim's hospice, twice ravaged by the Turks, had been restored for a third time by Abbot Grunbeck of Heiligenkreuz, the great Cistercian abbey a few miles to the east. Early in 1887 Rudolf purchased the buildings from the white monks for conversion into a hunting lodge. By Christmas his personal stationery carried the letterhead 'Schloss Mayerling' beneath the embossed antlers of a deer. Outside the lodge walls a Holy Sepulchre chapel kept faith with the pilgrim past.

His son's acquisition of Mayerling was of little concern to Francis Joseph, who never visited the Schloss until after Rudolf's death. Yet this indifference to Rudolf's activities did not spring from any conflict of generations, and it would be a mistake to assume that relations between father and son were constantly strained. The Emperor continued to be impressed by Rudolf's wide range of interests. When Count Samuel Teleki wished to give Rudolf's name to the huge lake he had discovered in East Africa, the Emperor gave his approval, seeing the Count's request as a tribute to his son's backing of scientific discovery. And Francis Joseph was well aware that he could not have opened Vienna's prestigious 'Electrical Exhibition' in August 1883 with a speech of such confident authenticity as his son. 'May an ocean of light radiate from this city, may new progress arise from it', were sentiments which encouraged Rudolf's generation; from his socially conservative father they would have seemed derisively insincere. The Crown Prince enjoyed a felicitous gift for public speaking denied to the Emperor and, indeed, to most Archdukes as well.

Francis Joseph welcomed Rudolf's initiative in encouraging the publication of *Die Osterreichisch-ungarische Monarchie in Wort und Bild*, a twenty-four volume encyclopaedic survey of the Habsburg realm 'in word and picture'. The Crown Prince made substantial contributions himself (including the rhapsodic passages on Lower Austria quoted earlier in this chapter). In December 1885 he presented the Emperor with the first printed volume of a project which, though always called 'the Crown Prince's work' was not finished until thirteen years after the Mayerling tragedy. Francis Joseph was also pleased by the publication in Austrian weekly periodicals of several travel articles in which his son showed a detailed knowledge of bird and animal life in the Holy Land (which he had visited shortly before his marriage) and in Corfu and Albania. But the extent of Rudolf's political journalism remained unsuspected by his father.

Despite these strangely varied intellectual pursuits, Rudolf still regarded himself as a professional soldier. Like his father he recognized that the army was the cement binding the provinces of the common Monarchy in an uncommon unity. But there was a marked difference in the attitude of the two men towards the function of the armed forces. The Emperor placed increasing emphasis on the traditional role of his officers as dynastic surrogates bringing a gold-braided splendour to distant towns scattered across a rambling Empire. By contrast, Rudolf sought to promote new ideas in the old regiments, striving for an alert wartime efficiency and encouraging such curious experiments as the creation in 1886 of a 'penny-farthing' bicycle corps. His father, distrusting all such novelties and irritated by his son's advocacy of a preventive war during the Bulgarian crises, thought Rudolf too immature to be entrusted with high military responsibility.

So, on other grounds, did the influential Inspector General of the common army. 'Uncle Albrecht' never ceased to regard the heir to the throne as a rebellious liberal. Rudolf's links with radical journalists both in Vienna and Budapest alarmed the Archduke and prime minister Taaffe, too, although neither man realized the full extent of his contacts. They seem to have thought, with good reason, that Rudolf's volatile temperament inclined him to careless conversation with his intimates, thus making him (in later parlance) a 'security risk'. Rudolf, however, always remained surprised by the hostility of 'the gentlemen who hold the reins of government'. In the spring of 1888 he expected to receive the command of the Second Army Corps, with headquarters in Vienna itself. Instead, he was made Inspector-General of Infantry, a specially created post with ill-defined duties which were carefully monitored by the supreme inspector, Uncle Albrecht. Already, on several occasions, Rudolf had complained privately of persecution by the Emperor's inner circle of military advisers: as he once wrote to Bombelles, 'they fear I may grow out of the common, comfortable pattern and thereby differ from most of my relations'. Now 'they' had shown their power. From March 1888 onwards the Crown Prince's outlook on political life was soured by a deep and bitter sense of frustration.

Much of his resentment was turned against his father. He always exaggerated Francis Joseph's detailed knowledge of the day-to-day life of his officers: there is an odd letter from him to Archduke Francis Ferdinand as early as November 1884, in which he warns his cousin to avoid military escapades, for 'the Emperor knows everything' about such matters. In this assumption Rudolf was totally wrong: Francis Joseph may have had the command structure at his finger-tips; he may regularly have examined requests from commissioned officers for permission to marry; but the meticulous study of reports laid before him gave the Emperor no real insight into garrison life. On the other hand the police chief in Vienna, Baron Alfred von Krauss, knew a great deal about the seamier activities of the younger Archdukes: Mizzi Caspar, the sultry cocotte dancer who for many years offered her favours to Rudolf and his fellow officers (including, on at least one occasion, Francis Ferdinand), found it useful to have among her protectors a skilful lawyer, Florian Meissner; and Meissner was a diligent police informer. Some of the intelligence reaching Krauss from Meissner and other spies was made known to Taaffe but, since the prime minister believed in seeking as quiet a life as politics permitted him to enjoy, he saw no reason to disturb his sovereign master with disagreeable scandal. Francis Joseph knew his son's conduct was far from chaste, but he cannot have realized what dangerous enemies the Crown Prince was making by compounding dissolute behaviour with the ruthless lash of a sarcastic tongue.

Rudolf could still exercise great charm, however. It showed itself in London, where in May 1887 he was his father's representative at Queen

Victoria's Golden Jubilee celebrations, and it frequently permeates his private letters, when he wishes to appear as the family man. He continued to treat Stephanie with indulgent affection, even if their marriage bonds had by now worn thin. The Crown Princess was unlikely to conceive another child despite frequent visits to Franzensbad, a spa in western Bohemia whose waters reputedly countered sterility. Yet she fulfilled all her official duties, often accompanying her husband to the provincial capitals. Stephanie was a woman of courage and determination; she insisted on being with Rudolf when, in June 1888, he defied death threats to visit Sarajevo and Mostar. But on one such journey – to Galicia at midsummer in 1887 – she fell in love with a Polish Count. For the next eighteen months she made as little effort to hide her feelings from her husband as he to conceal his lapses from her. Gossip maintained that late in 1888 Rudolf was seeking divorce, or a papal annulment of his marriage. He is said to have quarrelled with his father over the matter; but there is no written evidence, and it is all unlikely. A tolerance of infidelities, and love for 'little Erzsi', kept the marriage together.

Stephanie remained concerned over Rudolf's health. As winter drew to a close in 1886 persistent bronchitis, together with rheumatic pains, had left him so weak that the Emperor insisted he should spend a month on the island of Lacroma, off Dubrovnik, to build up his strength. But he never made a full recovery. A few months later he told Stephanie, 'I am keeping the cough under control with morphine, although it is a dangerous drug'. Ever since his boyhood fall from a tree, he experienced occasional blinding headaches; their incidence now increased. Soon he seemed dependent on morphia, and began drinking far too much. His handwriting, which in contrast to that of his father and grandmother was always bold and well-formed, deteriorated rapidly. By the time of his visit to Bosnia he looked seriously ill. It is probable that he had contracted gonorrhoea.

There is, however, no convincing evidence for much of the gossip embellished in reminiscences after the Mayerling tragedy. Legend has, for example, perpetuated rumours of serious rifts within the imperial family. Rudolf certainly did not conceal his disapproval of his sister Valerie's determination to marry her childhood friend, Archduke Francis Salvator, from the Tuscan branch of the Habsburgs; although it is by no means clear why Rudolf was so hostile to their distant cousin. But over this question Francis Joseph agreed with his son: the Emperor would have preferred Valerie to seek marriage with the heir apparent of either Portugal or Saxony rather than with a penniless kinsman. Francis Joseph sought to understand all three of his children, but it was hard for a father who was shy of carefree human contacts to attain any intimacy with a son of such unpredictable temperament. Yet, although their personal interests were for the most part so different, Francis Joseph and Rudolf often went stalking together. On one such expedition, made shortly before he acquired Mayerling, the Crown Prince allegedly disobeyed the safety rules; he fired a shot at distant stags which wounded his father's gun-bearer in the arm and narrowly missed the Emperor's head. For such irresponsible behaviour Rudolf is said to have been banned from sub-sequent imperial shooting parties. This tale, however, was not made public until forty years later; even if true in substance, it seems much exaggerated. Only four weeks before his death Rudolf was hunting beside his father in Styria – 'and in the most cheerful spirits', as Francis Joseph sadly recalled in the following autumn.

The Crown Prince's interest in high politics intensified rather than diminished during the years when his health seemed to be deteriorating. He was by now more critical of the Czech political leaders than in his years of residence at Prague and he included among his boon companions several prominent Hungarians. But it would be a mistake to assume he was in any way sympathetic to Magyar claims for independence or for changing the structure of the imperial–royal army. Moreover he was critical of Hungary's treatment of her minorities; he particularly sym-pathized with the Croats, whose past services to the Habsburg dynasty he stressed during a visit to Zagreb in 1888 at which he received a warm welcome. The Crown Prince was more interested in the European balance of power than in the internal affairs of the Monarchy. In April 1888 'Julius Felix' – Rudolf's final pen-name – published in Paris a 15,000 word German language 'Open Letter to His Majesty Emperor Francis Joseph I' on 'Austria-Hungary and its Alliances'. The pamphlet argued that the Dual Monarchy was in danger of destruction in a war caused by Prussian militarism and that the most effective way of keeping peace in Europe was by cultivating the friendship of France and Great Britain. The pam-phlet ended with a patriotic clarion call: 'Away with Prussia! May Austria and the Habsburgs flourish!'

The authorship of the 'Open Letter' was a well-kept secret and there is no indication that Francis Joseph ever read it. Had he done so, he would hardly have agreed with his son's reasoning: 'I believe that, over all political and military questions, the lynchpin of our policies must be the broadest of agreements and the greatest solidarity with Germany', he wrote in a private letter to his old friend, King Albert of Saxony. But Rudolf thought differently: as William II recalled in exile nearly forty years later, 'his soul revolted from the Prussian idea'. On 11 March 1888, four days before Rudolf arrived in Berlin for William I's funeral, Szeps's *Neues Wiener Tagblatt* printed an anonymous obituary, which the Crown Prince had drafted a few years before: it paid grudging tribute to 'a Prussian through and through' who was 'convinced that all his actions, no matter how unjust they might be, were in obedience to God's will ... He saw himself as the protector of all sound conservative ideas, but even so he stole land from his neighbours. Neither his son nor his grandson have any resemblance to him', Rudolf's article concluded, 'With Emperor William died the last of his kind'.

Within a hundred days, there was a second royal funeral in Berlin. Emperor Frederick, gravely ill with cancer at his accession, died on 15 June. His successor, William II – the 'Kaiser Bill' of First World War propaganda – was only six months younger than Rudolf, and the two princes had known each other well since 1873 when 'Willy' accompanied his father and mother on their visit to the World Exhibition in the Prater. On that occasion the German Crown Princess thought her son seemed an uncouth 'bear or a schoolboy beside Rudolf'; but both sets of parents assumed the two fourteen-year olds would become firm friends. They did not; in temperament and outlook on politics they remained poles apart. William deplored Rudolf's 'faults of character', his failure to 'take religion at all seriously': conversely the Crown Prince thought him an unctuous humbug. Rudolf took pleasure in re-telling how, not long before his accession, Germany's new master came on a courtesy call to Austria and borrowed 3,000 florins from him 'for an indefinite time' in order to pay for dubious pleasures in Vienna – a tale which much amused Francis Joseph when he heard of it. More seriously, both father and son regarded the young William II with some suspicion. Francis Joseph could not fail to notice the enthusiasm with which Austria's Pan-Germans welcomed the change of sovereign in Berlin, but he hoped to maintain the close dynastic links forged in William I's final years. Rudolf was less sanguine: he was convinced of William's hostility towards Austria in general and the Habsburgs in particular. 'William II will do well; probably he will soon stir up deep trouble in old Europe', he wrote to Szeps on 24 August with perceptive irony, 'Quite likely in the course of a few years he will cut Hohenzollern Germany down to the size it deserves'.

Yet was Rudolf more depressed than this tone of cynical resignation suggests? On one occasion in that summer he had a strange conversation with Mizzi Caspar, who was then living in the Feldgasse at Mödling, a few miles from Mayerling. The Crown Prince proposed she should accompany him to the 'Hussar Temple', a neo-classical memorial to the bravery of officers who died at Aspern in 1809 which stands on a promontory in the wooded hills south of Mödling. Would she, Rudolf asked, be prepared to die with him? They would, he explained, make a fine gesture, shooting themselves in front of the monument dedicated 'To

Emperor and Fatherland'. Mizzi laughed, dismissing the suggestion as preposterous: for a Crown Prince to dash off Viennese dialect lyrics for tavern songs which lauded a girl's 'dark charms' was flattering, but an invitation to strengthen his wavering courage by sharing the last shots of his revolver was a terminal honour she could not believe he offered in earnest. She was a vivacious extrovert, too excited by life to end it prematurely (though, sadly, her health was to give way and she died at 42). Mizzi maintained that she put the conversation at the back of her mind until she was alarmed by his odd behaviour four months later. Yet did she never mention his strange proposal to any of her close acquaintances that summer? Not all were Rudolf's drinking companions: a ruthless enemy, hearing of his frailty of resolve, might seek and find a young romantic so infatuated with the Crown Prince that she would allow her flame of passion to sear the senses and accept the suicide pact Mizzi had scorned.

Rudolf's soul-searching was totally alien to his father's mode of thought and action. Far lesser problems perplexed Francis Joseph that autumn. How was he to entertain three foreign visitors, the Prince of Wales, the German Emperor and the King of Serbia, as well as his personal friend, Albert of Saxony? The Prince, an attentive host to the Crown Prince in England, reached Vienna on 10 September and spent much of his time with Rudolf, who in a letter to Stephanie admired 'the indefatigability . . . of the old boy'. The imminent arrival of William II cast a shadow before it. 'I am glad to have Wales as a guest', Rudolf wrote to Stephanie, 'but I would invite William only in order to arrange a discreet hunting mishap'. Together Rudolf and the Prince went to the races at Freudenau; they hunted evasive bears in Transylvania; and they shot thirty chamois in seven hours on the crags of Styria. More commendably, with fine contempt for the mounting anti-semitism of the capital, they lunched at the most famous of Vienna's restaurants with the Jewish philanthropist and financier, Baron Moritz Hirsch. They also accompanied the Emperor on a shoot at Gödöllö and joined him for the army manoeuvres in Croatia. Francis Joseph was less appreciative of his guest's company than his son: 'By trotting and galloping I went to some pains to shake off the Prince of Wales but I could not do it', he wrote to Katharina Schratt after the manoeuvres were over, 'The fat man was always with me and held out quite unbelievably, only he got very stiff and tore his red Hussar trousers and, as he was wearing nothing underneath, that must have been very uncomfortable for him'. When 'the fat man' discovered that William II would arrive in Vienna on 3 October, he wished to be there to greet his nephew: they had, after all, been in the city together at the time of Rudolf's wedding. Now, however, their relative ranks were different: the Prince

had spoken privately but unwisely of his contempt for William's pretensions; and the German embassy in Vienna made it clear that their
sovereign was not prepared to meet his uncle during the state visit. The
Prince of Wales, somewhat affronted, withdrew temporarily to Roumania.

For Francis Joseph it was tediously embarrassing. And there was, too,
the problem of Schönerer's noisy followers. The Emperor agreed with
Taaffe that strict precautions should be taken to prevent the Pan-Germans
exploiting the visit of their 'hope for the future, the beacon light of
the German people'. On 29 September Rudolf informed Kálnoky, with
evident satisfaction, that 'the Emperor ordered me today' to make certain
'... the German Emperor should not walk about alone in Vienna' for fear
of the excitement his presence might arouse, but 'the matter should be
handled with extreme care so that the real intention cannot be discerned'.
At the same time Francis Joseph summoned Archduke Francis Ferdinand
to the capital in order to support the Crown Prince as he trod the
Hohenzollern trail.

William II's visit was not a success: after attending an Austrian military
review he had the effrontery to criticize in conversation with Francis
Joseph and Elizabeth the turn-out of the infantry and the effectiveness of
its chief inspector, Crown Prince Rudolf. William was only in Vienna for
three days, followed by five wet days at Mürzsteg, but Francis Joseph
found 'the festivities' hard to 'survive', especially once the Empress
escaped to the peace and sunshine of Corfu. His guest's aggressive
ebullience left him ill at ease. With candid relief he let Katharina Schratt
know on 5 October that 'My toast at yesterday's dinner, of which I was
extremely nervous, I managed to deliver without getting stuck and without
a prompter'. After William's departure for Rome, he awaited the return
of the 'fat man' and the coming of the King of Serbia with equanimity.

On 14 October the Emperor and his royal guests went to the gala
opening of the new Burgtheater on the Ringstrasse. In the audience the
Prince of Wales noticed a seventeen-year old girl whom (as he later told
Queen Victoria) he had 'met frequently at Homburg and Vienna' and
whose mother, aunts and uncles he had known 'for the last 16 years'; by
the Prince of Wales's reckoning Baroness Mary Vetsera was 'a charming
young lady and certainly one of the prettiest and most admired in Vienna'.
Others would have agreed with him in London, where Mary had been
with her mother earlier that year. Most enthusiastic race-goers in England
knew of the family, especially Mary's uncles, Hector and Aristide Baltazzi,
one of whom had owned the Derby winner of 1876, 'Kisber'. Although
Francis Joseph had recently warned Katharina Schratt to be wary of
Hector, since he did 'not have an entirely correct reputation in racing and
money matters', the Prince of Wales knew nothing to their social det-

riment. At the Burgtheater he duly 'pointed out' Mary Vetsera to his neighbour, the Crown Prince, 'and said how handsome she was'. To the Prince's surprise Rudolf 'spoke I thought disparagingly of her'. Yet, though the Crown Prince knew her by sight and had been hotly pursued by her mother in his bachelor days, he seems never to have met Mary socially, and his comments were either prompted by hearsay or from the distant assessment of a cynically roving eye. Within three weeks of the Burgtheater gala they had become intimate acquaintances, and it is possible the Prince of Wales first aroused Rudolf's interest in Mary; but it is unlikely that he introduced them to each other, as one of Rudolf's journalist friends maintained. For that fateful connection the Crown Prince's first cousin, Marie Larisch, was responsible.

Countess Marie Larisch was the daughter of Empress Elizabeth's eldest brother, who in 1857 renounced his rights in order to marry, morganatically, the actress Henriette Mendel (created Baroness von Wallersee two years later). The Empress, who treated Henriette with more kindness than other members of the family, grew fond of her niece at an early age; she particularly admired Marie's horsemanship, which was far superior to that of Elizabeth's own children, and in 1875 she invited Marie to become an attendant Lady of the Imperial and Royal Household at Gödöllö, where her musicality and vivacity soon made her welcome. But ambition tempted Marie to overstep the mark. With boundless confidence she threw herself at her cousin, Rudolf, with whom by 1877 she was flirting outrageously. Even more rashly she turned her siren charm on her Aunt Sisi's favourite riding companions. In that autumn the Empress encouraged – or ruthlessly arranged – Marie's marriage to the wealthy Lieutenant Count Georg Larisch von Moennich, the best-natured nitwit in Francis Joseph's army. Thereafter, though the Countess outwardly remained a dutiful niece, she lost all sympathy or gratitude towards her aunt: from scattering spiteful gossip around the outer fringe of high society she graduated in later years to the writing of inventive memoirs in which her malicious venom spared neither Elizabeth nor Francis Joseph.

Yet in a fitful way Marie Larisch was clever. More readily than his closer relatives she perceived the swift changes of Rudolf's temperament. She was also sensitive to the gnawing hopes of others eager for social advancement: indeed, to satisfy them became the mainspring of her oddly warped vocation. In this role she befriended the recently widowed Baroness Helene Vetsera and became the confidante of her daughter Mary, who made no secret of her infatuation for the Crown Prince. In the late autumn of 1888 Marie Larisch arranged a casual meeting between Mary and the Crown Prince in the Prater. Soon afterwards – on Monday, 5 November – the Countess took Mary 'shopping' with her in Vienna, visiting a photographer. In the evening she brought Mary to Rudolf's rooms in the Hofburg, using the back stair entrance to gain admission from the ramp leading up to the Albertina.

Mary Vetsera left a record of that Monday in a private letter which her mother subsequently transcribed and published. It mentions the visit to the photographer and their arrival at the Crown Prince's apartments. The letter continues, 'Marie introduced me, and he said, "Excuse me, but I would like to talk to the Countess privately for a few minutes". Then they withdrew to another room. I looked around me. On his desk was a revolver and a skull. I picked up the skull, raised it between my hands and looked at it from all sides. Suddenly Rudolf returned and took it from me with deep concern. When I said I wasn't afraid, he smiled'. Other clandestine meetings followed over the next few weeks. Yet, however deep Mary's passion, for two months she can have meant little more to Rudolf than earlier women whom the trusted Nehammer led up the back stairs of the Hofburg. Not until 13 January did Mary know the fearful delight of love fulfilled, as more than one of her pathetic letters testifies. By then their lives had only a fortnight to run.

The Emperor was in Hungary on the Monday, Marie Larisch took Mary Vetsera to the Hofburg, and the Empress was still in Corfu. After what he considered a light day's work – 'a mere 50 audiences' in the old royal palace at Buda – Francis Joseph went back to Gödöllö that evening. Snow showers ruled out all prospect of hunting and, as he wrote to Katharina Schratt, 'I found time to get much pleasure' from reading the 'extremely handsome and fascinatingly written' book she had sent him – *Vom Nachtswachter zum türkishchen Kaiser* (From Night Watchman to Turkish Emperor), reminiscences of theatrical life in Vienna by Karl Sonntag. A few years previously he would never have opened such a book. Now, in the absence of the Empress, he was entranced by the backstage world of the theatre, its feuds, rivalries and superstitions. While Elizabeth sought refuge in the classical past, throughout much of the last quarter of the year her husband also escaped from present realities by 'reviving in my memory so much that I had long forgotten . . . particularly about the Burgtheater', and by discovering in 'what lively and peculiar ways things were done in the theatre' where 'almost everything seems possible'. It was not simply Sonntag's book which sustained Francis Joseph's interest. He continued to seek information on stage affairs, as intrigued by what was likely to happen as a modern devotee of some television soap-opera. 'You make me especially happy when you write to me about the theatre', he told Katharina; characteristically he then felt bound to add, 'That is not very high-minded of me; but it is true, just the same'.

As yet, there were no pressing political problems calling for attention that winter. For the past two years there had, however, been a groundswell of discontent in Hungary after a series of insensitive actions by senior non-Magyar officers of the Budapest garrison (who were publicly defended by Archduke Albrecht). It was therefore clear that when Tisza's proposed Army Bill was ready for presentation to parliament early in 1889, any clauses which favoured Germanic traditions and practices were likely to receive rough treatment from Hungarian nationalists – including Count Pista Károlyi, who was a friend of both Rudolf and the Prince of Wales. But during his long stay at Gödöllö the Emperor was not embarrassed by political demonstrations and received a loyal and royal reception from all the great landowners, including Károlyi. The danger of serious unrest in Budapest seemed less acute than in Vienna, where police agents kept a close eye on the street politicians: Schönerer's Pan-Germans were a noisy threat, but there was also strong following in the capital for the anti-semitic Christian Union, founded by Karl Lueger in November 1887; and the socialists were active, with plans to unify the social democrat factions at a congress to be held at Hainfeld, in Lower Austria, on New Year's Day. More immediately Francis Joseph was worried by family matters and especially by his wife's peace of mind; for he suspected that Valerie would soon wish to marry, and he knew that the prospect of losing Valerie's companionship would sadden Elizabeth. He had to telegraph bad news to the Empress from Munich. Her father, who suffered a stroke in the summer, died on 15 November. It was impossible for her to return to Bavaria for the funeral, but the Court was plunged into mourning. The Emperor and Empress were reunited on 1 December at Miramare where, next day, they quietly celebrated the fortieth anniversary of his accession.

Amid all this relative calm, a political storm gathered around the Crown Prince, for which he was largely responsible. On the last day of October, when Francis Joseph was already in Hungary, a new weekly, *Schwarzgelb*, went on sale in Austria. The name showed impeccable Habsburg loyalty; but the journal was strongly hostile to the Pan-Germans and their Hohenzollern idol; and the tone of the articles echoed the Crown Prince in his more unguarded moments. Foreign observers rightly assumed that *Schwarzgelb* had Rudolf's backing, and there was an inevitable response from beyond the frontier. A scandalous book by the extreme anti-semite Charles Drumont had been published in Paris in October, with a preface which denounced Rudolf's alleged links with Jewish high finance. Early in November, immediately after the first issue of *Schwarzgelb*, Drumont's attack was taken up in two German newspapers with a relatively small readership; they claimed to have knowledge of the Crown Prince's long concealed love affair with 'a Jewess'. On 28 November, when the fourth issue of *Schwarzgelb* appeared, two influential Prussian dailies associated with Bismarck went into action, emphasizing not simply the Crown Prince's involvement with Jewish big business, but the 'envious hatred' which he showed toward Germany's new ruler. Meanwhile the Italian paper *L'Epoca* also joined the fray, with a prurient titbit on 15 November informing readers that the heir to the Habsburg throne 'led a most dissolute life'.

Francis Joseph must have been aware of the general course of this international press war, for semi-official newspapers in Vienna and Budapest responded by printing articles extolling the Crown Prince's virtues. He also knew Rudolf's prejudices too well to believe he was the innocent victim of journalistic spite. But he does not seem to have realized that his son was behind the launching of *Schwarzgelb*; nor can he possibly have imagined the depth of Rudolf's willingness to smear William II's reputation. For, three days after his first meeting with Mary Vetsera in the Hofburg, Rudolf sent Szeps what he called 'an unsavoury article on William II'. This racily written contribution gave details of William's private behaviour during his visit to Austria in 1887; his affair with a former lady-in-waiting to the Queen of Württemberg, their evening rendezvous 'in the Catholic cemetery at Mürzsteg', the attempts of the German ambassador to hush up the scandal when a claim for alimony was subsequently put forward, and the name of the lawyer ('Dr Meissner') upon whose discretion the ambassador relied – almost certainly the same Florian Meissner to whom Mizzi Caspar turned for legal protection, and who had close contact with police chief Krauss. There was nothing sensational about William's alleged sexual ethics; they conformed to the standard casually observed by many officers, Archdukes included. But his conduct was ill-suited to the mood of Providential mission in which he had exalted since his accession. Szeps knew that in Vienna he dared not use such explosive information. At the Crown Prince's suggestion, Szeps forwarded the 'unsavoury article' to Paris, where he had close friends working for *Figaro*: they, too, thought the scoop too hot to print; 'the story' (as Rudolf called it) was not made public until all concerned in it were dead. Yet did no one other than the editors read the unsavoury article? For the Crown Prince it was a dangerous tale to have put in circulation at such a time.

It is difficult to discover who knew what in Vienna during Rudolf's last ten weeks of life. On 19 November he had a bad fall from his horse but insisted on keeping news of the accident secret; and yet it was so serious that, according to a close friend, it 'brought his brains into disorder, at least he complained frequently of headache and stomach trouble'. Francis Joseph did not hear of the fall, nor was he aware of the interest Krauss's agents had begun to take by early December in the secret assignations of Mary Vetsera. So convinced was Krauss that the Crown Prince's affections had shifted from Mizzi Caspar to Mary that when – at Florian Meissner's prompting – Mizzi reported to him further talk of suicide, as well as Rudolf's original conversation in the previous summer, the chief of police merely filed away her sworn statement, cautioning her to keep the matter to herself; Krauss believed she was a cast-off lover over-dramatizing incidents in order to boost her falling esteem. Francis Joseph does not seem to have had any warning of his son's troubled state of mind, and he ignored any physical manifestations of his illness. On one occasion, apparently before Christmas, Crown Princess Stephanie broke the conventions by insisting on seeing the Emperor privately in order to draw his attention to her husband's poor health. Could he not, she asked, be sent away from Vienna on a goodwill voyage around the world? Francis Joseph was unperturbed. 'There is nothing the matter with Rudolf', he replied, 'He is rather pale, rushes about too much, demands too much of himself; he should stay at home with you more than he does'.

The Christmas festivities at the Hofburg were brief that year, for on 26 December the Empress had arranged to go to Munich to console her widowed mother, taking Archduchess Marie Valerie with her. Gifts were exchanged at half past four on Christmas Eve – Elizabeth's 51st birthday – in (as Francis Joseph wrote) 'an intimate family circle, just our children and our little granddaughter'. Rudolf presented his mother with eleven autograph letters by Heine, which he had commissioned Szeps to bring back for him from Paris. That evening the family celebrated Valerie's betrothal to Francis Salvator, with the Crown Prince in his most benign mood. His parents' thoughts were concentrated on their daughter's immediate future. Francis Joseph was sorry for himself; with Elizabeth's departure he was, as he wrote, 'a grass-widower again'. He could not even talk theatre with Katharina Schratt, for she was in quarantine, her son having caught measles; she was not allowed to write to the Emperor, only to send him telegrams. On 29 December, to ease his loneliness, Francis Joseph paid, for the last time, a purely social call on Anna Nahowski in Hietzing.

By the second week in January 1889 his gloom was lifting. He had spent some days at Mürzsteg, hunting not very profitably but in the company of Rudolf, who was outwardly in good spirits; and the Empress and Valerie were safely back from Munich, though he thought Elizabeth tired herself by working too hard at modern Greek. He was himself busy with routine paperwork, notably reports from Hungary on Tisza's army bill, which included a controversial proposal requiring reserve officers to pass a new examination in German. Yet Hungary was not a pressing problem; Tisza could take care of the linguistic nationalists. For Francis Joseph the worst cloud on the horizon was William II's birthday on Sunday, 27 January; he was expected to attend a soirée at the German embassy ('it pleases me little') and preside over a state dinner ('could last too long').

Would the Crown Prince join in the celebrations? The question aroused wide speculation at Court and in the diplomatic corps that week. Rudolf held honorary rank in the 2nd Prussian Lancers; courtesy obliged him to appear at the Embassy reception in his German uniform. On 16 January, however, the twelfth issue of *Schwarzgelb* carried on its front-page 'Ten Commandments of an Austrian': they included 'Thou shalt have no Emperor other than thine own Emperor' and 'Thou shalt not make an idol of Prussia, nor of the Germany over which Prussia rules'. Both in Austria and abroad this decalogue of dynastic patriotism was openly associated with Rudolf, who may well have drafted it. During the following week British, French and Russian diplomats all commented on the Crown Prince's renewed hostility towards Germany; and newspaper articles suggested that he favoured a reversal of alliances, with Austria-Hungary abandoning Germany and Italy in favour of France and Russia. Not surprisingly, Francis Joseph summoned his son to an audience on the morning before the birthday celebrations.

There is no record of what was said. Did the Emperor insist that Rudolf should cut his links with journalism? Did the Crown Prince urge a change of policy at home and abroad? Were 'unsavoury' aspects of his private life questioned? Nobody knows. Voices were certainly raised, one court dignitary maintaining that he heard the Emperor shout at his son, 'You are not worthy to be my successor'; and Rudolf appeared to be angry when he left the Hofburg that Saturday morning. It is probable that his father's obduracy threw him into a black mood of frustrated depression from which he never emerged. But he was at the embassy reception next evening, properly turned out as a Prussian Lancer, although complaining that 'the whole uniform is distasteful to me'. Lady Paget, the British ambassador's wife, noticed that, when Francis Joseph arrived, Rudolf 'bent low over his father's hand, touching it almost with his lips'. It was the last meeting between father and son.

Contemporaries who were not at the reception maintain that there were dramatic scenes, with the Emperor pointedly turning his back on his son, and with the Crown Princess and Mary Vetsera glaring at each other 'like tigers ready to spring'. Lady Paget saw no such confrontation and nor did General Beck, though he recognized Mary Vetsera: she left early, he noted, having barely taken her eyes off the Crown Prince, while Beck saw him looking intensely at her on several occasions. That night, however,

Rudolf was with Mizzi Caspar until three in the morning. He had already told his servants he would leave the Hofburg before noon on Monday for Mayerling, having arranged for a small shoot in the neighbouring woods on Tuesday. By 11.50 a police agent spotted the Crown Prince's carriage well south of the city.

Soon afterwards an agitated Countess Larisch sought out the chief of police. She told Krauss that, while she was settling an account at a shop in central Vienna, her companion Mary Vetsera had stepped out of the carriage in which they had been travelling and was driven away by another coachman. The Countess contacted one of Mary's uncles who thought the Crown Prince might be involved: was he, perhaps, at Mayerling? Krauss, who was not unfamiliar with the escapades of Archdukes and their ladies, insisted that his authority extended to neither the Hofburg nor Mayerling. Not until early on Tuesday afternoon, after further visits from Marie Larisch and Mary's family, did Krauss make a report to Taaffe: he had suggested to Alexander Baltazzi that he should travel out to Mayerling, find if Mary was there, but keep the whole affair as quiet as possible, for no uncle would wish to give journalists the chance to sully a niece's reputation. Though Baltazzi ignored this advice and did not go to Mayerling, Taaffe backed Krauss's handling of the problem; as prime minister he welcomed decisions involving him in no action whatsoever.

That Tuesday evening Francis Joseph was disconcerted when Rudolf failed to arrive at the Hofburg in time for a family dinner party. An explanation by the Crown Princess mollified him: she had received a telegram from Mayerling; Rudolf was suffering from a sudden feverish cold and sent his apologies. This thin tale was confirmed by Stephanie's brother-in-law, Prince Philip of Coburg, who had just arrived from Mayerling and was due to return there by the early morning train to Baden. He told Francis Joseph that Rudolf had felt so unwell after breakfast that he declined to go shooting with his two guests, the Prince of Coburg and Count Hoyos, the Court Chamberlain. Somewhat sourly, Archduke Albrecht remarked that the Crown Prince had been expected to take the chair at a meeting of the directors of the proposed Army Museum that Tuesday. The visitor's book for 1889, showing the Crown Prince's titles beside a blank space where he was to sign his name, is now an exhibit at the Heeresgeschichtliches Museum.

On Wednesday morning (30 January) the routine of life at the Hofburg slipped naturally into a familiar pattern. By 10.30 the Empress was learning Greek, the Crown Princess practising singing, the Emperor finishing the day's second session of desk work; he was anticipating an hour's relaxation in Katharina Schratt's company, for Elizabeth had invited their 'good friend' to join them at eleven. A cab from the Sudbahnhof arrived at the inner courtyard. From it Count Hoyos stepped down; he sought out the Emperor's adjutant and told him how, a few hours earlier, he and the Prince of Coburg had found the Crown Prince and Mary Vetsera dead in a locked room at Mayerling. Neither Hoyos nor the adjutant wished to break the terrible news to the Emperor – that, they decided, was a wife's responsibility, even though Francis Joseph himself always insisted that Elizabeth should be spared emotional shocks. The Greek lesson was interrupted; and the Empress, though momentarily in a state of collapse, drew on her latent inner strength of character and went to Francis Joseph. Their son lay dead at Mayerling, poisoned by Mary Vetsera, she told him; for that was what she had been led to believe. Soon afterwards, Elizabeth had to receive Mary's distraught mother who, knowing nothing of events at Mayerling, had come to the palace seeking news of her daughter: now she too learnt the grim truth from Elizabeth. Not, of course, the whole truth, for scandal must be avoided: no mention of a second body at Mayerling; no mention of poison. 'Remember' Elizabeth insisted, as she left Helene Vetsera to her grief, 'Rudolf died of heart failure'.

So, too, reported the special editions of newspapers which went on sale in Vienna in the late afternoon. No one believed the announcement: a heart-attack at thirty in a sturdy family with no record of thrombosis? Even before the court physician reached Mayerling for his autopsy, suspicion of an official cover-up was rife; it was compounded by the evasions and contradictions of the following days. On 2 February a revised statement, admitting Rudolf's suicide, did nothing to re-assure the public. Had the liberal-minded reformer prince been murdered by political enemies, it was asked? Had a cuckold husband taken revenge on him, others wondered?

Not all the blame for the initial confusion rests with the Emperor. For twenty-four hours he remained misinformed over what had happened; Hoyos, who had spent Monday and Tuesday nights at an outer annex rather than in the Schloss and knew nothing of Mary's presence until the bodies were found, did not examine the corpses before leaving for Vienna, nor did he see Rudolf's revolver – only an empty glass which he assumed had contained cyanide. Early on Tuesday morning Francis Joseph heard a report from his physician and realized, with horror, that his son had shot himself and, almost certainly, his mistress, too. For advice Francis Joseph turned to his prime minister and friend, Taaffe. At their first meeting it was agreed to keep three objectives in mind: to secure papal permission for a full Christian burial, despite the stigma of suicide; to conceal the presence of Mary Vetsera and her fate from press and public;

and to delve deeply into the immediate past to see if Rudolf's friends in any way shared responsibility for the tragedy.

When the dreadful news first broke, the Empress showed 'fortitude and courage which surpassed the power of words to describe', as the British ambassador reported to London. The aftermath was too much for her. The autopsy indicated some abnormality in Rudolf's skull, suggesting he had shot himself 'while in a state of mental derangement'. This statement was sufficient for the Pope, under some pressure, to approve the full rites of burial; but it distressed Elizabeth. She feared she had brought into the family the strain of insanity which haunted the Wittelsbachs: might she herself become certifiably mad, she wondered? Her desire to hide herself away from the public intensified. Neither Elizabeth nor Valerie went to Rudolf's funeral on 5 February: for one and a half hours they remained in prayer, secluded in a private chapel.

For support in 'accompanying the best of sons, the loyalest of subjects to his last resting place' in the Kapuzinerkirche Francis Joseph turned to his elder daughter, Gisela. *The Times* reported:

'During the service the Emperor stood perfectly calm, looking about him with quick movements of the head, as his custom is. After the chanting of the *Libera*, however, His Majesty stepped out from his place, walked up to his son's coffin, knelt down beside it, and with clasped hands remained for a moment or two in prayer. This was a moment of poignant emotion for all present. Not a sound was heard. Nobody coughed, not a dress rustled, not a scabbard clanked on the flagstones. An entire stillness prevailed till the Emperor rose from his knees and walked back calmly to his place'.

'I bore up well', Francis Joseph told Elizabeth and Valerie after the funeral, 'It was only in the crypt that I could endure it no longer'.

Five months after the Crown Prince's funeral the Austrian socialist leader Viktor Adler described the Dual Monarchy as 'despotism softened by casualness'. The famous phrase mocked the working of the government system as a whole; but it might well have applied specifically to the handling of the Mayerling tragedy. The macabre conveyance at dead of night from Mayerling to the Heiligenkreuz graveyard in an ordinary carriage of Mary Vetsera's fully dressed corpse, propped up between two of her uncles, was intended by the authorities to frustrate the probing eyes of journalists already suspicious of what lay concealed behind the Schloss's shuttered windows. As soon as Mary had been secretly buried at Heiligenkreuz, Taaffe visited Helene Vetsera to insist that the family ignore the grave 'while so many reporters infested the district', though later she might exhume her daughter's body for burial elsewhere; meanwhile, on the Emperor's orders, she was temporarily to leave the capital.

This command she was prepared to obey, though protesting that she had every intention of letting her daughter's remains lie in peace. Once away from Vienna she could express herself more freely; and she did. Nothing could halt mounting speculation in the capital, in Budapest and the great provincial cities, or across frontiers where Rudolf was better known than any previous Archduke. Emergency censorship, carrying threats to suspend editors and their journals, was employed to stifle the Austrian press. Clumsy attempts were also made to confiscate foreign newspapers – which then, of course, went on sale at black market prices. Within a week a Munich daily paper was linking Mary Vetsera's name with the Mayerling tragedy: but, to the end of Francis Joseph's reign and beyond, the government in Vienna never acknowledged the connection.

Police-chief Krauss, who had been suspicious from the start of Marie Larisch's role, gained an early success. A note from the Countess, apparently referring to Mary's proposed 'disappearance' from the Larisch carriage, was found crumpled in the pocket of a tunic which, a few days previously, Rudolf had left with an artist who was painting his portrait in uniform. Consequently Marie Larisch found herself permanently banished from Court even before the funeral. Other 'discoveries' were less revealing, however. The police investigations assembled a mass of facts, many of questionable relevance. At the same time, on Taaffe's instructions, the credentials of the Crown Prince's friends were critically examined. Even such trusted servants of the Emperor as Bombelles and Latour came under scrutiny: Bombelles produced a letter written by the Emperor Maximilian in the last days before his execution as testimony to his personal probity, and it is now filed away among Rudolf's surviving papers. So, too, are transcripts from books on Russian history, including an account of the coup which brought Tsar Alexander I to the throne and in which his father was, contrary to the son's instructions, murdered. But it would be wrong to assume from such evidence that Rudolf was studying the technique of palace coups; he had been preparing for a projected trip to St Petersburg, for he had never before visited Russia.

At times it seems as if, like an accomplished crime writer, the police allowed red herrings to float on the surface of the evidence so as to make the search for a solution even harder. Why, for example, did they give such attention to Hungarian affairs? Probably because, during the first weeks of the investigation, hostility to Tisza's Army Bill became increasingly vocal and more violent than at the start of the year. Rudolf, who conscientiously took the trouble to speak Magyar in Hungary, was popular in Budapest. In the summer of 1882 he had briefly thought that, like his great-uncle Ferdinand, he might be crowned King of Hungary during his father's lifetime. Archduke Albrecht, however, strongly opposed such a move, arguing that coronation would necessitate a binding oath to uphold the constitution which would hamper Rudolf if he wished, in later years, to reform the character of the Monarchy as a whole; and Rudolf had recognized the strength of this argument. Never would he support any political agitation seeking to broaden the distinction between Hungary and Cisleithania. In the last weeks of his life the Crown Prince was puzzled by the conduct of his friend, Count Károlyi, who spoke out against the Army Bill in parliament after (so the Budapest press said) receiving a letter from Rudolf. The police investigation discovered that, on the fateful 30 January, Károlyi was travelling to Vienna by train to see the Crown Prince when he heard of his death; at once he turned back for Budapest. But were Károlyi's activities worth intensive scrutiny? Clearly he had sought a personal meeting in order to clarify a misunderstood speech and perhaps to give warning of a mounting crisis and it was natural for an eminent magnate to return home when the kingdom was plunged into mourning. A 'Hungarian conspiracy', tempting the Crown Prince into treason, is a figment of the historical imagination.

That particular exercise of the mind continues to find in the Mayerling tragedy a tempting source of speculation, just as it does in the Jack the Ripper murders which took place in London that same winter: the body of the seventh victim of 'the Monster of the East End' was, in fact, found dismembered in Spitalfields at the end of the week in November 1888 when Mary Vetsera made her first visit to the Crown Prince in the Hofburg. It is no coincidence that these contemporaneous mysteries should have aroused sustained interest for so long; they came at a time when, in continental Europe and in Britain, there was a rapid spread of cheap newspapers, with competing rival editors seeking means of gratifying a new appetite for sensation – as, indeed, Taaffe feared and clumsily sought to combat. Each mystery mixed sex and violent death; each echoed disturbing undertones of anti-semitism; each remained 'unsolved'. Soon they passed into lurid folklore, spawning plays and films, novels and ballets. From time to time they are spiced with new theories based on fresh revelations or fashionable taboos: once political 'reasons' for Rudolf's death lost immediate relevancy, there were hints of incest belatedly discovered and, more recently, of a disastrous abortion.

Much about both mysteries is still puzzling; and over the Mayerling tragedy unanswerable questions remain. Why, for example, was there so long a gap between the arrival of the lovers at the Schloss on Monday afternoon and their deaths on Wednesday morning? Why in a farewell letter to Stephanie – written in his old, firm clarity of hand – did Rudolf tell her that he went to his death 'calmly' and as 'the only way to save my good name'? And why did his note to his sister Valerie say 'I do not die willingly'? The British prime minister, Lord Salisbury, at first believed the Crown Prince had been murdered, a notion hastily scotched by Queen Victoria (who was kept remarkably well-informed, both by the Prince of Wales and by Philip of Coburg). Rudolf fired the fatal shots. Yet it is possible that among the many political enemies he made, some were prepared to seek ways of tempting him to kill himself, surrendering to one of the moments of black despair which his illness engendered. Three near certainties stand out: the Mayerling deaths sprang from a suicide pact, agreed before the couple set out from Vienna; Mary Vetsera was devotedly infatuated with her partner in death, whatever the emotions torturing his brooding mind; and the Crown Prince wretchedly accepted that he could never match up to the standards he believed his father expected from him. Rudolf left messages for his wife, mother and sister, as well as for several friends. But, to Francis Joseph's distress, there was no letter of contrition or farewell for him.

The Crown Prince's premature death made as little difference to Austro-Hungarian political history as the anonymous booklets and articles in which he had preached dynastic patriotism. For the diseases eating him away were so grave that he could no more have become a liberal reformer than Germany's enlightened Emperor of a hundred days, Frederick III. But the Mayerling tragedy left a deeper mark on Francis Joseph's personal life than any earlier misfortune. At first he sought to put pained memories aside, resuming his desk-bound routine while telling Katharina Schratt of his worries for the health of the Empress, 'whom I can see is filled with a deep, silent agony'. He talked personally, with sympathy and a measure of understanding, to many sorrowing members of Rudolf's household, trying through them to make sense of the incomprehensible. 'All this does no good at all', he confessed to Frau Schratt on 5 March, 'But one cannot possibly think of anything else, and talking at least brings a certain relief ... The time may come when it is possible to have other thoughts'. Eleven days later he began to exchange theatre news with her: 'You see I am once more taking a certain interest in gossip', he added. From Ischl on Palm Sunday he wrote that in the afternoon he would go grouse shooting – 'and so I am drifting back into old habits and taking up the old life, though things can never be the same'.

One decision Francis Joseph had already taken: Mayerling was to be demolished immediately. As an act of atonement, a chapel was to be built on the site, with a convent of Carmelite nuns. There the Sisters would follow a contemplative life, devoted to intercession by prayer and penance. On All Souls Day (2 November) Francis Joseph travelled out to Mayerling, heard Mass in the new chapel, 'inspected' the cloisters and communal buildings, and was awed by the strict ascetism of the Carmelites. In contrast to the stern simplicity of the conventual buildings, the chapel was intentionally planned to emphasize the devotional unity of the imperial family. Francis Joseph commissioned the Viennese artist Joseph Kastner to paint an ornate fresco above the high altar, which was erected where had stood the room in which Rudolf and Mary Vetsera went to their deaths. Kastner was to show the patron saints of those dearest to Francis Joseph, grouped in adoration of the Holy Trinity. The boy-martyr St Rudolf is prominent in the fresco. So, too, are St Elizabeth of Hungary (whom history recognizes), with St Sophie (whom history does not) behind her; kneeling are the scarcely less obscure St Gisela and St Valery. Kastner also included in the fresco saints associated with the Carmelites and with Habsburg history, as well as the Emperor's own patrons, Joseph and Francis of Assisi. The fresco was (and is) a minor triumph in neo-baroque for, like the craftsmen of Vienna's greatest churches, Kastner's grouping helps focus the eye on the cross, the symbol of expiation. Kastner's fresco is unlikely to have been completed when the Emperor made his first visit. But though Francis Joseph returned to Schönbrunn sorrowful, he was satisfied, conscious that the purpose of his bequest was being truly fulfilled: 'Over everywhere there was a comforting, soothing peace in that lovely countryside', he wrote.

Chapter 17

SPARED NOTHING?

Mayerling left Francis Joseph stunned and shocked. He did not, however, relax the routine of daily business. To pace the treadmill of state was to him a solace for frayed nerves, as his private letters show. Yet there were some problems of government he could not bring himself to discuss. Who, for example, would succeed him on the throne now that his only son was dead? Not a direct descendant, for Habsburg dynastic convention ruled out the possibility of female succession. Technically the Emperor's 55-year-old brother, Charles Ludwig, was the new heir-presumptive but nobody believed he would ever become Emperor-King. Charles Ludwig was as amiably ineffectual and as devoid of ambition as his father had been, though more devout. For the past twenty-eight years he had taken little part in public life and it was assumed that, should Francis Joseph die, he would follow his father's precedent and step aside in favour of his eldest son, Francis Ferdinand, who was born at Graz in December 1863. In fact, the problem of renouncing the succession never arose, for Charles Ludwig died in May 1896 from typhoid contracted on a pilgrimage to the Holy Land; the sacred waters of Jordan might be sprinkled in baptism, but they were not to be imbibed, even in piety.

The Emperor gave no clear indication that he regarded Francis Ferdinand as his successor, either before or after Charles Ludwig's death. The Archduke was not a favourite nephew: while still very young he had added 'Este' (the family name of the former rulers of Modena) to 'Habsburg' in order to inherit the fortune of a distant kinsman, the last Duke of Modena; and, when he was a junior officer, his wild escapades incurred the displeasure of 'Uncle Albrecht', who felt it his duty to inform the Emperor of such matters. Moreover, though Francis Ferdinand might look as strong as an ox, he had inherited from his Bourbon-Sicilian mother the weak lungs which caused her death from consumption when her eldest son was nine years old. The Archduke was first granted sick leave to winter in Egypt in 1885 and not until the spring of 1898 did his doctors finally declare him cured from the last of several tubercular relapses. With such uncertainty over Francis Ferdinand's health, it is small wonder if there were moments when the Emperor seemed to regard his brother Otto as a more likely successor. Nevertheless, within a few months of Mayerling the Archduke was fulfilling official engagements which would normally have been entrusted to the heir to the throne: he travelled to Stuttgart for the silver jubilee celebrations of King Charles of Württemberg, and he accompanied Francis Joseph on a state visit to Berlin. Eventually, in 1891, he undertook the goodwill mission to St Petersburg for which Rudolf had begun to prepare himself shortly before his death.

By then, however, the Emperor had grave doubts over his nephew's temperament. When the news of Mayerling broke, Francis Ferdinand was a major serving with an infantry regiment in Prague and living – like the Crown Prince before him – in the imperial apartments of the Hradčany palace. But a year later he was given command of a Hungarian Hussar regiment at Sopron, a garrison town in western Hungary barely 50 miles from Vienna. The Archduke was sad to leave Prague. By Habsburg standards he was a poor linguist: he had mastered some Czech, but Magyar utterly defeated him. To his fury he found the Hussar officers ignoring army regulations which made German the language of command for the Monarchy as a whole. They persisted in speaking Magyar 'even in front of me', he complained to a friend: 'Military terms were translated into long-winded Hungarian phrases. In short, throughout the regiment, not a word of that German language so detested by the Hungarians'. A responsive, astute colonel might have charmed the less truculent officers into co-operation. But not Francis Ferdinand. He reacted like a frustrated child; his rage knew no bounds. Archduke Albrecht sympathised with him, but he emphasized the need for members of the dynasty to cultivate the trust of every nationality. Such counsel was wasted: Francis Ferdinand's experiences at Sopron left him with a firm impression that all Hungarians, irrespective of social stature, were treasonable rogues. This conviction he never lost. His incandescent temper soon made the prejudice public, with ominous consequences for the dynasty as a whole: for, over a period of some twenty years, the personal authority of the Emperor-King among his Hungarian subjects was diminished by their fear that his heir would remain a rabid anti-Magyar once he came to the throne.

Hungary was in political turmoil during much of the last decade of the old century. Throughout 1889 Kálmán Tisza's army bill continued to provoke unrest in the capital. As a concession to Magyar nationalism, on 17 October Francis Joseph authorised two changes of name: the Imperial-Royal War Ministry of the Empire in Vienna would henceforth be known as the 'Imperial and Royal War Ministry', while the Imperial-Royal Army similarly became the Imperial and Royal Army. These trivial changes, replacing a hyphen by a conjunction and omitting the word 'empire', were regarded by Francis Joseph as 'almost laughable' but in Budapest they were interpreted as confirmation that the sovereign regarded the two parts of his Monarchy as linked solely by mutual consent. This gesture helped secure the passage through parliament of the unpopular army bill and brought a momentary calm to the streets of the capital. But Kálmán Tisza knew that his days of power were over. He no longer commanded the political following of earlier years. When, in March 1890, a further storm broke in parliament he decided to leave office.

Francis Joseph was in residence at Budapest throughout February and well into March that year. He found the politicking of the Magyar parliamentarians around him 'disagreeable': 'The Opposition deputies attack the prime minister with extraordinary rudeness and there is a colossal uproar at times', he wrote to Katharina Schratt. After a relatively stable fifteen year association with the same prime minister he found it hard to accustom himself to a new man. He appointed Count Gyula Szapáry, a cautious conservative, to succeed Tisza, but with little hope of any lasting political calm for Szapáry had no great support in parliament. His gloom was justified. The era of strong Magyar leadership – first Andrássy and later Tisza – was at an end. To Francis Joseph's dismay, over the next fifteen years, he had to find a new Hungarian prime minister on no less than six occasions.

He arrived back in Vienna on 17 March to face fresh problems. In the previous summer the Paris Congress of the Second International summoned socialists and trade unionists on both sides of the Atlantic to observe May Day as a proletarian festival of unity. Since May Day had long been celebrated in the German lands as a spring festival it was easy for Viktor Adler, the Jewish intellectual who led the Austrian socialist movement, to implement the Paris Congress's resolution. He urged trade unionists to hold meetings of 'a popular character open to the public' on 1 May 1890, though only in the morning: in the afternoon everyone should enjoy 'Nature's springtime'. Adler's innocuous call alarmed the Emperor, who could never forget the spring events of 1848 and the ease with which street demonstrations sparked off revolution. Francis Joseph summoned several meetings of ministers in Vienna, presiding over them himself and insisting that Taaffe should take strong action to check the spread of dangerous beliefs. Troops and police were put on the alert in every major city.

As May Day drew nearer, there was a flutter of apprehension in the capital: windows were shuttered; food hoarded for fear that roads from the countryside into the markets might be cut; in the Prater iron railings were removed so as to give cavalry horses freedom of manoeuvre if the mood of the demonstrators turned ugly. Yet the day passed as peacefully as in earlier years. A show of anti-capitalist solidarity brought thousands out to the Prater, processing down the Hauptallee behind a cluster of red flags. But troops and police reserves were kept discreetly in their barracks; with holiday sunshine in such a place at such a time the miasma of protest did not hang long in the air. There was no trouble in the smaller industrial towns of Austria, while in Bohemia and Moravia the response to Adler's call for peaceful demonstrations was lessened by an uneasy Czech awareness that the social democratic movement remained overwhelmingly Germanic in leadership. Francis Joseph's fears proved groundless.

Yet, though he exaggerated the risk of socialist upheaval, the Emperor was right to alert Taaffe's government to the threat posed by mass politics taking to the streets. For it was by now clear that the Reichsrat was no longer an effective safety-valve: the two chambers were too limited in composition and the deputies easily tempted to indulge themselves in rarefied rhetoric over matters remote from public concern. On the other hand, beyond the confines of parliament Schönerer's followers missed no opportunity to flaunt their Pan-German enthusiasm: even the announced intention of ex-Chancellor Bismarck to come to Vienna for his son's wedding was enough to worry the Emperor: 'I hope that Schönerer and company will not make too much trouble for us', he wrote to Katharina Schratt as the arrival of 'the devilish old Imperial Chancellor' drew nearer. But, far more pernicious than all this Pan-German rowdiness, was the rapid spread of anti-semitic feeling at a time when thousands of Jewish families, persecuted in Tsarist Russia and Roumania, were seeking refuge in Austria. The Emperor had no hesitation in condemning all attacks on Jewry: his great-great uncle, Joseph II, had issued patents of toleration in the 1780s; and the Jews were formally emancipated in Austria and in Hungary for the past quarter of a century. Now Francis Joseph looked with particular misgiving at the increased support given to Karl Lueger and his Christian Social Party. 'Every anti-Semitic movement must be nipped in the bud at once', the Emperor told Taaffe, after reading early reports of racial unrest, 'You will immediately have any anti-Semitic assembly dissolved. The Jews are brave and patriotic men who happily risk their lives for emperor and fatherland'.

But Taaffe, like Tisza in Hungary before him, was losing his grip on government: the 'Iron Ring' coalition was twelve years old and showing rust around the edges. His ideal political balance always rested on reconciliation between Czechs and Germans, first in Bohemia and Moravia, later in Cisleithania as a whole. A complicated educational and legal compromise (the *Punktationen* of 1890), settled with the 'Old Czech'

Party, seemed to bring the prime minister's plans to fruition. Taaffe, however, miscalculated: he had ignored the pace of social change in the Czech provinces. The Old Czechs had become yesterday's men: the initiative lay with the 'Young Czechs', radical militants ready to respond in kind to Schönerer's provocation, both in Bohemia-Moravia and in Vienna. They rejected the *Punktationen* and all talk of further compromise. In 1891 they began to win striking electoral successes. Both Taaffe and the Emperor were alarmed, not so much at changes in party affiliation as at the increase of nationalist feeling shown each time Czech and German townsfolk prepared to vote.

At this point Taaffe's minister of finance, Emil Steinbach, put forward an ingenious proposal: he urged the prime minister to broaden the franchise in elections for the lower house of the Reichsrat. Steinbach argued that in Cisleithania intensive nationalism was a middle class phenomenon and to give the working classes a voice in parliament would thus constrain the nationalistic antagonism which threatened the structure of the Monarchy. Taaffe was not easy to convince but, early in 1893, he was won over. To his surprise he found Francis Joseph not simply prepared to listen, but readily receptive: he welcomed the proposed extension of the franchise; in both the countryside and the smaller towns, the Emperor had always found loyal support from the least sophisticated of his subjects. Steinbach was accordingly instructed to prepare a suffrage bill which would have given the vote to almost every literate male in Cisleithania over the age of twenty-five. But Steinbach was not allowed a free hand: he was to draw up the bill in great secrecy, so as to prevent a protracted political crisis; and he was to preserve the complicated electoral system by which the proportion of deputies was stacked heavily in favour of the large landowners and the chambers of commerce.

The Emperor did not expect Steinbach's draft proposals to cause trouble; he was in Hungary again when the franchise reform was announced in Vienna. It was ill-received. Taaffe found every existing parliamentary group opposed to the scheme – except, strangely enough, the Young Czechs – and his coalition partners resigned from the government. There was resentment that the proposals were sprung unexpectedly on the party leaders, who were afraid that a wider suffrage would destroy old established power bases. Might it not advance the socialist cause, they argued? As the links in the Iron Ring began to fall apart, Francis Joseph hurried back to Vienna on 28 October. Taaffe, who had recently celebrated his sixtieth birthday, was a tired man. Technically, the Emperor dismissed the Count from office – an action for which Francis Joseph has been accused of deep ingratitude towards an old friend who had served him for fourteen years. But this charge is unmerited. Although Taaffe was in no hurry to go, he recognized that, sooner or later, he would have to tender his resignation, for he had no hope of forging a new coalition 'ring'. Significantly, after his fall, Taaffe showed no bitterness towards the Emperor; only towards ministerial colleagues who deserted him.

Francis Joseph's reactions to the crisis are interesting. He would have liked to appoint another 'Emperor's Minister', with no party affiliation whatsoever, and both Archduke Albrecht and General Beck recommended the Governor of Galicia, Count Casimir Badeni, who had pleased the generals by his strength of purpose during the Russian war scares of the previous decade. The Emperor, however, felt bound to allow the political leaders who broke the Iron Ring an opportunity to form a coalition of their own; and on 5 November 1893 Prince Alfred zu Windischgraetz, a grandson of the 'emperor-maker' of 1848, accepted the challenge. Once again, however, Francis Joseph imposed a condition: the Steinbach plan must not be dropped, for he was convinced that when an emperor accepted the principle of a reform it ought never to be cast aside in response to criticism in the Reichsrat. Instead, Steinbach's draft bill was referred to a parliamentary committee for close scrutiny and discussion.

In the end, the Windischgraetz coalition achieved little. Confusion between the party leaders led to a dispute in Styria which stirred up latent antagonism between the chief nationalities over the funding of Slovene language classes for secondary school pupils in the predominantly German town of Cilli. This affair, magnified out of all proportion to its significance, split the government and forced Windischgraetz out, after a mere twenty months in office. A stop-gap prime minister, Count Erich Kielmansegg, barely had time to soothe the Slovenes before belatedly making way in September 1895 for the much-respected Governor of Galicia, Count Badeni.

But, to Francis Joseph's dismay, by the middle of the decade Austrian politics were caught in a cycle of change as dramatic as in Hungary; after Taaffe's downfall, there were eight different heads of government in Vienna in seven years. Had the Emperor followed the advice of Albrecht and Beck and appointed Badeni to succeed Taaffe in 1893, the Polish aristocrat might well have emerged as a strong, non-party prime minister, for he possessed considerable personal skills. As it was, however, Badeni's prospects for extricating Francis Joseph from the parliamentary morass were hampered by two unexpected developments: the fall of Kálnoky, and his replacement as foreign minister by a Polish aristocrat; and the rapid rise in influence of Karl Lueger, both in the affairs of the capital and the political life of Austria as a whole.

By the spring of 1895 Gustav Kálnoky had been foreign minister for thirteen and a half years, almost as long a time-span as the premierships of Taaffe or Tisza. The Moravian landowner seemed a solid pillar of the state; he was automatically the chairman of ministerial conferences in the absence of the Emperor and principal arbiter of differences between the two governments of the Monarchy. Kálnoky was not popular with his colleagues nor with the diplomatic corps, for his aristocratic haughtiness never thawed in human contact, nor did he make much effort to conceal his clericalist political sympathies. But in his years at the Ballhausplatz Kálnoky achieved much: a strengthening of the alliances with Germany and Italy; closer co-operation with Britain over the problems of the eastern Mediterranean; and, above all, the maintenance of good relations with Serbia, Roumania and Bulgaria so as to limit the spread of Russian influence in the Balkans. He was, however, exasperated by the confused internal politics of the Monarchy. Neither the Emperor nor Taaffe told him of Steinbach's proposed franchise reforms; Kálnoky heard of them first from the King of Greece in a casual conversation. And for several years he was in conflict with the parliamentarians in Budapest, for the Magyars thought his policies encouraged Serbian and Roumanian irredentism. His contempt for Hungary's politicians, often expressed aloud, brought him an open rebuke from the prime minister in Budapest in May 1895. Kálnoky at once tendered his resignation to Francis Joseph, who accepted it with unflattering alacrity.

In Kálnoky's place, the Emperor appointed Count Goluchowski, son of the wealthy Polish aristocrat responsible for the October Diploma thirty-five years before. In domestic politics Goluchowski 'the Younger' (born four months after Francis Joseph's accession) was as conservative as his predecessor and no less suspicious of Hungarian party politics; but there was much to be said in his favour, notably his personal charm of manner. Nevertheless, Goluchowski's presence at the centre of affairs in Vienna made Badeni's task more difficult. When Badeni included in his ministry two more compatriots – one of whom became Austrian minister of finance – it is hardly surprising if the Viennese Press began to hint at a Polish takeover of government. That at least was the contention of Karl Lueger and his Christian Social Party. And by the autumn of 1895 what Lueger said was of considerable importance in Austrian politics.

To Francis Joseph, Lueger came as a new and unwelcome phenomenon. He was a vote-catching demagogue who exploited the hopes and prejudices of the 'little man in the street' to climb to the top in municipal affairs and, from a narrow power base in the capital, sought to make or brake successive governments. In 1895 he was fifty-one, a radical Catholic lawyer from the Landstrasse district of Vienna, a city councillor for the past twenty years and a deputy in parliament for ten. Though at first a

German Liberal, he won support from a wealthy group of clericalists, headed by Prince Liechtenstein. Their patronage enabled Lueger to build up the Christian Social Party on a basis of loyalty to the Habsburgs as a German-Austrian dynasty, hostility towards 'Jewish capitalism', and respect for the five encyclical letters of Pope Leo XIII which updated the social teachings of Roman Catholicism. 'Handsome Karl' was as good a rabble-rouser as Schönerer, over whom he had three advantages: a more positive programme; an efficient party machine; and a constituency in the capital, whereas Schönerer represented the Waldviertel, the Pan-German district which was the boyhood homeland of Adolf Hitler (born at Braunau-am-Inn in 1889, eleven weeks after Mayerling).

Under Lueger's leadership, the Christian Socials gained an inconclusive municipal electoral victory in June 1895. A second election, three months later, proved more decisive; they won twice as many seats on the Vienna City Council as the German Liberals, who had dominated the capital's politics for several decades. Francis Joseph was appalled: he feared that inflammatory speeches against the Jews would cause greater violence in the streets than Schönerer's followers ever provoked – and he had no doubt that the Schönerer mob would back any mass anti-semitic demonstrations Lueger might encourage. So serious was the prospect that several wealthy Jewish financiers hinted that a Lueger municipal regime in the capital would force them to move their financial institutions away from Vienna to Hungary. The Emperor had the constitutional right to refuse to confirm the election of a Mayor of Vienna if he thought him a danger to the well-being of the state; and in the early autumn he made it clear to Kielmansegg, the outgoing premier, that 'so long as I rule, Lueger will never be confirmed as mayor of my imperial capital'. He rejected a second mayoral victory by Lueger in late October. Badeni, the new prime minister, had shown scant respect for democratic votes in his seven years as Governor of Galicia; his advice strengthened the Emperor's own inclinations. On 13 November he again vetoed Lueger's re-election: the council was dissolved and the city's administration entrusted to an imperial commission of fifteen nominees.

On that November evening, there was some risk of bloodshed in the streets of the capital. One group of supporters wished to storm the Rathaus but were restrained by Lueger himself; ominously another group headed for the Hofburg, but were turned away by the police. The demonstrators were not hostile to the Emperor in person; they seem to have thought he was badly advised: 'Out with foreigners', 'Back to Galicia' were popular slogans. Even so, for the next few days, when Francis Joseph drove down the Mariahilferstrasse on his way to and from Schönbrunn, the customary 'hurrahs' and polite salutes were missing; he made the journey in a silence he had not experienced since the dark weeks which followed Solferino. The stock exchange in Vienna remained nervous, with the worst panic selling since the *Krach* of 1873. New municipal elections would be held in February or March and there would be parliamentary elections a year later. Despite his repeated assurances that he would protect all his subjects, would a staunch Catholic like Francis Joseph continue to resist the growing strength of the Christian Social Party?

He was certainly puzzled. 'Among the highest social circles anti-semitism is an extraordinarily widespread disease and the agitation is unbelievable', he wrote to Elizabeth in Munich at the end of December 1895; he enclosed letters which he had received from their younger daughter and from one of the older aristocratic families 'in which Lueger and his party were recommended to me most warmly'. He admitted that 'the basic foundation' of Lueger's beliefs 'is intrinsically good', but 'the excesses are terrible'. Badeni, too, was under pressure; and both he and Lueger were troubled by the mounting support for Adler's Social Democrats as parliamentary elections came nearer. At a secret meeting between the two men it was agreed that the prime minister would ask the Emperor to receive Lueger in a private audience at which he would affirm the movement's loyalty and his personal intention to act with restraint as Mayor.

Francis Joseph and Lueger talked at great length on 27 April 1896, at a time when Francis Joseph was primarily concerned with Hungarian affairs. A tacit understanding was reached: the Emperor would appoint one of Lueger's lieutenants as interim Mayor, to hold office until the Christian Socials had shown their administration to be constructive and not discriminatory. Lueger would then become Mayor. Meanwhile the Christian Socials would maintain only formal opposition to Badeni's proposals in parliament, notably over the passage of the modified version of Steinbach's franchise reform, to which the Emperor continued to attach great importance. The Christian Social council duly took office in Vienna in the last week of May 1896 and eleven months later Francis Joseph at last ratified Lueger's appointment as Mayor. By then, Badeni's franchise bill had become law, and elections in March 1897 gave Austria a new Reichsrat, containing 425 deputies from 25 political parties. The franchise reform was hardly democratic: it allowed five and a quarter million male voters over the age of twenty-four and with a fixed residential qualification of six months to elect 72 deputies to the lower house; the remaining 353 members were returned by one and three quarter million electors voting in their four traditional privileged spheres.

Party politics, whether in Vienna's city council, in the Reichsrat, or in Hungary's parliament, remained distasteful to Francis Joseph. Not least, they tied him even longer to his desk and entailed more and more audiences for him. His daily routine was formidable: a first session spent in reading reports in his study at five in the morning, followed at eight o'clock by a series of meetings with the head of his military chancellery, the foreign minister or a senior official from the Ballhausplatz and with other ministers concerned with topical problems. Twice a week, at ten o'clock, whether he was in Vienna or Budapest, the Emperor held a general audience: on these occasions, on the average, he would speak to a hundred people individually. Further audiences would continue in the afternoons, after he had studied police reports and a digest of the morning newspapers. As in earlier years of the reign, Francis Joseph dutifully attended official functions in both parts of the Monarchy, his duties increased by the absence of a Crown Prince and the ill-health of Francis Ferdinand. He continued to study the details of military exercises, even adding to the obligations which he felt bound to accept. For he now made a point of joining his ally William II at German manoeuvres, a gesture which William reciprocated, sometimes coming to Austria-Hungary three or four times in the year. These attentions of his German ally were an additional burden; Frances Joseph remained ill-at-ease when exposed to the neo-Hohenzollern swagger and bombast which William affected during the first years of his reign. When Archduke Albrecht died in February 1895 Francis Joseph was sad at losing a kinsman on whose counsel he relied heavily for over thirty years. The grandeur of the state funeral moved him deeply, but he admitted ruefully to Katharina Schratt that preparations for the ceremony were exhausting: 'I had to drive five times to different railway stations to receive foreign guests, clad four times in foreign uniform and once in Austrian ... With the constant putting on and putting off, I could vividly imagine just how agreeable a play must be with many costume changes in it!'.

It would have been unthinkable to shirk the duties of kingship and yet, sadly, the Emperor was left increasingly to sustain them on his own. After Mayerling the Empress Elizabeth allowed the darkness of grief to blanket her world. Melancholia stifled the poetic imagery of the previous decade. Her elder daughter, Gisela, was so alarmed that she warned Valerie to take especial care of their mother when visiting the waterfalls at Gastein, in case she should throw herself into the torrent. But such fears misunderstood Elizabeth's temperament. She wished the world to know of her self-reproach, her regret that she had never understood her son's needs; intruders into the privacy of her soul should find contrition in as much of her fading beauty as she revealed to probing eyes. Always she dressed in mourning, though she rarely appeared at ceremonial functions and was reluctant to sit as a hostess at dinner with visiting state dignitaries.

At the first Court reception graced by the Empress – two years after Rudolf's death – the wife of the British ambassador noted that she was dressed almost like a nun, heavily veiled, with a necklace of black beads which seems to have resembled a rosary, although with the cross replaced by a medallion containing a lock of her son's hair.

In the first shock of the Mayerling tragedy Elizabeth curtailed her foreign wanderings, seeking rest in Hungary or the Dolomites until after the marriage of Archduchess Marie Valerie – a quiet affair at Ischl on 30 July 1890. But, once Valerie had settled with her husband near Wels (where he was serving in a dragoon regiment), the Empress saw no reason to keep up the pretence of Court life. She travelled, not simply to Bavaria or down the Adriatic to Corfu, but to Switzerland, the French Riviera, the Azores and north Africa. She dreamt of setting out on a world cruise in a chartered sailing ship: someone had told her she would find Tasmania attractive. But, to the relief of her faithful household, she accepted that such a voyage was now beyond her physical strength.

Ever since her visit to the Isle of Wight in 1874 the Empress repeatedly urged Francis Joseph to join her on a vacation, shaking off the last coils of Court life for once. At last, in March 1893, she persuaded him to join her for a fortnight in Switzerland, staying in a hotel at Territet, near Montreux. Yet, though they enjoyed walks together, out to the Castle of Chillon or up the mountain foothills behind the lake, the Territet visit was not really a holiday for him. His hopes of remaining incognito were dashed within twenty-four hours, when the hotel proprietor proudly flew the black and gold imperial standard from his flagpole; and, a day later, the Emperor had to spend the whole morning in the hotel dealing with the official papers a courier brought him from Vienna. Moreover, though the Swiss holiday momentarily lifted his flagging spirits, he was sad at the thought that, on leaving Territet, he would not see Elizabeth again for at least six weeks. 'No joy, only loneliness awaits me in Vienna', he admitted in a private letter sent a few hours before setting out on his homeward train journey.

During these long and increasingly frequent weeks as a grass-widower, Francis Joseph was dependent on the companionship of Katharina Schratt, though she was herself often away from the capital. In the bitter aftermath of Mayerling her good sense and sympathy had steadied the Empress's nerves as well as giving him a certain comfort and, with Elizabeth's agreement, he responded gratefully and generously to her gestures of support and understanding. A codicil added to Francis Joseph's will in March 1889 pledged a legacy of half a million florins to the Court actress Katharina Kiss von Itebbe (neé Schratt) 'to whom I am bound by the deepest and purest of friendships and who has always been loyally and faithfully at my side and at that of the Empress during the hardest moments of our life'. At the same time, with the Emperor's support, she purchased a delightful villa at Hietzing overlooking the botanical gardens of Schönbrunn, in what was then the Gloriettegasse. The house was only four doors uphill from the Nahowski home, a source of occasional embarrassment; but it was close enough to the palace for the Emperor frequently to follow the practice which he had begun at Ischl of inviting himself to breakfast, after which the two friends would stroll in the grounds of Schönbrunn itself. As the Empress went out of her way to show her approval of 'the friend', these walks and talks were not in themselves a source of scandalous gossip. Only Archduchess Marie Valerie strongly disapproved of the way in which her father exchanged confidences with '*die Schratt*', and her mother treated her as a family friend.

Relations between Emperor and actress were not always smooth. He was uneasy at her continued friendship with Ferdinand of Bulgaria and irritated by her occasional attempts to secure a more rewarding post in the diplomatic service for her, discreetly distant, husband – who in 1892 was at last transferred from the consulate in Tunis to Barcelona. Most of all Francis Joseph was angered by Katharina's insistence on making a balloon flight over Vienna in June 1890, which received much publicity in Austrian newspapers. He thought the flight dangerous, and he was particularly displeased that her companion should have been Alexander Baltazzi: 'That you made the aerial trip under his auspices means nothing to me, I assure you', Francis Joseph wrote to her from Hungary, 'but in the eyes of the malicious world it will harm you, for the newspaper concentration on his presence underlines the fact that the Baltazzi family is not welcome in all circles since our disaster'. Though he was momentarily afraid that this scolding might end their friendship, he need not have worried; with disingenuous sincerity Katharina assured him that, when next she took to the air, she would keep the matter secret so as to cause him no disquiet.

There were other troubled moments, too. On one occasion in June 1892 – a time when the Emperor was concerned over the Pan-German response to Bismarck's visit to the capital – Francis Joseph 'could hardly sleep at night' after hearing from Katharina that her 12-year old son, Toni Kiss, had received at school an anonymous obscene letter slandering his mother. The Vienna police chief was alerted; the financier Eduard Palmer asked to serve as a discreet go-between, interviewing Toni (who did not understand the implications of the letter), his mother, and the police chief; and the Empress was at once consulted by letter. No prosecution followed; and it was the Empress who responded most sensibly to the whole affair; for when Francis Joseph and Elizabeth were in residence at Ischl that summer and Frau Schratt and her son were invited to take tea at the imperial villa, the Empress took Toni Kiss aside for a walk through the gardens, praising his mother and emphasizing the value of the support she gave the Emperor and herself in the saddest months of their married life.

Unlike his mother and his younger daughter Francis Joseph did not keep a detailed journal. As a substitute for a daily record of this character, he would send long letters to the two women closest to his heart. To the Empress he normally wrote every other day during her travels. Between September 1890 and September 1898 no less than 474 of these letters have survived, clear testimony both to his diligence as a correspondent and to the frequency of her absence from Court. Few make interesting reading: they record the weather, the statistics of his audiences, the seating plan of the formal dinners which she was so relieved not to attend, his comings and goings, news of their daughters and of much loved 'little Erzsi', who lived with the Crown Princess out at Laxenburg and is mentioned on more than seventy occasions. In considerable detail, the letters describe visits to *die Freundin* in the Gloriettegasse, the walks they took together, the progress of Toni Kiss (more than 30 mentions), his meetings with Katharina's cousins and aunt, and all the intimacy of the bourgeois existence which meant so much to him. Occasional entries suggest that the Emperor's interests were broader than many writers concede: he was, for example, fascinated by the invention of the 'Edison phonograph', on an early version of which he heard, very clearly, a German band playing the *Radetzky March*. His theatre visits were not limited to the plays in which Katharina Schratt appeared. Most unexpectedly, on 19 January 1897, he wrote: 'At five o'clock I dined alone and afterwards I went to the second performance of *The Wild Duck* by Ybsen (*sic*), a curious modern piece, uphill work, but excellently presented'. Did the title tempt the marksman in Francis Joseph to the theatre that evening? The letter says nothing of the actors, but 'a new 16-year-old actress, Fraulein Medelski playing a 14-year old maiden showed a remarkable talent and acted very well'. Did he, one wonders, stay for the last scene, in which 'the maiden' shoots herself in her inner sanctuary?

His other correspondent, Katharina Schratt, received more than two hundred letters from the Emperor during the same eight year period (September 1890 to September 1898). They are lighter in character and tinged with mocking self-pity but they reveal more about his inner feelings. Surprisingly they show the onset of a timidity he did not possess before the buffeting of misfortune in his middle years: 'The Empress restarts the sea-voyaging – for me a constant anxiety and worry', he wrote in the autumn of 1890; and he was to warn Katharina, not only against balloon ascents, but against excursions to the glaciers, against mountaineering ('let me remind you that, for safety's sake, you promised me not to climb to the peak of the Dachstein') and, in April 1897, against the risks of falls when bicycling, which was 'a real epidemic' that spring and a pastime much favoured by his daughter, Gisela, three years Katharina's junior.

These letters also preserve his sense of incredulity at what he saw around him during holidays with the Empress on the French Riviera. He first joined her at Cap Martin, near Menton, for a fortnight in March 1894; they were there for a week in February 1895, and for nearly three weeks a year later. A fourth visit in March 1897 was, he said 'ruined by anxiety about the Empress's health' but the earlier vacations were happy affairs; they brought liveliness and colour back to his daily existence.

As at Territet he was fascinated by hotel life, though he contributed little to it: 'I dined in our suite at 7 o'clock', he wrote on arrival in 1896, ... and soon went to bed, lulled to sleep by music from the hotel lounge'. He visited the gambling rooms at Monte Carlo in 1894, but he thought there were too many onlookers for him to chance his luck. Best of all on the Riviera he liked the 'wonderful gardens' at Cannes. A year later he thought the Riviera 'full of Englishmen' and caught sight of Mr and Mrs Gladstone walking in the hotel grounds, but he showed no desire to meet one of Austria's consistently stern critics: why darken a holiday?. 'We try all kinds of restaurants and are really eating far too much and too varied a fare', he told Katharina at the close of the first holiday at Cap Martin, 'After all, the prime purpose of life here consists only in eating. With which sparkling observation I end my letter'.

Inevitably business of state intruded on the holiday mood in March 1896, when the Emperor met the head of a republic for the first time, exchanging visits with President Felix Faure, who was on an official tour of the Alpes Maritimes. Francis Joseph admired the bearing of the Presidential escort of cuirassiers, 'with trumpeters blowing'. He enjoyed watching the French fleet at sea from the Corniche and amused himself by scrambling up to a vantage point for a surreptitious assessment of Alpine infantry as they carried out field exercises with live ammunition. He found, with apparent surprise, that this stretch of the Third French Republic's coastline provided a winter haven for many royal dignitaries: among them he entertained members of his own family, Romanov Grand Dukes, the Prince of Wales, and his old friend, the Empress Eugenie. Queen Victoria was there, too. On 13 March 1896 Francis Joseph and Elizabeth visited her at Cimiez, the only occasion in her life when she 'received the Emperor and Empress of Austria' together. It was, the Queen reported to her prime minister, a 'cordial' meeting: she noted, with satisfaction, the Emperor's confidence in Goluchowski as a foreign minister and his optimism at the prospects for lasting peace in Europe.

Soon after the visit to Cimiez Francis Joseph returned to Vienna, ready once more to face the problems raised by Lueger's meteoric rise in popularity. At the same time Elizabeth sailed to Corfu, still intent on mastering modern Greek, but anxious also to build up her strength in order to meet the challenge of a formidable programme of royal events in the months ahead. For the year 1896 marked the thousandth anniversary of the coming of the Magyars to the Danubian plain and Budapest remained en fête from spring to autumn.

These millennial celebrations, originally planned during the primacy of Kálmán Tisza, were of crucial political importance to the stability of the Dual Monarchy as a whole. They could either confirm Hungary's economic self-sufficiency and cohesion or spark off even worse friction between the master nation and the kingdom's Roumanian and Slav minorities. Tension had grown during 1895 after the appointment in January of a Hungarian Liberal Government headed by a convinced believer in Magyarization, Baron Bánffy. At the same time, the ascendancy of Lueger's Christian Socials in Austria threatened the economic Ausgleich on the eve of its decennial re-assessment, which was due in 1897; for the Christian Socials in Vienna constantly attacked 'greedy Magyar politicians', whom they alleged were in the pay of 'Jewish bankers', hostile to the Catholic church. On every count it was essential for Hungary's King and Queen to tread warily during the weeks of grandiose celebration. And this they did well.

The festivities began on 2 May 1896, when Francis Joseph and Elizabeth opened the Millennial Exposition of Hungarian achievement in the Városliget, the town park of Budapest. The setting recalled the World Exhibition of 1873 in the Vienna Prater, although the most striking building erected for the occasion was not a great rotunda but the Vajdahunyad Castle, an architectural mélange of more than twenty different 'Hungarian' styles, from Romanesque to Baroque. To convey visitors from the inner city to the park the municipal authorities made proud use of a technological innovation, unknown in Europe outside London – an underground railway, running for the most part only a few feet below the surface of Budapest's smartest boulevard, Andrássy-Út, and stopping at eight stations. Francis Joseph made the journey, in a specially decorated imperial carriage, on 6 May, four days after the first trains ran, but Elizabeth did not accompany him. She had felt overwhelmed by 'all that splendour and pomp' at the opening of the exhibition and, as she wrote to her daughter, she was saddened by memories of earlier grand occasions, when she had Rudolf beside her. King and Queen attended a thanksgiving Mass in the coronation church that same week and Francis Joseph stayed on in the city for other festivities. Early in June they were together again for the opening of a new wing to the royal palace in Budapest and for a solemn procession in which the Holy Crown of St Stephen and the coronation regalia were borne across the Danube to the Parliament House and back to the Crown Room beneath the palace dome. In September, when Francis Joseph joined the Kings of Roumania and Serbia at Orsova for the opening of the canalised section of the Danube through the Iron Gates, some attention was paid to the sensitivities of Hungary's minority nationalities, but for the most part the celebrations boosted Magyar nationalism. Bánffy's Liberals easily won a general election in the late autumn, but it was an ugly campaign, with more than thirty people killed in riots or scuffles.

The millennial festivities re-affirmed their Queen's unique hold on the affections of the Hungarian people. Francis Joseph, however, still did not trust Magyar loyalty, especially at a time when there was such widespread commemoration of Kossuth's activities fifty years before. A conflict over the relative contributions of the two halves of the Monarchy to the common budget continued throughout 1897: the Delegation from the Reichsrat in Vienna argued that, since the Milleniary Exhibition had emphasized the great economic progress made by Hungary, parliament in Budapest should now meet 42 per cent of common expenses rather than the 31.5 per cent agreed in 1867 by the original Ausgleich. The Hungarians, on the other hand, maintained that the 1867 level was always too high and they resented the possibility of having to subsidise backward areas of Cisleithania. A powerful rearguard action by the Hungarian Liberals delayed settlement of this tiresome question until the closing months of 1898, with the Hungarian quota finally raised to a mere 34.4 per cent of total expenses. Gloomily Francis Joseph noted that the Bánffy Government expected the anniversaries of the Hungarian revolution to be marked by public holidays. It was an odd situation; for the Emperor-King himself still had paintings on his palace walls which showed the valour of Austria's whitecoats in crushing Kossuth and his rebels during the first year of the reign.

There was, too, the delicate problem of how to celebrate the Golden Jubilee of Francis Joseph's accession, which would fall on 2 December 1898. Here he had at least hoped he would have backing from a firm government in Vienna, especially when in the spring of 1896 Badeni and Lueger reached their informal agreement over the franchise bill. But Badeni made an appalling political miscalculation. In order to win Czech support in the contest with Hungary over the tax quota, he issued language ordinances for Bohemia and for Moravia in April 1897: from July 1901, every civil servant in each of these provinces would have to be bi-lingual in German and Czech; and in lawsuits, the language of the plaintiff was to be used at every level, from magistrate's hearings to the supreme court of appeal.

The Badeni Ordinances gave an enormous advantage to educated Czechs, most of whom spoke and wrote German as well as their native language. On the other hand few Germans, irrespective of their home province, spoke any of the minority Slav languages. What if the Language Ordinances were extended to other provinces? Would German bureaucrats have to become proficient in Slovene or Ruthene or Polish or Italian? To say that the Badeni Ordinances were fought tooth and nail in the Reichsrat is almost literally true: sometimes punches were thrown, sometimes inkpots. A Pan-German deputy who described the ordinances as 'a piece of Polish rascality' accepted a challenge from the prime minister, and in the subsequent duel wounded Badeni in the arm. Most of the disorder was in central or suburban Vienna, but there was serious rioting in Graz, where the Slovene minority was conscious of racial kinship with the Czechs. Lueger led 'Out with Badeni' demonstrations in the capital; and by the last weekend in November military guards patrolled the Ringstrasse and the inner city. If the German ambassador is to be believed, 'Frau Kathi' Schratt – who normally avoided political matters – implored Francis Joseph to get rid of Badeni before the troubles worsened. At all events, the Emperor decided to sacrifice the prime minister for the sake of good order on the streets. On 28 November 1897 Badeni was dismissed, the only minister forced from office by public opinion during the reign.

Yet, though the Emperor might sack a particular man under popular pressure, he obstinately refused to concede changes in the law. Two more years went by before he admitted that the Language Ordinances were administratively impossible to observe and withdrew them. The effect of all this political skirmishing was to weaken the central authority in Vienna. Instead of approaching the critical anniversary year of 1898 with a strong government, as he had hoped, Francis Joseph was forced to work with stopgap administrations, headed by five different incumbents in some twenty-five months.

The only wise inner counsellor to whom the Emperor could turn in 1897–98 was Count Goluchowski, the second of his chosen Polish aristocrats, in the Ballhausplatz. As foreign minister, Goluchowski patiently worked for improved relations with Russia, establishing the principle that Vienna and St Petersburg would work in harmony in the Balkan lands rather than take advantage of each other's problems to destabilise so sensitive a region. In his secondary role, as de facto chairman of ministerial councils held in the sovereign's absence, the easy-going Goluchowski was of great service to the dynasty, since he was able to reduce the chronic tension between the successive prime ministers of the two parts of the Monarchy. Goluchowski's hostility towards the Language Ordinances are more likely to have tipped the balance of Francis Joseph's judgment against Badeni than any prompting from Katharina Schratt.

One important decision, however, probably owes more to Vienna's Mayor than to any individual minister: the Golden Jubilee was to be celebrated in anticipation, not simply left for a winter's day in December; the festivities would begin in the spring, thereby ensuring that attention was drawn to the dynasty during months when more radical spirits might wish to recall the deeds of the 1848 revolutionaries. In mounting commemorative festivals Vienna sought to outshine Budapest. Thousands could flock to the newly completed Volksprater amusement park, where Francis Joseph and Lueger stood side by side as the great Ferris Wheel began its first majestically slow rotation. On 7 May the Emperor opened a Jubilee Exhibition in the Prater itself; he came again on six other days before midsummer; and on 9 May, accompanied by both the Mayor and Cardinal-Archbishop of Vienna, he inaugurated the *Stadtbahn*, a more extensive urban railway system than in Budapest, though not technically an 'underground'. Seventy thousand schoolchildren paraded down the Ringstrasse to greet their Emperor on 24 June: 'It was a joy to see how they smiled at me and to hear the enthusiasm with which they shouted', he wrote to Katharina. A few days later he was hailed by 4,000 huntsmen gathered at Schönbrunn. Yet there was one striking difference between these celebrations and the millennial festivities in Budapest: the Empress took no part in them. The last state occasion which she graced with her presence was a gala dinner at the Hofburg in honour of Tsar Nicholas II and his Empress on 27 August 1896, during a visit which promoted Goluchowski's ideal of an Austro-Russian entente. Thereafter Elizabeth's doctors insisted that, for the sake of her health, she should retire into private life.

For two years Francis Joseph was constantly uneasy over his wife's health and well-being. She was anaemic, and yet insisted on rigorous dieting, sometimes eating no more than half a dozen oranges in the course of a day. There were new anxieties, too: her face was pocked with a rash she found impossible to conceal and doctors who examined her were concerned at an apparent dilation of the heart. When Katharina Schratt was about to visit the Empress at Cap Martin in March 1897, Francis Joseph warned their friend in advance: 'If you should be shocked by her appearance, which unfortunately is very bad, please do not show it'.

A few weeks later tragedy again struck Elizabeth. On 4 May 1897 her youngest sister Sophie, married to the Duke of Alençon, perished in the fire which swept through a charity bazaar at the Rue Jean-Gujon in Paris, killing 200 people: 'In all its circumstances' the fire 'is more terrible than anything that has happened this century', the British prime minister wrote to Queen Victoria. The shocking news from Paris, and the grisly newspaper reports which followed it, almost unhinged Elizabeth; once more her mind seems to have turned round upon itself, bringing to the surface of her consciousness old griefs and past remorse. She travelled more restlessly than ever – to Biarritz, to the Riviera, to the German spas. In the spring of 1898 Francis Joseph joined her at Kissingen for ten days. They were together for a fortnight at the height of summer in Ischl. But on 16 July Elizabeth set out for a new cure at Bad Nauheim. They never saw each other again. Fittingly their romance ended where it began, in the mountain valleys of the Salzkammergut.

Francis Joseph remained at Ischl until the last week of August. Then, after a brief visit to Schönbrunn and a sad walk in the gardens of the Villa Hermes worrying about the health of its chatelaine, he was off to southern Hungary, to watch autumn manoeuvres along the Danube frontier with Serbia. Still he found time to write every other day to Elizabeth, the letters following her from Nauheim into Switzerland. He was back in Vienna on Friday, 9 September, attending to urgent Austrian affairs, for he planned to leave for Gödöllö the following evening. Early on Saturday morning he wrote to Katharina letting her know that he had 'thank God, really good news from the Empress', who was 'enjoying ... the pure, invigorating mountain air' of Switzerland. But at half-past four that afternoon his adjutant arrived with a telegram: it contained, he said, 'very bad news'. At once, the Emperor assumed it was from Geneva, for worry over Elizabeth's health remained uppermost in his mind. The message, however, reported not the Empress's sudden collapse, but that she had been 'injured'. Francis Joseph was both alarmed and puzzled: what could have happened? Within minutes a second telegram arrived and the terrible truth broke upon him: Sisi had been stabbed by an Italian anarchist as she walked to a lake steamer in front of the Hotel Beau Rivage at Geneva; she lost consciousness and died within minutes of the attack. '*Mir bleibt doch gar nichts erspart auf dieser Welt!*', Francis Joseph exclaimed in deep grief: 'So I am to be spared nothing in this world!'. And then, so the adjutant reported, he said softly, as if speaking to himself, '*Niemand weiss, wie sehr wir uns geliebt haben*': 'Nobody knows the love we had for each other'.

Chapter 18

THE BELVEDERE

'With whom better can I speak of the lost one than with you?', Francis Joseph wrote to Katharina Schratt on 12 September, thanking her for cutting short a holiday to hurry back to Hietzing and visit him in Schön-brunn. Throughout that autumn his grief was so deep that he went through the daily routine of administration like an automaton, waiting for the hours when he could talk and talk and talk about the Empress, sometimes to his daughters, more often to the friend. Inevitably, the festivities to celebrate the Golden Jubilee were cancelled, as mourning enveloped Court life. His daughters sought to sustain their father; but 'faced with such pain I am powerless to help', Valerie wrote in her journal. She was, of course deeply saddened herself and, being extremely devout, she was worried by the thought that her mother had lost consciousness before receiving the last rites. With encouragement from a Jesuit chaplain, she urged her father to go regularly to confession, dedicating himself anew to God for the sake of the Empress's immortal soul. Of this practice, the family friend did not approve. 'They never stop worrying the poor old gentleman', Katharina Schratt told Philip Eulenburg, the German ambassador, who was fast becoming her confidant: 'All this talk about prayer and repentance gets on his nerves ... I say to him, "There's little point in Your Majesty going to confession when you have no sins on your conscience to confess"'.

No sins, perhaps; but the continued relationship with *die Schratt* was in itself ambiguous; and his strait-laced younger daughter and her husband had every intention of discouraging it. Over the past decade the openness of Elizabeth's friendship with Katharina to some extent curbed slanderous gossip. The Empress invariably treated their friend generously. Earlier that year, she had told her that, to mark the Golden Jubilee, a special medal – the Elizabeth Order – would be struck: and she would be among the first to receive it. The medal was, indeed, struck; but when the list of recipients was published it did not include Frau Schratt's name.

Katharina raised the question with the Emperor, reminding him of the Empress's promises. She should have known her sovereign better. Over such matters Francis Joseph was adamant. Blandly he explained that what would have been natural when the Empress was alive was now out of the question; he could not himself bestow on her an Order honouring his wife without setting tongues wagging so viciously as to cause her pain. Katharina was hurt, much more deeply than Francis Joseph realized since she made some effort to conceal her sense of injury, inwardly blaming Archduchess Marie Valerie for the humiliating disappointment. By the end of the year a rift had opened in the long friendship.

Over the following eighteen months, the rift became a chasm, with the Emperor declining to intervene in rows between the Court actress and the director of the Burgtheater. In July 1900 she sent from Paris a letter of resignation from the Burgtheater company: to her surprise it was accepted. She was in her forty-seventh year; her nerves were shattered and her absent husband still running her into debt. Moreover the disapprobation of the Archduchess's household froze the spontaneous warmth which had brought such enchantment to meetings with the Emperor in earlier years. The letters of Eulenburg, a waspish commentator on any social scene, even gave the impression she was finding 'the poor gentleman' rather a bore. At last, in Ischl immediately after Francis Joseph's seventieth birthday celebrations, she told him that she felt their close companionship must come to an end. Almost immediately she left for Gastein, going on to Munich and Paris and Lucerne and Florence; faithful letters pursued her across Europe. Occasionally she replied to him – as when she let him know that in the Pavilion of Sport at the Paris Exhibition he was accorded a life-size photograph, together with an updated tally of his marksmanship: 48,345 head of wild game had fallen to the sharpness of his eye and the steadiness of his hand. But for much of the time the Emperor was left to gather news of his 'dearest friend' from other sources, such as Eduard Palmer or even her son, Toni Kiss. He was at times a very lonely old gentleman.

Rather surprisingly, Archduchess Marie Valerie seems to have hoped that her father would re-marry. An Empress at Court would focus high society on the imperial family once again; he might even still have a son to succeed him. Many earlier Habsburgs had declined to remain widowers; and both his grandfather, Emperor Francis, and his own brother, Charles Ludwig, married three times, with the last nuptials in both instances celebrated on the eve of their fortieth birthdays. There is, however, a difference between nearly forty and nearly seventy. Although embassy gossip induced Eulenburg to take the possibility of re-marriage seriously, it was never likely and when, long before her voluntary exile,

Katharina Schratt passed the rumours on to the Emperor, Francis Joseph was amazed at such credulity. 'You can tell Count Eulenburg from me that, whatever people may say, I have no intention of marrying again', he said firmly. At seventy Francis Joseph wished life to run smoothly along familiar grooves, like the electric tramcars Lueger was bringing to Vienna's streets; no jumping of tracks through a sudden switch of points; just a steady journey to the terminus, with a bell ringing to clear the path ahead.

Sometimes, however, the journey was impeded by an unexpected obstacle. One such hazard, encountered at high summer in 1899, was the Archduchess Isabella. For several years this formidable wife of his second cousin, the Duke of Teschen, had convinced herself that the heir presumptive sought marriage with her eldest daughter; for why otherwise should Francis Ferdinand so often fish for invitations to her castle at Bratislava? Isabella was flattered: to have a daughter groomed as the next Empress-Queen would at once lift the standing of the parents in Europe's spas and capital cities. But when, in that July, the doting mother could not resist the temptation to open a locket hanging from the chain of a gold watch which the Archduke had left beside her tennis court, she made an unwelcome discovery: she was confronted with a miniature picture, not of her daughter, but of her lady-in-waiting, Countess Sophie Chotek, his occasional doubles partner. Indignantly Archduchess Isabella at once informed the Emperor of such scandalous deception.

To Francis Joseph her complaint was most unwelcome. Private affairs were already intruding on public business: the widowed Crown Princess Stephanie wished to marry a Hungarian nobleman, Count Lonjay. The Emperor did nothing to impede her re-marriage, which was celebrated at Miramare in March 1900, but it posed difficult legal problems, not least concerning Stephanie's status. While he was personally sympathetic towards his widowed daughter-in-law, Francis Ferdinand remained antipathetic to him. Moreover, the fuss over Sophie Chotek erupted at a particularly bad time, politically: she came from Bohemian nobility, and he was under pressure from several aristocratic families to scrap Badeni's Language Ordinances and come down firmly in support of his German subjects in their fight against Czech linguistic claims. Not unnaturally Francis Joseph was inclined at first to dismiss the whole Chotek affair as the passing infatuation of an Archduke with a wandering eye for a demure woman with a warm smile and a good figure. But it was more serious than that. To the Emperor's consternation, Francis Ferdinand insisted he had been in love with Countess Chotek for five years. He wished to marry her. Over the autumn and winter months no peremptory summons to the Hofburg or sharp letters from his brother Archdukes could persuade him otherwise.

Dynastically the marriage was out of the question, by Francis Joseph's reckoning. The Countess's family were good, loyal Bohemian aristocrats; her father was the diplomat in Brussels who had helped negotiate the marriage settlement for Rudolf and Stephanie; but the Choteks were not of sufficiently high social ranking to give the Monarchy its next Empress. At last Francis Ferdinand's step-mother interceded with the Emperor, inducing him to accept the only way in which his nephew could remain heir-presumptive and marry the woman he loved. With a heavy heart, the Emperor reconciled his conscience to accepting the principle of a morganatic marriage, excluding any offspring from succession to the throne. On 28 June 1900, at a ceremony in the Hofburg, the Emperor summoned fifteen senior Archdukes, the papal nuncio, the Cardinal-Archbishop, foreign minister Goluchowski and all the senior court officials to hear Francis Ferdinand solemnly renounce under oath all claims of his proposed wife and children for the rights of status or inheritance accorded to 'a marriage between equals'. The wedding took place a few days later at the castle of Reichstadt, in Bohemia: it was attended by neither the Emperor nor any of the Archdukes. Francis Ferdinand and his 32-year old wife made their principal home at Konopischt, a fortress thirty-four miles outside Prague, which the Archduke had purchased in 1887 and converted into a delightful home with rose gardens famous throughout the continent; they looked best, it was said, from the window of Francis Ferdinand's lavatory, on the third floor of the castle.

Once the morganatic settlement was legalized, the Emperor behaved perfectly correctly towards his heir-apparent. He gave the bride a diadem and raised her to princely (but not royal) rank as Princess von Hohenberg. Francis Ferdinand, more fortunate than poor Rudolf, was given the loveliest of Vienna's baroque palaces, the Upper Belvedere, as an official residence; and he had the personal wealth to allow 'Soph' (as he called the Princess) to create within this splendid museum piece rooms in which it was possible to enjoy family life. Two months after the wedding Francis Joseph officially received 'my nephew's wife' for the first time: he thought her 'natural and modest, but ... no longer young'. Three weeks later he returned the visit, to see Prince Eugene's garden palace – Vienna's counterpart to Blenheim – acquiring the comforts of domesticity. The marriage was an extremely happy one: a daughter, born a year after the wedding, was given her mother's name; a son, Maximilian, followed in September 1902 and a second son, Ernest, in May 1904. That summer Francis Ferdinand could write contentedly to his step-mother: 'By far the wisest thing I ever did was to marry my Sophie. She is everything to me: my wife, my doctor, my adviser – to put it in one word, my whole happiness'. And he went on to describe evenings 'spent at home': 'I smoke my cigar and read the papers, Sophie knits, and the children tumble about, pulling everything off the tables – it's all so delightfully cosy'.

Yet, despite such rare family happiness, official protocol inflicted a series of humiliations on the Princess von Hohenberg. A year after their marriage she could not attend a gala dinner given by her husband at the Belvedere in honour of the German Crown Prince. When the Archduke was within the Belvedere, sentries stood guard at the gates: when he left the palace, the sentries were withdrawn, even though his wife and eventually his children, remained in residence. While he was driven about Vienna in an imperial 'Viktoria' or 'Mylord' with gold-rimmed wheels, his wife and children had to make do with an ordinary carriage. At the opera or the theatre the Archduke would be seated in a separate box from Sophie, and he could never escort her into a state dinner or ball. These social restraints cannot have surprised Francis Ferdinand, for when he accepted the limitations of a morganatic union he well knew the rigidity of convention and protocol at the Habsburg Court; but it was natural for him to look with sympathy on foreign princes who treated Sophie with the respect which he was sure she deserved. When William II – at the prompting of his Chancellor, Prince Bülow – went out of his way to flatter the Princess von Hohenberg during a visit to Vienna in the autumn of 1903, the German Emperor ensured that he could count on the Archduke's friendship and support during the remaining eleven years of his life.

The trivialities of protocol which governed the family's daily existence at the Belvedere were part of a fossilized routine followed by the Court as a whole. Little had changed at the centre of affairs in the last twenty years. In particular, as the nineteenth century came to an end, the isolation of the dynasty from the cultural life of the capital became more and more apparent. The break was made dramatically clear in 1898 when a young architect, Adolf Loos, writing in the *Neue Freie Presse*, attacked Ringstrasse Vienna as an architectural fake, a false facade giving a Renaissance splendour to buildings which lacked a character of their own. In that same year of the Golden Jubilee, barely a quarter of a mile across the Ringstrasse from the Opera, the *Sezession* building was opened; it was (and is) a defiantly modern 'Grove of Art' built in a neo-Assyrian style to house the works of young artists who had 'seceded' from the conventional work favoured by the Academy of Fine Arts. 'To the age its art, to art its freedom' ran the gilt lettered inscription above the main entrance to the *Sezession* exhibition hall.

Yet although the young artists gloried in the modernity of free expression, bringing to Vienna some of the individualism and vitality of the Impressionists, their recognized leader was Gustav Klimt; he was thirty-six in the year of the first exhibition, and had made his name under imperial patronage, assisting Makart at the Hermes Villa and completing several frescoes for the main stairway of the Burgtheater. It is hardly surprising if Francis Joseph had little interest in the innovative work of the *Sezession* artists, and even less for their younger and angrier successors; but, probably because he had always been artistically a detached and slightly puzzled outsider, he accepted *art nouveau* as a phenomenon which might please others, though not himself. While Francis Ferdinand puffed and fumed at the scandalous lascivious lines in Klimt's later work, the Emperor made no protest. He was prepared to spend an hour and a half examining 'applied modern art' at a museum in Vienna before deciding that 'my taste' did not extend to exhibits 'tinged with the *Sezession*'. Many times as his carriage brought him into the city from Schönbrunn he must have seen the *Sezession* exhibition hall, yet it never seems to have aroused his anger. He accepted, too, the functionalism of Otto Wagner's Stadtbahn stations. Only in 1911 was his architectural taste seriously offended: for he intensely disliked Adolf Loos's 'house without eyebrows', the plain fronted building which had no window frames and no ornamentation, built on the corner of the Michaelerplatz. Nothing disturbed his faith in the enduring qualities of all that was familiar to him so much as this '*Looshaus*', standing provocatively across the road from the windows of one of the Hofburg's newer wings: 'Pull the curtains', he ordered, as if turning his back on the future.

At the start of the century it had looked as if he wished to turn his back on parliament, too. 'We are the laughing-stock of Europe' he remarked sharply after an unedifying outburst of fighting between rival nationalists in the Reichsrat. There is a well-known picture of deputies in Vienna's lower chamber banging gongs, clashing cymbals and blowing trumpets in order to silence spokesmen with whom they disagreed. In order to secure the passage of legislation in Cisleithania, the Emperor was forced to make use of emergency decrees, originally proposed by Schmerling but authorized by Article XIV of the 'December Constitution' in 1867: the sovereign could enact measures essential to maintain effective government in the absence of Reichsrat approval. Nevertheless, Francis Joseph was by now sufficiently versed in the art of ruling not to hanker for the autocracy of earlier years, however much the parliamentary system might appear paralysed.

The Emperor favoured a double approach to the protracted political crisis: administration by a dexterous non-party prime minister, who would reduce nationalistic tension by offering material improvements; and a gradual movement toward genuine universal male suffrage. He seems to have accepted the belief that national sentiment was an indulgence practised by the educated middle classes and of little relevance to the lives of the majority of his subjects. If in some industrialized regions, there was an increase in socialist representation, a 'red peril' bogey would frighten the nationalistic parties into co-operation with the dynasty.

The most successful of Austria's bureaucrat prime ministers was Ernst von Koerber, to whom Francis Joseph turned in January 1900 after the final withdrawal of Badeni's Language Ordinances. Koerber at once launched a public works programme which brought new roads, railways and canals to districts whose parliamentary deputies were induced to give him their support in the chamber. At the same time, there was a rapid spread of social welfare projects and a drastic reduction in police surveillance and press censorship. But Koerber was no parliamentarian. Sniping attacks on him in the chamber by rival German and Czech groups, each complaining he favoured the other, left him exhausted. At Christmas in 1904 after five years of improvisation, Koerber stepped out of politics. Francis Joseph began the new year by assessing seriously the prospects for electoral reform and looking for another non-party prime minister to carry it through.

From much that has been written about the septuagenarian Francis Joseph, it seems remarkable he mustered the energy to seek new policies at such a time. Legend represents him as a tired old man living in the past. For this image, he was himself partly responsible; not surprisingly, the buffetings of misfortune often plunged him into deep self-pity. 'You will find me aged a lot and feebler in mind', he wrote to Katharina Schratt in the spring of 1902, when there was a prospect of her returning to the Gloriettegasse, 'My one pleasure in your absence has been my seven grandchildren who, with Valerie, have spent some weeks with me at Schönbrunn. The older one gets the more childlike one becomes, and so I am coming closer and closer to them and their company'. Soon afterwards the old friendship was renewed. Katharina had the doubtful delight of again entertaining her sovereign to breakfast in Ischl at a time when sensible actresses were soundly asleep. As a concession to advancing years – hers rather than his – the breakfast hour at Hietzing was subsequently pushed back to nine.

Physically Francis Joseph was still a fit man. Mentally he was no less and no more receptive than at the height of the reign. To his satisfaction he was able to stay 'long in the saddle' during the autumn manoeuvres of 1902; and it is clear he continued to insist that all army matters and the general conduct of foreign affairs were questions for him to study in detail alone and decide for himself. He retained an elevated concept of the dynasty's role in Austria's past, sharply defined in his mind and, as he believed, incapable of comprehension by nobility or commonalty alike.

The letters to Katharina Schratt show that he was glad to hear his friend would make guest appearances on the stage; but he received icily the news that she had accepted the title role in a new play about his revered ancestor, Maria Theresa, to be presented at the Deutsches Volkstheater in Vienna. Someone leaked the good publicity that 'our Kathi' – as the *Oesterreichische Illustrierte Zeitung* called her – would wear her own jewellery, which was said to comprise gifts from the Emperor. Although the play had a glittering first night in the third week of October 1903, it was not a great success. Pointedly Francis Joseph did not visit the theatre during its short run.

For much of that autumn of 1903 he remained in Hungary, where hopes of raising more recruits to the army by a revised military service bill were running into serious trouble. Over the preceding seven years party loyalties had changed considerably in the kingdom. The Liberals, the government party since their formation in 1874–5, were challenged by the rapid rise of a Party of Independence, led by Ferencz Kossuth, son of the great revolutionary (who, from exile, had remained an influence on politics right up until his death in 1894). By 1903 the Independence Party was concentrating its activities on creating a national Hungarian army which would be controlled from Budapest rather than Vienna, with no regiments quartered outside the kingdom, and with Magyar as the language of command; meanwhile, the Party was disinclined to allow more Hungarians to be called up for service in the joint army. So vociferous was the Opposition that it provoked scenes in the Budapest parliament reminiscent of the recent unrest in the Reichsrat. In June and August 1903 two successive Hungarian prime ministers were forced to resign because they could not conduct parliamentary business in such an atmosphere.

At this point Field Marshal Beck, the Emperor's military confidant for more than a third of a century and Chief of the General Staff since 1881, drew up the first plans for *Fall U[ngarn]* 'Case U.': Austrian troops from Vienna and Graz would move swiftly into Hungary and occupy Budapest, while other units from Przemysl, Zagreb and Lvov converged on central Hungary. Archduke Francis Ferdinand, though in conflict with the General Staff over many matters, warmly supported the proposed military coup. His uncle, however, saw in 'Case U.' the torch which would ignite Hungary and revive the tragic conflicts with which his reign had opened; Beck's contingency plan was put into cold storage, to receive serious consideration again two years later. But while the Emperor shrank from the risk of civil war, he did not intend to loosen his grip on the imperial and royal army, which he regarded as the keystone of the Dual Monarchy.

It was for this reason that, on 16 September 1903, he issued an Order of the Day from Chlopy, his headquarters for autumn manoeuvres in Galicia. The Chlopy Order emphasized the unity of the army: 'Loyal to its oath, my entire army ... must be imbued with that spirit of unity and harmony which respects national characteristics and stands above all antagonism so as to make use of the qualities of each *Volksstamm* (racial group) for the benefit of all'. Unfortunately the Magyar version of the Chlopy Order used *néptörzs* (tribal group) for *Volksstamm*; and the sensitive Hungarian nation resented being downgraded as a tribe. So angry were the subsequent scenes in the Hungarian parliament that Francis Joseph had to spend several weeks in residence at Budapest and Gödöllö, papering the cracks in the Ausgleich settlement with exemplary patience. He conceded the authorization of Hungary's national flag to be flown alongside the imperial flag over military establishments and he allowed Hungarian officers the right to transfer to regiments stationed within the kingdom. In desperation Francis Joseph turned to István Tisza, son of the former Liberal prime minister, and on 31 October 1903 he was able to form an administration pledged to uphold a reformed settlement with Vienna. But, despite Tisza's good intentions, the Opposition's filibustering tactics continued to make a mockery of parliamentary government, although it did at least accept a compromise over the recruitment proposals.

There was no Article XIV in the Hungarian Constitution, permitting rule by emergency decrees. Tisza was therefore at a loss as to how to prevent the country from falling into anarchy. He thought the Opposition parties had discredited themselves by their behaviour in the chamber and would be rejected in a snap election. But this device, tried in January 1905, rebounded disastrously against Tisza: the Liberals were defeated. The Party of Independence emerged as the largest single group in a 'Coalition of National Parties'. Their terms for forming a government involved a greater change in the character of the Monarchy than the Emperor-King was prepared to accept.

Again Francis Joseph came under strong pressure to stage a military coup. But he would not give his assent to 'Case U'. In June 1905 he ordered the formation of a non-parliamentary government under a Hungarian soldier of unquestionable loyalty, the former commandant of the Royal Guard, General Geza Fejérváry. But the crisis dragged on. Ominously, four days after his birthday, Francis Joseph broke precedent by presiding over a council of ministers at Ischl, where detailed study was made of the military options. On 23 September he summoned the Hungarian politicians to Schönbrunn and told them bluntly that, if they wished to constitute a government, they would have to drop from their programme all legislation concerned with language of command or changes in the army structure: these matters, he emphasized once more, remained strictly the concern of the sovereign. They would also have to pledge themselves to pass the proposed budget, to approve a new army bill providing more recruits, and to modify the economic relationship between Hungary and Cisleithania only after agreement in the Delegations, as stipulated in past negotiations. Francis Joseph would not discuss these matters with the Hungarian delegates; they were to see Goluchowski, since he was the responsible co-ordinating government minister. The meeting ended five minutes after it began.

Despite such tough talk, Francis Joseph was uncertain how these over-excited Hungarian politicians would react to what was virtually an ulti-matum. Nine days after the 'five minute audience' he was still in doubt, writing from Schönbrunn to Katharina Schratt (in Baden-Baden) to complain that he had been unable to go hunting in Styria, as he planned: 'Unfortunately I must stay on here and worry and fret about Hungary: but I am not going to give way ...' Two months later he authorized the next step forward. Fejérváry's minister of the interior published the text of a proposed reform bill. It would have raised the size of the Hungarian electorate from one million to two and half million, thereby swamping Magyar voters under a flood of newly enfranchised Roumanians, Slovaks, Serbs and members of other minorities. Such a measure meant the end of the built-in Magyar majority in Hungary's parliament.

The threat was taken seriously by the Coalition leaders. Rather than face such a future, they chose to come to terms with their king. A Hungarian government of all-the-talents was formed in April 1906 under Alexander Wekerle, a Liberal of no strong party commitment. The elec-toral reform bill was not enacted. An appropriate, dignified calm returned to Budapest's impressive parliament house. Bluff, and a strong hint of political blackmail, had given the seventy-five year old Emperor-King a sound victory. Yet he was neither elated nor confident. 'I have been busier than ever with the makeshift solution of the crisis over Hungarian rights and am very tired and cannot prevent my nerves from being on edge', he wrote to Katharina Schratt on the Wednesday in Holy Week, with two days of penitential observance ahead of him; 'God will help us further, but I see still more fights looming up', he added.

By now he had a new cause for concern: the heavy shadow of the heir-apparent darkened the political scene. Francis Ferdinand was too forceful a personality to be content with deputizing for the Emperor on state occasions. Yet, though an admirable family man, he lacked those easy graces which win popular acclaim. Basically he mistrusted people: 'On first acquaintance I look upon everyone I meet as being a scoundrel', he told the Chief of the General Staff. After his marriage his prejudices intensified, despite his wife's calmly reasonable outlook on life: he remained anti-Semitic, anti-Magyar, anti-Italian. It is hard to escape the feeling he would have become a disastrous Emperor had he succeeded to the throne. Yet he prepared for that day more assiduously than poor Rudolf. From 1901 onwards he built up a personal intelligence service at the Lower Belvedere, the lesser of the complementary palaces built for Prince Eugen and originally intended as administrative offices. In January 1906 he persuaded the Emperor to accept the machine he had created as a Military Chancellery. Under Major von Brosch's supervision it grew into a team of fourteen officers who prided themselves on greater knowledge than the Emperor's Military Chancellery and on smoother efficiency than the General Staff. They recognized – Brosch in particular – the need for 'finesse and tact' in working with a man of such 'explosive energy'.

Though Francis Joseph was frequently exasperated by his nephew and irritated by his bustling restlessness, he treated Francis Ferdinand with punctilious respect: he knew from his own early months with Grünne that an heir to the throne needed access to official papers and, from the spring of 1906 onwards, copies of all important documents and despatches were sent regularly from the war ministry, and often from the Ballhausplatz, to the Lower Belvedere. Not that the Archduke was often in Vienna to receive them: Brosch later calculated that Francis Ferdinand was away from the capital for 200 days a year, on the average. He expected his office to feed him with paperwork wherever he might be. His particular interests were in the armed services (and notably in the navy), in maintaining good relations with Berlin and St Petersburg, in what he regarded as the nefarious intrigues of Hungary's politicians, and in preserving historic churches and buildings. At the same time, Francis Ferdinand turned for political guidance to a circle of advisers including right-wing representatives of the Czech, Roumanian and Croat minorities. In Austria itself the Archduke's sympathies were with Karl Lueger, whom at one time he was expected to appoint as prime minister or even as Chancellor, should he succeed in changing the political structure of the Monarchy.

Francis Joseph welcomed the Archduke's interest in military affairs. He was relieved that Francis Ferdinand seemed pleased to don an Admiral's uniform (the Emperor never had one himself) and launch battleships in Trieste or visit fleet anchorages down the Adriatic. But Francis Joseph was suspicious of the Archduke's politics, which were as conservative as his own beliefs but more narrowly clericalist and far more aggressively authoritarian. It was disconcerting for the Emperor to find, after all these years, a shadow court functioning in Vienna, with ambassadors discreetly keeping in touch with the man whom they believed must surely soon be called to the throne. Francis Joseph treated the emergence of the Belvedere as an alternative political centre as if it challenged his whole concept of the Monarchy. He had no intention of sharing the responsibilities of government with Francis Ferdinand. Sometimes he seems deliberately to have looked for an alternative policy to anything which the Archduke was believed to favour.

Yet it was obvious that men of talent with an eye to the future would be drawn towards the Belvedere. Not all, however, were young, for Francis Ferdinand himself was forty-two at Christmas in 1905. One of the Archduke's earliest associates and wisest counsellors during the crisis over his marriage was Baron Max von Beck (who was totally unrelated to his namesake, the distinguished soldier). Max Beck had such obvious gifts as a constitutional lawyer and patient negotiator that in June 1906 the Emperor invited him to head the Austrian government, an appointment made without consulting Francis Ferdinand, who was abroad at the time. Beck successfully carried through the electoral reforms in Cisleithania which Francis Joseph had long contemplated: universal male suffrage was instituted in January 1907, in time for the Christian Socials and their allies to emerge as the largest single party at the May general election for the Reichsrat. He also succeeded in working out an acceptable commercial Ausgleich with the Hungarians in 1907. But neither of these achievements pleased Francis Ferdinand: he mistrusted universal suffrage in the 'Austrian' half of the Monarchy as opening a door for socialism; and he regarded even the slightest concessions to Hungary's politicians as tantamount to treason. Francis Joseph seems to have hoped that in appointing an old friend of the Archduke as prime minister he would have a tactful intermediary between the Hofburg and the Belvedere. In this he was disappointed: Francis Ferdinand never forgave Max Beck's apparent apostasy. The so-called 'Belvedere Cabal' joined the Christian Social politicians in November 1909 to force the ablest of Francis Joseph's later prime ministers out of office.

Over military affairs Francis Ferdinand showed a sounder judgment than in politics. To some extent he became what 'Uncle Albrecht' had once been, a prodder-general to the military establishment, seeking to combat stagnation in a decade of rapid change. The Archduke's activities did not endear him to Field Marshal Beck, who shared the Emperor's slightly contemptuous assessment of the Archduke's qualities. There was, for example, a wide difference in their attitudes to the significance of the internal combustion engine. Francis Ferdinand early saw the advantages of a car during his indefatigable travelling between isolated garrison towns and along distant frontiers. To Field Marshal Beck, on the other hand, the motor-car was 'a pretty pastime for aristocratic lazybones and Jewish sportsmen; no use for the army'. Francis Joseph's innate conservatism inclined him to agree with Beck: the Emperor visited the Sixth Automobile Exhibition in Vienna in 1906, but he only drove in a car for the first time in August 1908, at King Edward VII's prompting during a visit to Ischl. A year later he sat beside William II in a half-open car at the last autumn manoeuvres they attended. At heart he was convinced that cars had no place with an army in the field: did they not, after all, frighten the horses? Yet Francis Joseph had seen so many changes in transport during his lifetime that he had no wish to reject the latest innovations out of hand. On 18 September 1910 he agreed to be driven by car thirty miles out to the Steinfeld flying field at Wiener Neustadt, where he inspected biplanes and monoplanes and talked to pioneer pilots. A photograph caught an expression of incredulity on the wizened face, as if he was as puzzled as sixty-five years earlier, when he stood beside Radetzky to watch military balloons ascend above the amphitheatre in Verona. Perhaps there was a future in military aviation: he was too open-minded to dismiss all of his nephew's proposals for modernizing the army.

On one particular occasion, four years before his visit to the flying field, the Emperor accepted that Francis Ferdinand was right and he was himself mistaken. In August 1906 the Emperor travelled to Teschen for cavalry manoeuvres in the foothills of the Beskid mountains. At the same time, Francis Ferdinand was sent as his uncle's representative to observe combined sea and land exercises in the northern Adriatic. While the Emperor was satisfied with all he saw, his nephew was shocked by the total lack of co-ordination between artillery, infantry and fleet. In a devastating report, carefully detailed with material fed to him by Brosch's staff in the Lower Belvedere, the Archduke recommended the dismissal of the war minister and Beck's retirement as Chief of the General Staff. Reluctantly the Emperor decided he must agree with his nephew. He would have to look for a new war minister; more importantly he must find for the first time in twenty-five years, a new Chief of the General Staff.

At almost the same time that autumn Count Goluchowski, a tired man exasperated by the attitude of Hungary's political leaders, let the Emperor know he had decided he must give up the foreign ministry. Francis Joseph had little doubt whom he wished to see as Goluchowski's successor; he had the highest opinion of Baron Aehrenthal, the ambassador at St Petersburg for the past seven years. With his attention thus concentrated on the Ballhausplatz, he was prepared to give his nephew a freer hand in finding incumbents for the two military posts than at a less pressing moment. For the war ministry the Archduke had a ready candidate in Baron von Schonaich (who, in fact, soon offended his patron by over-leniency towards Hungary); but General Conrad von Hötzendorf, the soldier whom he wished to take Beck's place, was reluctant to give up a field command and assume the greatest of all staff responsibilities. Only after being browbeaten by the Archduke in two long audiences at the Belvedere did Conrad accept that it was his duty to take up the post. The Emperor formally gazetted him Chief of the General Staff on 18 November 1906, three and a half weeks after Aehrenthal took up his duties as foreign minister. Not for over thirty years had Francis Joseph made so momentous a change of personnel at the head of affairs as in his appointments of Aehrenthal and Conrad. With a semblance of dignity restored to Hungarian politics and parliamentary government refurbished in Vienna, it seemed as if a new dynamism was beginning to power the old Monarchy. But how soon would it blow a fuse?

Chapter 19

TWO JOURNEYS TO
SARAJEVO

By 1906 it was forty years since Francis Joseph had been at war. His subjects were enjoying a longer period of external peace than under any previous Habsburg rulers. Few serving officers could remember the fluctuating fortunes of a military campaign, those dashed hopes which their Emperor recalled all too vividly. Yet there were signs that these halcyon days might already be numbered. From about 1900 onwards a new mood crept into the politics of the Balkan states: young, ambitious army officers – first in Serbia, later during the decade in Bulgaria, Greece and even Turkey – banded together in pressure groups which imposed nationalistic policies on their respective governments. Goluchowski warned Francis Joseph of the mounting danger from Belgrade at the turn of the century, though he assumed that any crisis could be localized. 'Should anything serious happen in the Balkans and the Serbs follow a policy we do not like, we shall simply strangle Serbia', he explained to the German ambassador as early as January 1901.

The first dramatic episode took Francis Joseph by surprise, though not perhaps his ministers. In the small hours of 11 June 1903 King Alexander Obrenović of Serbia and his Queen were butchered by a group of rebel army officers and their naked, mutilated bodies thrown from the palace window in Belgrade. The conspirators invited the head of the rival dynastic clan, Peter Karadjordjević, to return from exile and ascend the throne. Great Britain and the Netherlands, shocked by the savage act of regicide, broke off diplomatic relations with Serbia and declined to renew them for three years. But Austria-Hungary, with posts along the Danube directly facing Belgrade, could not treat the change of dynasty with such lofty disdain. Francis Joseph hesitated. Were the Serbs about to embark on policies Vienna would 'not like'? Had the time come to 'strangle Serbia'? Or would Peter, who was almost sixty in 1903, prove a strong ruler, willing to reject the dangerous policies advocated by the younger generation? The Emperor decided to give the new regime in Belgrade an opportunity to form a stable government. He became the first monarch to recognize Peter I as King of Serbia.

Francis Joseph believed that the surest way of maintaining peace in the Balkans was to work closely with St Petersburg, preserving the Austro-Russian entente attained at the end of the old century. A meeting between the Austrian and Russian rulers, with their foreign ministers, at Mürzsteg in October 1903 agreed to put joint pressure on Sultan Abdulhamid to accept international policing and administrative reform in Macedonia, the most troubled of his Balkan provinces. By 1906, however, Francis Joseph could wonder if the loose understanding with Russia had gone far enough. He was becoming increasingly suspicious of the Belgrade government and the influence of Pan-Serb agents operating beyond Serbia's frontiers. In the autumn of 1905 meetings of Croatian politicians at Rijeka and leaders of Austria-Hungary's Serbian minority at Zadar passed resolutions in favour of Serbo-Croat collaboration against 'the anti-Slav Habsburg dualists'; and sympathy for these resolutions was expressed in Belgrade, much to the irritation of both the Austrian and Hungarian prime ministers. The Serbian government seemed determined to lessen the kingdom's dependence on Austria-Hungary and affirm a sense of Slav, Orthodox brotherhood. A customs union between Serbia and Bulgaria, made public in January 1906, was seen in Vienna as a breach of Austro-Serbian agreements which had long regulated commerce. To Francis Joseph's indignation, the Serbs then placed a huge arms order with the French firm of Schneider-Creusot rather than with Skoda in Bohemia, as in the past. The Serbs, it was decided, must be brought to heel: the Emperor approved the imposition of economic sanctions; Austria-Hungary's frontiers were closed to imports of Serbian pigs and cattle, living or slaughtered.

This 'pig war' proved a disastrous shift of policy, hardening the two government's mutual hostility. Although 80 per cent of Serbia's exports had gone to Austria-Hungary, the sanctions did not bite: the Serbs found new markets and alternative routes, notably through Salonika. The pig war dragged on for four years: anti-Habsburg feeling intensified among the Serbian peasantry inside and outside the Dual Monarchy, particularly in occupied Bosnia-Herzegovina. The incoming Chief of the General Staff, Conrad von Hötzendorf, had seen active service against the Muslim militia in 1878 and brought to his new post a sabre-rattling belligerence. He chafed at the continuance of these ineffectual sanctions: the Balkan problem, he wrote a week before Christmas in 1907, 'must be resolved in grand style by the annexation of Bosnia-Herzegovina and Serbia'.

Francis Joseph did not agree with Conrad. Under no circumstances would he risk a protracted and expensive military campaign. His new foreign minister, Aehrenthal, also stopped short of advocating armed intervention, but he regarded some re-ordering of the Monarchy's Balkan policies as essential. Long-nurtured plans for railway construction were made public in January 1908 and, with the Sultan's assent almost certain, Aehrenthal announced in Budapest that a line would be built through the Sanjak of Novibazar linking Bosnia with the main Turkish trunk routes and eventually with the port of Salonika, then the second largest city of Turkey-in-Europe. At the same time Aehrenthal was giving close attention to the possible incorporation of Bosnia-Herzegovina in the Monarchy. To make the political transference of sovereignty and the railway project palatable abroad he favoured the withdrawal of army units from the towns they had occupied in the Sanjak for thirty years. Yet for Aehrenthal to carry through these radical changes, three pre-conditions were essential: an agreement with Russia; the concurrence of Conrad and the army chiefs; and the formal approval of the Emperor.

In Andrássy's day Francis Joseph followed expedient twists of policy during the Eastern Crisis with minute attention, even if he failed to understand issues in dispute. Now, in 1908, he believed he was still consulted as much as ever, for there was no diminution in the number of papers requiring attention on his desk and his ministers and generals reported personally to him whether he was in Vienna, Budapest or even Ischl. 'Today I am absolutely in no position to ask you to visit me', he told Katharina Schratt in May; 'in the trouble, excitement and rush these days', he explained, 'I cannot find a moment to set aside in advance for me to talk quietly with you'. Yet, though Aehrenthal and Conrad might ply the Emperor with memoranda, they increasingly behaved as if he were in virtual retirement. Conrad in particular consulted the 'alternative Court' at the Belvedere before submitting proposals to his sovereign; and the foreign minister seems to have assumed that the Emperor would automatically approve action already agreed around the ministerial council chamber. But Aehrenthal knew that the Emperor expected to be well briefed on major adjustments to the balance between the Great Powers. In early July 1908 he therefore kept Francis Joseph carefully informed of an apparent change in Russian policy, a diplomatic 'bargain offer' from Alexander Izvolsky, Nicholas's foreign minister for the past two years: if Aehrenthal supported Izvolsky's attempts to secure revision of the Straits Convention (so that Russian warships might pass through the Bosphorus and Dardanelles in time of peace), Russia would not object to the annexation of Bosnia-Herzegovina and the Sanjak of Novibazar.

At first, both Francis Joseph and his minister were suspicious of the proposed bargain. But events in Constantinople caused second thoughts.

In late July the Young Turk revolution, which had begun in Macedonia and spread to the Sultan's capital, induced Abdulhamid to restore the Constitution of 1876, a short-lived experiment in parliamentary government. Aehrenthal was immediately alarmed: what would happen if the Young Turks announced the holding of elections in Bosnia and in Herzegovina for an Ottoman assembly? And how far would the balance in the Balkans be changed if they called for the return of deputies from tributary states such as – in Europe – Bulgaria? When faced by these uncertainties, Aehrenthal recommended the annexation of Bosnia-Herzegovina. He also advocated a change in Balkan patronage, by which Austria-Hungary would back Russia's traditional client, Bulgaria, in any disputes with Serbia. Francis Joseph approved: Aehrenthal was to sound out Izvolsky privately.

On 19 August Aehrenthal told his ministerial colleagues that he could carry through the annexation without arousing the hostility of Russia and with support from Austria's German and Italian allies. Although the two prime ministers were hesitant, Aehrenthal brushed all objections aside, confident of the Emperor's support. He met more opposition from the Belvedere; Archduke Francis Ferdinand doubted if the Dual Monarchy was sufficiently unified in purpose to absorb two provinces with so many conflicting races and religions. He made the important stipulation that Bosnia-Herzegovina must become the joint responsibility of both partners in the Dual Monarchy: 'If Hungary claims the territories for the Crown of St Stephen (as will certainly happen) this must under no circumstances be conceded, even at the cost of abandoning annexation and leaving things as they are', Francis Ferdinand wrote from army manoeuvres, after talks with the Chief of the General Staff. Significantly the Archduke added a further warning: 'I am utterly opposed to all such shows of strength, in view of our sorry domestic affairs ...', he wrote, 'I am against mobilization, and I think we should merely heighten our military readiness'. These were not the views of the Archduke's former protégé, General Conrad.

Aehrenthal met Izvolsky at Buchlau, a shooting-lodge in Moravia, on 15 September, taking up the Russian's earlier 'bargain' terms. No written record was made of their conversations; later accounts by the two participants show discrepancies – to which historians have, perhaps, given undue attention. Izvolsky certainly did not realize that the Austrians were in a hurry because they were worried by the new political vitality in Constantinople. Similarly, Aehrenthal failed to appreciate Izvolsky's difficulties, not knowing that the Russian foreign minister was acting virtually on his own, without backing from the Tsar or the government in St Petersburg, and without consulting Russia's ally, France, or the new

Entente partner, Great Britain. Francis Joseph for his part did all that Aehrenthal expected from him. He even received Prince Ferdinand of Bulgaria with full royal honours in Budapest in late September, though nothing could overcome his basic mistrust of 'the Coburg' as a person. But it was on 6 October 1908 that the Emperor took the decisive step, signing a proclamation addressed to the peoples of Bosnia-Herzegovina; they were told that, as they deserved an autonomous and constitutional government, he had decided to extend his sovereignty so as to include their two provinces within his Empire. At the same time he sent a letter to Aehrenthal, intended for immediate publication, in which he announced that 'to show the peaceful intentions which have inspired me to take this inevitable step' he was ordering the immediate withdrawal of his army from the Sanjak of Novibazar. Meanwhile, in Sofia, Prince Ferdinand had jumped the gun by asserting his country's total independence of the Ottoman Empire on 5 October and proclaiming himself 'Tsar of the Bulgarians' (a title downgraded to 'King' under Austrian pressure).

By annexing Bosnia-Herzegovina the Emperor at last acquired two provinces, his only territorial gains in a long reign. The cost was greater than he had anticipated. For the timing of the annexation left Francis Joseph out of step with every other ruler in Europe, except the precipitate Foxy Ferdinand. The German Emperor, William II, was appalled: 'I am deeply offended in my role as an ally not to have been taken into His Majesty's confidence!', he wrote stuffily in a marginal note to a despatch drafted by Chancellor Bülow. Reaction elsewhere was more dramatic. There were anti-Austrian demonstrations in several Italian cities; the Turks withdrew deposits from Austrian banks, refused to unload Austrian ships, and boycotted goods imported from the Monarchy. Five days after the annexation was announced, ten thousand people demonstrated against Austria-Hungary and Bulgaria in the streets of Salonika, the port which Aehrenthal hoped to develop as the Trieste of the Aegean. The British complained of Aehrenthal's recklessness, the Russian press and people maintained a bitter campaign against the government in Vienna, while Izvolsky insisted that Aehrenthal had deceived him at Buchlau. The Serbian heir-apparent and the most influential Serbian Radical politician, Nikola Pašić, travelled to St Petersburg to win support from Russia's Panslavs; in Belgrade itself 120,000 reservists were mobilized and a national defence organization (*Narodna Odbrana*) established to sustain the Serb loyalties of compatriots in Bosnia-Herzegovina by subversive propaganda and sabotage. Politically the annexation left the Dual Monarchy isolated in Europe.

Francis Joseph backed every move made by Aehrenthal to keep the peace. The Turks were offered money for the loss of two provinces which had long been developed as virtual colonial protectorates. The Emperor gave personal assurances to Nicholas II and to William II that he 'cherished no designs of conquest at the expense' of Serbia and Montenegro, even should one or other of the kingdoms violate his territory and provoke a punitive expedition. Tension gradually relaxed; and the crisis was finally resolved in March 1909 by quiet diplomacy, in which Aehrenthal himself and British and Italian intermediaries all played their part, though much of the credit was claimed by Chancellor Bülow in Berlin.

Ultimately the whole affair strengthened rather than weakened the Austro-German connection, as had seemed likely when William complained of lack of consultation, back in October. The external threat, especially from Russia, favoured close co-operation between the Austro-Hungarian and German chiefs of staff, a link neglected during the past eighteen years. Exchanges between Conrad and the younger Moltke, which began in January 1909, continued long after the crisis was over. More immediately, however, it was the intervention of the German foreign ministry which left an impact on events. For, at almost the last moments in the crisis, while Izvolsky was prevaricating, a telegram in Bülow's name demanded from St Petersburg a clear 'yes' or 'no' response; did Russia recognize the annexation? This near ultimatum was unnecessary. Consent would soon have come, once the Russians devised ways of saving face. Now they were denied any such consolation: Izvolsky appeared to give way under threats from Germany's 'mailed fist'.

William II was well-satisfied. He believed he had checked Austria's drift into dangerous isolation; and he did not intend to release Francis Joseph from the bonds of Hohenzollern friendship. Eighteen months later, William made an impromptu speech in the Rathaus during a visit to Vienna: the Austrian people were told that they, and Europe with them enjoyed peace that year because he had stood 'shoulder to shoulder . . . in shining armour' beside their 'august and venerable' monarch during the crisis over Bosnia. The speech irritated Francis Joseph; he did not seek a close relationship with militaristic Prussia. Privately he remarked that, in 'this ostentatious display of the sharp blade of Germany's sword' he sensed danger.

After twenty years of partnership, Francis Joseph still found his German ally personally antipathetic. William tried to endear himself to his brother sovereign, though at times with a patronizing manner almost discourteous in its impact. Unfortunately his frequent presence in Vienna often recalled a past which intruded uneasily on Francis Joseph's peace of mind, particularly the last twelve months before Mayerling and Rudolf's anger at the poses struck by Germany's Emperor on his accession. There were, too, other sad echoes: in 1907 William purchased the Achilleion for a million marks from Archduchess Gisela, who could find no delight in the marble palace among the cypresses and ilex trees which she had inherited from her mother. It became natural for him to sail back from Corfu to Trieste or Pola and break his journey in Vienna. Occasionally his guest's enthusiasm for his island refuge grated on the old widower's sensitivities, opening sore wounds in a starved heart. Yet William was ready to pay homage to Francis Joseph as the head of a great dynasty. On 7 May 1908 he led a deputation of German rulers who travelled to Schönbrunn to greet the Emperor on his Diamond Jubilee. After William conveyed their joint congratulations, Francis Joseph received each prince individually. As he felt obliged to change into the uniform of any of their regiments in which he enjoyed honorary rank it proved to be a long ceremony.

The princes' visit anticipated the anniversary of his accession by seven months, for once again the festivities began in the spring rather than in the gloom of short winter days. On 21 May 82,000 schoolchildren – 12,000 more than in 1898 – gathered on the lawns of Schönbrunn: 'The older I become the more I love children', Francis Joseph remarked, as he waved to them from the balcony. Three weeks later there was a historical pageant along the Ringstrasse, which evoked for the Emperor poignant memories of the silver wedding festivities nearly thirty years before. By early December, with the uncertainties of the Bosnian Crisis weighing on his mind, Francis Joseph looked weary, but he acknowledged a further round of tributes. On 1 December the younger members of the dynasty serenaded him with garlands and bouquets in the private theatre at Schönbrunn; and on accession day itself Francis Ferdinand conveyed the joint congratulations of the Archdukes and their families assembled in the Hofburg, much as had William II for the German princes seven months before. When a few hours later the Emperor attended a short gala at the Opera, the Viennese hailed a father figure they held in affectionate respect. By contrast in Bohemia there were violent demonstrations against the dynasty, with cries of 'Long live Serbia' in a menacing show of Slav solidarity. For twelve days Prague remained under strict martial law.

Yet police reports of increased unrest among the national minorities left Francis Joseph unperturbed. The Emperor never showed any fear of sudden death, treating the threat of assassination as an occupational hazard. No Austrian Habsburg, whether ruler in Vienna or heir to the throne, had fallen a victim to the politics of murder. Accordingly when, in February 1910 General Marijan Varešanin, the Governor of Bosnia, proposed that an imperial dignitary might pay a state visit to the newly annexed provinces, the Emperor himself was anxious to make the journey, even in his eightieth year. Early in March it was announced in the Press that Francis Joseph would visit Bosnia-Herzegovina between 30 May and 5 June. Would-be assassins were thus given eleven weeks in which to complete their plans.

Rumours of a conspiracy reached the Austro-Hungarian embassy in Paris in mid-May: a police informer claimed to have overheard southern Slav anarchists talking of a plan to kill the emperor at Mostar, the capital of Herzegovina. A similar report, again mentioning Mostar, was received at the legation in Sofia. Some precautions were taken, but the authorities still believed that any attempt on Francis Joseph's life would be made in Sarajevo rather than any other town. Close surveillance of travellers into the city was ordered, more than a thousand uniformed police were in the streets, together with a double line of troops along the Emperor's route. Before leaving Vienna, Francis Joseph approved of the arrangements. 'It is to be hoped it will not be too hot in Bosnia', he wrote to Katharina Schratt on the eve of his departure, 'You will see from the arrangements . . . that the rush could be worse and that my decrepitude has been taken into consideration . . . I commend myself to your prayers throughout the whole Bosnian expedition'.

Francis Joseph arrived at Sarajevo at mid-afternoon on 30 May 1910, his train having stopped at several small stations in Bosnia so that his new subjects could see their Emperor from a respectful and safe distance. He stayed in the Bosnian capital for four nights, driving through the city in an open carriage on four occasions and out to the spa at Ilidze in a car. There was a military review, at which he took the salute sitting superbly upright in the saddle. He watched torchlit festivities for the young from the balcony of the Konak, Governor Varešanin's official residence, and left for Mostar elated by the apparent enthusiasm of his new subjects.

He was at Mostar for only a few hours on 3 June, before boarding the specially decorated imperial coach of the Bosnian Railways for Vienna. 'It all went better than I had expected', he told Katharina Schratt with relief and characteristic understatement on his return. Others concerned with organizing the visit preferred to use superlatives. 'A triumphal progress', reported General Appel, commander of 15 Corps, in a letter to the head of Francis Ferdinand's military chancellery. The Emperor's success prompted Appel to an afterthought: why should not the Archduke come to Sarajevo, the general suggested in a postscript? He could bring his wife and children with him and stay at Ilidze. It would 'give the population great joy', Appel wrote, adding confidently, 'I will vouch for the security of such a visit with my head'.

Within ten days of Appel's letter and Francis Joseph's return home, shots were fired at Governor Varešanin as he rode back to the Konak after opening the newly instituted provincial assembly in Sarajevo. Vare-šanin was unhurt and his assailant, a law student named Bogdan Žerajić, killed himself with his last bullet. Investigations showed that Žerajić had tracked the Emperor throughout his visit and was himself trailed by three suspicious detectives in Sarajevo while Francis Joseph was in the city. One of Žerajić's friends said that Bogdan had told him he was so close to Francis Joseph at Mostar railway station that he could almost have touched him; and yet the inner compulsion to pull out his revolver and turn it on the Emperor at that moment was lacking. Subsequently Žerajić was so disgusted with himself, and so unable to account for his hesitancy, that he made his futile attempt to kill Governor Varešanin instead of his sovereign and chose suicide as an act of martyrdom. In death Žerajić did, indeed, become a hero of *Mlada Bosna* (Young Bosnia), a militant force linked with the *Narodna Odbrana* movement which attracted support from schoolboys and students.

By now, except in these southern regions and in Prague, Francis Joseph enjoyed more personal popularity than at any time in his reign; he had the rare distinction that summer of unveiling statues of himself. Foreign visitors, too, recognized him as a 'presence that pervades the entire feeling of life' in Vienna. A distinguished American observer, ex-President Theodore Roosevelt, was able to judge for himself the reality behind the popular image of 'the old gentleman'. It was seven weeks before his journey to Bosnia that the Emperor met a President of the United States for the only time in his life. He received Theodore Roosevelt in private audience on 15 April 1910, when he is said to have called himself 'the last monarch of the old school'. The ex-President's account of the conversation is slightly different: he 'did not strike me as a very able man, but he was a gentleman', Roosevelt recalled soon afterwards; 'He talked very freely and pleasantly, sometimes about politics, sometimes about hunting; ... he said that he had been particularly interested in seeing me because he was the last representative of the old system, whereas I embodied the new movement'. Roosevelt was invited to dine at Schönbrunn: an interesting occasion, he wrote, marred by 'one horrid habit'; for when 'fingerbowls were brought on, each with a small tumbler of water in the middle, the Emperor and all the others proceeded to rinse their mouths and empty them into the fingerbowls'.

Archduke Francis Ferdinand, meeting the President at King Edward VII's funeral a month later, complained in a letter to his uncle that 'Rooseveldt' (*sic*) lacked 'court manners'; he was 'enormously witty, or to put it more clearly – impertinent'. Francis Joseph, on the other hand, has left no criticism of his visitor's behaviour. Long experience of other nation's customs gave him a certain tolerance. He respected the United States as a federation of peoples functioning effectively without any need for a unifying dynasty. By emphasizing the solemn bonds of a historic flag and a secular constitution, the American nation had already made 'the new movement' traditional. But such ideas were not, he thought, for Europe. He could not hope to explain to Theodore Roosevelt his conviction that 'the old system' which he exemplified rested on divine sanction. For Francis Joseph, dynasty and supranational Empire remained twin pillars of a just society based upon a predominantly Christian moral order.

In this sunset of the reign he was, perhaps, 'an anachronism' – as he once himself admitted. Politicians whom he consulted complained that proposals they advanced were countered by preconceptions dating back to Schwarzenberg's time. But this was a superficial criticism; long experience and common sense gave him a more detached insight into human problems than his younger ministers or generals, particularly in matters referred to him by the courts of justice. Yet the world around him was changing rapidly, and not every visitor to Vienna was a respectable champion of the established order. Adolf Hitler, a thin and hungry bearded drop-out, was standing in the Ringstrasse when in March 1910 the Emperor rode to St Stephen's Cathedral for the funeral of Karl Lueger. Also in Vienna in these years was Leon Bronstein (alias Trotsky), who was to be joined briefly by an ex-seminarist with the revolutionary pseudonym of 'Stalin'. But, though the authorities showed a passing interest in 'Herr Bronstein', the two more ominous names in this sinister trio went unnoticed in the crowd.

Despite his attachment to the 'old system', Francis Joseph allowed his mind to recognize that familiar certainties of belief were being called in question throughout this first decade of the century. He had himself received in special audience Dr Sigmund Freud, when the University of Vienna belatedly found a professorship for the pioneer champion of psychoanalysis. He knew, too, that among intellectuals there was a strong current of sceptical agnosticism: a newly commissioned army officer now had the right to declare himself '*konfessionslos*', unattached to any denomination. Nevertheless, the decennial census of 1910 showed that 65.9 per cent of his subjects were Roman Catholics. So, demonstratively, was their sovereign. Each summer successive rulers in Vienna had followed the Holy Sacrament as it was born in procession through the Graben to St Stephen's Cathedral on the Feast of Corpus Christi. That tradition Francis Joseph maintained with great solemnity as late as the summer of 1912. However deep the intellectual ferment of new ideas in his capital might be, there was no wavering in the Emperor's public affirmation of the baroque Catholicism he had inherited from an earlier age.

In August 1910 he celebrated his eightieth birthday, like so many other ones, among the mountains of the Salzkammergut. Seventy-two members of the dynasty joined him at Ischl – officially *Bad* Ischl for the past four years. There was a family dinner in the principal salon of the Kurhaus, for the two-storeyed yellow ochre Kaiservilla was too compact for such a gathering; it was a relaxed country house, with balustraded wings and a colonnaded portico looking out across a single jet fountain and neat lawns to rising parkland filled with conifers and the steeper slopes of the Jainzenberg, with an unbroken line of higher peaks behind. Antlers and stuffed trophies recalled hunting forays; even the waste-paper basket beside the Emperor's bureau seemed to be held steady by the paws of a small bear he had once shot. At eighty Francis Joseph was almost resigned to hanging up his guns. Almost, but not quite; he still hoped to rise again to the silent challenge of stalking the Alpine slopes.

During his visit to Sarajevo, old Turks who knew and respected good horsemanship admired his skill in the saddle; surely, they insisted, he could not be so old as they were told; their Emperor rode like a man in his fiftieth year, not his eightieth. Physically, however, he was frailer than he appeared to distant onlookers. He had long suffered occasionally from bronchial asthma and in April 1911 he fell seriously ill. Immediately after Easter, he travelled to his daughter Marie Valerie's home at Wallsee, on the upper Danube. The weather was cold; he had recently followed a Lenten abstinence by his customary observance of the full Holy Week discipline of fasts; and, with damp mists drifting in from the river, he lacked the strength to throw off a persistent cough. Soon he was forced to remain in bed. His doctors were alarmed. Archduke Francis Ferdinand, as heir apparent, was alerted.

Even while confined to a sick room at Wallsee, the Emperor insisted on having official papers brought to him each morning. His Austrian lands were in political turmoil in this summer of 1911 with the conflict of Czechs, Poles and Germans forcing an early and indecisive election in mid-June. For the first time since 1905 the government had to resort to Article XIV of the constitution, imposing essential legislation on this occasion at the decree of a sovereign who many believed would not survive the onset of winter. At the same time there was a new vitality in the political life of Budapest, where István Tisza had emerged as Hungary's strong man, although he did not become prime minister again until June 1913. Tisza's 'Party of Work' favoured reforms, closer collaboration between German-Austrians and Magyars, and no concessions to national minorities or to the southern Slavs in autonomous Croatia. Although critical of Tisza's sternly Calvinistic style of government, Francis Joseph appreciated his qualities of leadership. Archduke Francis Ferdinand did not; the head of his military chancellery in the Belvedere recommended that, should he succeed to the throne, he must delay swearing to uphold Hungary's rights until he had imposed a revised constitution on the kingdom. Such proposals were not made public but it was with genuine relief that Tisza welcomed his king to Hungary when, in June, Francis Joseph exchanged convalescence at Wallsee for recuperation at Gödöllö.

By October 1911 he was fit to travel the forty miles from Vienna to Schwarzau, where his great-nephew (and eventual successor), Archduke Charles, was to marry the 19-year old Princess Zita of Bourbon-Parma. An early newsreel shows the Emperor in good spirits, caught in lively conversation with the bridegroom's mother, though he stoops forward to hear what she is saying and, in profile, his face is deeply lined. The early camera work may accentuate the jerk of his head, the appraising glance with which he looks about him, but he smiles readily and the film conveys an impression of surprising alacrity: here is a great-uncle at ease, and thoroughly happy. Perhaps Francis Joseph enjoyed himself too much that Saturday in the deceptive autumn sunshine at Schwarzau, where the wind came down the valley from the slopes of the Raxalpe; for he caught a chill which lingered through the remaining weeks of the year. Archduke Francis Ferdinand decided that his family should spend Christmas at the Belvedere rather than in distant Konopischt.

Francis Joseph's relapse came at a critical moment in world affairs. Three weeks before the Schwarzau wedding the Italians, complaining of Turkish maltreatment of their merchants, invaded Libya, the Ottoman provinces of Tripolitania and Cyrenaica. Austria-Hungary, as an essentially conservative Great Power, deplored the colonial adventure of its ally: war with Turkey might soon spread to the Adriatic, for the Italian port of Brindisi was nearer to Ottoman Albania than southern England to Normandy; and a campaign in Albania would ignite the Balkans. Conrad von Hötzendorf at once proposed an immediate Austro-Hungarian attack on Italy, seeking quick victories in order to advance the southern frontiers to Verona and the line of the River Piave and to assert the Monarchy's role as arbiter of affairs in the Balkans and eastern Mediterranean.

Aehrenthal was aghast at Conrad's folly. On the day after the Schwarzau wedding the foreign minister drafted a formidable indictment of the Chief-of-Staff which he presented to the Emperor, who had already taken Conrad to task more than once for his bellicose views. On 15 November, as soon as his health was up to the strain of renewed argument, Francis Joseph summoned Conrad to a private audience. Attacks on Aehrenthal for his attitude towards Italy and the Balkans were attacks on himself, he told Conrad: 'These pinpricks, I forbid them! ... Policy? It is *I* who make it ... *My* Minister for Foreign Affairs conducts *my* policy ... a policy of peace'. Conrad did not give up the fight but when he returned a fortnight later for another audience, the Emperor relieved him of his post as Chief-of-Staff. He was succeeded by General Blasius Schemua, a competent officer of limited experience, free from his predecessor's obsessive Italophobia.

Yet while Francis Joseph was prepared to re-affirm his authority in a man-to-man confrontation with a difficult general, he did not feel able to summon a meeting of ministers to co-ordinate policy. In the critical weeks of the Franco-Prussian War of 1870 the Emperor had presided over five ministerial conferences in twelve days, but he never attended any of the thirty-nine meetings of the Council of Ministers for Common Affairs convened during the last three and a half years before the First World War. When, on 6 December, the council met for the first time since Conrad's dismissal it was Aehrenthal who emphasized the need 'to stand should to shoulder with our alliance partners', Germany and Italy. The ministers were not impressed by the military capabilities of their southern ally since three army corps were needed to subdue Tripolitania and the Turks were still offering vigorous resistance. The principal purpose of the council meeting was to determine the military budget for the following year. It was acknowledged that the long period of European peace was coming to an end but the ministers sought, so far as possible, to keep expenditure down; they hoped to economize by ignoring Conrad's earlier pleas for arms and re-deployment at the head of the Adriatic.

By the time that Francis Joseph finally approved the ministers' decisions – on 7 January 1912 – he knew he would soon have to find another foreign minister; Aehrenthal was losing a courageous fight against leukaemia. Remarkably, the minister battled on to the end, seeking especially to prevent war coming to the Balkans. Individual diplomats warned Vienna that the Balkan States themselves would form a league, backed by Panslav agents independently of official Russian policy. Aehrenthal discounted this possibility: he thought the hostility between Serbs and Bulgars too deep, and the mistrust of the Balkan politicians too explosive, for such an alliance.

When on 17 February 1912 Aehrenthal died, the Emperor chose as his successor Leopold von Berchtold, ambassador in St Petersburg for four years. The new minister was more naturally at ease escorting society ladies from the paddock to the grandstand at Freudenau racecourse, with field glasses bumping the left hip, then seated in his Ballhausplatz study ready to receive an ambassador. He lacked the expertise of Goluchowski or Aehrenthal, and he knew it. 'When I took over the ministry I had no notion of the southern Slav question', he frankly admitted to the German ambassador in Vienna shortly before Christmas, 'One must have lived here to understand it'. Almost too eagerly he would turn for advice to senior officials in the ministry, have second or third thoughts, and pirouette on an agreed policy. Yet Francis Joseph never realized Berchtold's limitations, possibly because (as with Taaffe) the Emperor interpreted a laid-back manner as a sign of competent mastery rather than concealed fumbling. At one time during the Balkan crises he thought so highly of his conduct that he shook Berchtold warmly by the hand, a rare gesture of confidence from a man who shunned human contact. Berchtold enjoyed one fortuitous advantage; his wife was a girlhood companion of Sophie Chotek (who, in 1909, the Emperor had created Duchess of Hohenberg). This friendship made the Berchtolds welcome guests at the Belvedere and Konopischt.

By the autumn Berchtold was immersed in the full complexity of Balkan politics. It was nearly forty years since Francis Joseph first entertained Nicholas of Montenegro at the World Exhibition in the Prater, receiving the down-at-heel princeling with condescending approval. In four decades Nicholas's fortunes had changed. He was now a ruler of stature, vain, sly and ambitious, a self-proclaimed King since August 1910 and patriarch of an impressive family; his sons-in-law included the Kings of Italy and Serbia and four Russian Grand Dukes. When in June 1912 Nicholas paid a three day visit to Austria, the Emperor was at the Sudbahnhof to welcome him with full royal honours. The Viennese public found it hard to accept Nicholas or his kingdom at face value: the 'Pontevedro' of *The Merry Widow*, Lehar's light-hearted triumph at the Theater an der Wien, seemed to parody the black mountain, while the operetta's hero, like Nicholas's predecessor and his heir, was named Danilo. Nevertheless at Schönbrunn and in the Ballhausplatz the Montenegrin question was taken very seriously indeed: a possible union between Serbia and Montenegro would give Belgrade a strong position on the Adriatic and also block Austrian railway projects through the Sanjak; and an invasion of Turkish Albania might gain Montenegro an expanded coastline and, in the lower Boyana River south of Scutari, a waterway which could be canalized and developed as a southern Slav port. Francis Joseph flattered Nicholas during his visit, even making him honorary colonel of an infantry regiment. But over his immediate intentions in the Balkans Nicholas kept his cards close to his chest.

Four months later the King played an ace. On 8 October 1912 Nicholas declared war on the Ottoman Empire, sent his small army into the Sanjak and Turkish Albania, and called on other Balkan governments to emulate

Montenegro. Serbia, Bulgaria and Greece followed suit, massing armies more than twice as large as the Sultan could hope to put into the field. Within five weeks the Turks were driven out of the whole of Europe except for Constantinople and its hinterland, Edirne (besieged by the Bulgarians), Ioannina (besieged by the Greeks) and Scutari in Albania (besieged by the Montenegrins). The Serbs won a victory at Kumanovo, the Bulgarians at Kircasalih, and the Greeks entered the coveted port of Salonika. No less alarming to the authorities in Vienna was the capture by the Serbs of two small Albanian ports, Durazzo and San Giovanni de Medua. On 3 December an armistice brought a halt to operations, except around Ioannina; within a fortnight peace talks opened at St James's Palace, London. Much credit for bringing the combatants to the conference table lay with Berchtold and Francis Joseph's ambassadors.

The Emperor was determined not to be hustled into any conflict. 'I don't want war', he told his ministers at the end of November 1912, banging his fist on the table, 'I have always been unlucky in wars. We would win, but lose provinces'. But there was a persistent military pressure group in Vienna, backed up by General Oskar Potiorek, who in May 1911 had succeeded Varešanin as Governor of Bosnia-Herzegovina. During the late autumn Potiorek pressed for mobilization and the despatch of more and more troops to the two provinces; and on each occasion Francis Joseph rejected his requests. Eventually, on 28 October, the ministerial council agreed to ask the Emperor for a gradual increase of troops, calling up certain reservists without intensifying the crisis by ordering mobilization. Priority was given to Bosnia-Herzegovina and southern Hungary but by late November the steady build up of troops in Galicia, facing the Russians, was causing alarm among civilians in Cracow and Lvov. In the Belvedere, Archduke Francis Ferdinand remained in favour of peace throughout October and November, but with the coming of the armistice he was alarmed by reports of patriotic belligerence in Belgrade and gave serious consideration to a pre-emptive strike. He had become critical of General Staff planning; on 7 December he induced Francis Joseph to re-instate Conrad von Hötzendorf as Chief of the General Staff. Both the Emperor and the Archduke were soon to regret the return of such a dangerous military schemer to the centre of affairs.

Berchtold, like Francis Ferdinand, was worried about the mood in Belgrade. He was also troubled by the war hysteria in several Austrian and Hungarian newspapers; and in particular by public indignation at the alleged atrocious behaviour of the Serbs towards the consul in Prizren, Oskar Prochaska. On 11 December, almost before the reinstated Conrad had unfolded his Balkan maps, Berchtold visited the Belvedere for a long discussion with the Archduke, whom he found in a state of great excitement and pressing for an immediate attack on Serbia and Montenegro. Later that same day, at Berchtold's request, the Emperor presided over a top-level meeting of ministers at Schönbrunn. Since neither Conrad nor the war minister (General Krobatkin) were present it was not technically a war council. In their absence the case for military action was put by the Archduke, while Berchtold argued against any adventures on the eve of the St James's Palace Conference and the Austrian finance minister complained of the expense of any campaign. The Emperor listened to the exchange of views in an 'unusually serious, composed and resolute' mood, according to Berchtold's diary entry. After an hour of concentrated discussion he took a firm decision: there must be no military adventures; full support should be given to the peacemakers in London.

Significantly Francis Ferdinand at once accepted his uncle's ruling. Throughout the following year he worked in harness with Berchtold. Conrad, however, remained obstinate. As soon as he heard of the meeting on 11 December, he refused to take the Emperor's decision as final: he insisted the Chief of the General Staff and the war minister repeat their conviction that only a short, victorious campaign against Serbia and Montenegro would allow Austria-Hungary to impose an acceptable settlement in the western Balkans, and the war minister agreed with him. Dutifully, Berchtold sought an audience two days after Christmas in order to clarify the Emperor's attitude. He found Francis Joseph unswerving in his commitment to peace. Conrad and Krobatkin were left fuming at what they considered a lost opportunity.

Bulgarian intransigence at the conference table led to a resumption of fighting in the Balkans from early February to mid-April 1913, when the diplomats once again began to try to patch up a peace settlement in London. To the Emperor's dismay, the Austrians found themselves consistently outvoted at the conference, receiving little support from Germany or Italy, despite a recent renewal of the Triple Alliance. Only over Scutari did the Austrians have any success: the Great Powers in conference assigned Scutari to an independent Albania. King Nicholas thought otherwise: neither Montenegrins nor Serbs would lift the siege of Scutari. Again Conrad wished to send the army forward, confident that Europe would allow the Monarchy to implement conference decisions: again he was restrained by the Emperor, the Archduke and Berchtold. However, to Francis Ferdinand's satisfaction, the Austro-Hungarian navy, of which he had long been a staunch patron, was allowed to flex its muscles: on 20 March three battleships, two cruisers and a flotilla of smaller vessels took up position off Ulcinj. But the blockade of a little used stretch of coast had no effect on the fighting around Scutari, nearly 20 miles up river. Nicholas was unimpressed; nor did he respond when at the end of the month three British and two Italian warships joined the squadron. To Vienna's chagrin, the Montenegrins and Serbs tightened the noose around Scutari and on the night of 22–23 April the Turkish commander surrendered the town to King Nicholas. There was intense fury in Vienna. For a week it seemed as if Conrad would be allowed to implement *Fall-M*, his plan to overwhelm Montenegro with 50,000 troops thrusting down the River Drina from Bosnia. Francis Joseph at once authorized Governor Potiorek to proclaim a state of emergency in Bosnia-Herzegovina, putting the army on a war footing in the two provinces.

Tripod masts on a distant horizon meant nothing to King Nicholas, but the rumble of gun carriages across the frontier and the glow from camp-fires in a night sky were warnings he understood. By 4 May Berchtold was able to tell Francis Joseph that the Montenegrins were pulling out of Scutari and he expected the Serbs to withdraw from Durazzo and San Giovanni di Medua. On 14 May a British colonel arrived in Scutari at the head of an international commission charged with delineating the frontiers of a newly independent Albania. To Conrad's intense annoyance it was assumed at Schönbrunn and the Belvedere that the war clouds had lifted. The Chief of the General Staff still believed he should be allowed to implement, not only *Fall-M*, but *Fall-B* as well, the plans he had first drawn up six years before, providing for a general offensive in the western Balkans to destroy both Serbia and Montenegro as independent kingdoms.

Fortunately for Francis Joseph's peace of mind during these taxing winter months, the conflict between the nationalities had become less intense. Much of the credit for this mellowing of old antagonisms lay with the Czech political 'realist' Thomas Masaryk, professor of philosophy at Prague university for a quarter of a century. Although Masaryk had virtually no party following in the Reichsrat, he was widely respected by intellectuals inside and outside the Monarchy for promoting a disciplined ethic of citizenship and a fundamentally federalist ideal of democratic government. Under his influence a political compromise had been achieved in Moravia in 1905, with Germans and Czechs accepting equal status in the provincial legislature and administration, and by the beginning of 1913 similar settlements gave some grounds for optimism in the Bukovina and Galicia. Personally Masaryk still had hopes of winning support for a Moravian-type compromise in neighbouring Bohemia and gradually educating the 'Austrian' politicians to accept reforms which would unify the Monarchy as a whole. The Emperor respected Masaryk's personal integrity and fundamental loyalty, though he recognized that anything achieved in the Austrian and Czech lands would have little effect on the nationality question within Hungary. There was, however, a certain tranquillity in 1913 within the Budapest parliament, imposed by István Tisza. Since out of nearly four hundred members of the lower house only 18 were non-Magyars, this appearance of calm did not reflect the general mood of the kingdom. Tisza was a man of intelligence who realized he needed to show a willingness for reform, if only to quieten the outcry against Magyar domination which he anticipated Francis Ferdinand would encourage on his accession. Yet Tisza offered few concessions: approaches to the Roumanians of Transylvania kept their politicians talking but achieved little, while a token gesture towards the Zagreb Diet met with no response from the deeply mistrustful Croats. For the moment, however Tisza's grip on affairs freed Francis Joseph from any pressing worries in Hungary.

Physically 'the old gentleman' needed any respite which the uncertainties of this troubled year might offer him. The strain of months of chronic crisis had been considerable. After a bad attack of bronchitis in the autumn of 1912 the Emperor remained under strict medical supervision from the court physician, Dr Joseph von Kerzl, who insisted that he should spend most of his time at Schönbrunn, where the air was clearer than in the city; and for the last four years of his life Francis Joseph travelled to the Hofburg only for official business and ceremonial occasions. Although he spent a few days at Wallsee with Marie Valerie and her family, he was rarely seen in public during the winter of 1912–13 or the early spring. Apart from his happiness at being with the youngest Habsburgs, he still found contentment in Katharina Schratt's companionship. By now she was a widow approaching sixty, and there were even silly tales that the Emperor had secretly married her. The memoirs of Francis Joseph's valet, Eugen Ketterl, originally published thirteen years after his master's death, show that the relationship between the retired Burg actress and her sovereign remained unchanged throughout these final years. Since Ketterl was writing while Frau Schratt was still alive, it is possible his account exaggerates her influence on the imperial household. But there is no reason to doubt Ketterl's picture of the lonely Emperor awaiting a visit from his old friend in pleasurable excitement, 'restlessly starting out of his chair to go to the bedroom and brush his hair or comb his side-whiskers'. Katharina Schratt gave him the material comforts he always neglected, such as a dressing gown or a rug to place beside his iron bedstead; and when Dr Kerzl banned strong cigars she found mild ones for him to smoke, in stubborn half-defiance of medical counsel. Summer evenings – again according to Ketterl – would bring the Emperor an invitation to a private dinner party at no. 9 Gloriettegasse, where his hostess would see that one of the popular quartets from the Grinzing *heurigen* was on hand to play familiar Strauss waltzes or newer tunes from Lehar's operettas in the seclusion of her terraced garden.

Yet there can have been few relaxed evenings of entertainment for him in this last full summer of peace. The news from the Balkans remained bad. Moreover he was shocked by a scandal at a high level in the institution upon whose absolute loyalty he set greatest store. In the early spring of 1913 Conrad was informed that German counter-intelligence believed there was a Russian spy in the Austro-Hungarian General Staff: and on 24 May he was told by senior officers, whom he had ordered to investigate the allegation, that the traitor had been identified as Colonel Alfred Redl, chief-of-staff to the 8th Army Corps in Prague. He ordered a small 'commission' of Redl's brother officers to provide the traitor with a loaded revolver and give him an opportunity to judge himself alone. Soon after midnight the officers confronted Redl in a room of an inner city hotel, the Klomser, no. 19 Herrengasse. Redl, left alone, shot himself forty minutes later.

Like Mayerling, the Redl Affair has been over-dramatized on stage and screen. Redl, a 49-year old bachelor from a German middle-class family in Galicia, had been a staff officer for nineteen years. Before going to Prague he was head of counter espionage in the *Evidenzburo* (Vienna's equivalent of London's MI5). A belated investigation revealed that because of his homosexual predilections and taste for a luxurious life style, Redl was blackmailed by the Russians, whom he supplied with information about staff plans and the identity of Austro-Hungarian spies; his activities may have contributed to the setback in Serbia and Galicia on the outbreak of war, though they did not make defeat certain.

Of more immediate consequence was the bungled attempt to hush up the scandal – again reminiscent of Mayerling. Redl was well known in society; a perceptive journalist, Egon Erwin Kisch, soon saw through the bland statements which followed the suicide, alerting newspapers in Berlin and Prague. Within a week of Redl's death alarming rumours of treachery, sexual perversion and corruption were circulating in Vienna, while in Budapest the Magyar press was especially hard on the army. 'The Colonel Redl treason case shocks public opinion', wrote the German-Austrian parliamentarian Joseph Redlich in his diary as early as 2 June. Conrad had given a full report of the affair to Francis Joseph on the previous day, after a preliminary conversation four days earlier. The Emperor agreed that it was right for Redl to have been encouraged to kill himself rather than for the authorities to bring him to trial and thereby undermine confidence in the military establishment – 'to save the army from worse dishonour', as Conrad explained to Joseph Redlich.

Francis Ferdinand, on the other hand, attacked Conrad for his bumbled handling of so explosive an issue. The Emperor supported the General, especially once it was clear that the Archduke's main complaint was over Conrad's complicity in urging Redl to take his life; what was a mortal sin to a devout Catholic was traditional in the army code of honour for which Francis Joseph always showed respect. There were other differences, too, between uncle and nephew. The German initiative in unmasking Redl particularly rankled with the Emperor; no action was taken against Redl's immediate superior, Colonel von Urbanski, a protégé of Conrad and later his biographer. Not unreasonably, the Archduke argued that Urbanski should have been aware that Redl was a security risk: where, after all, did the Colonel acquire money to purchase a Daimler touring phaeton motor car which was the envy of his colleagues? But Francis Joseph sympathized with Urbanski. He disliked probing inquiries into private affairs: serving officers could not marry without their sovereign's permission, Urbanski himself spending several years on a waiting list because the regulations stipulated that, at any one time, half the officers on the General Staff must be celibate; but so long as officers did not compromise themselves with rankers or neglect their duties for the favour of dubious mistresses, the Emperor saw no reason to question their behaviour.

Francis Joseph was anxious to limit the demoralizing effect of the Redl scandal on his army. Officers and rank-and-file must continue to project imperial grandeur, accepting him as a paterfamilias, stern and exacting, but also protective of their way of life. Throughout the summer and autumn he once more emphasized the links of army and dynasty, taking care to give public affirmation of his confidence in the heir apparent, whatever his private doubts. In August he therefore appointed Francis Ferdinand as his military surrogate, making him Inspector General of the Army, a post held by only one previous incumbent, Archduke Albrecht. But as the centenary of the battle of Leipzig drew near, the Emperor made it known that he would himself take the salute in the Schwarzenbergplatz at a parade to commemorate the allied triumph over Napoleon. Thoughtfully on 16 October, a raw autumnal morning in Vienna, a small Persian carpet was spread on the pavement at a corner of the square. Such coddling did not meet with his approval. Photographs, taken as the regiments filed by, show Francis Joseph standing erect, with drawn sword lowered at the salute – and his feet disdainfully placed well behind the carpet.

The Leipzig centenary celebrations, though arranged long before October 1913, fortuitously acquired a topical significance: in that week, for a third time in ten months, it seemed likely that the troops on parade would soon be entrained for the South, marching into Serbia or Montenegro. During the summer the balance of Balkan power had shifted decisively in Serbia's favour when the recent allies fell out over the partition of Macedonia. In early July Bulgaria was defeated in a brief campaign rashly initiated by King Ferdinand and entangling his strategically divided forces with his ex-allies (Serbia and Greece), with Roumania in the north, and with rejuvenated Turkish troops, determined to recover Edirne. Victory made the Serbs overreach themselves. Success on the battlefields intensified the influence of the Black Hand, a secret society established in May 1911 among young army officers in Belgrade and pledged to bring about the union of Serb minorities in the Habsburg and Ottoman Empires with their kinsfolk in independent Serbia. With the army having already doubled the size of the Serbian kingdom, it was difficult for any government in Belgrade to urge caution and restraint. The Black Handers had established a newspaper of their own, provocatively called *Piedmont*, to give Vienna due notice of the role they envisaged for Serbia in creating a unified southern Slav state. The warning was not lost on an Emperor whose formative years coincided with Piedmont's bid for primacy in the Italian *Risorgimento*.

Yet was Nikola Pašić, prime minister and foreign minister in Belgrade from 1910 onwards, Serbia's Count Cavour? In the first days of October the policy makers of Vienna had an opportunity to judge for themselves, for Pašić travelled to the Austrian capital, ostensibly to re-assure Berchtold and the Emperor over alleged Serbian subversion in Croatia. The visit was not a success: the Serbs had still not evacuated Albania, and in the early autumn it was reported they were reinforcing their regular troops in the disputed territories. Pašić showed no wish to talk about Albania; and his evasiveness was exploited by Conrad and the militarists among the ministers. Significantly the 'war party' was now reinforced by István Tisza, who saw Pašić's journey as a sign of appeasement; the time had come, he thought, for harsher measures against Serbia.

On 13 October an informal meeting of ministers in Vienna, with Conrad co-opted so as to give military advice, recommended a short and sharp action which would bring the Serbs to heel. Archduke Francis Ferdinand, deeply mistrustful of Tisza, urged caution; but his uncle, who was rapidly losing patience with the whole affair, agreed with Tisza. On the day after the Leipzig centenary parade, at a time when newspaper editorials in Vienna and Budapest struck a warlike tone, Francis Joseph authorized Berchtold to send an ultimatum to Belgrade, handed over to Pašić on 18 October: the Serbs were given eight days in which to evacuate Albanian territory or face unspecified consequences. Pašić, finding no support for any concept of Slav solidarity from St Petersburg, speedily gave way and by 26 October the Serbs were out of Albania. The crisis had a twofold consequence: in Belgrade it intensified the hidden conflict between the Black Handers and the prime minister whom they now accused of weakness; and in Vienna it showed that armed threats – the 'brinkmanship' of a later generation – brought a swift response from a government which tended to treat the pleas and prods of cautious nego- tiation with contempt. Neither Francis Joseph nor his foreign minister knew of Pašić's difficulties with the Black Hand; but the effectiveness of diplomacy by ultimatum was too self-evident for them to ignore in any future Balkan crisis.

Foreign observers, and some Austrian members of the Reichsrat, assumed that Francis Ferdinand and his 'Belvedere circle' favoured war. The Archduke, however, was in many ways better informed than his uncle, though his judgment was always clouded by Magyarophobia. He knew that there were deficiencies in the army, and he no longer held the high opinion of Conrad which had first brought the General to the key post he retained so long. The Archduke had such a thundering row with his former protégé during the autumn manoeuvres of 1913 that Conrad went on sick leave. Although the General's apologists maintain that the dispute was caused by his failure to hear Mass during manoeuvres rather than by any military matter, relations between the two men remained strained throughout the winter. Yet there was no doubting the tenacity of purpose with which the Archduke fulfilled his duties as Inspector General of the Army. Even before the October war crisis, he had accepted an invitation from Governor Potiorek to go to Bosnia in the summer and watch army exercises in the newly acquired provinces. Francis Joseph welcomed the proposed visit. In mid-March 1914 it was confirmed that the Archduke would attend manoeuvres of 15th and 16th Army Corps in the Bosnian mountains in June; he would then pay a state visit to Sarajevo, accompanied by his wife, the Duchess of Hohenberg. In 1911 when the Archduke had considered making such a journey he sought advice from a leading Croat who warned Francis Ferdinand's envoy, 'I know the Serbs. I know that they will wait for him in ambush as murderers'. Now, three years later, the Serb students were given a clear three months in which to contact the Black Handers and co-ordinate their plans.

Throughout the winter of 1913–14 Francis Joseph's health caused no particular alarm, although his obstinacy must have exasperated Dr Kerzl. On one occasion, having heard that his exact contemporary General Beck had broken an arm, the Emperor visited his old confidant at his apartment in Vienna and insisted on climbing three flights of stairs rather than make use of the lift. By now, however, excursions of any kind were rare. But he did visit the annual exhibition in the Wiener Künstlerhaus on the first day of spring. Two days later he rode in a carriage from Schönbrunn to Penzing Station with Emperor William II who, as usual, had broken his journey to Corfu in Vienna. But, as three years before, Francis Joseph fell seriously ill with chronic bronchitis immediately after Easter. The first medical bulletin was issued on 20 April; not until 23 May did Dr Kerzl decide that daily reports were no longer necessary. For the last ten days of April Archduke Francis Ferdinand, who was with his family at Konopischt, kept an engine under steam at the nearest railway station, ready to take him to the capital should his uncle's condition worsen. By the third week in May Montenuovo, the Lord Chamberlain, could tell the controller of the Archduke's household that 'if everything develops normally, by the end of June' the Emperor's 'health will be completely recovered'. Yet the illness left Francis Joseph weak. For once, even the routine business of government suffered. Normally he would read, annotate and approve reports of ministerial council meetings within a fortnight; but he was unable to complete work on the papers for the 24 May session until 11 July. The meeting had discussed ways of keeping control of proposed Balkan railway routes in the newly enlarged Serbia; by the second week of July, the topic was a historical irrelevancy.

In mid-May Archduke Francis Ferdinand seriously considered cancelling his journey to Bosnia-Herzegovina because of 'the state of His Majesty's health'. By 4 June, however, Francis Joseph was fit enough to receive the Archduke in audience at his customary early hour; and they appear to have met again on 7 June, once more at a quarter to eight in the morning, when they talked for some forty-five minutes. Ought the Sarajevo visit to be postponed? Francis Ferdinand's own health was suspect and he was having second thoughts over the wisdom of a state occasion, requiring ceremonial uniform, under Bosnia's midsummer heat. Moreover, as on the eve of the Emperor's journey to the two provinces, reports were coming in from several sources of a conspiracy and plans for assassination. No one knows what was said between uncle and nephew. According to Francis Ferdinand's elder son, the Emperor was against the visit but his father felt duty bound not to disappoint the army commanders; according to the later Empress Zita, 'the Emperor made it quite clear that he desired the Archduke to go'; but the most likely reaction is that recorded by General Conrad, who states that Francis Joseph merely told his nephew, 'Do as you wish'.

Emperor and Archduke did not meet again. Francis Joseph was eager to set out for Bad Ischl, but he was still in residence at Schönbrunn on 18 June, when he presented new colours to the Wiener Neustadt military academy. By then Francis Ferdinand was at Konopischt, where he had received in the previous week both Emperor William II and, immediately afterwards, Count Berchtold and his wife. Later commentators have read a sinister significance into these meetings, seeing them as evidence that the German Emperor had written off Francis Joseph and was re-shaping a future Europe with his sabre-rattling Austrian friend. Francis Ferdinand and William did, indeed, discuss Balkan affairs as well as the beauty of the Konopischt rosarium. Since the Tsar's armies were not yet ready for war, it might be well for Austria-Hungary to pursue a firm policy in the Balkans before the situation deteriorated again, William thought; but his general observations were strangely oblique. He took greater trouble in explaining away remarks made to his host at Miramare a few weeks earlier when, having been poorly briefed on the Archduke's prejudices, he had gone out of his way to commend the statesmanlike qualities of István Tisza.

After the visits of the German Emperor and Berchtold, the Archduke enjoyed a few days of family peace. The gardens of his estate were opened for the first time to the people of Bohemia. In his role as squire of Konopischt, he moved easily among his visitors, pleased by the appreciation of both Czechs and Germans for the roses of which he was so proud. But by Tuesday, 24 June, he was at Trieste: that morning he boarded SMS *Viribus Unitis* to sail down to Metković, while Francis Joseph was preparing to set off at the end of the week for Bad Ischl and the good mountain air of the Salzkammergut. In Sarajevo a group of young assassins were studying the detailed itinerary of the coming visit, which the authorities had circulated several days before. Security precautions were far slacker than for the Emperor's visit. Care had been taken to make sure that a quartet was on hand to play 'light Viennese music' for the state visitors at lunch; but there is no evidence that Governor Potiorek realized the significance of the date chosen for the Archduke's processional drive through the heart of Sarajevo: Sunday, 28 June, was Serbia's National Day.

By noon on Saturday the military exercises in Bosnia were over. In the late afternoon a telegram from Ilidze, the small spa a few miles outside Sarajevo, reached Bad Ischl: the Archduke was glad to let the Emperor know that the bearing and efficiency of both army corps had been 'outstanding beyond all praise'. 'Tomorrow I visit Sarajevo, and leave in the evening', the telegram ended. Some eighteen hours later, in the bright sunshine of a Sunday morning, a telephone message reached the Kaiservilla. It was received by Count Paar, who had been duty adjutant at the Hofburg in 1889 when Hoyos arrived from Mayerling and who in 1898 had broken to the Emperor the 'grave news' from Geneva. Now Paar brought him grave news from Sarajevo: the Archduke and the Duchess of Hohenberg had been killed by pistol shots. Later reports gave more details: the visitors had survived a bomb attack earlier in the morning; and on this second occasion their chauffeur, having taken a wrong road on the quayside by the river, was about to reverse when, with the car stationary, a Bosnian Serb student was able to fire at his victims from less than five feet away. Subsequently it was discovered that the student, Gavrilo Princip, was only one of six assassins roaming the streets of Sarajevo that morning.

On hearing of the murders the Emperor is said to have 'slumped in the chair at his desk' before pacing the room in great agitation and saying, almost to himself, 'Terrible. The Almighty is not to be challenged ... A higher power has re-established the order which I, alas, could not pre-serve'. This familiar tale derives from what Count Paar, the sole witness of his master's grief, told Colonel von Margutti, his deputy, who then wrote up his account ten years later. The harsh comment, with its echo of old worries over the intrusion of a morganatic marriage in what the Emperor regarded as a divinely ordained line of dynastic descent, seems so artificially stilted as to be apocryphal. On the other hand, the news broke on a Sunday, at a time when the unfathomable workings of Provi-dence may have been close to the surface of his shocked mind. Next day he was back at Schönbrunn, sad but self-composed, gratified at being met at the railway station by his great-nephew, Archduke Charles, now heir to the throne, the fifth of the reign. Archduchess Marie Valerie hurried to Schönbrunn to be with her father. She found 'Papa amazingly fresh', as she wrote in her journal, though he was 'shocked, with tears in his eyes ... when he spoke of the poor children'; but he had more confidence in the tact and skills of the new heir than in the murdered Archduke. 'For me it is a relief from a great worry', he admitted to his daughter, thinking of the fate of the dynasty. No one in the family circle foresaw that the event which they mourned as a personal tragedy was for Europe as a whole a cataclysmic disaster.

Chapter 20

WAR

'Terrible shock for the dear old Emperor', King George V commented in his journal on 28 June 1914: 'Poor Emperor, nothing is he spared', echoed his consort, Queen Mary, a few days later. 'The horrible tragedy', as the Queen described the Sarajevo murders, appalled the European courts. In London the Duke of Connaught, Queen Victoria's surviving son, made ready to set out for the funeral. In Brussels King Albert I proposed to go in person. So, too, did Emperor William II who put an abrupt end to the Elbe regatta, ordering his warships to lower their ensigns to half-mast as soon as the news broke. The general dismay abroad was in sharp contrast to reaction within Austria-Hungary. 'No mood of mourning in the city; in the Prater, and here with us at Grinzing, music everywhere on both days!', Joseph Redlich noted in his diary on Monday, 29 June; and the indifference of Vienna was surpassed in Budapest, where little attempt was made to disguise the widespread relief at the death of an Archduke notorious for having hated everything Magyar.

The coffins of the victims reached Trieste aboard SMS *Viribus Unitis* on the evening of 1 July. By then embassies and legations in Vienna had been advised that the Emperor's poor health precluded his acting as host to any gathering of European sovereigns; the funeral ceremonies in the capital would therefore be limited to a single day. In accordance with the Archduke's instructions interment would follow not in the Kapuzinerkirche but at Artstetten, his estate in Lower Austria, where in 1909 he had supervised the building of a 'light and airy' family crypt. The coffins reached the Sudbahnhof from Trieste at 10 p.m. on 2 July and left the Westbahnhof again shortly after ten on the following night for Pöchlarn, a country railway station two miles from Artstetten, but on the opposite bank of the Danube. The obsequies in Vienna were therefore compressed within a mere twenty-four hours.

Francis Ferdinand's secretary, Baron Morsey, and several members of the Belvedere circle were incensed that the Archduke and his wife had been given a 'third class burial'. For this final insult they blamed the Lord Chamberlain, Prince Montenuovo, an old personal enemy of the dead couple and himself descended from a morganatic marriage – his grandmother was the widowed Empress Marie Louise who had not been buried beside his grandfather, Count Neipperg. The unimaginative Montenuovo was a stickler for protocol and, in this instance, had no precedent to follow. He refused to concern himself with what happened after the special funeral train pulled out of the Westbahnhof, since Artstetten was a private residence, outside the Chamberlain's jurisdiction; and no one could blame Montenuovo or anybody else for the violent thunderstorm which so terrified the horses in the funeral cortège between Pöchlarn and Artstetten that they almost plunged the coffins into the Danube. Moreover, while the Lord Chamberlain might legitimately be criticized for limiting the lying-in-state at the Hofburg chapel to a mere four hours, it is hard to see what other action he could have taken once it was conceded that the Emperor's physical frailty made it essential to act as speedily as dignity permitted. But, as early as 5 July, the *Reichspost* (a daily newspaper sympathetic to the Archduke's political views) asked in an editorial 'why, according to the original arrangement, the funeral was so startlingly simple, and so insulting to a grieving people?'. Two days later the *Wiener Zeitung* published a letter from Francis Joseph to the Lord Chamberlain in which he commended Montenuovo's handling of the 'extraordinary duties' which followed 'the passing away of my beloved nephew'. Did Francis Joseph feel that he was himself to blame for denying the murder victims full honours? There could, of course, be no public criticism of the Emperor's conduct. Privately, however, one of Francis Ferdinand's aides-de-camp noted that, during the fifteen minute Requiem, Francis Joseph glanced around the chapel 'with complete indifference and the same unmoving glacial expression he showed towards his subjects on other occasions, too'.

Berchtold, who had seen Francis Joseph for the first time since the tragedy on 30 June, thought the Emperor deeply shaken. His eyes were moist and, unusually, he greeted the foreign minister with a handshake and invited him to sit down beside him. Something would have to be done about the Serbs, the Emperor conceded, for the first reports from Governor Potiorek in Sarajevo suggested the involvement in the conspiracy of military officials in Belgrade. Francis Joseph told Berchtold that he wanted to know from István Tisza how the Hungarians would react to a military confrontation; and he wondered how far Vienna could rely on support from Berlin. Tisza, whom the Emperor saw later that Tuesday, favoured forceful diplomatic pressure on Serbia, taken after consultation with the other leading European Powers but he deplored any moves which involved a risk of war. On reflection, Francis Joseph thought 'the time for military action not yet ripe'. Nevertheless, he sent a personal letter to Emperor William II, blaming Panslavism for the murders; the letter also sought German support in keeping King Carol I of Roumania loyal to his secret attachment to the Triple Alliance and in securing the collaboration of Bulgaria, so that 'the band of criminal agitators in Belgrade' should not go 'unpunished': 'Serbia must be eliminated as a political power-factor in the Balkans', Francis Joseph wrote.

Significantly, however, he avoided any use of the word 'war'. The Emperor's letter was entrusted to a personal envoy, the young Count Alexander Hoyos (the only German-Austrian among senior officials in the Ballhausplatz that year) who also took with him to Berlin a long memorandum on general policies over Balkan affairs, completed by one of Berchtold's senior advisers four days before the assassination and hurriedly updated. The letter was presented to William II by the Austro-Hungarian ambassador at Potsdam on Sunday, 5 July, almost a week to the hour after the Sarajevo murders. Hoyos remained in the German capital for two days of discussion with senior policy makers in the Wilhelmstrasse. His remarks, which were supplemented by reports reaching Berlin from the ambassador in Vienna, suggested that Berchtold was more warlike than his sovereign and may have strengthened the feeling in Berlin that if a general European conflict was unavoidable, it must come 'now or never', at a time when Germany could rely on Austria-Hungary to accept the full commitments of the military alliance. On the evening of 6 July Berchtold duly learnt by telegram from Berlin that 'over Serbia' Austria-Hungary could 'always count' on German support as 'a faithful ally and friend'; and this German offer of 'a blank cheque' was confirmed by the young and enthusiastic Hoyos when, soon afterwards, he arrived back at the Ballhausplatz.

Next morning Francis Joseph resumed his interrupted holiday at Bad Ischl. He remained in the Salzkammergut throughout these three weeks of mounting tension in Europe. There is no clearer illustration of the extent to which age had withered the hand of autocracy than the Emperor's withdrawal from the centre of affairs at such a time. When war loomed in 1859 and 1866 he kept in constant touch with his generals and ministers, and in the summer of 1870 he presided over five Crown Council meetings in twelve days while weighing the merits of neutrality or intervention in the Franco-Prussian War. Now, in July 1914, he was absent from every conference of ministers. He had with him at Bad Ischl only a small personal staff. They were accustomed to conducting urgent business by telegraph during the annual sojourn at the Kaiservilla and, unlike their sovereign, they were even prepared to make use of the telephone. But if a minister or general sought an audience with the Emperor he had to allow five hours for the journey from the capital to Bad Ischl, and another five hours to travel back and report to his colleagues. Berchtold, Conrad and the two prime ministers therefore had greater freedom to shape policy in July 1914 than any of their predecessors earlier in the reign. Moreover, there was no 'shadow court' to influence policy, for the Belvedere circle disintegrated as soon as Francis Ferdinand was killed, and Archduke Charles was too young to have built up a following of his own.

Yet no decisive step towards war could be taken without the Emperor's written consent. Berchtold therefore found it necessary to travel down to Bad Ischl as early as Wednesday 8 July, barely twenty-four hours after Francis Joseph left Schönbrunn. For on the Tuesday on which the imperial railway train was heading south the foreign minister presided over a vital meeting of the 'Council of Ministers for Common Affairs' at the Ballhausplatz. There, despite opposition from Tisza, it was decided to prepare a harsh ultimatum to be sent to Serbia in full expectation that the terms would prove unacceptable and war follow along the middle Danube and the mountainous borders of Bosnia.

Berchtold spent Thursday, 9 July, at the Kaiservilla discussing Tuesday's council meeting in great detail. Francis Joseph at once saw the significance of Tisza's continued striving for peace. He therefore pressed Berchtold to settle the disagreement with Hungary, for he wished his ministers to agree on a united policy at such a time of crisis. Personally the Emperor agreed with Berchtold's 'opinion that a peaceful solution of the crisis would be worthless without positive guarantees that the Pan-Serbian movement will ... be suppressed on the initiative of Belgrade'. He was not prepared for a long series of diplomatic exchanges; but, like Tisza, he refused to rule out the possibility of a peaceful solution if the Serbian authorities had the good sense to fulfil the conditions laid down in Vienna. Neither the Emperor not his ministers seem to have realized that, four days before the Sarajevo murders, Nikola Pašić secured the dissolution of parliament in Belgrade and announced that the first general election in the recently enlarged kingdom would be held early in August. Throughout the July crisis Pašić was therefore fighting an election campaign among a proud people who would certainly reject his Radical Party if its leader bowed to foreign demands.

Tisza, too, was sensitive to public opinion, even though elections were not imminent in Hungary. The 'Austrian' prime minister, Karl Sturgkh, could take decisions without worrying about parliament, for the Reichsrat had been prorogued in March 1914, mainly because of obstructionism by Ruthene and Slovene deputies, and it was not to meet again until after

Francis Joseph's death. But the lower chamber in Budapest sat throughout July, making it necessary for István Tisza to spend an increasing number of days in Hungary. He spoke in parliament on several occasions and was therefore able to sense for himself the mounting desire of the people for some decisive move against the Serbs. At the same time, Tisza knew that most Magyar magnates agreed with him in arguing against the inclusion of more Slavonic peoples in the Monarchy: ideally Karadjordjević Serbia would be crushed and a puppet 'colonialized' kingdom created, ruled either by an Austrian Archduke or a German prince sympathetic to Hungary's commercial needs. So delicate was the political balance among the Hungarian parties that Tisza preferred to keep a personal envoy in Austria, someone who could represent his views to Berchtold and Conrad in Vienna and, when necessary, take the royal road to Bad Ischl.

This task Tisza entrusted to Count István Burian, for nearly ten years before 1912 the common finance minister, a post with special responsibilities inside Bosnia-Herzegovina; he understood the problems posed by Pan-Serb agitation in the provinces and sympathized with Governor Potiorek. But Burian, who possessed the mind of an obstinate legalist and had no liking for compromise, did not agree with Tisza's stand against a harsh ultimatum. Hardly had Berchtold returned to Vienna from the Kaiservilla than Burian set off in the opposite direction. He reported to Tisza – back in Vienna from Budapest by 14 July – that he found Francis Joseph ready to judge the situation calmly and firmly, 'holding out to the bitter end'. Burian's account of the mood at Bad Ischl swayed Tisza's assessment of the crisis, inclining the Hungarian prime minister towards acceptance of a military rather than a diplomatic solution. At the same time Tisza was impressed by the repeated assurance of support received by Berchtold from Berlin. There was no danger of Austria-Hungary being left in isolation, as in 1908, after the announcement of the annexation of the provinces. By the start of the third week in July the foreign minister could see that Hungarian opposition to his war policy had evaporated.

On Sunday, 19 July, Berchtold convened a council of ministers at his home. The meeting agreed that a strongly worded ultimatum should be presented in Belgrade on the following Thursday afternoon, giving the Serbs forty-eight hours to accept the Austro-Hungarian demands, and providing for mobilization in a week's time. By then the harvest would be gathered in and regiments, depleted by 'harvest leave', up to strength again. Yet Tisza still showed an independence of spirit. He insisted that, as soon as the victory was won, no Serbian territory would be annexed by the Monarchy; he still hoped that, if a public declaration was given in Vienna that 'we have no intention of annexing any territory', Russia might be persuaded to stand aside.

First reports of the council's resolutions reached the Kaiservilla on Monday morning, by telephone or telegram. Francis Joseph discussed them at length with Count Paar, his principal adjutant. Colonel von Margutti's account suggests that both men remained convinced throughout the week that any war could remain localized. The Emperor seems to have assumed Serbia would give way under pressure, as in the Balkan Wars. There is, however, also evidence that Francis Joseph believed Berchtold was gambling on Russia's reluctance to risk a war which would spread like a grass-fire from the Balkans to the Baltic and that, as an ex-ambassador in St Petersburg, he knew the limits of official backing for Panslavism.

Yet when, on Tuesday, Berchtold arrived at the Kaiservilla and handed Francis Joseph a copy of the ultimatum, the Emperor was surprised by the severity and precision of the demands. The Serbs were required, not merely to condemn and forbid 'the propaganda directed against Austria-Hungary' and dissolve 'the society called *Narodna Odbrana*', but also to consent that Imperial and Royal officials should 'assist in Serbia in suppressing the subversive movement'. If, on receiving the ultimatum, Pašić should turn for support to the Russian Government and be rejected, the world would see that Panslavism was an empty sentiment, politically of no value whatsoever. Francis Joseph at once saw that St Petersburg's reaction to the ultimatum was of great significance. 'Russia cannot possibly swallow a note like this', he remarked. Yet he did not question the soundness of Berchtold's judgment or the collective wisdom of his ministers. If they were untroubled by the Russian threat, why should he be? No attempt was made to tone down the demands. At six o'clock on the evening of Thursday 23 July, the Austro-Hungarian envoy in Belgrade handed to the deputy prime minister a 48-hour ultimatum which would have virtually reduced Serbia to an Austro-Hungarian dependency. London, Paris and St Petersburg were officially notified by Francis Joseph's ambassadors on Friday morning, some fifteen hours later. That afternoon there was in these distant capitals, for the first time, an apprehension that a general European war was imminent. The Serbian Government had received, as Churchill wrote, 'an ultimatum such as never had been penned in modern times'.

No answer from Belgrade reached Bad Ischl (or, indeed, Vienna) on that Friday, nor on Saturday morning. The Emperor followed his customary routine, busying himself with trivialities of etiquette, even on holiday. The Duke of Cumberland, once Crown Prince of Hanover, was expected to luncheon on that Saturday and Francis Joseph insisted on giving his staff precise written instructions on the Court courtesies to be observed for the elderly exile and his family. But he was ill-at-ease, pacing the terrace of the villa with his hands behind his back. When his guest arrived he was unable to keep conversation flowing at the luncheon table, for he had resolved not to talk of the crisis and no topic other than the uncertainty of the passing hours filled his mind.

Others waited anxiously in Bad Ischl, too. Katharina Schratt was at the Villa Felicitas, her summer home for a quarter of a century. General Krobatkin, the war minister, and Leon von Bilinski, the common finance minister, had made the journey down from Vienna so as to give the Emperor advice at this crucial time; and Berchtold was on hand, staying at the Hotel Bauer, on the lower slopes of the Kalvarienberg, a hill half a mile from the Kaiservilla, across the Ischl River. At a quarter past six the foreign minister decided that no news would come that evening and left the hotel for a walk on the hills. But before seven o'clock the war ministry telephoned from Vienna. Margutti took the message: the Serbs had rejected the ultimatum; the staff of the Legation in Belgrade had crossed the Danube to the safety of Zemlin, twenty minutes away in Croatia. 'So that's that,' Francis Joseph sighed, when Margutti handed him the message. For a few moments he sat dim-eyed at his desk, silently brooding: then, as if clutching at one last straw, Margutti heard him mutter to himself, 'Now that is a break of diplomatic relations; it doesn't necessarily mean war'. He stood up and called for 'the foreign minister – at once, at once'. Hurriedly Berchtold was brought back from his stroll on the hillside. Krobatkin and Bilinski joined him at the Kaiservilla, but they brought Francis Joseph little comfort; he agreed to sign the order for mobilization against Serbia. 'Later than usual' on that Saturday evening Katharina Schratt looked out from the verandah of the Villa Felicitas and saw the Emperor was crossing her private bridge, haltingly and with a weary stoop. 'I have done my best but now it is the end', he told her.

Still, however, Francis Joseph lingered in Bad Ischl. On Sunday he was told that Marshal Radomir Putnik, Serbia's most distinguished soldier and likely commander in the field, had been detained in Budapest while seeking to return home from a spa in Bohemia where he had been taking the waters. The Emperor's sense of chivalry was affronted by the news: orders were immediately sent to Budapest for Putnik to be released, provided with a special train, and allowed back across the frontier to take up his duties in Belgrade. Was there still an element of make-believe in the whole crisis? It is possible that had Francis Joseph returned to Vienna when war clouds closed in he would have seen, as did William II in Berlin, that the Serbian reply to the ultimatum was not unreasonable; the only point firmly rejected was the participation of Austrian officials in policing activities on Serbian soil – an issue scarcely providing a pretext for even a localized war. Yet had Francis Joseph been at Schönbrunn could he have held back his ministers and generals? A quarter of a century later William II explained that in 1914, 'the machine ... ran away with me'. Why should Francis Joseph have fared better in dealing with Conrad than William II with the German Chief-of-Staff, Moltke? The one person who, in an earlier crisis had shown the strength and stature to apply brakes to the machine, lay dead in the crypt at Artstetten.

War was declared on Serbia on Tuesday, 28 July. Next morning two monitors from the Austro-Hungarian flotilla on the Danube began to bombard Belgrade. Only on that Wednesday did Francis Joseph order preparations to be made for the Court's return to the capital. For him it seemed unthinkable to take a holiday when his subjects were at war. Yet he left Bad Ischl early on Thursday, 30 July, with a great inner sadness; he knew it was unlikely that his senses would ever again sharpen to the fresh morning beauty of the mountains or allow the rising mist rolling back up the valley to lift the burden from an aching heart.

The illusion that the war might remain localized as an expanded Balkan conflict persisted in Vienna, despite ominous reports of troop movements around Moscow and Kiev. Except for the token participation of an auxiliary corps on the flank of Napoleon's *Grande Armée* in 1812, the Habsburg armies had never been at war with Russia and there was a reluctance to accept Tsar Nicholas II as an enemy. But war plans, long prepared and well matured, precluded diplomatic improvisation which might have called a halt to the war after a punitive assault on Belgrade. When, on 30 July, Russia ordered general mobilisation behind the long frontier from the Baltic to the Black Sea, neither Germany nor Austria-Hungary could ignore the threat and next day both governments put their armies on a war footing. Fighting broke out along Germany's eastern frontier on 1 August, followed by an invasion of Luxembourg and Belgium and, on 3 August, a German declaration of war on France. Only under German pressure did Francis Joseph agree to go to war with Russia on 6 August. To the Emperor's dismay the tightening of the bonds between the entente partners led Great Britain to join France in declaring war on Austria-Hungary on 12–13 August, even though there was little sympathy for Serbia in London and no clash of interests between Vienna and the Western Powers. Both Italy and Roumania stayed neutral, insisting that their treaty commitments obliged them to support Germany and Austria-Hungary only if these empires were the victims of aggression. Early in November 1914 the Ottoman Empire entered the war on the side of the Central Powers, although as a junior partner – or client – of Germany rather than of Austria-Hungary.

By temperament and conviction Francis Joseph always regarded himself as a soldier. Age, however, necessarily diminished his exercise of military authority: 'if only *I* could have been with my army', he was to remark to Field Marshal von Mackensen in the last year of his life. Since the Emperor believed that a member of the dynasty should lead his troops into battle, he appointed as commander-in-chief, Archduke Frederick, the 58-year old nephew of Archduke Albrecht. Two other Habsburg Archdukes, Eugen and Joseph, also held the rank of Field Marshal, while the heir to the throne, Archduke Charles, gained military experience as an itinerant staff-officer, his soldiering hampered by strict orders from the Emperor that he should not be posted to any sector where his life would be in danger. Effective leadership of the army was entrusted to the Chief of the General Staff, Conrad von Hötzendorf, an over-rated strategist with an obsessive desire to take the offensive. Supreme army headquarters (AOK) were established by Conrad in the fortress of Przemysl. At Schönbrunn the Emperor retained a skeleton military chancellery, which was still headed (after twenty-five years in the post) by General Alfred Bolfras. Apart from the narrowly bureaucratic routine of administration, there was little for Bolfras or the Emperor to do, except to study and assess reports from the two battle fronts, in Serbia and Galicia.

They made sorry reading. As Francis Ferdinand had repeatedly warned, the *k-und-k Armee* lagged behind the armies of the other great continental powers; it was especially weak in artillery. Moreover Conrad gravely bungled his original war plans: on 25 July he ordered maximum concentration against Serbia, even though he had assured his German allies that, in the event of war with Russia, most troops would be sent to Galicia and, on 1 August, this promise was repeated by Francis Joseph in a personal message to William II. The effect of Conrad's 'adjustment' to the war plans was to deprive both fronts of the Second Army in the first weeks of the war: the twelve infantry divisions of the Army were already heading southwards for the Danube when, on 31 July, Conrad sought to recall them for service in Galicia, an about-turn rightly described by the railways section of the General Staff at the time as 'causing endless complications'. Eventually six divisions of the Second Army arrived on the north-eastern frontier to help cover Lemberg (Lvov), the fourth largest city in the Monarchy and capital of Galicia; the other six divisions were engaged in the south, some 600 miles away, probing Serbian defences along the River Sava. General Potiorek, now field commander of the Austro-Hungarian forces in the Balkan sector, originally hoped to present a defeated Serbia to Francis Joseph as a birthday gift on 18 August. By then, however, his troops were no longer making progress against the Serbs and within a few days he was forced to pull every division back across the frontier. In Galicia initial successes by the First Army and the

Fourth Army were soon offset by three weeks of heavy losses in the battle of Lemberg, which on 3 September fell to the Russians.

For the 'old gentleman' in Schönbrunn the news from the battle fronts came like some nightmare recollection from a past he would rather have forgotten. He was bitterly pessimistic, even from the earliest days. When, on 17 August, the Archduchess Zita spoke enthusiastically to him of hopeful reports from the River Bug he replied, cynically, 'My wars have always begun with victories only to finish in defeats. And this time it will be even worse and they will say of me, "He is old and cannot cope any longer". The revolutions will break out and it will be the end'. Next day he received a telegram of birthday congratulations in French from the Roumanian chief-of-staff who hoped he 'will bear up against the shocks inherent to all wars, even the happiest ones'. 'Well meant, of course,' Francis Joseph commented, 'But is it going to be a happy war for us? Already all the signs seem to point the other way'.

Experience, on the other hand, emphasized the need for patience. Five days after the shock fall of Lemberg the Emperor sent a warning to Archduke Frederick: he should not punish defeated senior officers too severely 'because today's unlucky commander may well be victorious tomorrow'. Yet, as winter succeeded autumn, it became clear that his armies were locked in disastrous campaigns in the south and the east. Belgrade fell on the sixty-sixth anniversary of Francis Joseph's accession, but the city was recaptured by the Serbs eleven days later as Putnik mounted a counter-offensive which threw the invaders back across the frontier for a second time. In Galicia a Russian advance on Cracow was brought to a halt and in the Bukovina Czernowitz was recaptured, but these successes were gained only at enormous cost. By the end of the year four-fifths of the pre-war trained infantry in the Austro-Hungarian army lay dead, or were recovering from wounds, or were held captive by the Russians.

During these grim months the Emperor rarely moved outside Schönbrunn. For security purposes the parkland close to the palace had been closed to the public and the Viennese saw so little of their sovereign that there were rumours he was dead or totally senile. In late September he visited, on separate occasions, hospitals hastily set up at the Augarten and within the inner city at the Fichtegasse. He was not greatly concerned over changes which strengthened the hands of military authorities at the expense of the civil courts; and he accepted the establishment of 'military zones' where the army exercised virtually all administrative powers. Not all these 'military zones' were near the front line; they included districts in Silesia and north-eastern Moravia where the greatest danger came not from invaders a hundred miles away but from 'unpatriotic' dissident demonstrators. Yet, though the Emperor was unconcerned over such matters, he was deeply conscious of the impact of war on his least fortunate subjects. The fighting in the East was ravaging one of the Monarchy's richest granaries, making industrialized Austria more and more dependent on food from Hungary. At the same time, fear of the Russian invader had forced many Jews in Galicia to flee westwards and seek safety in the capital, a migration which caused Mayor Richard Weiskirchner to propose that the refugees should be moved to camps in Moravia. The Emperor, however, was adamant: 'If Vienna has no more room for refugees', he told Weiskirchner, 'I shall make Schönbrunn available for my Jewish subjects'. Nothing further was said of camps in Moravia.

Christmas, Francis Joseph remarked to Katharina Schratt with typical simplicity, was a wretched occasion that year, for he could not help thinking of the 'jolly' days of old. Yet it was not only nostalgia which saddened him. He was convinced that the war was going to spread: soon, he told Count Paar, 'Italy will join our enemies', setting an example for Roumania to follow. Even in the first week of the war the Italians had sought cession of the Trentino as compensation for Austria-Hungary's anticipated expansion in the Balkans, a request disdainfully rejected in Vienna. By the coming of the new year Sonnino, Italy's foreign minister, was seeking Istria as well as the Trentino. Berchtold recommended concessions in order to prevent Sonnino striking a bargain with the Entente allies, but Francis Joseph and Conrad were united in their refusal to 'buy off' Italy. The Emperor had reverted to the attitude he assumed in early 1866 when, as Bismarck drew a tighter noose around the Monarchy, he would not consider handing over Venetia so as to save his army from a two-front war. In despair Berchtold resigned office on 11 January 1915, and went on active service as a staff-captain. On 8 March, for the last time, Francis Joseph presided over a ministerial council, summoned to discuss the threat from Italy; he backed Berchtold's successor, István Burian, in refusing to surrender 'one square metre'. Sonnino followed his earlier inclination of striking a bargain with London, Paris and St Petersburg. The secret Treaty of London of 26 April 1915 offered Italy such great gains in the Trentino, along the Adriatic and in Asia Minor that, a month later, Sonnino persuaded King Victor Emmanuel III to go to war with Austria-Hungary. The *k-und-k Armee* was thus given a third front to defend from invasion; and the Emperor focussed weary eyes on maps of the Dolomites, the Venetian plains and the head of the Adriatic: it was more natural to be fighting Italians than Russians. Rivers and mountain contours were all too familiar to him, though there were railway junctions where he had changed horses in earlier years and the Quadrilateral was now in enemy hands. Yet two fortresses, Peschiera and Verona, were within thirty miles of the Austrian frontier and marked on the map beyond them were the names of Custozza (for victory) and Villafranca (for peace).

Archduchess Zita, who with her two children had moved into Schönbrunn when her husband Charles went to the wars, found Francis Joseph increasingly looking back to the early years of the reign. Many years later she recalled that 'he confessed to a feeling that, ever since 1848, the Empire was like a volcano which was uneasily sleeping'. By the spring of 1915 there were ominous signs of imminent eruption. The civil authorities in Prague suspected the existence of an extensive network of secret societies linked with exiles in the West and, in particular with Masaryk, by now a dedicated antagonist of the Habsburgs. The Russians, too, were exploiting Czech and Ruthene dissidence. Propaganda leaflets had been circulating in Bohemia and Moravia throughout the winter and in mid-April the Emperor learnt with dismay that almost all the officers and men in the 28th Prague Infantry Regiment had gone over to the enemy during a battle around the village of Stebnicka Huta at the beginning of the month. There was a steady flow of deserters from Slav units fighting in the Carpathians that spring.

But the volcano did not erupt after all. Militarily the summer of 1915 held out some prospect of final victory. The Italians, whom London and Paris hoped would open up a new front of major strategic significance, made scant impact on the war: in two thrusts towards the River Isonzo they gained little territory, for the Austrian defences were sound. By contrast, an offensive launched in Galicia by the German and Austro-Hungarian armies on 2 May was so successful that in ten weeks the Russians were forced to evacuate almost all the Habsburg lands gained over the previous eleven months. The good news from the East was a tonic to morale in the capital. On 24 June 1915 Francis Joseph came out on to the palace balcony at Schönbrunn to acknowledge cheers from a crowd celebrating the re-capture of Lemberg: press photographs show the Emperor looking happily down on a throng of civilians, dressed as if about to enjoy a summer's day in the Prater, while army officers mingle with them in service uniform: sharing the balcony with the Emperor are Mayor Weiskirchner and Archduchess Zita who holds aloft her two-year-old son Otto, next in line of succession to his father as heir to his great-great uncle's throne.

Later that year came more news of victory. In the third week of October Bulgaria entered the war on the side of the Central Powers and, by the end of November, German, Austro-Hungarian and Bulgarian armies had overrun Serbia, thus fulfilling Vienna's original war aim. Francis Joseph knew, however, that these triumphs, in the East and the Balkans, had been achieved only with German collaboration and under German leadership. An attempt by Conrad to boost Austro-Hungarian pride by gaining a further victory against the Russians in a 'solo' campaign – the *Schwarzgelbe* autumn offensive – ended in disaster on 14 October: the AOK reported 130,000 casualties; significantly, another 100,000 men were taken prisoner, though it is impossible to establish how many defected voluntarily. And to add to the winter's gloom there had been a poor harvest in Hungary. It was enough to feed the kingdom but not to supply regions of the Monarchy already denied Galician wheat; and the Austrian provinces were made dependent on Germany for bread.

The Emperor realized earlier than his ministers the significance of these events: military necessity and economic restraint were robbing the Monarchy of all independence of action. There was a genuine danger that Austria-Hungary might soon become tied as closely to Germany as Bavaria to the North German Confederation under Bismarck's primacy in the four years separating Sadowa from Sedan. This new, satellite status for the Monarchy was first shown clearly in a hardening of attitude in Berlin against earlier proposals from Vienna for a Habsburg solution of the Polish Question. As late as January 1916 a meeting of the council of ministers, discussing the Monarchy's war aims, still assumed that, when the Tsar's Empire collapsed, most of Russian Poland would be united with pre-war Austrian Galicia in a Catholic Polish Kingdom, incorporated in the Dual Monarchy. Such hopes were soon frustrated by Germany's frankly annexationist programme in the East and over the following ten months Francis Joseph was forced to agree to plans for the establishment of an 'independent' Polish kingdom, administered by Prussians though protected by a Hohenzollern-Habsburg condominium.

Two brief successes in January 1916 bolstered Conrad's diminishing authority in Vienna: Montenegro was overrun and a firm foothold established in northern Albania; and in the Bukovina the Austrians could claim a defensive victory when a Russian attack was repulsed with heavy enemy losses. Conrad, always an Italophobe, now argued that the Monarchy stood to gain more in Italy (where there would be no competition from German interests) than in the East. Accordingly he gained hesitant support from the Emperor for a spring offensive in Trentino, designed to strike southwards to the plain of Vicenza and cut off the main Italian armies concentrated between the rivers Tagliamento and Isonzo. Nine experienced divisions were taken out of the line in Galicia and the Bukovina and transported across the Monarchy in early March for concentration in the Sugana valley, at the head of the railway route from Trent to Padua.

Such movement of men and equipment could not be kept secret. The Italian High Command knew of the military build up as early as 22 March. Russian intelligence, too, discovered that élite troops were no longer facing the South-West Army Group on the River Dniester, information of great interest to their staff planners and at once invalidating Conrad's assurance to Francis Joseph that he had no cause for worry over the re-deployment of his army. Heavy snowfalls made Conrad postpone his much-advertised offensive until 15 May. At first all seemed to go well. A massive concentration of heavy guns blasted a path ahead for the best troops remaining in Francis Joseph's army. Within a fortnight the gunners were training their sights on Italian positions in the last foothills before the open plain. But there, on 2 June, the advance ground to a halt. The artillery had only enough shells left for a few days of action. Before fresh supplies of ammunition could complete the journey down a single track railway through the mountains, the Italian commander, Marshal Cadorna, had re-deployed half a million men for a counter-offensive which by 1 July won back much of the lost ground. More dramatically, on the night of 4 June, Conrad's headquarters heard that the Russians had launched a great offensive, stretching from the Pripet Marshes southwards to the Bukovina and striking at that weakened sector of the Front over which the Emperor expressed the deepest concern. Conrad had committed the greatest military blunder of any Austrian commander since Gyulai abandoned Milan after the battle of Magenta. In its consequences his decision to withdraw nine divisions from the Eastern Front surpassed his folly in having left the Second Army divided and train-bound during the first weeks of war. A Crown Council meeting in Vienna on 29 June, showed the hostility of the ministers towards the Chief-of-Staff. Remarkably, however, Conrad remained at his post until after Francis Joseph's death. He survived, not because he retained his sovereign's confidence, but because the Emperor was too old and too out of touch with the officer corps to find a successor.

The Russian assault in Galicia and the Bukovina – 'Brusilov's Offensive', as it is remembered in history – almost brought Austria-Hungary to final defeat. Within a month Brusilov had established a corridor 200 miles wide and in places 60 miles deep, bringing the Russians back to the eastern slopes of the Carpathians before, in September, the offensive lost its momentum. The change of fortune tempted Roumania into the war in August, fighting in Latin solidarity with Italy and France against the Central Powers who had been her allies for so many years during the long peace. Briefly Roumanian troops invaded Transylvania, penetrating some fifty miles across the frontier and threatening an advance into the Hungarian Plain. But, once again, all was reversed by German intervention.

By the late autumn, order was restored on the Eastern Front: General Falkenhayn mopped up the Roumanian units that had so rashly entered Transylvania; Field Marshal von Mackensen struck swiftly northwards from Bulgaria to the heart of the Roumanian kingdom. Francis Joseph admired Mackensen as a strategist and respected him; it is probable he would have accepted him as Conrad's successor. As it was, the Emperor agreed on 6 September to a unified command for the Central Powers with ultimate military authority entrusted to Hindenburg and Ludendorff.

Though desperately tired by now, Francis Joseph tried to follow in detail all the changing fortunes of war and its impact on his peoples. He may have suspected that the Austrian prime minister, Count Stürgkh, was concealing from him the deep distress in the capital, the lack of bread and milk and potatoes. From Katharina Schratt he knew that food supplies were uncertain and that distribution was far from perfect. A curious natural disaster led him to unburden his mind to his military aide, Baron von Margutti. At the beginning of July, with bad news coming constantly from the Eastern and the Italian Fronts a whirlwind swept through the town of Wiener Neustadt causing havoc to several military establishments, the airfield and factories. At once Francis Joseph sent Margutti to the town, with orders to give him a detailed report that evening.

On his return, however, Margutti found the Emperor with more on his mind to discuss than the damage in Wiener Neustadt. He seems to have treated the whirlwind as an omen, and he found relief in discussing the day-to-day problems of the Monarchy with a brother officer, thirty-nine years his junior. 'Things are going badly with us', he said in the end, looking deeply depressed, 'perhaps even worse than we suspect. A starving people cannot put up with much more. Whether and how we get through the coming winter remains to be seen. But I am determined to call a halt to the war next spring. I will not let us drift into irretrievable rack and ruin'. To Katharina Schratt the Emperor spoke, too, of his determination to seek peace before it was too late to hold the Empire together. Yet did he believe he would still possess the freedom of action within the alliance to impose peace? Above all, did he really believe he had the time and strength to check the drift into ruin? For the Emperor who spoke with such certainty to Margutti was only five weeks away from his eighty-sixth birthday.

Chapter 21

SCHÖNBRUNN 1916

In the late afternoon of 21 October 1916 Emperor Francis Joseph received the first reports of yet another violent death, though not on this occasion in his own family. Shortly before half-past two Friedrich Adler, who was the son of the veteran socialist leader, had gone up to Count Stürgkh's table at the Hotel Meissel-und-Schadn in Vienna's Neuermarkt as the prime minister was finishing lunch and fired three shots from a revolver at his head, killing him instantly. 'Down with absolutism! We want peace!', Adler shouted out before being seized and handed over to the police by another diner in the restaurant, Franz Aehrenthal, brother of the late foreign minister. Friedrich Adler – in personal life the gentlest of men – had every intention of being arrested and, at his trial, securing the widest possible publicity for his views.

The Emperor was shocked by the news. He did not hold Karl Stürgkh in particular esteem: the Count was a pedantic bachelor in his late fifties, with nothing to mark him off from other senior servants of the state except his height, for he was 2 metres tall (6 feet 7 inches). What troubled the Emperor was that a young, well-known intellectual should have felt the need to assassinate a minister of such little personal significance. He began to wonder if his darkest fear was now an imminent possibility. Were 'the things', of which he had spoken to Margutti, much worse than he suspected? Was Adler releasing the blind fury of anarchy? Would revolution paralyse the Monarchy while his armies were at war? Desperately Francis Joseph sought reassurance from his ministers. They convinced him that poor Stürgkh's chief failing was his refusal to contemplate the recall of parliament, thereby denying the political opposition a forum to express doubts over the conduct of the war; he had even boasted of having put the Reichsrat to good use at last – as a hospital. His murder was a terrible protest against rule by decree, as permitted by the notorious 'Article XIV' of the 1867 Constitution. In the evening the Emperor turned to the ablest political manipulator among Stürgkh's immediate predecessors, Ernst von Koerber, who had shown how to strike bargains between Germans and Slavs a dozen years back. Koerber was not, like Tisza in Hungary, a skilled parliamentarian but he would clear the hospital beds from the chamber and pump a little oxygen into Austria's constitutional life.

Winter came early that year over most of central Europe: at Schönbrunn there were damp days in late October, and a bitter wind. With the turn of the month, the first snow clouds swept in from the Marchfeld. It was a fortnight before Koerber had completed his talks with party leaders from the Reichsrat elected in 1911, and in the palace long political discussions, following each morning's assessment of reports from AOK and individual field commanders, left the Emperor exhausted. On his desk each day there was a mass of paperwork, including detailed proposals for an independent Polish kingdom and a new autonomous status for Galicia. It is probable, too, that there were dark moments for him in his inner life for, as earlier letters show, Francis Joseph always observed one solemn occasion in this fortnight – All Souls Day – in a mood of intense spiritual contrition, his thoughts deeply concerned with the 'departed ones', especially Rudolf and Elizabeth. Not surprisingly, under the shock, strain and introspection of these long wintry weeks his health began to fail once more. Persistent bronchitis in the last days of October led to fits of coughing, followed by a fever on 6 November and intense weariness. Dr Kerzl recognized similar symptoms to the post-Easter illnesses of 1911 and 1914. By the end of the week there was little doubt that the Emperor was suffering from pneumonia. On the afternoon of Saturday, 11 November, a warning telegram was sent to the heir to the throne who was in eastern Saxony, after visiting Hindenburg's headquarters on the Eastern Front. By Sunday evening Archduke Charles was at Schönbrunn, only to find the Emperor in much better health. As in 1914, he seemed to be shaking off the fever. On Wednesday the improvement was so marked that his daughters hesitated over coming to Schönbrunn in case the gathering of the family should lower their father's will to fight. But Wednesday's gleam of hope was too feeble to throw a clear light forward. His temperature began to climb again on Friday night and Dr Kerzl sought urgent advice from pulmonary specialists in Vienna's famous hospitals.

Sunday, 19 November, was the festival of St Elizabeth of Hungary, Sisi's patron saint. Sixty-three years ago that day a special envoy from Vienna had arrived in Munich with a diamond brooch, shaped like a bouquet, as a gift from Francis Joseph to the princess he was to marry in the spring; and other presents followed on each St Elizabeth's Day of her life. This year her widowed husband heard Mass in his study, for he was not well enough to go down to the chapel. In the afternoon Katharina Schratt came to visit him from Hietzing, where she presided over a convalescent home for officers wounded at the Front. The 'dear good friend' talked of the past, and especially of the Empress. At times she found Francis Joseph too weak to follow her conversation or reply to her. As she left for the short walk back to her villa, Dr Kerzl asked her not to come back on Monday, as the Emperor needed a day of complete rest. By now the wings of death cast lengthening shadows on Schönbrunn.

Archduchess Marie Valerie was at the palace, intent on ensuring that her father received the Church's full spiritual ministrations. Also with him was his granddaughter, Erzsi, the 36-year old Princess von Windischgraetz, whose company had cheered him in the lonely years after Mayerling and Geneva. He refused to be confined to bed: he coughed less if he sat upright, he said. Despite Kerzl's pleas for rest and quiet, the Emperor was determined to continue with his daily tasks. Archduke Charles and Archduchess Zita visited Francis Joseph's study shortly before midday on Tuesday, causing him passing concern because he had no opportunity to put on his military tunic before the Archduchess entered the room; he remained a stickler over conventions of dress. He commented on good reports he had received from the Roumanian Front, but his visitors were surprised to find him studying recruitment papers, even though his body temperature was 102°F (normal 98.4F), or 39.5C (normal 37°C). The work, however, was too much for him. In the early evening he admitted feeling extremely ill and he was persuaded to allow his valet, Eugen Ketterl, to help him to bed. But there was, he thought, much paperwork which still required his scrutiny and signature; perhaps it could wait for one more day. 'Has Your Majesty any further orders?', Ketterl asked before withdrawing. '*Morgen früh um halb vier Uhr*', a failing voice replied with indomitable insistence ('Tomorrow morning, at half past four').

They were not, however, his last words. As Ketterl helped him sip some tea, the Emperor faintly mumbled one final question, 'Why must it be just now?' He was barely conscious when a Court chaplain administered the rite of extreme unction. Half an hour later a fit of coughing shook the frail body, and then all was silent. Emperor-King Francis Joseph I died at five minutes past nine in the evening of 21 October 1916, only one long corridor and eighty-six years from the room in which he was born.

Joseph Redlich, entering up his journal out at Grinzing, could see no signs of sorrow for the deceased nor of joy in welcoming his successor: 'A deep tiredness, akin to apathy, hovers over Vienna', he wrote. Every day brought tidings of death to families in the city and there were fears for food and fuel supplies as the third winter of war tightened its grip on a hungry people. But they mourned the passing of 'the old gentleman', nevertheless. The Emperor's loyal subjects filed out to Schönbrunn, where for three days his body lay in simple state. On the Monday after his death they stood silently in streets covered with thin snow as eight black horses with trim black plumes between their ears hauled the massive funeral hearse into Vienna to rest, in full magnificence, in the Hofburg chapel.

Court ceremonial prescribed that a sovereign's body should not be buried until nine days after his death and Montenuovo, the Lord Chamberlain, was there to ensure that what was hallowed by tradition should be observed, even under the exigencies of war. A peace time funeral would have brought Europe's crowned heads to Vienna and won for Francis Joseph more charitable obituaries than the French and British Press chose to publish that November: in London Northcliffe's *Weekly Dispatch* even rebuked Fr Bernard Vaughan (brother of the late Cardinal-Archbishop) for praying for the soul of an enemy emperor at Mass in Westminster Cathedral. Germany's ruler, William II, came to Vienna on 28 November and joined the new Emperor Charles in prayer beside the bier, but he did not remain in the city for the final obsequies two days later.

Few troops could parade on 30 November, the day of the funeral, for the Imperial and Royal Army was heavily engaged on three battle fronts. Apart from the Life Guards detailed to escort the hearse, there was only a single battalion of infantry in the city. It was therefore decided, that in the absence of the army, the people of the imperial capital should have one last opportunity to salute the sovereign who had re-shaped the city's outer form. Instead of conveying the coffin directly from the Hofburg chapel to the cathedral, the great hearse followed a route which recalled, on that grey November afternoon, finer days of past pageantry. From the Hofburg the funeral procession moved out through the Burgtor, where Francis Joseph had stood on *Makart-Festzug* in 1879, turned left in front of the statue of Maria Theresa he had unveiled, passed the Opera House, crossed the innermost side of the Schwarzenbergplatz, where he had taken the salute at the Leipzig centenary, and completed a half-circuit of the Ringstrasse, which he had opened with Elizabeth beside him on May Day in 1865. At last the procession turned up the Rotenturmstrasse to the metropolitan cathedral of St Stephen for a final blessing from Cardinal-Archbishop Piffe. After the short service in the cathedral Emperor Charles, Empress Zita and Crown Prince Otto were joined by three kings – Ludwig III of Bavaria; Frederick Augustus of Saxony; Ferdinand of Bulgaria – to follow on foot the funeral chariot as it moved slowly from the cathedral by way of the Graben and the streets of the inner city to the

Kapuzinergruft, the crypt of the Capuchin Church in the Neuermarkt, where more than 140 members of the dynasty were entombed in the imperial vault. Tradition required Montenuovo, as Lord Chamberlain, to knock on the closed door of the crypt, which a Capuchin monk refused to open so long as Montenuovo craved admission for the Emperor-King's body, proclaiming Francis Joseph's full sovereign dignitaries on the first occasion and his more compact title of Emperor-King on the second. Only at the third knocking ceremony, when dynastic pretensions were laid aside and entry to the crypt sought for 'Francis Joseph, a poor sinner who begs God for mercy', did the great door swing open and pall-bearers carry the coffin to rest between the tombs of the Empress Elizabeth and Crown Prince Rudolf.

This final humbling moment of any Habsburg interment has always attracted most comment, and Montenuovo made certain that the age-old ritual was duly fulfilled. Yet the 'poor sinner' had ruled the Monarchy longer than any predecessor and in one respect Francis Joseph's obsequies acknowledged the unique character of the reign. For they did not end with the departure of the last mourners up the stairs from the imperial crypt. The 68th anniversary of his accession at Olmütz fell on 2 December 1916, just two days after the funeral, and a final Solemn Requiem was said in the Hofburg chapel, attended by the imperial family and the Court dignitaries. Only then did his subjects accept that the reign of Francis Joseph I was at an end and an era of Europe's history drawing to a close. Few could remember any other sovereign at the head of affairs in Vienna.

Chapter 22

INTO HISTORY

Within two years of Francis Joseph's death the Dual Monarchy became a cast-off relic of history. The good intentions of Emperor Charles – his proposals for a federalist restructuring of his realm and, in particular, his desire for an early negotiated peace – were frustrated by the sheer weight of powerful interests massed against their attainment. Austria-Hungary was so closely integrated militarily with Germany that Vienna lost all independent diplomatic options. Charles was to see his armies gain striking victories, when backed by Germany, on the Italian Front and against Russia. But after August 1918, when the allies and their American associates broke the German army in the West, Hindenburg and Ludendorff could spare neither men nor material for other theatres of war: General Franchet d'Espérey's multinational army in Salonika knocked out Bulgaria and began to advance from Macedonia into Serbia and Hungary; the Italians regained the military initiative along the River Piave. The governments in Vienna and Budapest had no answer to the sustained propaganda of their enemies in favour of self-determination and of new frontiers drawn 'along clearly recognizable lines of nationality'. The volcano of fanaticism, which Francis Joseph had feared since 1848, finally erupted almost seventy years to the day after the Habsburg Court found refuge from revolution at Olmütz.

On 11 November 1918 Emperor Charles signed at Schönbrunn a message to his peoples renouncing all participation in the affairs of state. He never abdicated, but retired with the Empress and their children to the shooting-lodge of Eckartsau, in the Marchfeld to the north-east of the capital; in March 1919 the family crossed into Switzerland. Members of the dynasty were excluded from Austria by law unless they gave a declaration of loyalty to the republic. Twice in 1921 Emperor-King Charles tried to regain his Hungarian throne from Admiral Nicholas Horthy, who in 1920 had been elected Regent by parliament in Budapest; he was defeated, in part by the hostility of Hungary's neighbours, but also by Horthy's reluctance to hand authority back to his King. Tragically, in the following spring, the exiled Emperor contracted pneumonia on Madeira and died on 1 April 1922, four months short of his thirty-fifth birthday. His eldest son, Archduke Otto (born in November 1912) became claimant to his titles.

By the time of Charles's death the lands he had inherited from Francis Joseph were shared out between seven independent states: the new republic of Czechoslovakia; a resurrected Poland; the kingdoms of Italy, Roumania and 'of the Serbs, Croats and Slovenes' (not called Yugoslavia officially until 1929); a kingdom of Hungary, reduced to a third of its area; and a rump republic of 'German' Austria, of which more than a quarter of the population lived in Vienna. In most successor states there were no regrets at the passing of the Monarchy: Habsburg properties were confiscated; insignia torn down. Yet a few officers of the Imperial and Royal Army remained attached to the dynasty, from both sentiment and a deep mistrust of nationalism. Thus the war hero Colonel Anton Lehar, younger brother of the composer Franz Lehar, could list Czechs, Hungarians, and German-Austrians among his immediate ancestors and denied that he possessed any single nationality: he was, he declared in 1921, a 'Habsburg subject'. Such loyalty made Colonel Lehar ready to stage-manage Charles's abortive bids to recover his crown in Budapest.

Sentiments elsewhere were shaped by different considerations. The reordering of Europe after the war brought unexpected hardship to many families in Vienna, especially those dependent on Habsburg state pensions or wage-earners made redundant when the imperial civil service withered away. New frontier barriers led to food shortages and carefully invested savings were hit by runaway inflation, with the cost of living multiplying twenty times between Christmas 1921 and Christmas 1922. Inevitably there was nostalgia for Francis Joseph's golden age of peace and security, back beyond the turn of the century. There were critics who argued that the Emperor's rigid conservatism, and especially his retention of the 1867 settlement virtually unchanged, had brought the Monarchy to disaster. But a spate of memoirs emphasized the good qualities of the 'old gentleman' at Schönbrunn – the compassion which he disciplined his emotions to conceal, choosing to appear callously indifferent rather than risk diminishing the grandeur of imperial sovereignty; the simplicity of his personal tastes and conduct; the sense of duty, which bound him to his desk as he sought expedient ways of guiding his subjects towards enlightened democracy. Margutti's detailed reminiscences of the Emperor's later years went on sale as early as the summer of 1921; they confirmed the widespread belief that he 'had long made the preservation of peace his sacred duty' and emphasized how 'horrified' he had been at his inability to control events in the wake of the Sarajevo murders. This was what a chastened generation, wistfully regretting a lost youth, wished to hear.

There was no orchestrated campaign reviling Francis Joseph. On the other hand, while respecting the person of the Emperor, it became fashionable to pour scorn on the structure of Imperial and Royal institutions. Robert Musil's novel *Der Mann ohne Eigenschaften* (The Man without Qualities), of which the first volume appeared in 1930, introduced the intellectuals of central Europe to 'Kakanien', an ironic name for the Dual Monarchy, based on the k.u.k (*kaiserlich und königlich*) abbreviation in common usage during the Ausgleich era. Musil's incomplete epic was a satirical portrayal of life in Vienna on the eve of the First World War. The book's anti-hero, Ulrich, is in 1913 appointed secretary of a committee given five years to prepare accession celebrations for Francis Joseph (seventieth anniversary) and William II (thirtieth anniversary). The main characters are meretricious social climbers and Kakanien an Empire kept in being only from force of habit, but Musil – an army captain who had distinguished himself on the Italian Front – stopped short of making the Emperor a figure of ridicule. Just as Queen Victoria's biographer Lytton Strachey blunted his iconoclastic pen in a growing respect for his subject, so Robert Musil became captivated by Francis Joseph's prestige in his later years. Nor was Musil the only writer to succumb to nostalgia for Imperial Austria. Joseph Roth, too, attacked the shallow decadence of Habsburg society throughout much of Francis Joseph's reign, but he believed its false values were held in check by the authoritative father figure at Schönbrunn. Roth went further than Musil in open admiration of the Emperor: Francis Joseph's sense of honour and soldierly obligations relieve the gloom of *Radetzkymarsch*, published in 1932; and he is, in effect, idolized in two of Roth's later novels, *Die Büste des Kaisers* and *Die Kapuzinergruft*.

The Emperor's younger daughter Archduchess Marie Valerie, who had pledged loyalty to the republic and settled in Lower Austria, did not live to see her father's memory enshrined in bitter-sweet legend: she died at Wallsee in September 1924. Her sister, Archduchess Gisela, remained in Bavaria, dying in Munich in July 1932, a fortnight after her seventy-sixth birthday. Francis Joseph's children were therefore spared the spectacle of Hitler's ascendancy over the German lands, Schönerer-ism run hideously rampant. Katharina Schratt, however, was in Vienna at the time of the Anschluss, defiantly ordering the blinds of her windows overlooking the Kartnerring to be kept closed on the day Hitler entered the city: she died in April 1940 at eighty-six, thus completing a span of life four months longer than the Emperor's. Two of his great-nephews – the tragic sons of Francis Ferdinand and Sophie Chotek – were sent to Nazi concentration camps; both survived, though neither lived to reach the age of sixty. Crown Prince Rudolf's widow, Stephanie (Princess Lonjay), settled with her second husband on his estate at Oroszvar, in western Hungary, until forced to flee from the advancing Red Army; they found sanctuary near Györ, in the Benedictine abbey of Pannonhalma, where Stephanie died in August 1945. Rudolf and Stephanie's daughter, the Emperor's favourite grandchild 'Erszi', divorced Prince Otto von Windischgraetz in 1924 and made her home in the Hutteldorf district of Vienna. There, in May 1948, she married Leopold Petznek, a socialist who served as Speaker of the lower chamber of parliament; she died at Hutteldorf in March 1963, in her eightieth year.

During the last quarter of her life Elizabeth Petznek saw her grandfather's capital both devastated and magnificently rebuilt. Five days of intensive fighting in April 1945 was followed by ten years of Four Power occupation, for the last allied troops did not pull out of Austria until October 1955. By the end of the decade, however, visitors flocked to Vienna in greater numbers than ever before, and the restored showplaces of Francis Joseph's reign – the Opera House, the Burgtheater, the magnificent facades along the Ringstrasse – were ready to welcome the tourist invasion which came with cheaper and speedier ways of travel. In 1906 a British traveller, Colonel Barry, had declared that no one could cross the inner square of the Hofburg 'without the heart for a moment standing still at the salute: for behind yonder windows lives the man who, as husband, father, emperor, presents to the world the noblest instance of a modern martyrdom'. Later sentiment, of course, does not brim over so readily with hyperbole, and if today's tourists glance up at the window from which Francis Joseph would catch a glimpse of his 'dear friend' on her way to Mass, they will find there only the empty reflection of car roofs from the courtyard below. But, though denied a live Habsburg peepshow, visitors to the Hofburg or Schönbrunn rarely fail to sense the aura of spacious splendour in the apartments through which they trail; even the Kaiservilla at Bad Ischl preserves an impression of majesty relaxed in tranquillity.

More than once, an anniversary or solemn occasion has conjured up a passing image from the Habsburg era. In 1982, for example, the exiled Empress Zita, who had spent long days with Francis Joseph during the war, was allowed to make three visits to Austria after sixty-three years abroad – and at the age of ninety. Tens of thousands of well-wishers greeted her in the capital after she attended a packed service of thanksgiving in St Stephen's Cathedral. When, seven years later, the Empress died from pneumonia in Switzerland, her body was brought to Vienna for a semi-state funeral on 1 April 1989. The coffin was conveyed from

St Stephen's to the Capuchin Church on Francis Joseph's massive funeral hearse, and the threefold ritual supplication for admitting the body of a 'poor sinner' to the crypt was heard for the first time in the republic. Then, the procession over, the hearse was taken back to Schönbrunn and trundled into the Wagenburg – the coach museum next to the palace – to go on show again as an artefact of history. Does contemporary Austria at times appropriate the spectacle of Francis Joseph's Empire to enhance its sense of national identity? At all events, though Maria Theresa may be the most respected of Habsburg monarchs, Francis Joseph continues to attract more personal sympathy than any other ruler in continental Europe since the Napoleonic upheavals. His cult matches the widespread appeal of Queen Victoria within Great Britain.

The Emperor would have been surprised at the durability of the legend, for he was a modest man, aware of his shortcomings. Cynics might say his name commands respect in today's Vienna because he remains good business (as he was in towns across the Monarchy throughout his later years). Yet there are better reasons than commercial gratification for honouring Francis Joseph's memory. Long experience of the eleven peoples grouped together under his rule gave him a deeper feeling for the dynasty's supranational mission than his critics admit. Margutti, serving as a Boswell to his Samuel Johnson, made notes of the table talk at breakfast in Gödöllö on an autumn morning in 1904: 'The Monarchy is not an artificial creation but an organic body', Francis Joseph claimed, 'It is a place of refuge, an asylum for all those fragmented nations scattered over central Europe who, if left to their own resources would lead a pitiful existence, becoming the playthings of more powerful neighbours'. Ninety years later, it is the eleven peoples who are fragmented and seek asylum.

NOTES AND SOURCES

Unless otherwise stated works in English are published in London. FJ throughout Notes and Sources stands for Francis Joseph.

Abbreviations of titles:

AHY: Austrian History Yearbook (Rice University, Texas, 1965–   )

Bourgoing: J. de Bourgoing (ed.) *Briefe Kaiser Franz Joseph an Frau Katharina Schratt* (Vienna, 1949)

Conrad: F. Conrad von Hötzendorf, *Aus meiner Dienstzeit 1906–1918* (Vienna, Berlin, 1921–25)

Corti, *Kind.*: E.C. Corti, *Von Kind bis Kaiser* (Graz, 1950)

Corti, *Mensch.*: E.C. Corti, *Mensch und Herrscher* (Graz, 1952)

Corti and Sokol: E.C. Corti and H. Sokol, *Der Alte Kaiser* (Graz, 1955)

Ernst: Otto Ernst, *FJ I in seinen Briefen* (Vienna, 1924)

FO: Foreign Office Papers in Public Record Office, Kew.

G-H: E. Glaise von Horstenau, *Franz Joseph Weggefährte. Das Leben des Generalstabchefs Grafen Beck* (Zurich, Leipzig, Vienna 1930)

GP: J. Lepsius, et al.: *Die Grosse-Politik der Europäischen Kabinette* (Berlin, 1922–27)

Ham. *El.*: Brigitte Hamann, *Elisabeth, Kaiserin wider Willen* (Vienna and Munich 1982)

Ham. *Rud.*: Brigitte Hamann, *Rudolf-Kronprinz und Rebell*, Revised paperback edition (Munich 1991)

Ham. *Schr.*: Brigitte Hamann (ed.), *Meine liebe, gute Freundin! Die Briefe Kaiser FJs an Katharina Schratt* (Vienna, 1992)

HHSA: Haus-, Hof-, und Staatsarchiv, Vienna.

HM: Adam Wandruszka and Peter Urbanitsch (eds) *Die Habsburgermonarchie 1848–1918:-(4)*: Vol. 4. *Die Konfessionen* (Vienna, 1985)

(5): Vol. 5. *Die bewaffenete Macht* (Vienna, 1987)

(6): Vol 6, pt. 1. *Die Habsburgermonarchie im System der internationalen Beziehungen* (Vienna, 1989)

Macartney: C.A. Macartney, *The Habsburg Empire, 1780–1918* (1968)

Margutti: A. von Margutti, *Vom Alten Kaiser* (Leipzig, Vienna, 1921)

Mitis: Baron von Mitis, *Life of Crown Prince Rudolph of Habsburg* (1930)

Nostitz: G. Nostitz-Rieneck (ed.) *Briefe Kaiser FJs an Kaiserin Elisabeth* Two volumes (Vienna, 1966)

OUA: L. Bittner and H. Uebersberger (eds) *Oesterreich-Ungarns Aussenpolitik von der bosnichen Krise 1908 bis zum Kriegsausbruch 1914*, 9 vols (Vienna 1930)

POM (i): H. Rumpler (Gen. ed.), *Die Protokolle des Österreichischen Ministerrates, 1848–1867* (Vienna 1973–   )

POM (ii): Gyözö Ember, (Gen. ed.), *Die Protokolle des gemeinsamen Minsterates der ö-u Monarchie*, 1867–1918 (Budapest, 1966–   )

Roth.: Gunther E. Rothenberg, *The Army of Francis Joseph* (West Lafayette, Indiana, 1976)

Rud. HHSA.: Papers of Crown Prince Rudolf in HHSA.

Schnürer: E. Schnürer (ed.), *Briefe Kaiser FJs an seine Mutter* (Salzburg, 1930)

Soph. Tb. HHSA: Diaries of Archduchess Sophie in HHSA

Chapter 1 Schönbrunn 1830

For Schönbrunn and Vienna in general in 1830 see chapters 2 and 3 of R. Waissenberger, *Vienna in the Biedermeier Era* (1986), pp. 29–91: Fertbauer's portraiture, ibid., p. 183. On the Duke of Reichstadt in Austria see J. Bourgoing, *Le fils de Napoleon* (Paris, 1950); his friendship with Archduchess Sophie, p. 343ff. Sophie's correspondence with her mother during pregnancy and on FJ's birth, see Corti, *Kind.* pp. 22–33, supplemented by Ernst, pp. 42–44. Metternich and 1830 revolutions: R. Metternich, *Mémoires . . . par le P. de Metternich*(Paris 1880–84, hereafter cited as Metternich Memoirs), Vol. 5, pp. 7–23; A. Palmer *Metternich* (1972), pp. 246–7; Macartney pp. 232–3. Corti, *Kind.* for Archduchess Marianna (pp. 133, 134), Sophie's reactions to Ferdinand's marriage (pp. 33–42), and for FJ's first visit to Ischl (pp. 43–44). For 'dear Ischl' in 1901, Ham., *Schr.* p. 471. Cholera epidemic, Corti, *Kind.* p. 43; and, in Hungary, Macartney p. 243 and István Deák, *The Lawful Revolution, Louis Kossuth and the Hungarians* (New York, 1979), pp. 21–22. For Coronation Diet of 1830: G. Barany, *Stephen Széchenyi and the Awakening of Hungarian Nationalism* (Princeton, N.J., 1968), pp. 269–70. On Reichstadt and birth of Maximilian: Corti, *Kind.* pp. 40–42, 55–60; Bourgoing, *Le fils.* pp. 350–1; J. Haslip, *Imperial Adventurer, Emperor Maximilian of Mexico and his Empress* (1971) p. 18. Marie Louise's visit to Francis Joseph's nursery: a contemporary letter in M.L.W. von Stürmfeder, *Die Kindheit unseres Kaisers* (Vienna 1910), p. 54, with other references to Reichstadt and his young cousin, pp. 15, 16, and 48.

Chapter 2 A Biedermeier Boyhood.

Many extracts from Archduchess Sophie's letters to her mother are in Corti, *Kind.* pp. 104–93, which also reproduces the Waldmüller portrait, facing p. 24. On Rauscher, HM (4), pp. 22–4, 52–3. Nursery recollections of the years 1830–

40 may be found in the letters in Louise von Stürmfeder's *Die Kindheit unserer Kaisers*, cited above; copies of this book are rare in England, but it is in the British Library. FJ's letters to his brother Maximilian, 1837–44, are printed in Ernst, pp. 55–75 and include facsimiles of some childhood drawings. Dismay at Emperor Francis's failing health in contemporary diaries: Kübeck, 6 October 1834, K. von Kübeck, *Tagebucher* vol I (ii) p. 532; Mélanie Metternich, 25–28 February 1835, Metternich Memoirs, vol. 5, pp. 645–8. Francis's death and testaments: A. Palmer, *Metternich*, pp. 268–9; Macartney p. 255. FJ and his grandfather's memory: Frances Trollope, *Vienna and the Austrians* (Paris, 1838), Vol 2., p. 300. On Bombelles, Macartney p. 409. For FJ's educational programmes, Ernst pp. 38, 48–51. Some letters in French from FJ to his mother are in Schnürer: in July 1838 p. 24; and the 'made us laugh' letter of May 1841, p. 32. For the 'loveliest valley I have seen', see Schnürer 9 September 1844, p. 44. Italian lithographs are reproduced in Corti, *Kind.* facing p. 241. 'Herr Lanner's music', 26 May 1841, Ernst p. 68. FJ's apparent enthusiasm for Jenny Lind's singing is noted in his mother's diary, Soph. Tb. HHSA, 20 February 1847. Fanny Elssler in 1846: Corti, *Kind.* p. 223; Ivor Guest, *Fanny Elssler* (1970), pp. 216–7; and for FJ's lasting admiration for her, Schnürer, 29 April 1851 no. 133, pp. 161–2. On Schreyvögel and Grillparzer see Ilsa Barea, *Vienna* (1966). Weissenberger's *Vienna in the Biedermeier Era* covers theatres on pp. 232–43 and also provides a copiously illustrated examination of Biedermeier culture in general. Archduke Albrecht's comment in 1844, Corti, *Kind.* p. 211. For Italian tour of FJ and his brothers in 1845: Schnürer, 7 September from Belluno, p. 55; 12 September from Verona ('balloon'), p. 59; 19 and 25 September from Venice, pp. 60–2; J. Haslip, *Imperial Adventurer*, pp. 28–31. On the *Staatskonferenz*: Macartney, p. 256; A. Palmer, *Metternich*, pp. 274–6; Alan Sked, *The Decline and Fall of the Habsburg Empire 1815–1918* (1989), pp. 26–30; and for Sophie's views on it, Corti *Kind.* p. 165. FJ's first train journey, Metternich Memoirs vol. 6, p. 242. FJ's diary entry on fifteenth birthday, Schnürer p. 57. Letters in Schnürer for FJ's boyhood friendships: Charly Bombelles in 1842 p. 34, and 1843 p. 41; Francis Coronini in 1845 p. 55; Albert of Saxony in October 1844 (p. 49) and warm September 1847 p. 82; Taaffe not mentioned until 1847 (p. 74), but, with Denes Széchenyi, he was FJ's close companion at Christmas 1845 (Corti, *Kind.* p. 229). FJ and Hungary, 1847: Schnürer 15 & 16 October, nos. 64 & 65 pp. 83–4; 'terrific agitation' 13 November, p. 85. On Sophie and FJ in closing months of 1847, Corti, *Kind.* pp. 244–5. Her diary (Soph. Tb. HHSA) for 20 December comments both on the preparations for *Wirrwarr* and the contrasting attitudes of her sons. Corti's *Kind.* reproduces the cast list of *Wirrwarr*, between pp. 272–3. For comments on performance: Soph. Tb. HHSA, 9–10 February 1848; Mélanie's journal, Metternich Memoirs, vol. 7, p. 534. A translation of the (1788) text of *Wirrwarr* was published in Cambridge in 1842, under title of *The Confusion, or The Wag*.

Chapter 3 Year of Revolution

Court faction: the American historian is Gunther Rothenberg, see Roth. p. 23; cf Metternich Memoirs vol. 7, p. 533. For Moehring and Sophie's role in these events, see Macartney p. 325 and Corti, *Kind*. p. 231; her pessimism is shown in diary entries for 2 and 31 December 1847 (Soph. Tb. HHSA). Political horoscope for 1848: Metternich Memoirs vol 7, pp. 569–72. On Kossuth and developments in Hungary: István Deák, *Lawful Revolution*, pp. 91–99 supplementing Macartney, pp. 323–5. Sophie's diary entries (Soph. Tb. HHSA): 9 March, parallels with French Revolution; 16 March, events of preceding four days; 2 April, drive with FJ in the Prater; 15 April, assessment after FJ's return from Pressburg; 19 April, meeting with Windischgraetz. Archduke John on Metternich and subsequent events, H. von Srbik, *Metternich, der Staatsmann und der Mensch* (Munich, 1925), vol. 2, pp. 263–82; Metternich's fall, A. Palmer, *Metternich*, pp. 309–11. FJ and Bohemia, Macartney pp. 349–50. Sophie's letter to Radetzky, 22 April 1848: Corti, *Kind*. p. 276. For FJ's 21 letters from the Italian Front in 1848 see Schnürer, pp. 88–109: 'eagle over Turin', no. 69 from Bozen, 27 April; 'cannon-balls', no. 76, from Verona, 6 May; cf. Oskar Regele, *Feldmarschall Radetzky* (Vienna and Munich 1957), pp. 285–87 and R. Kiszling, *Die Revolution in Kaisertum Oesterreich* (Vienna, 1949), vol. 1, pp. 116–21. On Vienna in May 1848: ibid., p. 128; Walter pp. 49–94; cf. contemporary warnings from Stratford Canning to Palmerston, 30 April 1848, FO 181/215. Further assessments from Canning at Vienna and Trieste in May, in FO 78/733. 'Mouse in trap' Soph. Tb. HHSA, 16 May 1848; escape to Innsbruck, Corti, *Kind*. pp. 289–91 and Kiszling, *Revolution vol*. 1 pp. 131–3. For Grünne's ascendancy, Corti, *Kind*., pp. 297–99. FJ and Bavarian cousins in Innsbruck: ibid., p. 300 and Corti, *Elizabeth, Empress of Austria* (1936), p. 24. Bohemia: Stanley Pech, 'The June Uprising in Prague, 1848', *East European Quarterly* (1968), vol. 1, pp. 341–70. Radetzky and Grillparzer, Macartney, p. 342; O. Regele, *Radetzky* pp. 464–6. For FJ's projected visit to England, Corti, *Kind*. pp. 304–5. FJ's eighteenth birthday, ibid., p. 306; 'that admirable Jellačić, ibid., p. 307. On Radetzky and Latour, HM vol. 5 pp. 8–9. For Batthyány and Jellačić, Macartney, pp. 387–92. Windischgraetz's contingency plan, Walter, p. 192 and Corti, *Kind*. p. 308; 'caravan', ibid., p. 313. Events of 6 October and murder of Latour, Kiszling, *Revolution* vol. 1, pp. 239–48. Army's attack on Vienna, R.J. Rath, *The Viennese Revolution of 1848* (Austin, Texas, 1957), pp. 355–8; WJR trinity, HM vol 5, pp. 1–10; Walter p. 224. Formation of a government: Kiszling, *Fürst Felix zu Schwarzenberg* (Graz-Cologne 1952), pp. 50–3; Macartney p. 406, for Hübner's assessment and Kremsier speech. Windischgraetz and the Empress, Walter pp. 262–4. On FJ's accession: Soph. Tb. HHSA, December 1848; Kiszling, *Revolution* pp. 311–20; Corti, *Kind*. pp. 328–32, including extracts from Ferdinand's journal. For Hungarian dissent: Deák, *Lawful Revolution*, pp. 205–6. On FJ's participation in glass-breaking: French quotation from Soph. Tb. HHSA; her fuller account in a letter to her brother is used by Corti, *Kind*. pp. 343–4.

Chapter 4 Apotheosis of the Army

On Schwarzenberg's policy in general see Kenneth W. Rock, 'Felix Schwarzenberg, Military Diplomat', AHY no. 11 (1975) pp. 85–100. For the invasion of Hungary: Kiszling, *Revolution* vol. 2, pp. 12–14. 'Grace of cannon' exchanges: Sked, *Decline and Fall*, p. 142–3, citing Walther and providing a good summary of events at Kremsier; and Macartney, p. 422. Novara campaign: HM (5), pp. 333–4; Kiszling op. cit., pp. 146–51. Battle of Kapolna and Hungarian counter-offensives, ibid., pp. 46–68. For the reluctant negotiation of the dynastic alliance against Hungary see K. W. Rock's article, 'Schwarzenberg versus Nicholas I, Round One', AHY no. 6/7, 1970/71, pp. 109–42 and Ian Roberts, *Nicholas I and Russian Intervention in Hungary* (1991), pp. 106–27. Fall of Windischgraetz: Kiszling, *Schwarzenberg*, p. 89; Kiszling *Revolution*, vol. 2, p. 77; FJ's letter of dismissal, J. Redlich, *Emperor Francis Joseph* (1929), p. 55. FJ's sentimentality: letter to his mother, Schnürer 19 April 1849, p. 111. FJ becomes supreme commander, Roth. pp. 39–40; and Nicholas I, E. Andics, *Das Bündnis Habsburg-Romanovv* (Budapest, 1963), pp. 372–5. FJ at Raab, Kiszling, *Revolution* vol. 2, pp. 187–88; Maxmilian's account, Corti, *Mensch.* pp. 33–34; Schnürer 29 June 1849, p. 119. On Vilagos, Roberts pp. 179–82; Macartney p. 430. On FJ and Haynau, ibid., pp. 431–2: Corti, *Mensch.* pp. 44–6. Radetzky fêted, Regele, *Radetzky*, pp. 466–7. On General Hess and Grünne, Roth. pp. 39–40, HM (5), p. 25, and FJ to his mother, 18 September, Schnürer, p. 131. 'Apotheosis of the army', F. Walter, *Aus dem Nachlass ... Kübeck* (Graz-Cologne, 1960), p. 34. Schwarzenberg's German policy: Sked, *Decline and Fall ...* pp. 150–7; F.R. Bridge, *The Habsburg Monarchy among the Great Powers, 1815–1918* (New York, Oxford, Munich 1990), pp. 45–8; Kiszling, *Schwarzenberg*, pp. 156–65. On Kübeck and the constitutional changes of 1851, Redlich, op. cit., pp. 83–8; Macartney, pp. 452–3; Walter pp. 438–42; Sked, op. cit., pp. 147–9; FJ to his mother, 26 August 1851, Schnürer p. 166. Provincial tour, 13 May 1850, Schnürer p. 136; 'mood grows worse' and 'church parade', 1 and 5 September, 1850, Schnürer pp. 139–40. FJ dancing, Corti, *Mensch.* pp. 69–70. Habsburgs and fleet: HM (5), pp. 687–92; FJ at sea May 1850, Schnürer, p. 137; storm of 1852, 6 March 1852 Schnürer, pp. 175–6 and Corti, *Mensch.* pp. 90–91. FJ visits Metternichs, Metternich Memoirs, vol. 8, p. 117; 'faithful pupil', Corti, *Mensch.* p. 87. Sylvester Patent; Macartney, pp. 454–6. Schwarzenberg's death: Kiszling, *Schwarzenberg*, pp. 202–3. 'My greatest minister', for FJ's use of the phrase in 1907, see Rock article, AHY no. 11 (1975), p. 87. FJ's comments to his mother, 6 April 1852, Schnürer, pp. 176–7.

Chapter 5 Marriage

For FJ's romantic attachments, Corti, *Mensch* pp. 101–3; Ham., *El.* pp. 24–25. 'elegant seat', J. Haslip, *The Lonely Empress* (1965) p. 37. Libényi: Corti, *Mensch.* pp. 106–7; J. Haslip, *Imperial Adventurer*, pp. 62–3; Archduchess Sophie's diary entries for late February 1853 and for anniversary references in later years, notably in 1871 and 1872, Soph. Tb. HHSA. Leopold I to Queen Victoria, 3

June 1853, *Letters of Queen Victoria*, First Series, Vol. 2, pp. 447–8. Sophie's invitation to her sister and the journeys to Ischl, Corti, *Elizabeth*, pp. 32–33; Ham. *El.* pp. 31–2. Both of these books cover the engagement, from Sophie's letters; the general course of events is confirmed by her diary entries (in French), 18–21 August 1853, Soph. Tb. HHSA; see also Corti, *Mensch.* pp. 121–5. 'Desk-bound existence', FJ to Sophie, September 1853, Schnürer p. 208. On Eastern Question problems in the background: Paul W. Schroeder, *Austria, Great Britain and the Crimean War* (Ithaca, 1972), pp. 77–82. FJ's letters to his mother for his courtship of Elizabeth in Schnürer: 17 October 1853, pp. 215–6; Christmas festivities, 27 December 1853, pp. 218–20; 'wonderful sunny day', 13 March 1854, p. 222. Background diplomacy; FJ at council of ministers: 23 and 31 January, 22 and 25 March, POM (i) vol 3 pt. 3, pp. 419–40; Paul Schroeder's article, 'A Turning Point in Austrian History in the Crimean War: the Conference of March 1854', AHY, vols, 4–5, (1968–9), pp. 159–202; the Austro-Prussian alliance of 20 April 1854, Bridge, op. cit., p. 54. Re-decoration of Vienna before the wedding: *The Times*, 26 April 1854. Mishap to crown: Soph. Tb. HHSA, 18 April 1854; Ham. *El.* p. 68 for repairs. Landing from Danube steamer, *The Times* 28 April 1854; Walter, *Aus ... Nach. Hübner*, vol. 1, p. 229. Wedding: *The Times* 2 May 1854; Soph. Tb. HHSA, 24 April 1854 (and for early married days entries of 25 and 27 April). For Renz: Corti, *Elizabeth* p. 54. Riding in Laxenburg, J. Haslip, *Lonely Empress*, p. 79.

Chapter 6 'It Is My Pleasure ...'.

FJ's council meetings in first weeks of marriage: POM (i) vol. 3. pt. 3, pp. 441–6. Elizabeth's later accounts of Archduchess's behaviour: in Marie Festetics's diary for 1872, Budapest archives, cited by both Corti (*Elizabeth*) and Brigitte Hamann (Ham. *El.*). Parrots: Corti, op. cit., p. 57. Corpus Christi procession: Soph. Tb. 15 June 1854 HHSA. FJ swimming: letter to his mother 28 June 1854, Schnürer, p. 225. Army preparations: HM (5) pp. 340–2; Roth. pp. 50–51. Ministerial conference of 19 May 1854: POM (i) loc. cit. and W. Baumgart (ed.), *Oesterreichische Akten zur Geschichte des Krimkriegs*, vol. 2, pp. 178–81; and diplomatic aftermath, HM (6) pt. 1, pp. 215–8. Nicholas I's disillusionment, Roberts, op. cit., p. 228 and p. 275; FJ to his mother, 'our future lies in the East', 8 October 1854, Schnürer, p. 232. Four Points and subsequent diplomacy: Schroeder, op. cit., pp. 182–226; Baumgart, *Akten* vol. 2, pp. 290–3; Bridge, op. cit., p. 55; A.J.P. Taylor, *The Struggle for Mastery in Europe* (1954), pp. 65–70; A. Palmer, *The Banner of Battle* (1987), pp. 185–6 and 192–3. Russell on FJ: Lord John Russell to Clarendon, 6 March, 1855, Public Record Office, Kew, 30/122/18. Pola as a naval base: HM (5) pp. 724–7. Maxmilian's views while in command of the fleet, chapter 5 of J. Haslip's *Imperial Adventurer*. For ministerial council on *Credit Anstalt* foundation, 9 October 1855, POM (ii) vol. 3 part 4, pp. 140–44. Bruck's achievements: Macartney, pp. 460–1 and 468–9, critically re-assessed by David F. Good, *The Economic Rise of the Habsburg Empire, 1750–1914* (Berkeley and Los Angeles, 1984), pp. 81–8. Re-building of Vienna: Ilsa Barea, *Vienna* pp. 234–9. Concordat: HM (4) pp. 25–34. Telegram on signing of Concordat, 18 August 1855: Schnürer, p. 243. Maximilian's quest for a bride and marriage: J. Haslip. op. cit. pp. 86–101; Corti, *Mensch*. p. 192. FJ criticizes his mother's possessive care for his daughters, 18 September 1856, Schnürer, p. 256. Visit to Lombardy-Venetia: ibid., pp. 258–63; Ernst, pp. 90–6. Visit to Hungary and death of eldest child: Schnürer, pp. 267–71 and p. 280; Corti, *Mensch*. p. 189; Ham. *El.*, pp. 118–21. Sophie on Charlotte's charm: Soph. Tb. 4 August 1857, HHSA. Birth of Rudolf: Ham. *Rud.* pp. 15–17; 'not exactly beautiful', 9 September, 1858. Schnürer p. 286.

Chapter 7 Italy without Radetzky

Radetzky's funeral: Horace Rumbold, *Recollections of a Diplomatist* (1902), vol. 1, pp. 263–4. 'Radetzky was disobedient': Maxmilian to his mother, W.A. Jenks, *Francis Joseph and the Italians* (Charlottesville, 1978), p. 146. The section in Jenks's book on Maximilian in Lombardy-Venetia is useful, especially pp. 140–9 which include extracts from FJ's letters to him. 'Counting on loyal support', Ernst p. 113. Events leading up to the war and FJ's excessive confidence in Buol: Roth., p. 52; Corti, *Mensch*. pp. 220–21. For FJ's hostility towards Prussia, see his letter to his mother, 16 June 1859, Schnürer p. 292. On Gyulai, HM (5) pp. 343–5. For FJ, Metternich and the appointment of Rechberg, A. Palmer, *Metternich*, p. 358 and Corti, *Mensch*. p. 223. On Sisi and FJ's departure for the wars: Soph. Tb. 29 May 1859 HHSA; Ham. *El.* pp. 131–3; Corti, *Elizabeth* p. 78. FJ's letters from the Italian Front to Elizabeth in Nostitz vol. 1, pp. 9–36: 'selfsame room', 31 May, p. 9; 'no place for women', 2 June, p. 11; dismissal of Gyulai, 17 June, p. 22; 'pull yourself together', 7 June, p. 14; no riding with Holmes, 13 June, pp. 19–20 (cf. Corti, *Elizabeth* p. 80); long meeting with Rechberg, 20 June p. 24 (see Corti, *Mensch*. p. 231 for the report Rechberg brought to FJ). FJ's account to Sisi of losing the battle of Solferino, letter of 26 June, Nostitz vol. 1, pp. 26–8; Maximilian's account to Charlotte. see J. Haslip, *Imperial Adventurer*, p. 119. Napoleon III's reactions to Solferino and his desire for peace: Jasper Ridley, *Napoleon III and Eugenie* (1979), pp. 450–5. Extensive coverage of Villafranca meeting by journalists: *The Times*, 19, 20, 21 July 1859. See also for the Italian campaign, Roth. p. 54 and the critical memoirs of Anton Mollinary, *Sechsundvierzig Jahre im österreich-ungarischen Heere*, vol. 2, pp. 45–7 and 60–4. FJ's return to Vienna and the depressed mood of the capital: Corti, *Mensch*. pp. 242–9.

Chapter 8 'Power Remains in My Hands'.

Viennese newspapers, cited Ham. *El.* p. 140. Laxenburg Manifesto and subsequent constitutional experiments: Macartney pp. 496–8 and Corti, *Mensch*. pp. 241–2. Bruck's suicide, ibid., pp. 256–7. FJ's hostility to constitutionalism, 1860: Macartney p. 499. For October Diploma, Corti, *Mensch*. p. 263. 'Power remains in my hands', FJ to his mother, 2 October 1850, Schnürer p. 300.

Archduchess Sophie at Empress's 22nd birthday celebrations: Soph. Tb. 24 December 1859, HHSA. Elizabeth's illness; Ham. *El.* p. 148; Corti, *Elizabeth*, pp. 84–7. Warsaw meeting 1860: W.E. Mosse, *The European Powers and the German Question* (1958), pp. 87–9. Extract from modern biographer on Empress's illness and outside physician: J. Haslip, *The Lonely Empress*, p. 141. 'Shattered by the news': Soph. Tb. 31 October 1860, HHSA. Empress at Antwerp: King Leopold to Queen Victoria, 22 November 1860, *Letters of Queen Victoria* (Series 1), vol. 3, p. 414. 'Eats dangerously little': Louis Rechberg in private letter, cited Corti, *Elizabeth* p. 88. Hungarian affairs and fall of Goluchowski: Macartney, pp. 509–11. FJ at council sessions preparing February Patent 1861; POM (i) vol. 5, pt. 1 pp. 3–5 and 32–61, with agreed text of Patent, pp. 61–6. FJ's insistence on safeguarding his prerogatives, 28 February 1861, ibid., p. 111. FJ and preparation of speech from throne: ibid., pp. 291–300 and 305–6. Empress's return from Madeira: Ham. *El.* pp. 156–7; Corti, *Elizabeth*, pp. 92–3. FJ, his ministers and troubles in Croatia and Hungary, councils of: 6 May 1861, POM (i) vol. 5, pt. 2, pp. 28–33; 9 September, ibid., pp. 360–66; 27 October, ibid., pp. 458–66; and ('disciplining Hungary') 1 November, ibid., pp. 469–73. FJ's Corfu visit of 1861, in letters to his mother: going to Corfu, 30 September, Schnürer p. 305; impressions of Corfu, 15 October, pp. 308–9. Hübner comment on FJ's happy married life at Venice, Corti, *Mensch.* p. 276. Countess Esterházy's dismissal: J. Haslip, *Lonely Empress*, p. 159; Soph. Tb. 27 January and 28 January 1862, HHSA; cf. Archduchess's comments in letters quoted in Ham. *El.* p. 164. Pictures of beautiful women: Corti, *Elizabeth*, p. 96. Dr Fischer's diagnoses and cures: Ham. *El.* pp. 164–8. Start of Mexican imbroglio: E.C. Corti, *Maximilian and Charlotte of Mexico* (1923); L.A.C. Schefer, *La grande pensée de Napoleon III* (Paris 1939); J. Haslip *Imperial Adventurer*, pp. 137–62; J. Ridley, *Napoleon III and Eugenie*, pp. 498–509. FJ 'hungry for mountain air', 11 August 1862, Schnürer, p. 311. Elizabeth's welcome in Vienna, Ham, *El.* pp. 172–3. FJ and Rudolf at Wiener Neustadt, Corti, *Mensch.* p. 282. Ball on 26 February 1863: Hans Pauer, *Kaiser Franz Joseph I, Beitrage zur Bild-Dokumentation seines Lebens* (Vienna and Munich, 1966), no. 1155, p. 164.

Chapter 9 In Bismarck's Shadow

For 1852 meeting of FJ and Bismarck: A. Palmer, *Bismarck* (1976), p. 50. 'Shift centre of gravity to Hungary', Karolyi to Rechberg, 5 December 1862, E. Brandenburg (ed.), *Die auswartige Preussens Politik* (Berlin 1930), vol. 3, no. 60, p. 100. Assessment of Bismarck's approach by FJ and ministers, 16 December 1862, POM (i) vol. 5, part 5, p. 117. Bismarck's vacillations: A. Palmer, op. cit., p. 81. The Frankfurt Congress of Princes; ibid., p. 86; Bridge, op. cit., p. 75; Corti, *Mensch.* p. 292–7. FJ's letters to his mother about the *Furstentag*: 'last chance for Germany's rulers' 13 August, Schnürer p. 320; a success, 2 September, ibid., pp. 322–4; FJ's difficult meeting with Queen Victoria, 11 September, ibid., p. 326. Military and naval action against Denmark: Roth. pp. 64–5; HM (5) pp. 345–6 and 694. FJ and Mexico, Corti, *Mensch.* pp. 299–300 (with Schnürer p. 302

for his continued mistrust of Napoleon III); Maximilian's problems, Corti, *Maximilian and Charlotte* (1928), pp. 384–99, J. Haslip, *Imperial Adventurer*, pp. 195–216. Alliance with Prussia 'the only sensible policy', FJ to his mother, 2 August 1864, Schnürer, pp. 333–4. Bismarck 'trying to frighten people with words', FJ to Albert of Saxony, 16 February 1864, Ernst, p. 160. On the Schönbrunn conversations: C.W. Clark, *Franz Joseph and Bismarck* (Cambridge, Mass. 1934), pp. 573–5 and the critical analysis of available evidence in H. von Srbik, '*Die Schönbrunnen Konferenzen von August 1864*', *Historische Zeitschrift* (Berlin-Munich, 1935–6), vol. 153, pp. 43–88. On Rechberg, Biegeleben and Mensdorff: Bridge, op. cit., pp. 77–9: HM (6) pt. 1 pp. 55 and 67; H. Friedjung, *The Struggle for Supremacy in Germany* (1935) pp. 64–8. FJ's talks with Deák, 1864–5, Macartney, pp. 537–9, 541. Convention of Gastein: A. Palmer, op. cit., pp. 104–5; Friedjung op. cit., p. 75; Clark, op. cit., p. 190. For military preparations and FJ's attitude to the needle-gun: Macartney p. 534; HM (5) pp. 56–7; O. Regele, *Feldzugmeister Benedek* (Vienna-Munich 1960), pp. 372–4. FJ and British ambassador: Bloomfield to Clarendon, 20 January 1866, FO 356/37, extracts in Corti, *Mensch.* p. 332. FJ and ministerial council, April 1866, POM (i) vol. 6, pt. 2, PP. 3–16, 36–40, 45–7, 57–61. Benedek and Krismanic, Regele, op. cit., pp. 396–405; Roth, pp. 67–73 (and for whole campaign). 'Must have a result', FJ to his mother, 11 May 1866, Schnürer, p. 355. FJ's stubbornness over Venetia and treaty with France: council of 11 June 1866, POM (i) vol. 6, pt. 2, pp. 135–9. Gordon Craig, *The Battle of Königgrätz* (1965), pp. 99–175 for the campaign and its climax. Regele, op. cit., pp. 385–447 for Benedek's unfortunate role. On Beck in 1866: G-H, pp. 99–132. For a critical comparison of the Italian and northern campaigns, see the diary and letters of General Karl Moehring, printed as an appendix to Adam Wandruszka, *Schicksaljahr 1866* (Graz-Cologne-Vienna 1966). Tegetthoff's victory at Lissa, HM (5) pp. 696–706. Ceasefire and preliminary peace with Prussia; FJ at ministerial councils of 26–27 July, POM (i) vol. 6 pt. 2, pp. 174–8 and 194–6; Bismarck's difficulties, A. Palmer, op. cit., pp. 122–4. 'We shall withdraw completely from Germany', FJ to Elizabeth, 23 July, 1866, Nostitz, vol. 1, p. 49. 'Refined double-dealing', FJ to his mother, 22 August 1866, Schnürer. p. 247.

Chapter 10 The Holy Crown of St Stephen

'Praise to God a thousand times over', Soph. Tb. 22 April 1865, HHSA. For Fanny Angerer, Ida Ferenczy, and Winterhalter portrait cf. Ham. *El.* pp. 199, 203–7, 218–9, 230–2; J. Haslip, *Lonely Empress* pp. 180–5; Corti, *Elizabeth* pp. 105–6, 171. Rudolf and wild boar: ibid., p. 110. Elizabeth's Ischl ultimatum of August 1865: mentioned, ibid., p. 111, printed in full from Munich archives, Ham. *El.* p. 181. Andrássy and Elizabeth in January 1866: ibid., pp. 226–7; Eduard von Wertheimer, *Graf Julius Andrássy, Sein Leben und seine Zeit* (Stuttgart 1910–13), vol. 1, p. 214. FJ to his mother on Elizabeth in Hungary, 3 and 17 February 1866, Schnürer, pp. 348 and 351. Elizabeth's letters to FJ during the 1866 War, pressing the Hungarian cause, Corti, *Elizabeth* pp. 126–27. FJ's reply to Elizabeth, 17 July,

Nostitz, vol. I, pp. 39–40. Exchanges between the imperial couple are summarized in Corti, *Elizabeth*, pp. 127–34, with FJ's letters printed in full, Nostitz, vol. I, pp. 40–67, notably his warning to her that he had no money to purchase Gödöllö (9 August; p. 58) and his concern over presence of 'Her Mexican Majesty' at Trieste (26 August, p. 65). For appointment of Beust, see FJ's council held at Prague, 28 October, POM (i) vol. 6, pt. 2, pp. 281–7, and F.F. Beust, *Memoirs* (1867) vol. I, pp. 313, 328, 339. 'No war for a long time ahead', Bridge, op. cit., p. 87. FJ at ministerial council of I February 1867: POM (i) vol. 2, pt. 6 pp. 300–10. On the agreed form of the Ausgleich and the settlement with Croatia: Macartney pp. 551–64 and, for an assessment of later commentaries, see Sked, *Decline and Fall* pp. 187–92. On the Holy Crown, its burial and later fate: Ian Roberts op. cit., p. 193; Wertheimer, op. cit., vol. I pp. 293–5. For the gift of Gödöllö: Corti, *Elizabeth*, p. 137; 'right good cheer', ibid., p. 139. Material showing the Crown Prince's boyhood idolization of Andrássy is preserved with his later papers, Rud. HHSA, K(arton) 12. Concern over fate of Maximilian at time of Hungarian coronation: Corti, *Mensch.* pp. 391–2; *The Times*, 3 June, 1867. Death of Archduchess Mathilde: Ham. *El.* p. 265; Corti, *Mensch.* pp. 392–3. Hungarian Coronation: *The Times*, 12 June 1867; French press quoted, J-P. Bled, *Franz Joseph* (English translation: Oxford, 1992) pp. 153–4; Crown Prince's account, B. Hamann, *Kronprinz Rudolf ... Schriften; Majestat, ich warne Sie* (Vienna and Munich, 1979, hereafter cited as 'Rudolf, *Schriften*') pp. 387–8. Elizabeth on the martyrs of Arad: Wertheimer op. cit., vol. I p. 271. FJ and news of Maximilian's death: Corti, *Mensch.* pp. 397–8. Sophie in mourning for 'my beautiful son', Soph. Tb. 31 December 1867, HHSA. 'Perhaps I am with child': Corti, *Elizabeth*, p. 145. Salzburg visit: *The Times*, 19–24 and 27 August 1867; Hans Wilczek, *Happy Retrospect* (1934), pp. 42–7; Beust, op. cit., vol. 2, pp. 33–6. Diplomatic significance: A.J.P. Taylor, *The Struggle for Mastery in Europe* (1954), pp. 185–6; Bridge, op. cit., pp. 88–9. Eugenie and Archduchess Sophie: Soph. Tb. 19 August 1867, HHSA. Elizabeth informs Eugenie of her pregnancy: H. Kurtz, *Empress Eugenie*, p. 223. FJ's letters from Paris, Nostitz, vol. I, pp. 68–79: beauty of Paris, p. 72; King Ludwig pp. 73 and 76; Prince Imperial and Crown Prince contrasted (postscript to 30 October letter), p. 75. For the December Constitution, Macartney pp. 560–2. Elizabeth's return to Hungary for her confinement: Corti, *Elizabeth* pp. 149–51. Birth of Marie Valerie, FJ's letter of 23 April 1868, Schnürer pp. 366–7.

Chapter 11 Facing Both Ways

FJ's pleasure in swimming: letter to his mother 3 August 1870, Schnürer, p. 374. Church-State relations and disruption of the Concordat: HM (4), pp. 38–9, 41–3, 51–7; F. Engel-Janosi, *Oesterreich und der Vatikan* (Graz-Vienna 1958), vol. I, pp. 145–50. Empress at opening of Vatican Council: Corti, *Elizabeth*, p. 163. FJ tells Sophie of ending of Concordat, 25 August 1870, Schnürer p. 377. Czech Fundamental Articles: Macartney, pp. 513–4; A.J. May, *The Hapsburg Monarchy 1867–1914* (Cambridge, Mass., 1965 edition), pp. 60–62; A.J.P. Taylor, *The Habs-*

burg Monarchy (1948 edition) pp. 145–8; fullest survey in A.O. Zeithammer, *Zur Geschichte der böhmischen Ausgleichversuche*, 1865–71 (Prague, 1913), vol. 2, pp. 4–59. Krisvosije Rising: Roth. p. 86; Theodor von Sosnosky, *Die Balkanpolitik Oesterreich-Ungarns seit 1866* (Stuttgart, 1913), vol. 1, pp. 71–90. On FJ's eastern tour: Beust, op. cit., vol. 2 pp. 126–62. For FJ's 12 letters 'from the East' see Nostitz, vol. 1, pp. 82–148: 'in Stamboul', pp. 84–7; Sultan's horse, p. 88; Hellespont, p. 96; Athens and Piraeus, pp. 97–9; in Holy Land, pp. 103–9; embarkation at Jaffa, p. 110; ball at Ismailia, pp. 125–6; climbing pyramid, pp. 140–1. For written exchanges between Empress Elizabeth and FJ during his tour: Corti, *Elizabeth*, p. 162. Report of opening ceremonies of Suez Canal: *The Times*, 30 November 1869. For an entertaining account of the festivities: Marie des Garets, *Auprès de l'Impératrice Eugénie* (Paris 1928) pp. 140–50. 'Resident guest in the Hofburg': long extract from *Neues Wiener Tagblatt* of 3 March 1870 in Ham *El.* p. 278. For Albrecht, Kuhn and Austro-French staff talks: most detailed account is in the reminiscences of the senior French officer, General B.L.J. Lebrun, *Souvenirs Militaires, 1866–70* (Paris 1895), pp. 69–172; but see also Roth. pp. 87–8, Bridge, op. cit., pp. 95–7 and G-H, pp. 162–73. See, in general, the article by F. Engel-Janosi, 'Austria in the Summer of 1870', *Journal of Central European Affairs*, volume 5 (Boulder, Colorado, 1945–46), pp. 335–53. FJ presides over council, 18 July 1870: minutes in HHSA, PA XL/285, a box which also contains accounts of the important council meetings of 9 August and 22 August (with Andrássy's insistence on being a 'bulwark against Russia'). Archduchess Sophie's sorrow at south German backing for Prussia: Soph. Tb. 27 July and 5 August 1870, HHSA. FJ to his mother on 'catastrophe in France', 25 August 1870, Schnürer, pp. 377–8. Archduchess on Napoleon III's vacillation: Soph. Tb. 3 September 1870, HHSA. FJ, Beust and ministerial council of 11 September 1870: minutes HHSA PA XL/285; and cf. Beust, op. cit., vol. 2 pp. 179–90. 'A very dark future.': FJ to his mother, 23 October 1870, Schnürer, pp. 380–1. Russia and Black Sea crisis: discussed by FJ and ministers at council of 14 November 1870, minutes in HHSA PA XL/285. Beust memorandum of 18 May 1871; quoted Corti, *Mensch.* p. 447; see also Bridge, op. cit., p. 100. Meetings of FJ and William I, ibid., pp. 101–2; Corti *Mensch.* pp. 448–50. Replacement of Beust by Andrássy: ibid., p. 453; Beust, op. cit., vol. 2, pp. 292–7. Merano sojourn and Rudolf: Soph. Tb. 5 October 1870 HHSA; for context, see Ham. *El.* p. 297. 'Worthless shining lights', Soph. Tb. 31 December 1871 HHSA. Gisela's betrothal: FJ's last letter to his mother, 7 April 1872, Schnürer pp. 384–5. Sophie's final days: entries in journal (Soph. Tb. HHSA) until 1 May 1872. For her death: Ham. *El.* pp. 304–6. Festetics record of Elizabeth's reminiscences, ibid., p. 308.

Chapter 12 A Glimmer of Light

On Strauss and the first performances of the Blue Danube: Peter Kemp, *The Strauss Family* (Tunbridge Wells, 1982), pp. 69–71; Ilsa Barea, *Vienna*, pp. 204–5. Spread of banking and commercial enterprise: May, op. cit., pp. 64–7; Macartney pp. 606–7; but cf. D.F. Good, op. cit., pp. 86, 170–9, 204–8. For economic penetration of Turkey-in-Europe: A. Palmer, *The Decline and Fall of the Ottoman Empire* (1992), p. 138. For Schäffle on FJ: A.E.F. Schäffle, *Aus meinem Leben* (Berlin 1904–05), vol. 2, pp. 69–70; and for Schäffle's theories, E. Crankshaw, *The Fall of the House of Habsburg* (1963), pp. 254–5. Gisela's wedding: Corti, *Elizabeth*, p. 184. For the World Exhibition: ibid., pp. 184–91 and cf. the contemporary diaries quoted by Corti, *Mensch*. pp. 466–7, 469–70. For Freud's interest in the World Exhibition, see Ronald W. Clark, *Freud, the Man and the Cause* (1980), p. 30; his description of the opening procession is cited by Clark (pp. 32–3) from an account in Freud's 'Early Unpublished Letters', *International Journal of Psychoanalysis*, vol. L. (1969), p. 423. 'Black Friday' in 1873: Corti, *Mensch*. p. 467; effects of the 'Crash', Macartney, pp. 608–9, 616–18 and the later chapters of Schäffle, op. cit. FJ's Silver Jubilee celebrations: Corti, *Mensch*. pp. 475–6; Brigitte Hamann, *Rudolf, Der Weg nach Mayerling* (Vienna-Munich, 1988), p. 34; J. Haslip, *The Emperor and the Actress* (1982), pp. 18–19; Ham. *Schr.* p. 19. FJ and Press criticism: Ham. *El.* pp. 323–4. FJ a grandfather: Corti, *Mensch*. p. 477; J. Haslip, *Lonely Empress*, p. 257. Confessional Laws of 1874; May, op. cit., pp. 63–4. Four letters from FJ to Elizabeth during his St Petersburg visit of February 1874: Nostitz vol. 1, pp. 149–56. The Gabrielle incident: fullest treatment in Corti, *Elizabeth*, pp. 198–205 (based on Fritz Pascher's papers). Empress on Isle of Wight, ibid., pp. 207–10; Roger Fulford (ed.) *Darling Child* (1976), p. 145. 'What a pity you cannot come': Corti, *Elizabeth*, p. 210 and Ham. *El.* p. 33. Prague and death of Ferdinand: Corti, *Mensch* p. 487. Domestic arrangements of Habsburg palaces: Princess Stephanie, *I Was to be Empress* (1937), pp. 151–2.

Chapter 13 The Herzegovina and Bosnia

General background, see Noel Malcolm, *Bosnia: A Short History* (1994). Mollinary's informative letters to his wife are the basis of the chapters in his second volume of memoirs, covering these events: A. von Mollinary, *46 Jahre.*, vol. 2, especially pp. 281–4. Two British Academy Raleigh Lectures clarify the Balkan crises: 1931 lecture by H.M.V. Temperley, 'The Bulgarian and other Atrocities 1875–8', *Proceedings of the British Academy*, Vol. 17, pp. 105–47; 1932 lecture by R.W. Seton-Watson, 'The Role of Bosnia in International Politics, 1875–1914' ibid., pp. 335–68. Military plans for seizing the provinces: Mollinary, vol. 2, pp. 305–6; Bridge, op. cit., p. 112. Starcević and Strossmayer: R. Kiszling, *Die Kroaten*, (Graz, 1956) p. 67. Andrássy's attitude: I. Dioszegi, *Hungarians in the Ballhausplatz* (Budapest, 1983), pp. 60–72; Wertheimer, *Andrássy*, vol. 2, pp. 258–61: German ambassador, L. von Schweinitz, *Denkwürdigkeiten des Botschafters General von Schweinitz* (Berlin 1927), vol. 1 pp. 309–10. Text of Schönbrunn Convention: Bridge, op. cit., pp. 381–2. On Kállay: Seton-Watson lecture cited above, pp. 342–4; Dioszegi, loc. cit.; his later career, Macartney, pp. 742–3. 'Blessed is the rifle' ballad: Temperley lecture cited above, p. 109. FJ's letters from his Dalmatian visit: Nostitz vol. 1, pp. 159–79. 'Local ... Panslavism': Consul Taylor to Lord Derby, 15 May 1875, FO 7/860/5. Spread of rising and Andrássy's attempts to calm down the crisis: R. Millmann *Britain and the Eastern Question*

1875–78 (1979), pp. 13–26; D. Harris, *Diplomatic History of the Balkan Crisis* (Stanford 1936), pp. 428–33. For Andrássy Note: B.H. Sumner, *Russia and the Balkans, 1870–1880* (Oxford, 1936), p. 152. FJ at Reichstadt: ibid., pp. 172–6 and 583–8; Wertheimer, op. cit., vol. 3, pp. 320–5. Text of Tsar Alexander's speech, 11 November 1876: Sumner, p. 227. Beck on war to avenge Világos: G-H p. 200. Albrecht and Beck appeal to FJ to maintain peace: ibid., p. 191 with background in HM (5), pp. 360–3. 'Compact Slav state . . . is out of the question': quotation from the Tsar's chancellor, Gorchakov, 5 December 1876, Sumner, p. 285. FJ on 'It is my policy': HM (6), p. 45. Tsar's tougher tone: Sumner pp. 428–32. Ministerial council of 15 January 1878: Wertheimer, op. cit., vol. 3, pp. 61–3; G-H pp. 196–8. Ministerial council of 24 February 1878: Wertheimer, vol. 3, pp. 76–9; G-H p. 201. Andrássy to Kálnoky on 'conflict or conference': 28 January 1878, GP. vol. 2, no. 303. Possible congress at Baden-Baden: Sumner pp. 434–5. Ignatiev in Vienna and FJ's comment on him: ibid., pp. 444–56; FJ to Albert of Saxony, 25 March 1878, Ernst, p. 175. FJ 'overjoyed': Rudolf to Latour, 13 August 1878, Rud. HHSA 16. 'Headed by a military band': Wertheimer, vol. 3, p. 153. Military plans and campaign problems in occupation of the provinces: Roth. pp. 101–2. For origin of 'Emperor never understand Eastern Question' remark, see Bridge, op. cit. p. 130. Andrássy insists on adhering to treaty terms: minutes of ministerial council on 24 August 1878, HHSA PA XL/290; and cf. his remarks at later council meetings on 11 October and 16 November, with minutes in same HHSA file. Andrássy's abortive attempt to resign, placed in a general context: Bridge, op. cit., p. 132. For Bismarck and Andrássy's resignation: Bruce Waller, *Bismarck at the Crossroads* (1974), chapter 8, especially pp. 190–3. Text of Austro-German Dual Alliance: appendix to Bridge, op. cit., pp. 382–4. Later Austro-Hungarian administration in Bosnia-Herzegovina: Macartney, pp. 740–8, supplemented by Robert Donia, *Islam under the Double Eagle 1878–1914* (New York, 1981), Peter Sugar, *The Industrialization of Bosnia-Herzegovina 1878–1918* (Seattle 1963), and Noel Malcolm, op. cit., pp. 136–55.

Chapter 14 Father and Son

A facsimile of the Crown Prince's military service record with 36th Infantry Regiment is in B. Hamann, *Rudolf, Der Weg nach Mayerling*, p. 57. An extract from *Funfzehn Tage auf der Donau* in Rudolf, *Schriften*, pp. 296–7. British royal family and Rudolf in 1877–78: Richard Barkeley, *The Road to Mayerling* (1958; hereafter cited as Barkeley), pp. 40–1, making use of the Royal Archives. Letter from Chester: Rudolf to Latour, 27 January 1878, Rud. HHSA, K16. His pamphlet on the Austrian Nobility: Rudolf, *Schriften*, pp. 19–52. His views on Joseph II, ibid., pp. 235–54. General Beck on Rudolf: G-H pp. 230–1. Crown Prince's Jewish romance in Prague: Ham. *Rud.* pp. 152–6; Barkeley pp. 52–3. His lecture on battle of Spicheren: see the military service record, cited above; Ham. *Rud.* p. 242; Rudolf to Latour, 4 April 1879, Rud. HHSA K16; for modern assessment of the battle, Michael Howard, *The Franco-Prussian War* (1960), chapter 3, pt. 2. 'All the beautiful women of Vienna.': Mitis, pp. 200–1. FJ's Silver

Wedding: Corti, *Mensch* pp. 526–7; Corti, *Elizabeth* p. 238; Ham. *El.* p. 358. Rudolf's satisfaction with regimental command: Mitis, p. 63. His letters to Latour in Rud. HHSA K16, cover Croat-Magyar relations (8 October 1878), Taaffe and the Czechs (13 October 1878), and social democracy (31 January 1879). Formation of Taaffe ministry and 'muddling through': Macartney pp. 611–15. FJ, Rudolf and Taaffe: Crown Prince to Latour, 30 October 1879, Rud. HHSA K16; Mitis, pp. 54–5; Ham. *Rud.* pp. 139–42, 146, 150–4. FJ and Helene Vetsera: Corti, *Elizabeth* p. 241, citing Marie Festetics's diary of 3 December 1879. FJ's meeting with Anna Nahowski: Ham. *Schr.* pp. 16–17; and Friedrich Saathen (ed.), *Anna Nahowski und Franz Joseph* (Vienna, 1986). On Rudolf's engagement, Princess Stephanie, *I Was To Be Empress*, pp. 89–90. Elizabeth receives telegram at Claridge's, Corti, *Elizabeth*, p. 244. Further correspondence of Crown Prince and Latour in 1880–81 in Rud. HHSA K16 includes: engagement telegram, 7 March; Stephanie 'comely', letter of 7 March; 'intoxicated with happiness', letter, 11 March; 'patriotism here is colossal', 5 April (cf. Mitis p. 202); Elizabeth at Red Cross meeting, 8 June (but for criticism of his mother, see Barkeley pp. 82 and 84); and his letter of 11 February 1881 attacking Taaffe and Cardinal Schwarzenberg and expressing his preference for a Jewish headmaster rather than a clericalist. Parts of this letter are in Barkeley and in Mitis; see also for his views, Ham. *Rud.* p. 166. Rudolf's wedding: ibid., p. 162; Corti and Sokol, pp. 14–15; Stephanie, op. cit., pp. 104–11, with Laxenburg references, pp. 112–3. Memorandum on situation in Austria: Rudolf: *Schriften*, pp. 56–78. The long letter to Latour of 2 December 1881, praising Stephanie and criticizing the views of FJ, is in Rud. HHSA K16; a translation forms an appendix to Mitis (pp. 205–7) and it is extensively quoted in Barkeley, pp. 81–4. The Haymerle years: Macartney, p. 594; Bridge, op. cit., pp. 136–49 (with text of Three Emperors' Alliance, pp. 384–6). Rudolf, Szeps and Clemenceau: Barkeley, pp. 113–7, 119–24, 125–6, 160–2; Mitis, pp. 203–5; Bertha Szeps, *My Life and History* (1938), pp. 94–7, 110–11. Rudolf's 'way of talking': Princess Louise of Belgium, *My Own Affairs* (1921), p. 106. 'Waclav' as possible child's name: Stephanie op. cit., p. 144. Birth of daughter 'Erszi', ibid., pp. 145–6: and FJ's reaction Barkeley p. 91.

Chapter 15 Golden Epoch

A comprehensive record of FJ's public duties is in Hans Pauer's, *Kaiser Franz Joseph I*, a chronological guide to the pictorial documentation of the reign: for the 1880s, pp. 191–205. FJ and Queen Victoria at Innsbruck; journal entry for 23 April 1888, G.E. Buckle, (ed.), *Letters of Queen Victoria*, Series 3, (1930), vol. 1, p. 400. For FJ's Kálnoky and the Skiernewice meeting: Corti and Sokol, p. 49; Bridge, op. cit., pp. 164–6; and correspondence between FJ and Kálnoky for July 1884 in HHSA PA 1/460 Liasse 22a. Milan of Serbia and his dependence on Vienna: A.F. Pribram, 'Milan IV von Serbien und die Geheimvertrage Österreich-Ungarns mit Serbien 1881–9', *Historische Blätter* (Vienna 1921), pp. 464–94; supplemented by material on Serbian problems, HHSA PA 1/456. Liasse 5. Italian state visit to Vienna: Stephanie memoirs, pp. 126–9; Ham. *El.* p. 212. FJ's visit to Trieste and the Oberdank affair; Corti and Sokol, pp. 30–1 and 34–5; Corti, *Elizabeth* pp. 256–8; Alfred Alexander, *The Hanging of Wilhelm Oberdank* (1977). FJ's reaction to Ringtheater fire: Corti and Sokol, p. 20. Villa in the Tiergarten at Lainz and the Titania theme: Ham. *El.* pp. 440–3. Susanne Walther (ed.) *Hermesvilla* (Vienna, 1986), an excellent brochure produced by Vienna's Historische Museum, with contributions by the editor, by Renates Kassal-Mikula on the architecture of the villa, and by Gunther Martin on the Empress and the villa. Elizabeth's excessive walks: Corti, *Elizabeth*, pp. 259–63; Stephanie memoirs, p. 173. 'Eagle' Ludwig and 'seagull' Elizabeth: see Ham. *El.* pp. 412–39. Dr Brigitte Hamann has edited Empress Elizabeth's 'poetic diary' for this period: *Kaiserin Elisabeth. Das Poetische Tagebuch* (Vienna 1984). FJ on Elizabeth in Ithaca: his letter to her of 1 November 1887, Nostitz, vol. 1, p. 190. FJ's first visit to the Hermesvilla: Ham. *El.* p. 443. FJ and purchase of the Achilleion: Corti, *Elizabeth*, p. 308. FJ's generosity to Helene Nahowski: Saathen (ed.), op. cit., pp. 118–9; Ham. *Schr.* pp. 159–60. Married and professional life of Katharina Schratt, 1873–83: J. Haslip, *Emperor and Actress*, pp. 20–34; Ham. *Schr.* pp. 19–25. FJ at Angeli's studio; ibid., p. 28; Kremsier meeting, Bridge, op. cit., pp. 167–8, 170; Crown Prince's reactions, Mitis, p. 247; Stephanie memoirs, pp. 188–9; Empress's view, Ham. *El.* pp. 533–5. The Bulgarian crisis of 1885: C. Jelavich, *Tsarist Russia and Balkan Nationalism* (Westport, Conn., 1978), pp. 315–43. Andrássy memorandum: Bridge, op. cit., p. 170. FJ and K. Schratt at Frauenstein 1886: Ham. *Schr.* pp. 31, 34, 37; J. Haslip, op. cit., pp. 38–40. 'Chatting ... at Frauenstein': reminiscence in FJ's letter to K. Schratt, 23 November 1886, Ham. *Schr.* p. 38. Anna Nahowski in 1886: ibid., p. 36 and Saathen, op. cit., pp. 110–1. Elizabeth and Ludwig's death: Ham. *El.* pp. 424–9; Corti, *Elizabeth*, pp. 279–84. Elizabeth visits Brundlfeld mental institution: ibid., p. 285. Kaulbars mission and its background: A. Palmer, *Chancelleries of Europe* (1983), pp. 192–3. 'Unthinkable for Austria-Hungary': Kálnoky cited by Aehrenthal in a 166 folio memorandum on Austro-Russian relations 1872–94, drawn up in May–June 1895, HHSA PA I/469. Contingency plans for war with Russia: G-H pp. 301–6. Strength of war party in Vienna: Roth. pp. 115–6; Rudolf and war party, G-H pp. 308–14. FJ's letters to K. Schratt, Christmas 1886: pleased to see her name on posters, 25 December, Ham. *Schr.* p. 39; 'the prospect is poor', 1 January 1887, ibid, p. 40. Elizabeth's New Year's Night poem, *Poetische Tagebuch*, pp. 138–9. FJ's views on Ferdinand of Saxe-Coburg: J. Haslip, op. cit., pp. 54–6. For the Prince generally: Stephen Constant, *Foxy Ferdinand* (1979), pp. 91–129. FJ's life at Ischl in 1887: Ham. *Schr.* pp. 60–5, with manoeuvre references in two later letters, pp. 65–7. Elizabeth at Cromer: recollection of Compton Mackenzie, *My Life and Times, Octave 1* (1963), p. 144; verses in *Poetisches Tagebuch*, pp. 216–39, with 'backward glance' from Ischl, p. 257. FJ's letters to K. Schratt 1887–8: 'champagne glasses' for Catherine's Day (25 November) and 'to see you would make me happy', 29 November 1887, Bourgoing p. 75, (extract in Ham. *Schr.* p. 69); 'looked up at my window', 6 January 1888, ibid., pp. 78–9; reply to 'letter of meditation', 14 February 1888, Ham. *Schr.* pp. 77–8; Bourgoing pp. 84–7 (cf. J. Haslip op. cit., pp. 69–70); 'frankness is best' and 'Tyrolean garden', 18 February

1888, Ham. *Schr.*, pp. 81–3. Rudolf to Stephanie on Szeps and the Schönerer troubles: Stephanie memoirs, pp. 223–6; supplemented by letter from Rudolf to Bombelles, 8 March 1888, Rud. HHSA K 16 in which he says he thinks Vienna is 'the right place to be at this time'; see also Ham. *Rud.* pp. 406–7; and Andrew G. Whiteside's penetrating study, *The Socialism of Fools; Georg Ritter von Schönerer and Austrian Pan-Germanism* (Berkeley, 1975). Unveiling of the Maria Theresa monument: Corti and Sokol, pp. 103–4; Corti, *Elizabeth* pp. 303–4; *Poetisches Tagebuch* pp. 339–44; F.J. to K. Schratt, 15 May 1888, Ham: Schr. p. 91.

Chapter 16 Mayerling and After

'Settle at Mayerling': Rudolf to Bombelles, 27 July 1887, Rud. HHSA K12. Descriptions of Wienerwald are from the 1888 Lower Austria volume of the Crown Prince's survey of Austria-Hungary: Rudolf, *Schriften*, pp. 351, 352. Opening of Electrical Exhibition: Hamann, *Rudolf, Der Weg . . .* p. 48. Army bicycle corps: ibid., p. 62; HM (5) pp. 434–5. Inspector-General of Infantry: ibid., pp. 365–6; Ham. *Rud.* pp. 259–62. 'Different from my relations': Rudolf to Bombelles, 4 April 1883, Rud. HHSA K12. FJ 'knows everything': Rudolf to Francis Ferdinand, November 1884, cited from Archduke's papers by Lavender Cassels, *The Archduke and the Assassin* (1983) p. 14; for military private affairs within FJ's cognizance, cf. I. Deák, *Beyond Nationalism*, p. 141 and p. 143. Mizzi Caspar: Judith Listowel's *A Habsburg Tragedy* (1978), gives a clear impression of her (notably pp. 123–5 and 246–7 and 253–4); Lady Listowel makes use of information from Dr Walter Hummelberger, who knew Mizzi's step-sister. See also the semi-official police compilation, *Das Mayerling Original* (Munich, Stuttgart, Vienna, Zurich, 1955), p. 45. Rudolf's mixed feelings towards Stephanie, critical but not unsympathetic: letter to Bombelles, 21 July, 1886, Rud. HHSA K16. For Rudolf and Stephanie in Galicia and Bosnia-Herzegovina: Hamann, *Rudolf: Der Weg . . .* pp. 90, 102–3, 106–8. For Stephanie on Rudolf's illness, his recuperation on Lacroma and his increasing dependence on morphine, see her memoirs, pp. 206–8. Shooting incident: Mitis, pp. 47–8; Barkeley (pp. 156–7) rightly points out that Mitis's version depends on testimony 40 years later; Listowel, pp. 168–70 emphasizes the event. Hunting in Styria in 1889: there is a hurriedly written letter from Rudolf at Mürzsteg on 2 January 1889 to the journalist Berthold Frischauer in Rud. HHSA K16 (fol. 52 of the Frischauer correspondence). 'In most cheerful spirits', FJ reminiscing to K. Schratt, 5 October 1889, Bourgoing p. 174. The 'Julius Felix' open letter: Rudolf, *Schriften*, pp. 191–227. 'Lynchpin of the German alliance': FJ to Albert of Saxony, 14 December 1887, Ernst p. 184. Rudolf's anonymous obituary of William I: Rudolf, *Schriften*, pp. 187–90. Boyhood relationship between William II and Rudolf: see the German Crown Princess's letters to Queen Victoria in 1873, R. Fulford (ed.), *Darling Child* pp. 73, 85, 88–9 and William II, *My Early Life* (1926), pp. 71–3. William borrows money from Rudolf on his visit to Vienna: Ham. *Rud.* p. 335; Stephanie's memoirs p. 143. Rudolf's ironic letter of August 1888 to Szeps about William II, cited from Rud. HHSA K17, Ham. *Schr.* p. 360. Hussar Temple episode: Barkeley, p. 218; Listowel, op. cit., p. 206. Lyrics of two *Heurigenlieder* for Mizzi: Rudolf, *Schriften*, pp. 276–7 (facsimile p. 278). Prince of Wales in Austria: Philip Magnus, *King Edward the Seventh* (1964), pp. 207–11; 'indefatigability', Stephanie's memoirs, p. 238; FJ and the 'fat man' on manoeuvres: letter to K. Schratt, 16 September 1888, Ham. *Schr.* p. 101. FJ and William II's state visit: Rudolf to Kálnoky, 29 September, 1888, Rud. HHSA K16; Stephanie's memoirs, p. 239; FJ 'extremely nervous', letter to K. Schratt, 5 October 1888, Ham. *Schr.* p. 103. Prince of Wales on seeing Mary Vetsera at Burgtheater gala: letter to Queen Victoria, cited from the Windsor archives by Barkeley, pp. 205–6, and written after the Mayerling tragedy. Marie Larisch, *My Past* (1913), pp. 170–208 give her version of events; on Larisch see Barkeley, pp. 209–11. Mary Vetsera's account of events on 5 November 1888 and subsequently, first appeared in Helene Vetsera, *Denkschrift*, (privately printed 1889, re-printed Reichenberg 1921); some of her manuscript is in facsimile in *Das Mayerling Original*, but Mary's original letters have never been made public. Sarah Gainham believes the Prince of Wales was misled (*Habsburg Twilight*, p. 16), deeply mistrusts the Vetsera *Denkschrift* (pp. 13, 25–6), and thinks the affair began earlier. For FJ's activities on 5 November 1888, see his letter to K. Schratt, 6 November, Ham, *Schr.* p. 111. For growing Hungarian army discontent: Macartney p. 695. FJ and Empress at Miramare 1888: Corti, *Elizabeth* p. 309. *Schwarzgelb* and Rudolf: Mitis, p. 109 plays down his role, but cf. Ham. *Rud.* pp. 372–8; see also Rudolf, *Schriften*, pp. 230–2. For Drumont's attack and *Epoca*: Barkeley, p. 198 and Ham. *Rud.* pp. 397–8. Rudolf's 'unsavoury article' about William II is printed in Rudolf: *Schriften*, pp. 228–9. Fall from horse; Barkeley p. 277. FJ does not believe Rudolf is ill: Stephanie's memoirs, pp. 240–1. Christmas at the Hofburg 1888: Corti, *Elizabeth*, pp. 310–11; FJ to K Schratt, 24 and 31 December, Ham, *Schr.* pp. 117–9; Saathen, *Nahowski*, p. 139; FJ to Elizabeth, 31 December, Nostitz, vol. 1, pp. 203–4. FJ's gloom at prospect of William II's birthday celebrations: letter to K. Schratt, 26 January 1889, Ham. *Schr.* p. 122. Title page of 12th issue of *Schwarzgelb* reproduced in *Hamann, Der Weg...* p. 120. For FJ's angry scene with his son and events of 29–31 January in Vienna and Mayerling, I have used books already cited by Barkeley and Listowel, together with: Corti and Sokol, pp. 116–8; Ham. *Rud.* chapter 14; Corti, *Elizabeth*, chapter 13; facsimiles in *Das Mayerling Original*; Walpurga Lady Paget, *Embassies of Other Days* (1923), vol. 2, pp. 464–6; and Hoyos's report, as printed in Mitis, pp. 273–86. Rudolf's funeral: *The Times*, 7 February 1889. For Victor Adler's speech of July 1889: Crankshaw, op. cit., p. 297, citing Adler's *Aufsàtze, Reden und Briefe*. Rud. HHSA K. 21 contains papers put together after the Mayerling tragedy; among them is material submitted by Bombelles to clear his name (including two letters from Maximilian, 1866 and 1867) and German language extracts from works on Russian history prepared for Rudolf in late 1888, including an account of the murder of Tsar Paul. Rudolf's farewell letter to his wife: Stephanie's memoirs, p. 248; facsimile in Hamann, *Der Weg...* p. 124. FJ to K. Schratt after the tragedy: 'talking brings relief', 5 March, Bourgoing, p. 135; 'interest in gossip', 16 March, Ham. *Schr.* p. 148; 'taking up the old life', 14 April, Bourgoing, p. 165. FJ described visiting Mayerling on All Souls Day 1889 in two letters: to K. Schratt, 3 November, Ham. *Schr.* pp. 189–90('soothing peace'); to Elizabeth, 6 November, Nostitz, vol. 1, pp. 205–6 (awed by Carmelite devotion).

Chapter 17 Spared Nothing

Fate of Charles Ludwig: Corti and Sokol p. 207. Francis Ferdinand's early life: L. Cassels, *Archduke and Assassin,* pp. 8–27; G. Brook-Shepherd, *Victims at Sarajevo* (1984) pp. 9–20. Relations between FJ and Francis Ferdinand after Mayerling: R. Kiszling, *Erzherzog Franz Ferdinand von Österreich-Este* (Graz-Cologne, 1953), pp. 18–20: Margutti, pp. 123–32. Francis Ferdinand's fury over use of Magyar language: G-H, pp. 476–7. Hungarian army bill: Deák, *Beyond Nationalism,* p. 66; Macartney, p. 698; Corti and Sokol, pp. 140–1. FJ on 'almost laughable' changes: letter to K. Schratt, 20 October 1889, Ham. *Schr.* p. 186. FJ on rudeness of Hungarian parliamentarians: letter of 26 February 1890, ibid., p. 210. May Day alarm: Barea, *Vienna,* pp. 311–12; and the detailed study by Harald Troch, *Rebellensonntag, Der 1 Mai zwischen Politik, Arbeiterkultur und Volksfest* (Vienna 1991). FJ and the Bismarck family wedding: letter to K. Schratt, 17 June 1892, Ham. *Schr.* p. 263; cf. A. O. Meyer, *Bismarck, der Mensch und der Staatsmann* (Stuttgart, 1949), pp. 691–93. FJ to Taaffe condemning anti-semitism: N. Vielmetti, *Das Österreichisches Judentum* (Vienna and Munich, 1974), p. 118. For the Czechs and the *Punktationen*: E. Wiskemann, *Czechs and Germans* (2nd ed. 1967), chapter 5, especially, p. 35. FJ, Taaffe's fall and suffrage reform: Macartney pp. 659–61; May, op. cit., p. 226. Cilli problem: ibid., p. 323; Macartney pp. 663–4. For FJ, the fall of Kálnoky and the rise of Goluchowski: Bridge, op. cit., pp. 205–8. On Karl Lueger's election and FJ's opposition; Richard S. Geehr, *Karl Lueger, Mayor of Fin-de-Siècle Vienna* (Boston, 1991), pp. 89–95; John W. Boyer, *Political Radicalism in Late Imperial Vienna* (Chicago, 1981), pp. 360–2 and 374–6; and for an objective assessment of Lueger's achievements, Gainham, *Habsburg Twilight,* pp. 65–90. FJ on anti-semitism as a 'disease': letter to Elizabeth, 30 December 1895, Nostitz, vol. 2, p. 111. FJ ratifies Lueger's appointment: Geehr, p. 99 and Boyer, pp. 409–10. Analysis of election: Macartney pp. 662–3. FJ on Albrecht's funeral: letter to K. Schratt, 27 February 1895, Ham. *Schr.* pp. 322–3. Gisela's warning to Valerie: Corti, *Elizabeth,* p. 329. Return of Empress to court life: J. Haslip, *Lonely Empress,* pp. 416–7. For FJ's reactions to life at Territet: Ham. *Schr.* pp. 273–6. FJ's codicil to his will, favouring Schratt: J. Haslip, *Emperor and Actress,* pp. 119–21. FJ and Baltazzi balloon flight: ibid., pp. 138–9 and Ham. *Schr.* pp. 213–4. FJ unable to sleep because of slanders on K. Schratt, ibid., pp. 264–7; fullest treatment of the affair in J. Haslip, *Emperor and Actress,* pp. 147–50. FJ mentions 'Edison phonograph' in letters both to K. Schratt (5 November 1889) and to the Empress (6 November): Ham *Schr.* p. 190 and Nostitz, vol. 1, p. 206. For FJ and Ibsen's *Wild Duck*: letter to Empress, 19 January 1897, Nostitz, vol. 2, p. 214; FJ anxious over Empress's sea voyages: 5 September 1890, Ham. *Schr.* p. 327; complains of bicycling mania, 13 April 1897, Ham. *Schr.* p. 364. FJ's Monte Carlo visit in 1894, ibid., p. 295; 'Soon to bed', 25 April 1896,

Bourgoing, p. 320; sees Gladstone, February 1895, ibid., p. 305 and Ham, *Schr.* p. 319; on Riviera eating habits, 12 March 1894, Bourgoing, p. 294 (with extract, Ham. *Schr.* p. 299). French fleet, Alpine infantry, presidential trumpeters, 5 and 7 March 1896: Ham. *Schr.* pp. 334–6. FJ and Empress to Cimiez: Queen Victoria to Lord Salisbury, 21 March 1896, *Letters of Queen Victoria* (3rd series) Vol. 3, p. 36. Hungarian millennial celebrations: Corti, *Elizabeth* pp. 357–8; Corti and Sokol, p. 206; May, op. cit., p. 363. Hungarian political crisis in 1897: Macartney pp. 700–01. Badeni Ordinance and subsequent unrest: ibid., pp. 663–4; May, pp. 325–8; P. von Eulenburg, *Erlebnisse an deutschen und fremden Höfen* (Leipzig 1934), vol. 2, pp. 210–12; J. Haslip, *Emperor and Actress* pp. 195–6. For FJ and Lueger at Stadtbahn opening: Hans Pauer, op. cit., p. 234. FJ. and schoolchildren: in 1898: letter to K Schratt, 26 June 1898: Ham. *Schr.* p. 384. Warning from FJ to K. Schratt about Empress's poor appearance, 3 March 1897, ibid., p. 358., 'More terrible than anything this century': Salisbury to Queen Victoria, 7 May, 1897, *Letters of Queen Victoria*, ser. 3, vol. 3, p. 159. Effect of fire tragedy on Empress: Corti, *Elizabeth*, p. 363. Elizabeth's visit to Geneva and her murder: ibid., pp. 365–84; Ham. *El.* pp. 596–600; see also Ham. *Schr.* p. 389. The earliest record of FJ's use of the phrase 'spared nothing' (in German) appears to be in an account of Goluchowski's conversation with the British ambassador, Rumbold to Queen Victoria, 11 September 1898, *Letters of Queen Victoria*, ser. 3, vol. 3, pp. 277–8.

Chapter 18 The Belvedere.

FJ's letter to K. Schratt of 11 September 1898: Bourgoing p. 367; Ham. *Schr.* p. 390. Marie Valerie's reaction; J. Haslip, *Emperor and Actress*, pp. 206–7. For Order of Elizabeth: ibid., pp. 208–9; Ham. *Schr.* pp. 396–400. FJ 'no intention' of marrying again: J. Haslip, p. 214. Archduchess Isabella and Sophie Chotek: the tennis-court incident was first printed by the Archduke's former secretary, Paul Nikitsch-Boulles, *Vor dem Sturm, Errinerungen an ... Franz Ferdinand* (Berlin, 1925), pp. 21–2; later treatment in Brook-Shepherd, *Victims at Sarajevo*, pp. 62–3. On Konopischt: ibid., p. 90. FJ and Archduke's marriage: ibid., pp. 78–81; Corti and Sokol pp. 252–61; and the biography of the Archduke's legal adviser, Max von Beck by J.C. Allmayer-Beck (Munich and Vienna, 1956), pp. 47–55. FJ thinks Sophie Chotek 'natural and modest': Corti and Sokol p. 263. Francis Ferdinand on 'wisest thing I ever did': T. von Sosnowsky, *Erzerhog Franz Ferdinand* (Vienna and Munich 1929), pp. 35–6 (and cf. Brook-Shepherd, p. 92). William II to Francis Ferdinand on his wife: Prince Bülow, *Memoirs*, 1892–1903 (London and New York 1931), p. 614. For Loos, FJ and the Sezession: Carl Schorske, *Fin de-siècle Vienna; Politics and Culture* (1979) pp. 217–20 and 338–40; A. Janik and S. Toulmin, *Wittgenstein's Vienna* (1973) pp. 90–8; Barea, *Vienna*, pp. 257–8; Gainham, *Habsburg Twilight*, pp. 201–2. Noisy scenes in Vienna parliament: May, op. cit., pp. 333–4. On Koerber: ibid., 334–7; Macartney, pp. 667–9. FJ 'aged a lot': letter to K. Schratt, 12 May 1902, Bourgoing, p. 438. FJ, K. Schratt and the Maria Theresa play: Ham. *Schr.* pp. 487–90; J. Haslip, *Emperor and Actress*, p. 242. Rise of Hungarian Independence Party: Macartney pp. 693, 695, 700 and 760–3; Tibor Zsuppan's contribution to Mark Cornwall (ed.), *The Last Years of Austria-Hungary* (Exeter, 1990), p. 69. Case U (*Fall U*): G-H 404–6; Roth. pp. 134–5. FJ's Chlopy Army Order of 1903: G-H p. 403; I. Deák *Beyond Nationalism* p. 69. FJ's 'five minute audience' and its background in Hungary: Macartney pp. 761–2; minutes of the ministerial conference at Bad Ischl, 22 August 1905, POM (ii) ser. 2 Vol. 5, pp. 445–60. FJ 'not give way' and 'busier than ever over Hungarian rights': letters to K. Schratt, 2 October 1905 and 11 April 1906, Ham. *Schr.* pp. 504 and 510 (cf. Bourgoing, pp. 383 and 385). Francis Ferdinand's mistrustful nature: Conrad, vol. 1. p. 338. On Brosch: Brook-Shepherd, *Victims at Sarajevo*, pp. 119–21; L. Cassels, op. cit., p. 80. There is a study of the archival material on the Archduke's military chancellery by Rainer Egger, *Mitteilungen des Österreichisches Kriegsarchivs*, vol. 28 (Vienna 1975), pp. 141–63. On Max Beck as prime minister: May, op. cit., pp. 338–9; Allmayer-Beck's biography (especially pp. 169–85) and Lother Höbelt 'Austrian Pre-War Domestic Politics' in Cornwall's *Last Years...*, pp. 52–4. Austrian internal politics: W.A. Jenks, *The Austrian Electoral Reform of 1907* (New York, 1950); and John W. Boyer, 'The End of the Old Regime: Visions of Political Reform in Late Imperial Austria', *Journal of Modern History*, vol. 58 (Chicago, March 1986), pp. 159–93. For FJ and cars: I. Deák, op. cit., pp. 70–1 (including F.M. Beck's comment). See also H. Pauer, *Kaiser FJ*: pp. 280–1 (Ischl, 12 August 1908); 294 (manoeuvres, 8 September 1909) and photograph 148 between pp. 336–7 for FJ at 1910 Air Show. Archduke's criticism of 1906 manoeuvres: HM (5) p. 133 and Brook-Shepherd, op. cit., pp. 138–9. Appointment of Aehrenthal and Conrad: Bridge, op. cit., pp. 268–9; Roth. p. 137–42; G-H 432–5; Conrad vol. 1. pp. 33–7.

Chapter 19 Two Journeys to Sarajevo

Goluchowski on 'strangle Serbia': Eulenburg to Bülow, 6 January 1901, GP Vol 18(i) no. 3443. Belgrade palace murders and diplomatic consequences: W.S. Vucinich, *Serbia between East and West, The Events of 1903–1908* (Stanford and London, 1904), pp. 46–60 and 75–80. Conrad's memorandum of December 1907: Conrad, vol. 1, pp. 522–3. On the Sanjak Railway: A.J. May, 'The Novibazar Railway Project', *Journal of Modern History* (Chicago, 1938), vol. 10, pp. 496–527; S Wank, 'Aehrenthal and the Sanjak of Novibazar Railway Project', *Slavonic and East European Review* vol. 42 (1964), no. 99, pp. 353–69. 'Trouble, excitement and rush': FJ to K. Schratt, Bourgoing, p. 470. FJ's reaction to Izvolsky's offer in July 1908 OUA vol. 1, no. 9; Bridge, pp. 279–80. For Young Turk Revolution: A. Palmer, *Decline and Fall of Ottoman Empire*, pp. 196–210. Ministerial Conference of 19 August, 1908, OUA vol. 1, no. 40. Francis Ferdinand on Hungarian claims: Brook-Shepherd, op. cit. p. 176, citing Chlumecky, *Wirken und Wollen*, pp. 98–9. On the Buchlau talks: Aehrenthal's version OUA vol. 1, no. 79; Bridge, op. cit., pp. 282–4, updates Taylor, *Struggle for Mastery*, pp. 451–2. FJ and Ferdinand of Bulgaria: OUA vol. 1, no. 87; J. Haslip. *Emperor and Actress*, p. 255.

FJ's formal annexation of provinces: OUA vol. 1, no. 146. William II 'deeply offended': minute written 7 October 1908, GP vol. 26, no. 8992. For FJ's denial of 'designs of conquest': FJ to Nicholas II, 28 January 1909, OUA vol. 1, no. 935. On Austro-German military talks: Norman Stone. 'Moltke and Conrad: Relations between the Austro-Hungarian and German General Staffs 1909–1914', in P. Kennedy (ed.) *The War Plans of the Greater Powers* (1979), pp. 222–51 (reproduced from *Historical Journal* vol. 9, no. 2). 'Yes' or 'no' telegram: Bülow to Pourtales, 21 March 1909, GP vol. 26 (ii), no. 9460. On FJ and William II: A. Palmer, *The Kaiser* (1978,) p. 139. FJ's diamond jubilee: Corti and Sokol, pp. 321–4. Prague protests: May, op. cit., p. 415. FJ's visit to Bosnia: V. Dedijer, *Road to Sarajevo*, pp. 236–41; L. Cassels, op. cit., pp. 110–12, 114–15, and her Chapter 12 in general. 'Not too hot in Bosnia': FJ to K. Schratt, 26 May 1910, Bourgoing, p. 47 (and Ham. *Schr.* pp. 518–9); J. Haslip, *Emperor and Actress*, p. 257. Appel's report to Francis Ferdinand's military chancellery cited, from the Vienna Kriegsarchivs, by L. Cassels, p. 112. FJ's pervading presence: J.P. Barry, *At the Gates of the East* (1906) p. 79. Roosevelt's audience with FJ: J.D. Bishop, *Theodore Roosevelt and His Times* (New York, 1920), vol. 2, p. 216 (cf E.F. Morris (ed.) *Letters of Theodore Roosevelt* [Cambridge, Mass. 1954] pp. 369–70). Archduke's criticism of Roosevelt: report of 25 May 1910, quoted from his papers in HHSA by Dedijer, p. 98 and dated in Brook-Shepherd, *Victims.*, p. 282. Hitler and Lueger's funeral: A. Hitler, *Mein Kampf* (first English translation, 1939), p. 113; see also Alan Bullock, *Hitler and Stalin, Parallel Lives* (1991) p. 44. For Bronstein/Trotsky see Berchtold, as quoted by Taylor, *Struggle for Mastery*, p.xxxiv. FJ and church festivals: Margutti, pp. 225–7. Religious observance census figures: I. Deák, *Beyond Nationalism*, p. 171. FJ celebrates 80th birthday: Corti and Sokol p. 356; illness, ibid., p. 368. Austrian domestic problems 1911: Lother Höbelt in M. Cornwall's *Last Years of Austria-Hungary*, pp. 54–7; Macartney, pp. 796–8; May, op. cit., pp. 428–30. Tisza and Hungary, ibid., pp. 439–45. FJ at Charles and Zita's marriage: Reinhold Lorenz, *Kaiser Karl und der Untergang der Donaumonarche* (Graz, Vienna, Cologne, 1959), pp. 92–5; G. Brook-Shepherd, *The Last Habsburg* (1968), pp. 22–4 and his *The Last Empress* (1991), p. 19. Conrad proposes attack on Italy, 24 September 1911, OUA vol. 3, no. 2644. Aehrenthal's response in memorandum to FJ, 22 October, OUA vol. 3, no. 2809. Conrad's audience with FJ, 15 November, and later dismissal: Conrad, vol. 2, p. 282; HM (5) p. 140. Ministerial Council, 6 December 1911, HHSA PA XL/310, extracts only in OUA vol. 3, no. 3057. (HHSA minutes show ministers critical of Italian ally, as 3 army corps were needed to subdue Tripolitania). FJ chooses Berchtold: Bridge, op. cit., p. 312; S. Wank, 'The Appointment of Count Berchtold as Foreign Minister', JCEA, vol. 23, July 1963. Berchtold professes ignorance of South Slavs: Tschirschky to Kiderlen-Waechter, 6 December 1912, GP vol. 33, no. 12487. Berchtold and Archduke's family: R.A. Kann, 'Francis Ferdinand and Berchtold, 1912–14', S.B. Winten (ed.) *Dynasty, Politics and Culture* (Boulder, Colorado 1991), pp. 105–50. Nicholas of Montenegro in 1912 J.D. Treadway, *The Falcon and the Eagle; Montenegro and Austria-Hungary* (West Lafayette, Ind., 1982), pp. 72–101. Balkan Wars: B. Jelavich,

History of the Balkans (Cambridge, 1983), vol. 2, *Twentieth Century*, pp. 95–100; A. Palmer, *Decline and Fall of Ottoman Empire*, pp. 215–8. FJ says 'I don't want war', Fritz Fellner (ed.) *Schicksalsjahre Osterreich, 1908–1919: Das Politische Tagebuch Josef Redlichs* (Graz, 1953–54; hereafter cited as Redlich *Tagebuch*), 29 November 1912, vol. 1, p. 183. Ministerial Councils of 28 October and 8 November, 1912, on war preparadness in annexed provinces: HHSA PA XL/310. FJ re-instates Conrad: his vol. 2, pp. 373–9. Prochaska affair: Bridge, op. cit., p. 318; HM (6)i p. 491. Berchtold on events of 11 December 1912, Hugo Hantsch, *Leopold Graf Berchtold* (Graz, 1963), vol. 1, pp. 360–4. His audience with FJ, 27 December: S.J. Williamson, *Austria-Hungary and the Origins of the First World War* (1991), P. 131, citing unpublished section of Berchtold's diary. Scutari crisis; ibid., p. 136; Redlich *Tagebuch*, (21 March 1913), vol. 1, pp. 192–3; Conrad vol. 3, pp. 226–30. Conrad wishes to implement earlier war plans: pp. 252–66. Attitudes of Masaryk, István Tisza: C.A. Macartney and A.W. Palmer, *Independent Eastern Europe* (1962), pp. 20–22; supplemented by Eva Schmidt-Hartmann, *Thomas G. Masaryk's Realism* (Munich, 1984). On FJ, Tisza and the Roumanians: Ottokar Czernin, *In the World War* (1919) pp. 76–86. FJ's concern for his appearance before visits of K. Schratt: E. Ketterl, p. 107; his relaxed moments with Grinzing musicians, ibid., p. 108. Basic to the Redl Case are E.E. Kisch, *Der Fall des Generalstafschef Redl* (Berlin 1924), and Robert Asprey, *The Panther's Feast* (New York, 1959); see also S. Gainham, *The Habsburg Twilight*, pp. 142–60; Conrad, vol. 3, pp. 338–80; Redlich *Tagebuch* (26 June 1913), vol. 1, pp. 201–2; and Norman Stone's chapter on the Austro-Hungarian intelligence services in Ernest May (ed.), *Knowing One's Enemies* (Princeton, NJ, 1984), especially p. 43. Conflict between FJ and the Archduke over Redl affair: Conrad, as cited above; and L. Cassels, *Archduke and the Assassin*, pp. 157–8. FJ increases Francis Ferdinand's military authority: ibid., p. 143; Roth. p. 170; HM (5) pp. 367–9. FJ and Leipzig centenary: see photographs in Franz Hubman, *The Habsburg Empire* (1972), p. 298. Serb officers' pressure group and Black Hand: A. Palmer, *The Lands Between* (1969), pp. 112–16, 116–7; Dedijer op. cit., pp. 371–81; and B. Jelavich's 'What the Habsburg Government knew about the Black Hand', AHY vol. 22, pp. 131–50, including five reports from the military attaché in Belgrade. Pašić in Vienna: Minutes of ministerial council 3 October, 1913: HHSA PA XL/311 (partly printed OUA vol. 7, no. 8779); Berchtold memorandum, OUA vol. 7, no. 8813; Griesinger to German Foreign Ministry, 7 October 1913, GP vol. 36 (i) no. 14157. Ultimatum to Belgrade, 17 October 1913; OUA vol. 7, no. 8850. Archduke and Conrad's non-attendance at Mass: L. Cassels, op. cit., p. 158. First proposals that Archduke should visit Sarajevo: ibid., pp. 143–44; Conrad, vol. 3, p. 445. FJ chooses to walk up the stairs: G-H, p. 442. FJ's illness in spring of 1914: Brook-Shepherd, *Victims.*, p. 259; Corti and Sokol, p. 408. Council of ministers on 24 May, 1914: HHSA PA XL/311. FJ's final audiences with Francis Ferdinand: Brook-Shepherd, *Victims.*, p. 222. William II and Archduke in 1914: ibid., pp. 228–32; A. Palmer, *The Kaiser* pp. 163–4; Dedijer, op. cit., p. 158; Williamson, op. cit., p. 164. Detailed accounts of the events in Sarajevo are in Brook-Shepherd, Cassels and Dedijer; see also

Joachim Remak, *Sarajevo* (1959), who cites (p. 106) telegram from the Archduke to FJ, 27 June. FJ informed of assassination: Margutti, pp. 147–8. Marie Valerie on her father's reaction: Corti and Sokol, p. 413.

Chapter 20 War

British royal sympathy for FJ: James Pope-Hennessy, *Queen Mary* (1959), pp. 485–6. 'No mood of mourning', Redlich *Tagebuch*, 29 June, vol. 1, p. 235. Baron Morse and the 'third class burial': Brook-Shepherd (*Victims.*, p. 261) writes that the phrase 'crops up repeatedly' in the manuscript diary of the Archduke's secretary, Morsey; and cf. Immanuel Geiss, *July 1914*, p. 56 for other use of the phrase. Brook-Shepherd (pp. 261–9) and Remak, op. cit., (pp. 166–81) give detailed accounts of the prolonged obsequies, from Trieste to Artstetten. Berchtold on FJ's reactions: Hantsch, *Berchtold*, vol. 2, p. 559. 'Time not yet ripe': Macartney p. 807; for Tisza and opinion in Hungary: N. Stone, 'Hungary and the Crisis of July 1914', *Journal of Contemporary History* (1966), vol. 1, pp. 153–170. 'Serbia must be eliminated': FJ to William II, 2 July 1914, OUA vol. 8, no. 9984. The Hoyos mission: S.R. Williamson, op. cit., pp. 195–6; Geiss, op. cit., pp. 70–81. Pledge of support to FJ from Berlin: Szögyeny to Berchtold, 6 July 1914, OUA vol. 8, no. 10076. Ministerial council of 7 July: minutes, OUA vol. 8 no. 10118 (excerpt, Geiss, pp. 80–7). FJ receives Berchtold at Ischl: Berchtold's diary entry for 9 July in Hantsch vol. 2, p. 570; Tschirsky to Jagow, 10 July, 1914, printed as document 16 in Geiss, op. cit., pp. 106–8. Ministerial council of 19 July: minutes, OUA, vol. 8 no. 10393; FJ's first response to report of meeting: Margutti, pp. 397–9. Austrian demands on Serbia, OUA vol. 8, no. 10395 (but see no. 10526 for final note handed to Serbia). FJ, Russia and ultimatum: R.A. Kann, 'Emperor Franz Joseph and the Outbreak of World War I' in S.B. Winters (ed.) *Dynasty, Politics and Culture*, pp. 283–310. Churchill's comment on ultimatum: Winston S. Churchill, *The World Crisis* (1938 edition), vol. 1, p. 155. Duke of Cumberland and other visitors to FJ: Margutti: pp. 401;2: 'That's that', ibid., p. 404. 'I have done my best': J. Haslip, *Emperor and Actress*, p. 267. William II unable to control events: A. Palmer, *The Kaiser*, pp. 170 and 224. FJ's departure from Bad Ischl: Margutti, p. 411. Bungling of war plans by Conrad: Stone, 'Moltke and Conrad' in P. Kennedy (ed.) *War Plans of the Great Powers*, pp. 237–40 and p. 249. 'My wars have always begun with victories': Empress Zita's reminscences of FJ as reported by Brook-Shepherd in *The Last Habsburg*, p. 29 and *The Last Empress*, p. 39. 'A happy war for us?': Margutti, pp. 417–8. FJ and Jewish refugees: A.J. May, *The Passing of the Hapsburg Monarchy*, 1916–18 (Philadelphia, 1968), vol. 1, p. 311. FJ at Christmas 1914: Margutti, p. 431. The Italian problem: L. Valiani, *The End of Austria-Hungary*, pp. 62–71 (1973), and his 'Italo-Austro-Hungarian negotiations 1914–15', *Journal of Contemporary History* (1966), vol. 1, pp. 113–36; Bridge, op. cit., pp. 348–52. FJ presides over his last council of ministers, 8 March 1915: M. Komjathy, *Protokolle des Gemeinsamen Ministerates ... 1914–18* (Budapest, 1966), pp. 215–32. FJ's 'volcano' metaphor: Brook-Shepherd, *Last Empress*, p. 37. Stebnicka Huta desertions:

Notes and Sources

Z.A.B. Zeman, *The Break-Up of the Habsburg Empire 1914–1918* (1961) pp. 55–7. FJ celebrates re-capture of Lemberg: Hans Pauer, *Kaiser FJ*, p. 327. Conrad's *schwarzgelbe* offensive: Roth. pp. 194–5. FJ and the Polish Question: Fritz Fischer, *Germany's Aims in the First World War* (1967), pp. 236–45; Zeman, op. cit., pp. 100–09. Frustrated Trentino offensive: Gerhard Artl, *Die österreichische-ungarische Sudtiroloffensive 1916* (Vienna, 1983), especially pp. 182–3. Effects of Brussilov's offensive: Macartney, p. 818; Roth. p. 198; Redlich *Tagebuch* (20 June 1916) vol. 2, p. 123. Germany imposes unified military command: 'Silberstein, *The Troubled Alliance; German-Austrian Relations, 1914–17* (Lexington 1970), chapter 13. Weiner-Neustadt whirlwind and FJ's determination to call a halt to the war: Margutti, p. 448.

Chapter 21 Schönbrunn 1916

Stürgkh's assassination is vividly described from contemporary sources and interviews: R. Pick, *The Last Days of Imperial Vienna* (1975), pp. 1–9. Archduke Charles's movements: K. Lorenz, *Kaiser Karl*, pp. 221–3; Brook-Shepherd, *Last Habsburg*, pp. 44–5. Last visit of Katharina Schratt: J. Haslip, *Emperor and Actress*, p. 270; Bourgoing p. 475. FJ's death: Corti and Sokol, pp. 467–9; Margutti, pp. 454–5; Ketterl, p. 251. Reaction to death: Redlich *Tagebuch* (21 November 1916), vol. 2 p. 156; in allied capitals, Harry Hanak, *Great Britain and Austria-Hungary during the First World War* (1962), pp. 211–13, citing *Weekly Despatch of 3 December 1916* for criticism of Fr. Vaughan. Burial processions: Margutti pp. 456–7; Lorenz, op. cit., pp. 227–8. Solemn Requiem on anniversary of FJ's accession: Margutti, p. 458.

Chapter 22 Into History

The second half of Barbara Jelavich's *Modern Austria* (Cambridge, 1987) covers the years 1916 to 1986. For the peace treaties of 1919–20 and their effect on central Europe: Macartney and Palmer, *Independent Eastern Europe*, pp. 97–198. On Anton Léhar's Habsburg loyalty: I. Deák, *Beyond Nationalism*, p. 219. Robert Musil's *Der Mann ohne Eigenschaften* was translated into English by Eithne Wilkins and Ernst Kaiser as *The Man without Qualities* (1953): David Luft's critical study, *Robert Musil and the Crisis of European Culture* (Berkeley, 1980) seems to suggest that Musil interpreted the mood of 1913–14 in terms of a highly individualistic Weimar-Vienna cultural Anschluss. An American edition of Joseph Roth's *Radetzkymarsch*, translated by Eva Tucker was published in Woodstock, New York, 1983. J.P. Barry, *At the Gates of the East* (1906), saluted the modern martyr in the Hofburg, p. 90. For Empress Zita's return to Austria in 1982: Brook-Shepherd, *Last Empress*, p. 323; her funeral in 1989, ibid., pp. 329–34. FJ's table-talk on the Monarchy as 'a place of refuge', Margutti, pp. 261–2.

ALTERNATIVE PLACE NAMES

The first name given below is the one normally used in the book. Abbreviations:–
A. Albanian; Cz. Czech or Slovak; E. English; G. German; H. Hungarian; I.
Italian; P. Polish; R. Roumanian; Rus. Russian; SC. Serbo-Croat; Slov. Slovene;
T. Turkish.

Bolzano (I): Bozen (G)
Bratislava (Cz); Pressburg (G);
 Pozsony (H)
Brno (Cz); Brünn (G)
Buda (H); Ofen (G)
Cracow (E); Kraków (P); Krakau (G)
Cilli (G); Celje (Slov)
Cluj (R.); Kolozsvár (H);
 Klausenburg (G)
Corfu (I); Kerkyra (Greek)
Czernowitz (G); Chernovtsy (Rus);
 Cernauţi (R)
Dubrovnik (SC); Ragusa (I)
Durrës (A); Durazzo (I)
Edirne (T); Adrianople (E from
 Greek)
Fiume (I); Rijeka (SC); Reka (Slov)
Franzensbad (G); Františkovy Lázňe
 (Cz)
Györ (H); Raab (G)
Komárom (H); Komorn (G);
 Komárno (Cz)
Königgrätz (G); Hradec Králové
 (Cz)
Konopischt (G); Konopište (Cz)
Kotor (SC); Cattaro (I)
Kremsier (G); Kromeriz (Cz)
Lemberg (G); Lwów (P); Lvov (Rus);
 Lviv (Ukrainian)

Lissa (I); Vis (SC)
Ljubljana (Slov); Laibach (G)
Merano (I); Meran (G)
Novi Sad (SC); Ujvidék (H); Neusatz
 (G)
Olmütz (G): Olomouc (Cz)
Pilsen (G); Plzeň (Cz)
Pola (I); Pula (SC); Pulj (Slov)
Prague (E); Prag (G); Praha (Cz)
Reichstadt (G); Zákupy (Cz)
Ruschuk (G and T); Ruše (B)
Salonika (E); Thessaloniki (Greek)
San Giovanni di Medua (I); Shengjin
 (A)
Scutari [in Albania] (I); Shkodra (A)
Sopron (H); Oedenburg (G)
Split (SC); Spalato (I)
Szeged (H); Szegedin (G)
Temesvár (H); Timişoara (R)
Tisza river (H); Theiss river (G)
Ulcinj (A); Dulcigno (I)
Vienna (E); Wien (G); Bécs (H);
 Videň (Cz); Dunaj (Slov)
Vlonë (A); Valona (I)
Vltava river (Cz); Moldau river (G)
Zadar (SC); Zara (I)
Zagreb (SC); Agram (G); Zágráb (H)
Zemun (SC); Semlin (G)
Znaim (G); Znojno (Cz)

INDEX

(abbreviations: FJ = Francis Joseph, E = Elizabeth, F. Ferdinand = Francis Ferdinand, A-H = Austria-Hungary, B-H = Bosnia Herzegovina, PM = Prime Minister)

Abdulaziz, Sultan: 160, 169, 170, 202
Abdulhamid II, Sultan: 160, 205, 209, 301, 303
Achilleion palace, Corfu: 235, 306
Adler, Viktor: socialist leader, 262, 269, 340
Aehrenthal, Count Aloys: foreign minister, 298–9, 302–5; and Italy, 311–12; dies, 312
Agriculture: Austro-Hungarian, 181, 187
Albania: 311; in Balkan Wars, 314–16, 320
Albert of Saxony, cousin of FJ: 23, 252
Albrecht, Archduke, cousin of FJ: 20, 103, 115, 188, 256; in 1848 revolt, 30–33; in Austro-Prussian war, 142–3, 145; and Franco-Prussian war, 173–4; and Eastern crisis, 204, 206; and Rudolf, 215, 247–8, 263–4; and F. Ferdinand, 267, 268; dies, 276
Alexander II, Tsar: 175, 176; meets FJ (1860), 120; FJ visits, 190–91; and Eastern crisis (1875–8), 203–6
Alexander III, Tsar: 240; meets FJ, 231, 237–8
Alexander of Battenberg, Prince: 238, 240
Andrássy, Count Gyula: 55, 174, 187; E supports, 150–52; Hungarian PM, 154, 156–9; and Czechs, 168; foreign minister of A-H, 177, 183, 190–91; and Eastern crisis (1875–8), 199–206; resigns, 211–12; achievements of,

212–13; and Balkan crisis (1885), 238
Angeli, Heinrich von, artist: 237
Angerer, Fanny, E's hairdresser: 148
Anna of Prussia, Princess: FJ and, 66
Anti-clericalism: Austrian, 189–90; Rudolf's, 222
Anti-semitism: 187, 270, 274–5; in Vienna, 244, 252, 256–7, 281
Army: FJ and, 20, 25; Italians in, 21; in Italian campaign (1848); 33, 35–7; FJ supreme commander of, 52, 56–7; mobilized, (1854–5) 73, 81–2, (1866) 142; in Italian war (1859), 103–4; FJ commands at Solferino 109–10; modernization of, 140, 141, 298; in B-H, 210; Hungarians in, 268–9, 293–5, Redl scandal in, 318–19, in World War I, 333–4
Army Bill (1889): 256, 258–9, 263
Augustinerkirche, Vienna: imperial marriages in, 77, 184–5, 222
Austria, empire of (1830): 5; and Crimean War, 81–5; in Italian war (1859), 102–13; in Schleswig-Holstein crisis, 133–4, 137–8; relations with Prussia, 140, 141–2
Austria-Hungary: Dual Monarchy established (1867), 154–9; and Franco-Prussian War, 174–6; and B-H, 197–8, 207–11, 213, 225, in Eastern crisis (1875–8), 201–7; relations with Italy, 231, 311–12; relations with Russia, 237–8, 283, 301–2; in Balkan crisis (1885–6), 238,

Austria-Hungary—*cont*
240, 241; relations with Serbia, 300–1,
304–5, 320–21; and German alliance,
305; and Balkan Wars, 314–16, 319–
20; in World War I, 332–41
Austrian Republic: 346–9
Austro-Prussian war (1866): 142–7
Autocracy: FJ exercises (1851–61), 62–
3, 80, 85, 117–18, 123; FJ prefers, 166

Bach, Alexander, minister of justice: 42,
45, 50, 59, 60, 89, 115
Badeni, Count Casimir: PM, 272–3, 275;
language ordinances of, 282–3
Balkan Wars, (1912–13): 313–16, 319–
20
Balkans, crisis in (1885–6): 238, 240, 241
Ballhausplatz, Austrian foreign ministry
in: 139, 177
Baltazzi, Alexander, uncle of Mary
Vetsera: 260, 262, 278
Baltazzi, Aristide, uncle of Mary Vetsera:
253
Baltazzi, Hector, uncle of Mary Vetsera:
253, 262
Banking: 87–8, 181–3; crisis in (1873,
186–7
Batthyány, Count Lajos, Hungarian PM:
37, 41, 42; executed, 55
Beck, Baron Max von, PM: 297
Beck, General Frederick von, CGS: 143–
4, 174, 197, 204, 321; and Rudolf,
215–16, 259; and Hungary, 293; and
F. Ferdinand, 297–8; retires, 298
Belcredi, Count, Richard, PM: 141, 152,
154
Belvedere palace, Vienna: F. Ferdinand's
home, 289–90
Benedek, General Ludwig von: 36; at
Solferino, 109–10; in Austro-Prussian
war, 142, 143–6
Berchtold, Count Leopold von, foreign
minister: 312, 322; and Balkan Wars,
313, 314–16; and declaration of war,
326, 328–9; resigns, 335
Berlin: Treaty of (1854), 74; Congress of
(1878), 206–9; Treaty of (1878), 207–
9; FJ's state visit to, 268
Beust, Count Ferdinand: foreign
minister, 153–4; PM, 154–5, 161–2,
168, 169, 176–7; and Franco-Prussian
war, 174, 175

Biedermeier culture: 18–20
Bismarck, Prince Otto von, German
chancellor: policy of to Austria, 130–
34, 137, 141–2, 145; visits Vienna, 130,
137–8, 270; policy of to A-H, 177,
212–13; and Congress of Berlin, 207
Black Hand, Serbian secret society: 320–
21
Blue Danube waltz: 180–81
Bohemia: 155; FJ governor of, 34; FJ
visits, 61, 192–3; FJ's 'assignations' in,
65; nationalism in, 167–8, 218, 270,
283, 306
Bombelles, Count 'Charly': 23, 26; and
Rudolf, 216, 263
Bombelles, Count Heinrich: FJ's tutor,
15–16, 24
Bosnia: 66, under Ottoman Empire,
195–7; F. Ferdinand visits, 321–4
Bosnia-Herzegovina: A-H and, 197–8;
unrest in, 199–200; A-H occupies,
207–11; annexation of, 213, 225, 301–
5; FJ visits, 306–8, and Balkan Wars,
314, 316
Bratislava: 8, 25, 29; 1848 revolt in, 32,
34–5
Britain: and A-H, 240–41; at war with A-
H, 332, 343
Brosch, Major von: F. Ferdinand's aide,
296, 298
Bruck, Baron Karl von: minister of
commerce (1849–50) 45; finance
minister (1855), 87, 115; suicide of,
117
Budapest: 24, 49; state visits to, (1857)
94–5, (1866) 141, (1896) 281–2; E at
(1866–7), 145, 151–2, 157, 163;
coronation in (1867), 157–9;
rebuilding of, (1883), 229, FJ in
(1889), 255; underground railway in,
281
Budapest Conventions (1877): 204–5
Bulgaria: 207, 303, 304; under Ottoman
Empire, 202; in crisis (1885–6), 238,
240–2: in Balkan Wars, 314–16, 320;
joins A-H in war, 336; collapses, 345
Bülow, Bernhard von, German
chancellor: 304–5
Buol-Schauenstein, Count Karl, foreign
minister, 66, 99; and Crimean War,
73, 82, 83–4; and Italian war (1859),
103–4

Burian, Istvan: finance minister and
foreign minister, 329, 335

Cap Martin, France: FJ and E stay at,
280
Carinthia: 5; state visits to, 92
Carol I, K. of Roumania: 242
Caroline Augusta, consort of Francis I:
3–4, 76
Caspar, Mizzi, dancer; and Rudolf, 248,
251–2, 258, 260
Cavour, Camille, PM of Piedmont: 93,
99–101, 102–3
Censorship: 30, 33
Charles Albert, K. of Sardinia-
Piedmont: 33, 39, 43, 51
Charles, Archduke, great-nephew of FJ:
marries, 311; becomes heir, 324; in
World War I, 333, 336; and FJ's last
illness, 341–2; Emperor, 343, 345;
dies, 346
Charles, Archduke, great-uncle of FJ: 15;
dies, 25
Charles Ludwig, Archduke, brother of
FJ: 13, 26, 161, 185, 217; and E, 38,
69; marries, 91, 287; dies, 267
Charlotte, Belgian Princess, 101, 102;
marries Maximilian, 92, 95–6; and
Mexican empire, 135–6, 153; mental
collapse of, 157
Cholera epidemics: (1831), 9; (1873),
186
Chotek, Count Bohuslav: Austrian
envoy in Brussels, 220, 289
Chotek, Countess Sophie: 313, marries
F. Ferdinand, 288–90; death of, 323–
4; burial of, 325–6; sons' fate, 347–8
Cisleithania: 155, 189
Clemenceau, Georges, French
statesman: and Rudolf, 225–6
Compromise (settlement of 1867): 154–
9
Concordat, Austrian: 88–91, 166;
annulled, 167
Conrad von Hötzendorf, General Franz:
CGS, 299; and Balkans, 301–3,
proposes attack on Italy 311–12;
reinstates as CGS, 314; and Balkan
Wars, 315–16; and Redl case, 318–19;
and Serbia, 320, 321: war plans of
(1914), 328; in World War I, 333–8
Constantinople: FJ visits, 169, 170

Constitutions, Austrian: proposed
(1848), 29–30, 34, 35, 37, 45;
'Stadion' (1849), 50–51, 57; 'Sylvester
Patent' (1851), 62; (1859–60), 115–
18; October Diploma (1860), 122;
February Patent (1861), 122–3;
December Constitution (1868), 162–
3: Austro-Hungarian: franchise
under, (1897) 271–2, 275, (1907) 297:
Hungarian: (1848), 29, 32, 47; (1849),
51; 1867 Compromise, 154–9
Corfu: E in, 123, 124; FJ visits, 124–5
Coronation, Hungarian: 157–9
Coronini-Cronberg, Count Johann: FJ's
chamberlain, 15
Cracow; 32, 57
Crenneville, Count Franz: 143, 144
Crimean War: Austria and, 73–4, 81–5
Croatia: in 1848 revolt, 32–3; 42,
disaffected, 124; and Yugoslav ideal,
198
Croats: in empire, 85; and 1867
Compromise, 155; and Serbs, 301;
and Hungary, 317
Cromer, Norfolk; E visits, 242–3
Custozza, battles of: (1848), 39; (1866),
143
Czech language: 282–3, 288
Czechs: in empire, 5; in 1848 revolt, 33,
34, 38–9; in Austrian army, 111; and
October Diploma, 122; and 1867
Compromise, 155; nationalism of,
167–8, 218, 270–71, 316

Dalmatia; 195, 197; FJ visits (1875), 200–
1
Danube, R., 34–5, 71, 73, 76, 83, 169,
209
Danubian Principalities (Moldavia and
Wallachia): 82–3, 176
Deák, Ferencz, Hungarian reformer: 41,
122, 139–40, 150–51, 154
Debrecen: 49, 51, 95
Dresden: Austro-Prussian conference in
(1850), 58–9
Dubrovnik: 200–1

Eastern crisis (1875–8): 199–207
Economy: Austrian, (1850), 58; (1855),
87–8; (1859) 102, 116–17; Austro-
Hungarian, flourishes, 181–2, 228; in
crisis (1873), 186–7; Hungary and, 282

Edward VII, K., as Prince of Wales: 189, 191, 214, 222, 280; visits Vienna, 185, 252–4; visits Ischl (as king), 298

Elise, Q. of Prussia, aunt of FJ: 69, 71

ELIZABETH, Empress and Queen:

Life (chronological): as child meets FJ, 38; wooed by FJ, 69–73; wedding, 73; dislike of court life, 77–8, 81, 123–4, 188–9; becomes mother, 91; accompanies FJ to Italy and Hungary, 93–4; mourns firstborn child, 95–6; birth of son, 96; and Italian War (1859), 105, 107, 112; first withdrawal from public life, 119, 123–4; resumes court life, 127–9; reconciliation with FJ, 148; likes Gödöllö, 152, 157, 170, 187; crowned Queen of Hungary, 157, 159; goes to Buda for birth of fourth child 163; declines to join FJ's tour in the East, 169–70; World Exhibition 187; Silver Jubilee 188–9; 'Gabrielle' escapade, 191; Silver wedding, 217; Rudolf's betrothal and marriage, 220–3; patronage of Red Cross, 221; shares dangers of FJ's Trieste trip, 231–2; delight in Hermes Villa 232–3; prefers Corfu, 235; commissions Schratt portrait for FJ, 237; visits Brundlfeld asylum, 240; Maria Theresa Monument, 245; 51st birthday, 258; breaks news from Mayerling to FJ, 261; reactions to the tragedy, 266, 276–7; constant travelling worries FJ, 279; in Hungary for Millenial Celebrations, 281–2; at last state function (1896), 284; shocked by sister's death, 284–5; murdered, 285

Appearance: 69, 70, 73, 77, 148–9

Character: 70–1, 72, 78, 219, 226, 232

Finances: 194

Health: 119–22, 125–7, 187–88, 233, 239–40, 241, 276–7, 284

Interests and pursuits: classical Greece 226, 233, 234, 235; fencing 233; Greek language (modern), 125, 258, 261, 281; Heine cult, 226, 234, 237, 242, 258; horses and hunting, 72, 78, 108, 193, 232; Magyar culture, 94, 125, 150, 151, 152; Titania fantasies, 232, 234; verse writing, 70–1, 234, 241, 242–3, 245; walking 233

Journeys abroad: Corfu, 123–4, 235, 243, 277, 281; England, 192, 215, 221, 233, 242–3; French Riviera, 280, 285; Ithaca, 234; Madeira, 121–2; Rome, 166, 173; Switzerland, 277, 285

Personal relations with: Andrássy, 150–1, 157; Fanny Angerer, 148; sister-in-law Charlotte, 95, 136–7; Eugenie 161, 169–70, 171; Ida Ferenczy, 148, 177, 191; Marie Festetics, 177, 179; daughter Gisela, 96, 125, 163–4, 177–8, 184–5, 189, 239, 276; Marie Larisch, 254; Ludwig II of Bavaria, 234, 239; Rudolk, 119, 125, 148–9, 157, 163–4, 221, 245, 265; Katharina Schratt, 237, 239, 243, 278–9, 286; Archduchess Sophie, 69–70, 73, 77–8, 81, 95–6, 105, 119–20, 126, 177–79; Stephanie, 221–3, 231; daughter Marie Valerie, 177, 192, 234, 239, 240, 243, 258, 277, 278; Queen Victoria, 192, 243, 280

Religion: 81, 166

Elizabeth, Archduchess, daughter of Rudolf: 227, 342, 348

Elizabeth of Modena, Princess: FJ and, 65–6

Elssler, Fanny, ballerina: 17–18

England: Rudolf visits, 214–15, 248

Eötvös, Baron Josef, Hungarian reformer: 122

Erfurt Union of German states (1850): 58

Esterházy, Count Moritz, Austrian minister: 139, 140, 141

Esterházy, Countess Sophie, Mistress of Robes: 71, 123, 126

Eugenie, French Empress: 161–2, 169–70, 171–2

Eulenburg, Count Philip zu, German ambassador in Vienna: 286–7

Faure, Felix, French President: 280

February Patent (1861); 122–3, 128, 141

Fendi, Peter, painter: 19–20

Ferdinand I, Emperor, uncle of FJ: 3, 31, 32, 34–5, 39, 42, 113, 134, 167; crowned K. of Hungary, 7–8; succeeds, 14–15; abdicates, 45–7; dies, 193

Ferdinand, K. of Bulgaria: 241–2, 278, 304, 343

Ferenczy, Ida, E's lady-in-waiting: 148, 177, 191
Festetics, Countess Marie, E's lady-in-waiting, 177, 219, 221
Fischer, Dr: E's doctor, 126, 127
France: and Habsburg empire, 1–2; revolutions in, (1830) 6–7, (1848) 29; in Italian war (1859), 103–13; relations with Austria, 142–3, 160–2; relations with A-H, 173; at war with Prussia, 175–6; at war with A-H, 332
Franchise, extension of: 271–2; (1897), 275; (1907), 297
Francis I, Emperor, 1–5, 287; dies, 14–15
Francis Charles, Archduke; father of FJ, 3–4, 10–11, 15, 22, 31–32, 47, 161; dies, 207
Francis Ferdinand, Archduke: 161, 248, 253, becomes heir, 267–8; anti-Hungarian, 268, 311; marries, 288–90; political activity of, 295–7; and armed forces, 297–9; and B-H, 303, and President Roosevelt, 308; and Balkan Wars, 314–15; and Redl case, 318–19; and visit to Sarajevo, 321; burial of, 325–6; sons' fate, 347–8
FRANCIS JOSEPH, Emperor and King
Life (chronological): birth, 4–5; nursery years, 7–15; formal education, 12, 15, 16, 19, 23; initiation into the army, 20–21; first train journey, 23; a reluctant actor, 26; and coming of 1848 revolutions, 30–5; admitted to inner government, 31; appointed Governor of Bohemia, 34; on active service under Radetzky, 35–7; with court at Innsbruck, 37–8, 40; meets E. as child, 38; proposed English visit abandoned, 40; reaches age of majority, 40; accompanies court to Olmütz, 43; accession, 46–8; and counter-revolution, 50–3, 55, 57; meets Nicholas I, 53–4; at 'burning bridge of Raab', 54; and Reichsrat proposals 1851, 59–60, 62; life endangered at sea, 61; mourns Schwarzenberg, 62–3; seeks a wife, 65–6; survives assassination bid, 66–7; betrothal to E., 68–71; marriage, 76–7; spoils E., 78; Crimean War, 82–5; re-building of Vienna, 88–9; becomes father, 91; eldest child dies, 95; Rudolf's birth,

96; Italian War (1859), 102–13; at Solferino, 109–11; at Villafranca, 112–13; abandons absolutism, 114–16, 118, 122–23; abrupt dismissal of Bruck, 117; rumoured attachment to a Polish countess, 120; and E's recuperation on Madeira, 121–2; and Hungarian moderates, 122, 139–40; Reichsrat, 122–3, 128, 140–1, 163, 205; and Mexico, 126–7, 134–7, 157–8; welcomes E's return to Vienna, 127–9; conclave of German princes (1863), 131–3; Schleswig-Holstein crisis (1863–5), 133–4, 137–8, 140;Schönbrunn talks (1864), 138; rise of Belcredi, 141; army modernisation, 141, 142, 146, 297–8; War of 1866 141–7; reconciled with E, 148; negotiation of 1867 Compromise, 151–6; and Beust 153, 154, 169, 176–7; Hungarian coronation, 156–9; Maximilian's death 160; Salzburg talks, 161; birth of Marie Valerie, 163–4; fails to secure agreement with Czechs, 167–8; significance of visit to the East, 169, 170, 173; Franco-Prussian War (1870) 173–6; and Andrássy as foreign minister, 177, 183, 199, 206–13; death of his mother, 179; learns economics from Schäffle, 182–3; World Exhibition of 1873, 183, 185–6; Vienna stock market crash, 186–7; Silver Jubilee, 188–9; becomes grandfather, 189; and anti-clericalism, 190; Dalmatian tour, 195; and Strossmayer's policies, 198–9; Eastern Crisis (1875–78), 201–10; and status of B-H, 209, 211, 213, 304; has Taaffe as head of government, 211, 218; Silver Wedding 217; Rudolf's marriage 222–3; Kálnoky as foreign minister, 225, 273; fulfils official duties, 230–1; Oberdank conspiracy, 231; presents E with villas in Tiergarten and Corfu, 232–5; Eastern Crisis of 1884–6, 238, 240; hostility to Pan-Germans, 244, 251, 256, 270; and Maria Theresa monument, 244–5; dislikes Baltazzi family, 253, 278; Tisza's Hungarian army bill, 256, 263, 268–9; last meeting with Rudolf, 259;

FRANCIS JOSEPH, Emperor and King
Life (chronological)—*cont*
    Mayerling tragedy, 261–5; at Rudolf's
    funeral, 262; hears Mass at Mayerling,
    265–6; reluctance to recognize new
    heir-apparent, 267–8; fears socialist
    May Day, 269–70; rise of Lueger 270,
    273–5; praises Jewish subjects, 270,
    335; supports wider suffrage, 271, 273,
    275, 291, 297; alleged ingratitude to
    Taaffe, 271–2; Hungarian
    Millennium, 281–2; Golden Jubilee,
    282–3, 284, 286; and fall of Badeni,
    283–4; learns of E's murder, 285;
    rejects idea of re-marriage, 287–8; and
    F. Ferdinand's marriage, 288–9; vetoes
    military action in Hungary, 293, 294–
    5; issues Chlopy Order of the Day,
    294; gives Hungarians 'five minute
    audience', 295; first car ride, 298; at
    flying show, 298; approves
    appointment of Aehrenthal and
    Conrad (1906), 298–9; reacts to Pan-
    Serb agitation, 301–2; welcomes
    acquisition of B-H, 302–5; Diamond
    Jubilee, 306; visits Sarajevo and
    Mostar, 307–8; entertains T.
    Roosevelt, 308; 80th birthday
    celebrated, 310; filmed at marriage of
    Archduke Charles, 311; asserts
    personal control over foreign policy,
    312; appoints Berchtold foreign
    minister, 313; opposes war in 1912,
    314, 315; respects Masaryk, 316; Redl
    Affair, 318–19; at Leipzig centenary
    parade, 319; threatens Serbia with war
    over Albania (1913), 320–1; approves
    F. Ferdinand's visit to Bosnia, 321,
    322; personal reaction to Sarajevo
    murders, 324, 325, 326; and
    archduke's burial, 326; in 1914 war
    crisis, 327–31; orders release of
    Putnik, 331; sceptical of war news,
    334, 336, 339; chairs war council over
    Italy (1915), 335; accepts Polish
    kingdom and unified command 337,
    339; hopes to end war in 1917, 339;
    and Stürgkh's murder, 340–41; last
    days and death, 342; funeral, 343–4;
    posthumous assessments, 346–9
Appearance: 9, 20, 25, 67–8, 130, 165,
    243–4, 312
Character: 19–20, 23, 52, 128, 166, 224,
    230, 239, 243–4
Finances: 193–4
Health: 9, 292, 310, 311, 317, 321, 332,
    341–2
Interests and pursuits: artistic patronage,
    19, 217, 230, 232, 235, 237, 291;
    dancing, 17–18; drawing, 17;
    horsemanship and hunting, 12, 20, 23,
    24, 66, 191, 194, 235; letter-writing,
    16–17, 105, 170, 279–80; rock-
    climbing, 127, 172; shooting wildlife,
    127, 194, 235, 250, 265, 287, 310;
    smoking, 40, 112, 194; swimming, 81,
    165; theatre, 17, 162, 229, 255, 279,
    293; touristic delights 170–72, 280;
    urban landscape 229–30
Personal relations with: Albert of Saxony,
    23, 153, 250; cousin FM Albrecht 20,
    22, 33, 174, 226, 260; Andrássy 151–
    2, 157, 168; Charles Ludwig, 23, 26,
    69, 217, 267; Prince of Wales (Edward
    VII), 191, 252; granddaughter
    Elizabeth ('Erzsi'), 227, 258, 277;
    Eugenie 162, 171–2; Francis I, 14–15;
    F. Ferdinand 251, 267–8, 288–9, 296,
    298, 308, 314, 315, 318–9, 321–4;
    Grünne, 38, 42, 56, 59, 115;
    Maximilian, 13, 17, 21, 23, 25–6, 54,
    61, 66, 86, 101, 102, 115–16, 126–7,
    134–7; Metternich family, 22–4, 26,
    62, 105; Anna Nahowski, 330, 235–6,
    239, 258; Reichstadt (Napoleon II),
    11; Rudolf, 128, 132, 150, 163–4, 214,
    218, 219, 223–4, 226–7, 247–50, 252–
    3, 257, 259, 265; Katharina Schratt,
    236–7, 238–9, 241, 242–5, 252–3, 255,
    258, 260, 265, 270, 276, 277, 279–80,
    283, 284, 286–7, 292, 293, 295, 302,
    307, 317, 331, 335, 339, 342;
    Archduchess Sophie, 9, 12–14, 25–6,
    31, 48, 52, 57, 68, 69, 60, 78, 81, 92,
    95, 96, 105, 118–19, 126, 133, 175–6,
    178–9; Stephanie 222, 258, 288; Taaffe
    family, 23, 25, 218, 271; daughter
    Marie Valerie, 249, 258, 310, 324;
    Queen Victoria, 133, 231; William II,
    251, 252–3, 257, 259, 276, 304–6
Religion: 16, 65, 88, 89–91, 166–7, 171,
    190, 261, 265–6, 286, 310, 324, 341,
    342
Journeys outside Empire: Bavaria, 72, 73,

74, 120, 123; Corfu, 124; 'the East' (Constantinople, Jerusalem, Athens, Suez Canal, Cairo), 169–73; French Riviera, 280; Paris 162; Russia 190–91; Territet, 277; Warsaw, 54, 72, 120; Views and ideas on: anti-semitism, 270, 275; 'applied modern art' (*Sezession*), 291; army officer's role in Empire, 247, 319; constitutional government, 60, 118, 224; Ibsen as dramatist, 279; organic composition of Monarchy, 349; parliamentary politics, 128, 205, 269, 270, 271, 275–6, 291; Southern Slav problem, 190, 199, 300–01; U.S. constitution, 311

Franco-Prussian war (1870–71): 174–6

Frankfurt: German princes meet at (1863), 132–3

Frederick III, German Emperor: 16, 133, 145, dies, 251

Frederick William IV, K. of Prussia: 28, 57–8; meets FJ, 72

Freud, Dr Sigmund: on World Exhibition, 184, 185; meets FJ, 309

Garibaldi, Riciotti: 172

Gastein, Convention of (1865): 140

Geneva; E killed at, 285

German Austrians: 5; in Austrian army, 110; and 1860 constitution, 122; anti-Czech, 168, 218, 270–71, 283

German Confederation: Austro-Prussian rivalry in, 131–4, 137–8, 141–2; dissolved, 146

German Empire: relations with A-H, 176–7, 212, 305

Germany: 1848–9 revolution in, 57; federalism in, 58; liberalism in, 124

Gisela, Archduchess, daughter of FJ, 91, 92, 95, 96, 123, 125, 163–4, 262, 276, 347; marriage of, 177–8, 184–5; daughter born to, 189

Giskra, Karl, minister for home affairs: 186

Gödöllö palace, Hungary: 152, 157, 167, 177, 187, 189, 255

Goito, battle of (1848): 33

Goluchowski, Count Agenor (elder), minister of interior: 115, 116–17, 122

Goluchowski, Count Agenor (younger), foreign minister: 273, 283–4, 295; resigns, 298; and Serbia, 300

Gondrecourt, Major-General Ludwig, Crown Prince Rudolf's tutor, 149–50

Gorchakov, Prince Alexander, Russian chancellor: 190, 202–3

Görgei, Arthur, Hungarian general: 50, 51, 54–5

Graz: FJ visits, 61

Greif, SIS, imperial yacht: 170–72

Grillparzer, Franz, Austrian poet: 2, 39, 68

Grünne, Count Karl: 35, 105; FJ's chamberlain, 38; advises FJ, 40, 51, 56, 59, 82, 85, 101, 104, 114–15; E and, 71, 124

Györ, battle of (1849): 54

Gyulai von Maros-Nemeth, Count Francis: 94, 101, in Italian campaign (1859), 103–4, 105–7

Habsburg dynasty: 5

Hauslaub, Colonel Franz von: 16

Haymerle, Baron Heinrich, foreign minister: 211, 223–4

Haynau, Baron Julius von: in Hungarian campaign, 52, 53–4; military governor of Hungary, 55, 57; recalled, 59

Heiligenkreuz Abbey: 246, 262

Heine, Heinrich, poet: 234, 237

Helen of Bavaria, cousin of FJ, 38, 66, 119, 124, 160; visits Ischl (1853), 69–70

Hermes Villa, Vienna: built for E, 232–5

Herzegovina: in Ottoman empire, 195–7 (*see also* Bosnia Herzegovina)

Hess, Baron Heinrich, army QMG: 56, 82–3, 104, 105, 107, 108

Hirsch, Baron Moritz: financier, 252

Hitler, Adolf: 274, 347; in Vienna, 309

Hofburg palace, 14; amateur theatricals in, 26–7; redecorated, 57; FJ's wedding festivities in, 77

Hohenwart, Count Charles von: and Czechs, 168

Holy Crown of St Stephen: 156–7, 158, 282

Honved (Hungarian national defence force): 42, 43, 50

Hoyos, Count Alexander, diplomat: 327

Hoyos, Count Joseph, Court chamberlain: 260–61

Hradčany castle, Prague: 10, 47, 167, 227

Hübner, Baron Joseph von; Austrian ambassador in Paris, 101, 125
Hungary: in empire, 8, 24–5, 85; kingdom of, 7–8, 47; 1848–9 revolt in, 29, 32, 41–2, 49–53, 55; state visits to (1857) 94–5, (1896) 281–2; nationalism in, 122, 124, 139–40, 256, 263–4, 268–9, 293–5; E visits (1866–7), 150–52, 157, 163; subject nationalities in, 189, 317; in Eastern crisis (1875–8), 198–9, 204; and coming of war 328–30

Ignatiev, General Nikolai, Panslav: 203–4, 206–7
Innsbruck: court at (1848), 37, 40
Ischl: FJ first visits, 9–10; FJ hunts at, 61, 235; FJ and E. betrothed at, 68–71; FJ's birthday at, 236; last visit of FJ and E to, 285; FJ's eightieth birthday at, 310; FJ at (1914), 327–332
Ismail, Khedive of Egypt: 169
Italians: in empire, 5, 20–21
Italy: in 1848 revolt, 29, 33, war of 1859 in, 102–13; Risorgimento in, 120; kingdom of established (1861), 125; allies with Prussia against Austria, 141–5; relations with A-H, 190, 231; invades Libya, 311–12; neutral (1914), 332; at war with A-H, 335
Izvolsky, Alexander, Russian foreign minister: 302–5

Jellaçić, Colonel Josip, Ban of Croatia: 57, 77, 198; in 1848–9 revolt, 33, 42, 43–4, 46, 49, 53
Jews: in empire, 116; in A-H, 270, 335; Rudolf and, 252, 256–7
John, Archduke, great-uncle of FJ, 15, 22, 30, 31, 38
Joseph Archduke, great-uncle of FJ: 8, 15; dies, 24
Juarez, Benito, President of Mexico: 126, 157–8, 160

Kállay, Count Benjamin: 199–200, 213
Kálnoky, Count Gustav, foreign minister: 225; and Russia, 237–8; and Balkans, 240–41; resigns, 272–3
Kapuzinergruft, Vienna: 25, 193, 262, 344, 347, 349

Karl Theodore of Bavaria, brother of E: 127
Károlyi, Count Alois, Austrian envoy in Berlin: 131
Károlyi, Count Pista, Hungarian nationalist: 256, 264
Kastner, Joseph, artist: 266
Kerzl, Dr Joseph von, FJ's doctor: 317, 321–2, 341, 342
Ketterl, Eugen, FJ's valet: 342; memoirs of, 317
Kisch, Egon, journalist: 318
Kiss von Itebbe, Nicholas, husband of Katharina Schratt: 236, 278, 287
Kiss von Itebbe, Toni, son of Katharina Schratt: 236, 278–9, 287
Kissingen: E at, 127, 148; E and FJ at, 285
Klimt, Gustav, artist: 235, 290–91
Koerber, Dr Ernst von, PM: 292, 341
Kolowrat-Liebsteinsky, Count Franz, minister of state: 22–3, 28, 32, 34
Kôniggrâtz, battle of (1866): 144–5
Konopischt castle, Bohemia: 289, 322–3
Kossuth, Ferencz, Hungarian nationalist leader: 293
Kossuth, Lajos, Hungarian revolutionary: 24–5, 29–30, 42, 47, 49, 51, 55, 110–11, 139, 156, 293
Kotor, Dalmatia: 169, 195, 201
Kotzebue, Augustus, dramatist: 26
Krauss, Baron Alfred von, Vienna police chief: 248, 257–8, 263
Kremsier: Reichstag at, 44, 49–51; Austro-Russian conference at (1885), 237–8
Krismanić, General Gideon: 142–4
Krobatkin, General, war minister: 315
Kübeck, Baron Karl von, Metternich's assistant: 46, 47, 57; drafts constitution, 59–60, 62
Kuhn, Baron Franz, war minister: 173–4, 175

Language Ordinances: 282–3, 292
Lanner, Joseph, composer: 17–18
Larisch, Countess Marie, niece of E: 254–5, 260, 263
Latour-Baillet, Count Theodore von, war minister: 36, 42–3
Latour von Thurnburg, General Joseph, Rudolf's tutor: 150, 214–15, 221, 223, 263

Laxenburg Manifesto (1859): 115–16
Laxenburg palace: 10, 114–15, 222–3; E
at, 78, 91, 95–6, 108, 123–4
Lehár, Colonel Anton: 346
Léhar, Franz, composer: 313, 318, 346
Leipzig, battle of, centenary: 319
Leopold I, K. of Belgians: 94, 121, 134;
visits Vienna, 67–8
Leopold II, K. of Belgians: 220
Leopold, Prince of Bavaria: 178, 184–5
Lesseps, Ferdinand de: 171
Libényi, Janos, assassin: 66–7
Lissa, naval battle of (1866): 145
Ljubljana: FJ visits, 61; state visits to, 92
Lobkowitz, Prince Joseph, FJ's adjutant-
general: 41, 42–3
Lombardy: in empire, 5; 1848 revolt in,
29, 33, 39; 1849 campaign in, 51; FJ
visits, 61; under Radetzky, 86; state
visits to (1857), 92–3; under
Maximilian, 99–100; ceded to
Piedmont (1859), 113, 138, 141
Loos, Adolf, architect: 290–91
Lower Austria: in empire, 5; in 1848
revolt, 30
Ludovika, Duchess in Bavaria, aunt of
FJ: 38, 66, 119, 126; visits Ischl (1853),
68–70; and daughter's marriage to FJ,
73, 74, 77–8
Ludwig II, K. of Bavaria: 226, 234;
suicide of, 239–40
Ludwig, Archduke, great-uncle of FJ: 15,
22, 31, 40
Ludwig Victor, Archduke, brother of FJ:
48, 91, 161, 186
Lueger, Karl, Mayor of Vienna: 256,
270, 272, 273–5, 283, 284, 296, 309

Macedonia: 301, 303, 320
Magenta, battle of (1859): 107
Magyar language: 8, 268, 293–4; FJ
learns, 24–5, E learns, 94, 150, 157
Magyar Millenium in Budapest (1896):
281–2
Makart, Hans, designer: 217, 235
Mantua: 36, 107, 113
Margaretha of Saxony, Princess: 91; dies,
101
Margutti, Albert von, FJ's aide: 330, 331,
339, 346, 349
Maria Anna of Savoy, consort of
Ferdinand I: 8, 31, 45, 47, 167, 193

Maria Theresa, Empress: 1, 293;
monument to, 244
Marianna, Archduchess, aunt of FJ:
disfigured at birth, 4, 81
Marie Louise, consort of Napoleon I: 2,
11; dies, 25
Marie, Q. of Naples, sister of E: 120,
191
Marie Valerie, Archduchess, daughter of
FJ: 163–4, 278, 317, 324, 342, 347;
accompanies E, 177, 192, 239, 241;
marriage of, 249, 256, 258, 277; after
E's death, 286–7
Masaryk, Thomas, Czech statesman:
316
Mathilde, Archduchess: 158
Maximilian, Archduke, brother of FJ: 11,
46; as child, 13; and Italy, 21; in
Hungarian campaign (1849), 54; and
navy, 61, 86, 134; and attempt on FJ's
life, 67; marries, 92, 95; governs
Lombardy-Venetia (1857), 94, 99–
101; and Italian war (1859), 111;
liberal views of, 115–16; and Mexican
empire, 126–7, 134–7, 152–3;
captured, 157–8; executed, 160
Maximilian, Duke in Bavaria, E's father:
71; dies, 256
Maximilian, Prince of Thurn and Taxis:
119, 124, 132, 160
Mayerling, Schloss: 246; tragedy of, 260–
5; convent of, 266
Meissner, Florian, lawyer: 248, 257
Mensdorff-Pouilly, Count Alexander,
foreign minister: 139, 141
Metternich, Prince Clemens von,
chancellor: 2, 6–8, 15, 22–25, 57, 60,
98–9, 168; resigns (1848), 28–32;
returns to Vienna, 61–2; advises FJ,
72, 104–5
Metternich, Princess Melanie von: 23,
25, 28, 61–2
Metternich, Richard von: 23–4, 26;
Austrian ambassador in Paris, 131,
143, 174
Mexico: Maximilian invited to rule, 134–
6, 152–3, 157–8
Milan: 21, 33; state visits to (1857), 93;
rebuilding of, 99, Austria loses (1859),
107
Miramare villa, Trieste: 86, 92, 123, 136,
157, 172–3, 231, 256, 288

Mollinary, General Anton: 195, 202
Moltke, Field Marshal Helmuth von, Prussian commander: 141, 146
Montenegro: 201–4; in Balkan Wars, 313–16
Montenuovo, Prince Alfred, Lord Chamberlain: 322, 326, 344
Moravia: 41, 43, 155, 270, 283; settlement in, 316
Mostar: FJ in, 307, 308
Munich: FJ visits E at, 72, 73
Murad V, Sultan: 160
Mürzsteg: 253, 257, 258
Musil, Robert, novelist: 347

Nahowski, Anna, friend of FJ: 220, 235–6, 239, 258
Napoleon I: 1–2
Napoleon II: *see* Reichstadt, Duke of
Napoleon III: 165, 171–2; and Italy, 100–101, 143, and Italian war (1859), 102–3, 109, 111–13; and Mexico, 126, 134, 135, 152–3; and Austro-Prussian war, 144, 145; visits Austria, 160–61; in Franco-Prussian war, 175
Napoleon, Prince Imperial: 162
National Guard, in Vienna: 37, 40
Navy: 61, 134, 145, 298; modernized, 86; in Albanian crisis (1913), 315–16
Nehammer, Karl, Rudolf's servant: 226
Neue Freie Presse: 290
Neues Wiener Tagblatt, liberal newspaper: 114, 185, 244; Rudolf and, 225, 250–51
Nicholas I, Tsar: 39, 58; intervenes in Hungary, 53–5, meets FJ (1849), 54, (1853) 72; relations with FJ, 62, 83
Nicholas II, Tsar, visits Vienna: 284
Nicholas, Prince (King) of Montenegro: 201, visits Vienna, 312; in Balkan Wars, 313–14
Novara, battle of (1849): 51
Novibazar, Sanjak of: 197, 209; railway in, 302; in Balkan Wars, 314

Obrenović, Alexander, K. of Serbia: 300
Obrenović, Milan, Prince (King) of Serbia: 199, 231, 253
O'Brien, Thomas, *Times* correspondent in Vienna: 74, 76
October Diploma (1860): 118
Olmütz: court at (1848–9), 43–9; FJ's

accession at, 47, 52; FJ meets Tsar at, 72; Austrian headquarters (1866), 143
Orsini, Count Felice, Italian terrorist: 100
Otto, Archduke, nephew of FJ: 161, 268
Otto, Archduke (Dr Otto von Habsburg): 343, 346
Ottoman empire: 66; Russia and, 71–2; and Eastern crisis (1875–8), 195–7, 202–9; A-H and, 209–11, 304–5; and Balkans, 303–3, 304–5; in Balkan Wars, 313–14, 320; in World War I, 332

Paar, Count Eduard: 323, 330, 335
Paget, Lady, British ambassador's wife: 259
Palmer, Eduard, banker: 236, 278, 287
Pan-German movement: 33, 34, 238, 253–4, 270; riot of, 244–5
Pan-Slav Congress (1867): 167
Panslavism: 38–9, 174, 200–1, 203–4, 327, 330
Papal States: 29, 113
Paris: FJ's state visit to, 161–2; Treaty of (1856), 85, 176
Parliaments: Austrian Reichstag, (1848), 39–40,44, 45, 47; (1849), 49–50 (after 1850 *see under* Reichsrat); Hungarian Diet, 24–5, 29, 32, 34–5, 39, 141; Hungarian (from 1867), 154, nationalists in, 293–5; provincial, 116, 118
Pascher, Fritz: with E at masked ball, 191
Pašić, Nikola, Serbian PM: 304, 320–21; in July crisis (1914), 328
Paskevich, Marshal Ivan, Russian commander: in Hungary, 54–5
Peschiera: 36, 37, 113
Peter I, K. of Serbia: 300–1
Philip, Prince of Coburg: and Mayerling, 260–61
Piedmont: at war with Austria (1859), 102–13
Pillersdorf, Baron Franz von, minister of interior: 34, 44
Pius IX, Pope: 21, 166, 190
Plener, Ignaz von, finance minister: 117
Polish Question: 7, 32, 122, 133, 337, 341
Possenhofen, Schloss, Bavaria: 72, 73, 119–20, 127

Potiorek, General Oskar, governor of B-H: 314; in war crisis (1914), 326; during war, 333

Prague: 10, 52; in 1848 revolt, 33, 38–9; martial law in (1849–53), 57, 67; nationalism in, 167; FJ visits, 167, 193; rebuilding of (1867), 182, (1883), 229; Rudolf serves at, 214, 218, 221–3; F. Ferdinand serves at, 268; Treaty of (1866), 146

Prater, Vienna: 6, 34, 35, 78; World Exhibition in, 184; FJ's Golden Jubilee in, 284

Princip, Gavrilo, Bosnian Serb assassin: 324

Prussia: relations with Austria, 57–8, 74, 103, 111, 130–33, 141–2; invades Schleswig, 133–4; at war with Austria (1866), 142–7, at war with France (1870–71), 175–6

Putnik, Radomir, Serbian Marshal: 331

Queretaro, Mexico: 160

Radetzky, Field Marshal Joseph: 20–21, 33, 40, 44, 77; in Italian campaign (1848–9), 35–7, 39, 51; takes Venice, 55–6; governs Lombardy-Venetia, 57, 84, 85–6, 93–4, funeral of, 98

Radetzky March: 56, 98, 279

Radowitz, General Joseph von, Prussian PM: 58

Railways: Balkan, 169, 197, 302, Budapest underground, 281; Vienna *Stadtbahn*, 284, 291; Vienna–Trieste (*Sudbahn*), 87

Rainer, Archduke, cousin of FJ, 115; PM, 122–3

Rauscher, Cardinal Joseph von, 12, 16, 90, 117, 166, 184; marries FJ and E, 77

Rechberg, Count Johann, foreign minister: 105, 108, 115–17, 131, 135–6; and Bismarck, 137–8; resigns, 139

Redl, Colonel Alfred: scandal of, 318–19

Redlich, Joseph, parliamentarian: on Redl case, 318; on news of Sarajevo, 325, on FJ's death, 342

Reichsrat: (1850–51), 59–60, 62; (1860), 116–18; (1861), 123; (1862), 128; dissolved (1865), 141; (1868), 163; and Eastern crisis (1875–8), 205, 211;

Bohemian parties in, 218; failure of, 270, 291; prorogued (1914), 328

Reichstadt: Agreement of (1876), 203–4, 205–6; F. Ferdinand's wedding at, 289

Reichstadt, Duke of, son of Napoleon I: 2, 10–11

Renz, Ernst, circus rider: 78

Revolutions: (1830), 6–7; (1848), 29–48

Rieger, Franz, Czech nationalist: 167

Risorgimento, Italian: 118, 120

Rodić, General, governor of Dalmatia: 195, 200, 201–2

Roosevelt, Theodore, US President: meets FJ, 308–9

Roth, Joseph, novelist: 347

Roumania: 209, 240, 241; allies with A-H, 238; in Balkan Wars, 320; in Triple Alliance, 326; neutral (1914), 332; at war with A-H, 338–9

Roumanians: 317; nationalism of, 169

Rüdiger, Bishop of Linz: 166

Rudolf, Crown Prince: born, 96; youth of, 119, 123, 125, 128, 163–4, 177–8, 185; education of 149–50; and Hungary, 157, 263–4; at Hungarian coronation, 158; army service of, 214–18, 222–3, 226, 247–8; intellectual pursuits of, 214–16, 247; sex life of, 216, 248–9; marriage of, 217, 220–23, 226–7; political writing of, 218–19, 223–6, 250–51, 256–7, 259; relations with parents, 188, 209, 223–4, 226–7, 240, 248–50, 258–9, 265; ill, 245, 249, 257–8; buys Mayerling, 246; and William II, 251, 257; suicide plan of, 251–2; and P. of Wales, 252–4; meets Mary Vetsera, 253–5; and Jews, 256–7; death, 260–6

Rumbold, Horace, British diplomat: 98

Ruschuk, Bulgaria, FJ at: 170

Russell, Lord John, British foreign secretary: 84, 94

Russell, William Howard, *Times* correspondent: 143, 145

Russia: relations with Austria (1854), 82–4; relations with A-H, 174–6, 212, 237, 283, 284, 302–5; FJ visits (1874), 190–91; and Eastern crisis (1875–8), 202–7; and Balkan crisis (1885–6), 240, 241; at war with A-H, 332

Russo-Turkish war (1877): 205–6

Saint Stephen's Cathedral, Vienna: 67, 343, 348–9
Salisbury, Robert, Marquis of, British foreign secretary: 207–8, 265
Salonika: 302, 304, 314
Salvator, Archduke Francis: 249, 258
Salvator, Archduke Johann: 210
Salzburg: 161, 177
San Stefano, Treaty of (1878): 206–7
Santa Lucia, battle of (1848): FJ at, 36
Sarajevo: 197; FJ visits, 307–8; F. Ferdinand's fatal visit to, 321, 322–4
Schäffle, Professor Albert, minister of commerce: 182–3
Schemua, General Blasius, CGS: 312
Schleswig-Holstein crisis (1864): 133–4, 137–8, 140
Schmerling, Baron Anton von, PM: 59, 122, 128, 131, 140–41
Schönaich, Baron Franz von, war minister: 298–9
Schönbrunn, Convention of (1873): 199
Schöbrunn palace: 1–2, 10–1, 40, 43, 53, 341–3, 345; Austro-Prussian talks at, 138; ministerial conferences at, 175
Schönerer, George von, Pan-German, 238, 244, 270, 274
Schratt, Katharina, actress: 188, becomes FJ's friend, 236–9; FJ writes to, 241, 243–5, 254–5, 265, 276, 280, 283, 285–6, 295, 302, 307; relations with FJ, 258, 277–9, 286–7, 292–3, 317–18; and coming of war, 331; last visit of to FJ, 342, last years of, 347
Schwarzau: Archduke Charles' wedding at, 311
Schwarzenberg, Prince Felix: 36, 39, 53, 55; PM (1848), 44; and Ferdinand's abdication, 45–7; policies of, 49–50, 57–9; and FJ, 52, 54, 59; dies (1852), 62
Schwarzenberg, Cardinal Frederick von: 90, 166, 221–2
Schwarzgelb, liberal weekly: 256–7, 259
Scutari (Albania): 314, 315–16
Serbia: 199, 209, 213; at war with Turks, 202–4; relations with A-H, 231, 301, 304–5, 320–21; at war with Bulgaria, 238; military coup in, 300–01; in Balkan Wars, 313–16, 319–20; in July crisis (1914), 326–8 (*see also* World War I)

Serbs: 169; in 1848 revolt, 41–2
Sezession, artistic movement: 290–91
Sidonia of Saxony, Princess: FJ and, 66
Silesia: 138, 143, 168
Slovenes: in empire, 5, 86, 283; and language question, 272
Socialism: 187, 238, 256, 269–70
Solferino, battle of (1859): 108–10
Sophie, Archduchess, daughter of FJ: 91, 92, dies, 95
Sophie, Archduchess, mother of FJ: 3, 6, 8, 23, 48; and children's births, 4, 11; and Duke of Reichstadt, 10–11; in FJ's youth, 9–10, 12–13, 15–17, 25–6; political activity of, 21–2, 28, 35, 37; in 1848 revolt, 30–31; 39, redecorates Hofburg, 56–7; and FJ's marriage, 64–6, 68–71, 73, 77–8; and E, 81, 105, 119, 127, 148, 177; and family marriages, 91–2, 95–6, 178; and Mexican empire, 134; and Maximilian's death, 160, 161; and Franco-Prussian war, 175–6; dies, 178–9
Sophie, Duchess of Alençon, sister of E: dies, 285
Staatskonferenz (Regency council): 22, 31
Stadion, Count Francis, interior minister: 45, 50–51, 59
Stalin, Joseph: in Vienna, 309
Steinbach, Emil, finance minister: 271
Stephanie, Crown Princess: marries Rudolf, 220–23; memoirs of, 226, 233; and Rudolf, 226–7, 249, 258, 260; remarries, 288; last years of, 348
Stephen, Archduke, cousin of FJ, Palatine of Hungary: 25, 32, 35, 41, 42
Strauss, Eduard, composer: 222
Strauss, Johann (elder), composer: 18, 56
Strauss, Johann (younger), composer: 180–81
Strauss, Joseph, composer: 96
Strossmayer, Bishop Joseph: 166, 198–9
Stürgkh, Dr Karl, PM: 328, 339, 340
Stürmfeder, Baroness Louise von: FJ's governess, 12–13
Styria: 5, 92
Suez Canal: FJ at opening of (1869), 169–70, 171–2

Széchényi, Dénes: 23, 26
Széchényi, Istvan, Hungarian statesman: 41
Szécsen, Count Nicholas, Hungarian politician: 118, 122
Szeps, Moriz, newspaper editor: 225–6, 244, 257

Taaffe, Count Eduard: early friend of FJ, 23–24; deputy PM, 154, 168; PM, 211, 230, 231; and Czech nationalism, 218–19, 222; and Rudolf's death, 261, 262, 263; resigns, 270–2
Tegetthof, Admiral Wilhelm von: 134, 145, 160, 197
Territet, Switzerland: FJ and E stay at, 277
The Times: on FJ's marriage, 74, 76–7; on Hungarian coronation, 158–9; on Rudolf's funeral, 262
Theresianum (palace and academy), Vienna: 74, 244
Three Emperors, League of: 199, 202–3, 211, 225, 231, 237–8, 241
Thun-Hohenstein, Count Leo, minister of education: 90, 101
Tisza, Istvan, Hungarian PM: and Serbia, 320, in war crisis (1914), 328–9
Tisza, Kálmán, Hungarian PM: 225, 240, 256, 268–9, 294, 317; reforms of, 310–11
Transylvania: 50, 155, 317; martial law in (1849–50), 57
Trieste: 153, 172, 229; Maximilian at, 61, 86; importance of, 86–7; state visits to, 92, 231
Triple Alliance (1882): 231, 241
Trotsky, Leon: in Vienna, 309
Tyrol: 5; FJ visits, 17

Umberto, K. of Italy: 231
Urbanski, Colonel: 319

Varešanin, General Marijan, governor of Bosnia: 306–8
Városliget Park, Budapest: Millennial Exposition in, 281
Vatican Council (1869–70): 166
Venetia: 5; FJ visits, 20–21, 61; 1848 revolt in, 29, 33; under Radetzky, 86; state visits to (1856–7), 92–3; under

Maximilian, 99–100; in Italian Confederation, 113, 125; and Italy (1866), 142–4, 146
Venice: 33; FJ visits, 20–21; surrenders to Austria (1849), 55–6; state visit to (1856–7), 93; E visits (1861), 125–6; FJ visits K. of Italy in (1875), 190
Ventnor, Isle of Wight: E at, 1927
Verona: 35–6; FJ visits, 20; FJ's headquarters (1859), 105–6, 108
Vetsera, Baroness Helene: 219, 254–5, 261, 262–3
Vetsera, Mary: 219; and Rudolf, 253–5, 259; death of, 260–3
Victor Emmanuel II, K. of Piedmont (Italy): 101–2, 107; visits Vienna, 186; FJ visits, 190
Victoria, Q.: 121, 165, 214–15, 231, 265; FJ visits at Coburg, 133; E and, 192; FJ and E visit in France, 280
Vienna: celebrates FJ's birth, 6; cholera in, 9, 186, theatre in, 18, 188; 1848 revolt in, 30–32, 34, 37, 40–1, 42–4; martial law in (to 1853), 57, 67; FJ distrusts, 61; attempt on FJ's life in, 66–7; FJ's marriage in, 74–7; peace talks in (1855); 84–5; rebuilding of (1857–88), 88–9, 182, 186–7, 229–30, 244; celebrates Rudolf's birth, 96–7; hostile to FJ (1859), 108, 113–14; sympathetic to E, 127–8; Opera House, 182; World Exhibition in (1873), 183–6; celebrates Gisela's wedding, 185; stock exchange crash in (1873), 186; FJ's Silver Jubilee in, 188; celebrates FJ's silver wedding, 217; music in, 228–9; Maria Theresa monument unveiled, 244–5; May Day (1890) in, 269–70; celebrates FJ's Golden Jubilee, 284; FJ's Diamond Jubilee in, 306; Leipzig centenary in, 319; after World War I, 346; after World War II, 348 (*see also* Lueger, Karl)
Vienna Press, 189, 318
Vienna, Treaty of (Dual Alliance, 1879): 212–13, 231
Villafranca: 107; Peace of (1859), 112–13
Votivkirche, Vienna: 67, 88

Wagner, Otto, architect: 291

Waldmüller, Ferdinand, painter: 13, 19
Wallsee: FJ ill at, 310
Warsaw: 54, 72, 118, 120
Wekerle, Alexander, Hungarian PM: 295
Welden, Baron von, army commander: 51–2, 53
Welden, Baroness Caroline von: Crown Prince Rudolf's nurse, 123, 125–6, 149
Weyl, Joseph, librettist: 180–81
Wiener Neustadt: military academy at, 128, 322; airfield at, 298; whirlwind devastates, 339
Wiener Zeitung, 50, 71, 326
William I, German Emperor: 103, 111–12, 130, 132–3, meets FJ, 120, 137–8, 177, 203, 231; visits Vienna, 186; dies, 244
William II, German Emperor: 222; and Rudolf, 250–51, 256–7; visits Vienna, 252–3, 321; visits A-H, 276; and F. Ferdinand, 290, 322–3; and B-H, 304; irritates FJ, 305–6; pays last respects to FJ, 343
Windischgraetz, Prince Alfred: 25, 77; in 1848 revolt, 31–32, 35, 41, in Prague revolt, 38–9; takes Vienna, 43–4,

political activity of, 43–6, 50; in Hungarian campaign (1848–9), 47–9, 50–52; fall of, 51–2
Winterhalter, Franz, painter: 148–9
World Exhibition, Vienna (1873): 183–8
World War I: July crisis (1914) and, 326–31; spreads rapidly, 332; Serbian campaigns in, 333–4, 336; Eastern Front in, 333, 336–7, 338; Italian Front in, 335, 337–8; Roumanian Front in, 338–9, 342; burden of on A-H people, 334–5, 339; aftermath of, 345–6

Yugoslav ideal: 198–9

Zagreb: 32–33, 198; rebuilt, 229; Rudolf visits, 250
Zerajić, Bogdan, Bosnian Serb terrorist, 308
Zita, Archduchess: 322, 336, 342; marries, 311; as Empress, 343, 348–9
Zollverein (German customs union): 58, 87
Zumbusch, Kaspar von: sculptor, 245
Zurich, Treaty of (1859): 116